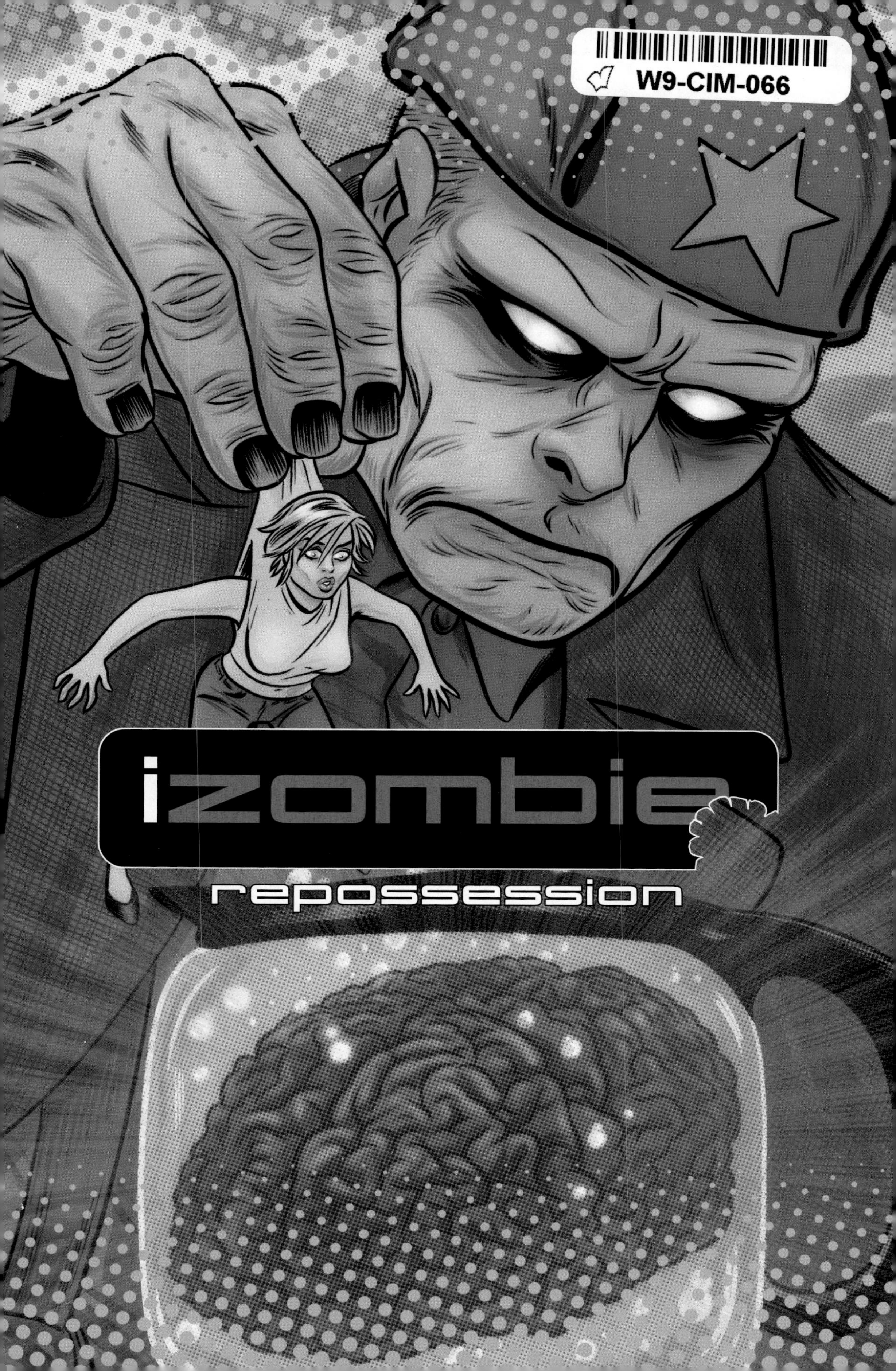
izombie
repossession

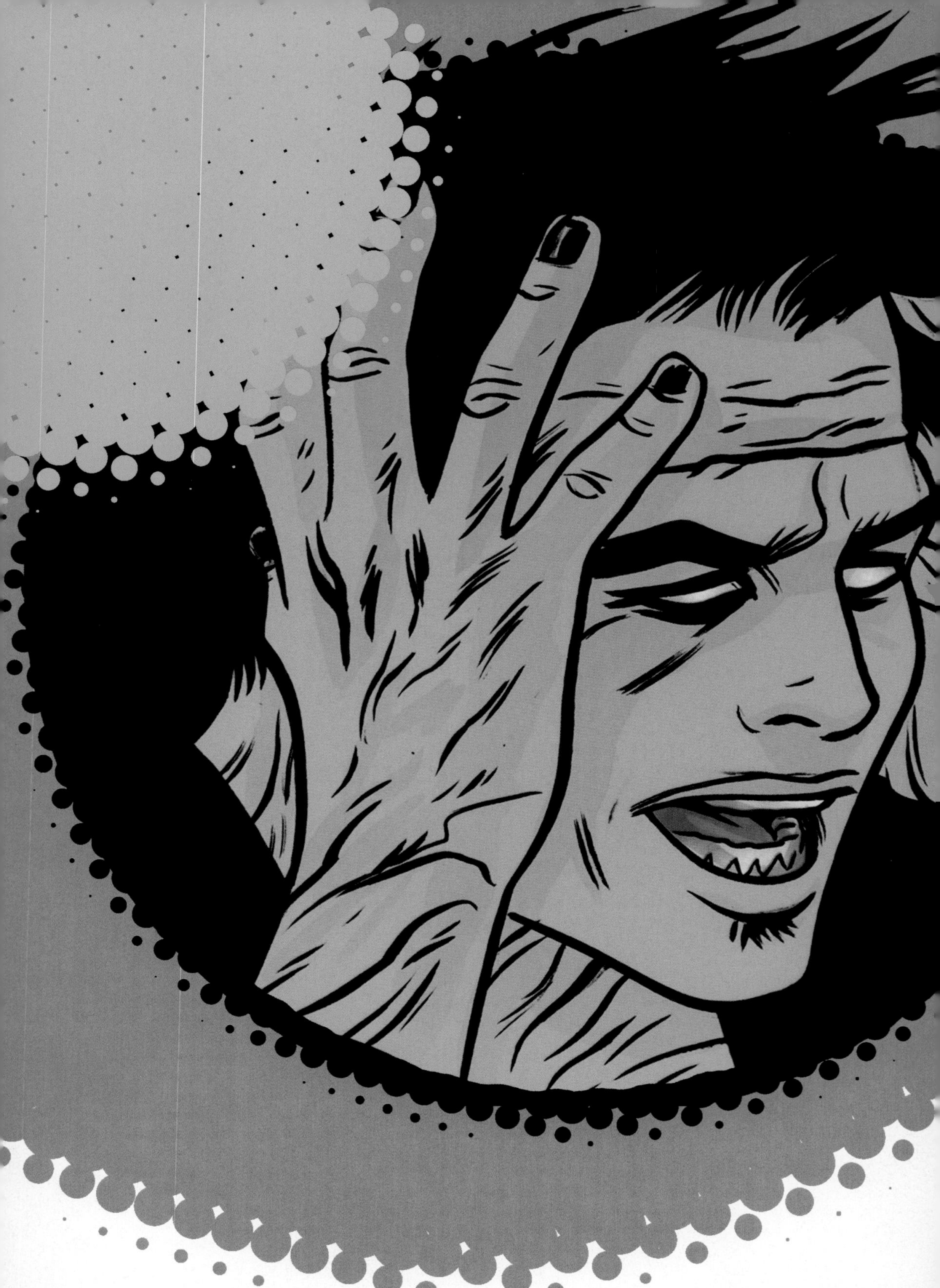

iZombie
repossession

Chris Roberson
Writer

Michael Allred
Art and Covers

J. Bone
Guest Artist – "Mix It Up"

Jim Rugg
Guest Artist – "Monsters of Rock"

Laura Allred
Colorist

Todd Klein
Letterer

iZombie created by **Roberson** and **Allred**

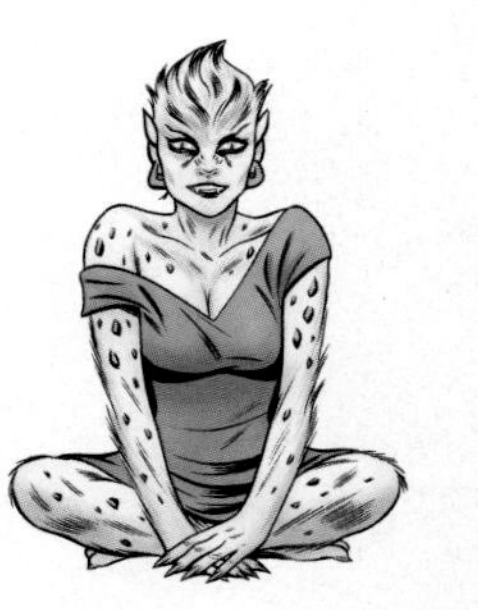

Shelly Bond Editor – Original Series
Gregory Lockard Assistant Editor – Original Series
Robin Wildman Editor
Robbin Brosterman Design Director – Books
Curtis King Jr. Publication Design

Karen Berger Senior VP – Executive Editor, Vertigo
Bob Harras VP – Editor-in-Chief

Diane Nelson President
Dan DiDio and Jim Lee Co-Publishers
Geoff Johns Chief Creative Officer
John Rood Executive VP – Sales, Marketing and Business Development
Amy Genkins Senior VP – Business and Legal Affairs
Nairi Gardiner Senior VP – Finance
Jeff Boison VP – Publishing Operations
Mark Chiarello VP – Art Direction and Design
John Cunningham VP – Marketing
Terri Cunningham VP – Talent Relations and Services
Alison Gill Senior VP – Manufacturing and Operations
Hank Kanalz Senior VP – Digital
Jay Kogan VP – Business and Legal Affairs, Publishing
Jack Mahan VP – Business Affairs, Talent
Nick Napolitano VP – Manufacturing Administration
Sue Pohja VP – Book Sales
Courtney Simmons Senior VP – Publicity
Bob Wayne Senior VP – Sales

iZOMBIE: REPOSSESSION
Published by DC Comics.

DC Comics, 1700 Broadway, New York, NY 10019
A Warner Bros. Entertainment Company.
Printed in the USA. 11/2/12. First Printing.

ISBN: 978-1-4012-3697-7

SUSTAINABLE FORESTRY INITIATIVE
Certified Chain of Custody
At Least 20% Certified Forest Content
www.sfiprogram.org
SFI-01042
APPLIES TO TEXT STOCK ONLY

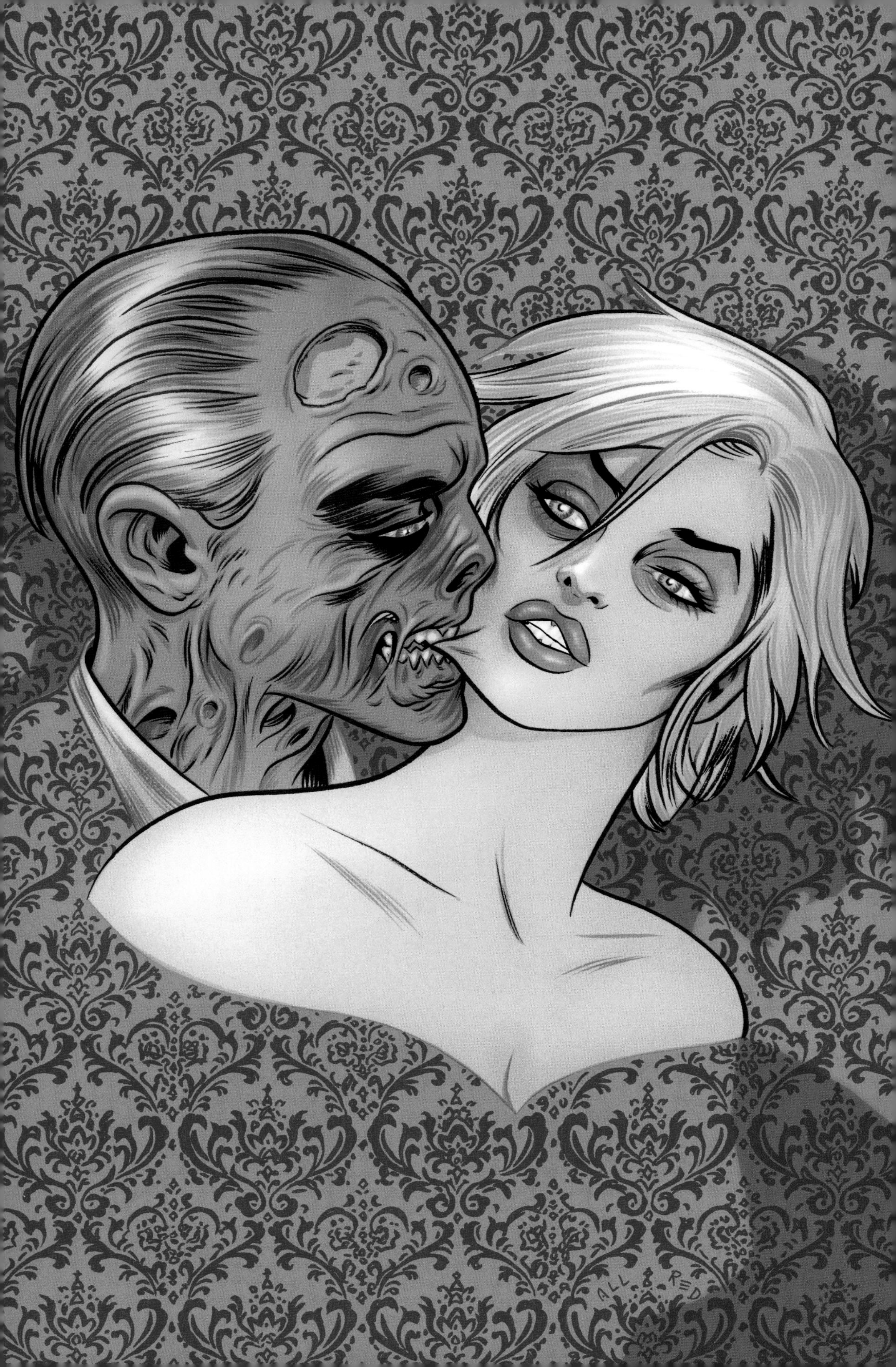
ALL
RED

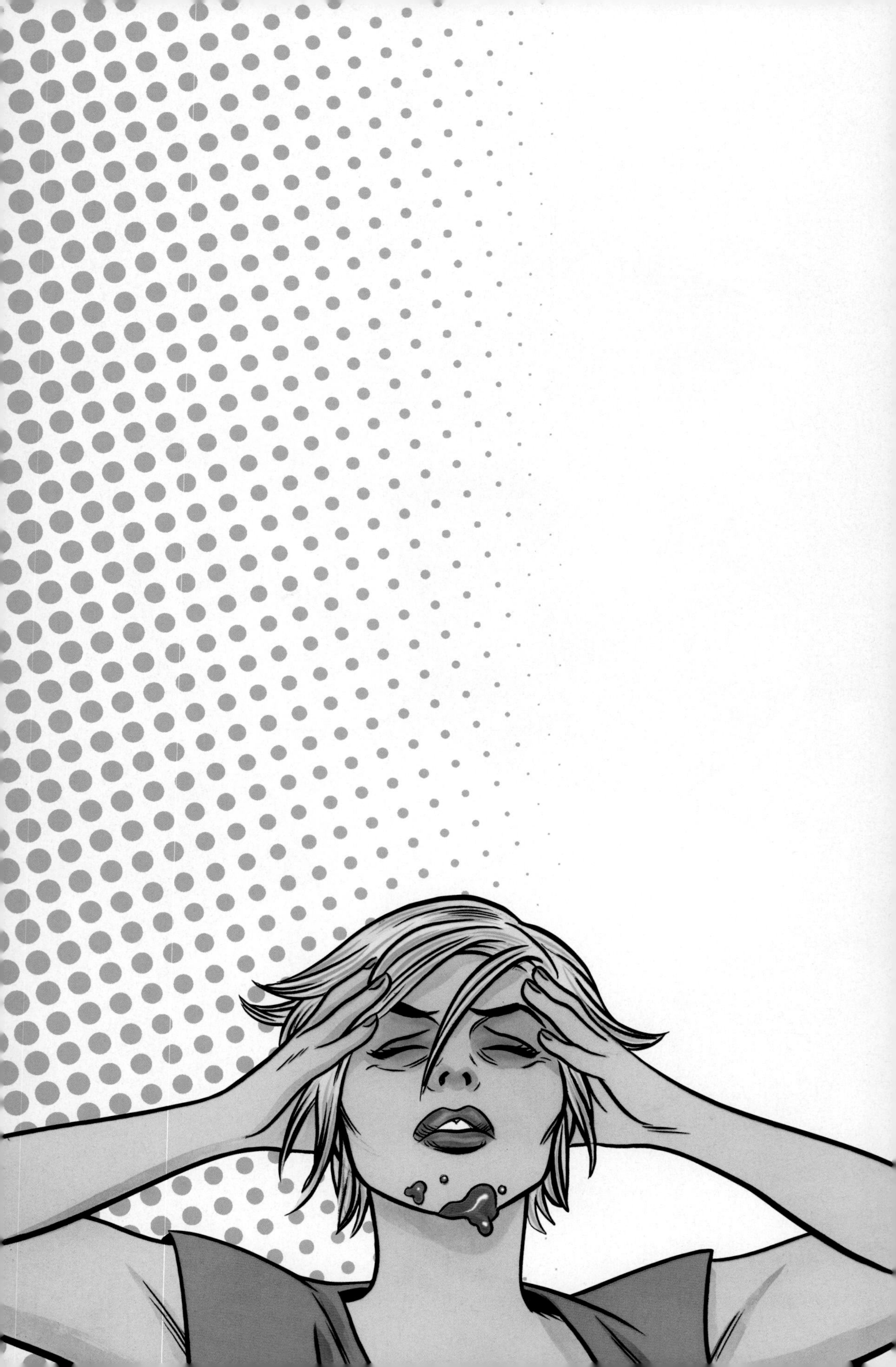

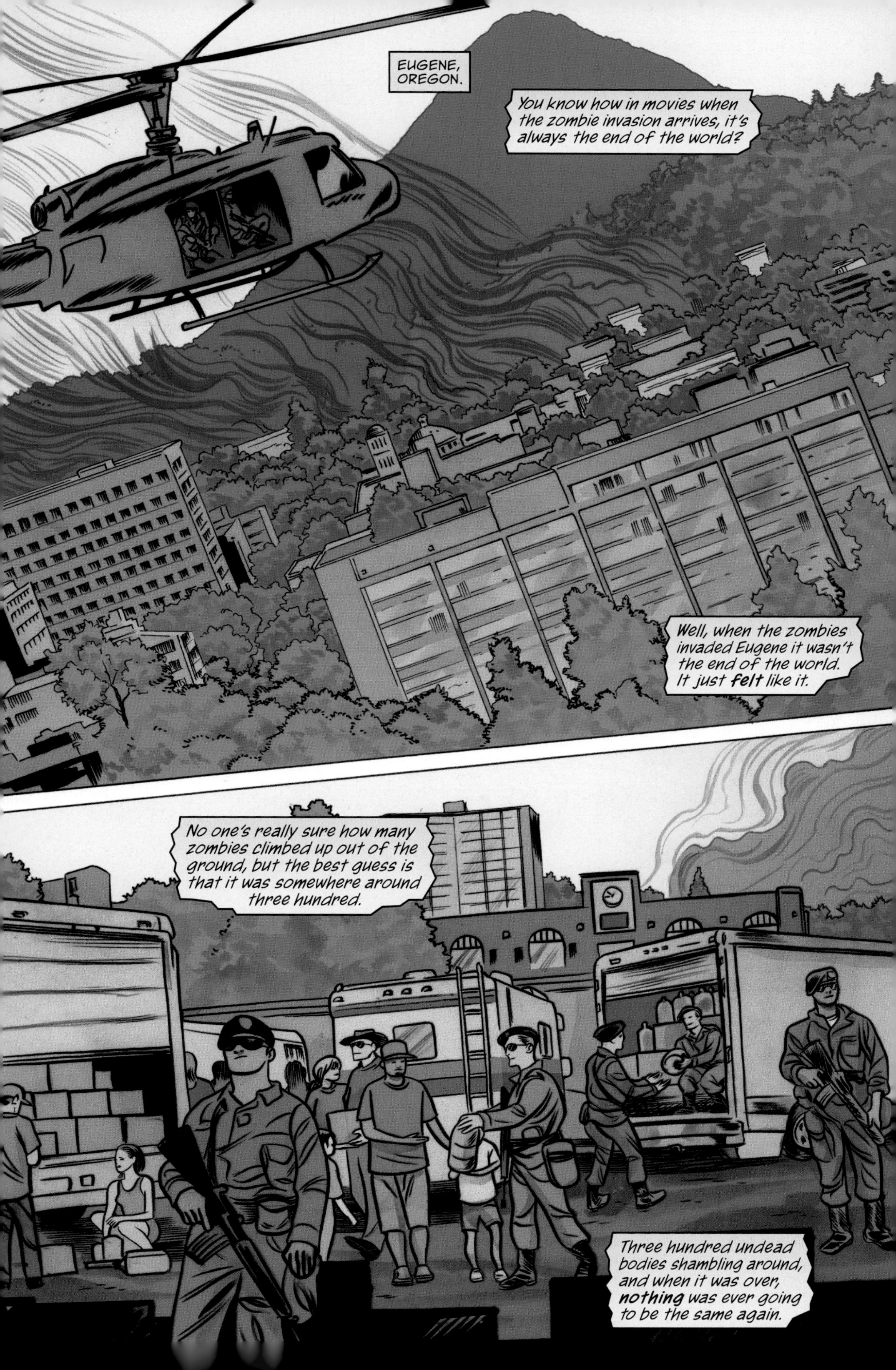
EUGENE, OREGON.
You know how in movies when the zombie invasion arrives, it's always the end of the world?
Well, when the zombies invaded Eugene it wasn't the end of the world. It just **felt** like it.
No one's really sure how many zombies climbed up out of the ground, but the best guess is that it was somewhere around three hundred.
Three hundred undead bodies shambling around, and when it was over, **nothing** was ever going to be the same again.

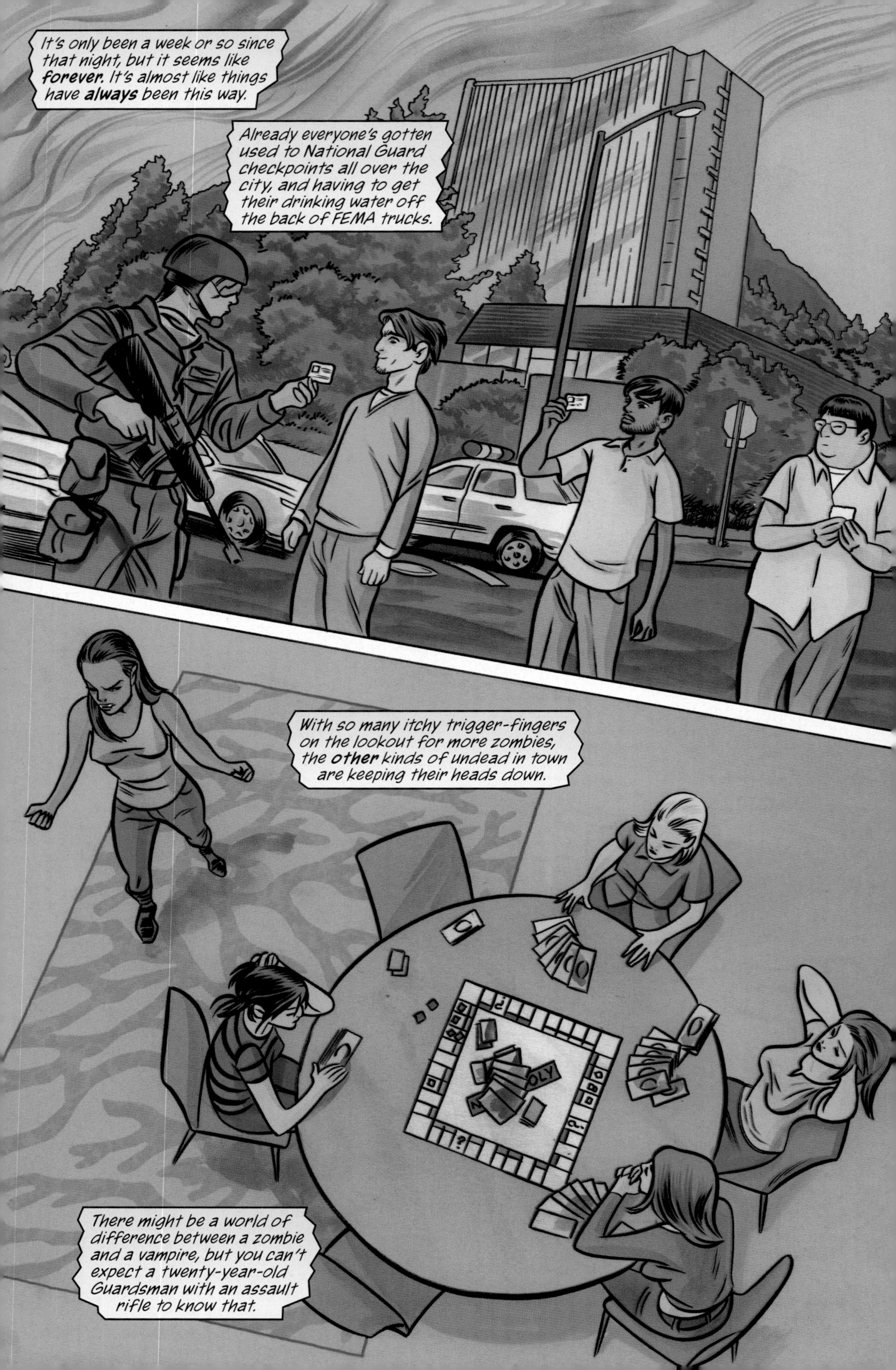
It's only been a week or so since that night, but it seems like **forever.** It's almost like things have **always** been this way.
Already everyone's gotten used to National Guard checkpoints all over the city, and having to get their drinking water off the back of FEMA trucks.
With so many itchy trigger-fingers on the lookout for more zombies, the **other** kinds of undead in town are keeping their heads down.
There might be a world of difference between a zombie and a vampire, but you can't expect a twenty-year-old Guardsman with an assault rifle to know that.

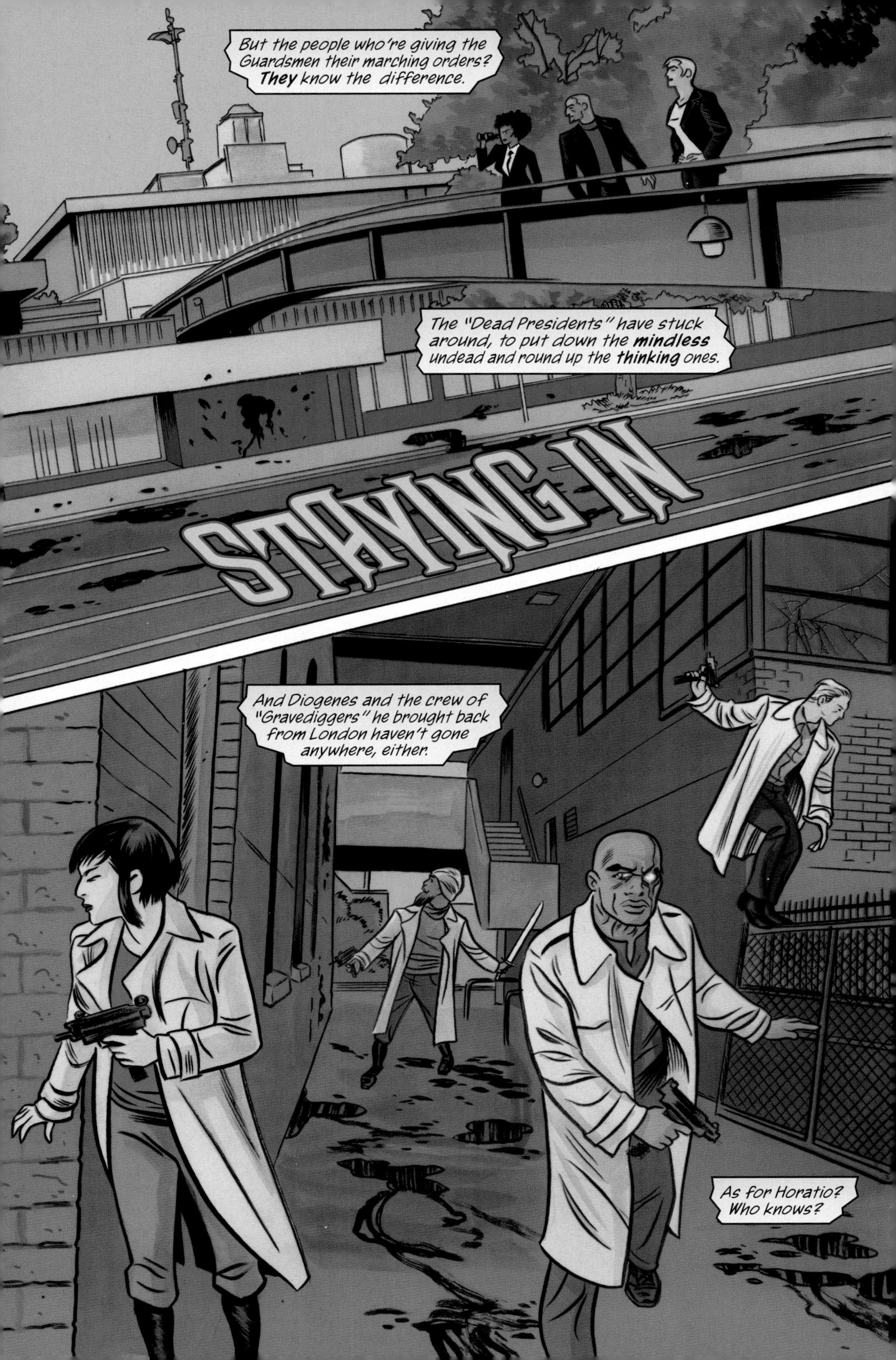
But the people who're giving the Guardsmen their marching orders? They know the difference.
The "Dead Presidents" have stuck around, to put down the mindless undead and round up the thinking ones.
STAYING IN
And Diogenes and the crew of "Gravediggers" he brought back from London haven't gone anywhere, either.
As for Horatio? Who knows?

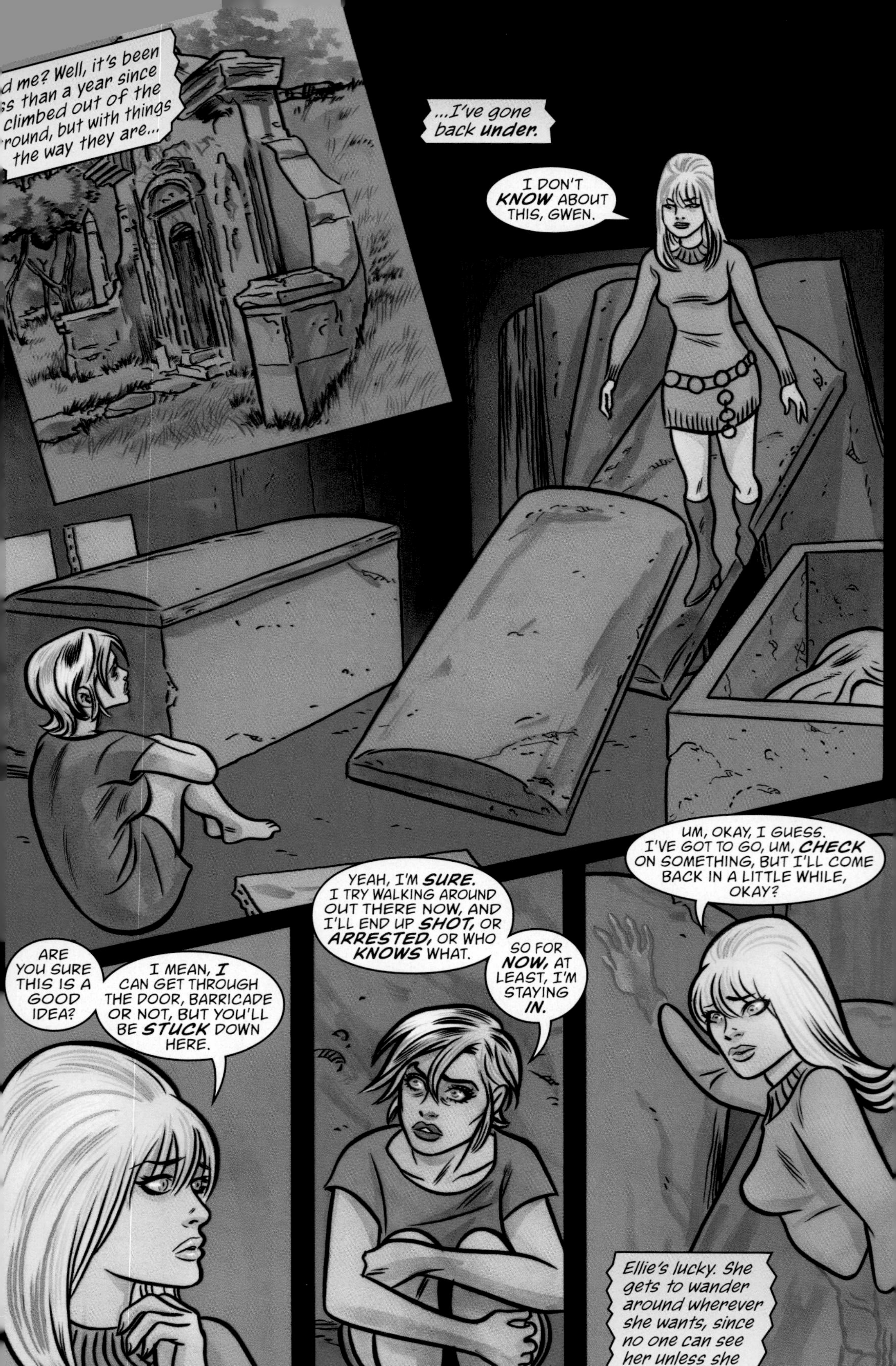

...d me? Well, it's been ...s than a year since ... climbed out of the ...round, but with things the way they are...
...I've gone back under.
I DON'T KNOW ABOUT THIS, GWEN.
ARE YOU SURE THIS IS A GOOD IDEA?
I MEAN, I CAN GET THROUGH THE DOOR, BARRICADE OR NOT, BUT YOU'LL BE STUCK DOWN HERE.
YEAH, I'M SURE. I TRY WALKING AROUND OUT THERE NOW, AND I'LL END UP SHOT, OR ARRESTED, OR WHO KNOWS WHAT.
SO FOR NOW, AT LEAST, I'M STAYING IN.
UM, OKAY, I GUESS. I'VE GOT TO GO, UM, CHECK ON SOMETHING, BUT I'LL COME BACK IN A LITTLE WHILE, OKAY?
Ellie's lucky. She gets to wander around wherever she wants, since no one can see her unless she wants them to.

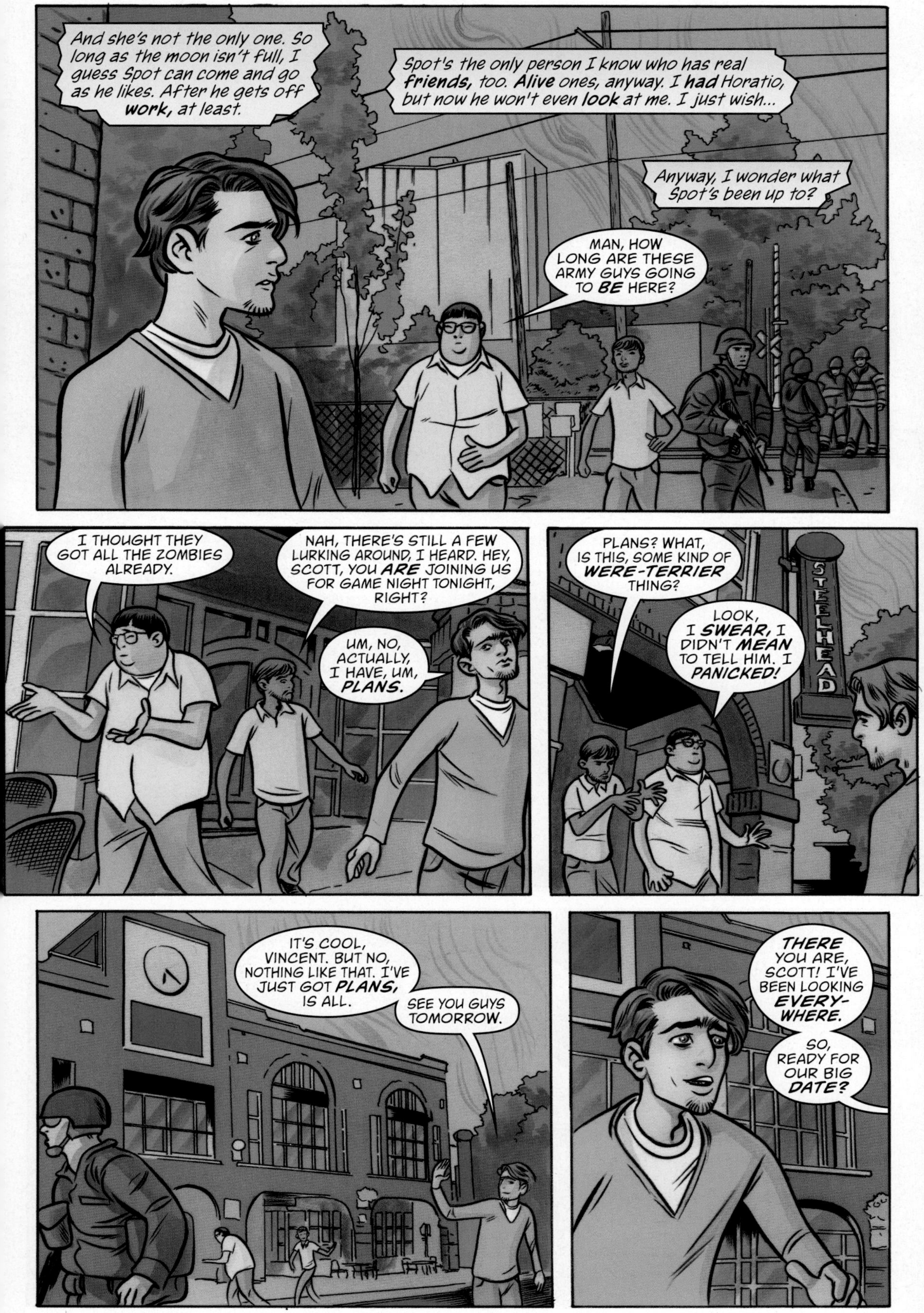

And she's not the only one. So long as the moon isn't full, I guess Spot can come and go as he likes. After he gets off **work**, at least.
Spot's the only person I know who has real **friends**, too. **Alive** ones, anyway. I **had** Horatio, but now he won't even **look** at me. I just wish...
Anyway, I wonder what Spot's been up to?
MAN, HOW LONG ARE THESE ARMY GUYS GOING TO ***BE*** HERE?
I THOUGHT THEY GOT ALL THE ZOMBIES ALREADY.
NAH, THERE'S STILL A FEW LURKING AROUND, I HEARD. HEY, SCOTT, YOU ***ARE*** JOINING US FOR GAME NIGHT TONIGHT, RIGHT?
UM, NO, ACTUALLY, I HAVE, UM, ***PLANS.***
PLANS? WHAT, IS THIS, SOME KIND OF ***WERE-TERRIER*** THING?
STEELHEAD
LOOK, I ***SWEAR,*** I DIDN'T ***MEAN*** TO TELL HIM. I ***PANICKED!***
IT'S COOL, VINCENT. BUT NO, NOTHING LIKE THAT. I'VE JUST GOT ***PLANS,*** IS ALL.
SEE YOU GUYS **TOMORROW.**
THERE YOU ARE, SCOTT! I'VE BEEN LOOKING ***EVERY-WHERE.***
SO, READY FOR OUR BIG ***DATE?***

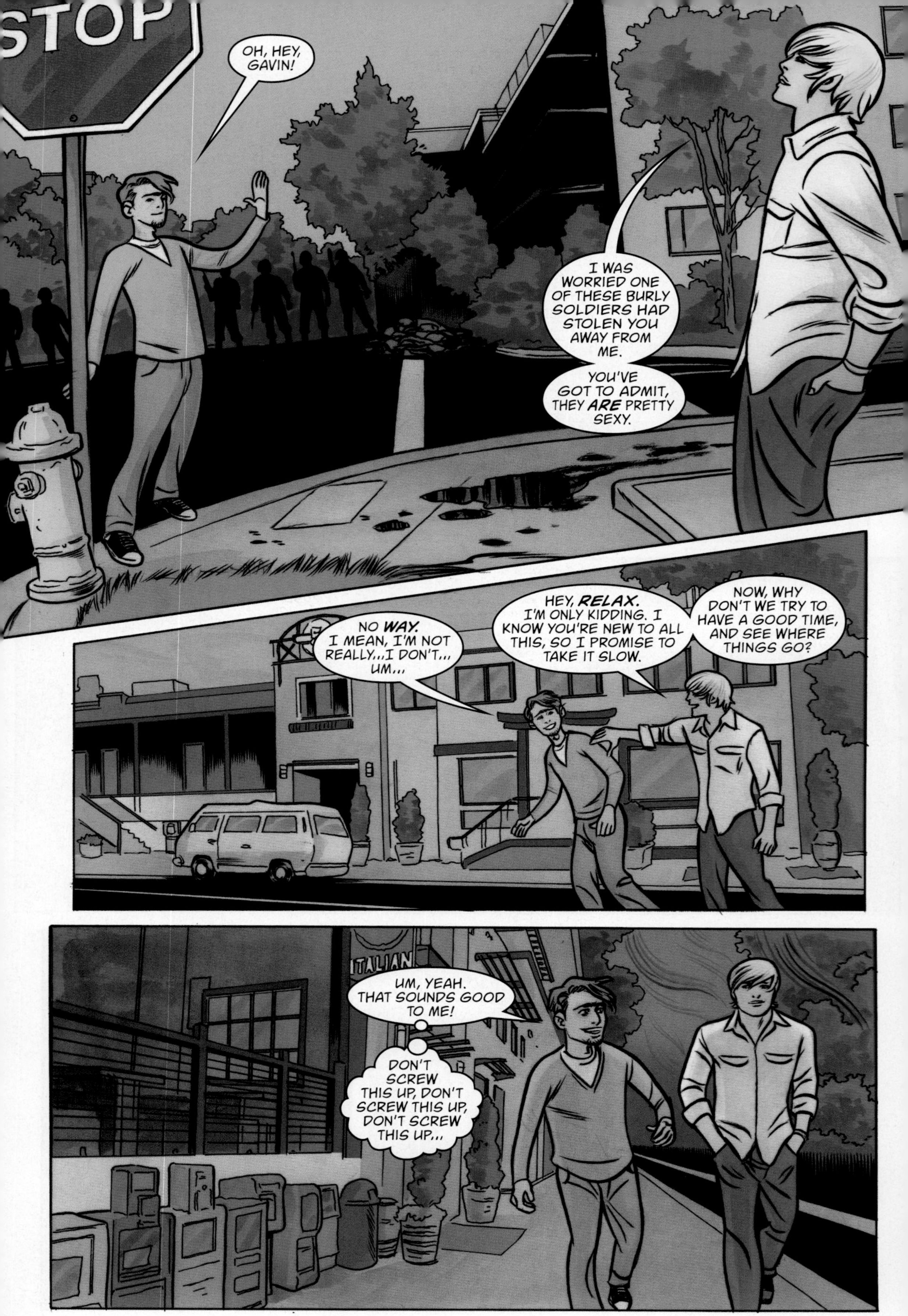
STOP
OH, HEY, GAVIN!
I WAS WORRIED ONE OF THESE BURLY SOLDIERS HAD STOLEN YOU AWAY FROM ME.
YOU'VE GOT TO ADMIT, THEY ARE PRETTY SEXY.
NO WAY. I MEAN, I'M NOT REALLY...I DON'T... UM...
HEY, RELAX. I'M ONLY KIDDING. I KNOW YOU'RE NEW TO ALL THIS, SO I PROMISE TO TAKE IT SLOW.
NOW, WHY DON'T WE TRY TO HAVE A GOOD TIME, AND SEE WHERE THINGS GO?
ITALIAN
UM, YEAH. THAT SOUNDS GOOD TO ME!
DON'T SCREW THIS UP, DON'T SCREW THIS UP, DON'T SCREW THIS UP...

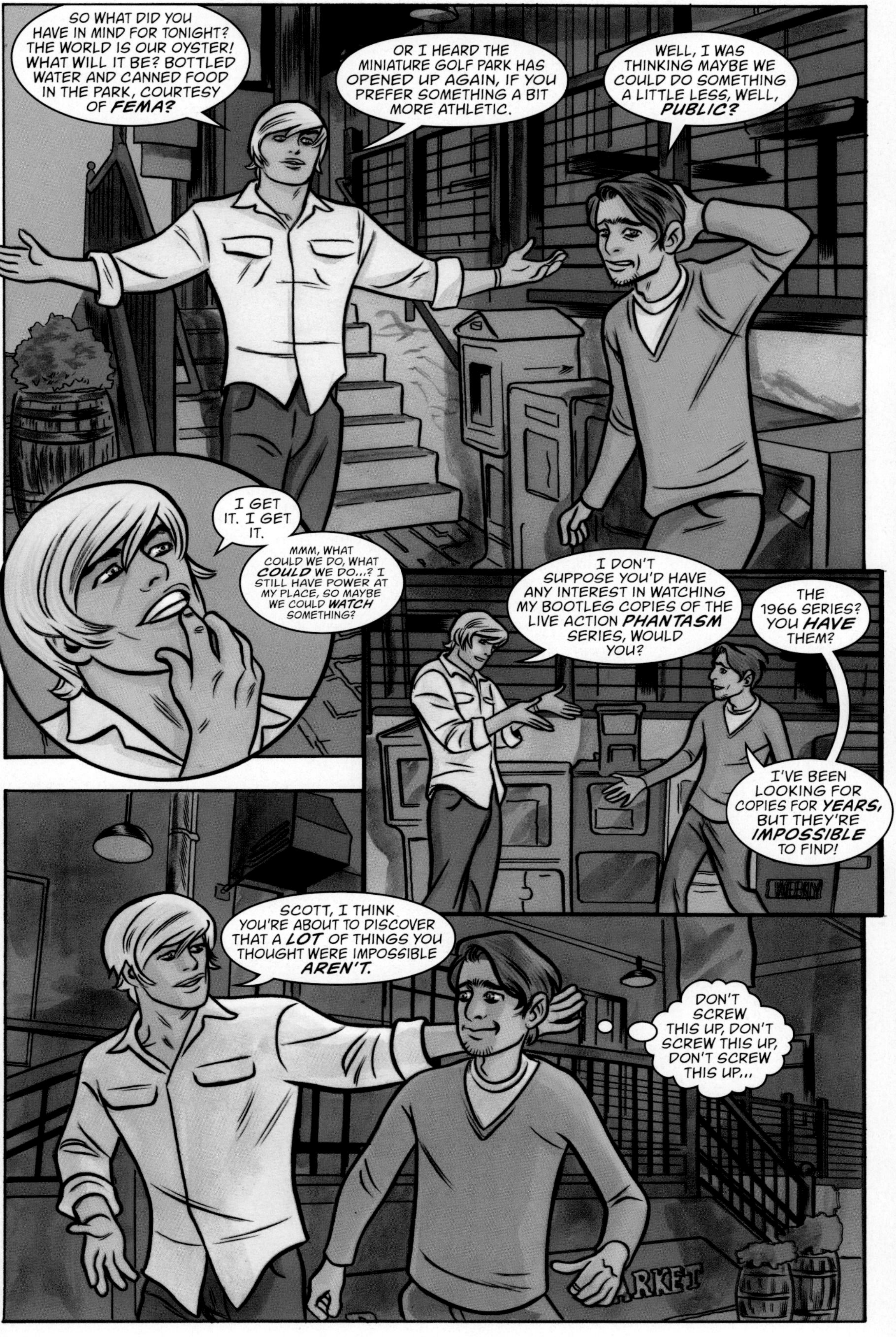
SO WHAT DID YOU HAVE IN MIND FOR TONIGHT? THE WORLD IS OUR OYSTER! WHAT WILL IT BE? BOTTLED WATER AND CANNED FOOD IN THE PARK, COURTESY OF FEMA?
OR I HEARD THE MINIATURE GOLF PARK HAS OPENED UP AGAIN, IF YOU PREFER SOMETHING A BIT MORE ATHLETIC.
WELL, I WAS THINKING MAYBE WE COULD DO SOMETHING A LITTLE LESS, WELL, PUBLIC?
I GET IT. I GET IT.
MMM, WHAT COULD WE DO, WHAT COULD WE DO...? I STILL HAVE POWER AT MY PLACE, SO MAYBE WE COULD WATCH SOMETHING?
I DON'T SUPPOSE YOU'D HAVE ANY INTEREST IN WATCHING MY BOOTLEG COPIES OF THE LIVE ACTION PHANTASM SERIES, WOULD YOU?
THE 1966 SERIES? YOU HAVE THEM?
I'VE BEEN LOOKING FOR COPIES FOR YEARS, BUT THEY'RE IMPOSSIBLE TO FIND!
SCOTT, I THINK YOU'RE ABOUT TO DISCOVER THAT A LOT OF THINGS YOU THOUGHT WERE IMPOSSIBLE AREN'T.
DON'T SCREW THIS UP, DON'T SCREW THIS UP, DON'T SCREW THIS UP...

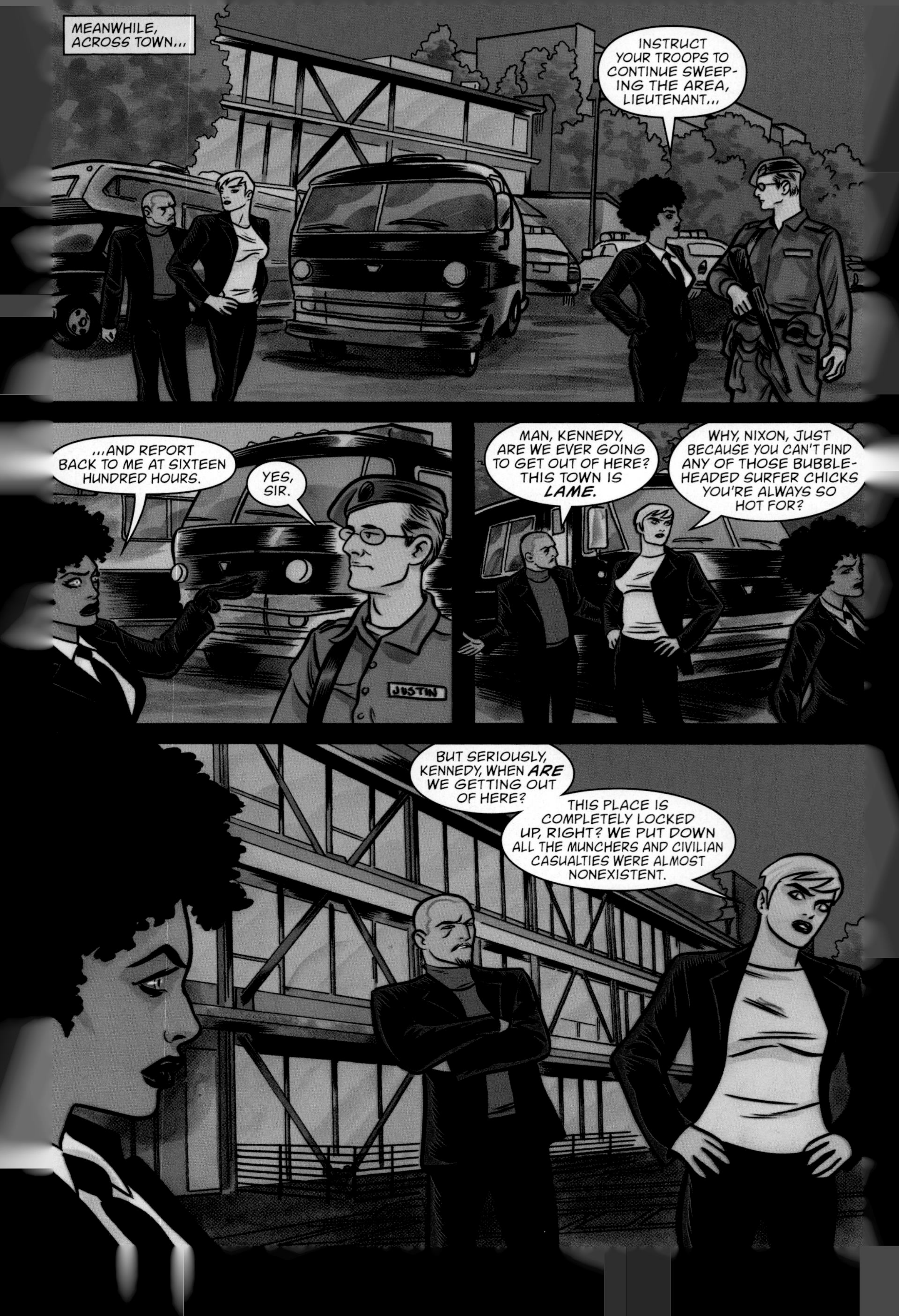
MEANWHILE, ACROSS TOWN...
INSTRUCT YOUR TROOPS TO CONTINUE SWEEPING THE AREA, LIEUTENANT...
...AND REPORT BACK TO ME AT SIXTEEN HUNDRED HOURS.
YES, SIR.
JUSTIN
MAN, KENNEDY, ARE WE EVER GOING TO GET OUT OF HERE? THIS TOWN IS *LAME.*
WHY, NIXON, JUST BECAUSE YOU CAN'T FIND ANY OF THOSE BUBBLE-HEADED SURFER CHICKS YOU'RE ALWAYS SO HOT FOR?
BUT SERIOUSLY, KENNEDY, WHEN *ARE* WE GETTING OUT OF HERE?
THIS PLACE IS COMPLETELY LOCKED UP, RIGHT? WE PUT DOWN ALL THE MUNCHERS AND CIVILIAN CASUALTIES WERE ALMOST NONEXISTENT.

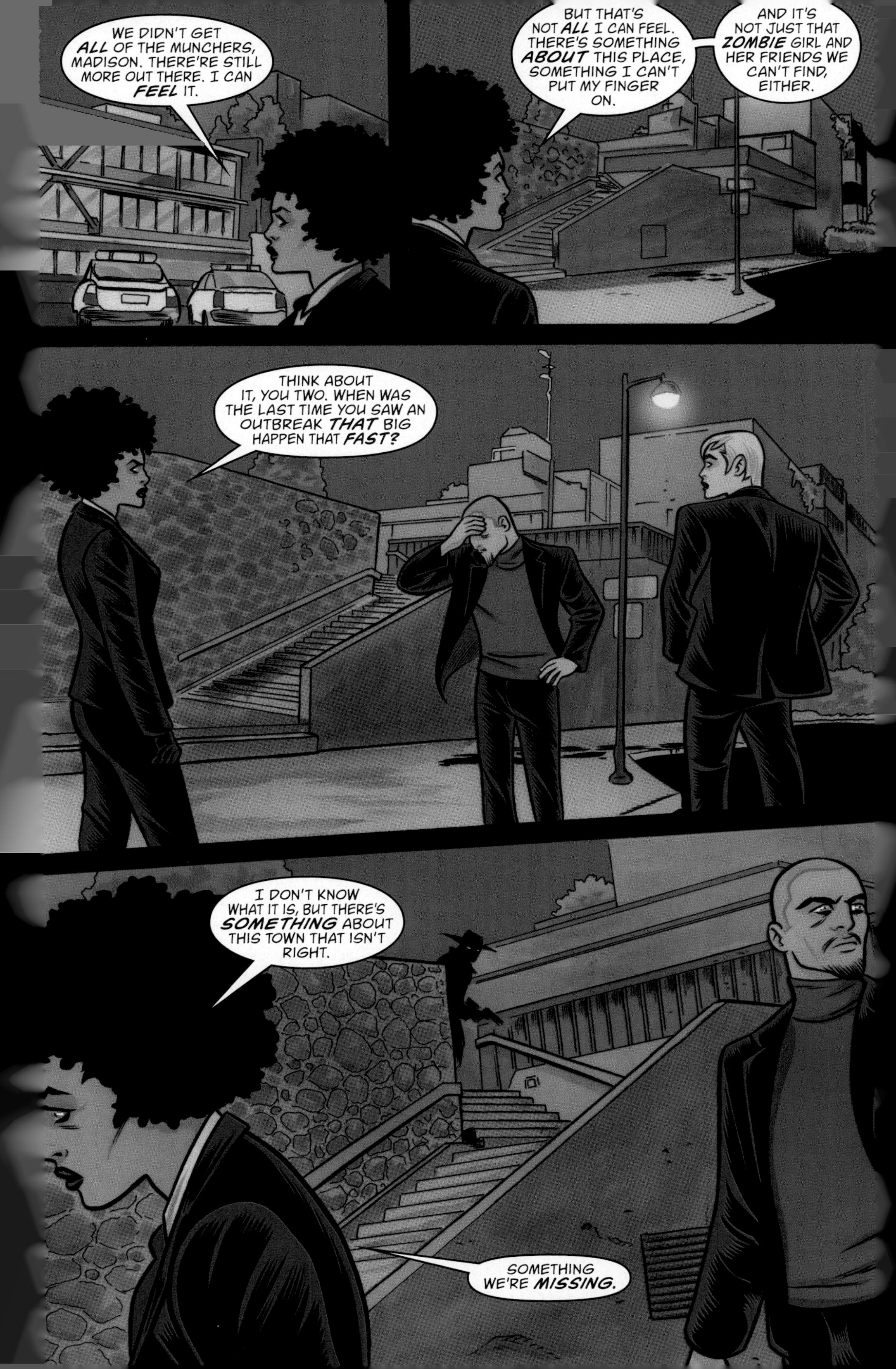
WE DIDN'T GET ALL OF THE MUNCHERS, MADISON. THERE'RE STILL MORE OUT THERE. I CAN FEEL IT.
BUT THAT'S NOT ALL I CAN FEEL. THERE'S SOMETHING ABOUT THIS PLACE, SOMETHING I CAN'T PUT MY FINGER ON.
AND IT'S NOT JUST THAT ZOMBIE GIRL AND HER FRIENDS WE CAN'T FIND, EITHER.
THINK ABOUT IT, YOU TWO. WHEN WAS THE LAST TIME YOU SAW AN OUTBREAK THAT BIG HAPPEN THAT FAST?
I DON'T KNOW WHAT IT IS, BUT THERE'S SOMETHING ABOUT THIS TOWN THAT ISN'T RIGHT.
SOMETHING WE'RE MISSING.

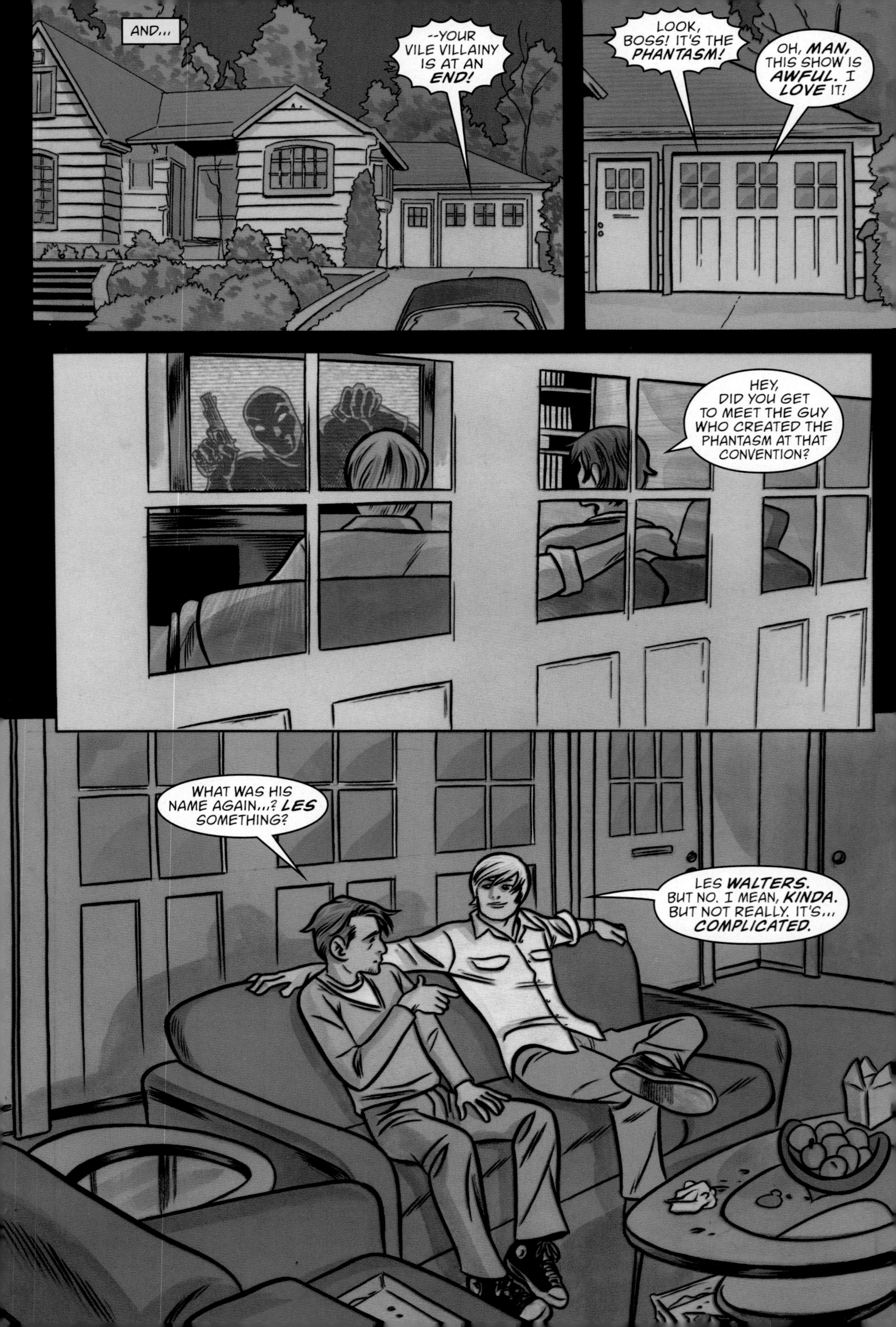
AND...
--YOUR VILE VILLAINY IS AT AN END!
LOOK, BOSS! IT'S THE PHANTASM!
OH, MAN, THIS SHOW IS AWFUL. I LOVE IT!
HEY, DID YOU GET TO MEET THE GUY WHO CREATED THE PHANTASM AT THAT CONVENTION?
WHAT WAS HIS NAME AGAIN...? LES SOMETHING?
LES WALTERS. BUT NO. I MEAN, KINDA. BUT NOT REALLY. IT'S... COMPLICATED.

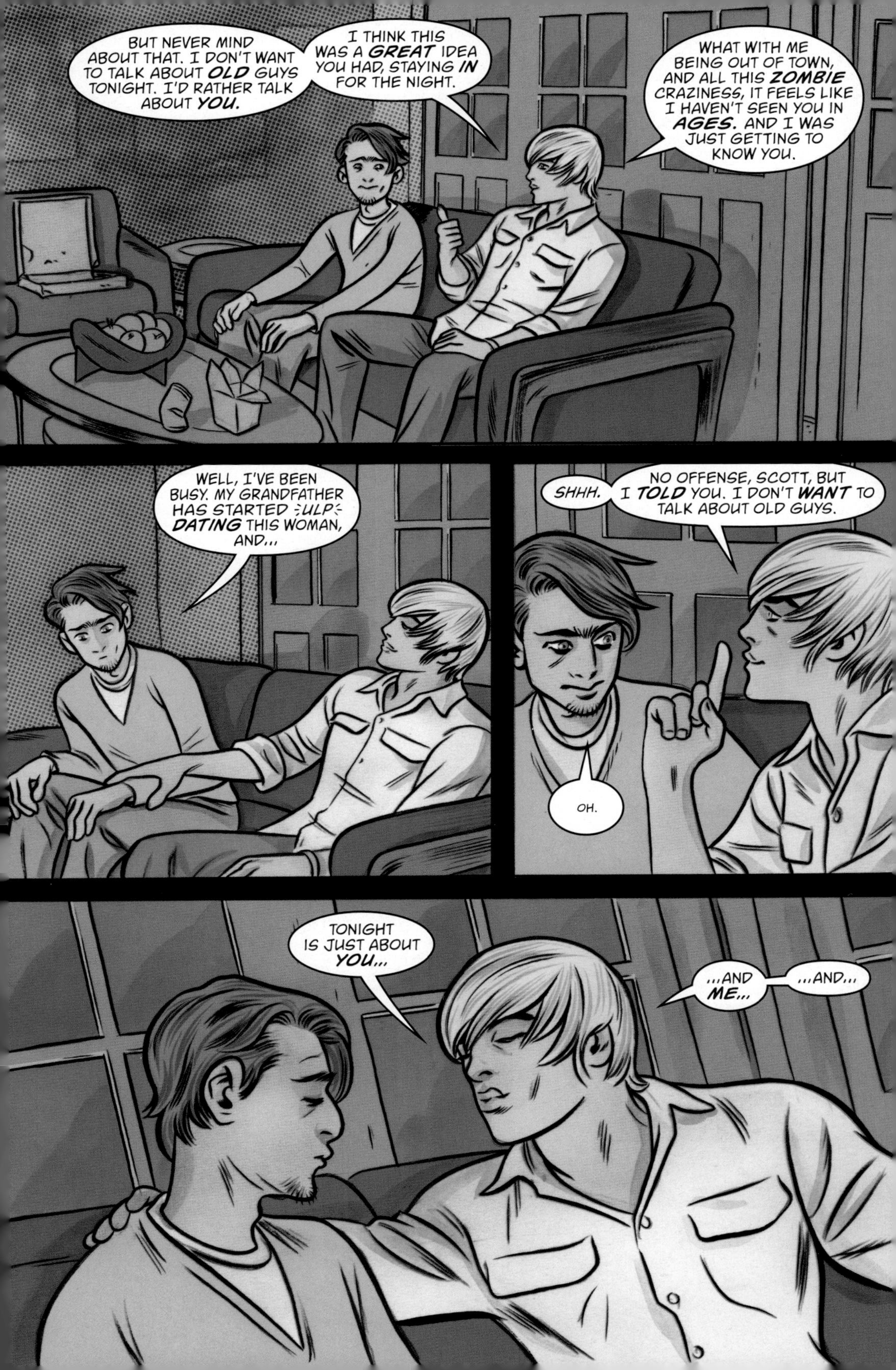
BUT NEVER MIND ABOUT THAT. I DON'T WANT TO TALK ABOUT OLD GUYS TONIGHT. I'D RATHER TALK ABOUT YOU.
I THINK THIS WAS A GREAT IDEA YOU HAD, STAYING IN FOR THE NIGHT.
WHAT WITH ME BEING OUT OF TOWN, AND ALL THIS ZOMBIE CRAZINESS, IT FEELS LIKE I HAVEN'T SEEN YOU IN AGES. AND I WAS JUST GETTING TO KNOW YOU.
WELL, I'VE BEEN BUSY. MY GRANDFATHER HAS STARTED -ULP- DATING THIS WOMAN, AND...
SHHH.
NO OFFENSE, SCOTT, BUT I TOLD YOU. I DON'T WANT TO TALK ABOUT OLD GUYS.
OH.
TONIGHT IS JUST ABOUT YOU...
...AND ME...
...AND...

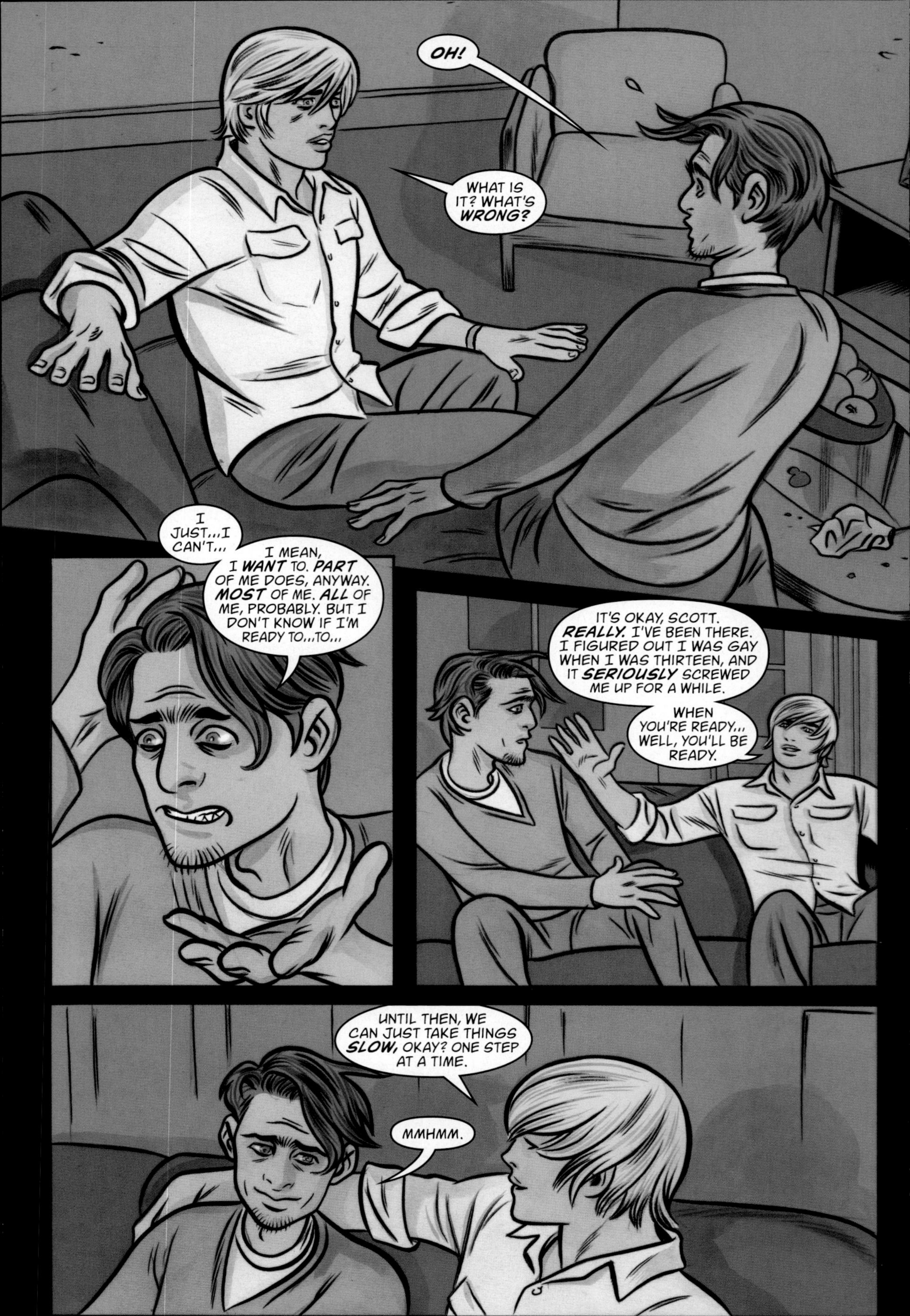
OH!
WHAT IS IT? WHAT'S WRONG?
I JUST...I CAN'T...
I MEAN, I WANT TO. PART OF ME DOES, ANYWAY. MOST OF ME. ALL OF ME, PROBABLY. BUT I DON'T KNOW IF I'M READY TO...TO...
IT'S OKAY, SCOTT. REALLY. I'VE BEEN THERE. I FIGURED OUT I WAS GAY WHEN I WAS THIRTEEN, AND IT SERIOUSLY SCREWED ME UP FOR A WHILE.
WHEN YOU'RE READY... WELL, YOU'LL BE READY.
UNTIL THEN, WE CAN JUST TAKE THINGS SLOW, OKAY? ONE STEP AT A TIME.
MMHMM.

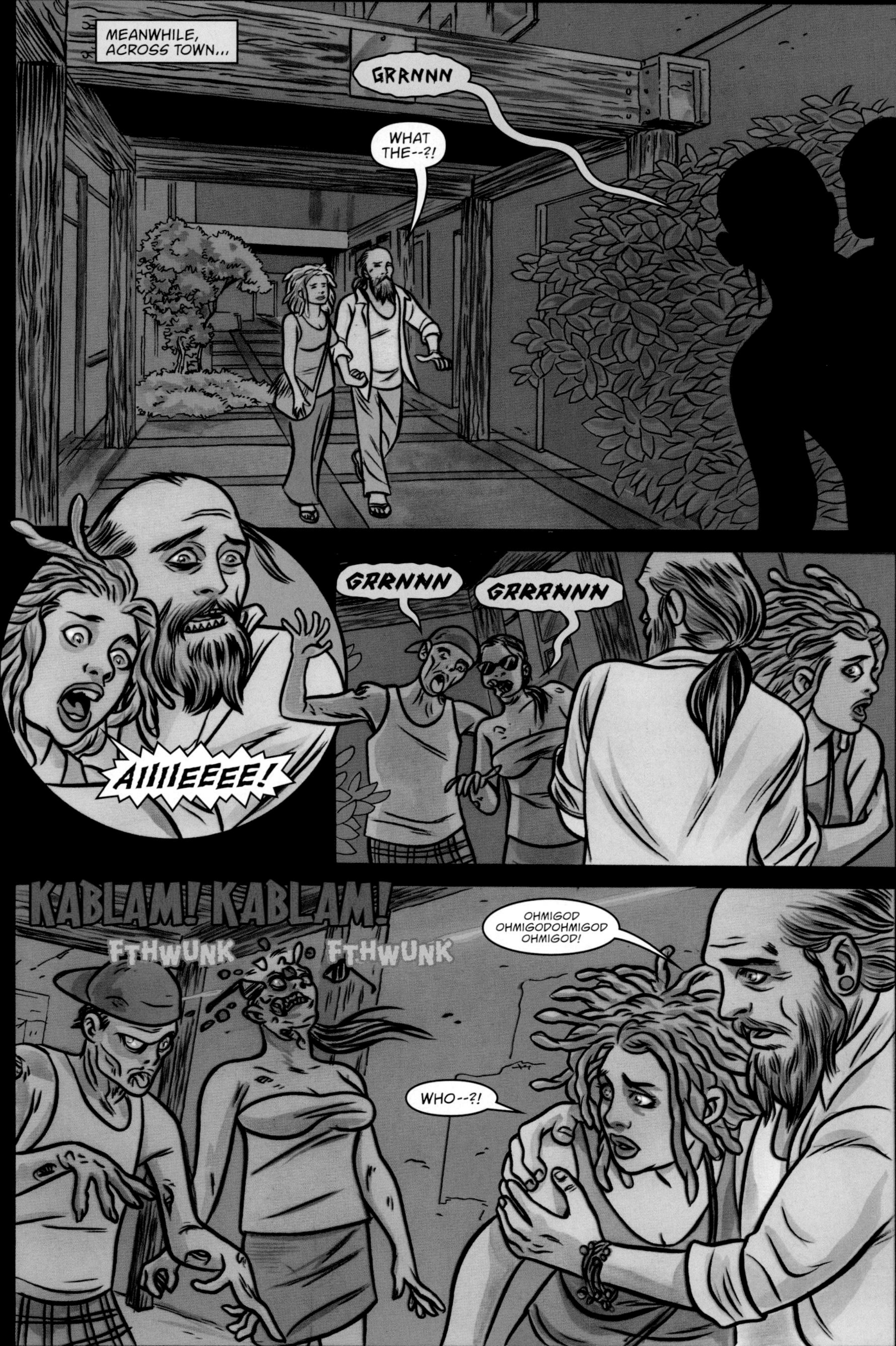
MEANWHILE, ACROSS TOWN...
GRRNNN
WHAT THE--?!
AIIIIEEEE!
GRRNNN
GRRRNNN
KABLAM! KABLAM!
FTHWUNK
FTHWUNK
OHMIGOD OHMIGODOHMIGOD OHMIGOD!
WHO--?!

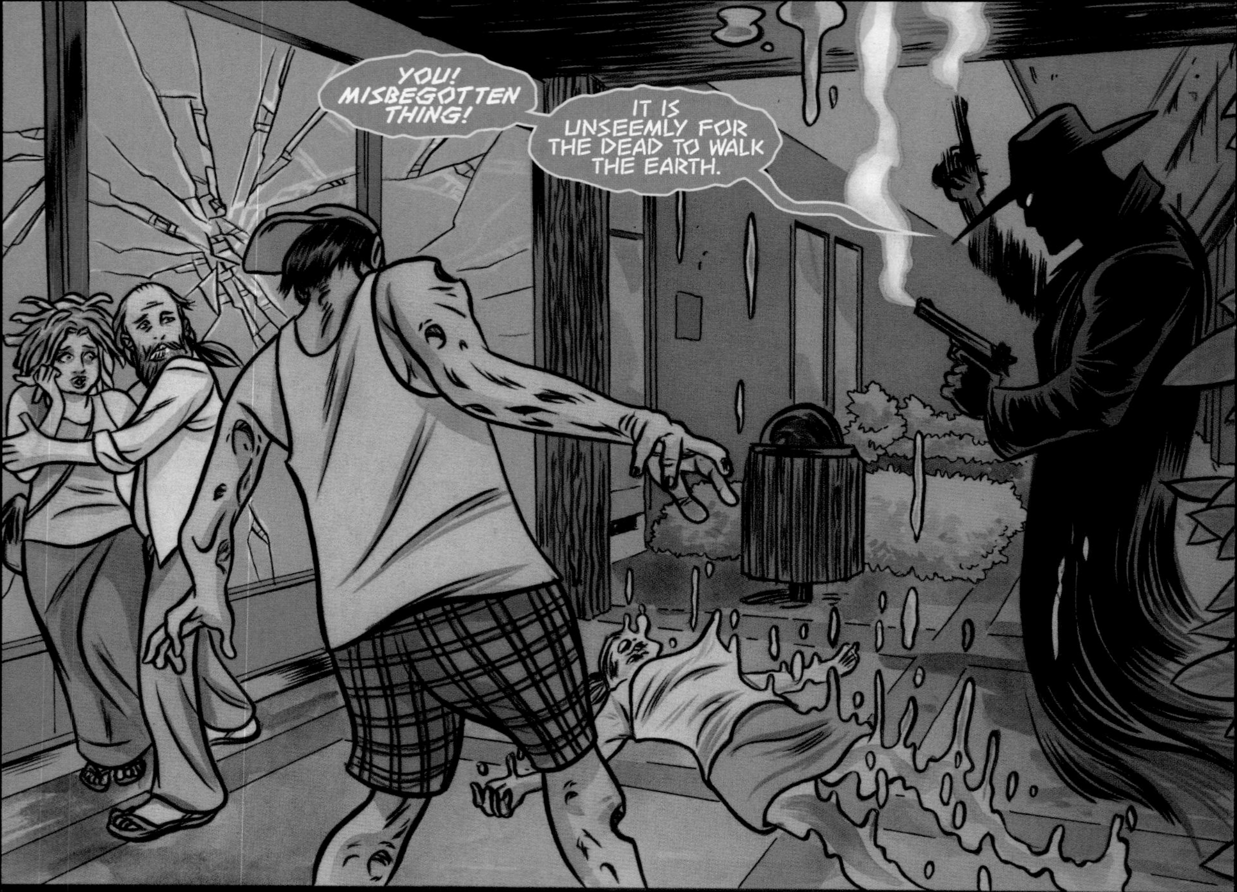
YOU! MISBEGOTTEN THING!
IT IS UNSEEMLY FOR THE DEAD TO WALK THE EARTH.

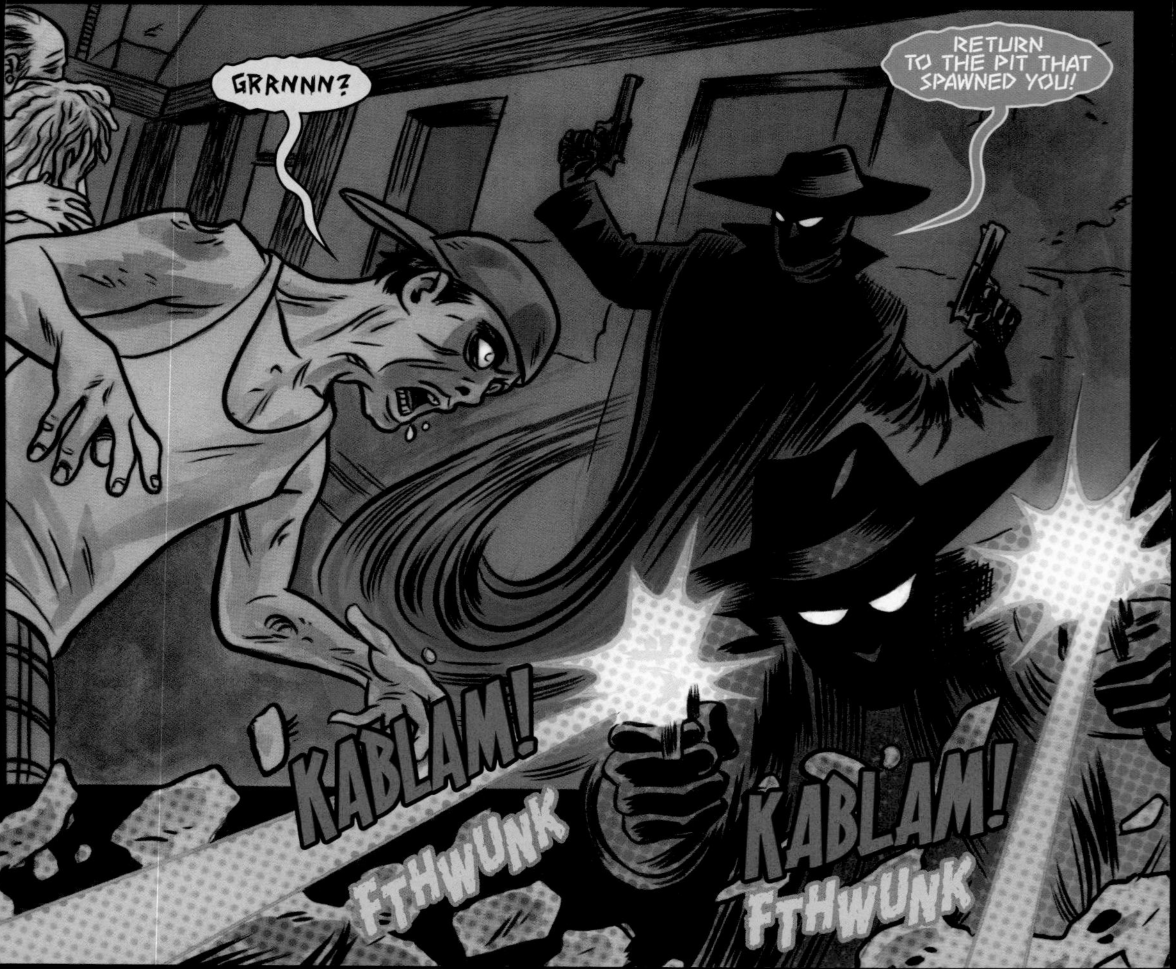
GRRNNN?
RETURN TO THE PIT THAT SPAWNED YOU!
KABLAM!
FTHWUNK
KABLAM!
FTHWUNK

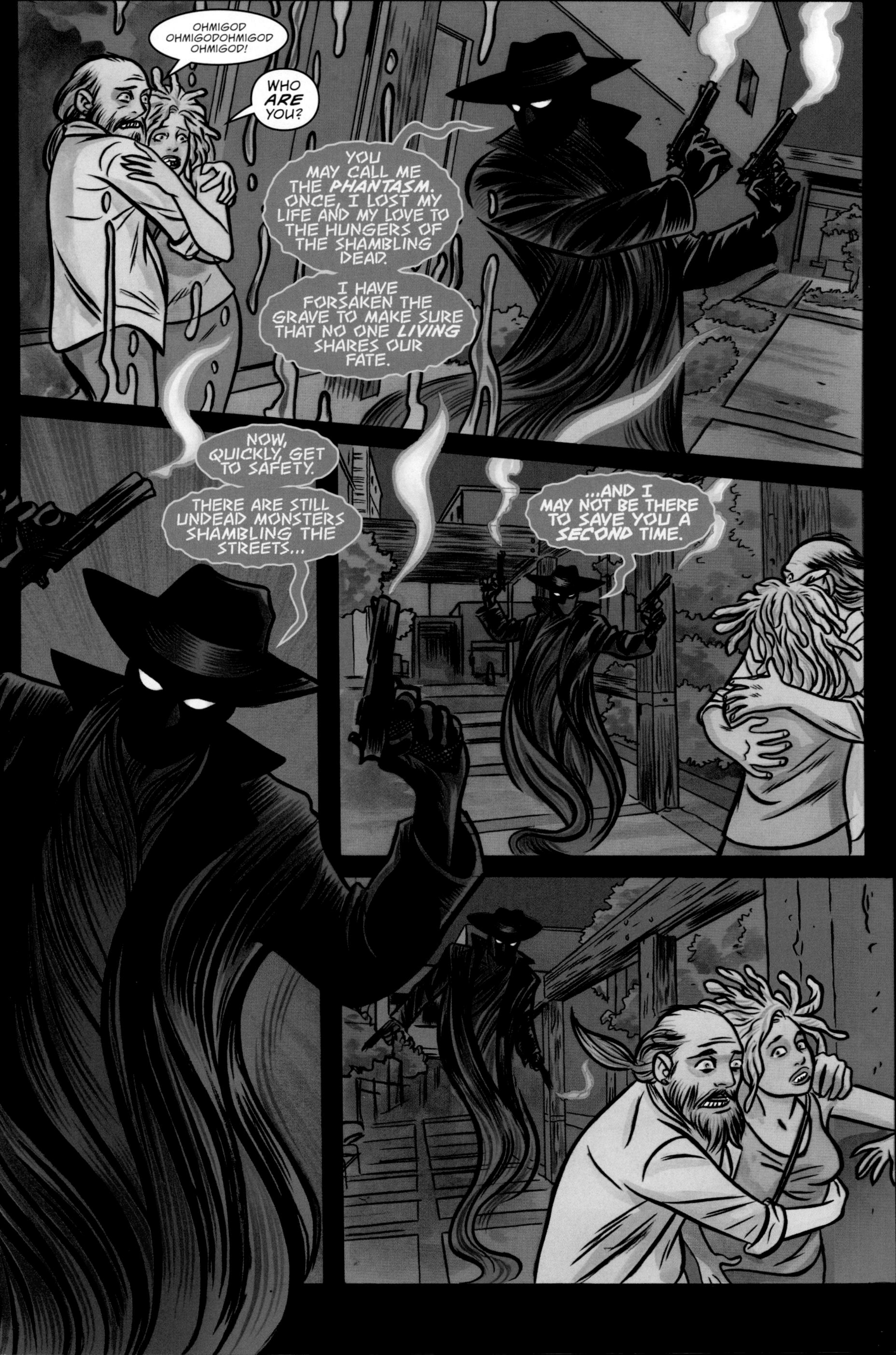
OHMIGOD OHMIGODOHMIGOD OHMIGOD!
WHO ARE YOU?
YOU MAY CALL ME THE PHANTASM. ONCE, I LOST MY LIFE AND MY LOVE TO THE HUNGERS OF THE SHAMBLING DEAD.
I HAVE FORSAKEN THE GRAVE TO MAKE SURE THAT NO ONE LIVING SHARES OUR FATE.
NOW, QUICKLY, GET TO SAFETY.
THERE ARE STILL UNDEAD MONSTERS SHAMBLING THE STREETS...
...AND I MAY NOT BE THERE TO SAVE YOU A SECOND TIME.

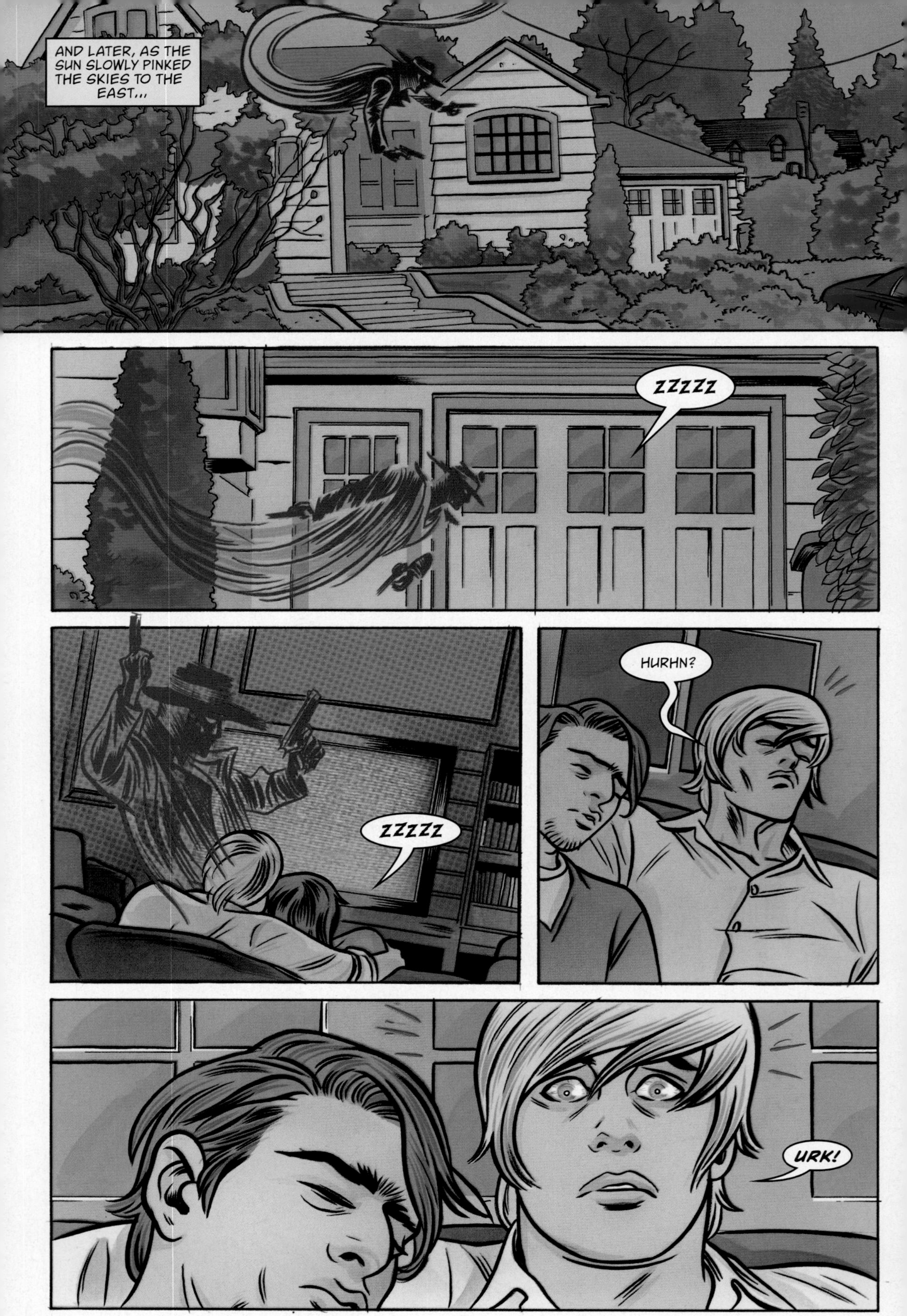
AND LATER, AS THE SUN SLOWLY PINKED THE SKIES TO THE EAST...
ZZZZZ
ZZZZZ
HURHN?
URK!

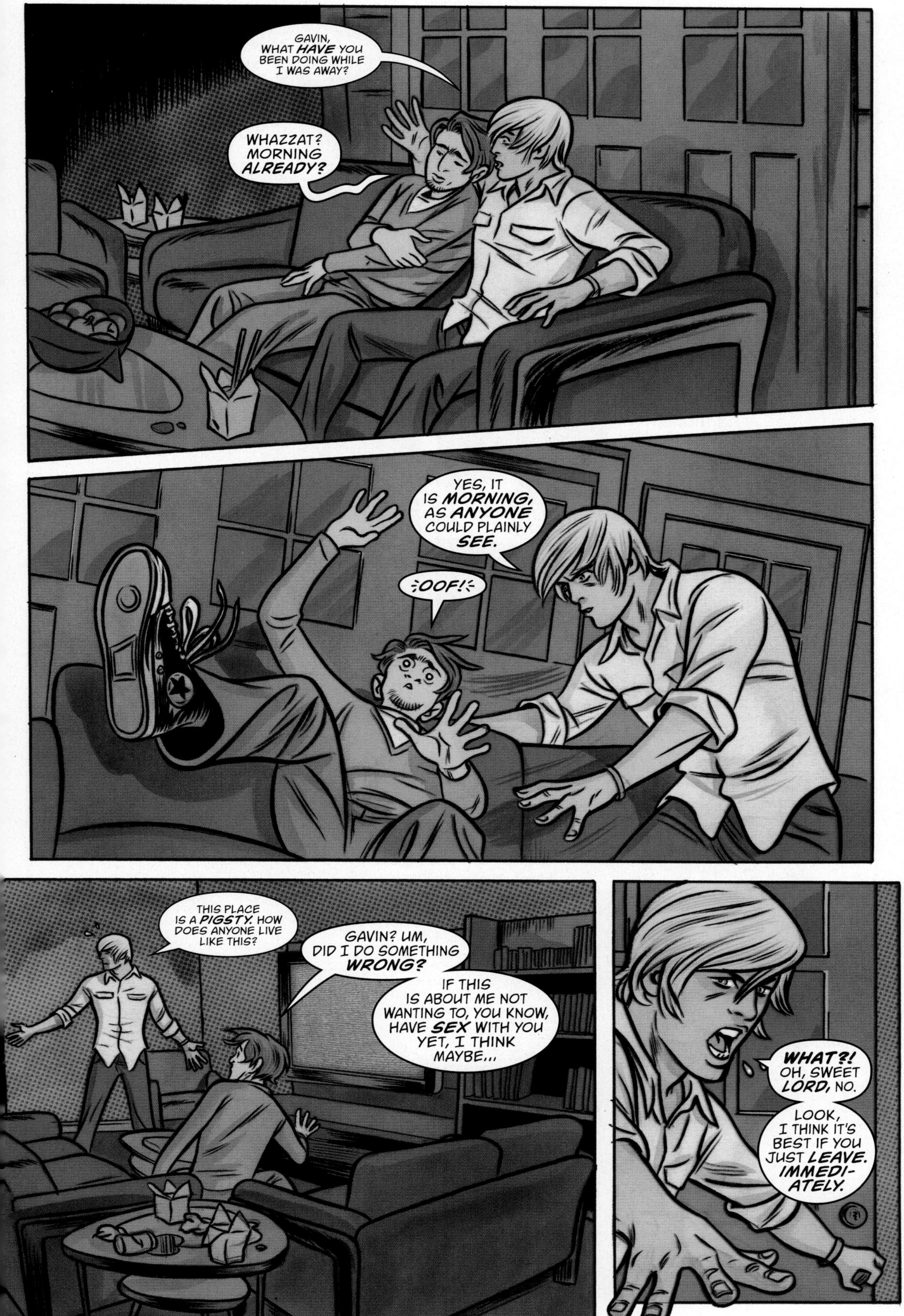
GAVIN, WHAT HAVE YOU BEEN DOING WHILE I WAS AWAY?
WHAZZAT? MORNING ALREADY?
YES, IT IS MORNING, AS ANYONE COULD PLAINLY SEE.
OOF!
THIS PLACE IS A PIGSTY. HOW DOES ANYONE LIVE LIKE THIS?
GAVIN? UM, DID I DO SOMETHING WRONG?
IF THIS IS ABOUT ME NOT WANTING TO, YOU KNOW, HAVE SEX WITH YOU YET, I THINK MAYBE...
WHAT?! OH, SWEET LORD, NO.
LOOK, I THINK IT'S BEST IF YOU JUST LEAVE. IMMEDI-ATELY.

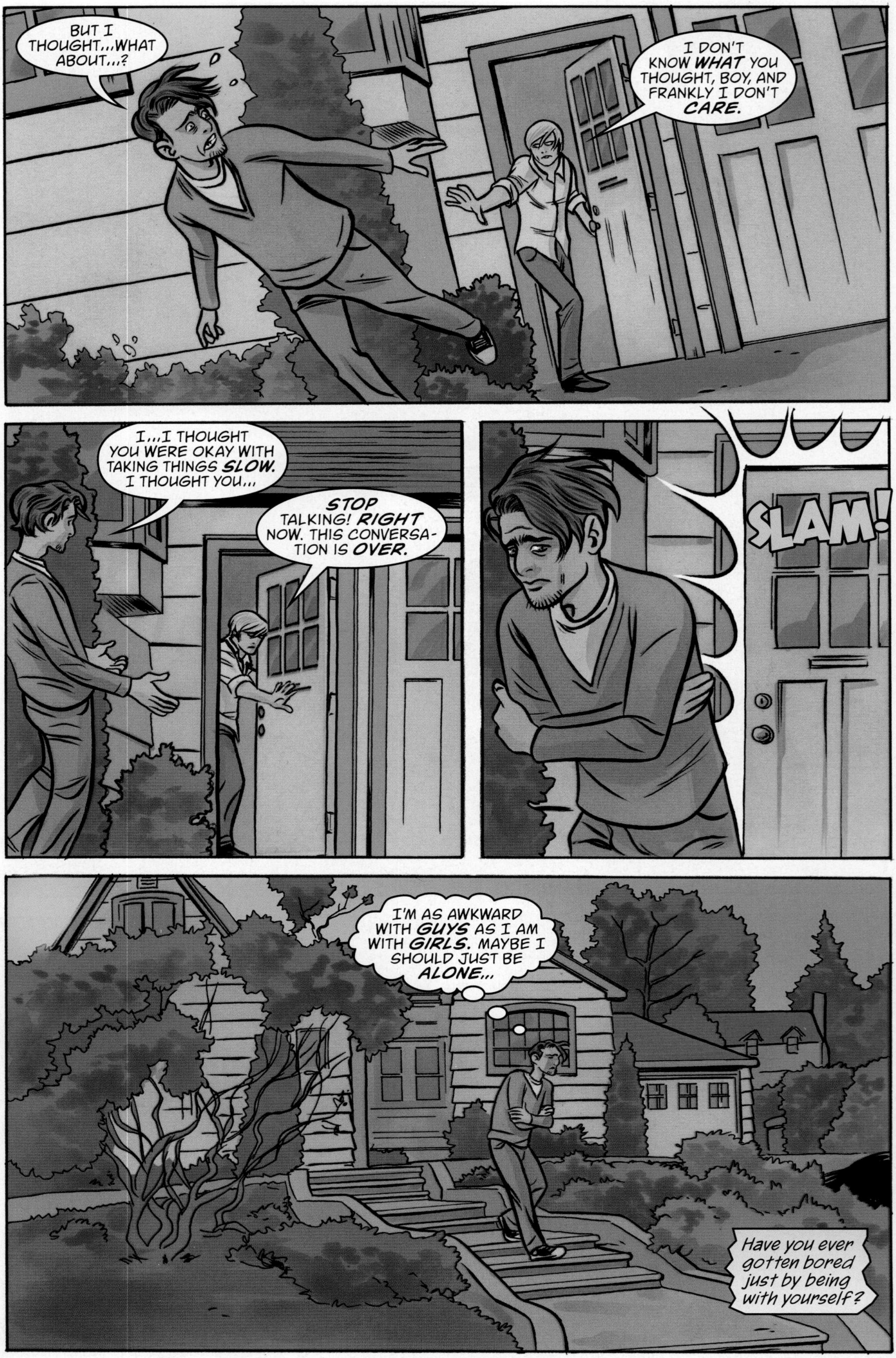

BUT I THOUGHT...WHAT ABOUT...?
I DON'T KNOW WHAT YOU THOUGHT, BOY, AND FRANKLY I DON'T CARE.
I...I THOUGHT YOU WERE OKAY WITH TAKING THINGS SLOW. I THOUGHT YOU...
STOP TALKING! RIGHT NOW. THIS CONVERSATION IS OVER.
SLAM!
I'M AS AWKWARD WITH GUYS AS I AM WITH GIRLS. MAYBE I SHOULD JUST BE ALONE...
Have you ever gotten bored just by being with yourself?

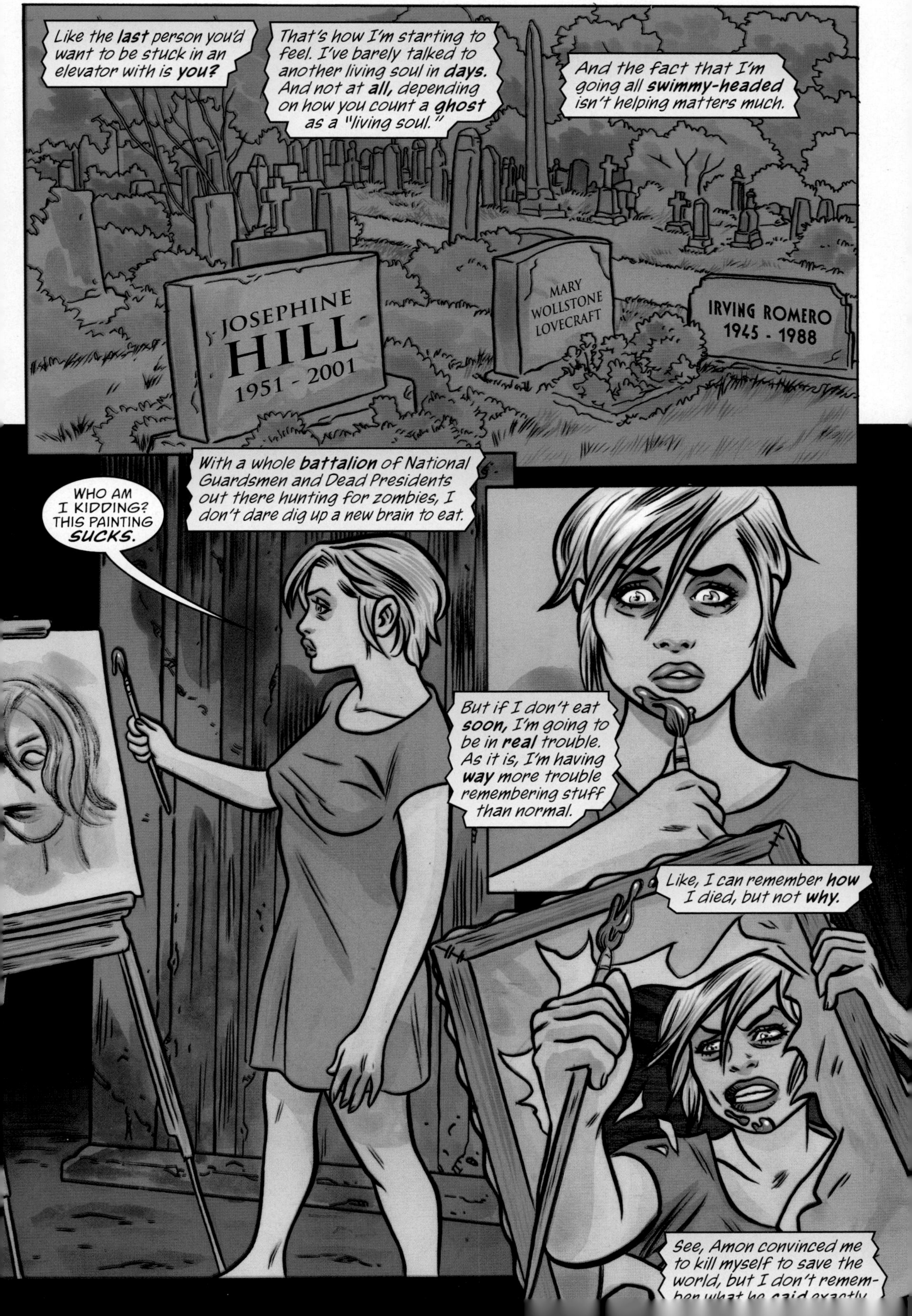
Like the last person you'd want to be stuck in an elevator with is you?
That's how I'm starting to feel. I've barely talked to another living soul in days. And not at all, depending on how you count a ghost as a "living soul."
And the fact that I'm going all swimmy-headed isn't helping matters much.
JOSEPHINE HILL 1951 - 2001
MARY WOLLSTONE LOVECRAFT
IRVING ROMERO 1945 - 1988
With a whole battalion of National Guardsmen and Dead Presidents out there hunting for zombies, I don't dare dig up a new brain to eat.
WHO AM I KIDDING? THIS PAINTING SUCKS.
But if I don't eat soon, I'm going to be in real trouble. As it is, I'm having way more trouble remembering stuff than normal.
Like, I can remember how I died, but not why.
See, Amon convinced me to kill myself to save the world, but I don't remem-

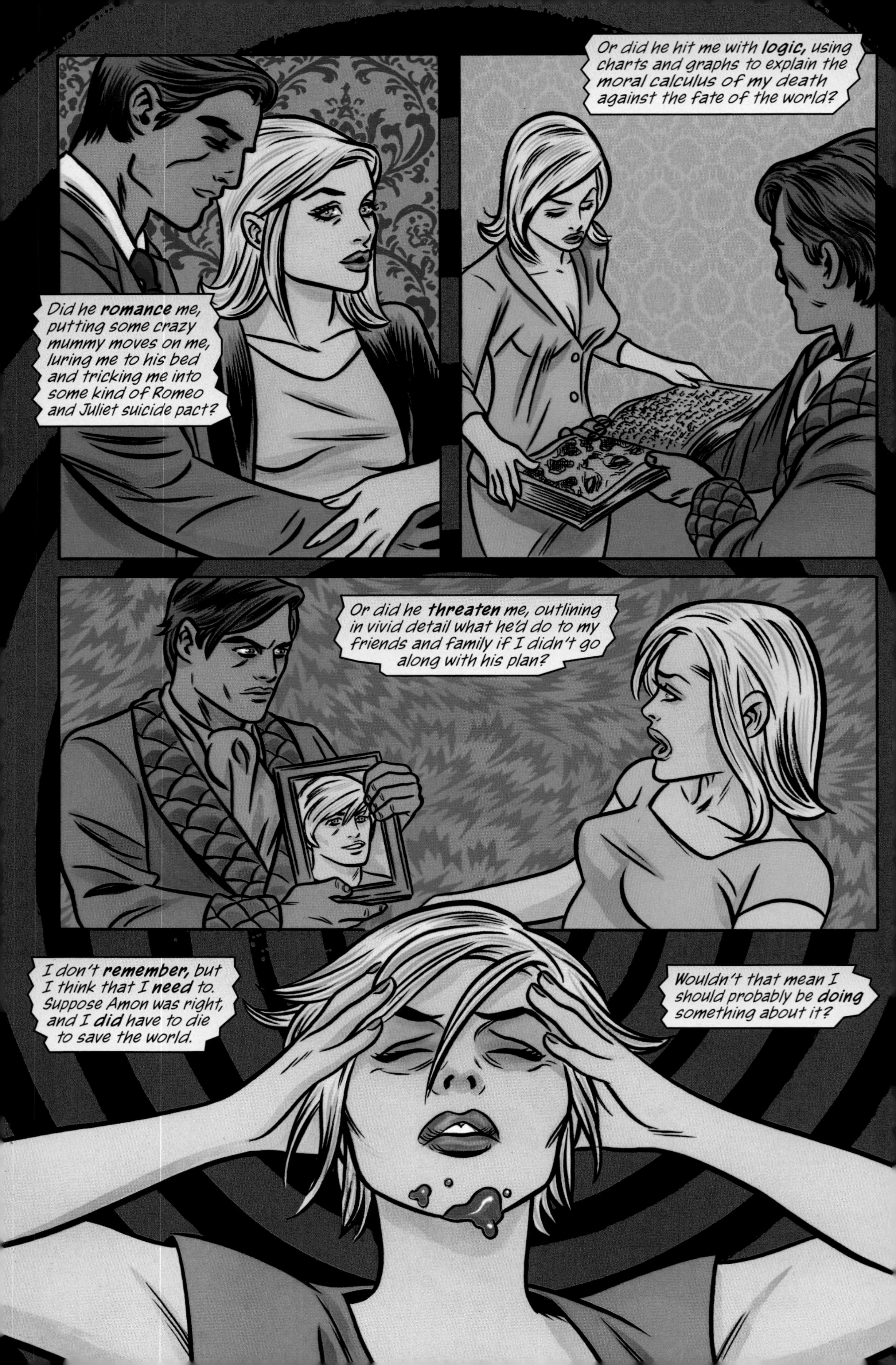
Did he romance me, putting some crazy mummy moves on me, luring me to his bed and tricking me into some kind of Romeo and Juliet suicide pact?
Or did he hit me with logic, using charts and graphs to explain the moral calculus of my death against the fate of the world?
Or did he threaten me, outlining in vivid detail what he'd do to my friends and family if I didn't go along with his plan?
I don't remember, but I think that I need to. Suppose Amon was right, and I did have to die to save the world.
Wouldn't that mean I should probably be doing something about it?

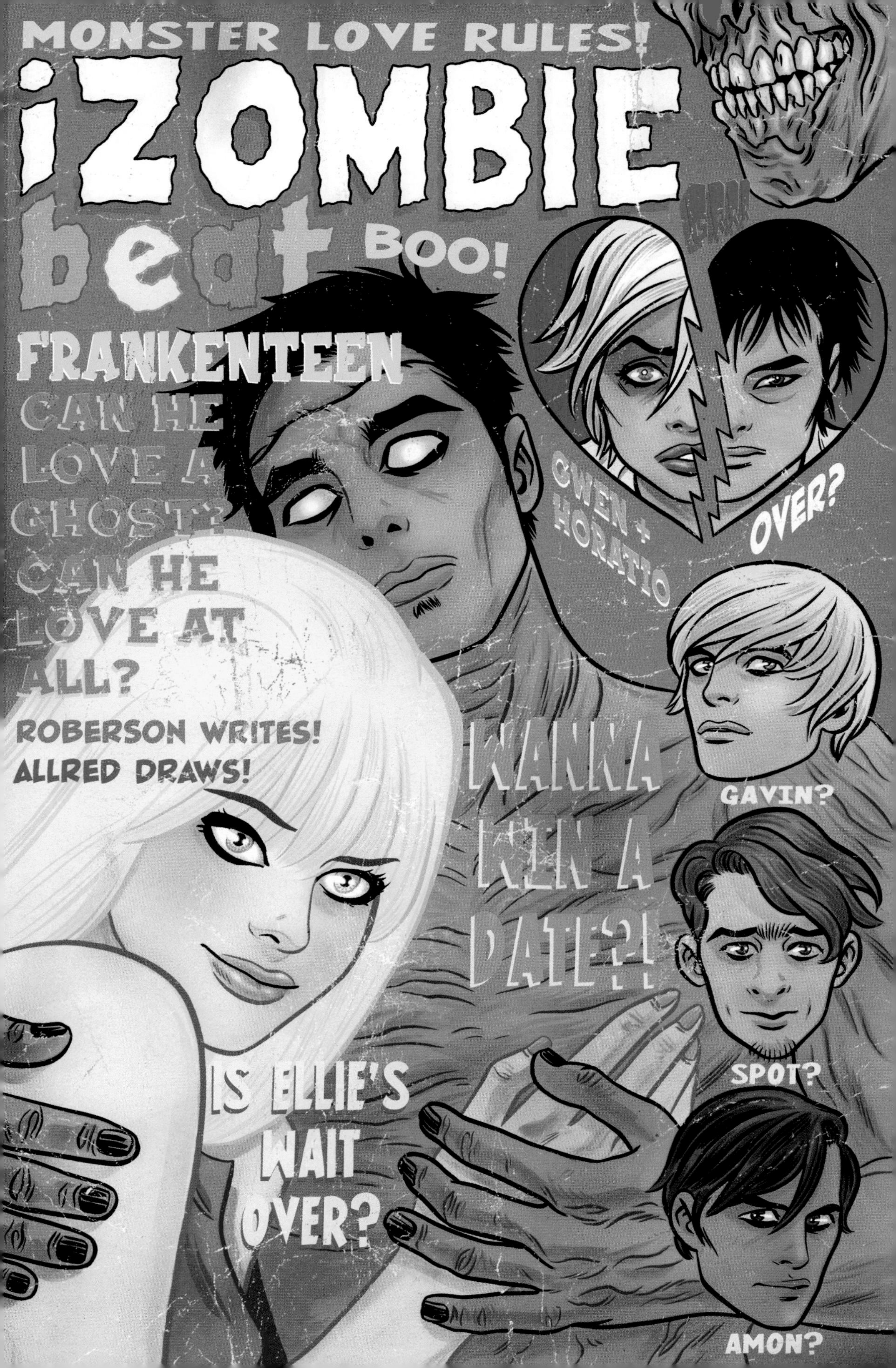
MONSTER LOVE RULES!
iZOMBIE
GRRR
beat
BOO!
FRANKENTEEN
CAN HE LOVE A GHOST? CAN HE LOVE AT ALL?
GWEN + HORATIO
OVER?
ROBERSON WRITES!
ALLRED DRAWS!
GAVIN?
WANNA KEN A DATE?!
SPOT?
IS ELLIE'S WAIT OVER?
AMON?

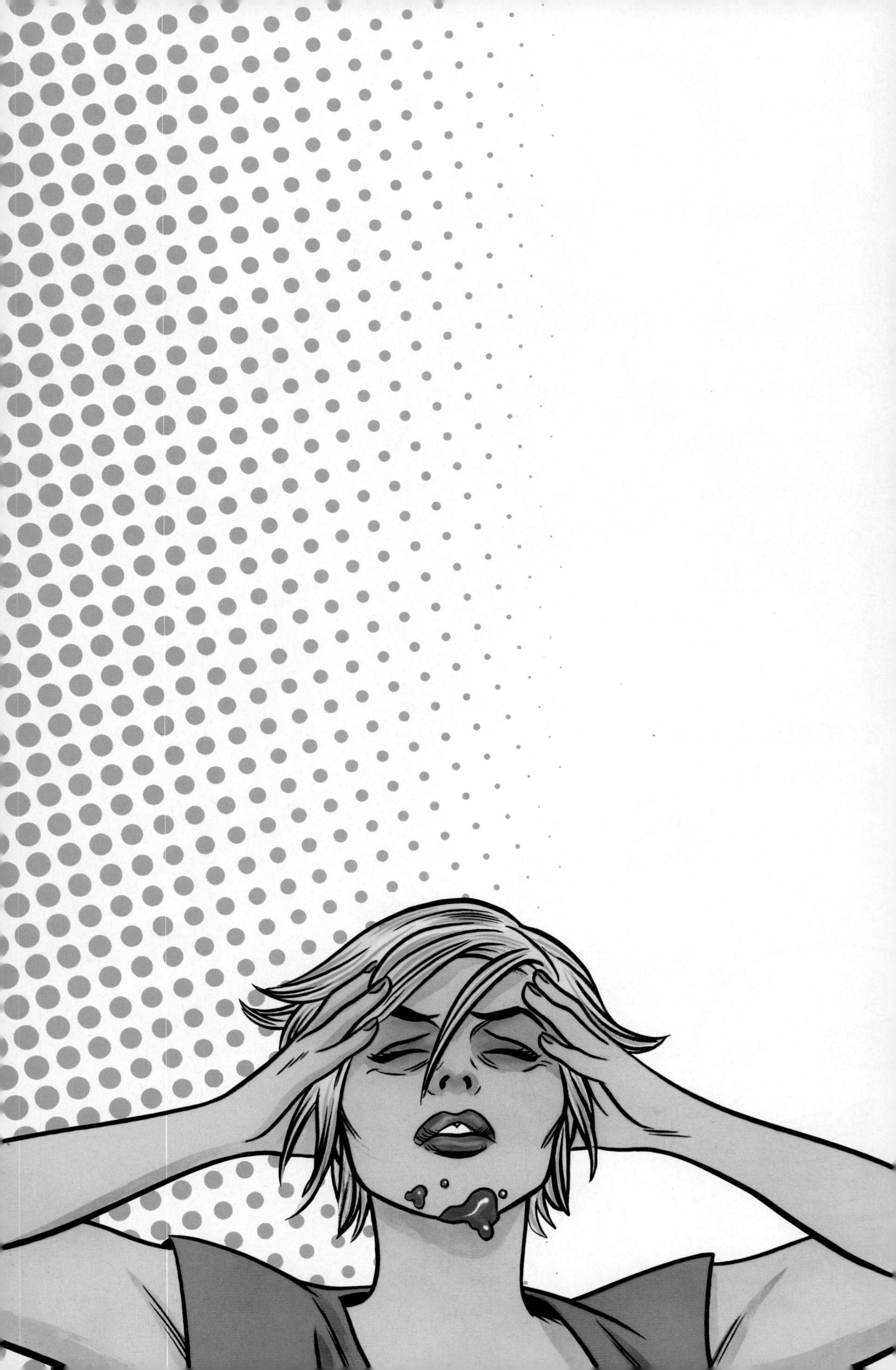

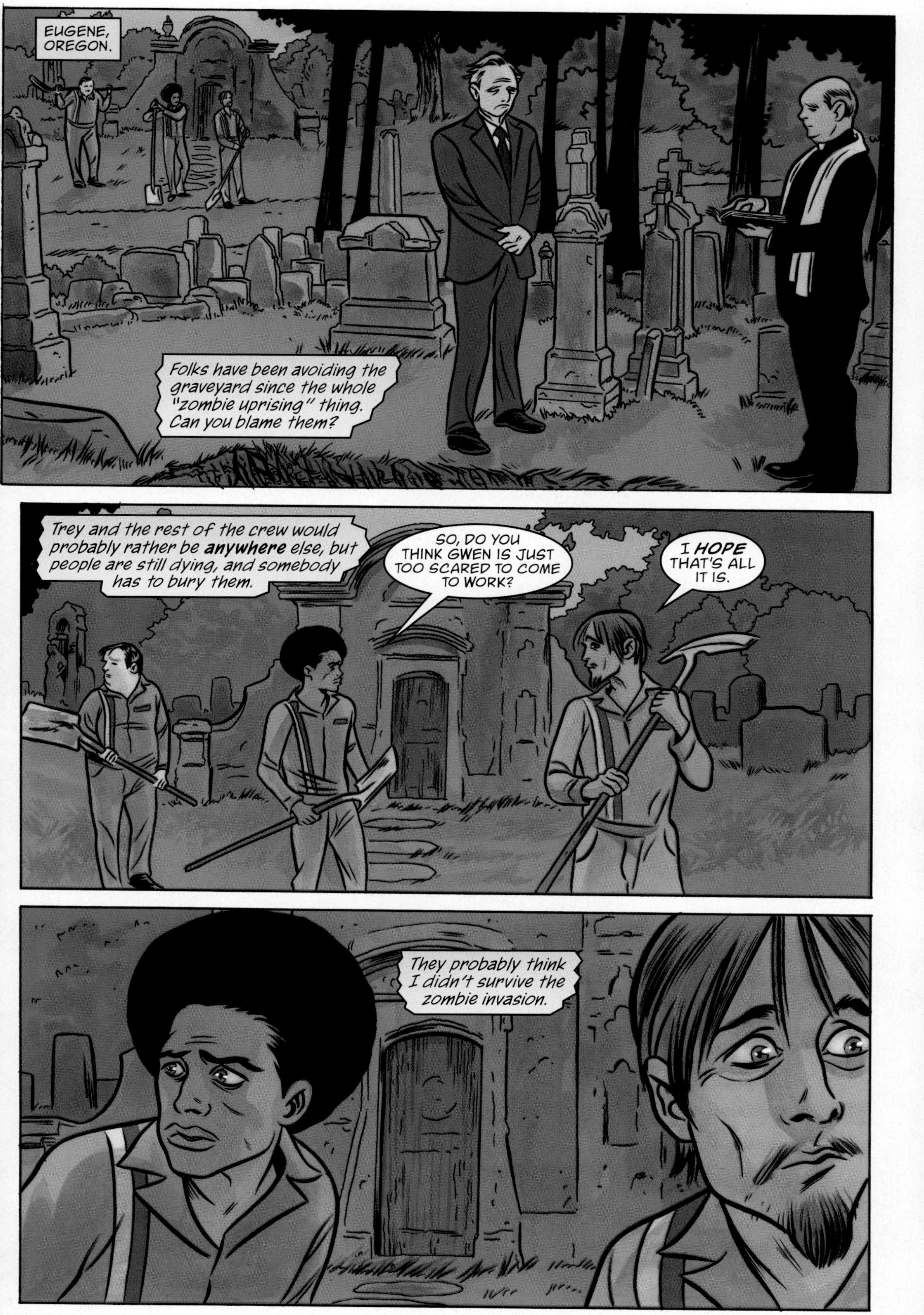
EUGENE, OREGON.
Folks have been avoiding the graveyard since the whole "zombie uprising" thing. Can you blame them?
Trey and the rest of the crew would probably rather be **anywhere** else, but people are still dying, and somebody has to bury them.
SO, DO YOU THINK GWEN IS JUST TOO SCARED TO COME TO WORK?
I **HOPE** THAT'S ALL IT IS.
They probably think I didn't survive the zombie invasion.

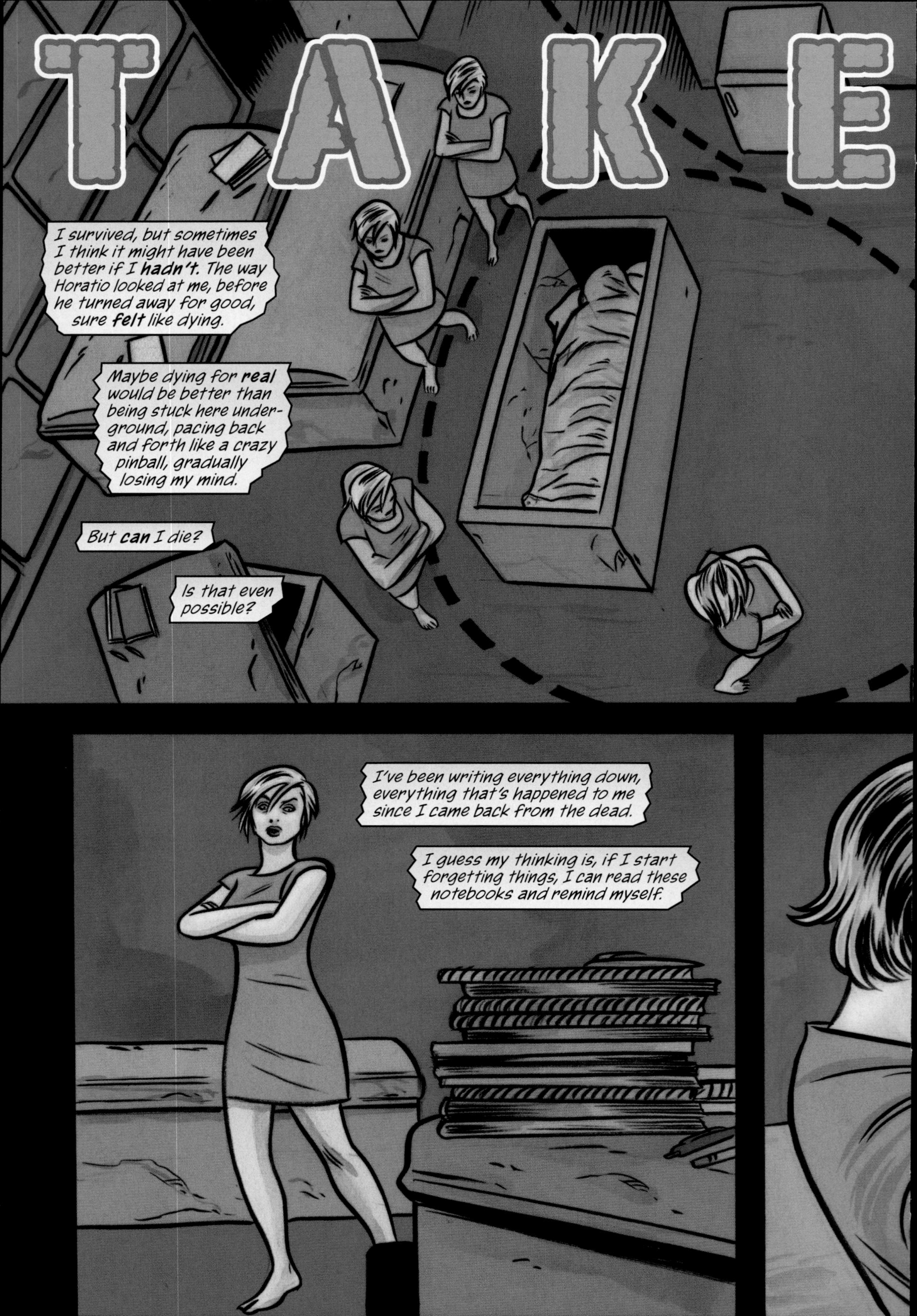
T A K E
I survived, but sometimes I think it might have been better if I hadn't. The way Horatio looked at me, before he turned away for good, sure felt like dying.
Maybe dying for real would be better than being stuck here underground, pacing back and forth like a crazy pinball, gradually losing my mind.
But can I die?
Is that even possible?
I've been writing everything down, everything that's happened to me since I came back from the dead.
I guess my thinking is, if I start forgetting things, I can read these notebooks and remind myself.

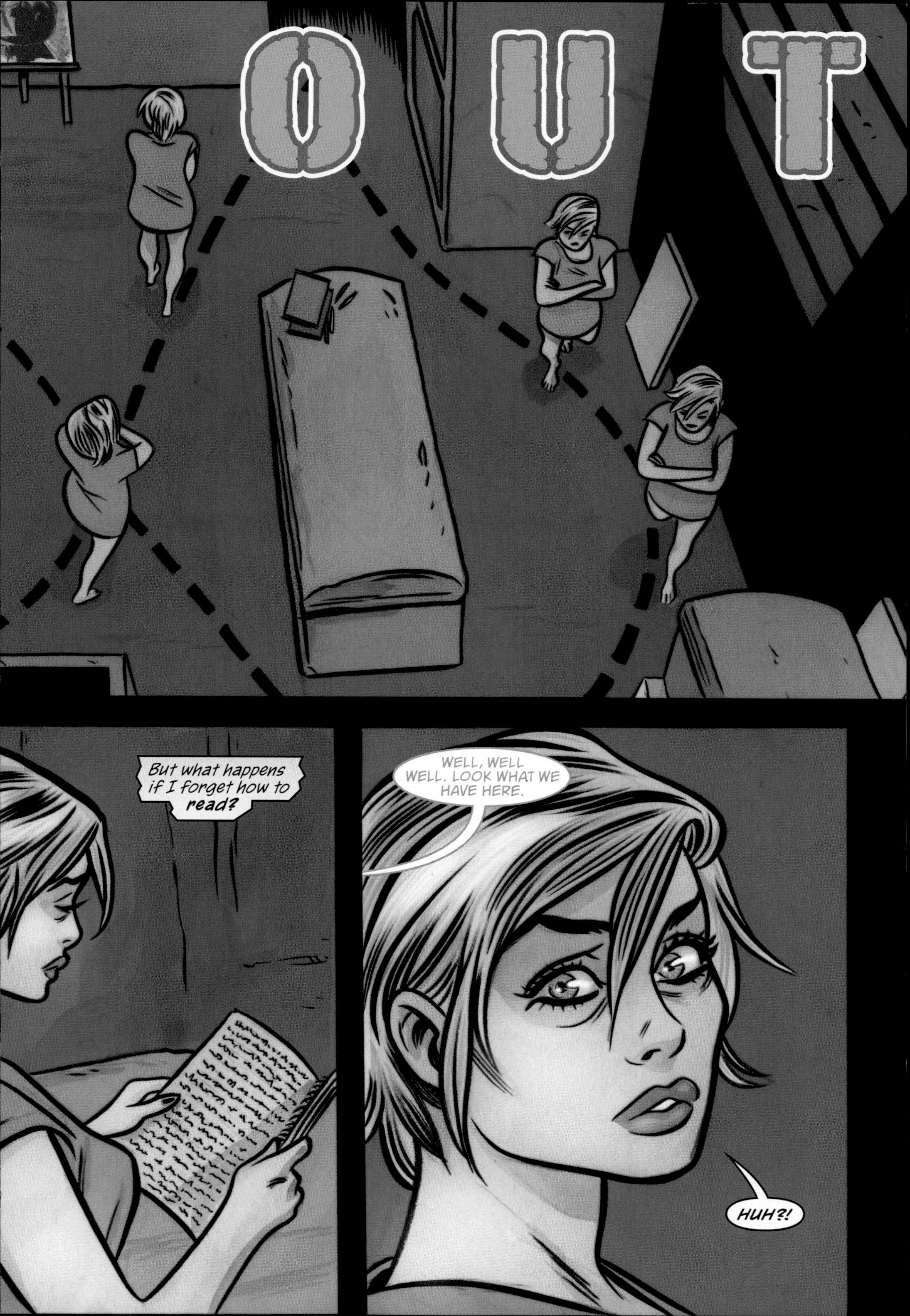
OUT
But what happens if I forget how to **read?**
WELL, WELL WELL. LOOK WHAT WE HAVE HERE.
HUH?!

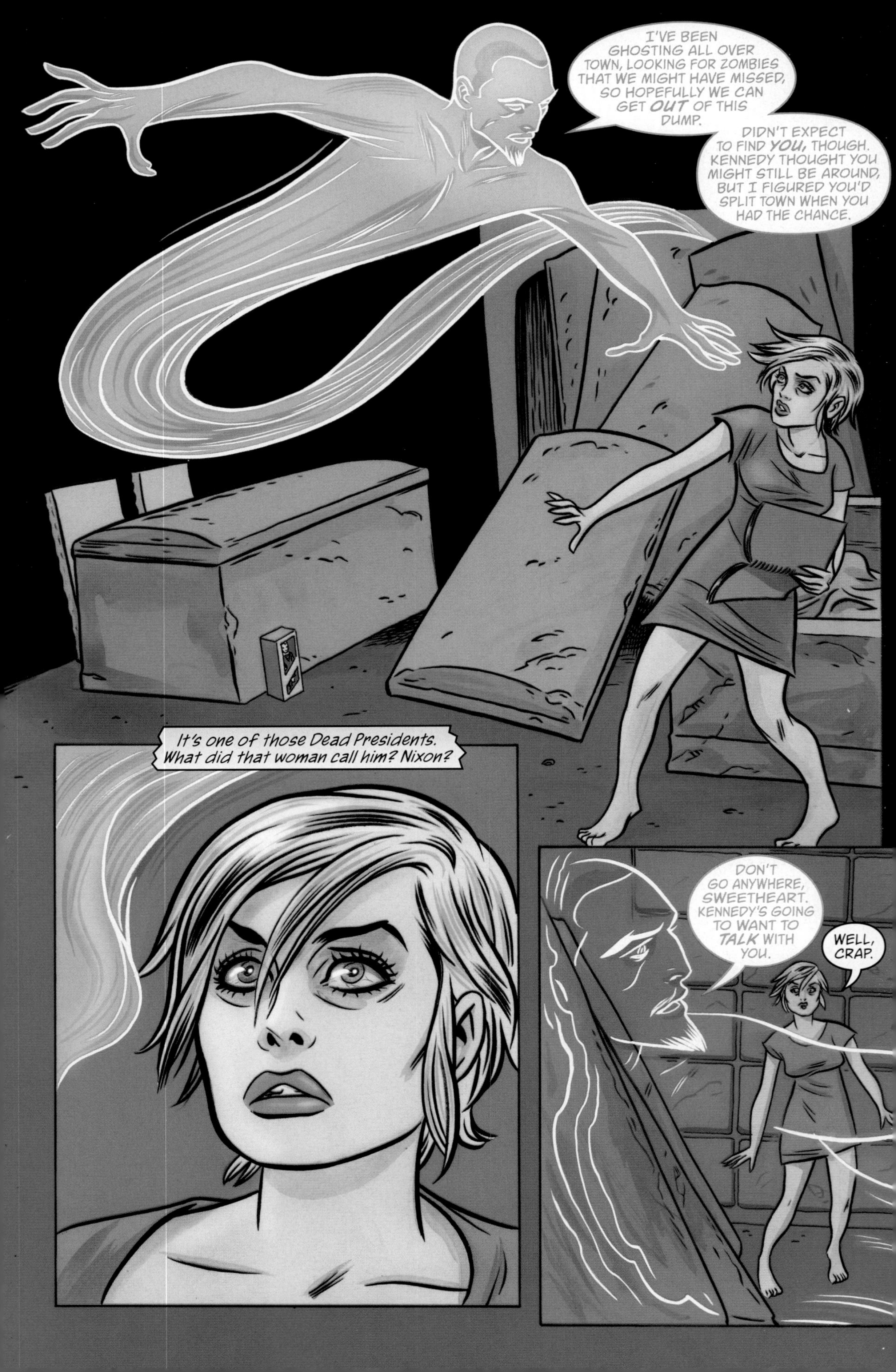
I'VE BEEN GHOSTING ALL OVER TOWN, LOOKING FOR ZOMBIES THAT WE MIGHT HAVE MISSED, SO HOPEFULLY WE CAN GET OUT OF THIS DUMP.
DIDN'T EXPECT TO FIND YOU, THOUGH. KENNEDY THOUGHT YOU MIGHT STILL BE AROUND, BUT I FIGURED YOU'D SPLIT TOWN WHEN YOU HAD THE CHANCE.
It's one of those Dead Presidents. What did that woman call him? Nixon?
DON'T GO ANYWHERE, SWEETHEART. KENNEDY'S GOING TO WANT TO TALK WITH YOU.
WELL, CRAP.

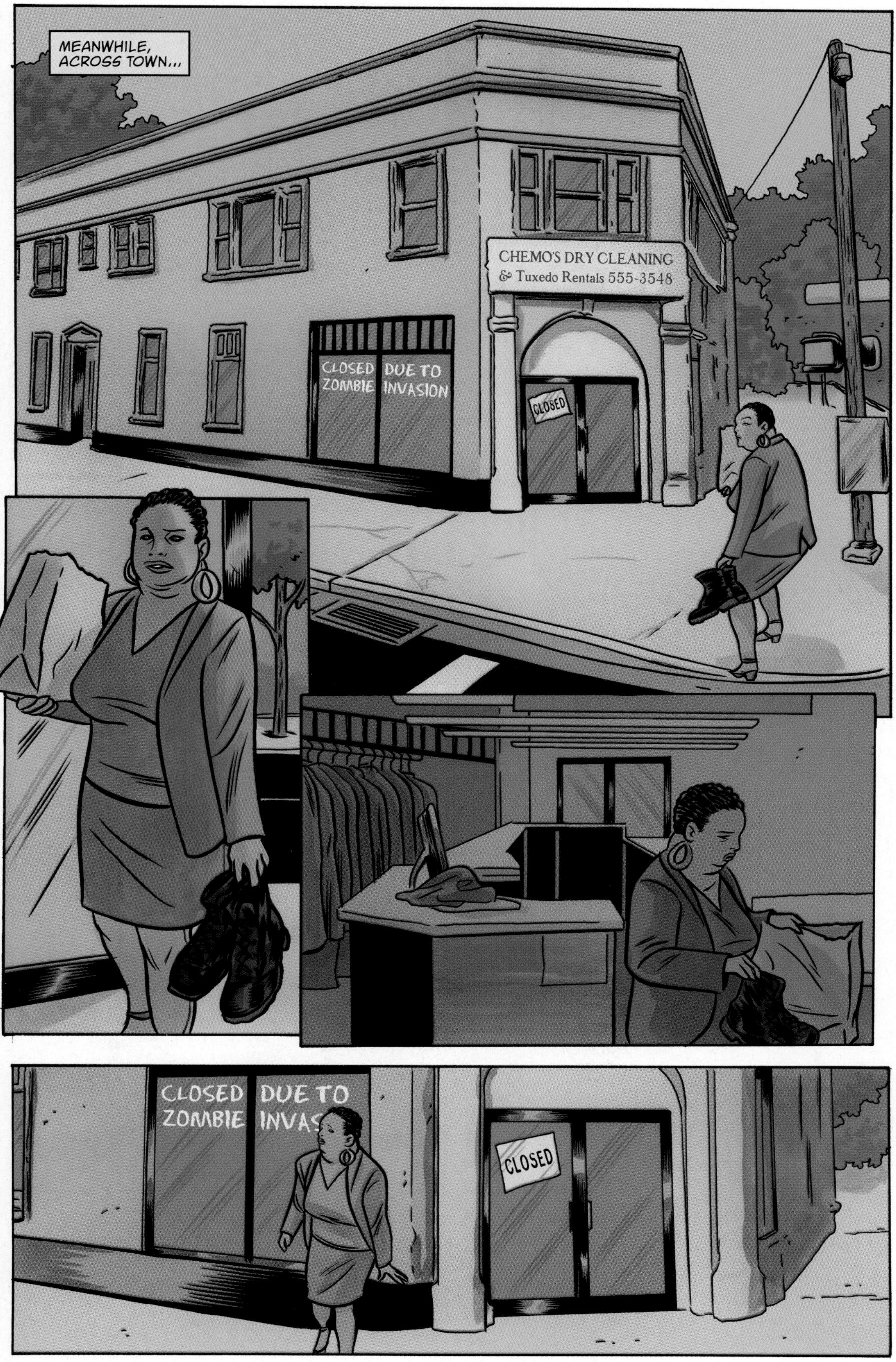
MEANWHILE, ACROSS TOWN...
CHEMO'S DRY CLEANING
& Tuxedo Rentals 555-3548
CLOSED DUE TO ZOMBIE INVASION
CLOSED
CLOSED
CLOSED DUE TO ZOMBIE INVAS
CLOSED

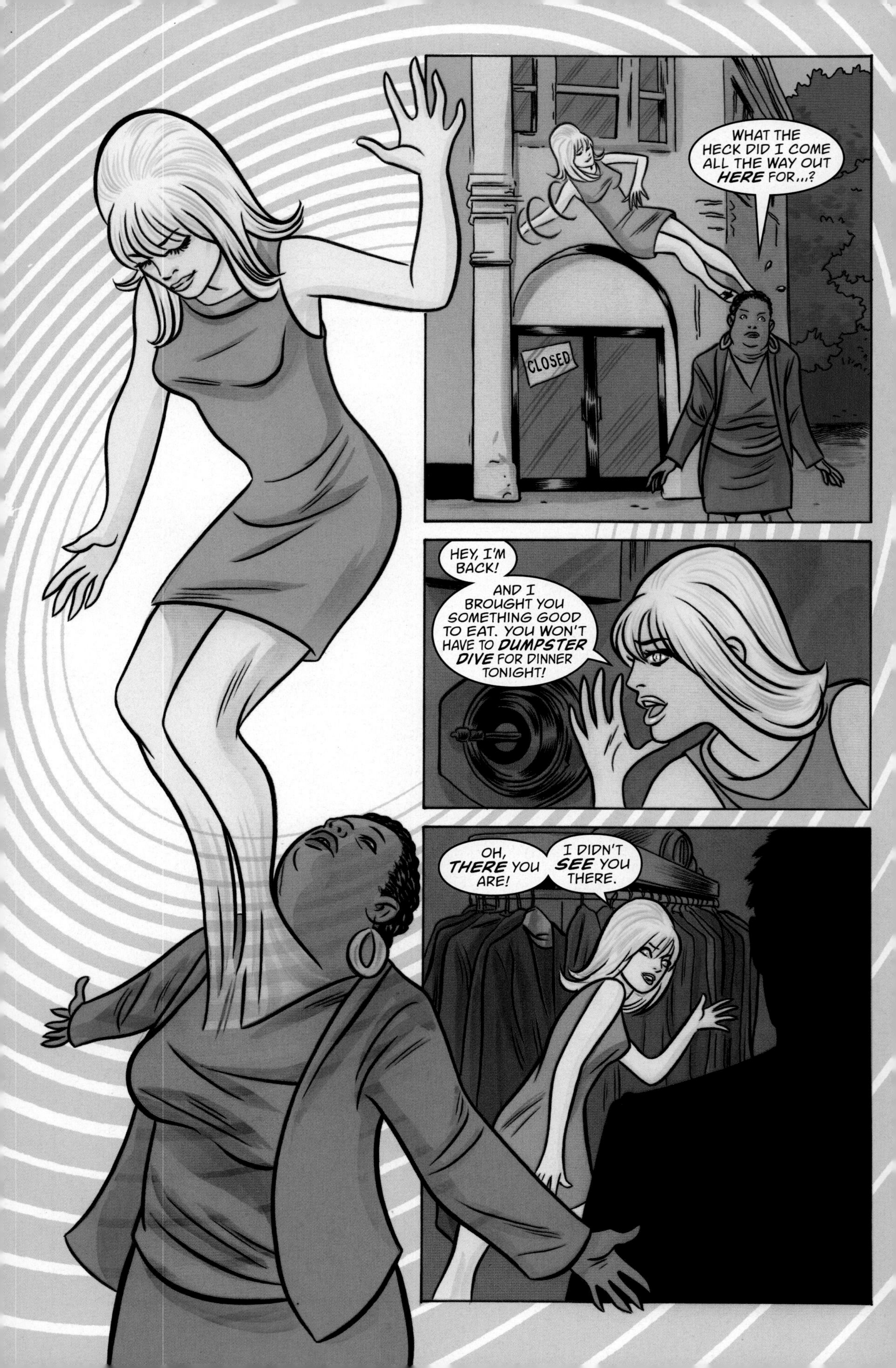

WHAT THE HECK DID I COME ALL THE WAY OUT HERE FOR...?
HEY, I'M BACK!
AND I BROUGHT YOU SOMETHING GOOD TO EAT. YOU WON'T HAVE TO DUMPSTER DIVE FOR DINNER TONIGHT!
CLOSED
OH, THERE YOU ARE!
I DIDN'T SEE YOU THERE.

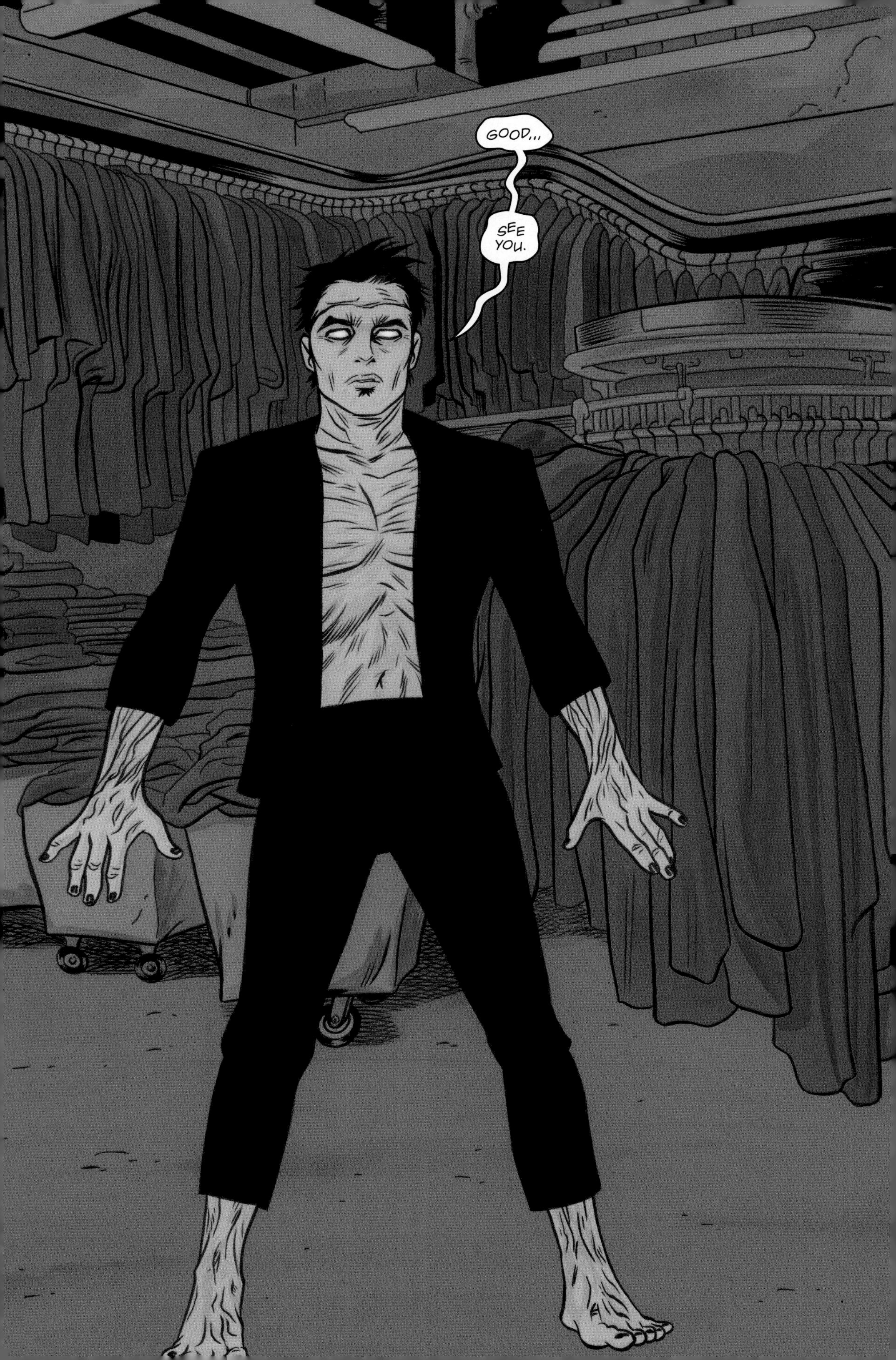
GOOD...
SEE YOU.

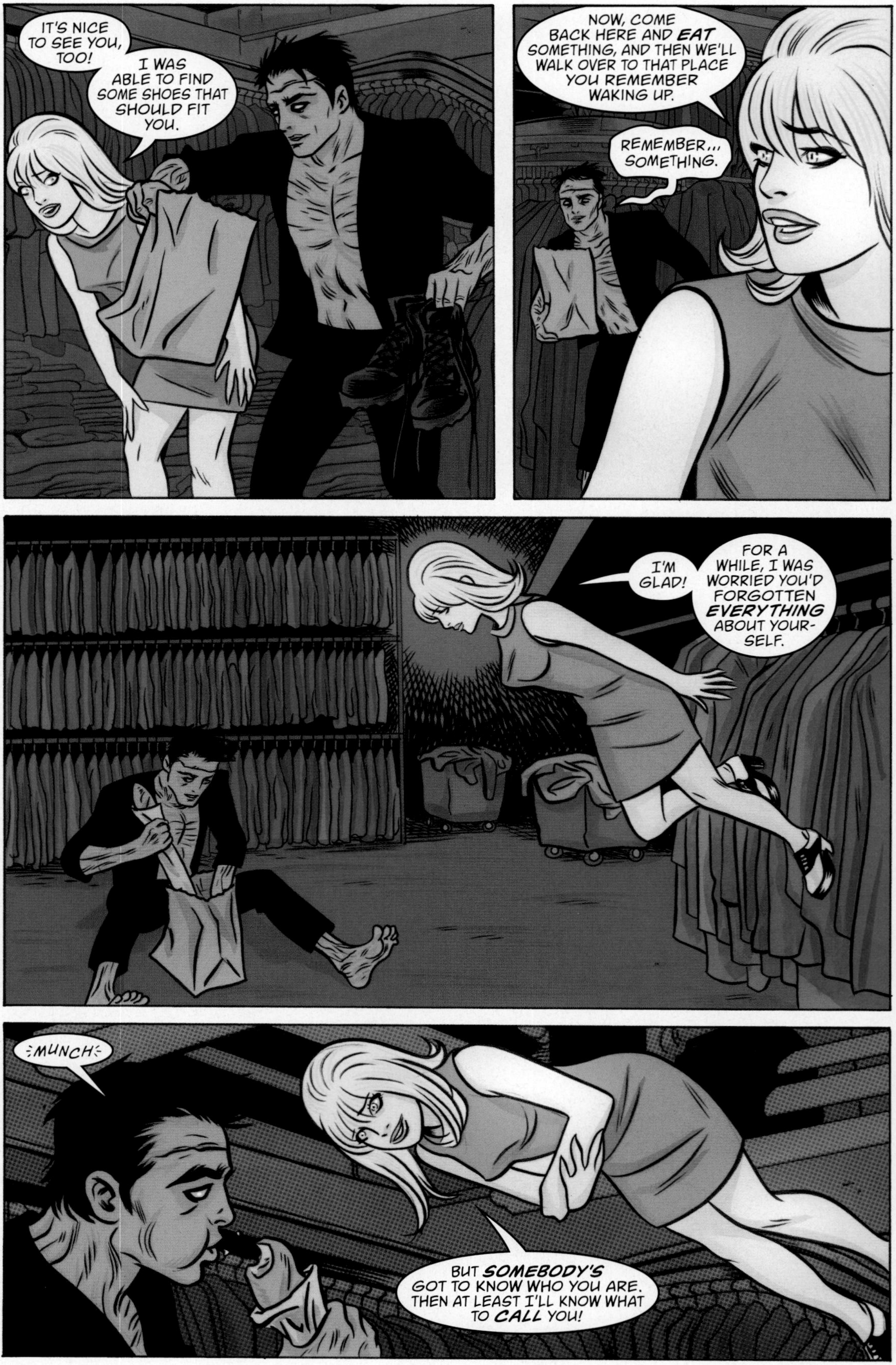
IT'S NICE TO SEE YOU, TOO!
I WAS ABLE TO FIND SOME SHOES THAT SHOULD FIT YOU.
NOW, COME BACK HERE AND EAT SOMETHING, AND THEN WE'LL WALK OVER TO THAT PLACE YOU REMEMBER WAKING UP.
REMEMBER... SOMETHING.
I'M GLAD!
FOR A WHILE, I WAS WORRIED YOU'D FORGOTTEN EVERYTHING ABOUT YOURSELF.
MUNCH
BUT SOMEBODY'S GOT TO KNOW WHO YOU ARE. THEN AT LEAST I'LL KNOW WHAT TO CALL YOU!

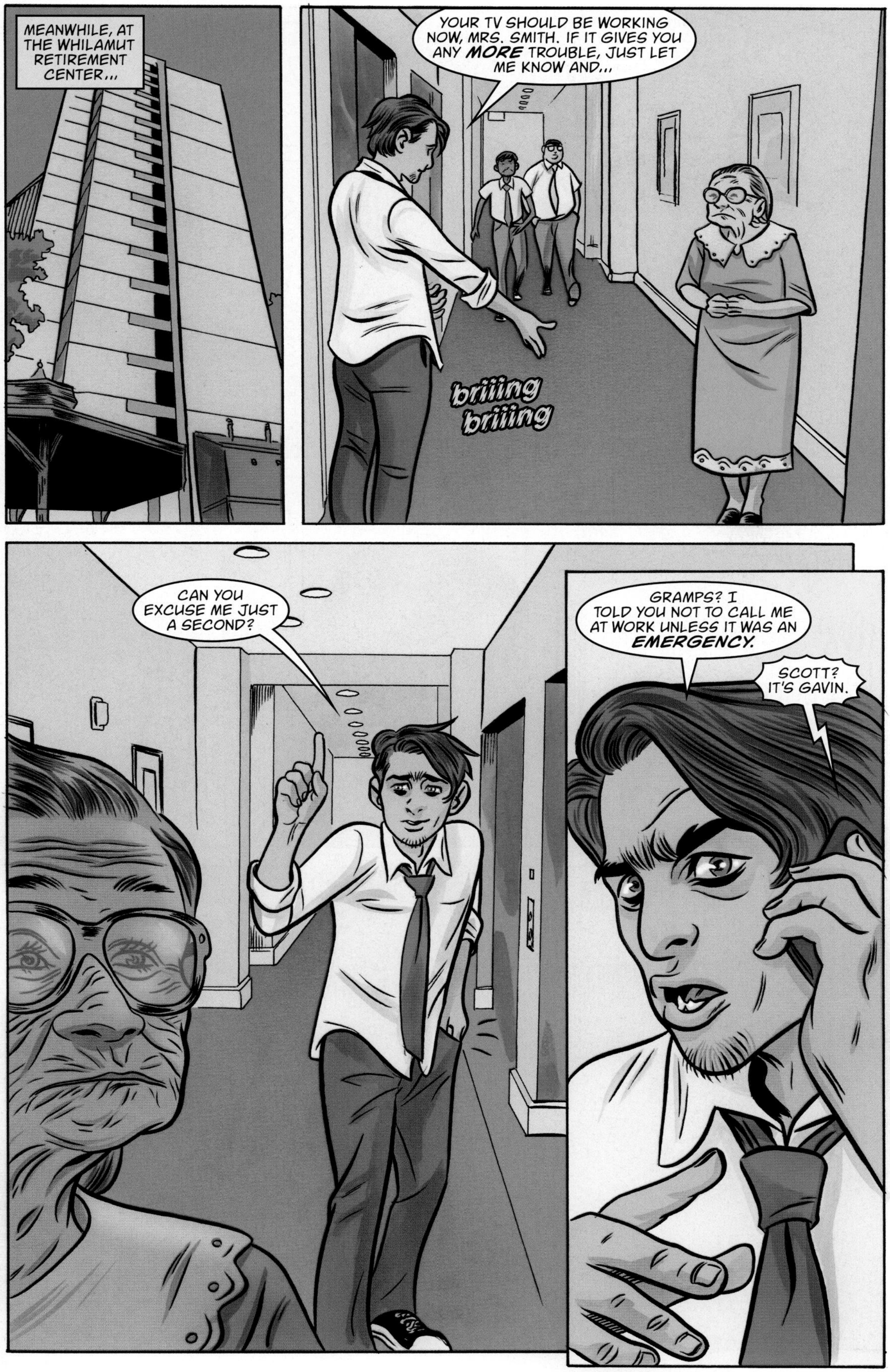
MEANWHILE, AT THE WHILAMUT RETIREMENT CENTER...
YOUR TV SHOULD BE WORKING NOW, MRS. SMITH. IF IT GIVES YOU ANY MORE TROUBLE, JUST LET ME KNOW AND...
briiing briiing
CAN YOU EXCUSE ME JUST A SECOND?
GRAMPS? I TOLD YOU NOT TO CALL ME AT WORK UNLESS IT WAS AN EMERGENCY.
SCOTT? IT'S GAVIN.

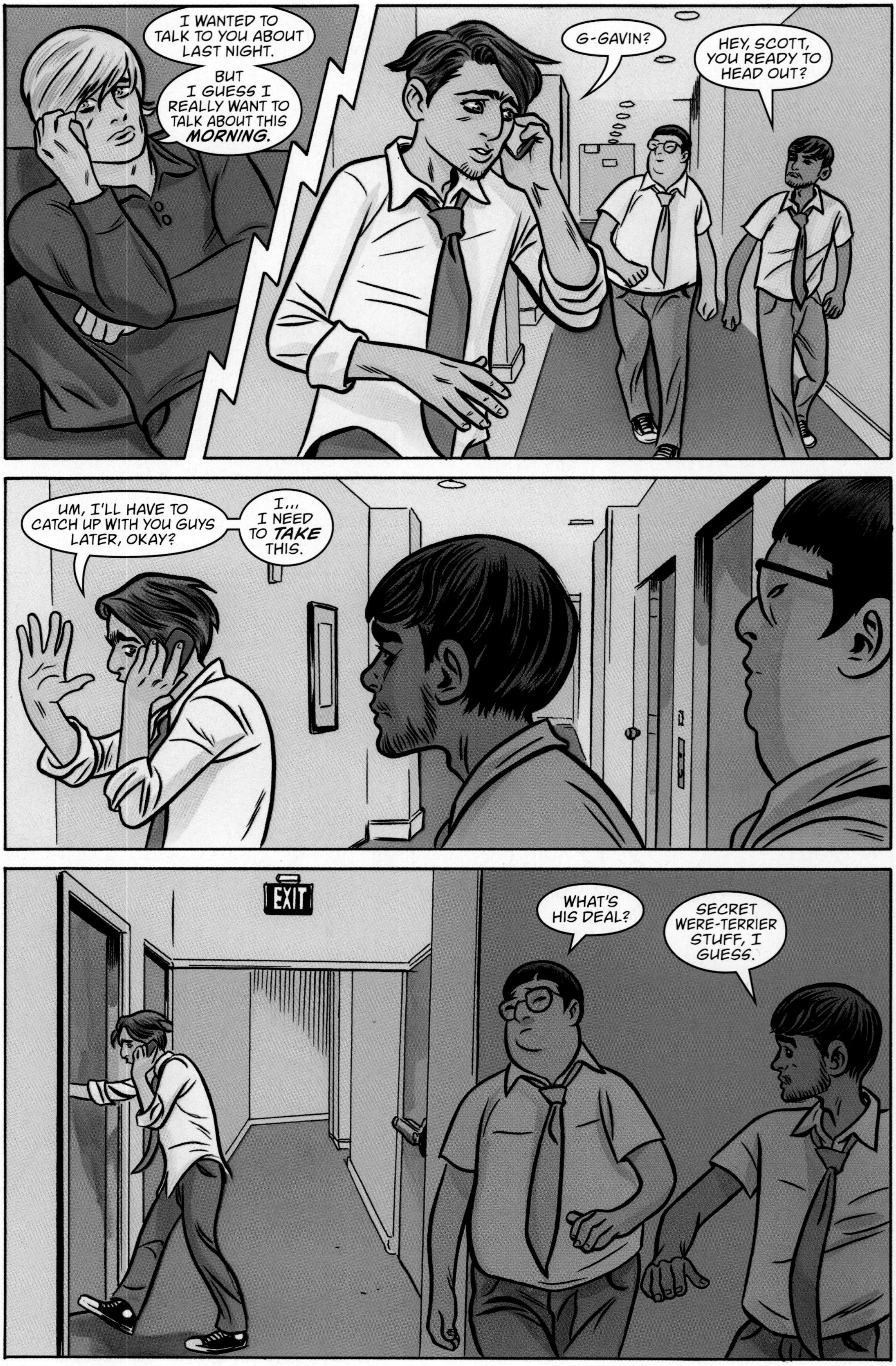
I WANTED TO TALK TO YOU ABOUT LAST NIGHT.
BUT I GUESS I REALLY WANT TO TALK ABOUT THIS MORNING.
G-GAVIN?
HEY, SCOTT, YOU READY TO HEAD OUT?
UM, I'LL HAVE TO CATCH UP WITH YOU GUYS LATER, OKAY?
I... I NEED TO TAKE THIS.
EXIT
WHAT'S HIS DEAL?
SECRET WERE-TERRIER STUFF, I GUESS.

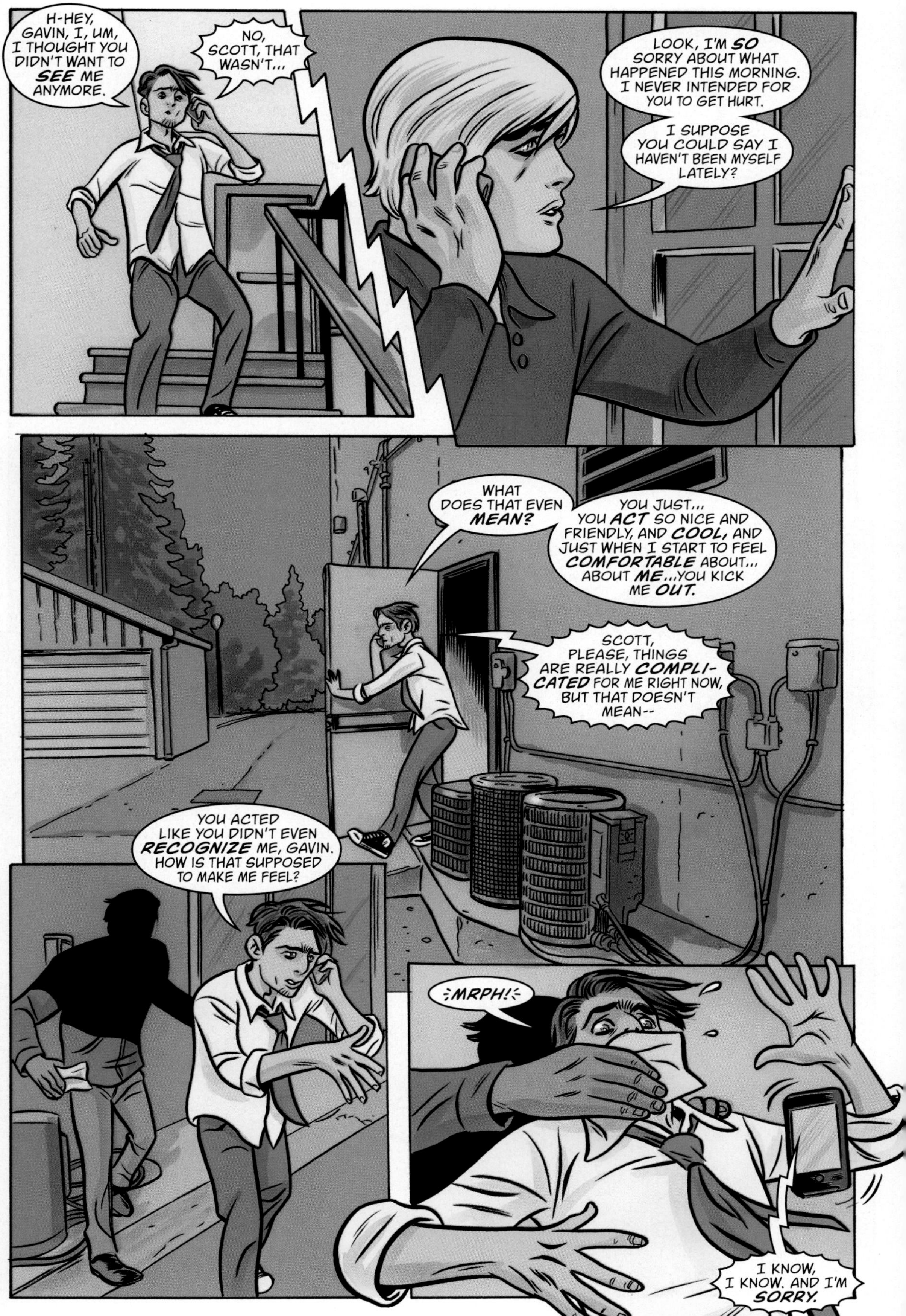
H-HEY, GAVIN, I, UM, I THOUGHT YOU DIDN'T WANT TO SEE ME ANYMORE.
NO, SCOTT, THAT WASN'T...
LOOK, I'M SO SORRY ABOUT WHAT HAPPENED THIS MORNING. I NEVER INTENDED FOR YOU TO GET HURT.
I SUPPOSE YOU COULD SAY I HAVEN'T BEEN MYSELF LATELY?
WHAT DOES THAT EVEN MEAN?
YOU JUST... YOU ACT SO NICE AND FRIENDLY, AND COOL, AND JUST WHEN I START TO FEEL COMFORTABLE ABOUT... ABOUT ME...YOU KICK ME OUT.
SCOTT, PLEASE, THINGS ARE REALLY COMPLI-CATED FOR ME RIGHT NOW, BUT THAT DOESN'T MEAN--
YOU ACTED LIKE YOU DIDN'T EVEN RECOGNIZE ME, GAVIN. HOW IS THAT SUPPOSED TO MAKE ME FEEL?
MRPH!
I KNOW, I KNOW. AND I'M SORRY.

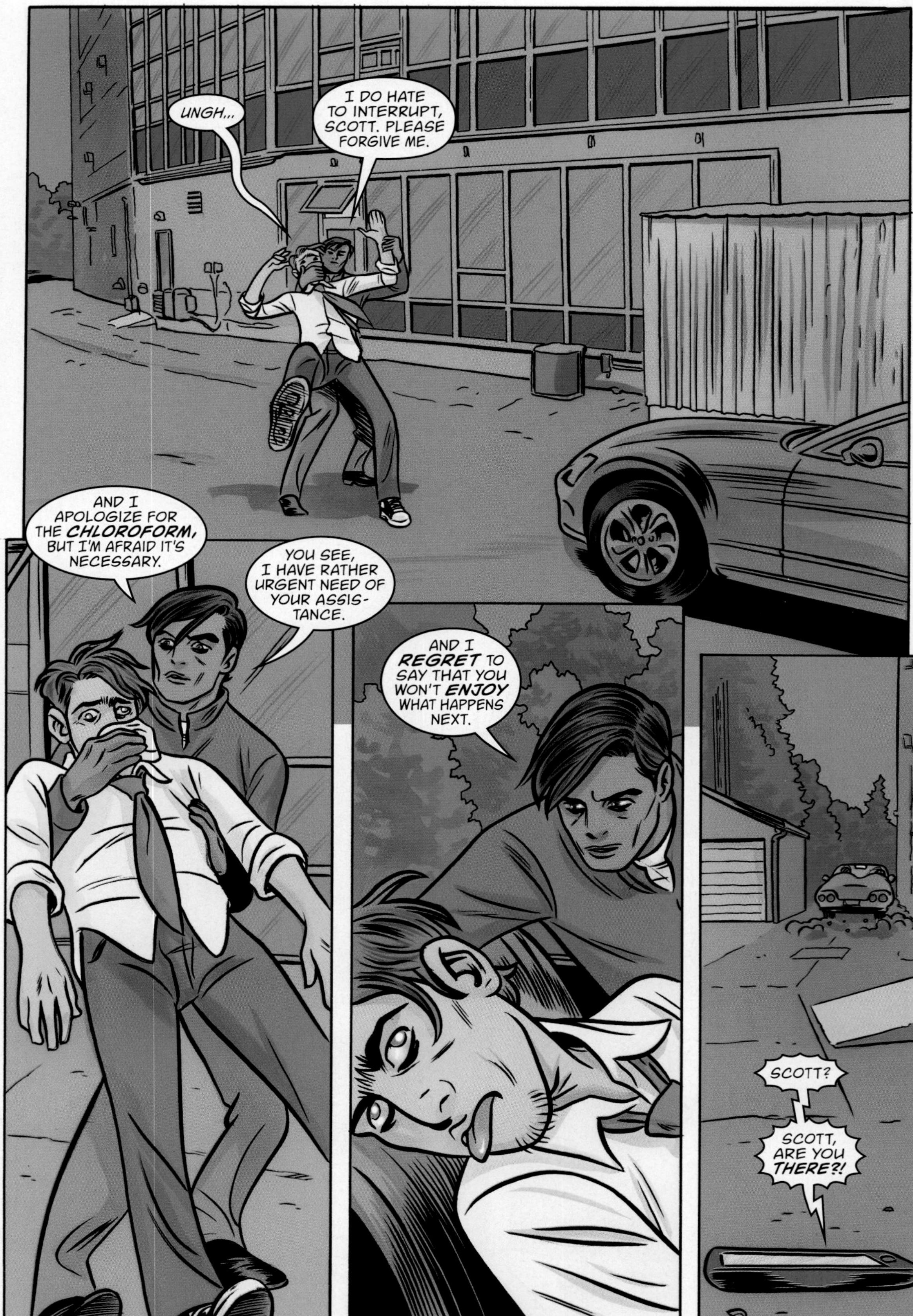
UNGH...
I DO HATE TO INTERRUPT, SCOTT. PLEASE FORGIVE ME.
AND I APOLOGIZE FOR THE CHLOROFORM, BUT I'M AFRAID IT'S NECESSARY.
YOU SEE, I HAVE RATHER URGENT NEED OF YOUR ASSISTANCE.
AND I REGRET TO SAY THAT YOU WON'T ENJOY WHAT HAPPENS NEXT.
SCOTT?
SCOTT, ARE YOU THERE?!

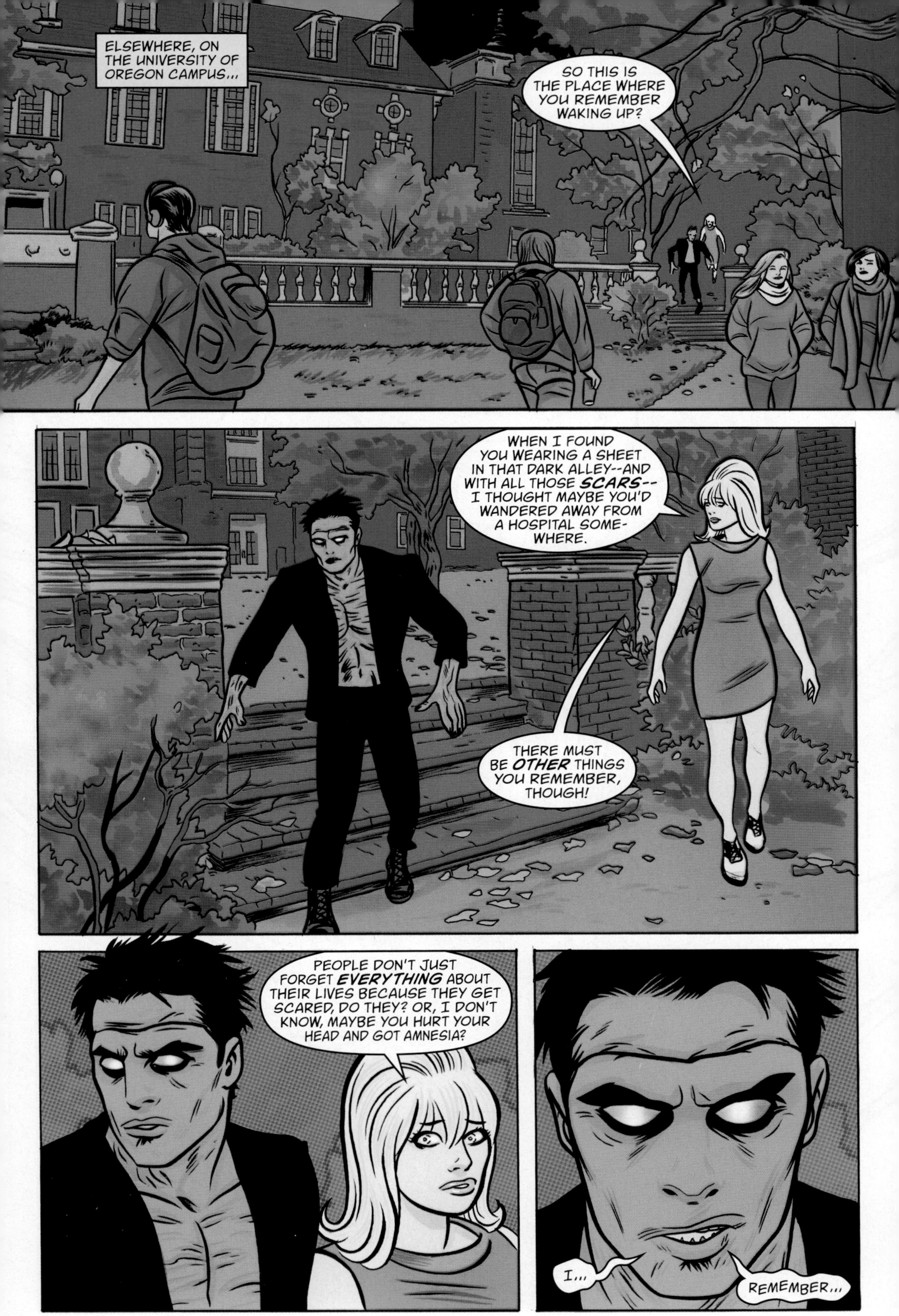
ELSEWHERE, ON THE UNIVERSITY OF OREGON CAMPUS...
SO THIS IS THE PLACE WHERE YOU REMEMBER WAKING UP?
WHEN I FOUND YOU WEARING A SHEET IN THAT DARK ALLEY--AND WITH ALL THOSE SCARS-- I THOUGHT MAYBE YOU'D WANDERED AWAY FROM A HOSPITAL SOME-WHERE.
THERE MUST BE OTHER THINGS YOU REMEMBER, THOUGH!
PEOPLE DON'T JUST FORGET EVERYTHING ABOUT THEIR LIVES BECAUSE THEY GET SCARED, DO THEY? OR, I DON'T KNOW, MAYBE YOU HURT YOUR HEAD AND GOT AMNESIA?
I...
REMEMBER...

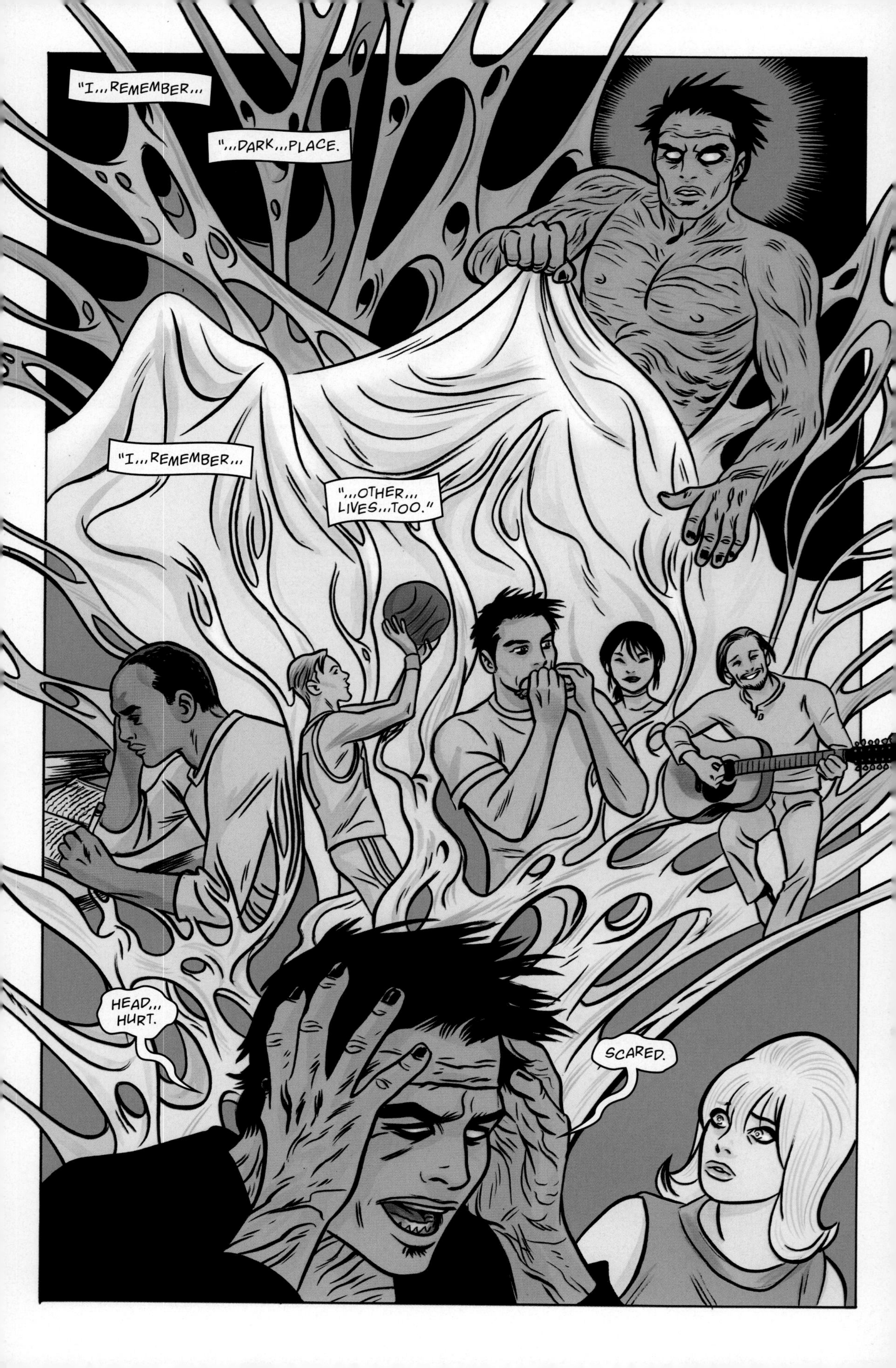
"I... REMEMBER...
"...DARK...PLACE.
"I... REMEMBER...
"...OTHER... LIVES...TOO."
HEAD... HURT.
SCARED.

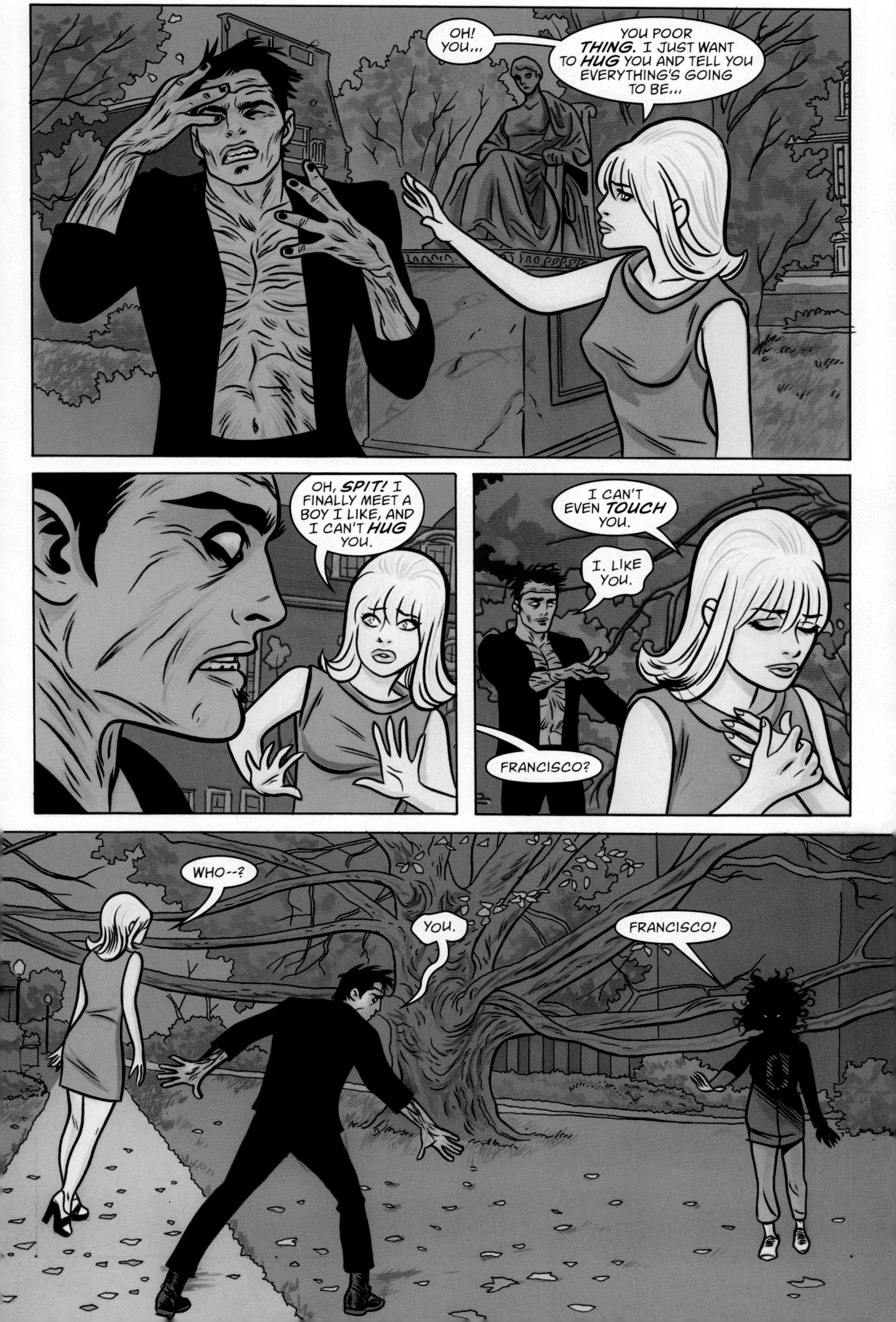
OH! YOU...
YOU POOR THING. I JUST WANT TO HUG YOU AND TELL YOU EVERYTHING'S GOING TO BE...
OH, SPIT! I FINALLY MEET A BOY I LIKE, AND I CAN'T HUG YOU.
I CAN'T EVEN TOUCH YOU.
I. LIKE YOU.
FRANCISCO?
WHO--?
YOU.
FRANCISCO!

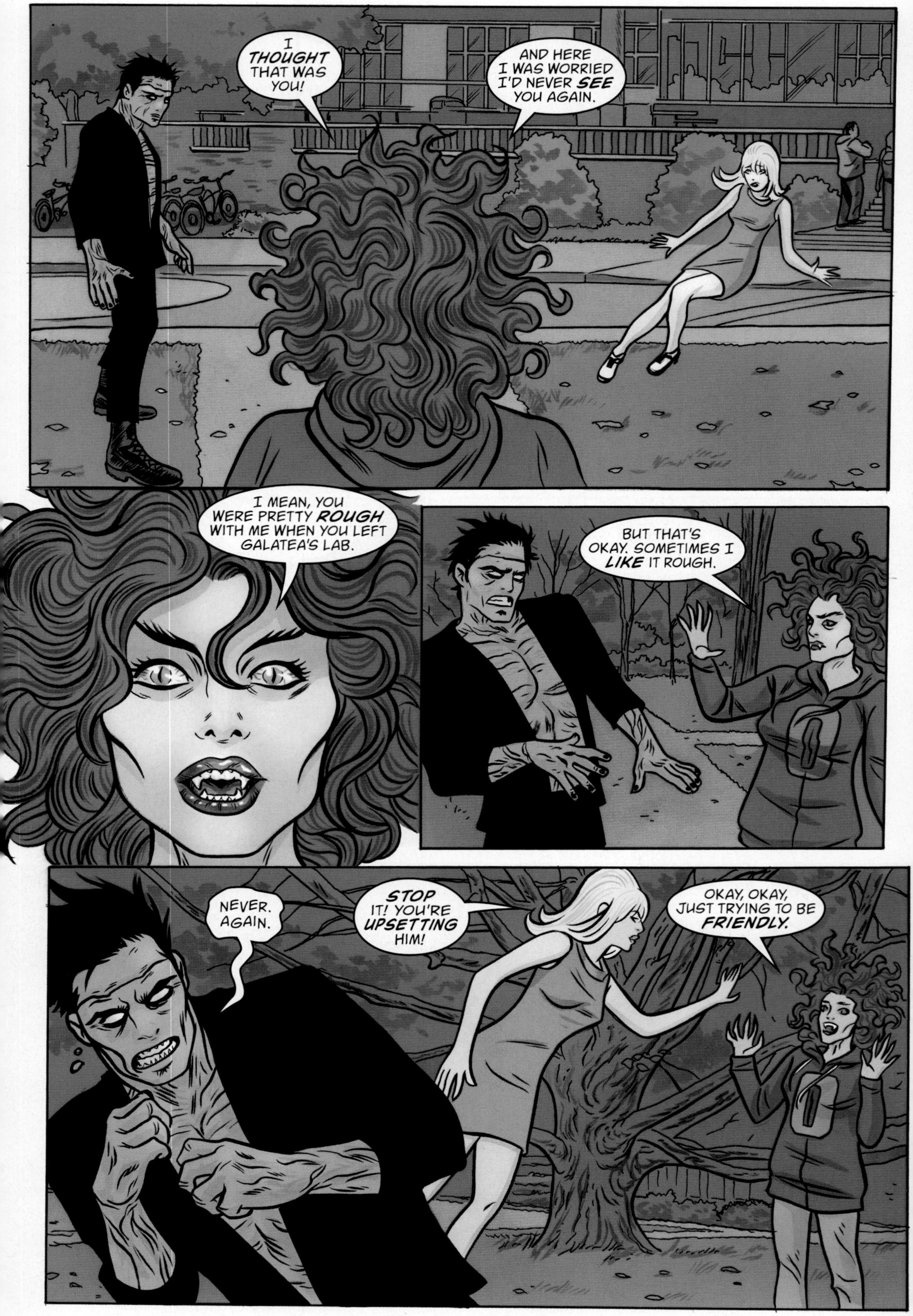
I THOUGHT THAT WAS YOU!
AND HERE I WAS WORRIED I'D NEVER SEE YOU AGAIN.
I MEAN, YOU WERE PRETTY ROUGH WITH ME WHEN YOU LEFT GALATEA'S LAB.
BUT THAT'S OKAY. SOMETIMES I LIKE IT ROUGH.
NEVER. AGAIN.
STOP IT! YOU'RE UPSETTING HIM!
OKAY, OKAY, JUST TRYING TO BE FRIENDLY.

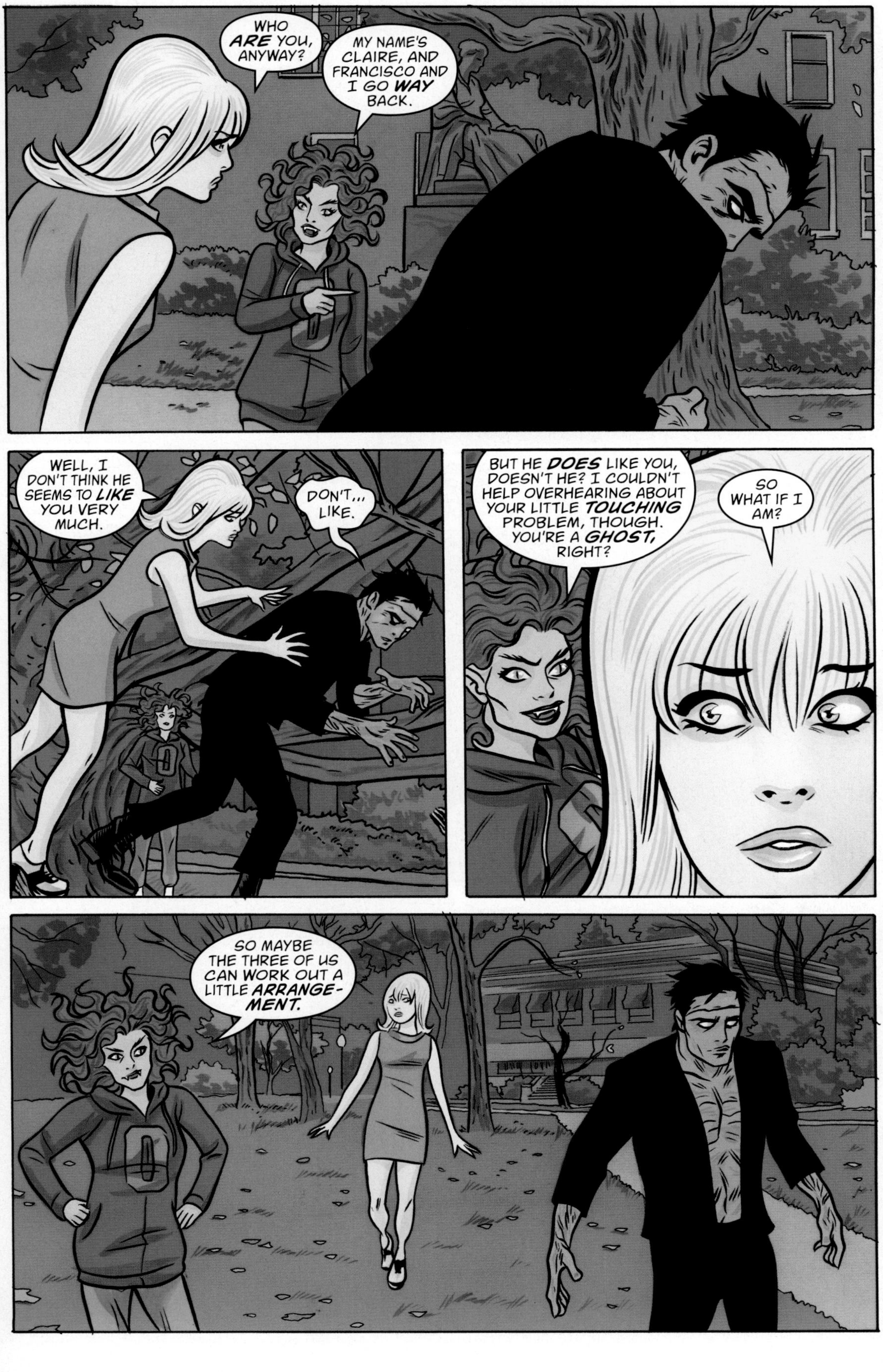

WHO ARE YOU, ANYWAY?
MY NAME'S CLAIRE, AND FRANCISCO AND I GO WAY BACK.
WELL, I DON'T THINK HE SEEMS TO LIKE YOU VERY MUCH.
DON'T... LIKE.
BUT HE DOES LIKE YOU, DOESN'T HE? I COULDN'T HELP OVERHEARING ABOUT YOUR LITTLE TOUCHING PROBLEM, THOUGH. YOU'RE A GHOST, RIGHT?
SO WHAT IF I AM?
SO MAYBE THE THREE OF US CAN WORK OUT A LITTLE ARRANGE-MENT.

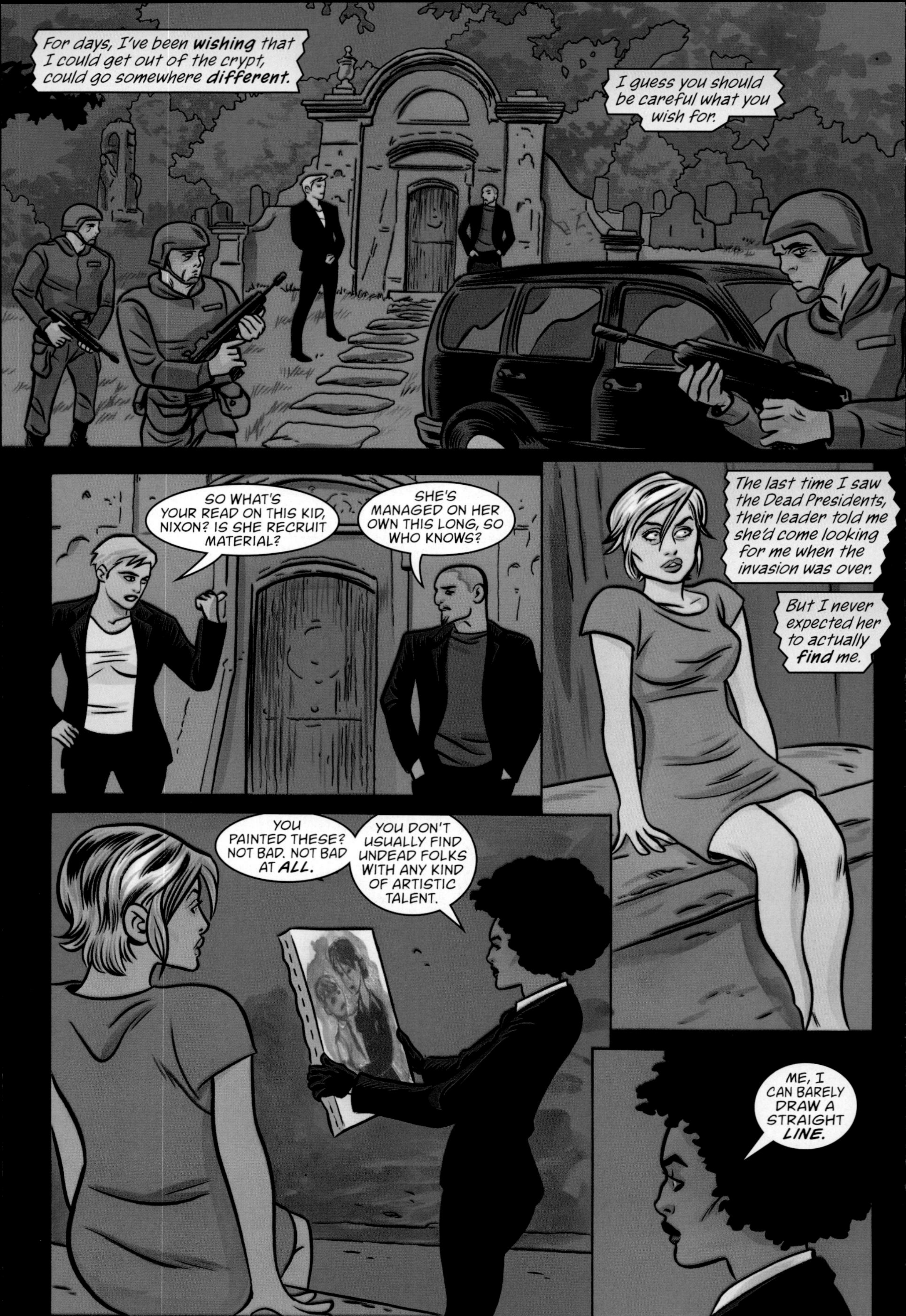

For days, I've been wishing that I could get out of the crypt, could go somewhere different.
I guess you should be careful what you wish for.
SO WHAT'S YOUR READ ON THIS KID, NIXON? IS SHE RECRUIT MATERIAL?
SHE'S MANAGED ON HER OWN THIS LONG, SO WHO KNOWS?
The last time I saw the Dead Presidents, their leader told me she'd come looking for me when the invasion was over.
But I never expected her to actually find me.
YOU PAINTED THESE? NOT BAD. NOT BAD AT ALL.
YOU DON'T USUALLY FIND UNDEAD FOLKS WITH ANY KIND OF ARTISTIC TALENT.
ME, I CAN BARELY DRAW A STRAIGHT LINE.

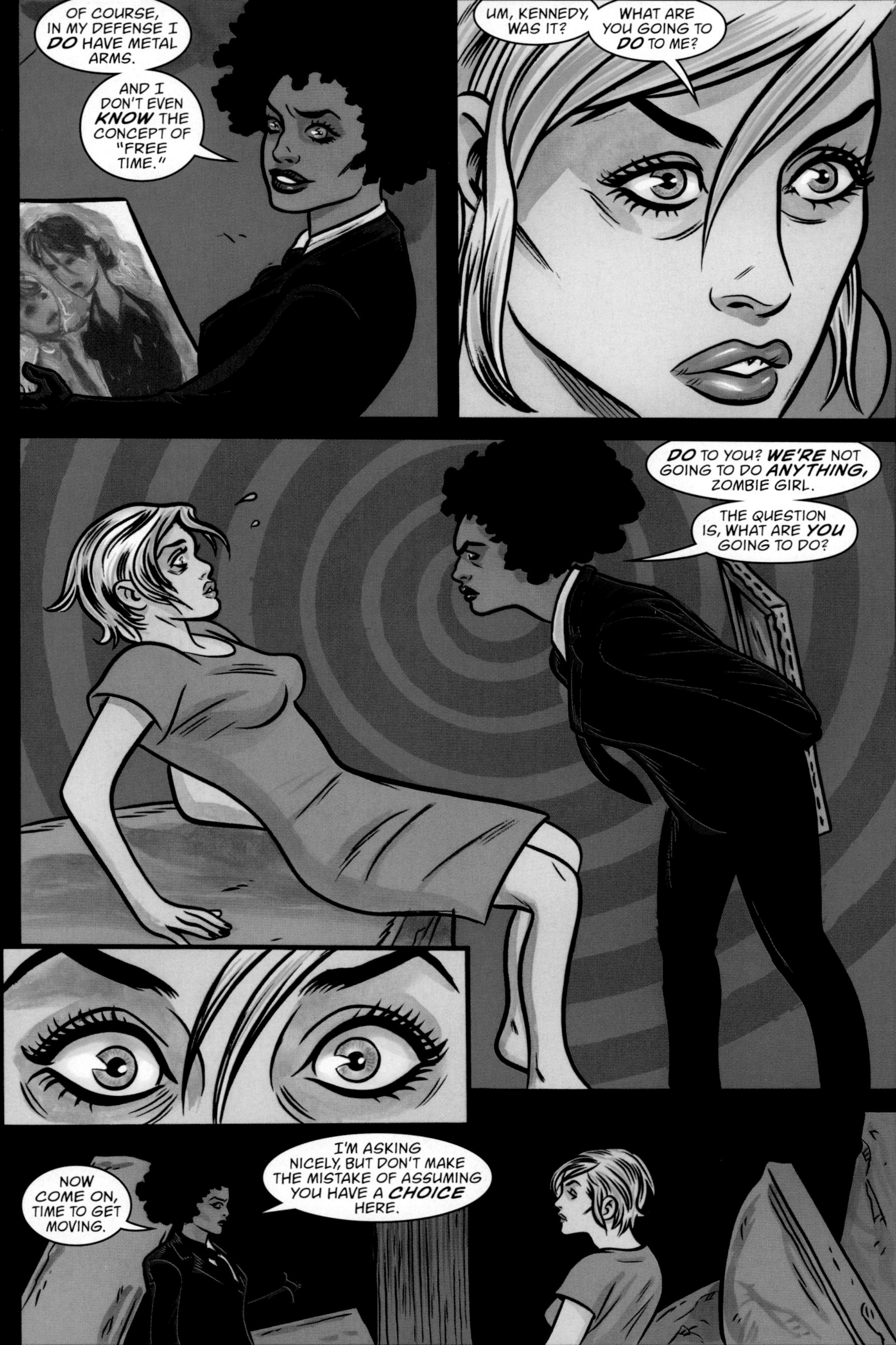
OF COURSE, IN MY DEFENSE I DO HAVE METAL ARMS.
AND I DON'T EVEN KNOW THE CONCEPT OF "FREE TIME."
UM, KENNEDY, WAS IT?
WHAT ARE YOU GOING TO DO TO ME?
DO TO YOU? WE'RE NOT GOING TO DO ANYTHING, ZOMBIE GIRL.
THE QUESTION IS, WHAT ARE YOU GOING TO DO?
NOW COME ON, TIME TO GET MOVING.
I'M ASKING NICELY, BUT DON'T MAKE THE MISTAKE OF ASSUMING YOU HAVE A CHOICE HERE.

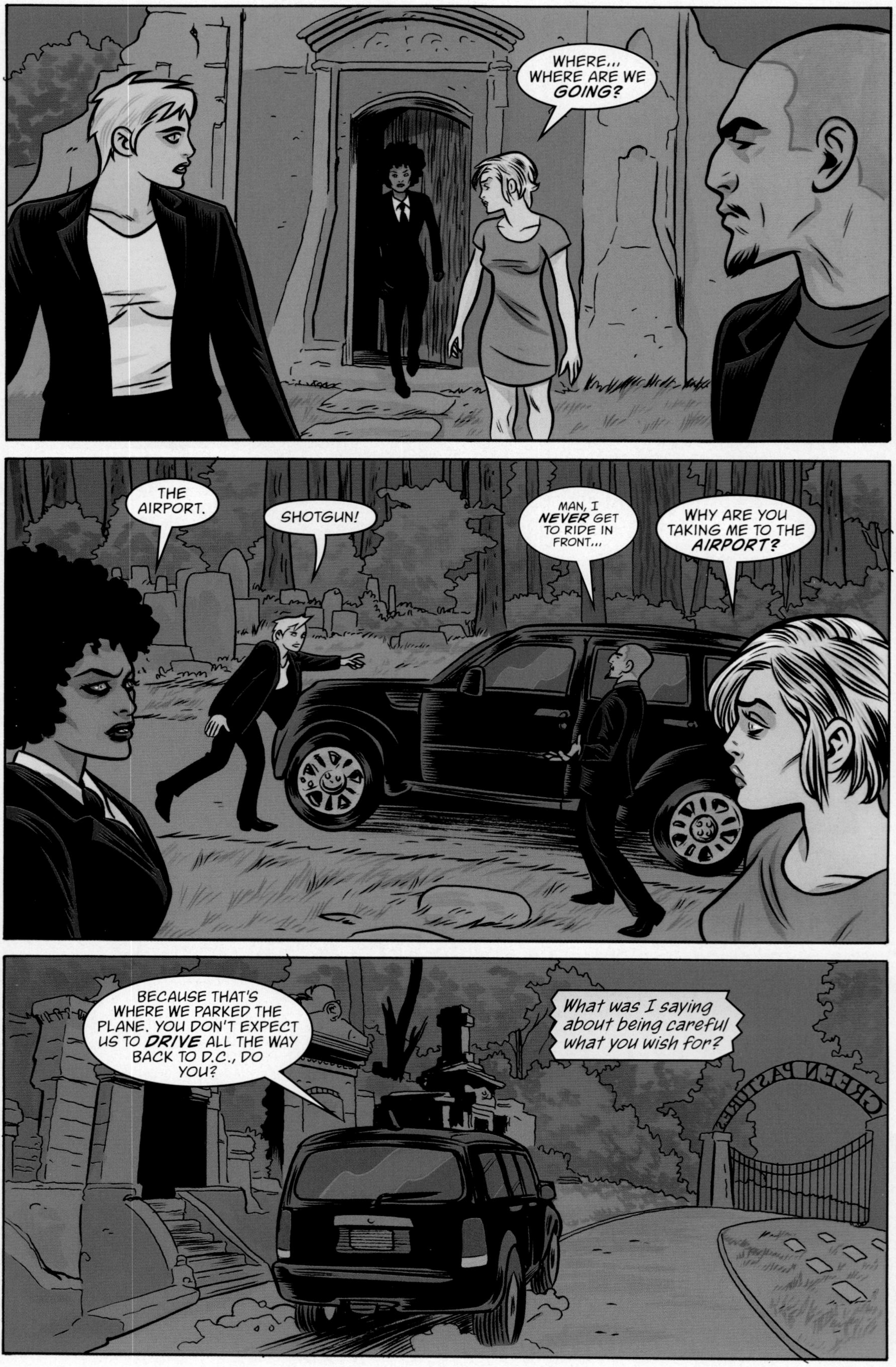
WHERE... WHERE ARE WE GOING?
THE AIRPORT.
SHOTGUN!
MAN, I NEVER GET TO RIDE IN FRONT...
WHY ARE YOU TAKING ME TO THE AIRPORT?
BECAUSE THAT'S WHERE WE PARKED THE PLANE. YOU DON'T EXPECT US TO DRIVE ALL THE WAY BACK TO D.C., DO YOU?
What was I saying about being careful what you wish for?

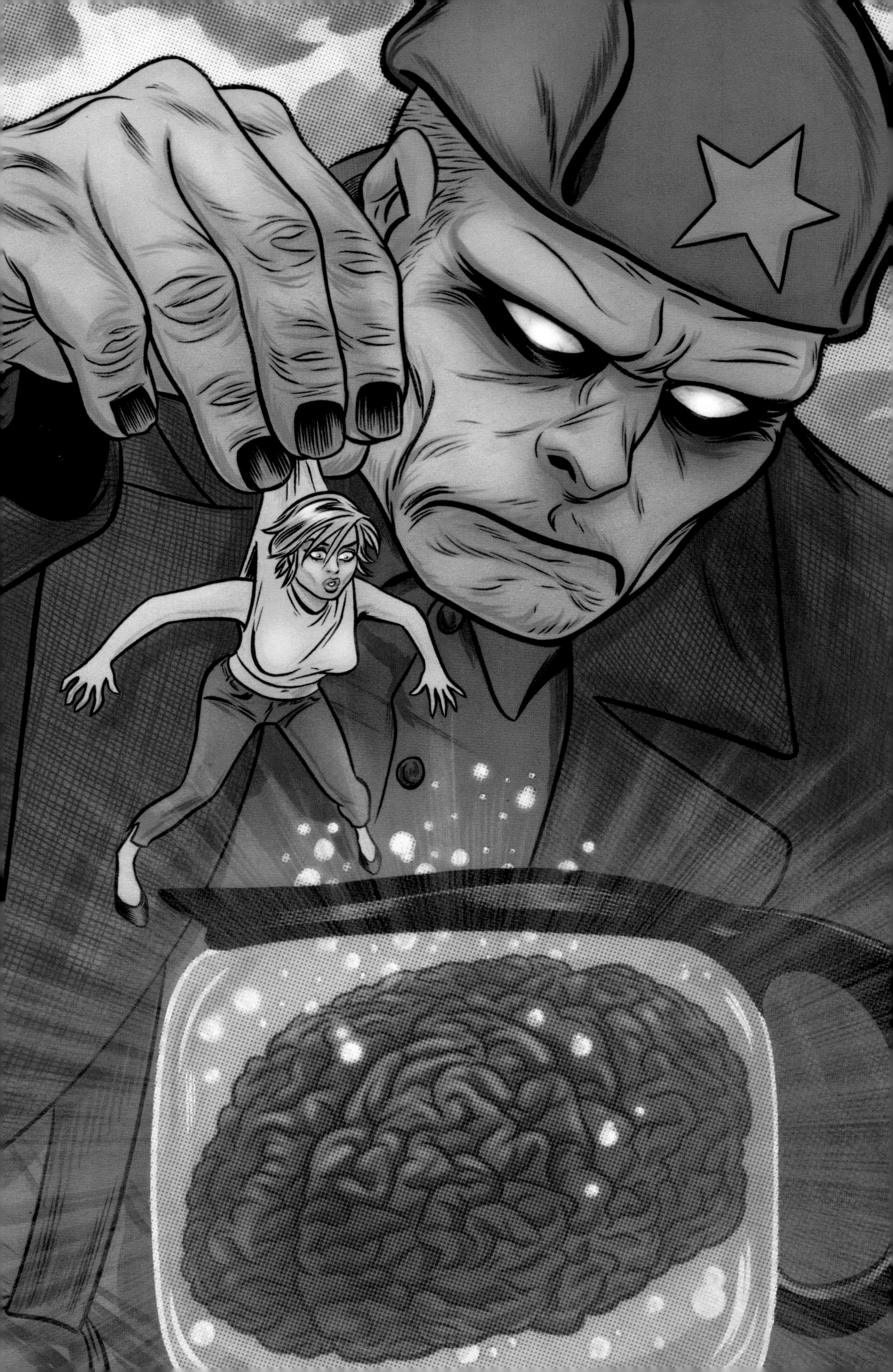

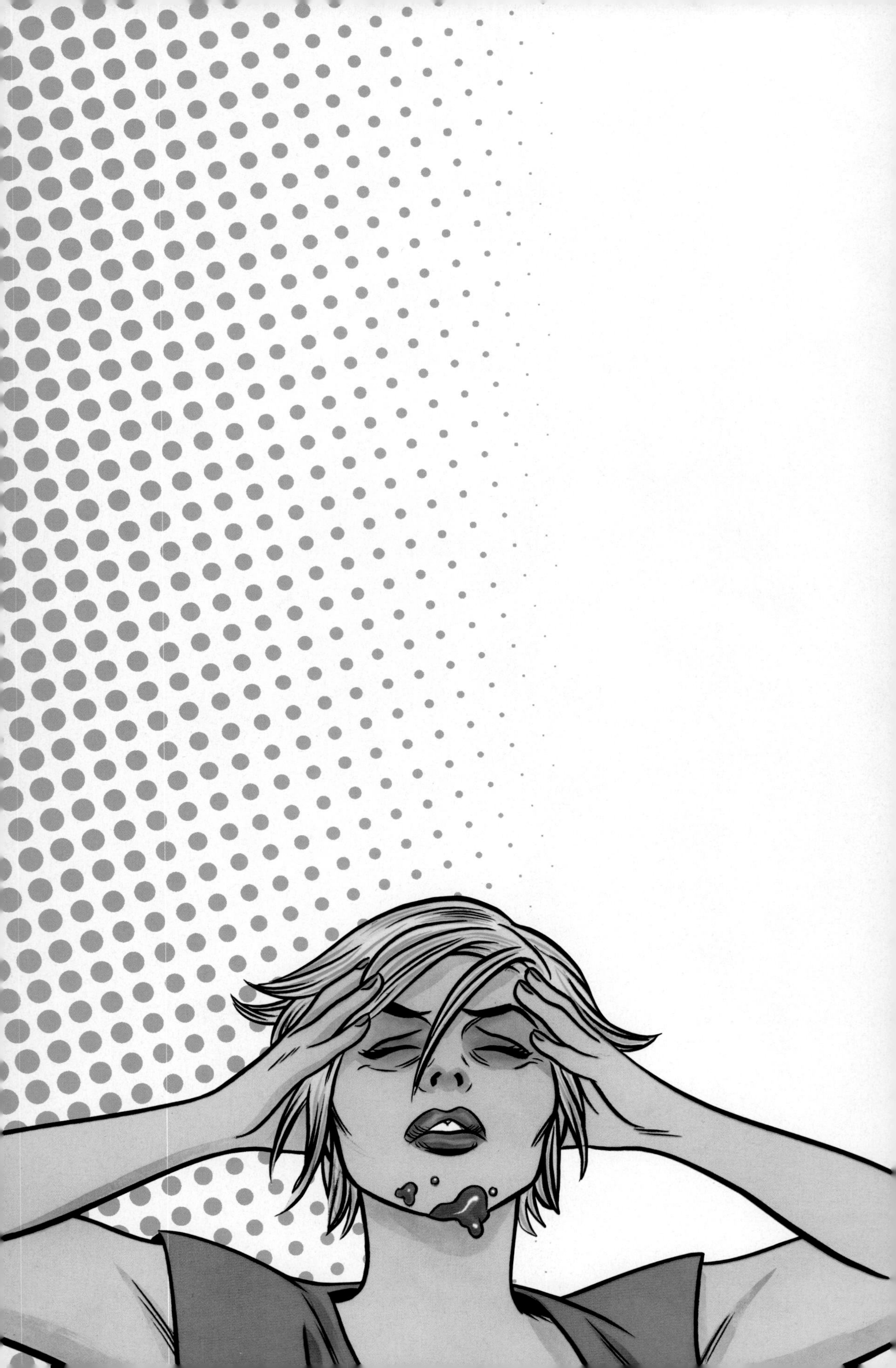

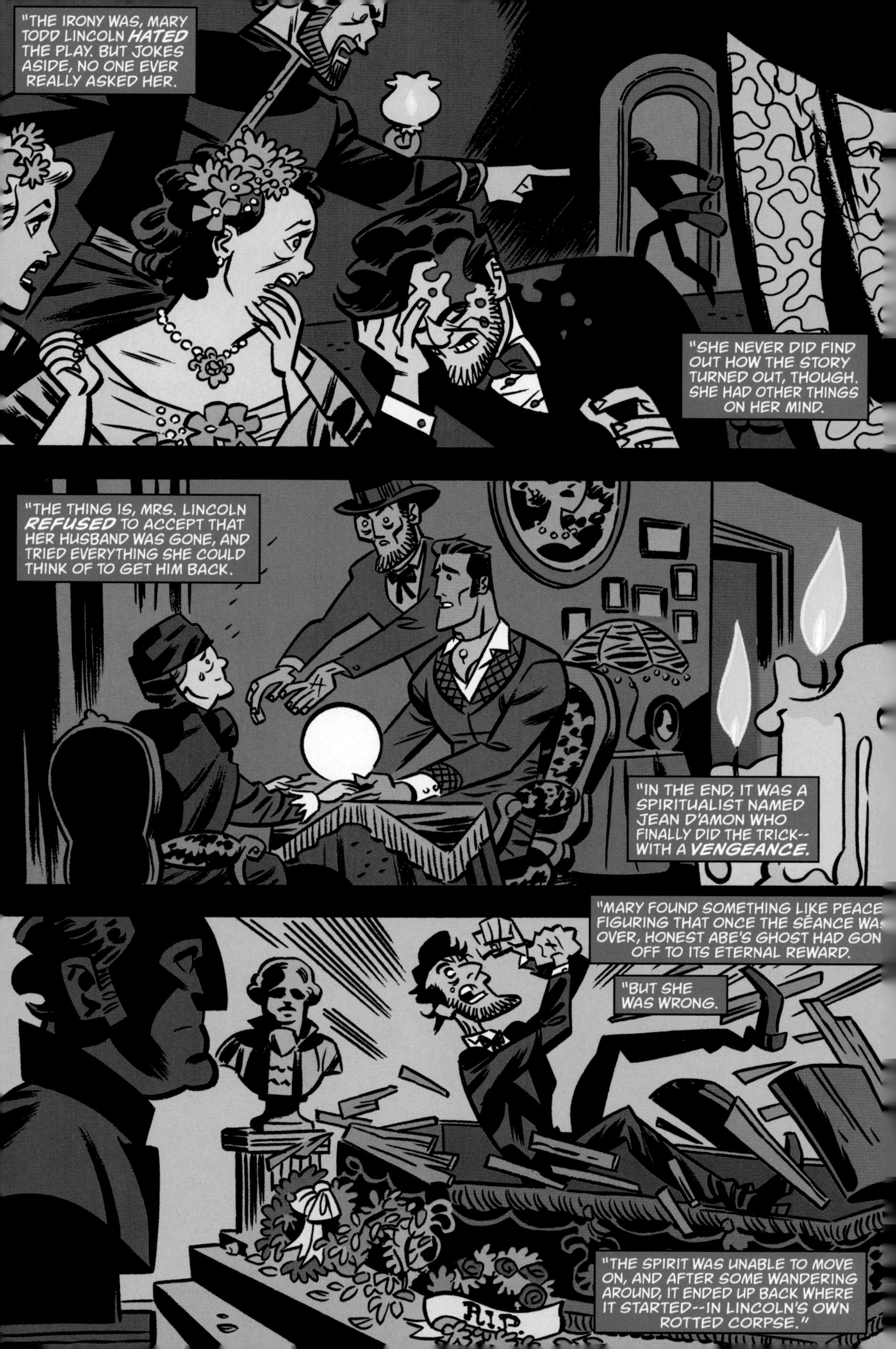
"THE IRONY WAS, MARY TODD LINCOLN *HATED* THE PLAY. BUT JOKES ASIDE, NO ONE EVER REALLY ASKED HER.
"SHE NEVER DID FIND OUT HOW THE STORY TURNED OUT, THOUGH. SHE HAD OTHER THINGS ON HER MIND.
"THE THING IS, MRS. LINCOLN *REFUSED* TO ACCEPT THAT HER HUSBAND WAS GONE, AND TRIED EVERYTHING SHE COULD THINK OF TO GET HIM BACK.
"IN THE END, IT WAS A SPIRITUALIST NAMED JEAN D'AMON WHO FINALLY DID THE TRICK-- WITH A *VENGEANCE*.
"MARY FOUND SOMETHING LIKE PEACE FIGURING THAT ONCE THE SÉANCE WA OVER, HONEST ABE'S GHOST HAD GON OFF TO ITS ETERNAL REWARD.
"BUT SHE WAS WRONG.
"THE SPIRIT WAS UNABLE TO MOVE ON, AND AFTER SOME WANDERING AROUND, IT ENDED UP BACK WHERE IT STARTED--IN LINCOLN'S OWN ROTTED CORPSE."
R.I.P.

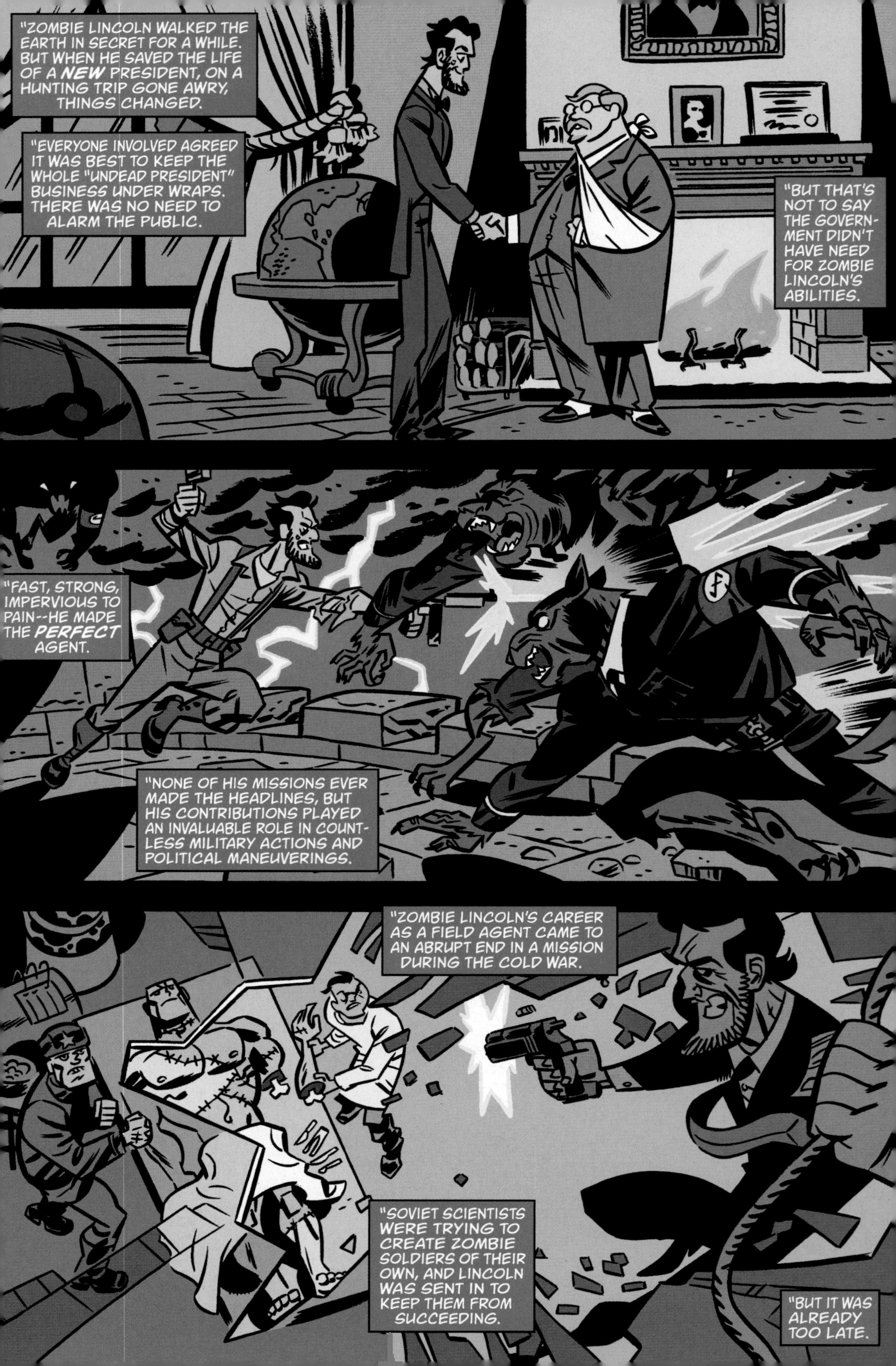
"ZOMBIE LINCOLN WALKED THE EARTH IN SECRET FOR A WHILE. BUT WHEN HE SAVED THE LIFE OF A *NEW* PRESIDENT, ON A HUNTING TRIP GONE AWRY, THINGS CHANGED.
"EVERYONE INVOLVED AGREED IT WAS BEST TO KEEP THE WHOLE "UNDEAD PRESIDENT" BUSINESS UNDER WRAPS. THERE WAS NO NEED TO ALARM THE PUBLIC.
"BUT THAT'S NOT TO SAY THE GOVERNMENT DIDN'T HAVE NEED FOR ZOMBIE LINCOLN'S ABILITIES.
"FAST, STRONG, IMPERVIOUS TO PAIN--HE MADE THE *PERFECT* AGENT.
"NONE OF HIS MISSIONS EVER MADE THE HEADLINES, BUT HIS CONTRIBUTIONS PLAYED AN INVALUABLE ROLE IN COUNTLESS MILITARY ACTIONS AND POLITICAL MANEUVERINGS.
"ZOMBIE LINCOLN'S CAREER AS A FIELD AGENT CAME TO AN ABRUPT END IN A MISSION DURING THE COLD WAR.
"SOVIET SCIENTISTS WERE TRYING TO CREATE ZOMBIE SOLDIERS OF THEIR OWN, AND LINCOLN WAS SENT IN TO KEEP THEM FROM SUCCEEDING.
"BUT IT WAS ALREADY TOO LATE.

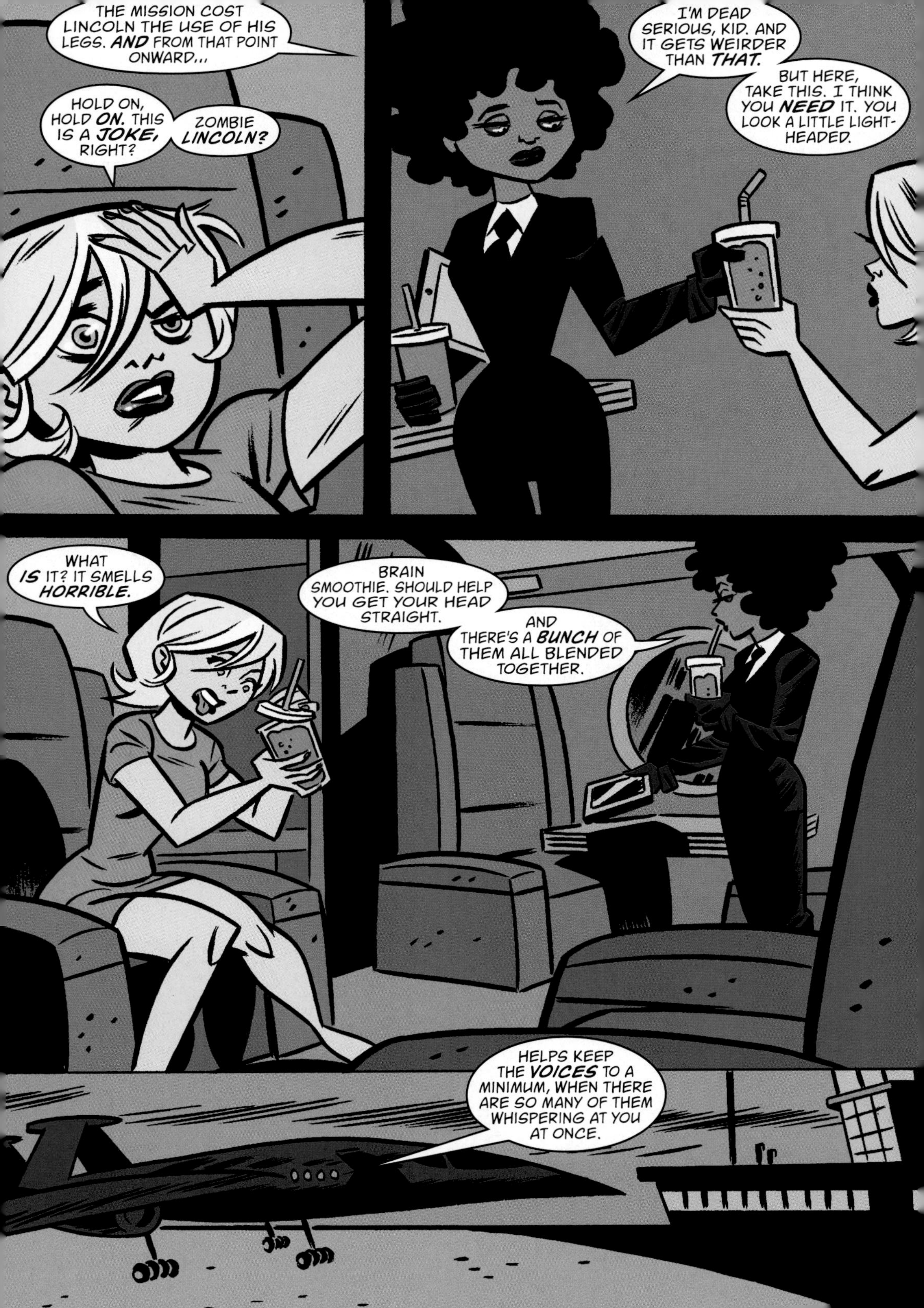
THE MISSION COST LINCOLN THE USE OF HIS LEGS. AND FROM THAT POINT ONWARD...
HOLD ON, HOLD ON. THIS IS A JOKE, RIGHT?
ZOMBIE LINCOLN?
I'M DEAD SERIOUS, KID. AND IT GETS WEIRDER THAN THAT.
BUT HERE, TAKE THIS. I THINK YOU NEED IT. YOU LOOK A LITTLE LIGHT-HEADED.
WHAT IS IT? IT SMELLS HORRIBLE.
BRAIN SMOOTHIE. SHOULD HELP YOU GET YOUR HEAD STRAIGHT.
AND THERE'S A BUNCH OF THEM ALL BLENDED TOGETHER.
HELPS KEEP THE VOICES TO A MINIMUM, WHEN THERE ARE SO MANY OF THEM WHISPERING AT YOU AT ONCE.

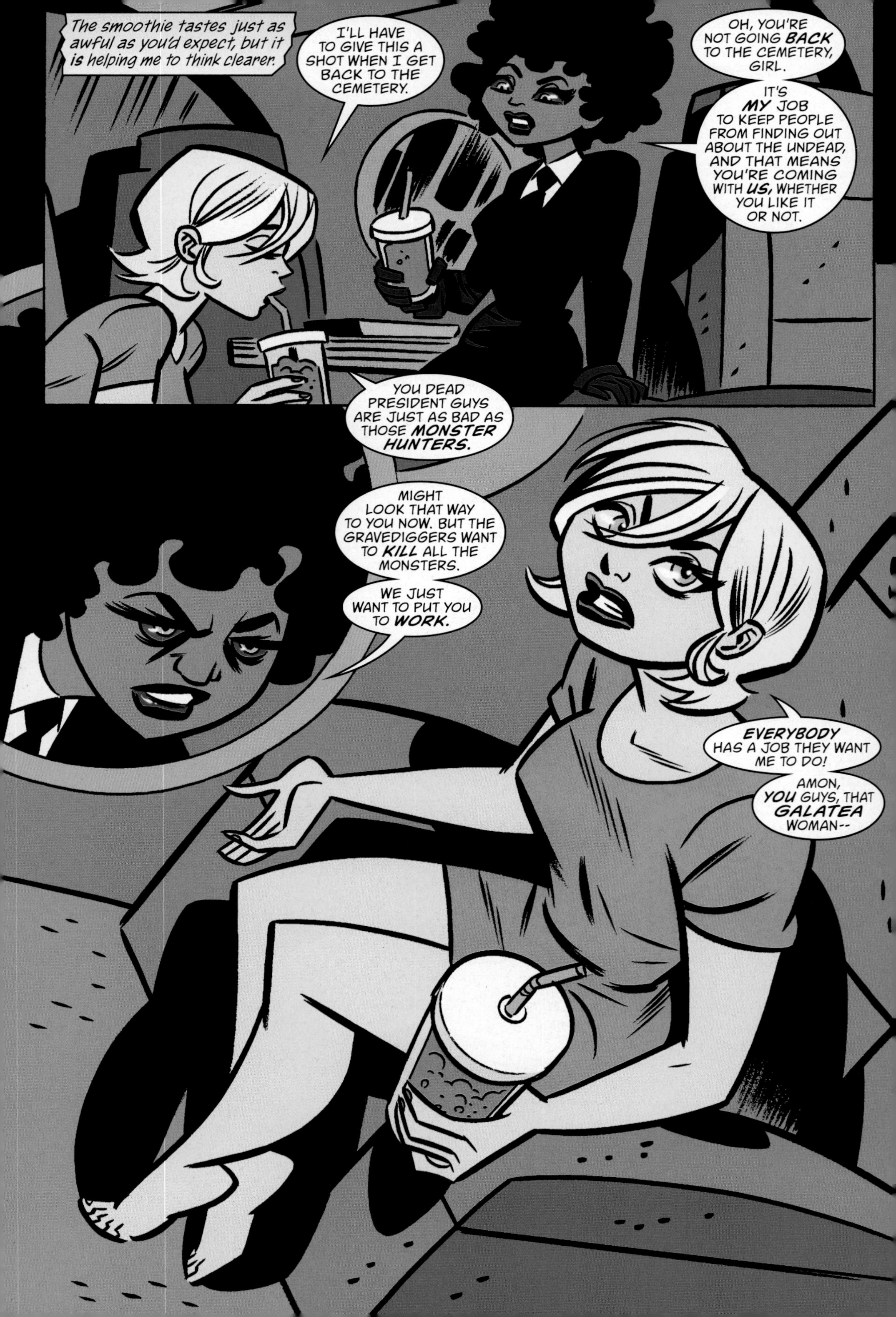
The smoothie tastes just as awful as you'd expect, but it is helping me to think clearer.
I'LL HAVE TO GIVE THIS A SHOT WHEN I GET BACK TO THE CEMETERY.
OH, YOU'RE NOT GOING BACK TO THE CEMETERY, GIRL.
IT'S MY JOB TO KEEP PEOPLE FROM FINDING OUT ABOUT THE UNDEAD, AND THAT MEANS YOU'RE COMING WITH US, WHETHER YOU LIKE IT OR NOT.
YOU DEAD PRESIDENT GUYS ARE JUST AS BAD AS THOSE MONSTER HUNTERS.
MIGHT LOOK THAT WAY TO YOU NOW. BUT THE GRAVEDIGGERS WANT TO KILL ALL THE MONSTERS.
WE JUST WANT TO PUT YOU TO WORK.
EVERYBODY HAS A JOB THEY WANT ME TO DO!
AMON, YOU GUYS, THAT GALATEA WOMAN--

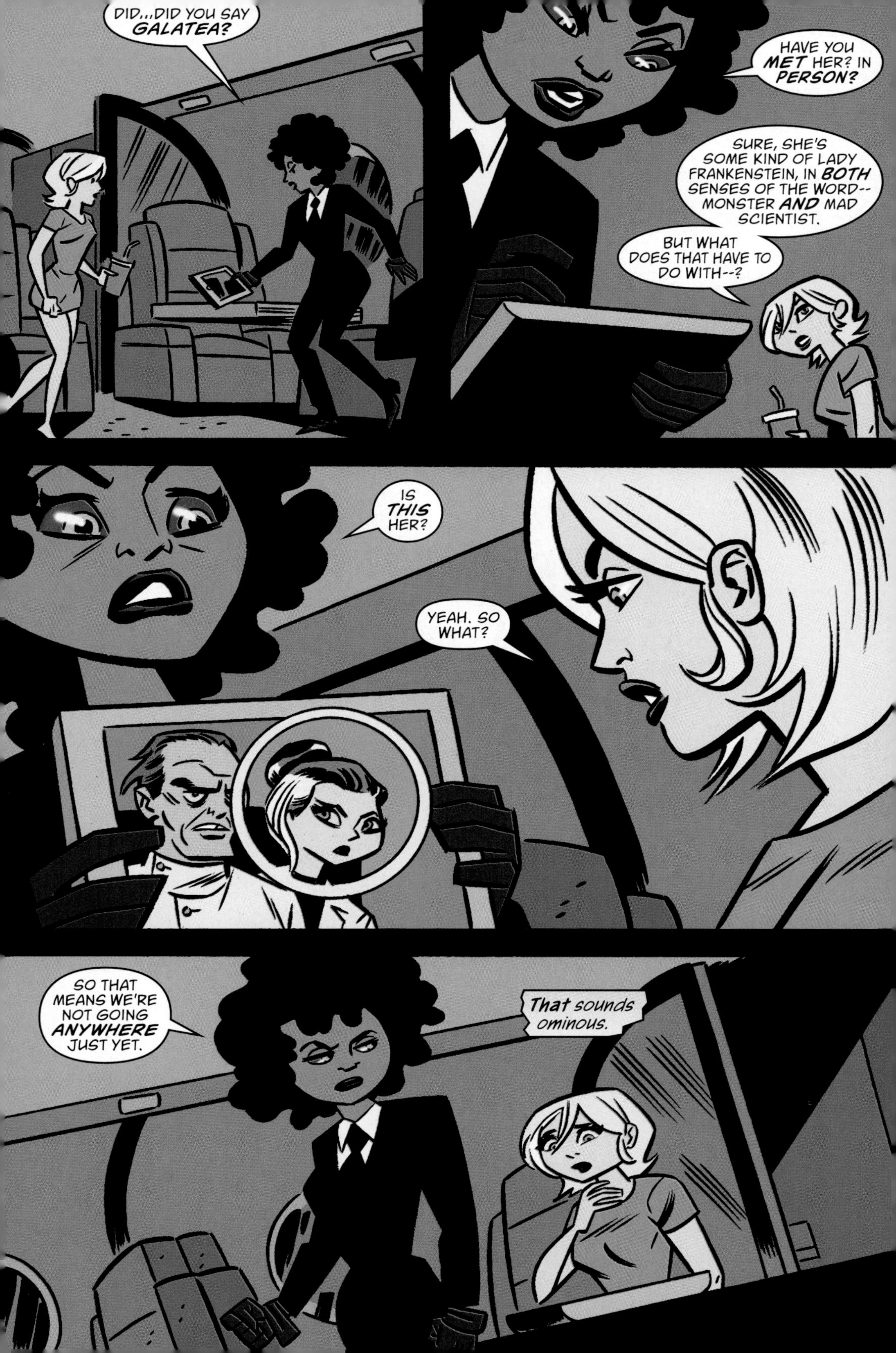
DID...DID YOU SAY GALATEA?
HAVE YOU MET HER? IN PERSON?
SURE, SHE'S SOME KIND OF LADY FRANKENSTEIN, IN BOTH SENSES OF THE WORD-- MONSTER AND MAD SCIENTIST.
BUT WHAT DOES THAT HAVE TO DO WITH--?
IS THIS HER?
YEAH. SO WHAT?
SO THAT MEANS WE'RE NOT GOING ANYWHERE JUST YET.
That sounds ominous.

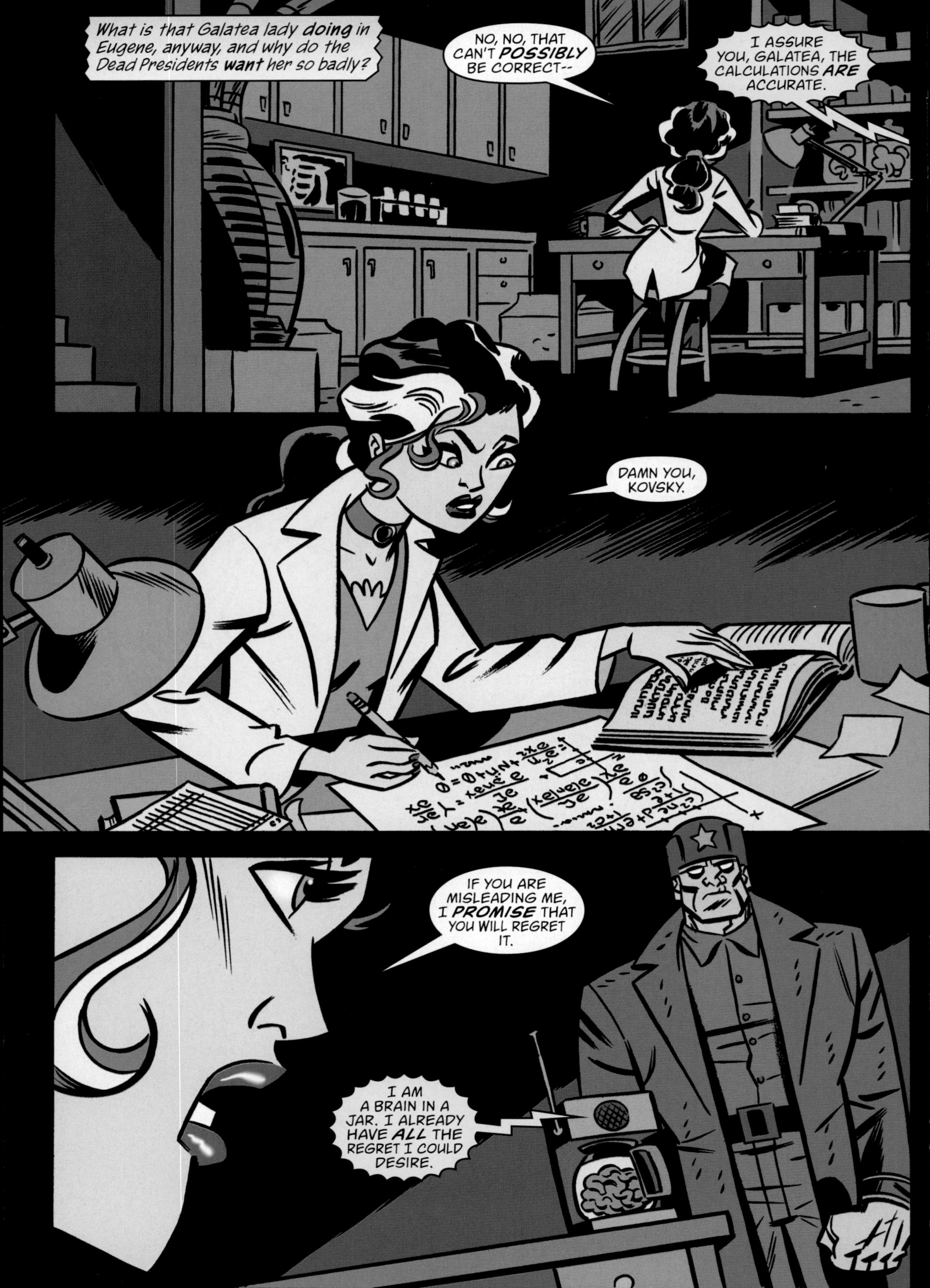

What is that Galatea lady doing in Eugene, anyway, and why do the Dead Presidents want her so badly?
NO, NO, THAT CAN'T POSSIBLY BE CORRECT--
I ASSURE YOU, GALATEA, THE CALCULATIONS ARE ACCURATE.
DAMN YOU, KOVSKY.
IF YOU ARE MISLEADING ME, I PROMISE THAT YOU WILL REGRET IT.
I AM A BRAIN IN A JAR. I ALREADY HAVE ALL THE REGRET I COULD DESIRE.

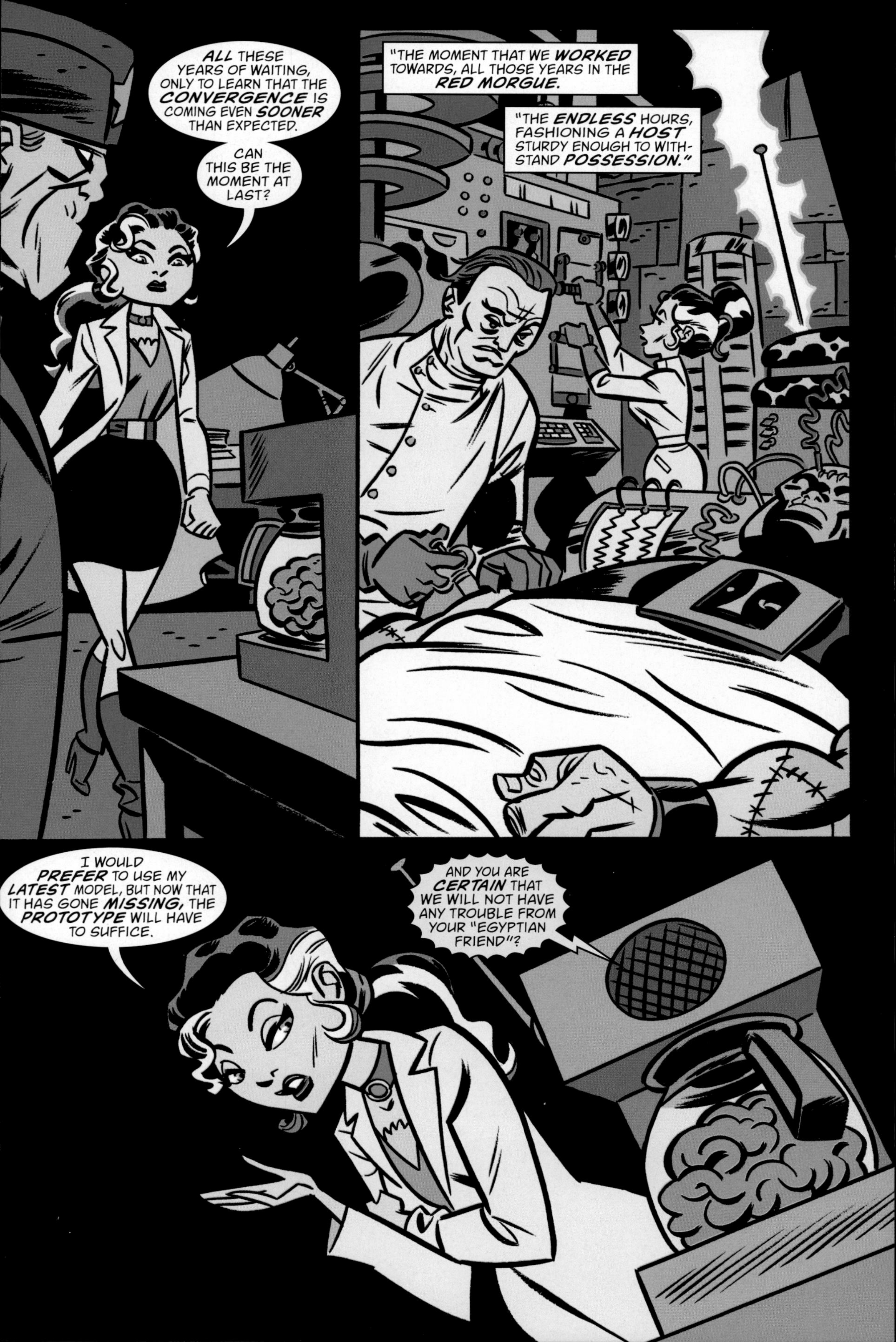
ALL THESE YEARS OF WAITING, ONLY TO LEARN THAT THE CONVERGENCE IS COMING EVEN SOONER THAN EXPECTED.
CAN THIS BE THE MOMENT AT LAST?
"THE MOMENT THAT WE WORKED TOWARDS, ALL THOSE YEARS IN THE RED MORGUE.
"THE ENDLESS HOURS, FASHIONING A HOST STURDY ENOUGH TO WITHSTAND POSSESSION."
I WOULD PREFER TO USE MY LATEST MODEL, BUT NOW THAT IT HAS GONE MISSING, THE PROTOTYPE WILL HAVE TO SUFFICE.
AND YOU ARE CERTAIN THAT WE WILL NOT HAVE ANY TROUBLE FROM YOUR "EGYPTIAN FRIEND"?

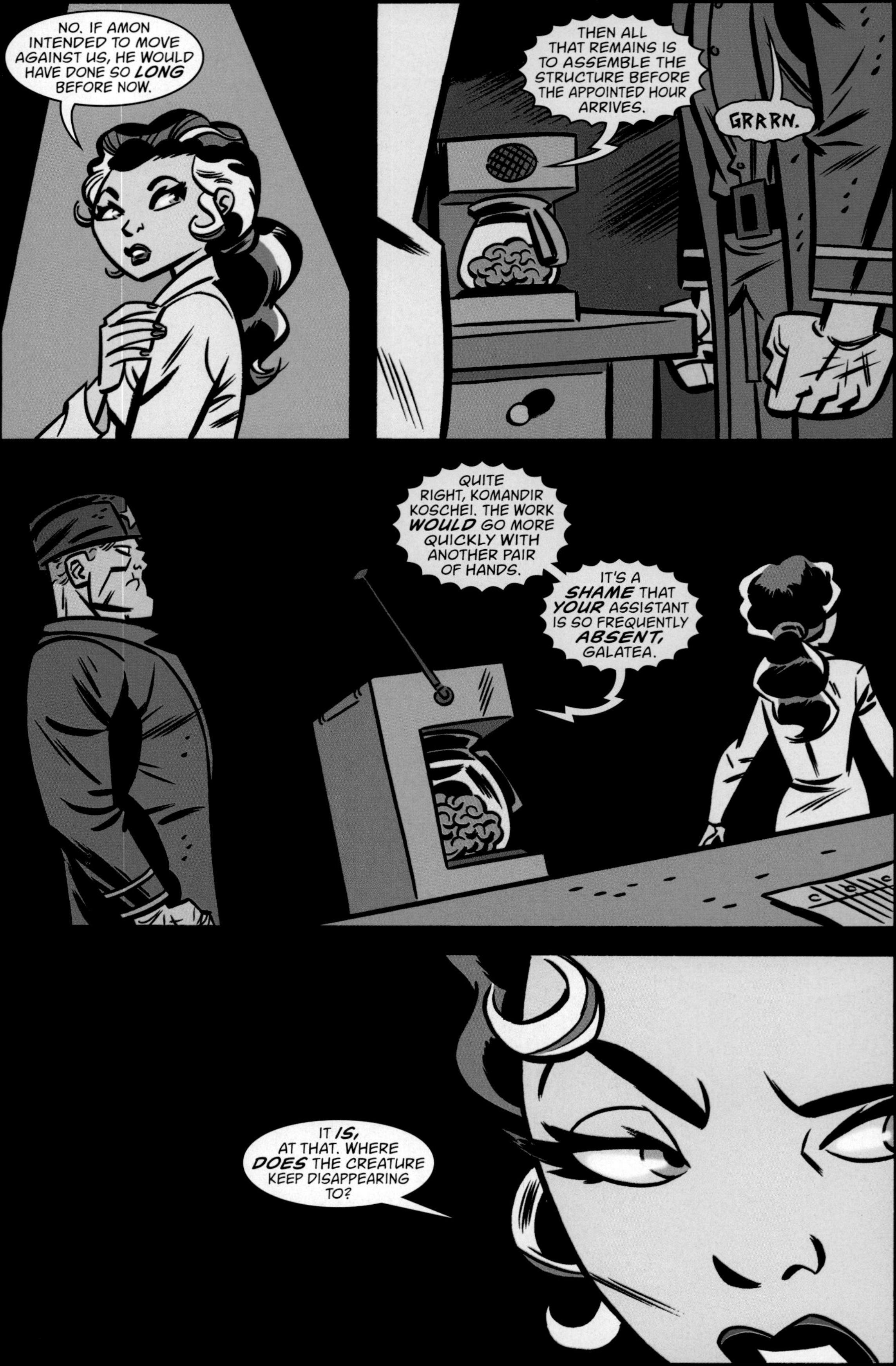
NO. IF AMON INTENDED TO MOVE AGAINST US, HE WOULD HAVE DONE SO LONG BEFORE NOW.
THEN ALL THAT REMAINS IS TO ASSEMBLE THE STRUCTURE BEFORE THE APPOINTED HOUR ARRIVES.
GRARN.
QUITE RIGHT, KOMANDIR KOSCHEI. THE WORK WOULD GO MORE QUICKLY WITH ANOTHER PAIR OF HANDS.
IT'S A SHAME THAT YOUR ASSISTANT IS SO FREQUENTLY ABSENT, GALATEA.
IT IS, AT THAT. WHERE DOES THE CREATURE KEEP DISAPPEARING TO?

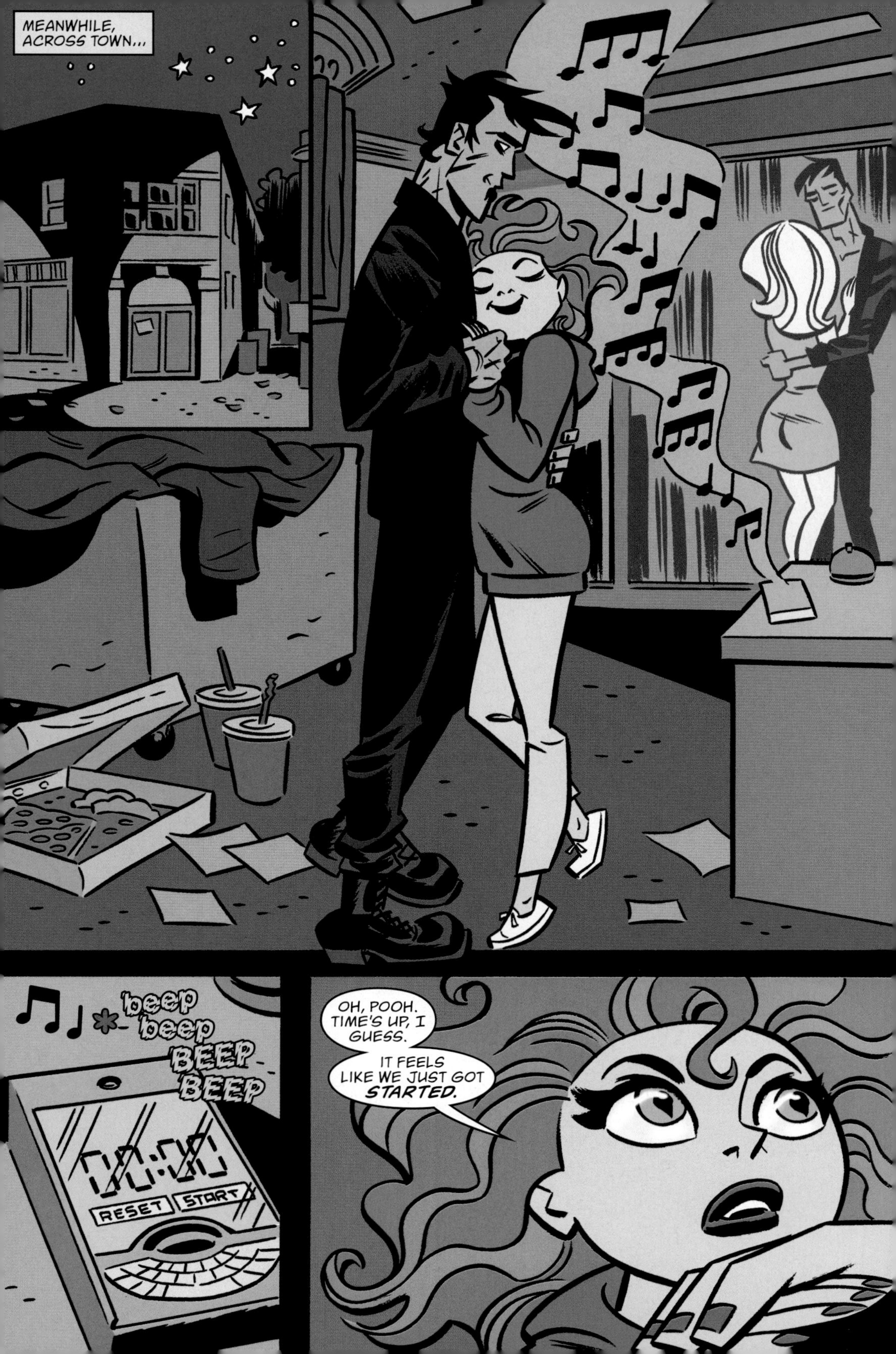
MEANWHILE, ACROSS TOWN...
'beep 'beep BEEP BEEP
RESET
START
OH, POOH. TIME'S UP, I GUESS.
IT FEELS LIKE WE JUST GOT *STARTED.*

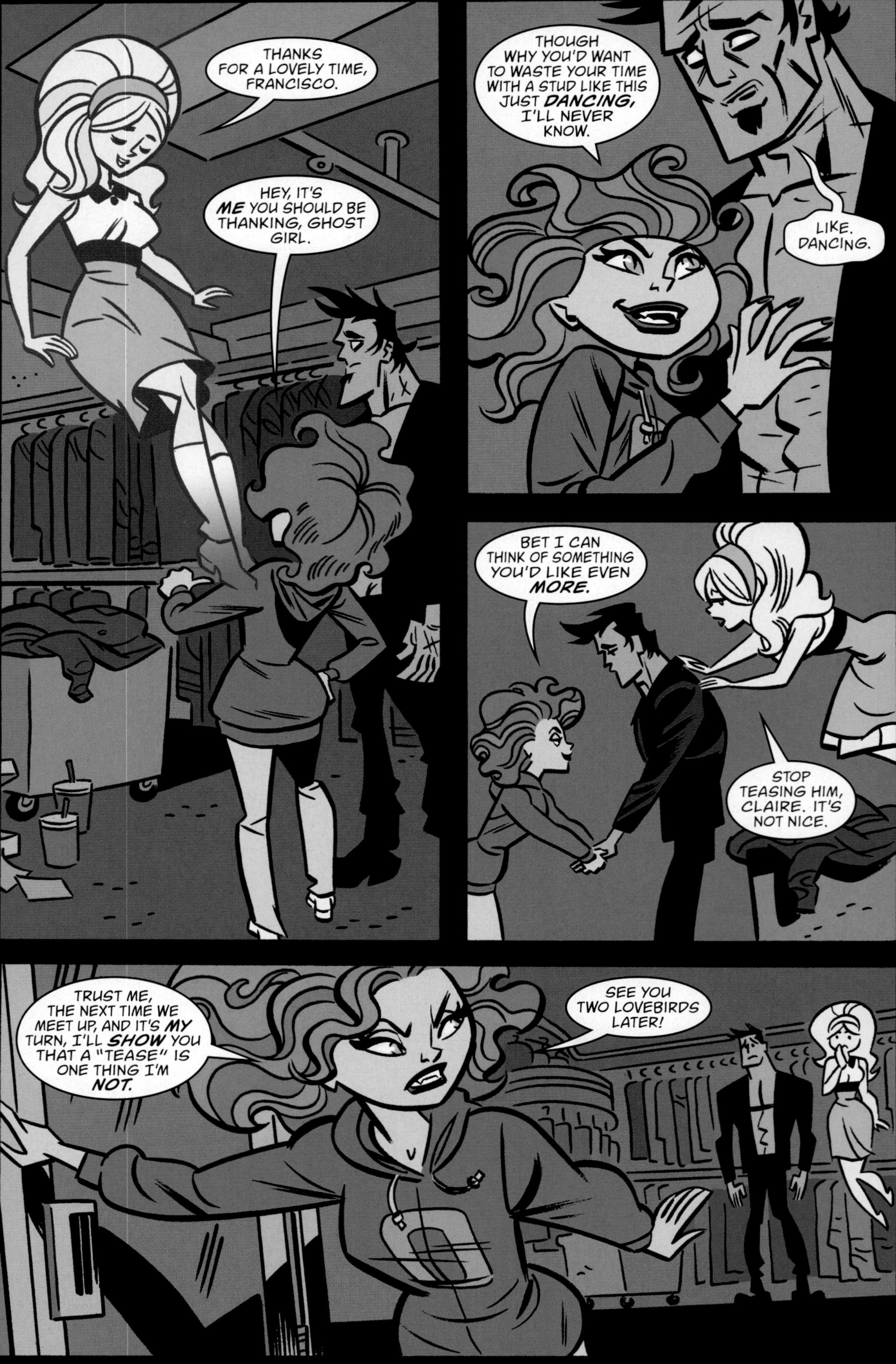
THANKS FOR A LOVELY TIME, FRANCISCO.
HEY, IT'S ME YOU SHOULD BE THANKING, GHOST GIRL.
THOUGH WHY YOU'D WANT TO WASTE YOUR TIME WITH A STUD LIKE THIS JUST DANCING, I'LL NEVER KNOW.
LIKE. DANCING.
BET I CAN THINK OF SOMETHING YOU'D LIKE EVEN MORE.
STOP TEASING HIM, CLAIRE. IT'S NOT NICE.
TRUST ME, THE NEXT TIME WE MEET UP, AND IT'S MY TURN, I'LL SHOW YOU THAT A "TEASE" IS ONE THING I'M NOT.
SEE YOU TWO LOVEBIRDS LATER!

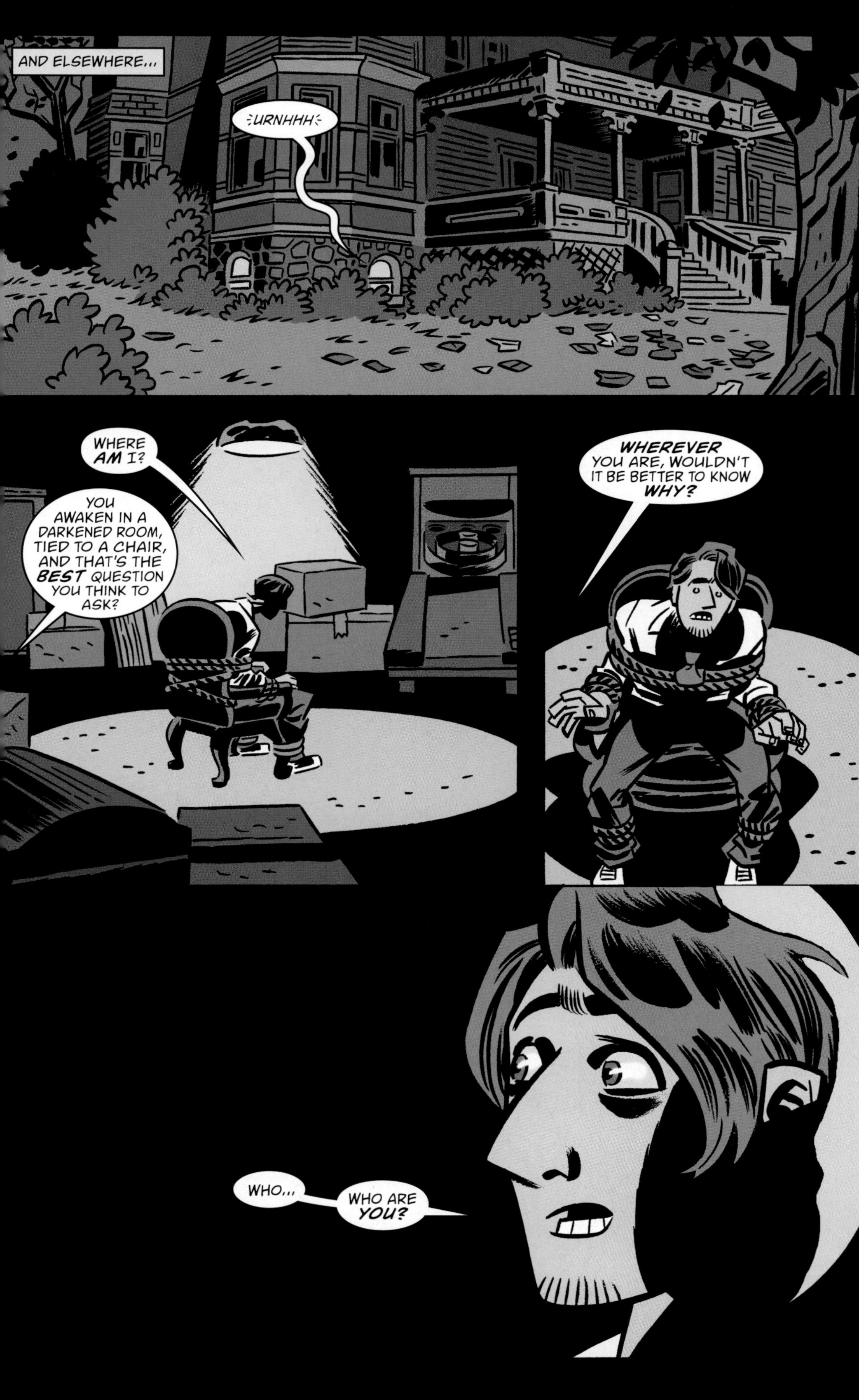
AND ELSEWHERE...
URNHHH
WHERE AM I?
YOU AWAKEN IN A DARKENED ROOM, TIED TO A CHAIR, AND THAT'S THE BEST QUESTION YOU THINK TO ASK?
WHEREVER YOU ARE, WOULDN'T IT BE BETTER TO KNOW WHY?
WHO...
WHO ARE YOU?

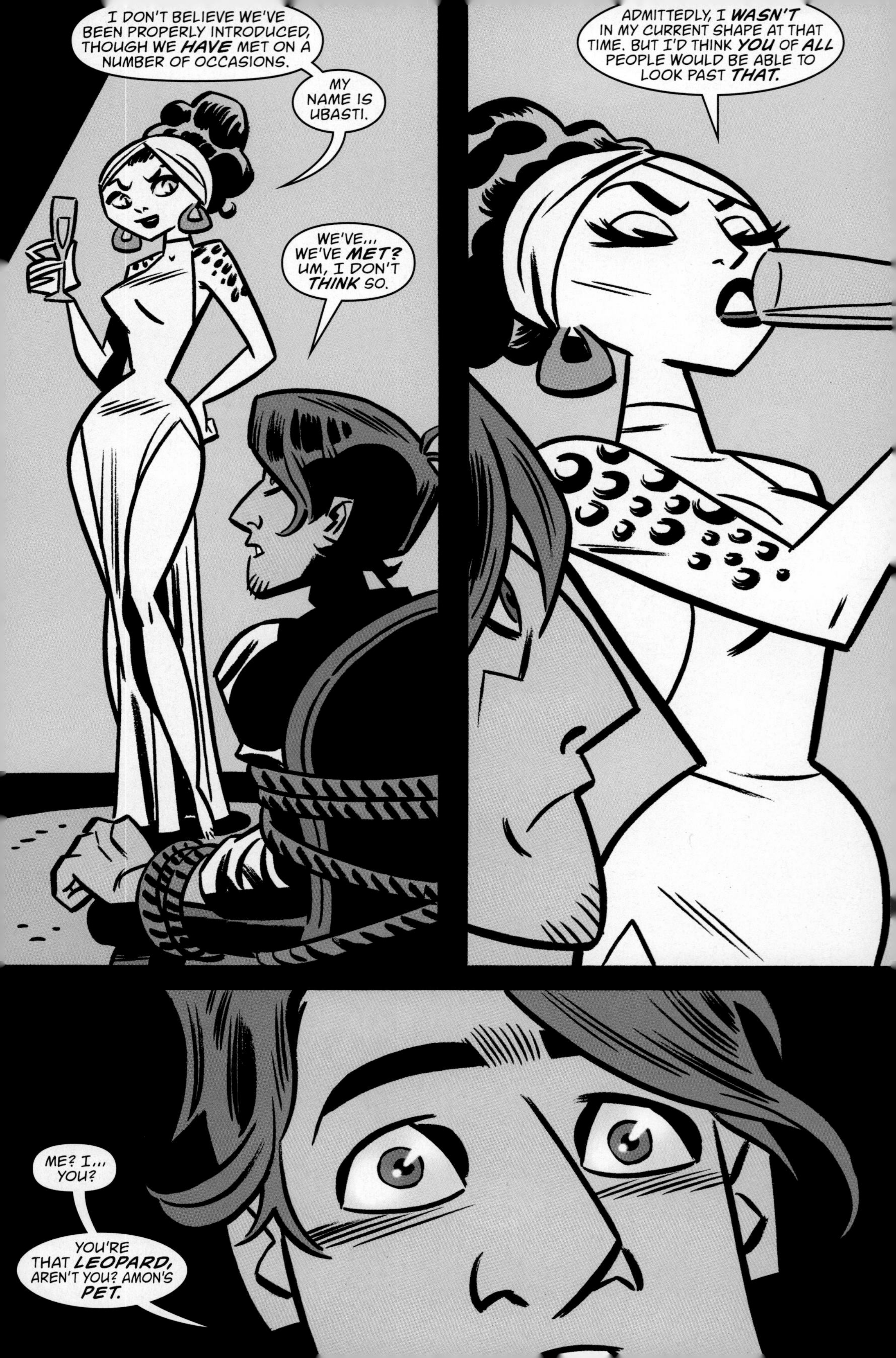
I DON'T BELIEVE WE'VE BEEN PROPERLY INTRODUCED, THOUGH WE ***HAVE*** MET ON A NUMBER OF OCCASIONS.
MY NAME IS UBASTI.
WE'VE... WE'VE ***MET?*** UM, I DON'T ***THINK*** SO.
ADMITTEDLY, I ***WASN'T*** IN MY CURRENT SHAPE AT THAT TIME. BUT I'D THINK ***YOU*** OF ***ALL*** PEOPLE WOULD BE ABLE TO LOOK PAST ***THAT.***
ME? I... YOU?
YOU'RE THAT ***LEOPARD,*** AREN'T YOU? AMON'S ***PET.***

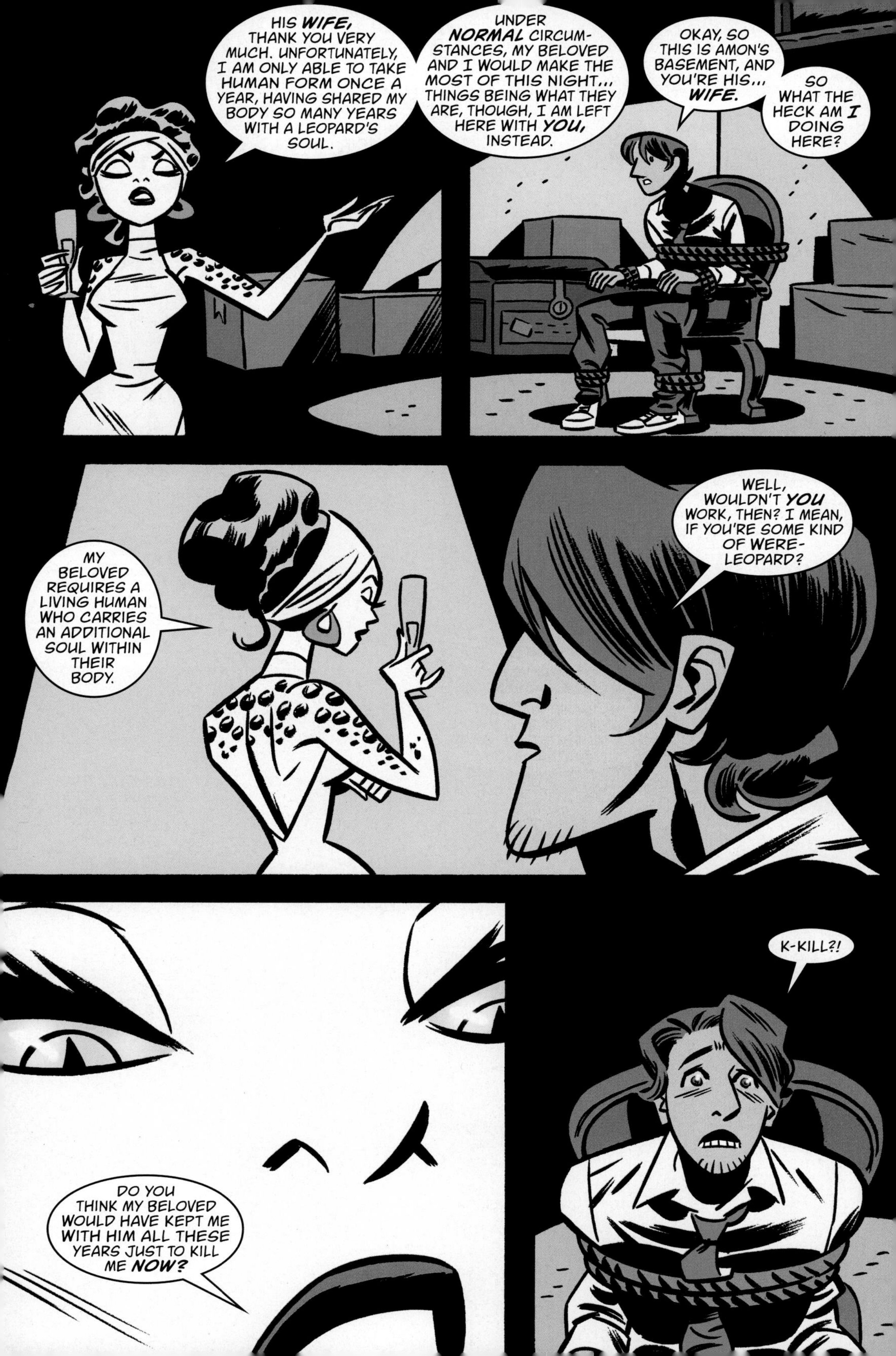
HIS WIFE, THANK YOU VERY MUCH. UNFORTUNATELY, I AM ONLY ABLE TO TAKE HUMAN FORM ONCE A YEAR, HAVING SHARED MY BODY SO MANY YEARS WITH A LEOPARD'S SOUL.
UNDER NORMAL CIRCUMSTANCES, MY BELOVED AND I WOULD MAKE THE MOST OF THIS NIGHT... THINGS BEING WHAT THEY ARE, THOUGH, I AM LEFT HERE WITH YOU, INSTEAD.
OKAY, SO THIS IS AMON'S BASEMENT, AND YOU'RE HIS... WIFE.
SO WHAT THE HECK AM I DOING HERE?
MY BELOVED REQUIRES A LIVING HUMAN WHO CARRIES AN ADDITIONAL SOUL WITHIN THEIR BODY.
WELL, WOULDN'T YOU WORK, THEN? I MEAN, IF YOU'RE SOME KIND OF WERE-LEOPARD?
DO YOU THINK MY BELOVED WOULD HAVE KEPT ME WITH HIM ALL THESE YEARS JUST TO KILL ME NOW?
K-KILL?!

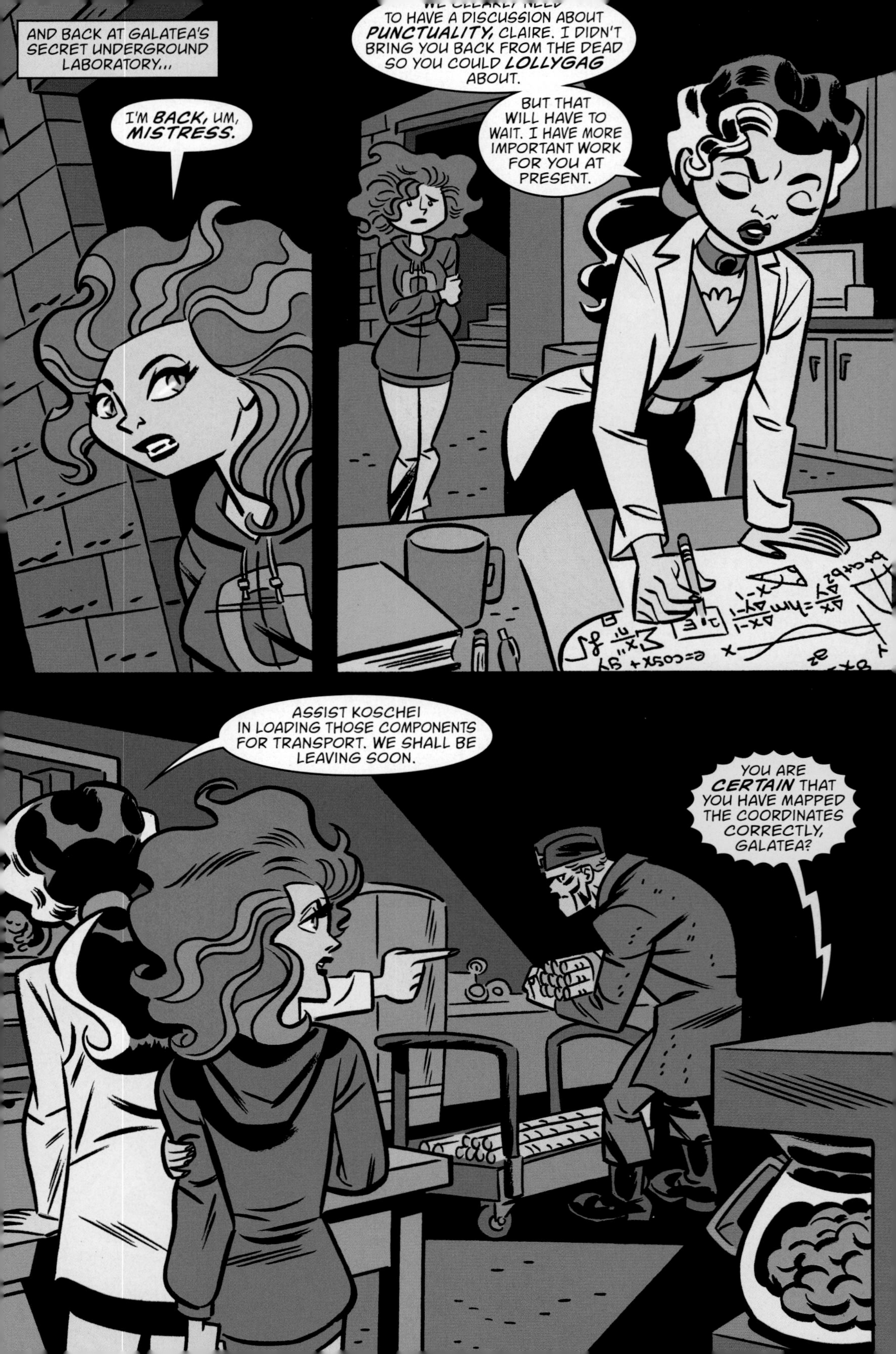
AND BACK AT GALATEA'S SECRET UNDERGROUND LABORATORY...
I'M BACK, UM, MISTRESS.
TO HAVE A DISCUSSION ABOUT PUNCTUALITY, CLAIRE. I DIDN'T BRING YOU BACK FROM THE DEAD SO YOU COULD LOLLYGAG ABOUT.
BUT THAT WILL HAVE TO WAIT. I HAVE MORE IMPORTANT WORK FOR YOU AT PRESENT.
ASSIST KOSCHEI IN LOADING THOSE COMPONENTS FOR TRANSPORT. WE SHALL BE LEAVING SOON.
YOU ARE CERTAIN THAT YOU HAVE MAPPED THE COORDINATES CORRECTLY, GALATEA?

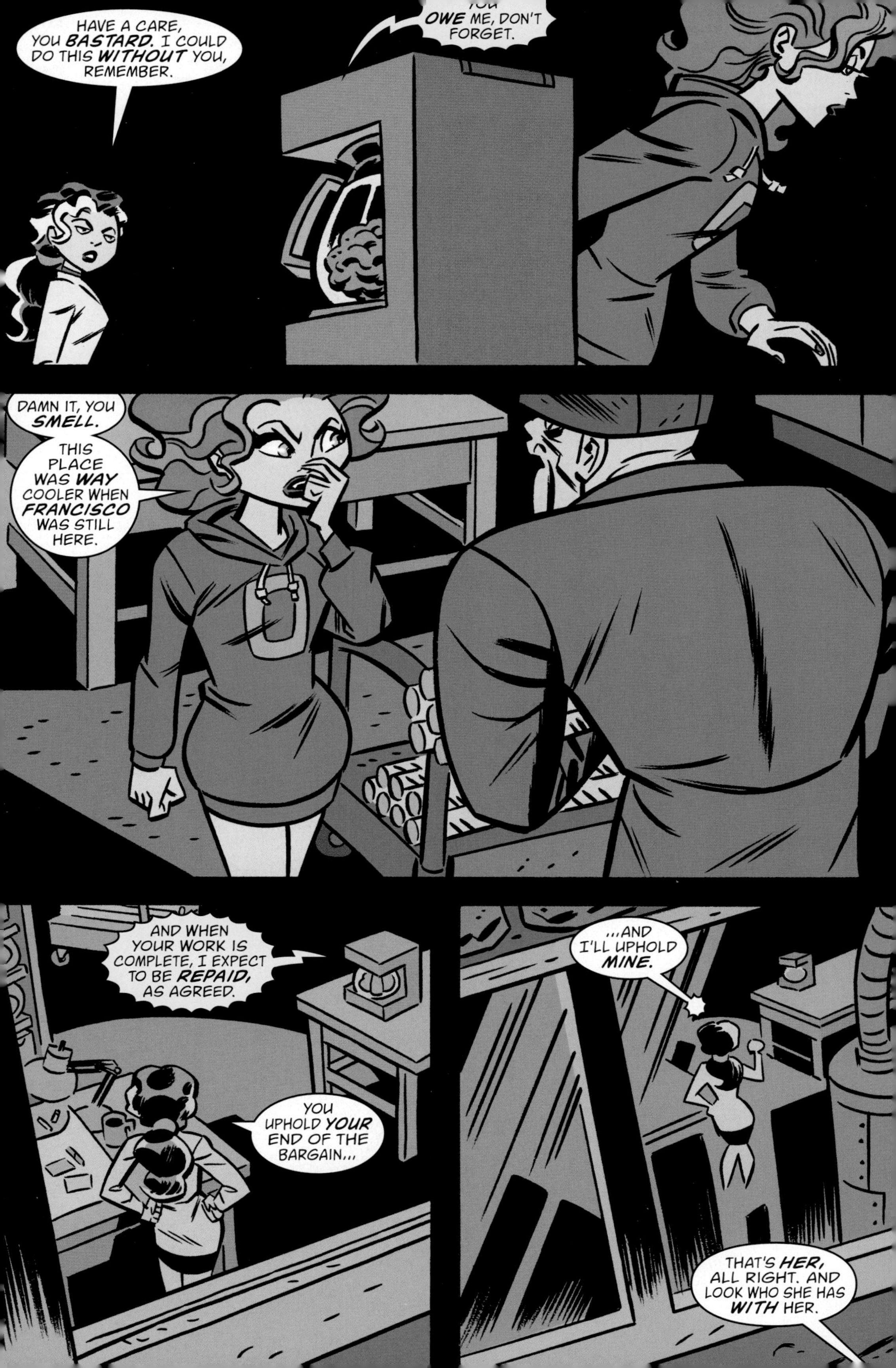
HAVE A CARE, YOU **BASTARD.** I COULD DO THIS **WITHOUT** YOU, REMEMBER.
OWE ME, DON'T FORGET.
DAMN IT, YOU **SMELL.**
THIS PLACE WAS **WAY** COOLER WHEN **FRANCISCO** WAS STILL HERE.
AND WHEN YOUR WORK IS COMPLETE, I EXPECT TO BE **REPAID,** AS AGREED.
YOU UPHOLD **YOUR** END OF THE BARGAIN...
...AND I'LL UPHOLD **MINE.**
THAT'S **HER,** ALL RIGHT. AND LOOK WHO SHE HAS **WITH** HER.

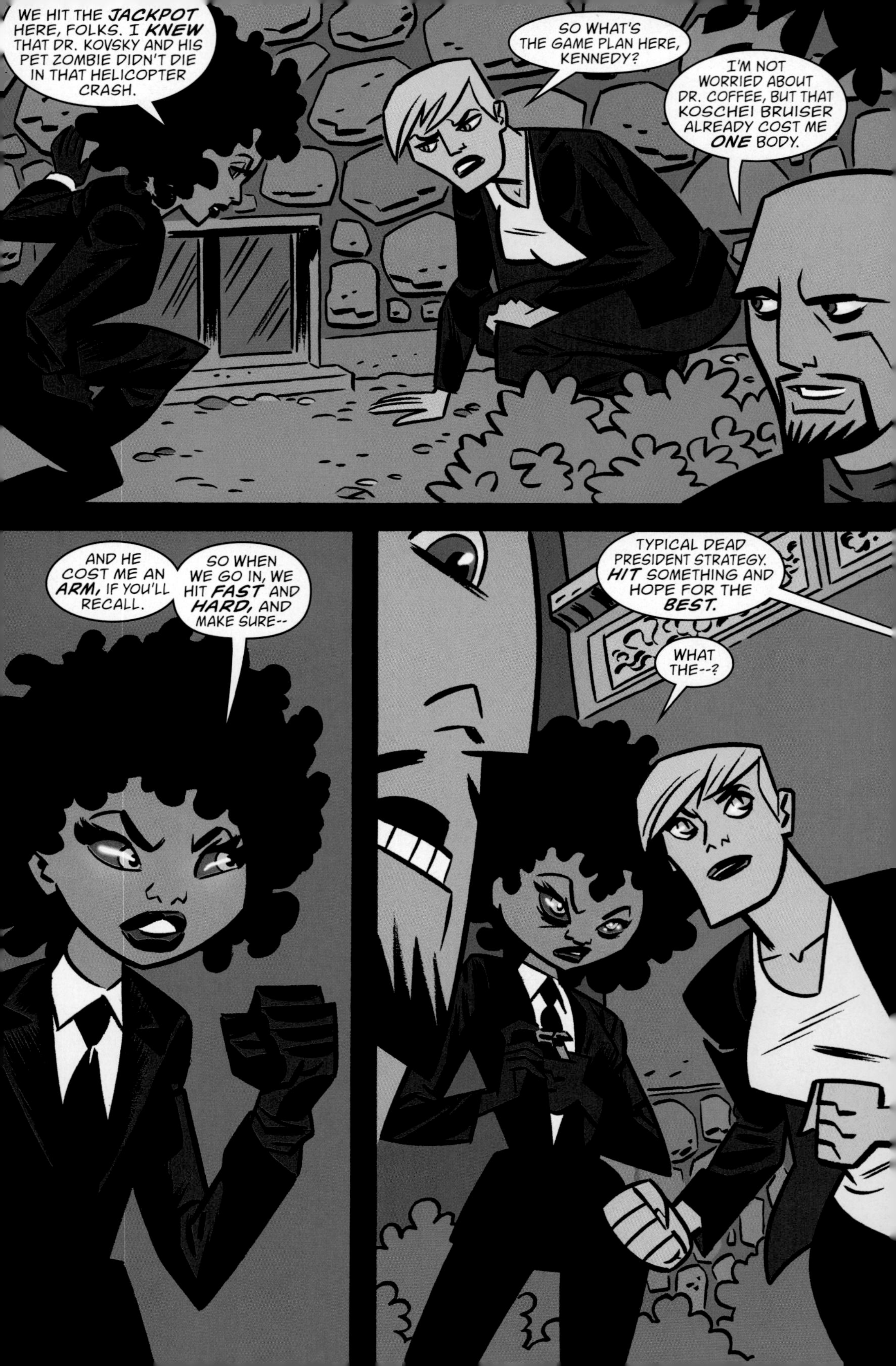
WE HIT THE JACKPOT HERE, FOLKS. I KNEW THAT DR. KOVSKY AND HIS PET ZOMBIE DIDN'T DIE IN THAT HELICOPTER CRASH.
SO WHAT'S THE GAME PLAN HERE, KENNEDY?
I'M NOT WORRIED ABOUT DR. COFFEE, BUT THAT KOSCHEI BRUISER ALREADY COST ME ONE BODY.
AND HE COST ME AN ARM, IF YOU'LL RECALL.
SO WHEN WE GO IN, WE HIT FAST AND HARD, AND MAKE SURE--
TYPICAL DEAD PRESIDENT STRATEGY. HIT SOMETHING AND HOPE FOR THE BEST.
WHAT THE--?

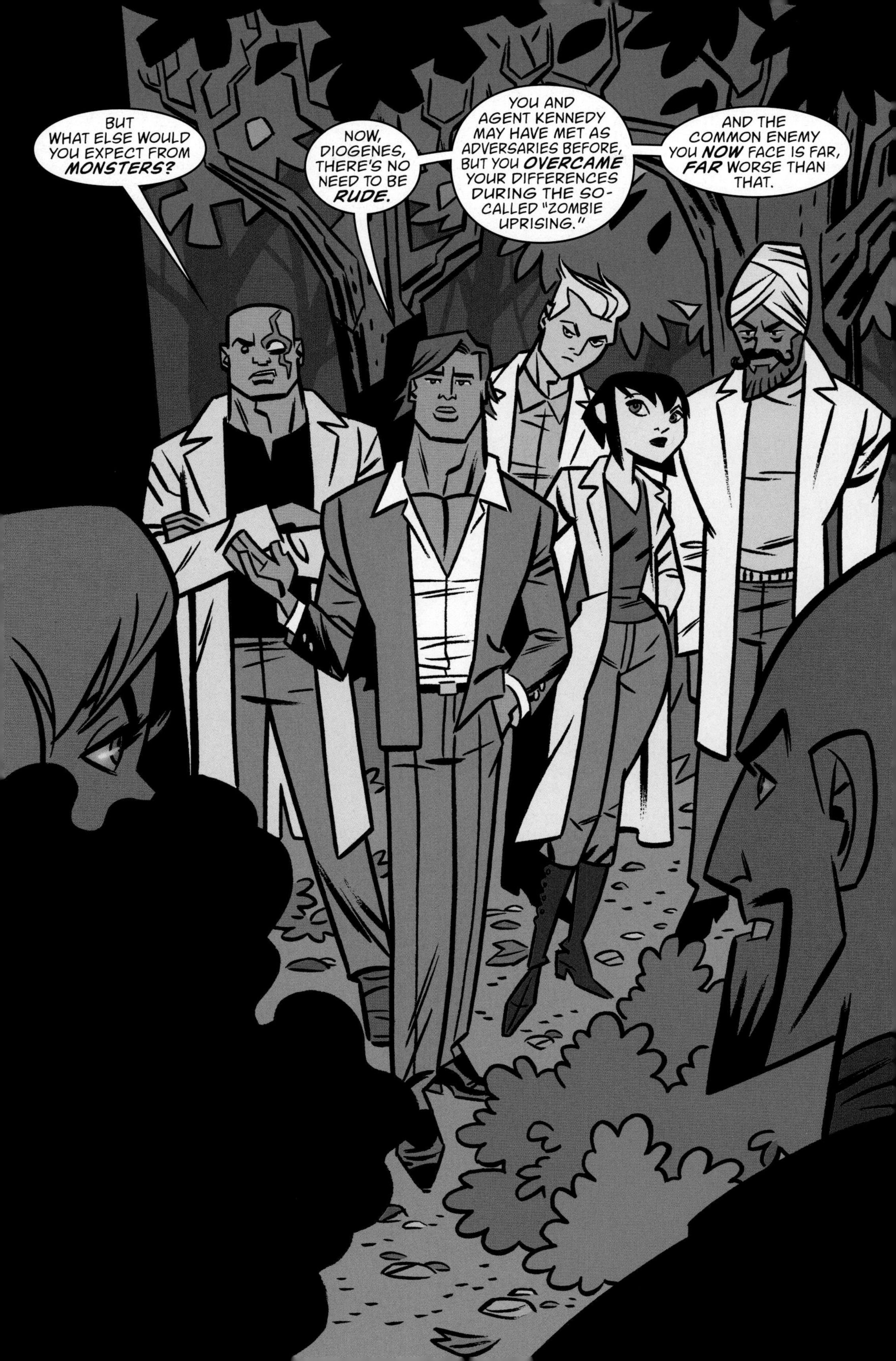
BUT WHAT ELSE WOULD YOU EXPECT FROM MONSTERS?
NOW, DIOGENES, THERE'S NO NEED TO BE RUDE.
YOU AND AGENT KENNEDY MAY HAVE MET AS ADVERSARIES BEFORE, BUT YOU OVERCAME YOUR DIFFERENCES DURING THE SO-CALLED "ZOMBIE UPRISING."
AND THE COMMON ENEMY YOU NOW FACE IS FAR, FAR WORSE THAN THAT.

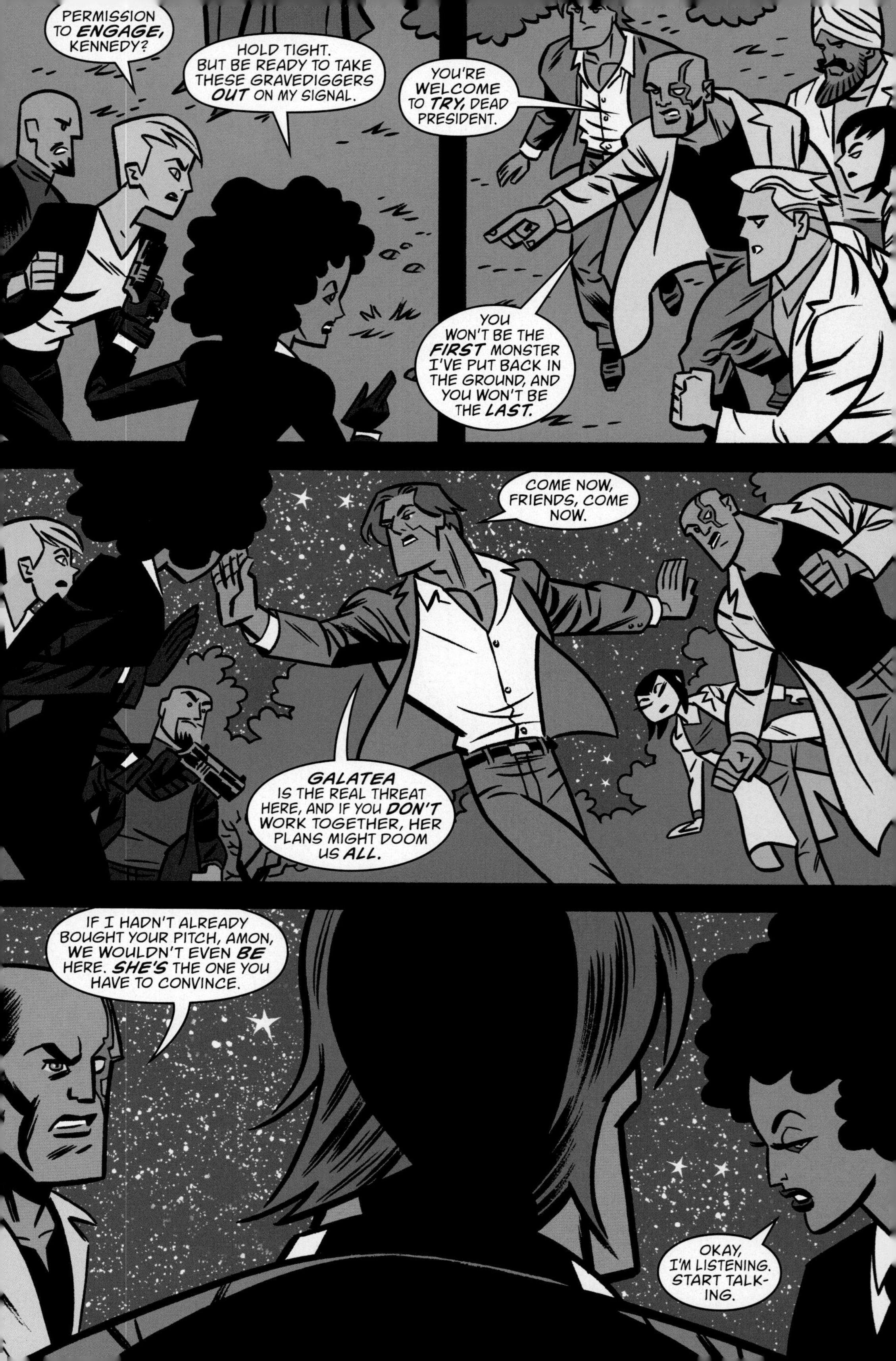
PERMISSION TO ENGAGE, KENNEDY?
HOLD TIGHT. BUT BE READY TO TAKE THESE GRAVEDIGGERS OUT ON MY SIGNAL.
YOU'RE WELCOME TO TRY, DEAD PRESIDENT.
YOU WON'T BE THE FIRST MONSTER I'VE PUT BACK IN THE GROUND, AND YOU WON'T BE THE LAST.
COME NOW, FRIENDS, COME NOW.
GALATEA IS THE REAL THREAT HERE, AND IF YOU DON'T WORK TOGETHER, HER PLANS MIGHT DOOM US ALL.
IF I HADN'T ALREADY BOUGHT YOUR PITCH, AMON, WE WOULDN'T EVEN BE HERE. SHE'S THE ONE YOU HAVE TO CONVINCE.
OKAY, I'M LISTENING. START TALK-ING.

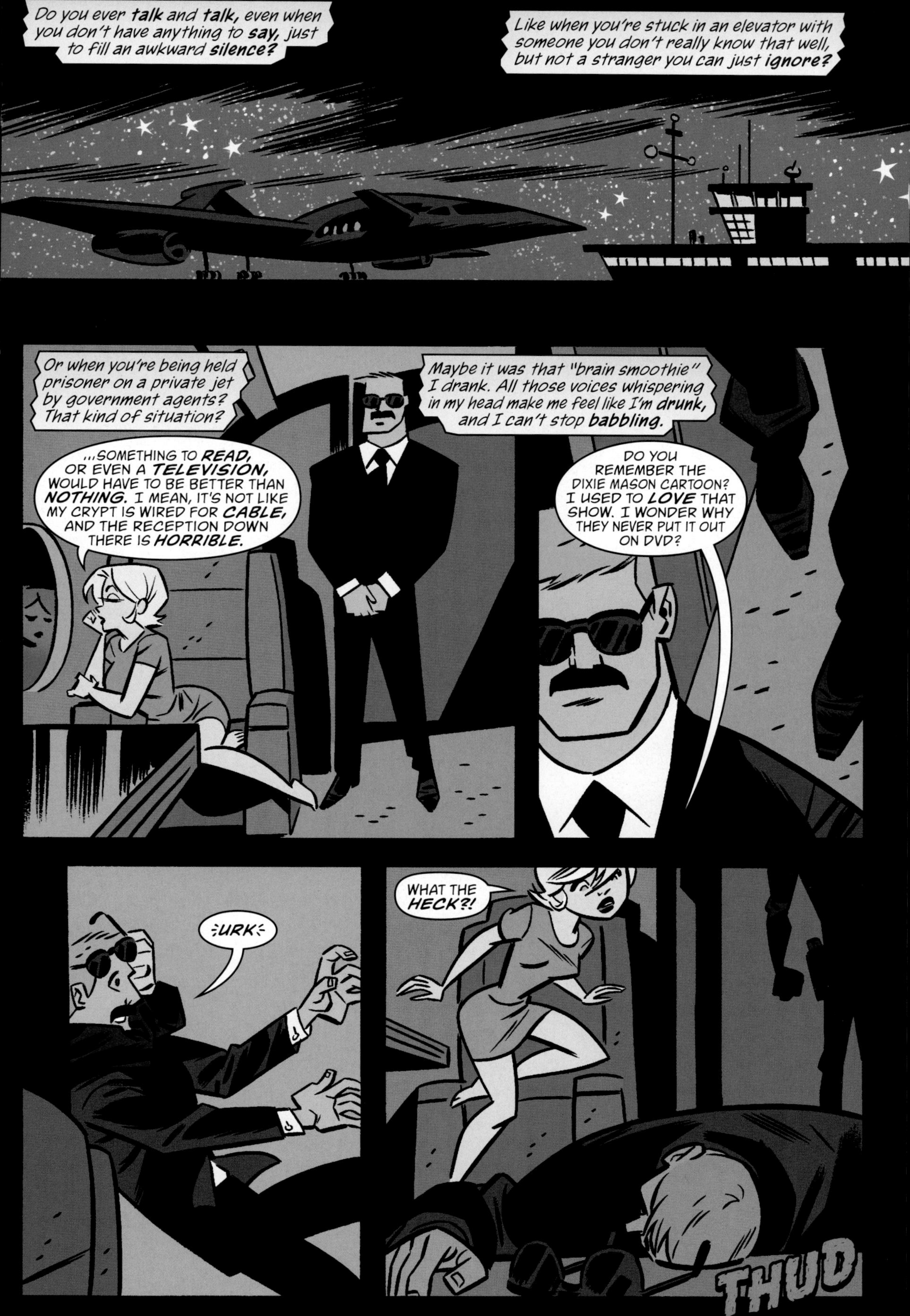
Do you ever talk and talk, even when you don't have anything to say, just to fill an awkward silence?
Like when you're stuck in an elevator with someone you don't really know that well, but not a stranger you can just ignore?
Or when you're being held prisoner on a private jet by government agents? That kind of situation?
...SOMETHING TO READ, OR EVEN A TELEVISION, WOULD HAVE TO BE BETTER THAN NOTHING. I MEAN, IT'S NOT LIKE MY CRYPT IS WIRED FOR CABLE, AND THE RECEPTION DOWN THERE IS HORRIBLE.
Maybe it was that "brain smoothie" I drank. All those voices whispering in my head make me feel like I'm drunk, and I can't stop babbling.
DO YOU REMEMBER THE DIXIE MASON CARTOON? I USED TO LOVE THAT SHOW. I WONDER WHY THEY NEVER PUT IT OUT ON DVD?
URK
WHAT THE HECK?!
THUD

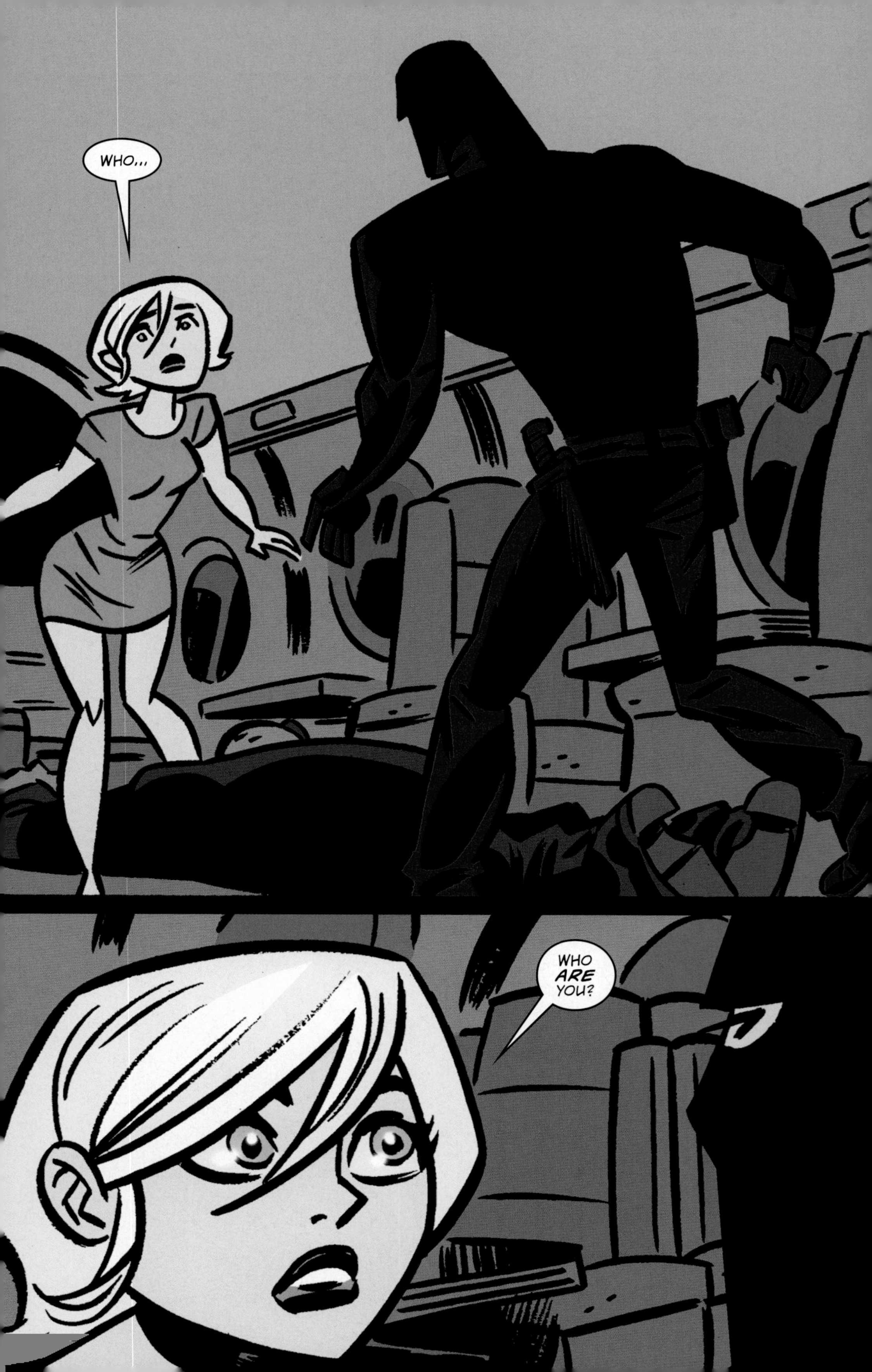
WHO...
WHO *ARE* YOU?

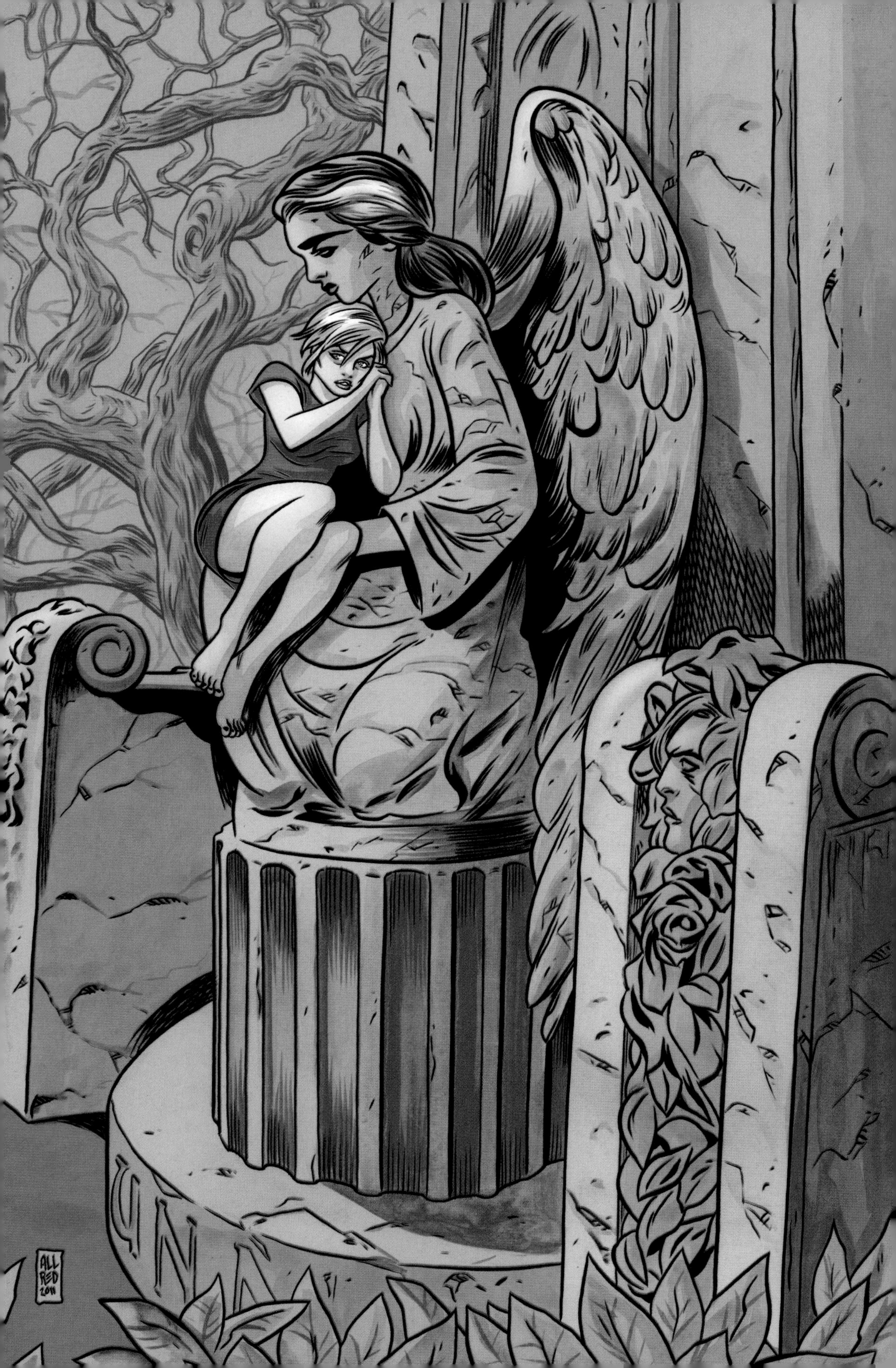
ALL
RED
2011

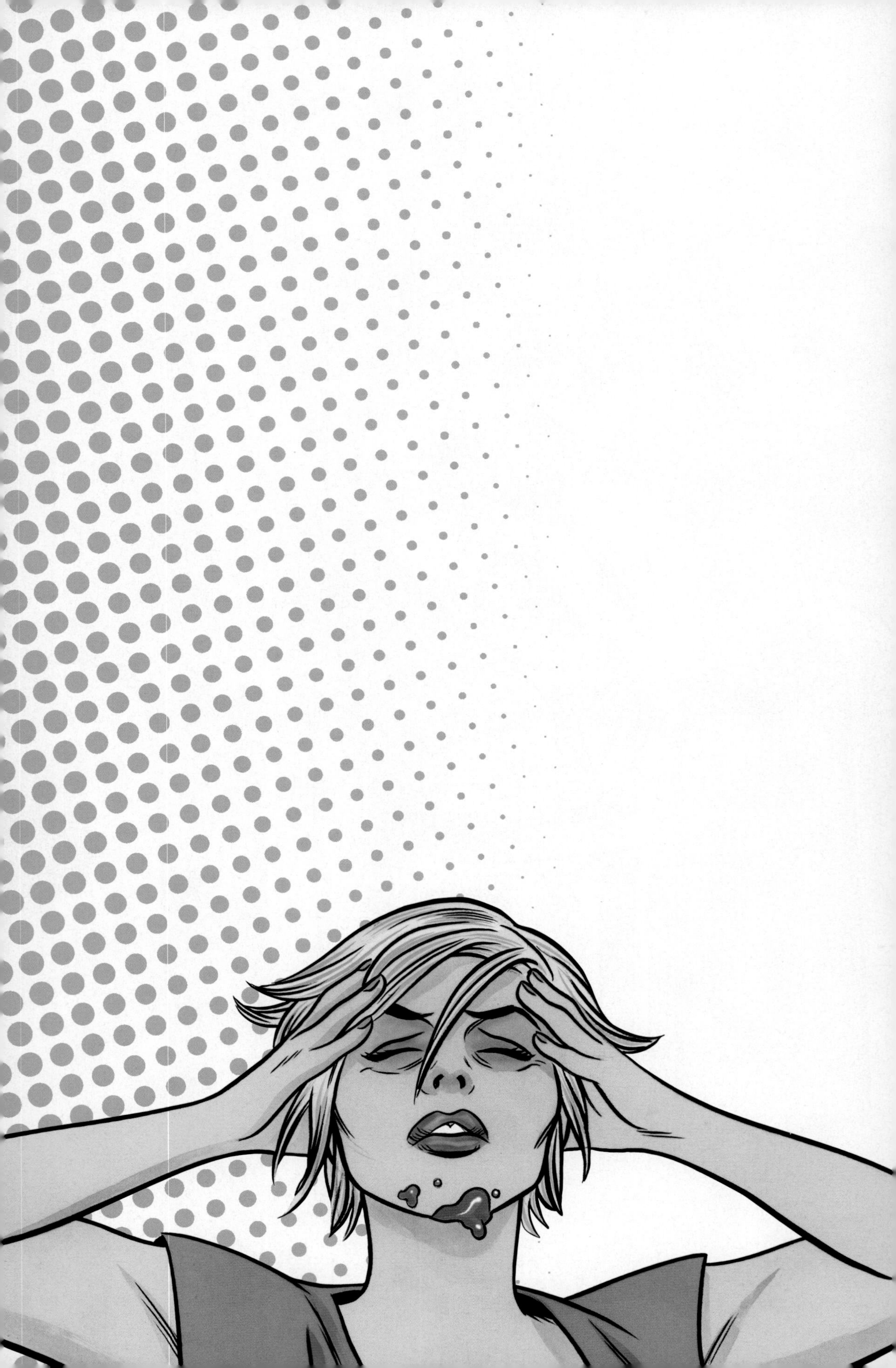

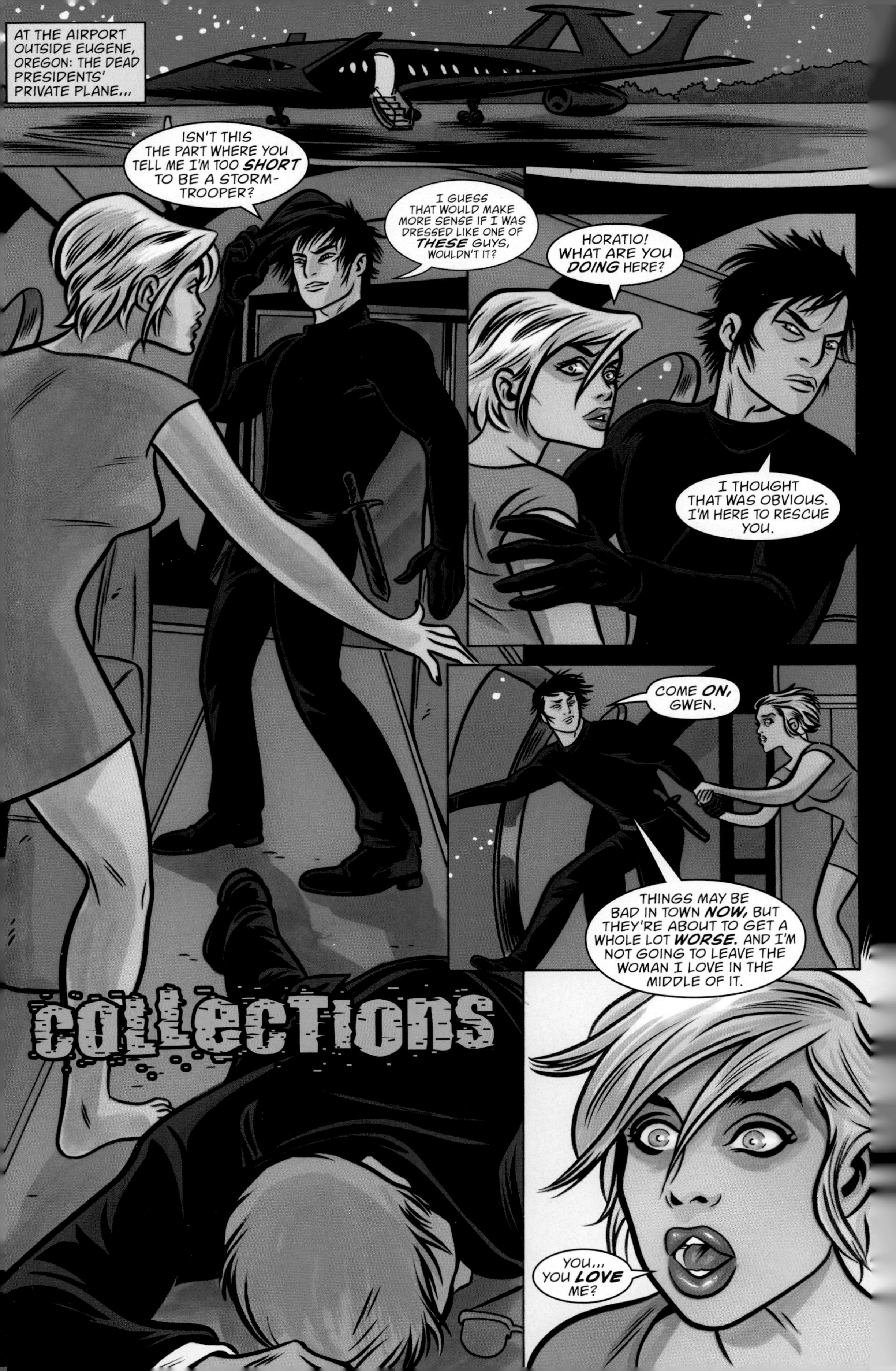
AT THE AIRPORT OUTSIDE EUGENE, OREGON: THE DEAD PRESIDENTS' PRIVATE PLANE...
ISN'T THIS THE PART WHERE YOU TELL ME I'M TOO SHORT TO BE A STORM-TROOPER?
I GUESS THAT WOULD MAKE MORE SENSE IF I WAS DRESSED LIKE ONE OF THESE GUYS, WOULDN'T IT?
HORATIO! WHAT ARE YOU DOING HERE?
I THOUGHT THAT WAS OBVIOUS. I'M HERE TO RESCUE YOU.
COME ON, GWEN.
THINGS MAY BE BAD IN TOWN NOW, BUT THEY'RE ABOUT TO GET A WHOLE LOT WORSE. AND I'M NOT GOING TO LEAVE THE WOMAN I LOVE IN THE MIDDLE OF IT.
collecTions
YOU... YOU LOVE ME?

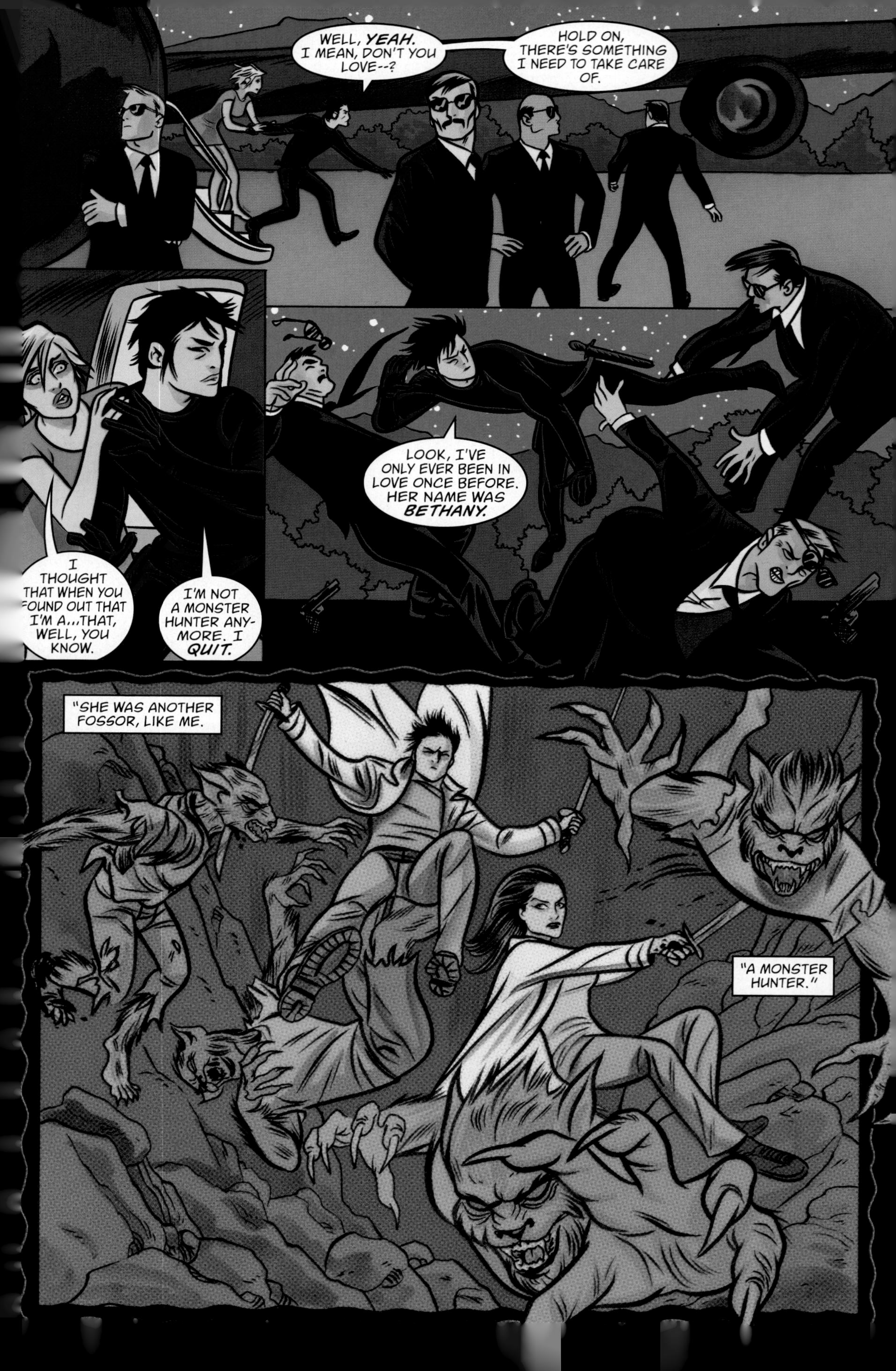
WELL, YEAH. I MEAN, DON'T YOU LOVE--?
HOLD ON, THERE'S SOMETHING I NEED TO TAKE CARE OF.
I THOUGHT THAT WHEN YOU FOUND OUT THAT I'M A...THAT, WELL, YOU KNOW.
I'M NOT A MONSTER HUNTER ANYMORE. I QUIT.
LOOK, I'VE ONLY EVER BEEN IN LOVE ONCE BEFORE. HER NAME WAS BETHANY.
"SHE WAS ANOTHER FOSSOR, LIKE ME.
"A MONSTER HUNTER."

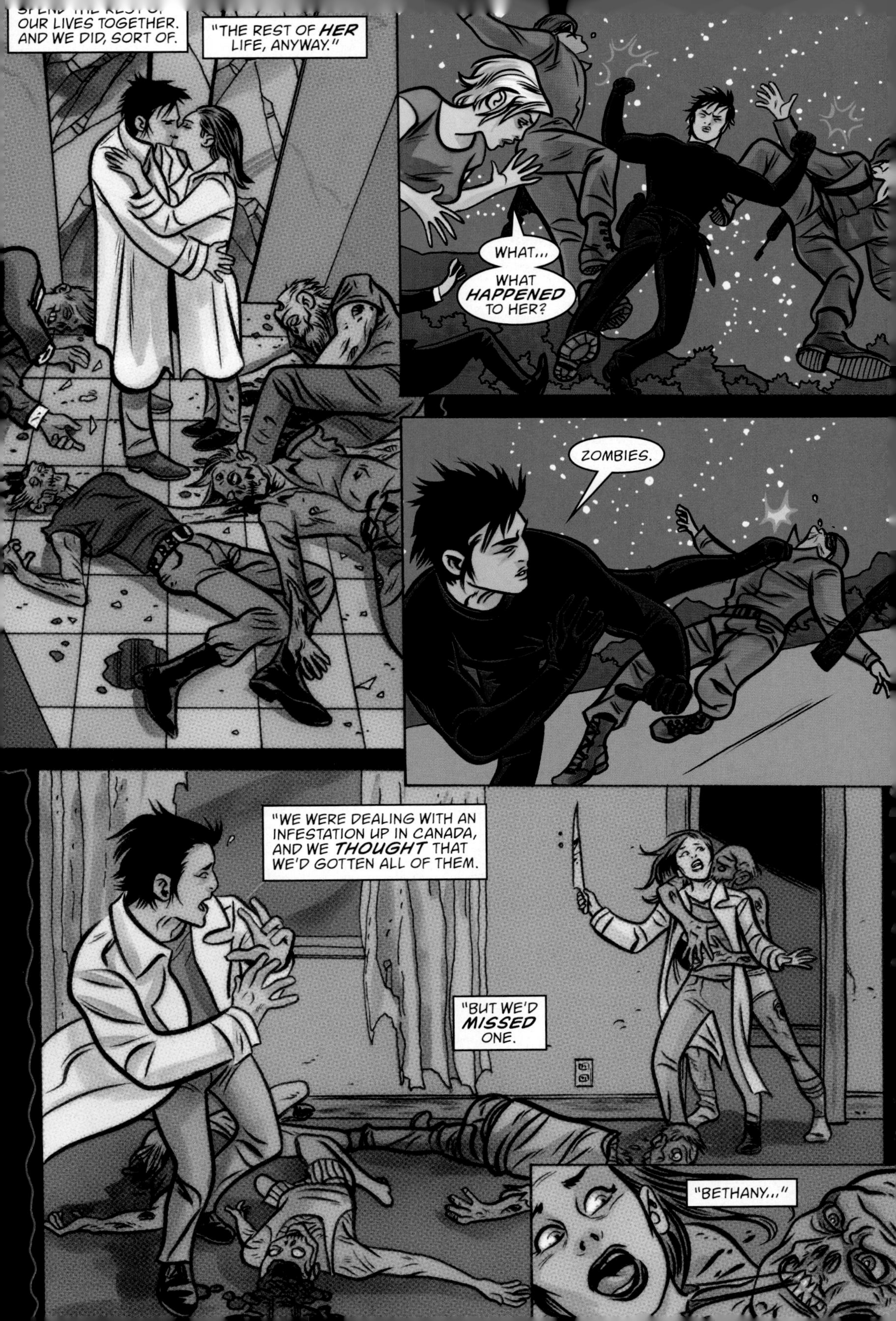

OUR LIVES TOGETHER. AND WE DID, SORT OF.
"THE REST OF HER LIFE, ANYWAY."
WHAT... WHAT HAPPENED TO HER?
ZOMBIES.
"WE WERE DEALING WITH AN INFESTATION UP IN CANADA, AND WE THOUGHT THAT WE'D GOTTEN ALL OF THEM.
"BUT WE'D MISSED ONE.
"BETHANY..."

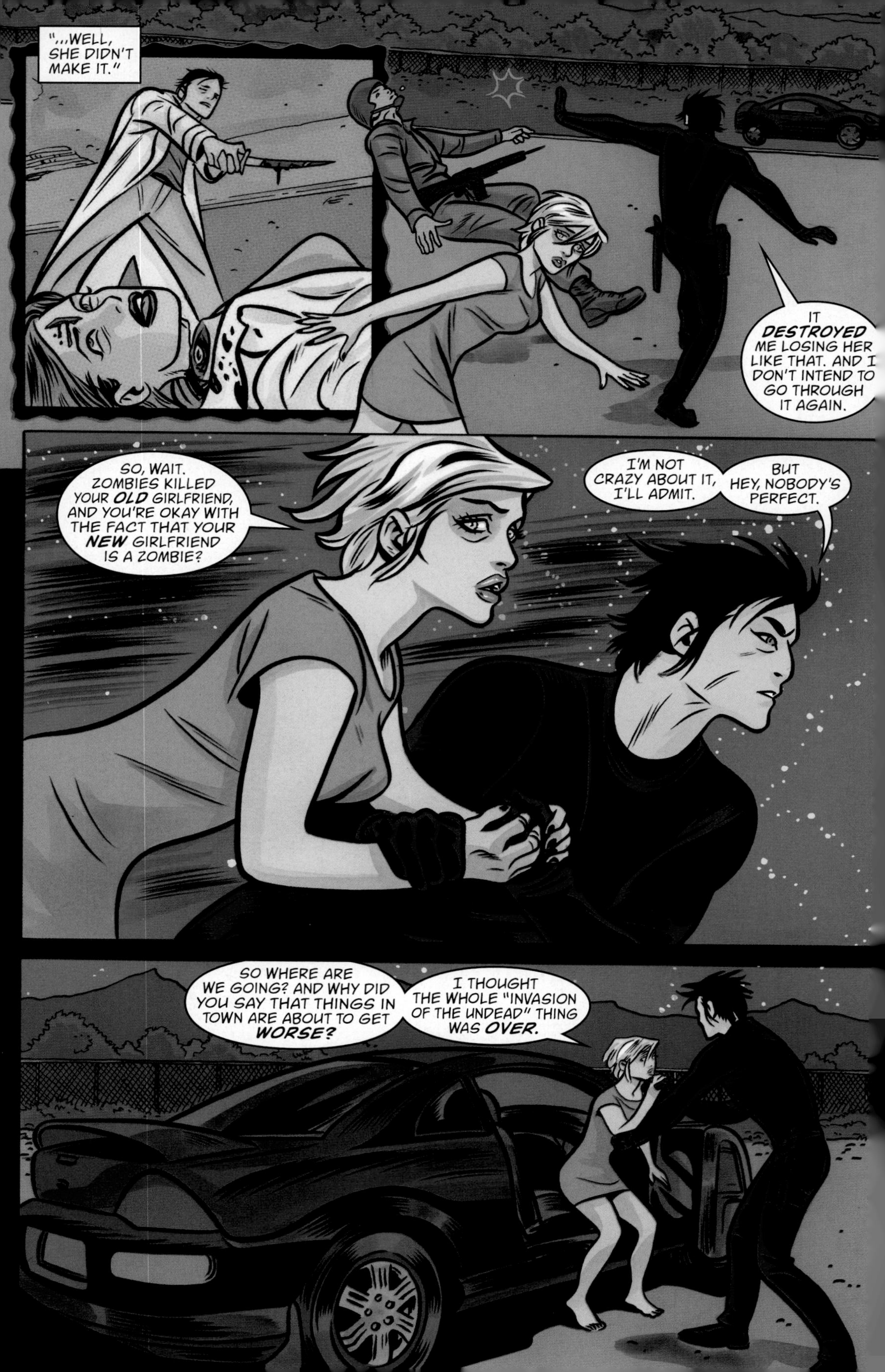
"...WELL, SHE DIDN'T MAKE IT."
IT *DESTROYED* ME LOSING HER LIKE THAT. AND I DON'T INTEND TO GO THROUGH IT AGAIN.
SO, WAIT. ZOMBIES KILLED YOUR *OLD* GIRLFRIEND, AND YOU'RE OKAY WITH THE FACT THAT YOUR *NEW* GIRLFRIEND IS A ZOMBIE?
I'M NOT CRAZY ABOUT IT, I'LL ADMIT.
BUT HEY, NOBODY'S PERFECT.
SO WHERE ARE WE GOING? AND WHY DID YOU SAY THAT THINGS IN TOWN ARE ABOUT TO GET *WORSE?*
I THOUGHT THE WHOLE "INVASION OF THE UNDEAD" THING WAS *OVER.*

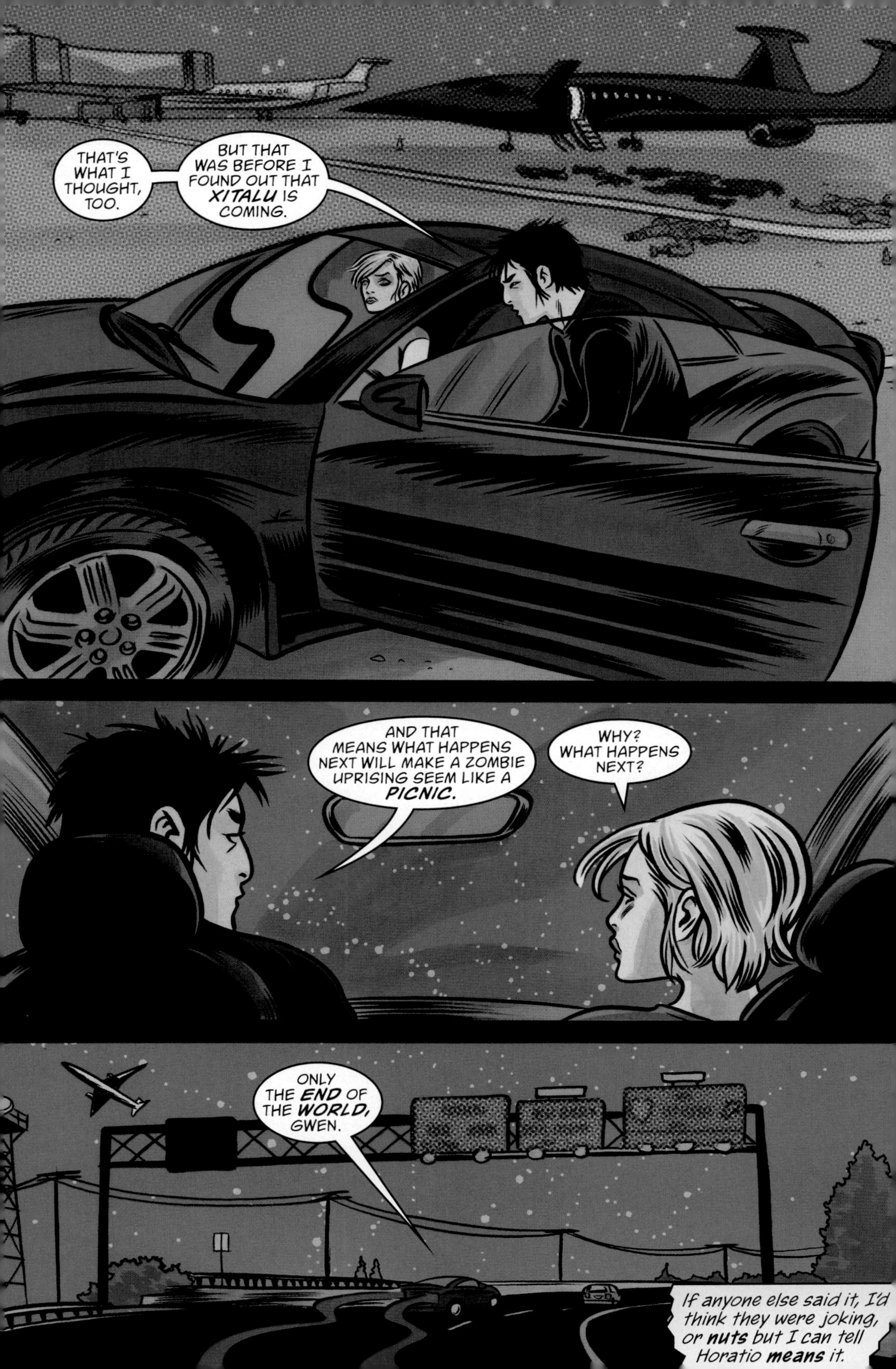
THAT'S WHAT I THOUGHT, TOO.
BUT THAT WAS BEFORE I FOUND OUT THAT **XITALU** IS COMING.
AND THAT MEANS WHAT HAPPENS NEXT WILL MAKE A ZOMBIE UPRISING SEEM LIKE A **PICNIC.**
WHY? WHAT HAPPENS NEXT?
ONLY THE **END** OF THE **WORLD,** GWEN.
*If anyone else said it, I'd think they were joking, or **nuts** but I can tell Horatio **means** it.*

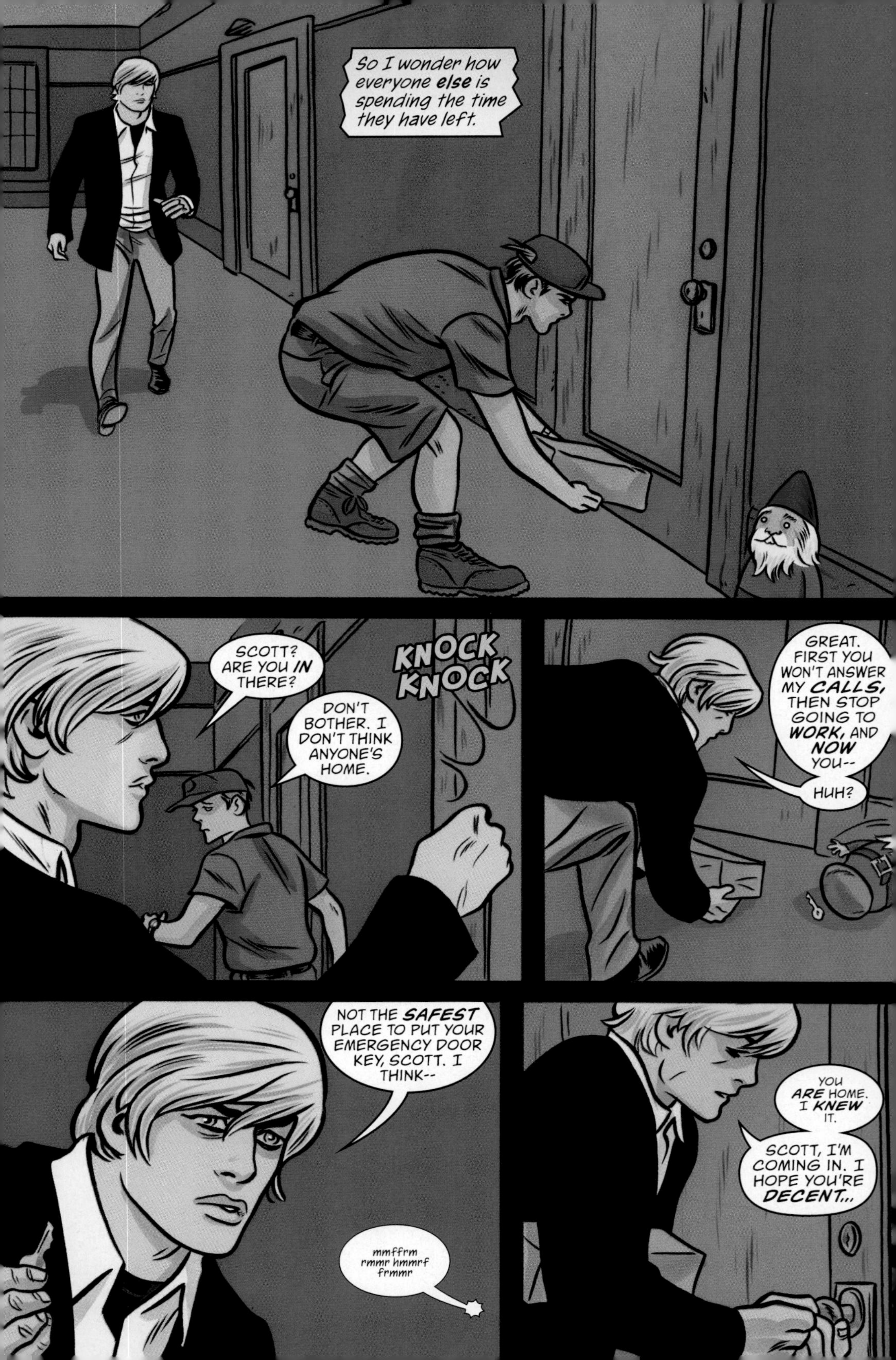
So I wonder how everyone **else** is spending the time they have left.
SCOTT? ARE YOU ***IN*** THERE?
KNOCK KNOCK
DON'T BOTHER. I DON'T THINK ANYONE'S HOME.
GREAT. FIRST YOU WON'T ANSWER MY ***CALLS,*** THEN STOP GOING TO ***WORK,*** AND ***NOW*** YOU--
HUH?
NOT THE ***SAFEST*** PLACE TO PUT YOUR EMERGENCY DOOR KEY, SCOTT. I THINK--
mmffrm rmmr hmmrf frmmr
YOU ***ARE*** HOME. I ***KNEW*** IT.
SCOTT, I'M COMING IN. I HOPE YOU'RE ***DECENT...***

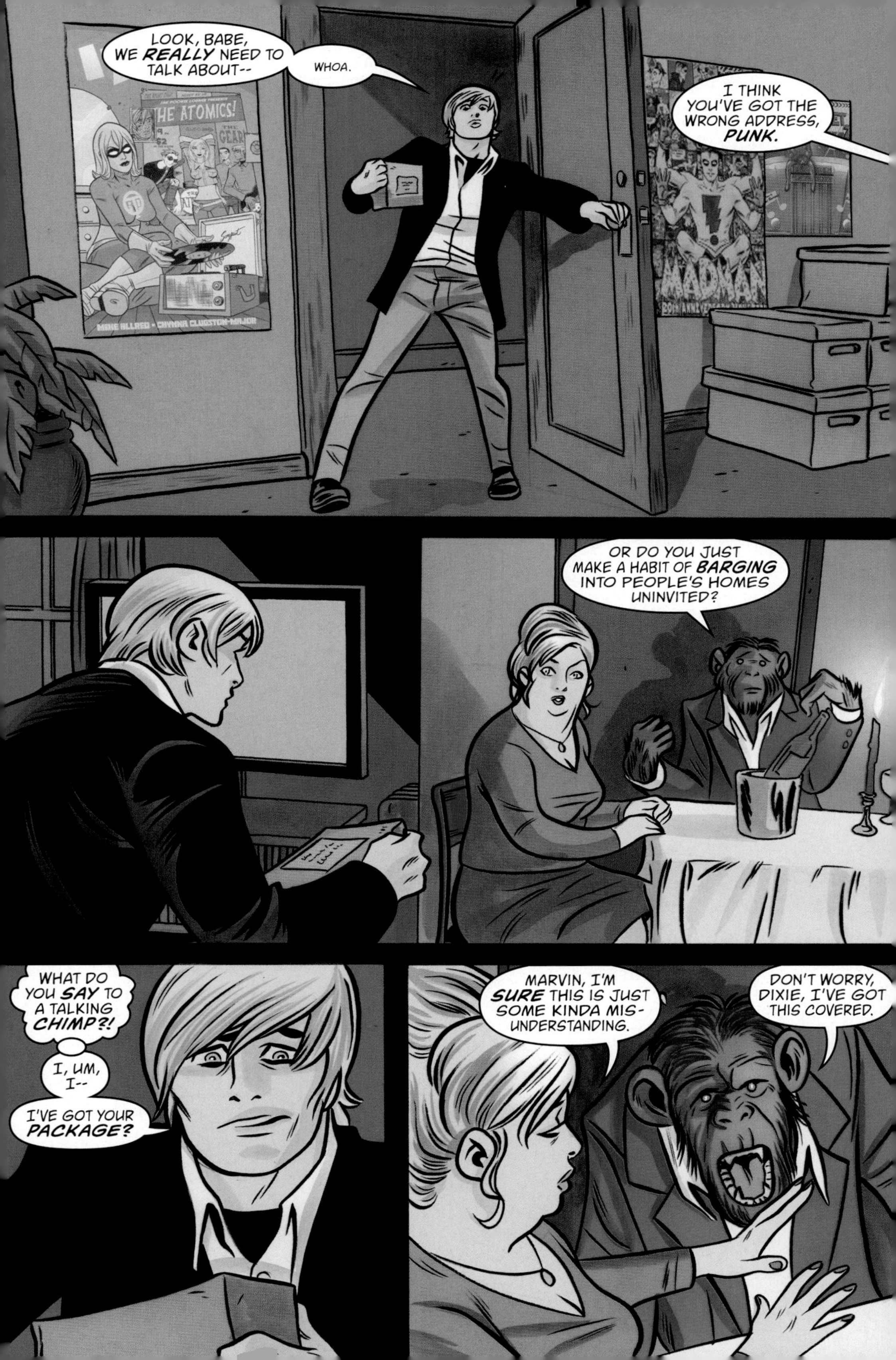

LOOK, BABE, WE REALLY NEED TO TALK ABOUT--
WHOA.
THE ATOMICS!
MIKE ALLRED • CHYNNA CLUGSTON-MAJOR
I THINK YOU'VE GOT THE WRONG ADDRESS, PUNK.
MADMAN
OR DO YOU JUST MAKE A HABIT OF BARGING INTO PEOPLE'S HOMES UNINVITED?
WHAT DO YOU SAY TO A TALKING CHIMP?!
I, UM, I--
I'VE GOT YOUR PACKAGE?
MARVIN, I'M SURE THIS IS JUST SOME KINDA MIS-UNDERSTANDING.
DON'T WORRY, DIXIE, I'VE GOT THIS COVERED.

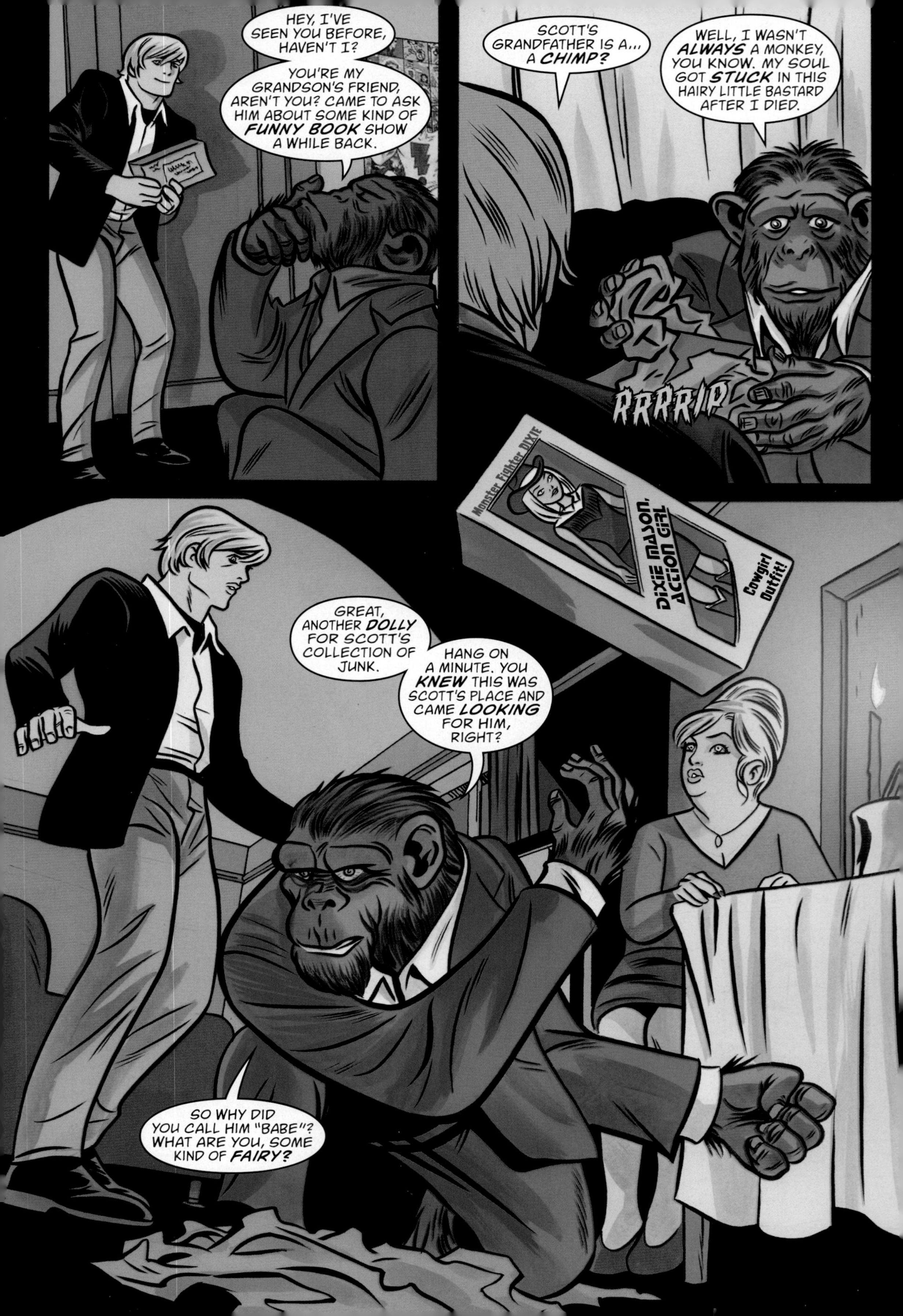
HEY, I'VE SEEN YOU BEFORE, HAVEN'T I?
YOU'RE MY GRANDSON'S FRIEND, AREN'T YOU? CAME TO ASK HIM ABOUT SOME KIND OF FUNNY BOOK SHOW A WHILE BACK.
SCOTT'S GRANDFATHER IS A... A CHIMP?
WELL, I WASN'T ALWAYS A MONKEY, YOU KNOW. MY SOUL GOT STUCK IN THIS HAIRY LITTLE BASTARD AFTER I DIED.
RRRRIP
Monster Fighter DIXIE
DIXIE MASON, ACTION GIRL
Cowgirl Outfit!
GREAT, ANOTHER DOLLY FOR SCOTT'S COLLECTION OF JUNK.
HANG ON A MINUTE. YOU KNEW THIS WAS SCOTT'S PLACE AND CAME LOOKING FOR HIM, RIGHT?
SO WHY DID YOU CALL HIM "BABE"? WHAT ARE YOU, SOME KIND OF FAIRY?

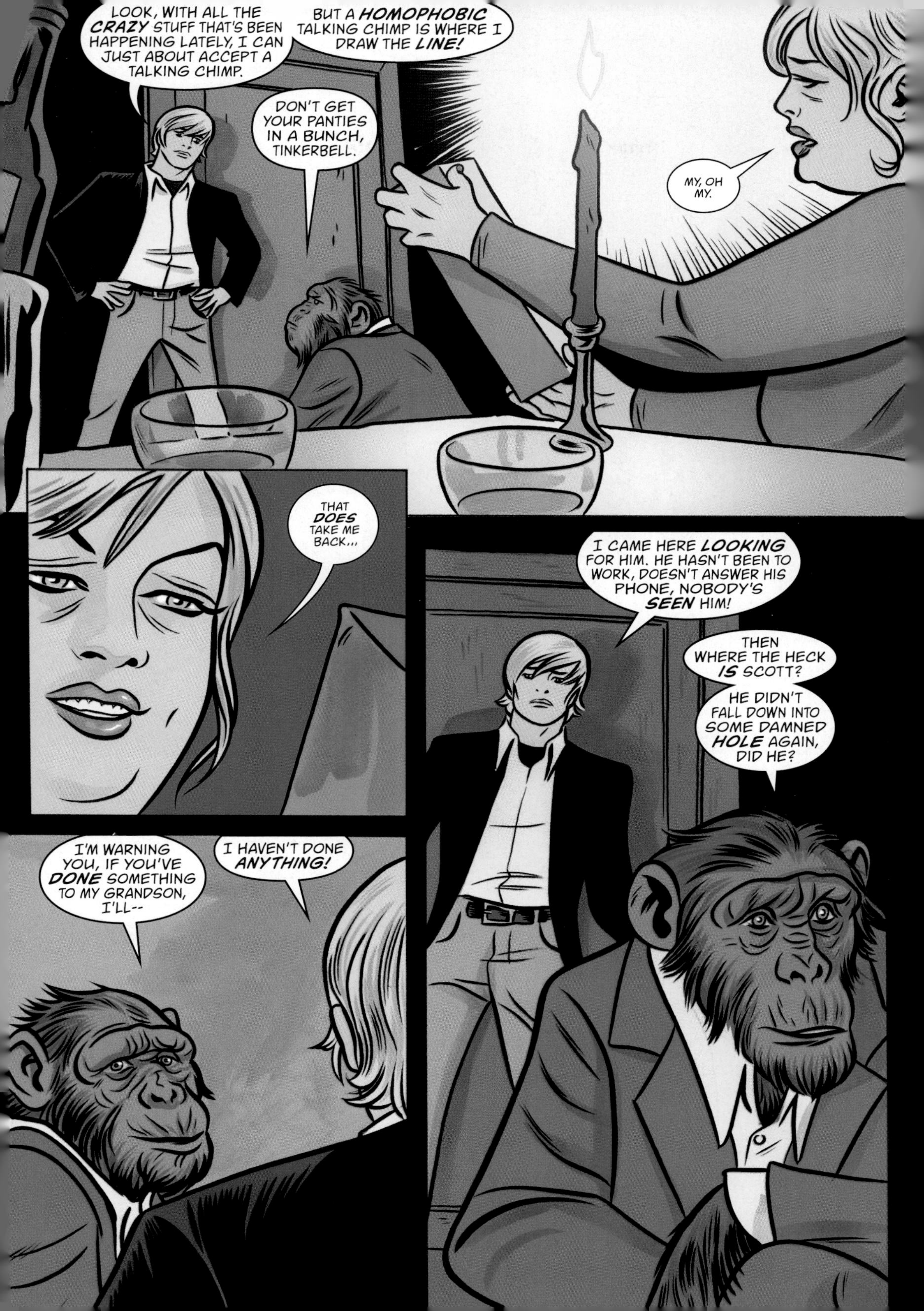
LOOK, WITH ALL THE CRAZY STUFF THAT'S BEEN HAPPENING LATELY, I CAN JUST ABOUT ACCEPT A TALKING CHIMP.
BUT A HOMOPHOBIC TALKING CHIMP IS WHERE I DRAW THE LINE!
DON'T GET YOUR PANTIES IN A BUNCH, TINKERBELL.
MY, OH MY.
THAT DOES TAKE ME BACK...
I CAME HERE LOOKING FOR HIM. HE HASN'T BEEN TO WORK, DOESN'T ANSWER HIS PHONE, NOBODY'S SEEN HIM!
THEN WHERE THE HECK IS SCOTT?
HE DIDN'T FALL DOWN INTO SOME DAMNED HOLE AGAIN, DID HE?
I'M WARNING YOU, IF YOU'VE DONE SOMETHING TO MY GRANDSON, I'LL--
I HAVEN'T DONE ANYTHING!

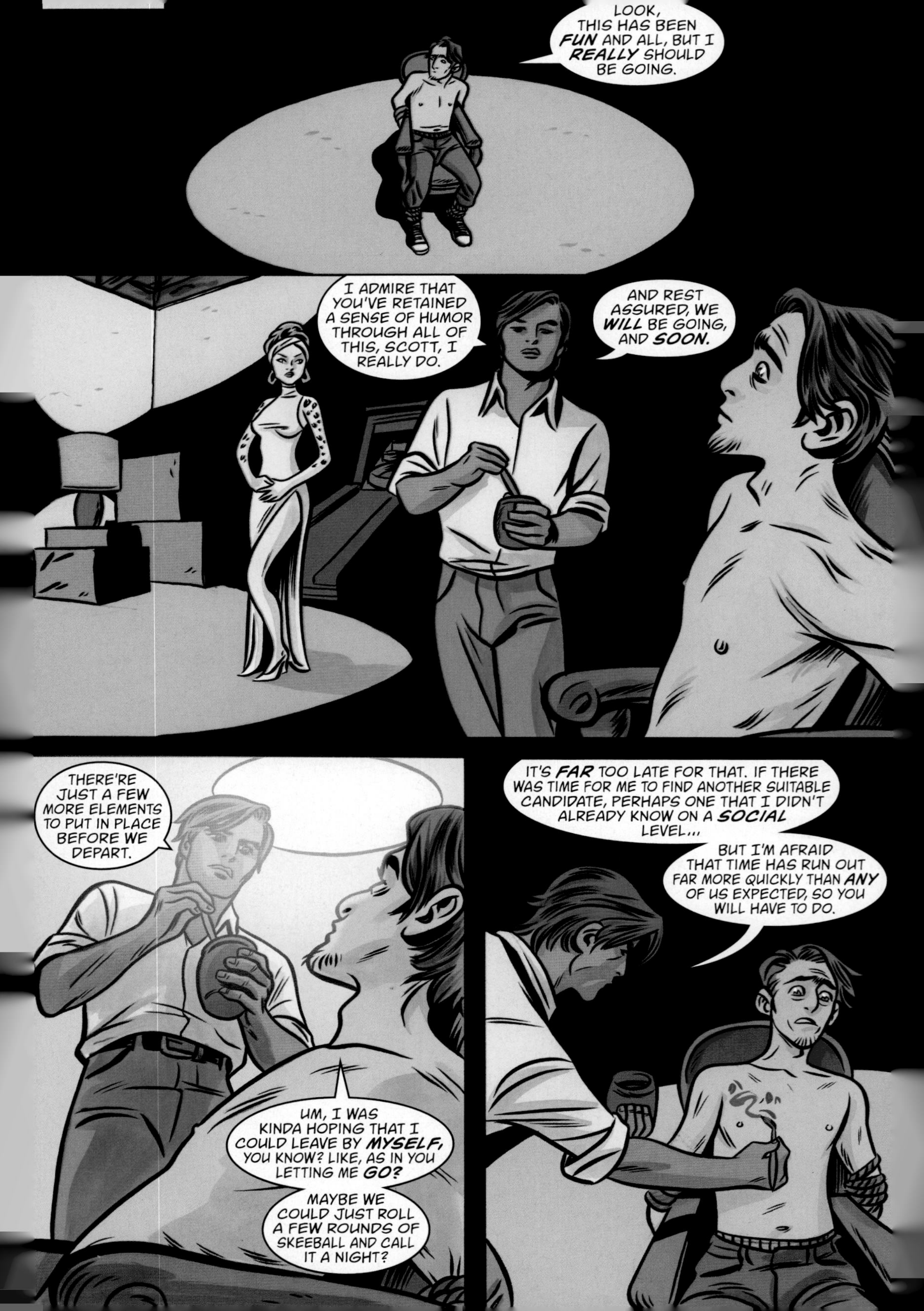
LOOK, THIS HAS BEEN FUN AND ALL, BUT I REALLY SHOULD BE GOING.
I ADMIRE THAT YOU'VE RETAINED A SENSE OF HUMOR THROUGH ALL OF THIS, SCOTT, I REALLY DO.
AND REST ASSURED, WE WILL BE GOING, AND SOON.
THERE'RE JUST A FEW MORE ELEMENTS TO PUT IN PLACE BEFORE WE DEPART.
UM, I WAS KINDA HOPING THAT I COULD LEAVE BY MYSELF, YOU KNOW? LIKE, AS IN YOU LETTING ME GO?
MAYBE WE COULD JUST ROLL A FEW ROUNDS OF SKEEBALL AND CALL IT A NIGHT?
IT'S FAR TOO LATE FOR THAT. IF THERE WAS TIME FOR ME TO FIND ANOTHER SUITABLE CANDIDATE, PERHAPS ONE THAT I DIDN'T ALREADY KNOW ON A SOCIAL LEVEL...
BUT I'M AFRAID THAT TIME HAS RUN OUT FAR MORE QUICKLY THAN ANY OF US EXPECTED, SO YOU WILL HAVE TO DO.

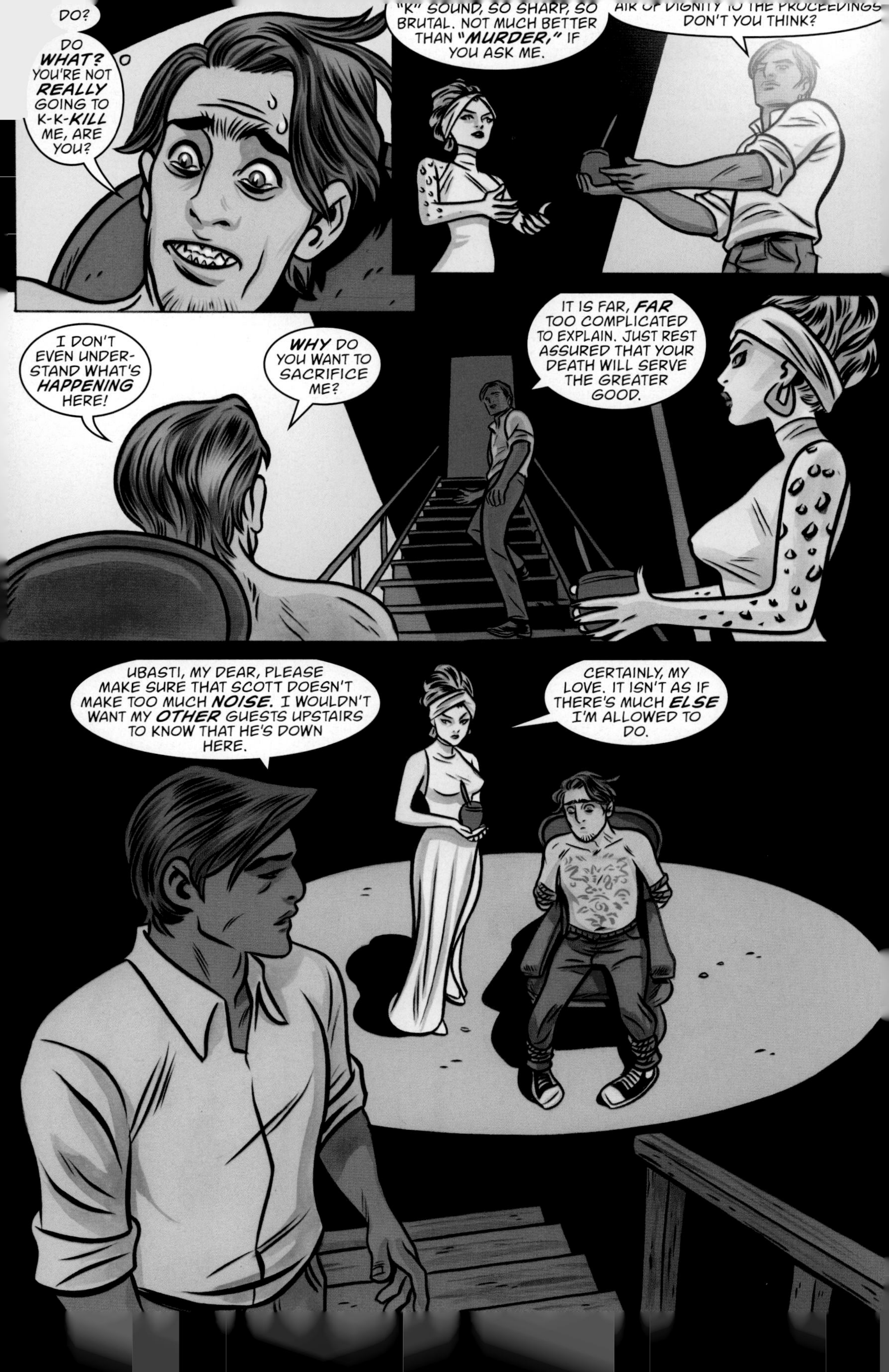
DO?
DO WHAT? YOU'RE NOT REALLY GOING TO K-K-KILL ME, ARE YOU?
"K" SOUND, SO SHARP, SO BRUTAL. NOT MUCH BETTER THAN "MURDER," IF YOU ASK ME.
AIR OF DIGNITY TO THE PROCEEDINGS. DON'T YOU THINK?
I DON'T EVEN UNDERSTAND WHAT'S HAPPENING HERE!
WHY DO YOU WANT TO SACRIFICE ME?
IT IS FAR, FAR TOO COMPLICATED TO EXPLAIN. JUST REST ASSURED THAT YOUR DEATH WILL SERVE THE GREATER GOOD.
UBASTI, MY DEAR, PLEASE MAKE SURE THAT SCOTT DOESN'T MAKE TOO MUCH NOISE. I WOULDN'T WANT MY OTHER GUESTS UPSTAIRS TO KNOW THAT HE'S DOWN HERE.
CERTAINLY, MY LOVE. IT ISN'T AS IF THERE'S MUCH ELSE I'M ALLOWED TO DO.

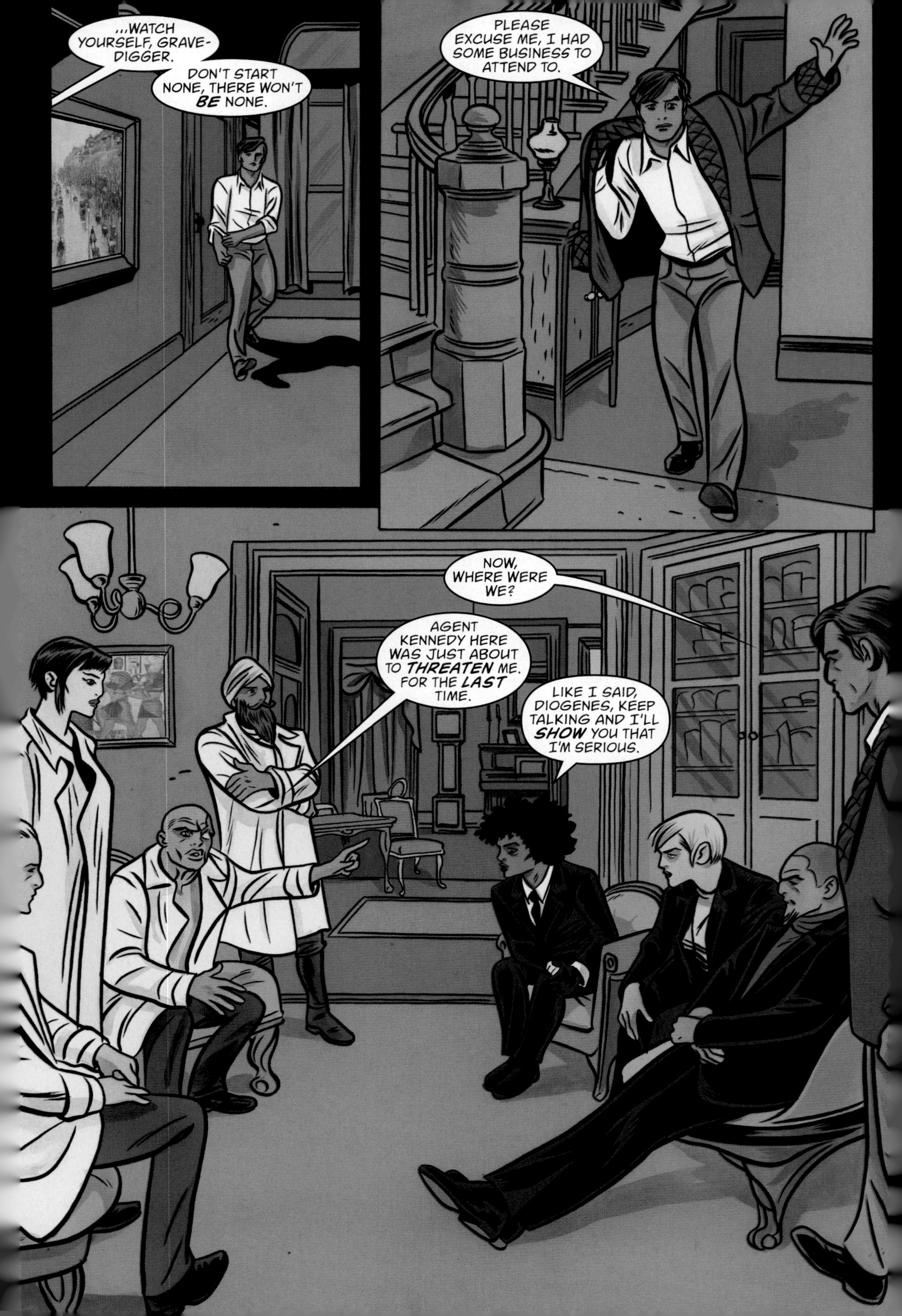
...WATCH YOURSELF, GRAVE-DIGGER.
DON'T START NONE, THERE WON'T BE NONE.
PLEASE EXCUSE ME, I HAD SOME BUSINESS TO ATTEND TO.
NOW, WHERE WERE WE?
AGENT KENNEDY HERE WAS JUST ABOUT TO THREATEN ME. FOR THE LAST TIME.
LIKE I SAID, DIOGENES, KEEP TALKING AND I'LL SHOW YOU THAT I'M SERIOUS.

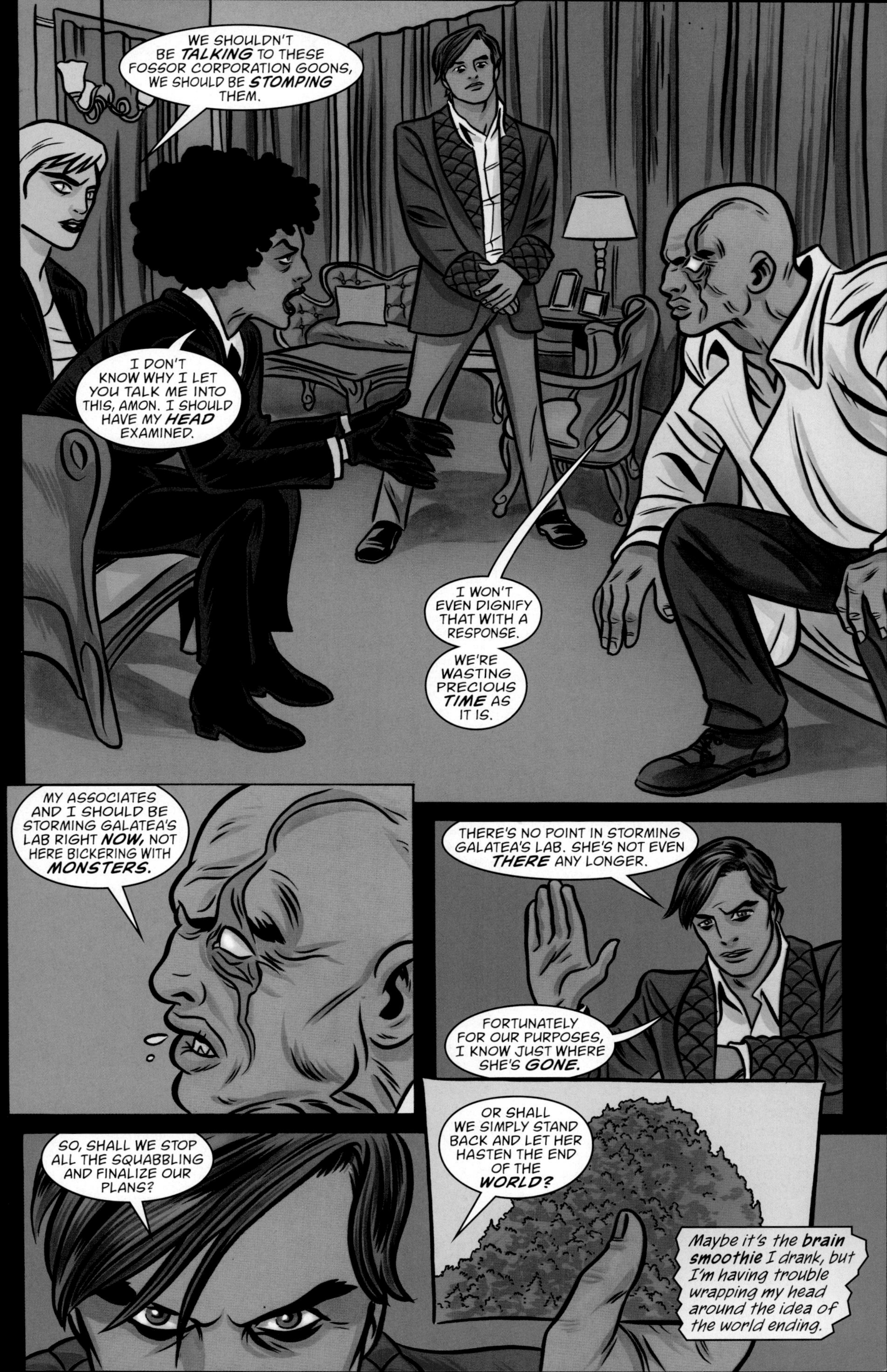

WE SHOULDN'T BE **TALKING** TO THESE FOSSOR CORPORATION GOONS, WE SHOULD BE **STOMPING** THEM.
I DON'T KNOW WHY I LET YOU TALK ME INTO THIS, AMON. I SHOULD HAVE MY **HEAD** EXAMINED.
I WON'T EVEN DIGNIFY THAT WITH A RESPONSE.
WE'RE WASTING PRECIOUS **TIME** AS IT IS.
MY ASSOCIATES AND I SHOULD BE STORMING GALATEA'S LAB RIGHT **NOW,** NOT HERE BICKERING WITH **MONSTERS.**
THERE'S NO POINT IN STORMING GALATEA'S LAB. SHE'S NOT EVEN **THERE** ANY LONGER.
FORTUNATELY FOR OUR PURPOSES, I KNOW JUST WHERE SHE'S **GONE.**
SO, SHALL WE STOP ALL THE SQUABBLING AND FINALIZE OUR PLANS?
OR SHALL WE SIMPLY STAND BACK AND LET HER HASTEN THE END OF THE **WORLD?**
*Maybe it's the **brain smoothie** I drank, but I'm having trouble wrapping my head around the idea of the world ending.*

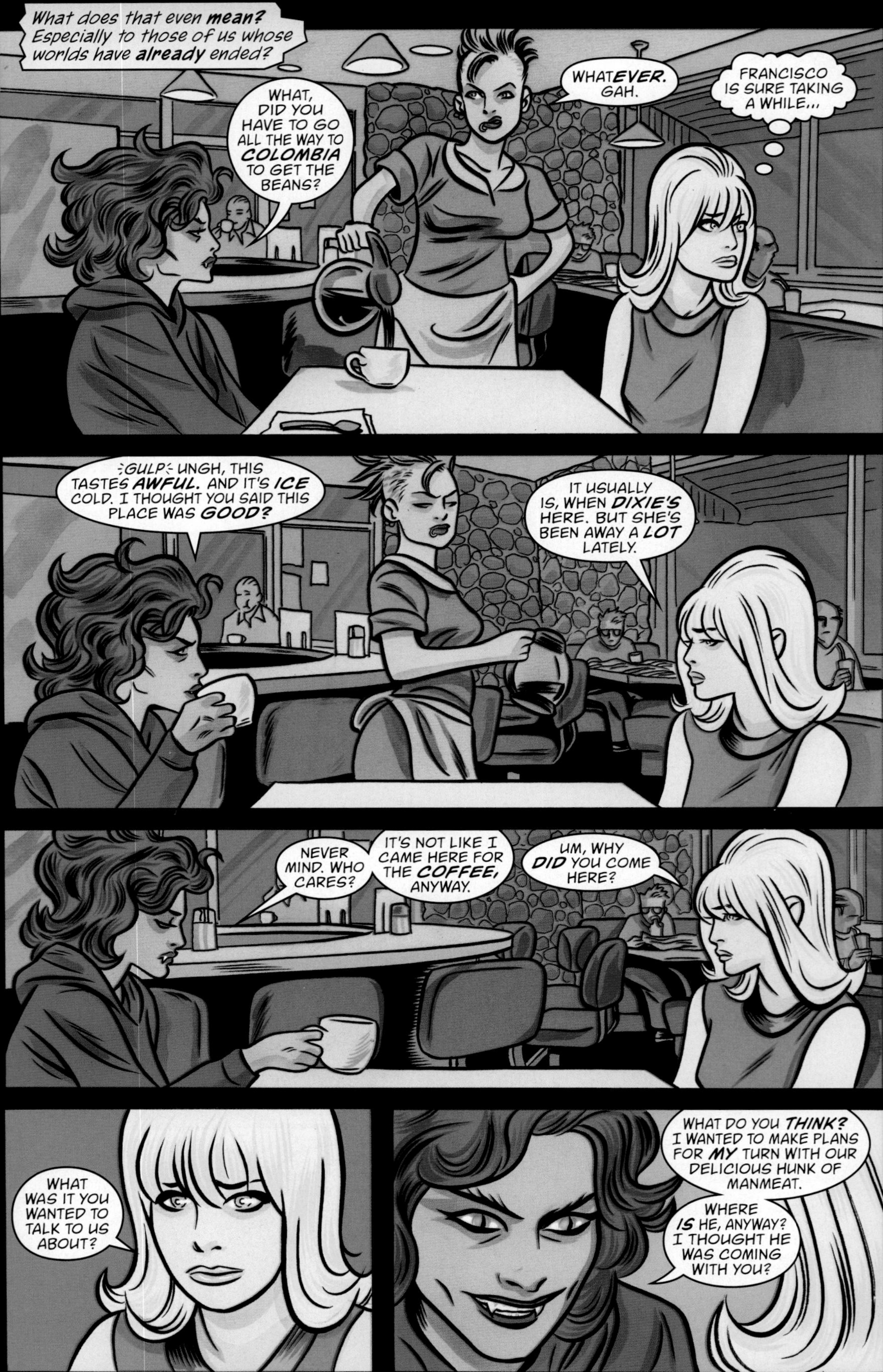
What does that even **mean?** Especially to those of us whose worlds have **already** ended?
WHAT, DID YOU HAVE TO GO ALL THE WAY TO **COLOMBIA** TO GET THE BEANS?
WHAT**EVER.** GAH.
FRANCISCO IS SURE TAKING A WHILE...
-GULP- UNGH, THIS TASTES **AWFUL.** AND IT'S **ICE** COLD. I THOUGHT YOU SAID THIS PLACE WAS **GOOD?**
IT USUALLY IS, WHEN **DIXIE'S** HERE. BUT SHE'S BEEN AWAY A **LOT** LATELY.
NEVER MIND. WHO CARES?
IT'S NOT LIKE I CAME HERE FOR THE **COFFEE,** ANYWAY.
UM, WHY **DID** YOU COME HERE?
WHAT WAS IT YOU WANTED TO TALK TO US ABOUT?
WHAT DO YOU **THINK?** I WANTED TO MAKE PLANS FOR **MY** TURN WITH OUR DELICIOUS HUNK OF MANMEAT.
WHERE **IS** HE, ANYWAY? I THOUGHT HE WAS COMING WITH YOU?

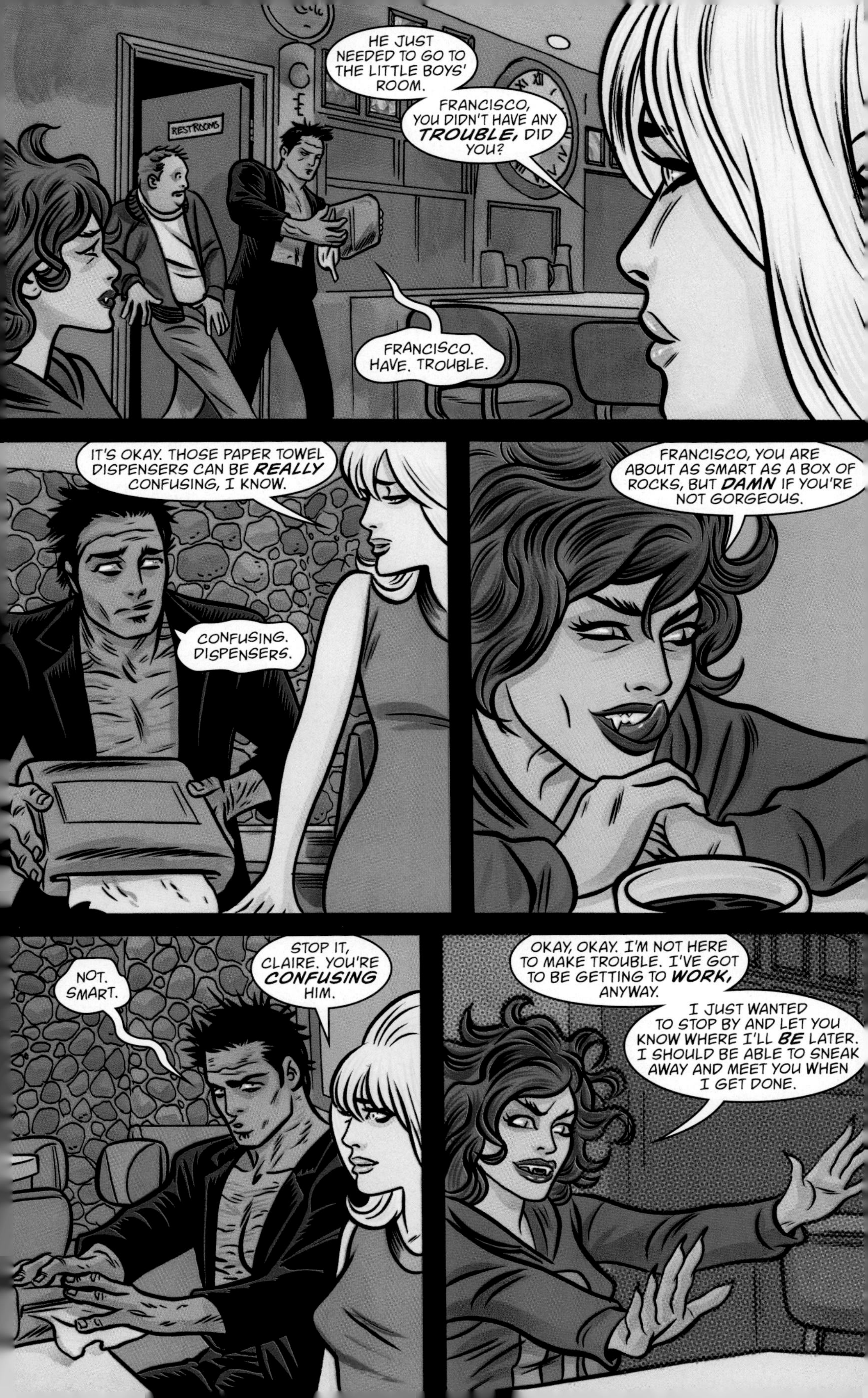

HE JUST NEEDED TO GO TO THE LITTLE BOYS' ROOM.
FRANCISCO, YOU DIDN'T HAVE ANY TROUBLE, DID YOU?
RESTROOMS
FRANCISCO. HAVE. TROUBLE.
IT'S OKAY. THOSE PAPER TOWEL DISPENSERS CAN BE REALLY CONFUSING, I KNOW.
CONFUSING. DISPENSERS.
FRANCISCO, YOU ARE ABOUT AS SMART AS A BOX OF ROCKS, BUT DAMN IF YOU'RE NOT GORGEOUS.
NOT. SMART.
STOP IT, CLAIRE. YOU'RE CONFUSING HIM.
OKAY, OKAY. I'M NOT HERE TO MAKE TROUBLE. I'VE GOT TO BE GETTING TO WORK, ANYWAY.
I JUST WANTED TO STOP BY AND LET YOU KNOW WHERE I'LL BE LATER. I SHOULD BE ABLE TO SNEAK AWAY AND MEET YOU WHEN I GET DONE.

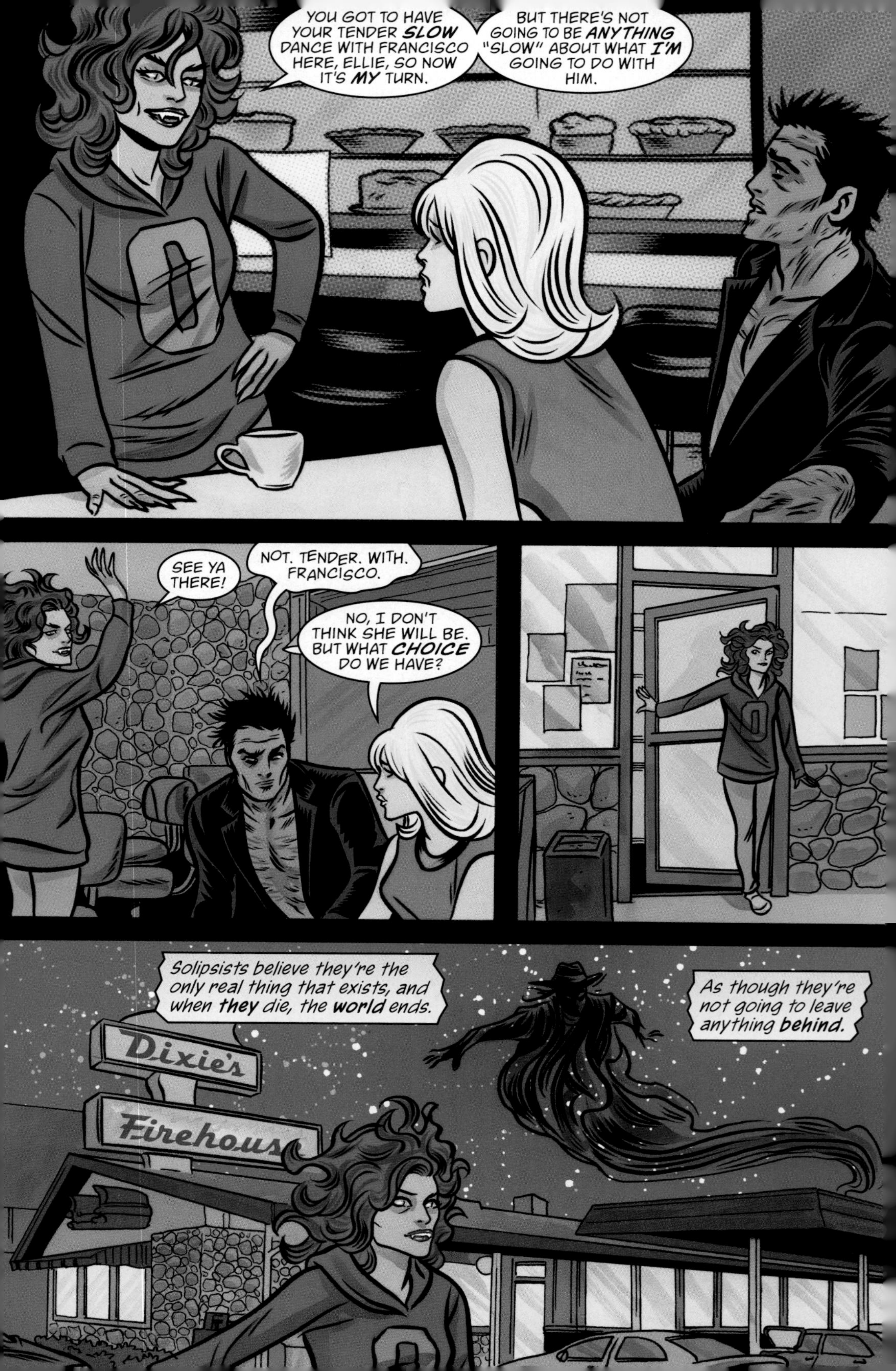
YOU GOT TO HAVE YOUR TENDER SLOW DANCE WITH FRANCISCO HERE, ELLIE, SO NOW IT'S MY TURN.
BUT THERE'S NOT GOING TO BE ANYTHING "SLOW" ABOUT WHAT I'M GOING TO DO WITH HIM.
SEE YA THERE!
NOT. TENDER. WITH. FRANCISCO.
NO, I DON'T THINK SHE WILL BE. BUT WHAT CHOICE DO WE HAVE?
Solipsists believe they're the only real thing that exists, and when they die, the world ends.
As though they're not going to leave anything behind.
Dixie's
Firehous

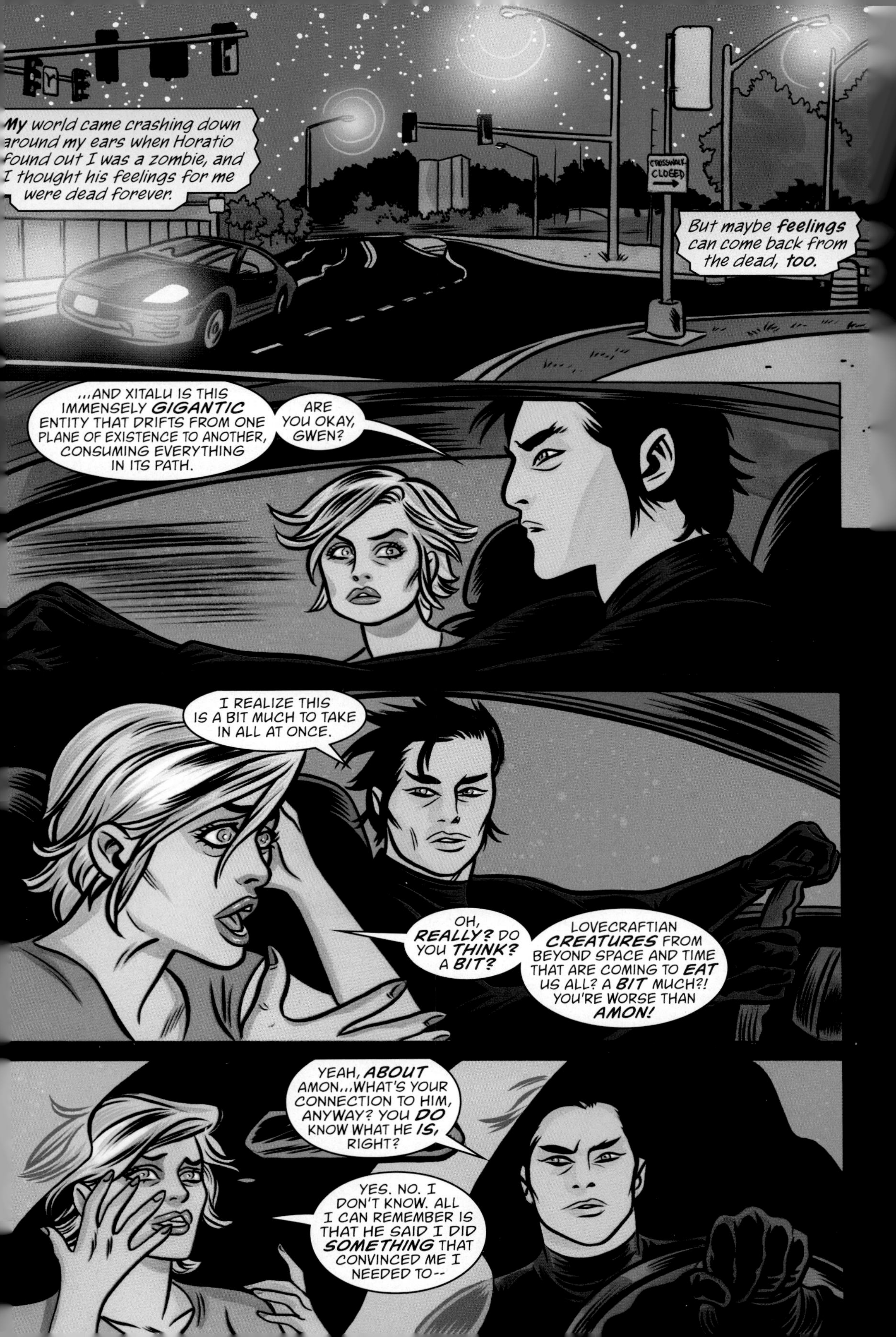
My world came crashing down around my ears when Horatio found out I was a zombie, and I thought his feelings for me were dead forever.
CROSSWALK CLOSED
But maybe feelings can come back from the dead, too.
...AND XITALU IS THIS IMMENSELY GIGANTIC ENTITY THAT DRIFTS FROM ONE PLANE OF EXISTENCE TO ANOTHER, CONSUMING EVERYTHING IN ITS PATH.
ARE YOU OKAY, GWEN?
I REALIZE THIS IS A BIT MUCH TO TAKE IN ALL AT ONCE.
OH, REALLY? DO YOU THINK? A BIT?
LOVECRAFTIAN CREATURES FROM BEYOND SPACE AND TIME THAT ARE COMING TO EAT US ALL? A BIT MUCH?! YOU'RE WORSE THAN AMON!
YEAH, ABOUT AMON...WHAT'S YOUR CONNECTION TO HIM, ANYWAY? YOU DO KNOW WHAT HE IS, RIGHT?
YES. NO. I DON'T KNOW. ALL I CAN REMEMBER IS THAT HE SAID I DID SOMETHING THAT CONVINCED ME I NEEDED TO--

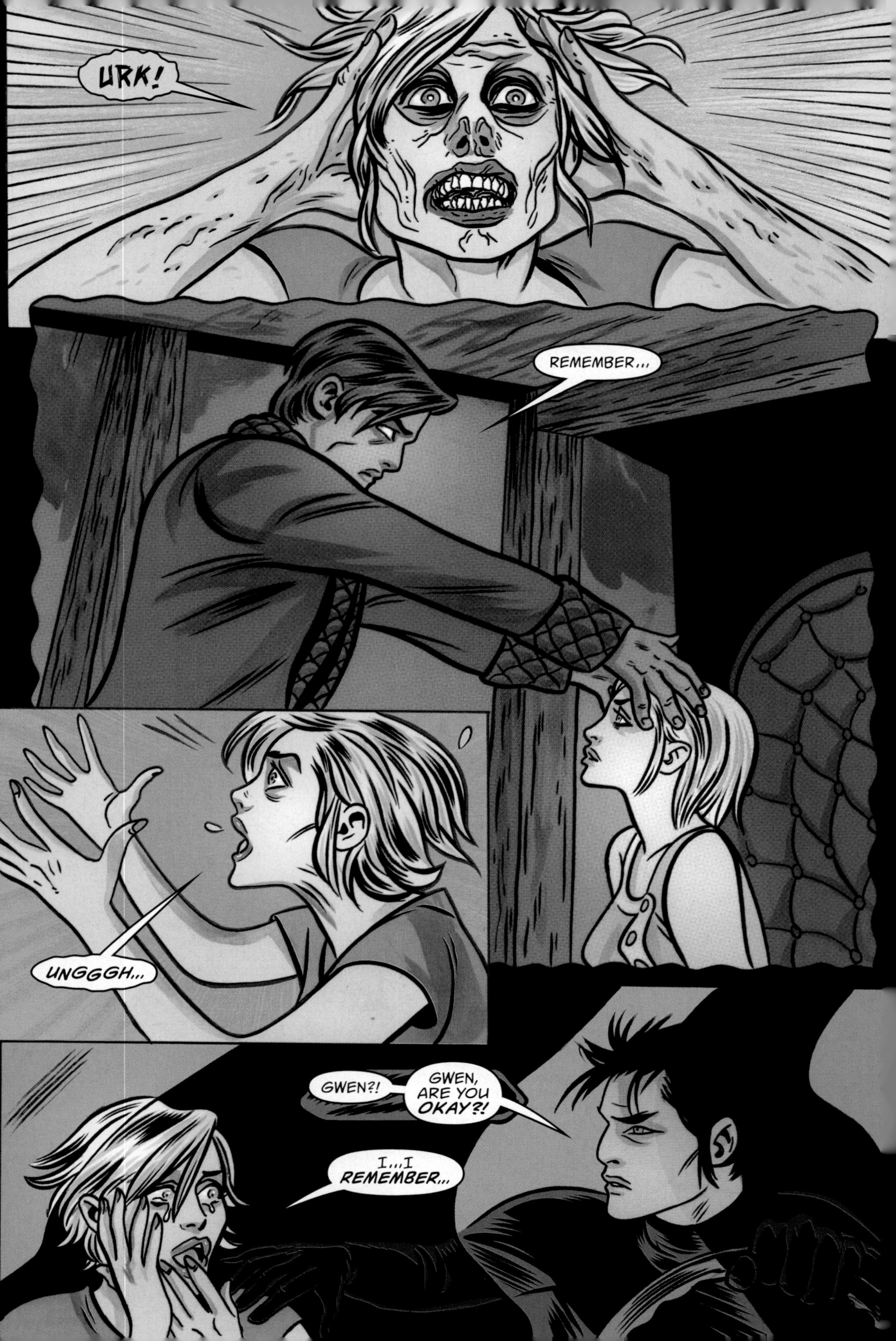
URK!
REMEMBER...
UNGGGH...
GWEN?!
GWEN, ARE YOU OKAY?!
I...I REMEMBER...

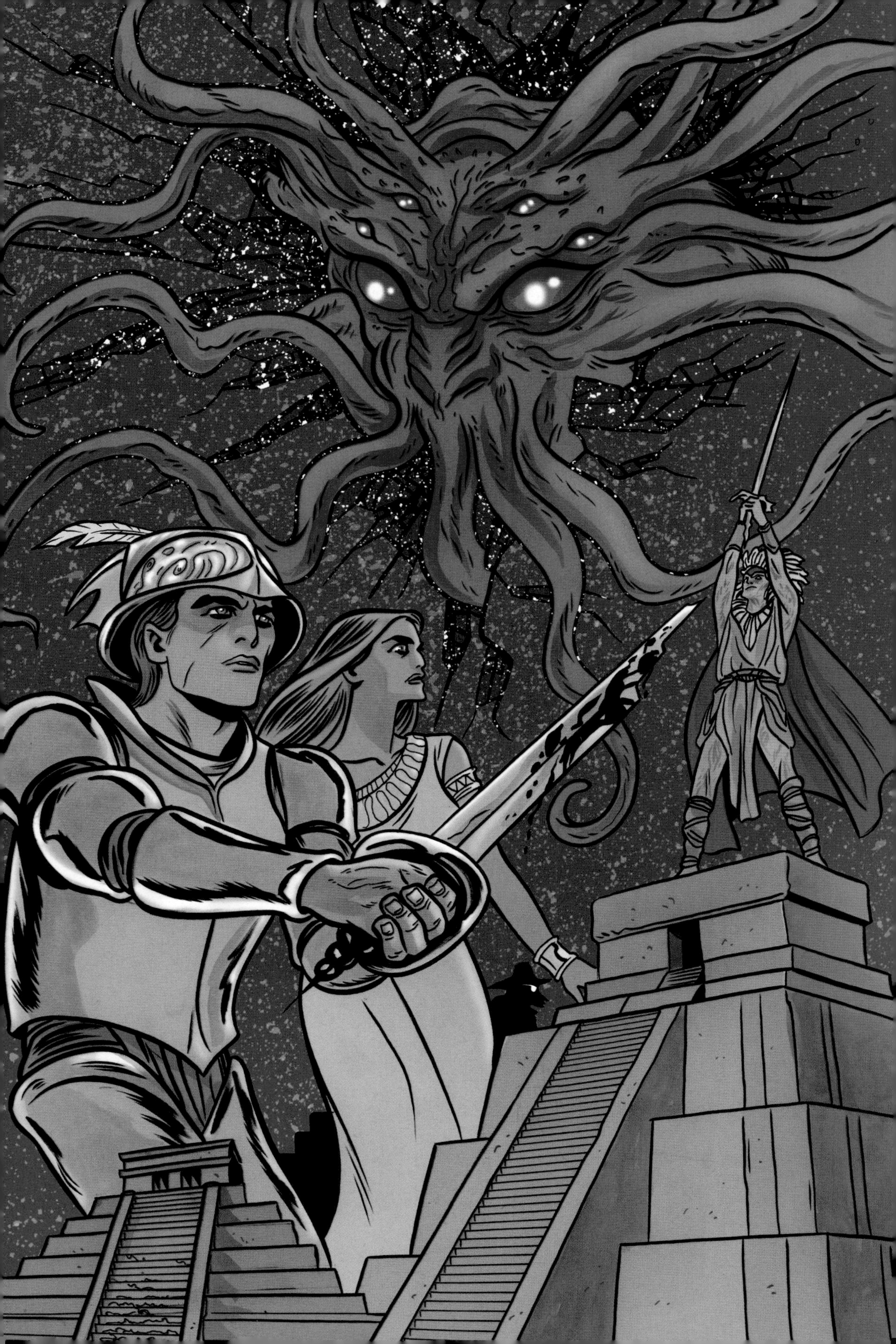

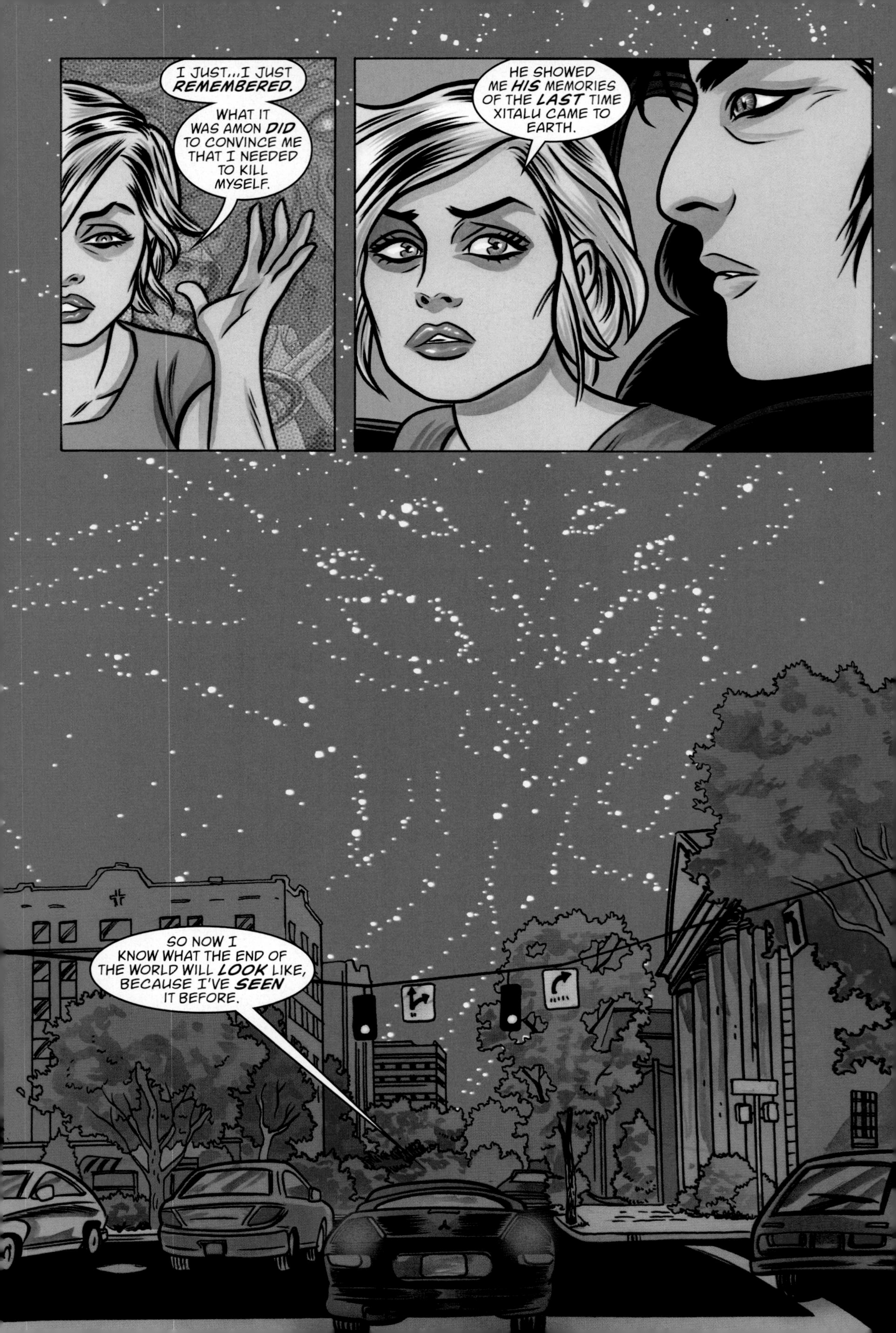
I JUST...I JUST REMEMBERED.
WHAT IT WAS AMON DID TO CONVINCE ME THAT I NEEDED TO KILL MYSELF.
HE SHOWED ME HIS MEMORIES OF THE LAST TIME XITALU CAME TO EARTH.
SO NOW I KNOW WHAT THE END OF THE WORLD WILL LOOK LIKE, BECAUSE I'VE SEEN IT BEFORE.

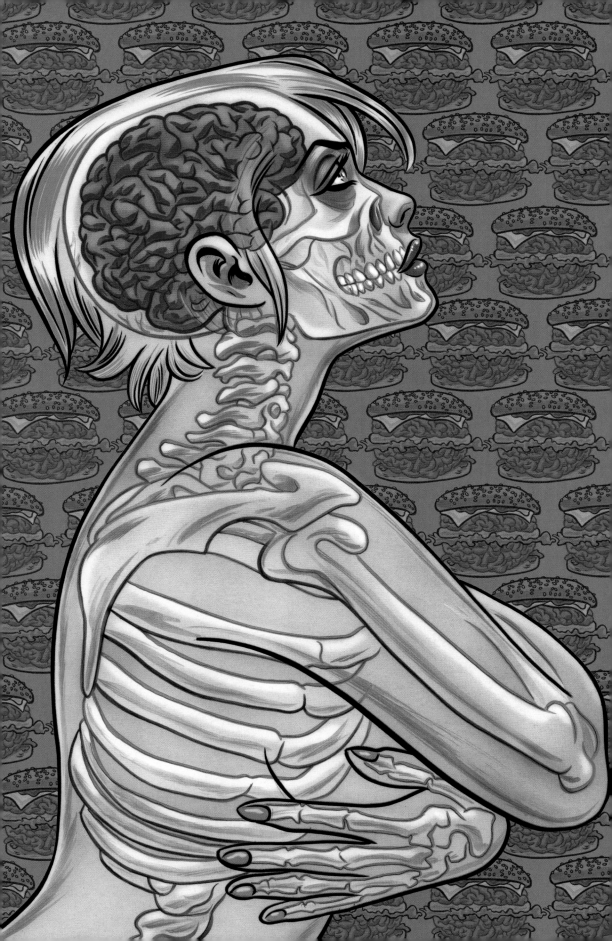

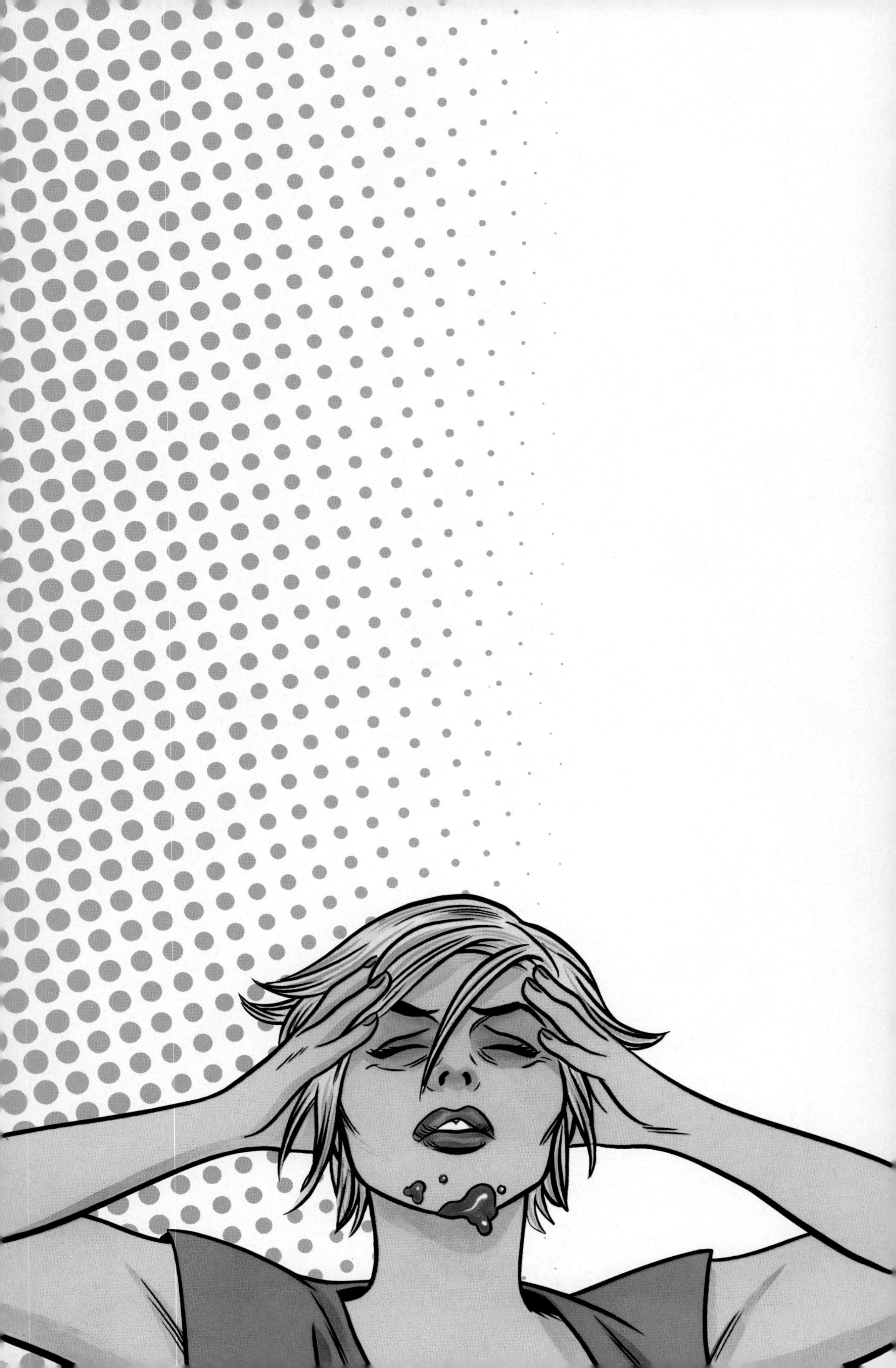

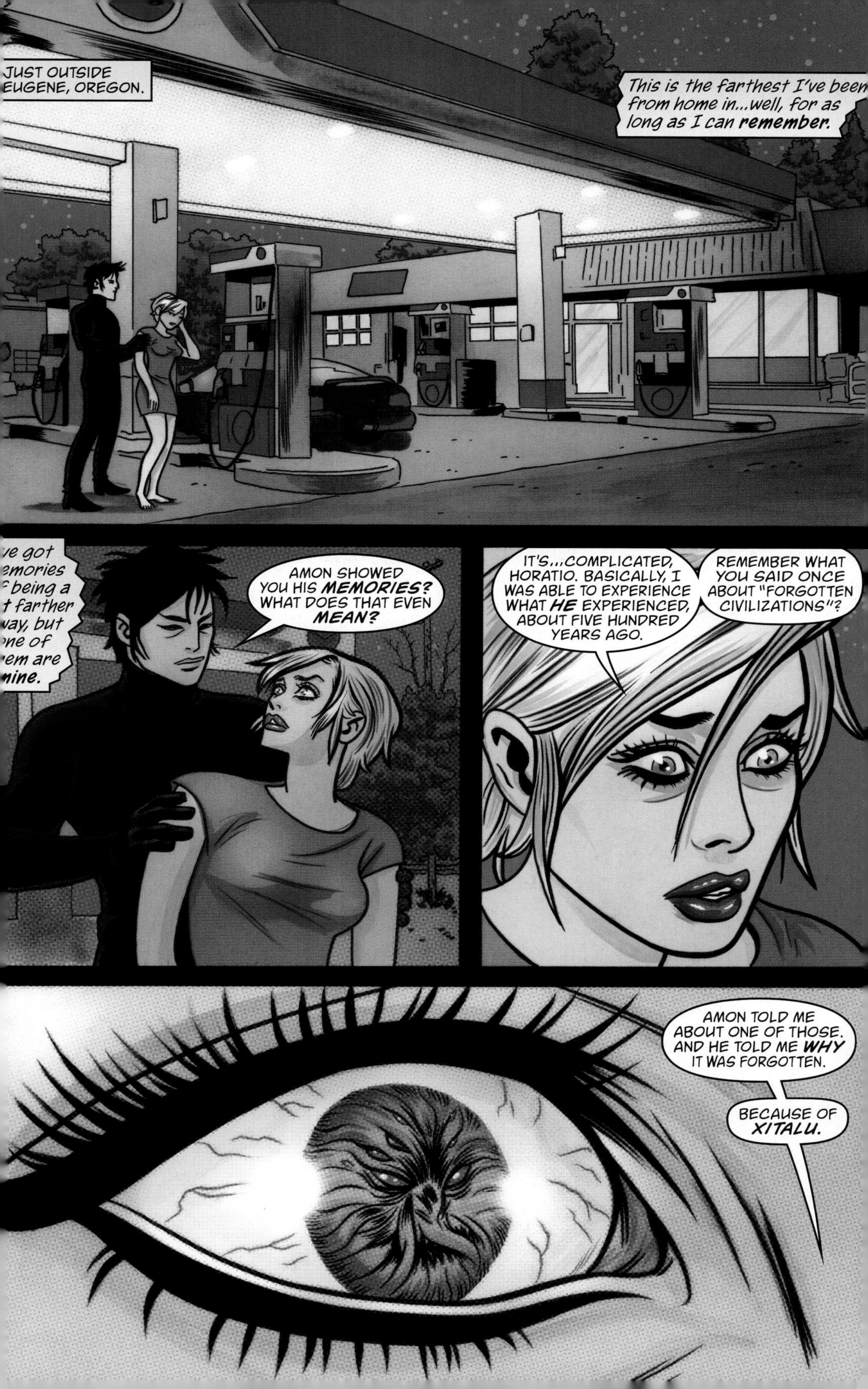

JUST OUTSIDE EUGENE, OREGON.
This is the farthest I've been from home in...well, for as long as I can **remember.**
ve got emories f being a t farther way, but one of em are mine.
AMON SHOWED YOU HIS **MEMORIES?** WHAT DOES THAT EVEN **MEAN?**
IT'S...COMPLICATED, HORATIO. BASICALLY, I WAS ABLE TO EXPERIENCE WHAT **HE** EXPERIENCED, ABOUT FIVE HUNDRED YEARS AGO.
REMEMBER WHAT YOU SAID ONCE ABOUT "FORGOTTEN CIVILIZATIONS"?
AMON TOLD ME ABOUT ONE OF THOSE. AND HE TOLD ME **WHY** IT WAS FORGOTTEN.
BECAUSE OF **XITALU.**

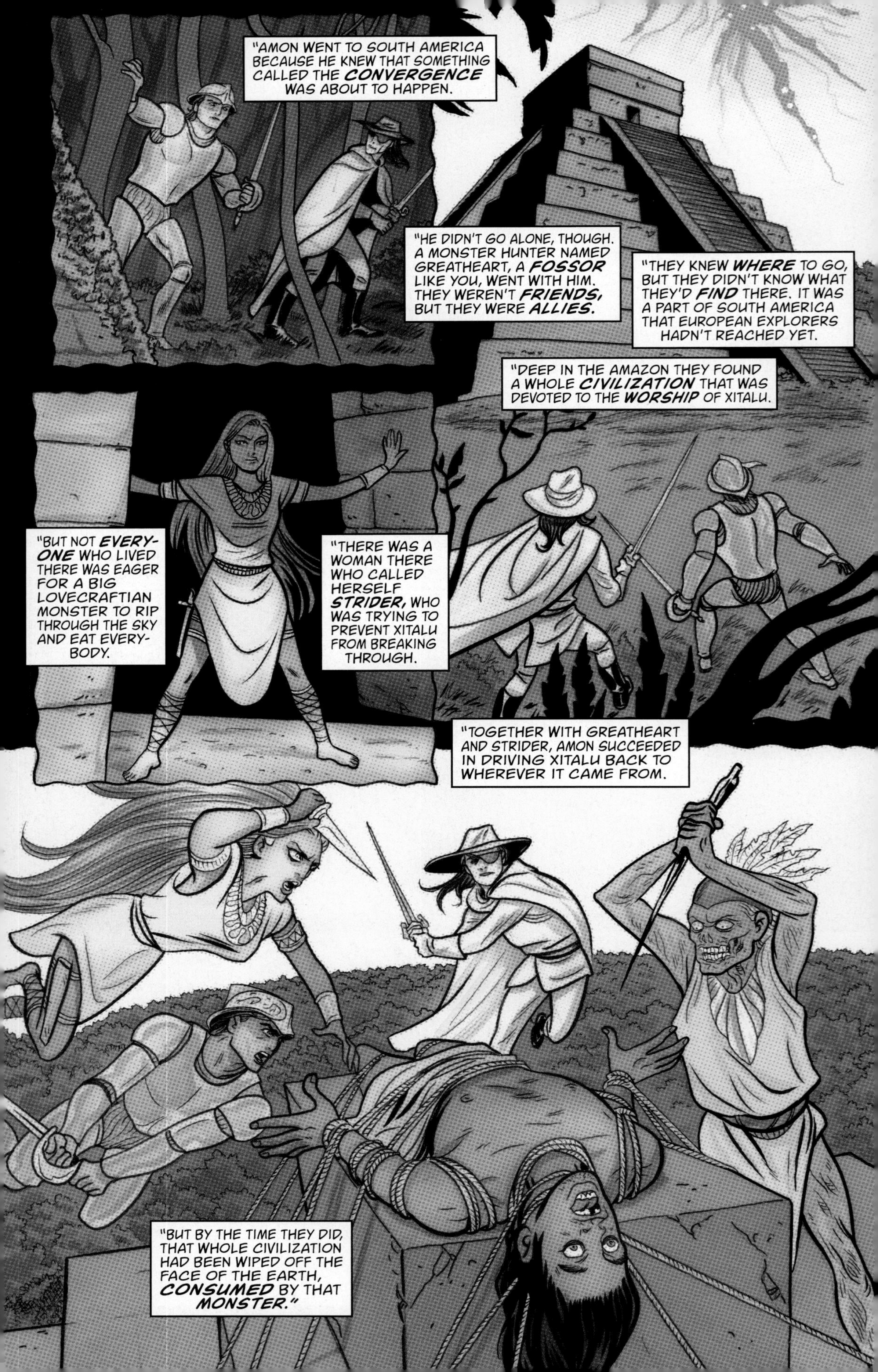
"AMON WENT TO SOUTH AMERICA BECAUSE HE KNEW THAT SOMETHING CALLED THE CONVERGENCE WAS ABOUT TO HAPPEN.
"HE DIDN'T GO ALONE, THOUGH. A MONSTER HUNTER NAMED GREATHEART, A FOSSOR LIKE YOU, WENT WITH HIM. THEY WEREN'T FRIENDS, BUT THEY WERE ALLIES.
"THEY KNEW WHERE TO GO, BUT THEY DIDN'T KNOW WHAT THEY'D FIND THERE. IT WAS A PART OF SOUTH AMERICA THAT EUROPEAN EXPLORERS HADN'T REACHED YET.
"DEEP IN THE AMAZON THEY FOUND A WHOLE CIVILIZATION THAT WAS DEVOTED TO THE WORSHIP OF XITALU.
"BUT NOT EVERYONE WHO LIVED THERE WAS EAGER FOR A BIG LOVECRAFTIAN MONSTER TO RIP THROUGH THE SKY AND EAT EVERYBODY.
"THERE WAS A WOMAN THERE WHO CALLED HERSELF STRIDER, WHO WAS TRYING TO PREVENT XITALU FROM BREAKING THROUGH.
"TOGETHER WITH GREATHEART AND STRIDER, AMON SUCCEEDED IN DRIVING XITALU BACK TO WHEREVER IT CAME FROM.
"BUT BY THE TIME THEY DID, THAT WHOLE CIVILIZATION HAD BEEN WIPED OFF THE FACE OF THE EARTH, CONSUMED BY THAT MONSTER."

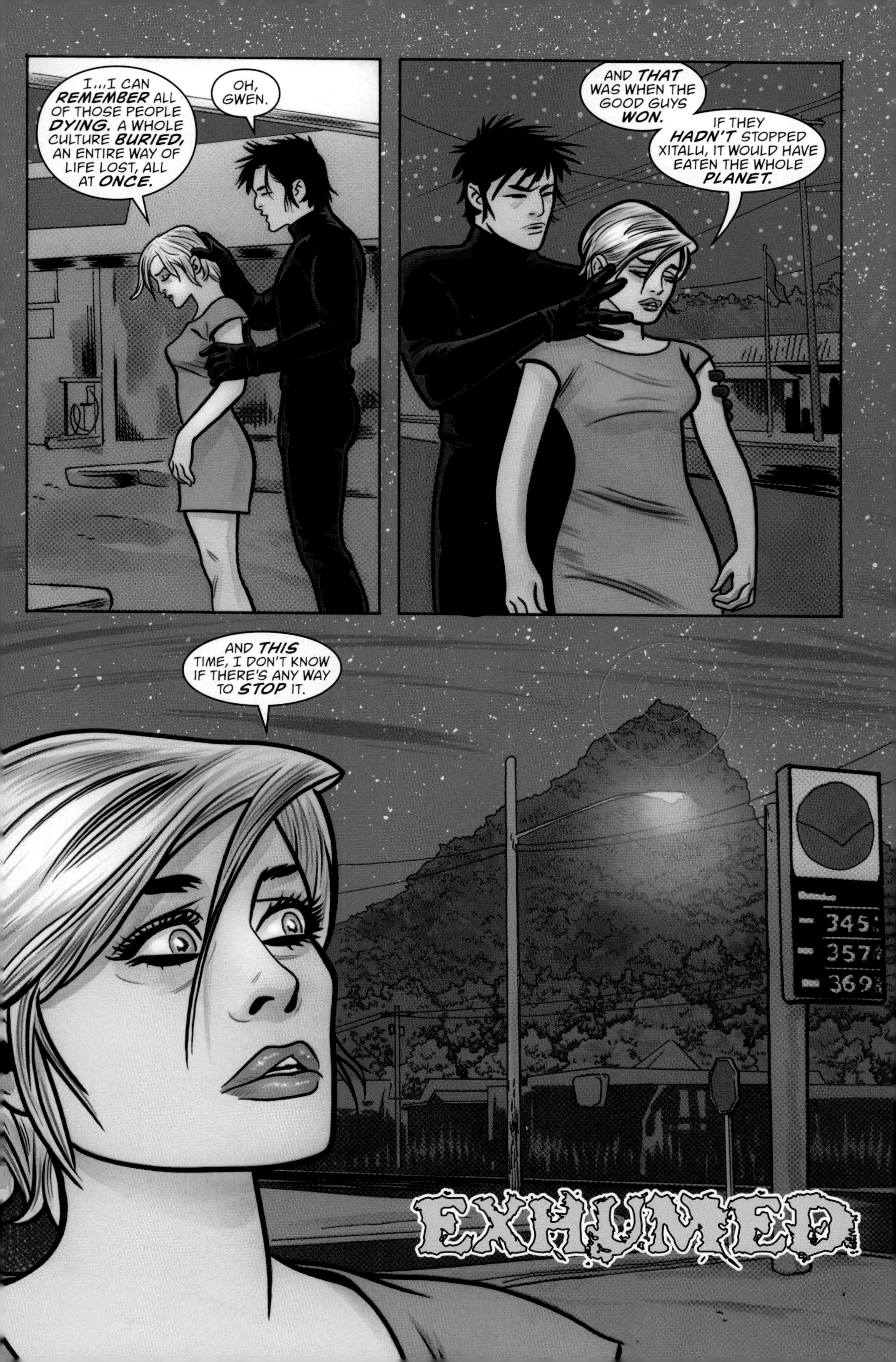
I...I CAN REMEMBER ALL OF THOSE PEOPLE DYING. A WHOLE CULTURE BURIED, AN ENTIRE WAY OF LIFE LOST, ALL AT ONCE.
OH, GWEN.
AND THAT WAS WHEN THE GOOD GUYS WON.
IF THEY HADN'T STOPPED XITALU, IT WOULD HAVE EATEN THE WHOLE PLANET.
AND THIS TIME, I DON'T KNOW IF THERE'S ANY WAY TO STOP IT.
345
357
369
EXHUMED

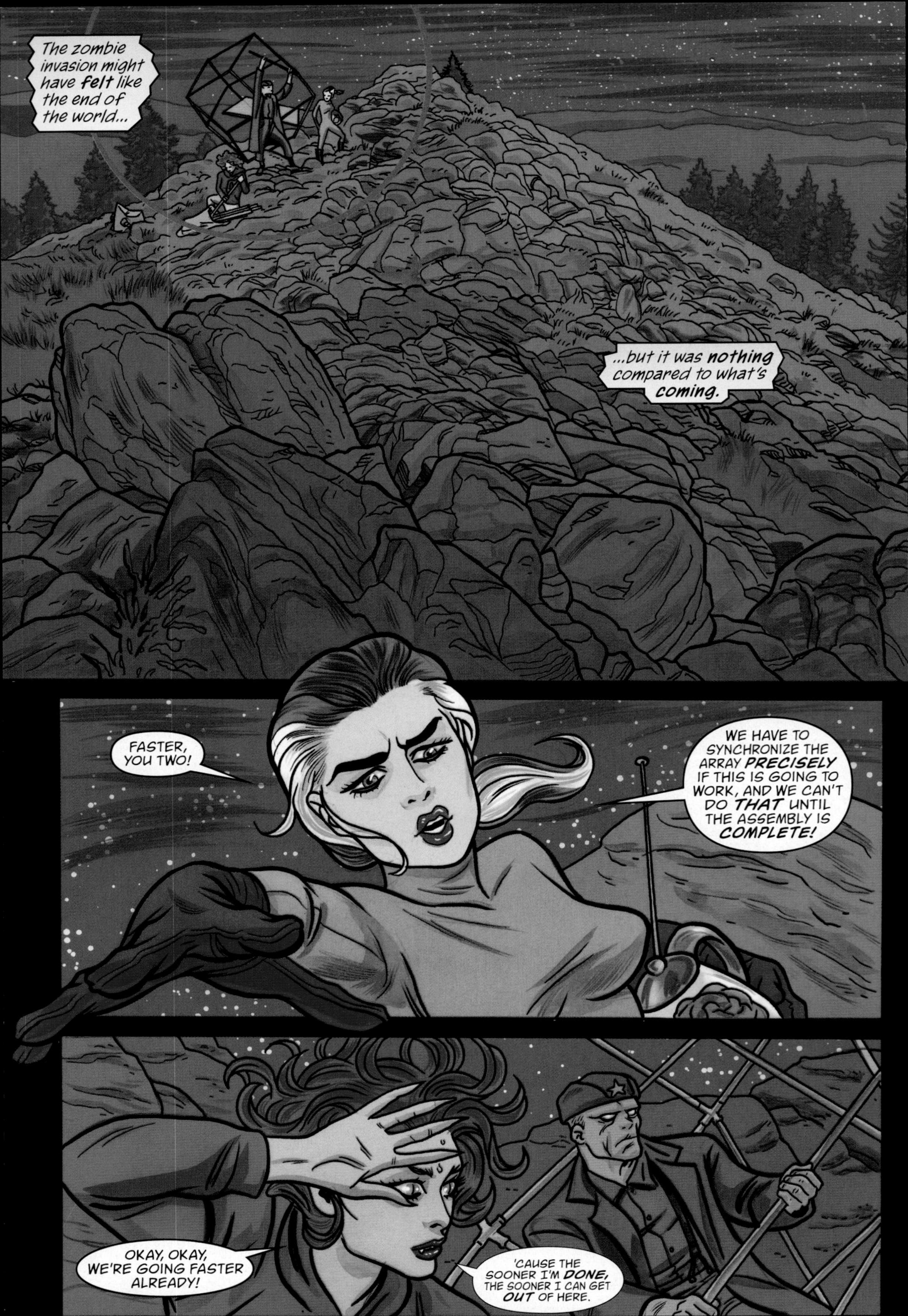
The zombie invasion might have felt like the end of the world...
...but it was nothing compared to what's coming.
FASTER, YOU TWO!
WE HAVE TO SYNCHRONIZE THE ARRAY PRECISELY IF THIS IS GOING TO WORK, AND WE CAN'T DO THAT UNTIL THE ASSEMBLY IS COMPLETE!
OKAY, OKAY, WE'RE GOING FASTER ALREADY!
'CAUSE THE SOONER I'M DONE, THE SOONER I CAN GET OUT OF HERE.

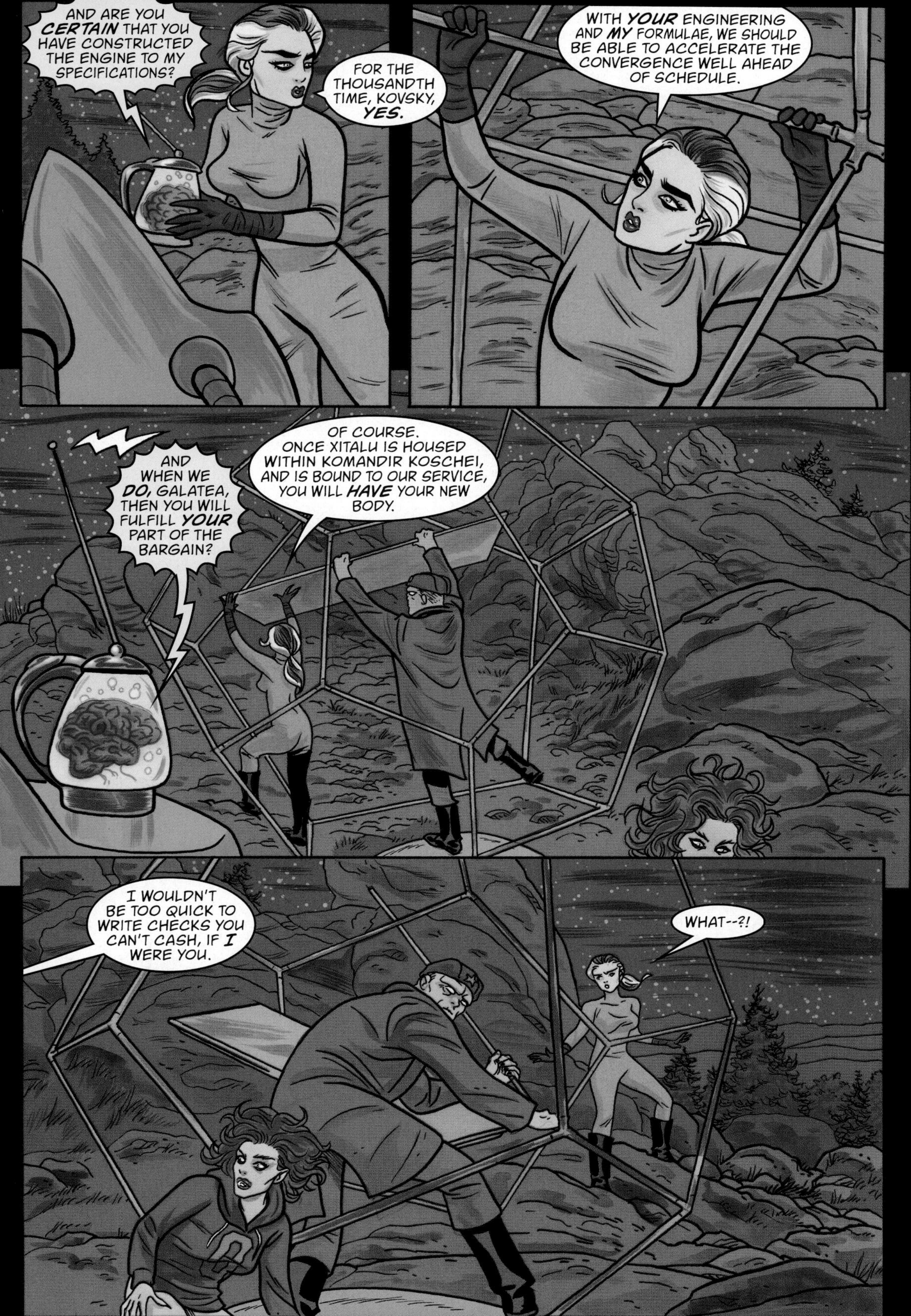
AND ARE YOU CERTAIN THAT YOU HAVE CONSTRUCTED THE ENGINE TO MY SPECIFICATIONS?
FOR THE THOUSANDTH TIME, KOVSKY, YES.
WITH YOUR ENGINEERING AND MY FORMULAE, WE SHOULD BE ABLE TO ACCELERATE THE CONVERGENCE WELL AHEAD OF SCHEDULE.
AND WHEN WE DO, GALATEA, THEN YOU WILL FULFILL YOUR PART OF THE BARGAIN?
OF COURSE. ONCE XITALU IS HOUSED WITHIN KOMANDIR KOSCHEI, AND IS BOUND TO OUR SERVICE, YOU WILL HAVE YOUR NEW BODY.
I WOULDN'T BE TOO QUICK TO WRITE CHECKS YOU CAN'T CASH, IF I WERE YOU.
WHAT--?!

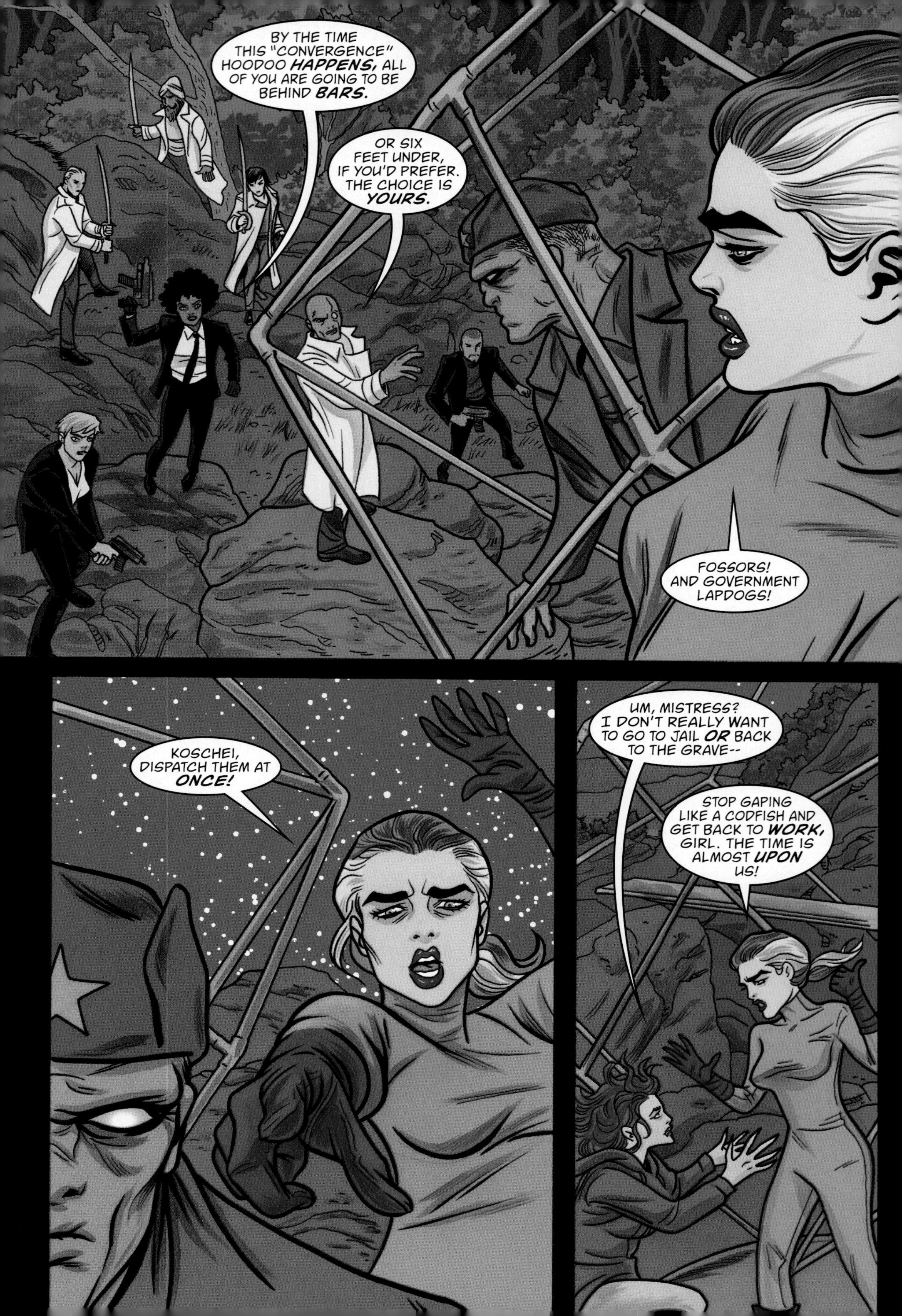
BY THE TIME THIS "CONVERGENCE" HOODOO HAPPENS, ALL OF YOU ARE GOING TO BE BEHIND BARS.
OR SIX FEET UNDER, IF YOU'D PREFER. THE CHOICE IS YOURS.
FOSSORS! AND GOVERNMENT LAPDOGS!
KOSCHEI, DISPATCH THEM AT ONCE!
UM, MISTRESS? I DON'T REALLY WANT TO GO TO JAIL OR BACK TO THE GRAVE--
STOP GAPING LIKE A CODFISH AND GET BACK TO WORK, GIRL. THE TIME IS ALMOST UPON US!

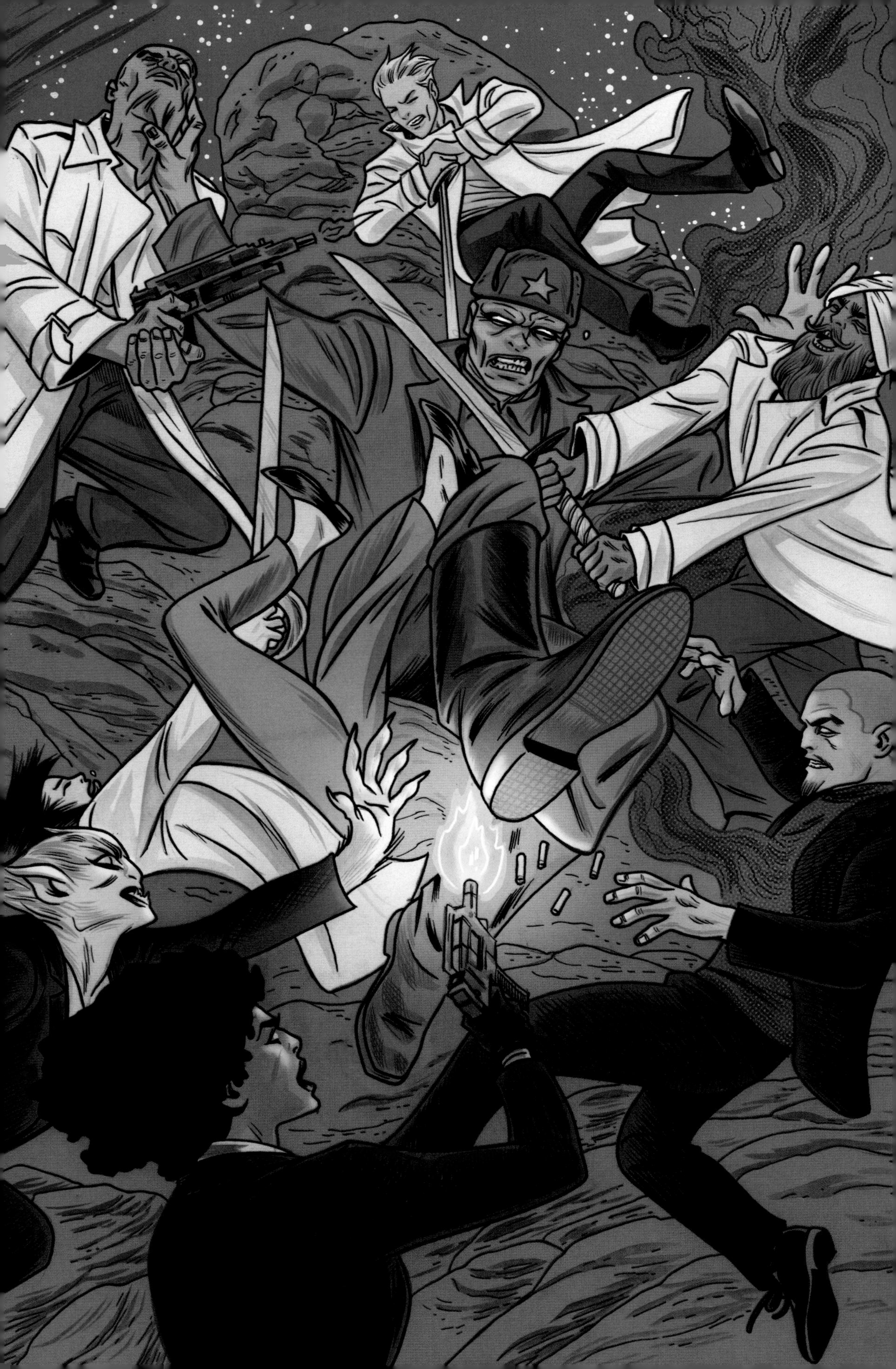

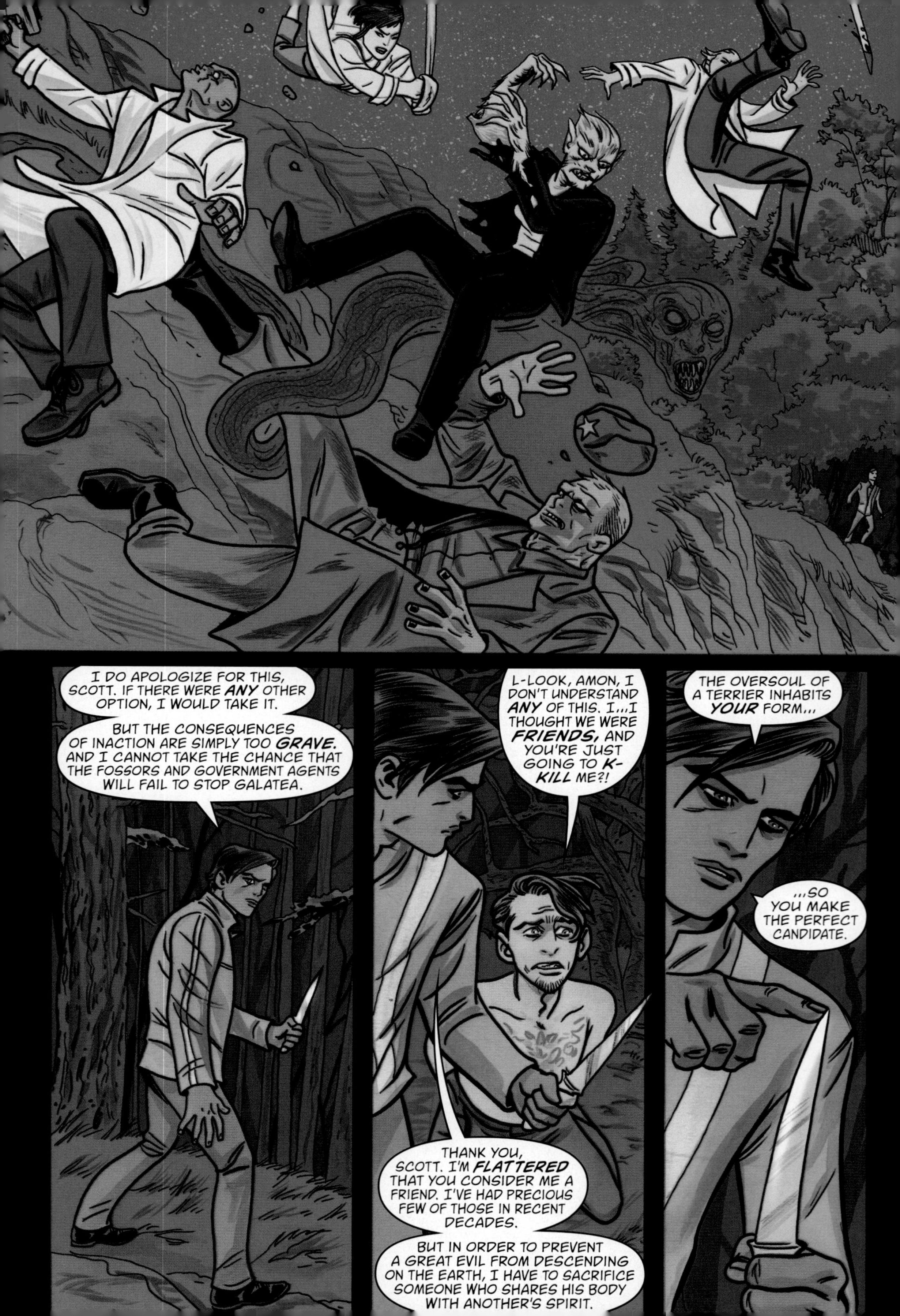
I DO APOLOGIZE FOR THIS, SCOTT. IF THERE WERE ANY OTHER OPTION, I WOULD TAKE IT.
BUT THE CONSEQUENCES OF INACTION ARE SIMPLY TOO GRAVE. AND I CANNOT TAKE THE CHANCE THAT THE FOSSORS AND GOVERNMENT AGENTS WILL FAIL TO STOP GALATEA.
L-LOOK, AMON, I DON'T UNDERSTAND ANY OF THIS. I...I THOUGHT WE WERE FRIENDS, AND YOU'RE JUST GOING TO K-KILL ME?!
THANK YOU, SCOTT. I'M FLATTERED THAT YOU CONSIDER ME A FRIEND. I'VE HAD PRECIOUS FEW OF THOSE IN RECENT DECADES.
BUT IN ORDER TO PREVENT A GREAT EVIL FROM DESCENDING ON THE EARTH, I HAVE TO SACRIFICE SOMEONE WHO SHARES HIS BODY WITH ANOTHER'S SPIRIT.
THE OVERSOUL OF A TERRIER INHABITS YOUR FORM...
...SO YOU MAKE THE PERFECT CANDIDATE.

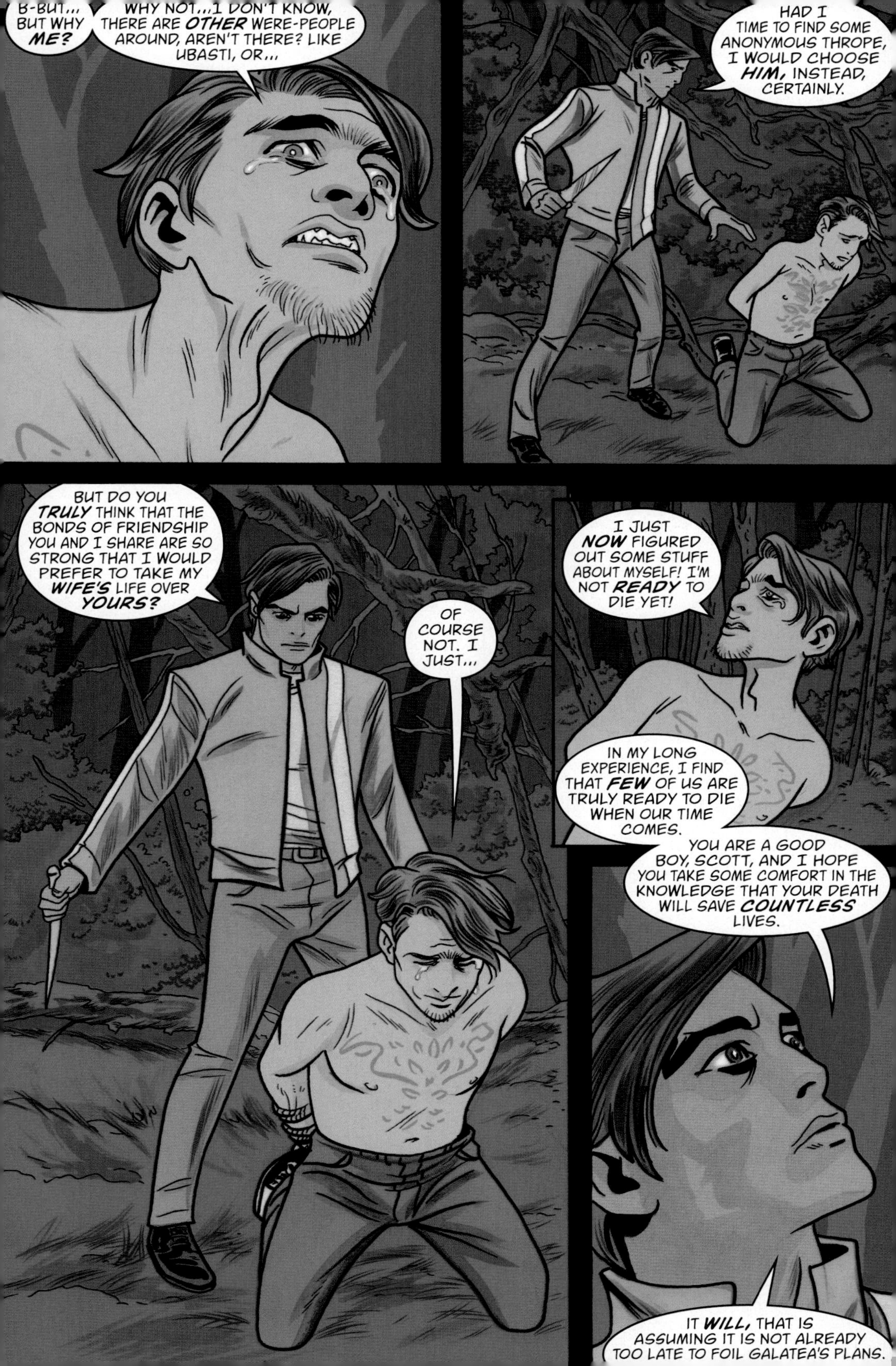
B-BUT... BUT WHY ME?
WHY NOT...I DON'T KNOW, THERE ARE OTHER WERE-PEOPLE AROUND, AREN'T THERE? LIKE UBASTI, OR...
HAD I TIME TO FIND SOME ANONYMOUS THROPE, I WOULD CHOOSE HIM, INSTEAD, CERTAINLY.
BUT DO YOU TRULY THINK THAT THE BONDS OF FRIENDSHIP YOU AND I SHARE ARE SO STRONG THAT I WOULD PREFER TO TAKE MY WIFE'S LIFE OVER YOURS?
OF COURSE NOT. I JUST...
I JUST NOW FIGURED OUT SOME STUFF ABOUT MYSELF! I'M NOT READY TO DIE YET!
IN MY LONG EXPERIENCE, I FIND THAT FEW OF US ARE TRULY READY TO DIE WHEN OUR TIME COMES.
YOU ARE A GOOD BOY, SCOTT, AND I HOPE YOU TAKE SOME COMFORT IN THE KNOWLEDGE THAT YOUR DEATH WILL SAVE COUNTLESS LIVES.
IT WILL, THAT IS ASSUMING IT IS NOT ALREADY TOO LATE TO FOIL GALATEA'S PLANS.

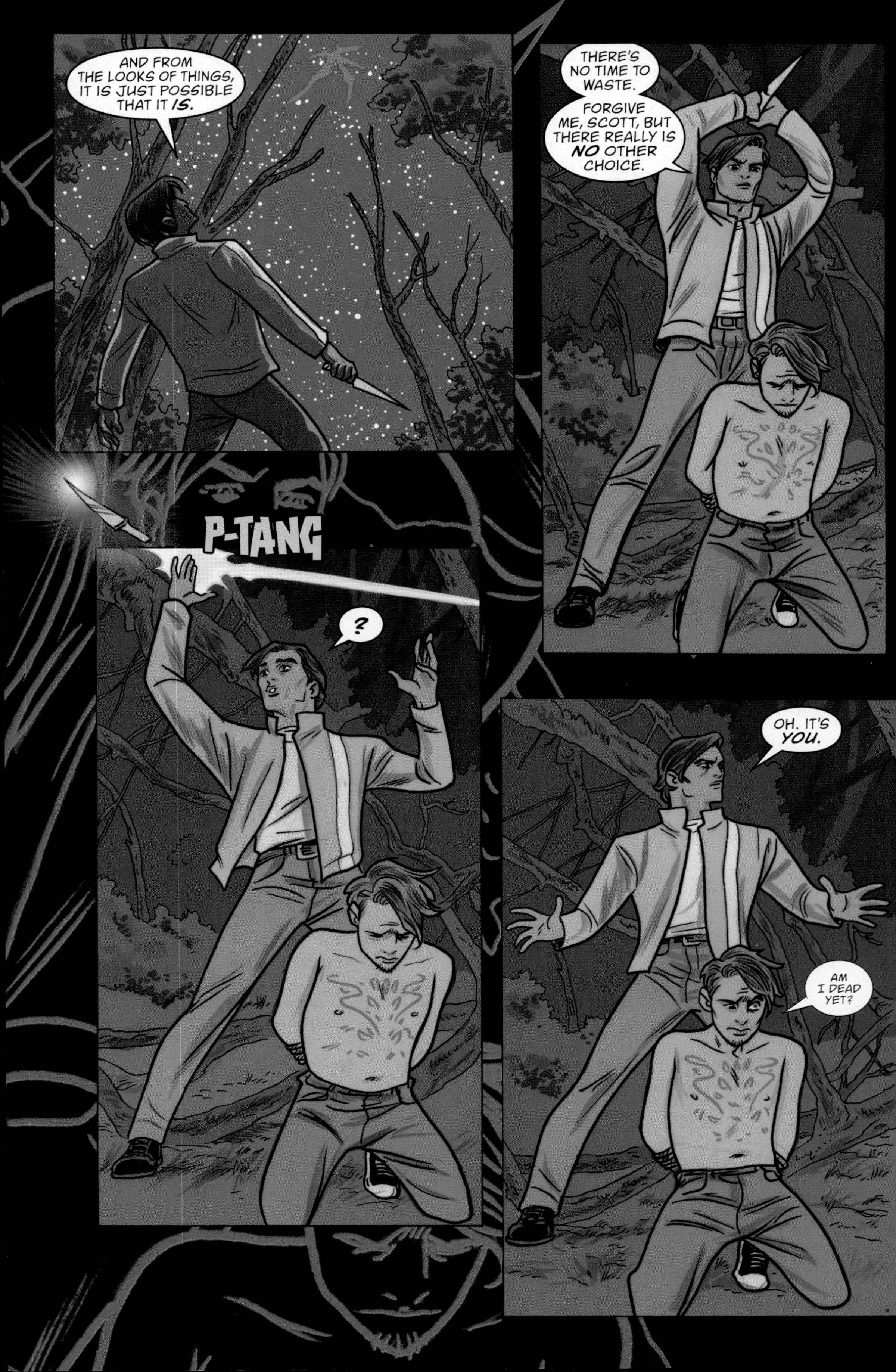
AND FROM THE LOOKS OF THINGS, IT IS JUST POSSIBLE THAT IT *IS.*
THERE'S NO TIME TO WASTE.
FORGIVE ME, SCOTT, BUT THERE REALLY IS **NO** OTHER CHOICE.
P-TANG
?
OH. IT'S *YOU.*
AM I DEAD YET?

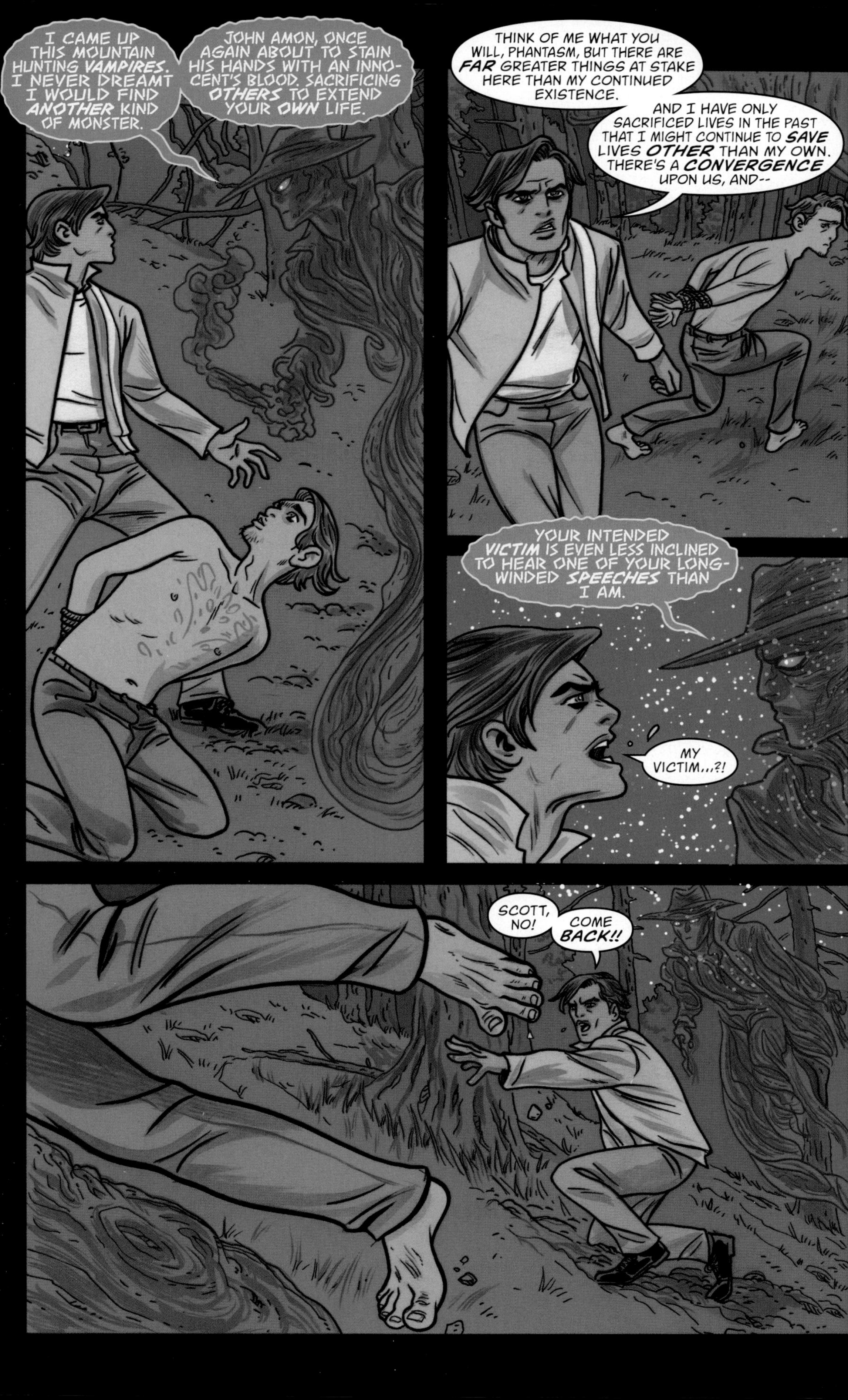
I CAME UP THIS MOUNTAIN HUNTING VAMPIRES. I NEVER DREAMT I WOULD FIND ANOTHER KIND OF MONSTER.
JOHN AMON, ONCE AGAIN ABOUT TO STAIN HIS HANDS WITH AN INNO-CENT'S BLOOD. SACRIFICING OTHERS TO EXTEND YOUR OWN LIFE.
THINK OF ME WHAT YOU WILL, PHANTASM, BUT THERE ARE FAR GREATER THINGS AT STAKE HERE THAN MY CONTINUED EXISTENCE.
AND I HAVE ONLY SACRIFICED LIVES IN THE PAST THAT I MIGHT CONTINUE TO SAVE LIVES OTHER THAN MY OWN. THERE'S A CONVERGENCE UPON US, AND--
YOUR INTENDED VICTIM IS EVEN LESS INCLINED TO HEAR ONE OF YOUR LONG-WINDED SPEECHES THAN I AM.
MY VICTIM...?!
SCOTT, NO!
COME BACK!!

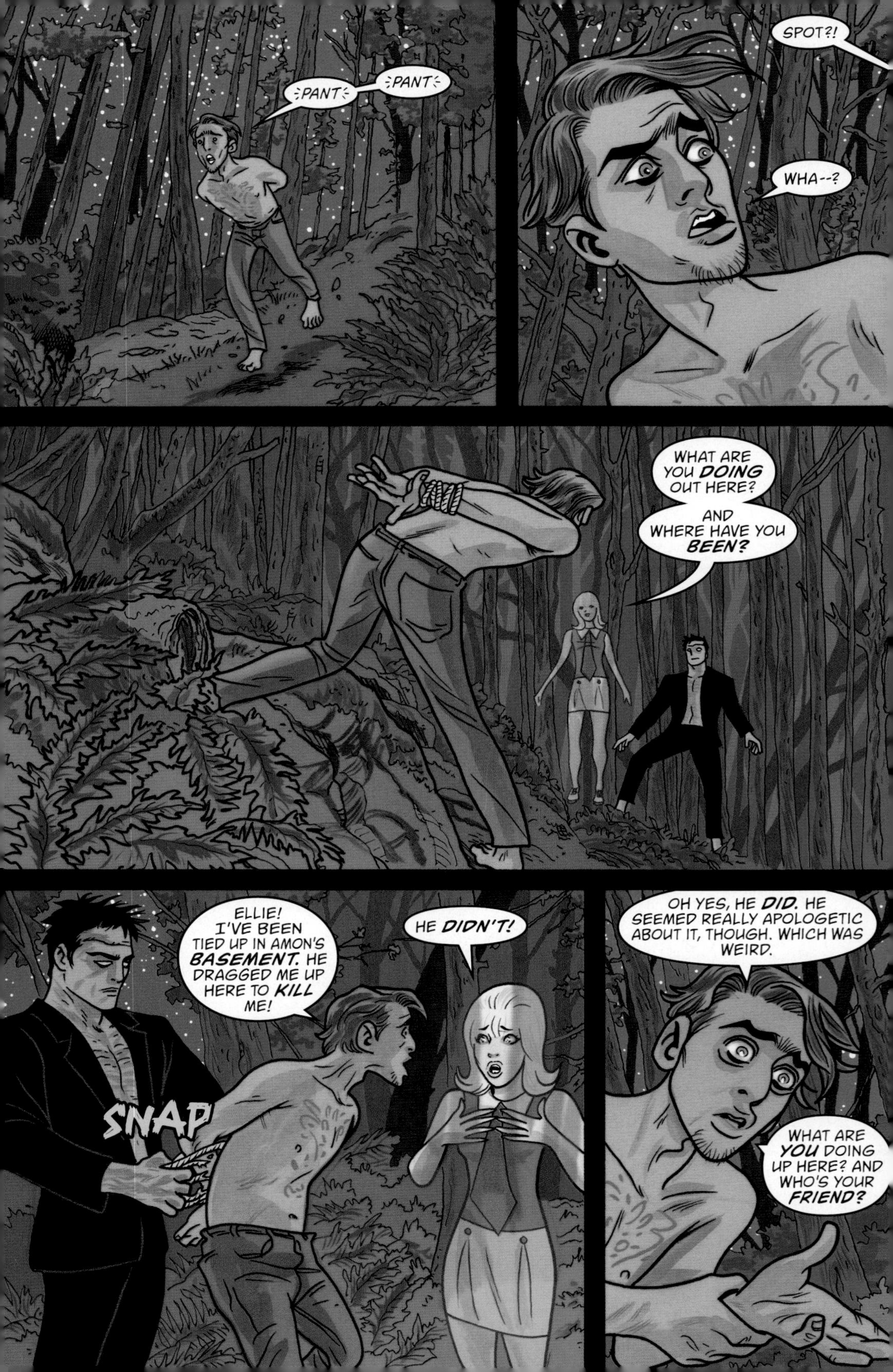
PANT
PANT
SPOT?!
WHA--?
WHAT ARE YOU DOING OUT HERE?
AND WHERE HAVE YOU BEEN?
ELLIE! I'VE BEEN TIED UP IN AMON'S BASEMENT. HE DRAGGED ME UP HERE TO KILL ME!
HE DIDN'T!
SNAP
OH YES, HE DID. HE SEEMED REALLY APOLOGETIC ABOUT IT, THOUGH. WHICH WAS WEIRD.
WHAT ARE YOU DOING UP HERE? AND WHO'S YOUR FRIEND?

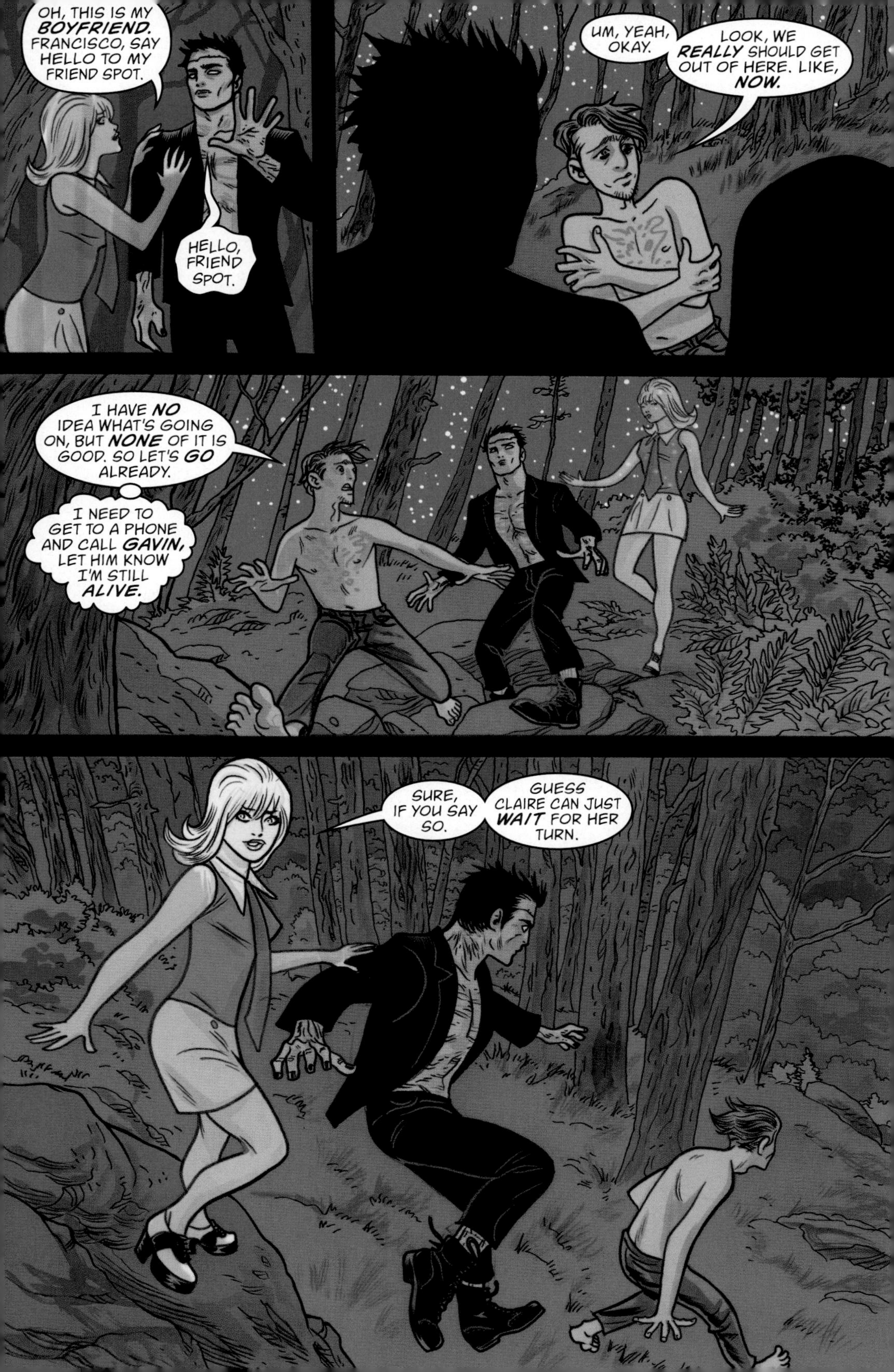
OH, THIS IS MY BOYFRIEND. FRANCISCO, SAY HELLO TO MY FRIEND SPOT.
HELLO, FRIEND SPOT.
UM, YEAH, OKAY.
LOOK, WE REALLY SHOULD GET OUT OF HERE. LIKE, NOW.
I HAVE NO IDEA WHAT'S GOING ON, BUT NONE OF IT IS GOOD. SO LET'S GO ALREADY.
I NEED TO GET TO A PHONE AND CALL GAVIN, LET HIM KNOW I'M STILL ALIVE.
SURE, IF YOU SAY SO.
GUESS CLAIRE CAN JUST WAIT FOR HER TURN.

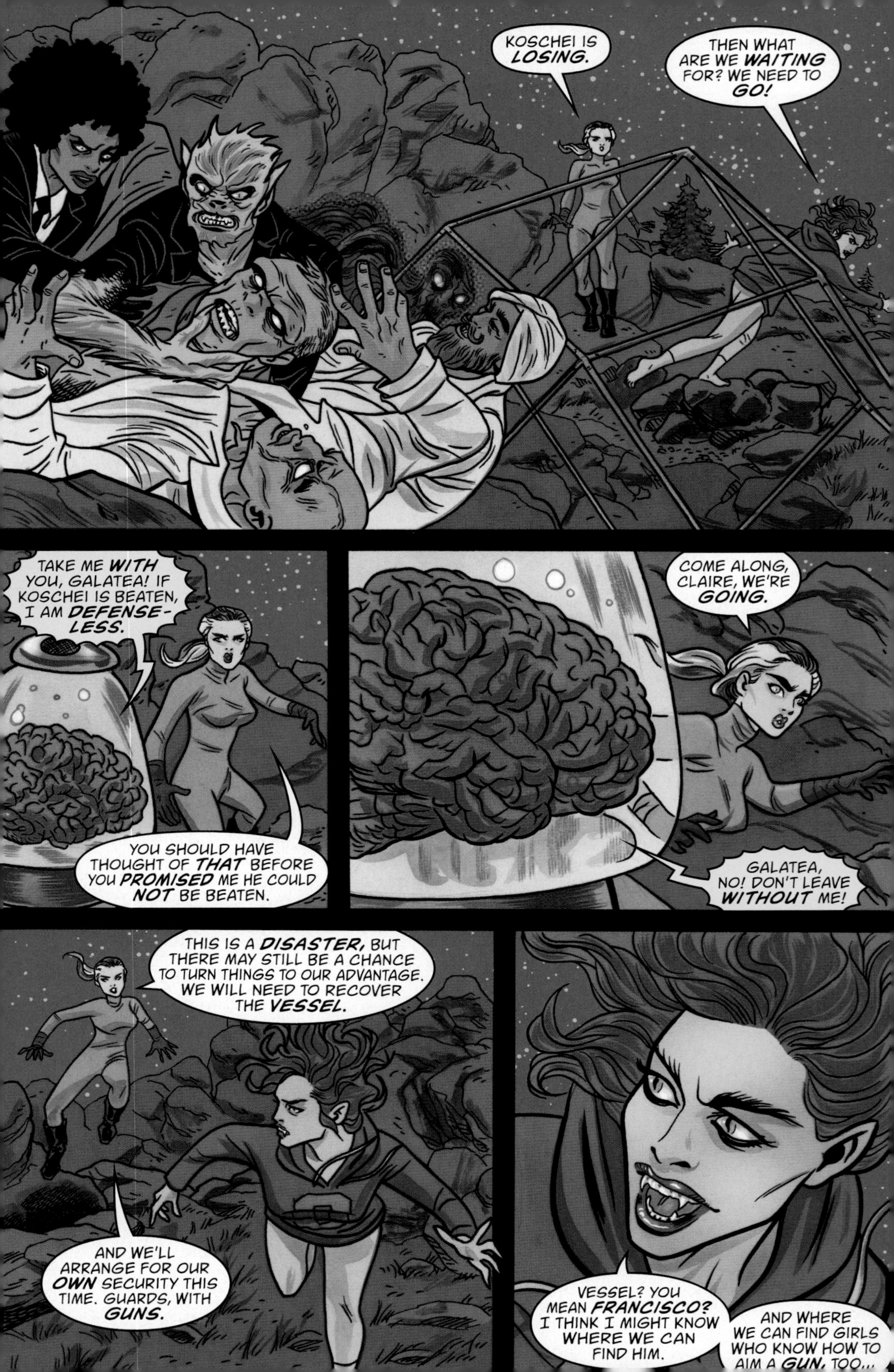
KOSCHEI IS LOSING.
THEN WHAT ARE WE WAITING FOR? WE NEED TO GO!
TAKE ME WITH YOU, GALATEA! IF KOSCHEI IS BEATEN, I AM DEFENSE-LESS.
YOU SHOULD HAVE THOUGHT OF THAT BEFORE YOU PROMISED ME HE COULD NOT BE BEATEN.
COME ALONG, CLAIRE, WE'RE GOING.
GALATEA, NO! DON'T LEAVE WITHOUT ME!
THIS IS A DISASTER, BUT THERE MAY STILL BE A CHANCE TO TURN THINGS TO OUR ADVANTAGE. WE WILL NEED TO RECOVER THE VESSEL.
AND WE'LL ARRANGE FOR OUR OWN SECURITY THIS TIME. GUARDS, WITH GUNS.
VESSEL? YOU MEAN FRANCISCO? I THINK I MIGHT KNOW WHERE WE CAN FIND HIM.
AND WHERE WE CAN FIND GIRLS WHO KNOW HOW TO AIM A GUN, TOO...

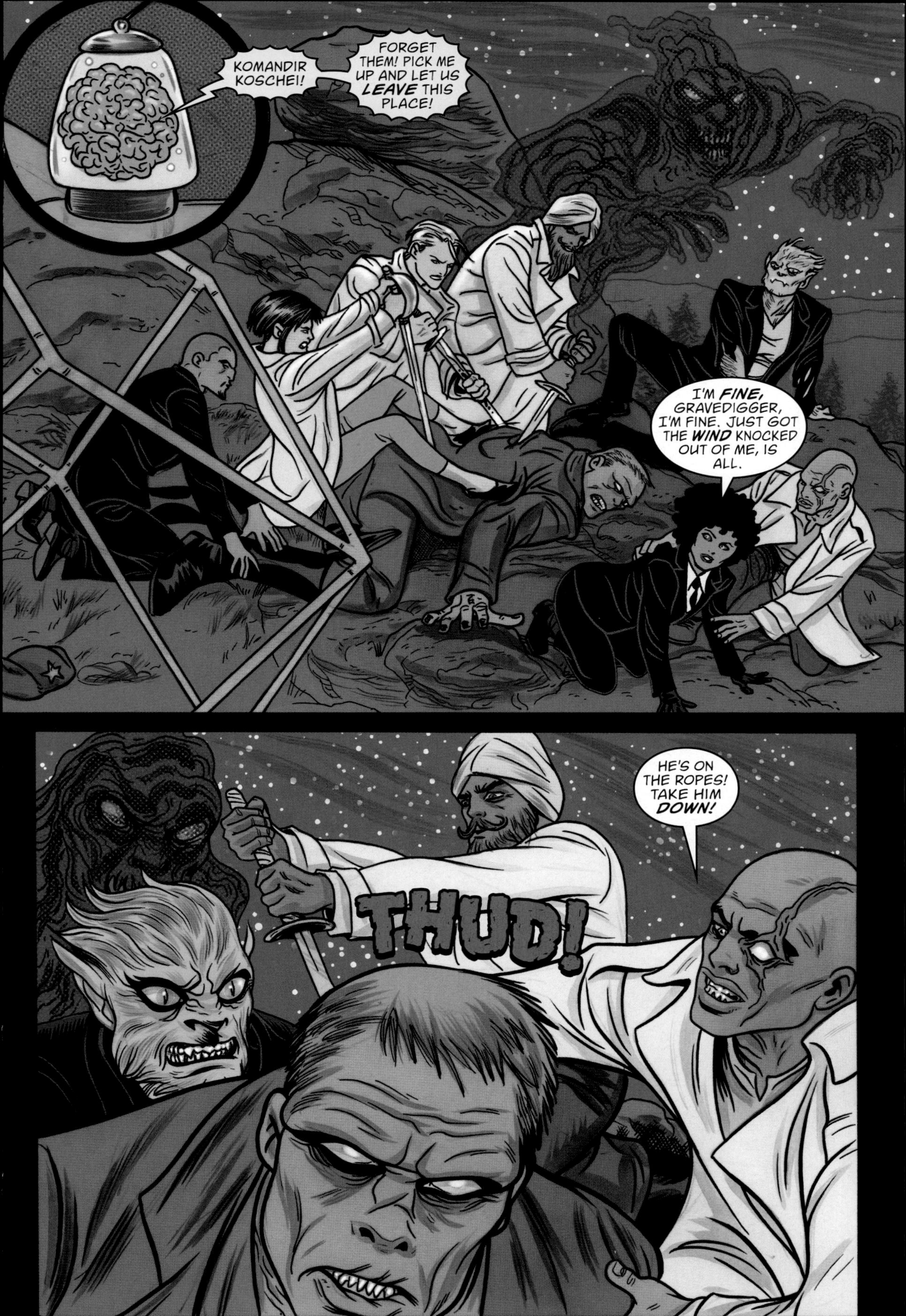
KOMANDIR KOSCHEI!
FORGET THEM! PICK ME UP AND LET US LEAVE THIS PLACE!
I'M FINE, GRAVEDIGGER, I'M FINE. JUST GOT THE WIND KNOCKED OUT OF ME, IS ALL.
HE'S ON THE ROPES! TAKE HIM DOWN!
THUD!

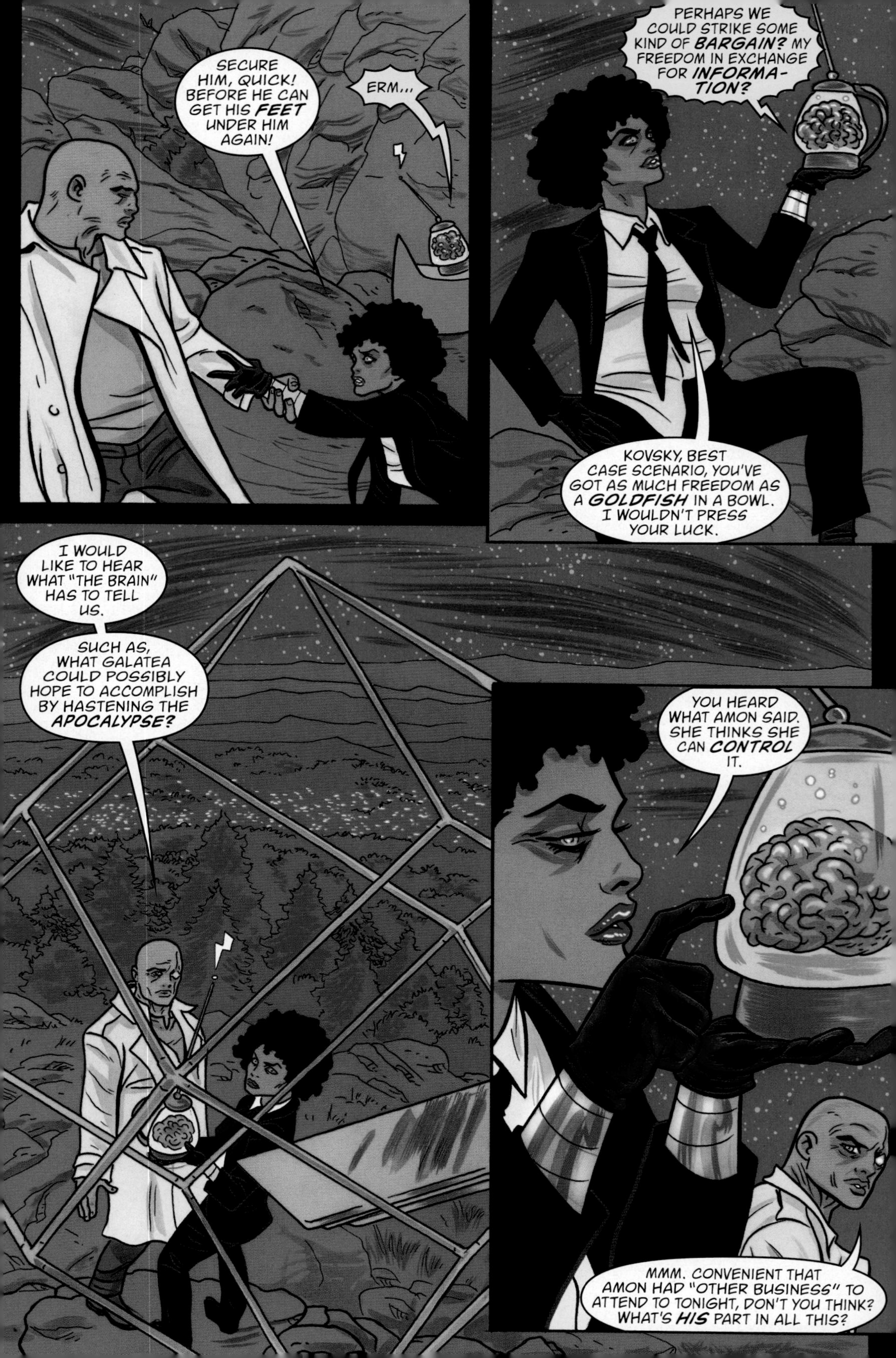
SECURE HIM, QUICK! BEFORE HE CAN GET HIS FEET UNDER HIM AGAIN!
ERM...
PERHAPS WE COULD STRIKE SOME KIND OF BARGAIN? MY FREEDOM IN EXCHANGE FOR INFORMATION?
KOVSKY, BEST CASE SCENARIO, YOU'VE GOT AS MUCH FREEDOM AS A GOLDFISH IN A BOWL. I WOULDN'T PRESS YOUR LUCK.
I WOULD LIKE TO HEAR WHAT "THE BRAIN" HAS TO TELL US.
SUCH AS, WHAT GALATEA COULD POSSIBLY HOPE TO ACCOMPLISH BY HASTENING THE APOCALYPSE?
YOU HEARD WHAT AMON SAID. SHE THINKS SHE CAN CONTROL IT.
MMM. CONVENIENT THAT AMON HAD "OTHER BUSINESS" TO ATTEND TO TONIGHT, DON'T YOU THINK? WHAT'S HIS PART IN ALL THIS?

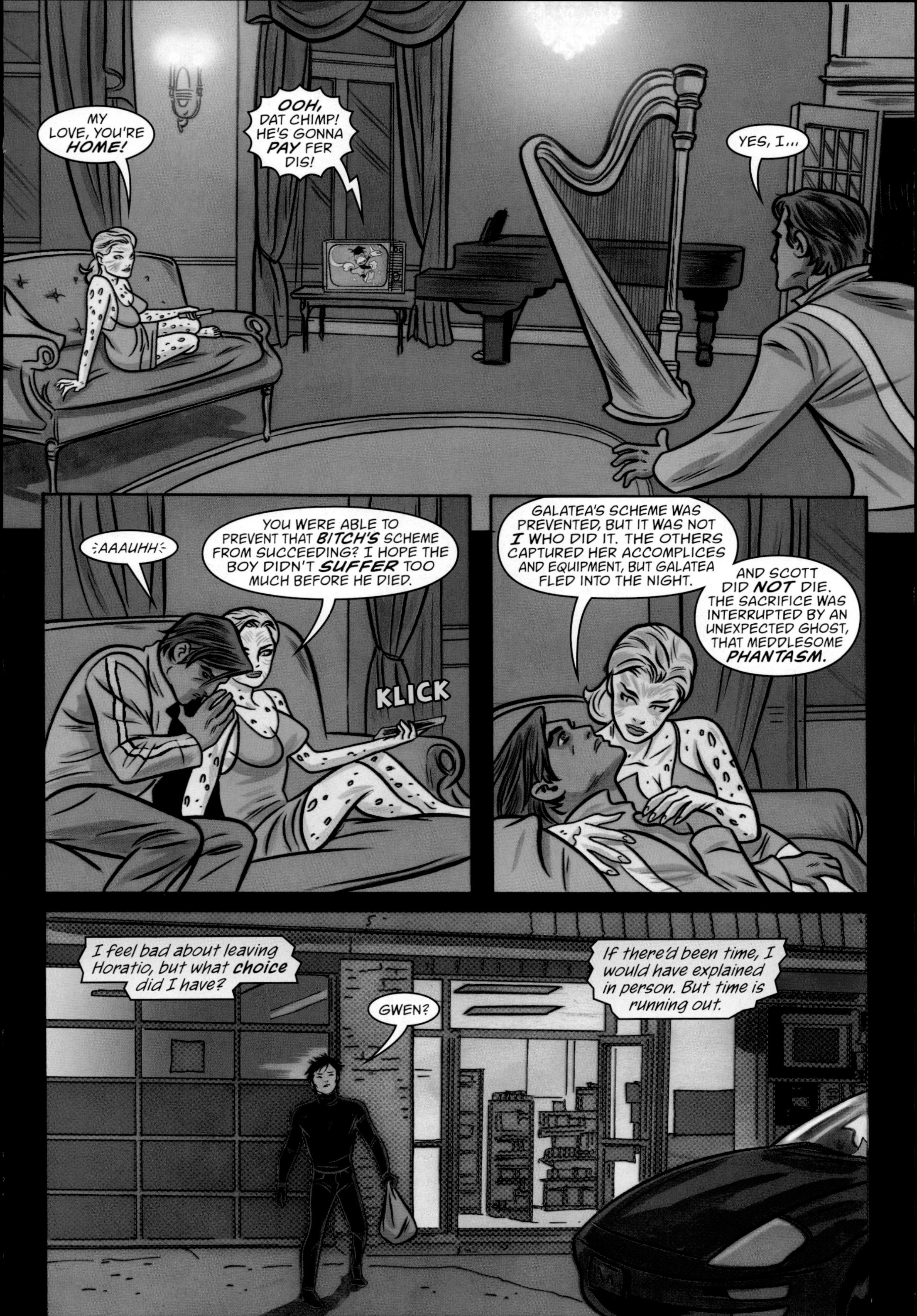

MY LOVE, YOU'RE HOME!
OOH, DAT CHIMP! HE'S GONNA PAY FER DIS!
YES, I...
AAAUHH
YOU WERE ABLE TO PREVENT THAT BITCH'S SCHEME FROM SUCCEEDING? I HOPE THE BOY DIDN'T SUFFER TOO MUCH BEFORE HE DIED.
KLICK
GALATEA'S SCHEME WAS PREVENTED, BUT IT WAS NOT I WHO DID IT. THE OTHERS CAPTURED HER ACCOMPLICES AND EQUIPMENT, BUT GALATEA FLED INTO THE NIGHT.
AND SCOTT DID NOT DIE. THE SACRIFICE WAS INTERRUPTED BY AN UNEXPECTED GHOST, THAT MEDDLESOME PHANTASM.
I feel bad about leaving Horatio, but what choice did I have?
GWEN?
If there'd been time, I would have explained in person. But time is running out.

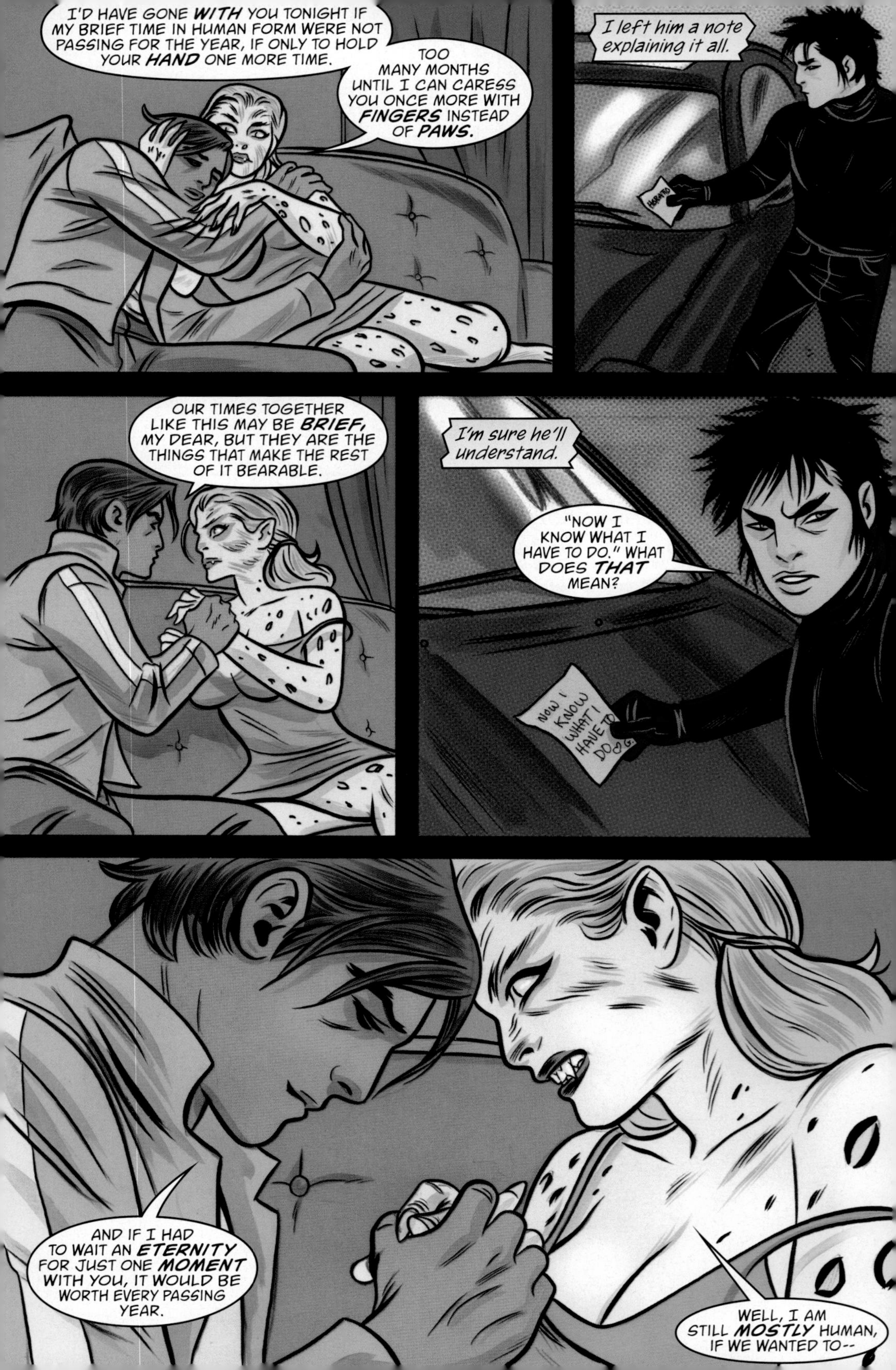

I'D HAVE GONE WITH YOU TONIGHT IF MY BRIEF TIME IN HUMAN FORM WERE NOT PASSING FOR THE YEAR, IF ONLY TO HOLD YOUR HAND ONE MORE TIME.
TOO MANY MONTHS UNTIL I CAN CARESS YOU ONCE MORE WITH FINGERS INSTEAD OF PAWS.
I left him a note explaining it all.
HORATIO
OUR TIMES TOGETHER LIKE THIS MAY BE BRIEF, MY DEAR, BUT THEY ARE THE THINGS THAT MAKE THE REST OF IT BEARABLE.
I'm sure he'll understand.
"NOW I KNOW WHAT I HAVE TO DO." WHAT DOES THAT MEAN?
NOW I KNOW WHAT I HAVE TO DO.
AND IF I HAD TO WAIT AN ETERNITY FOR JUST ONE MOMENT WITH YOU, IT WOULD BE WORTH EVERY PASSING YEAR.
WELL, I AM STILL MOSTLY HUMAN, IF WE WANTED TO--

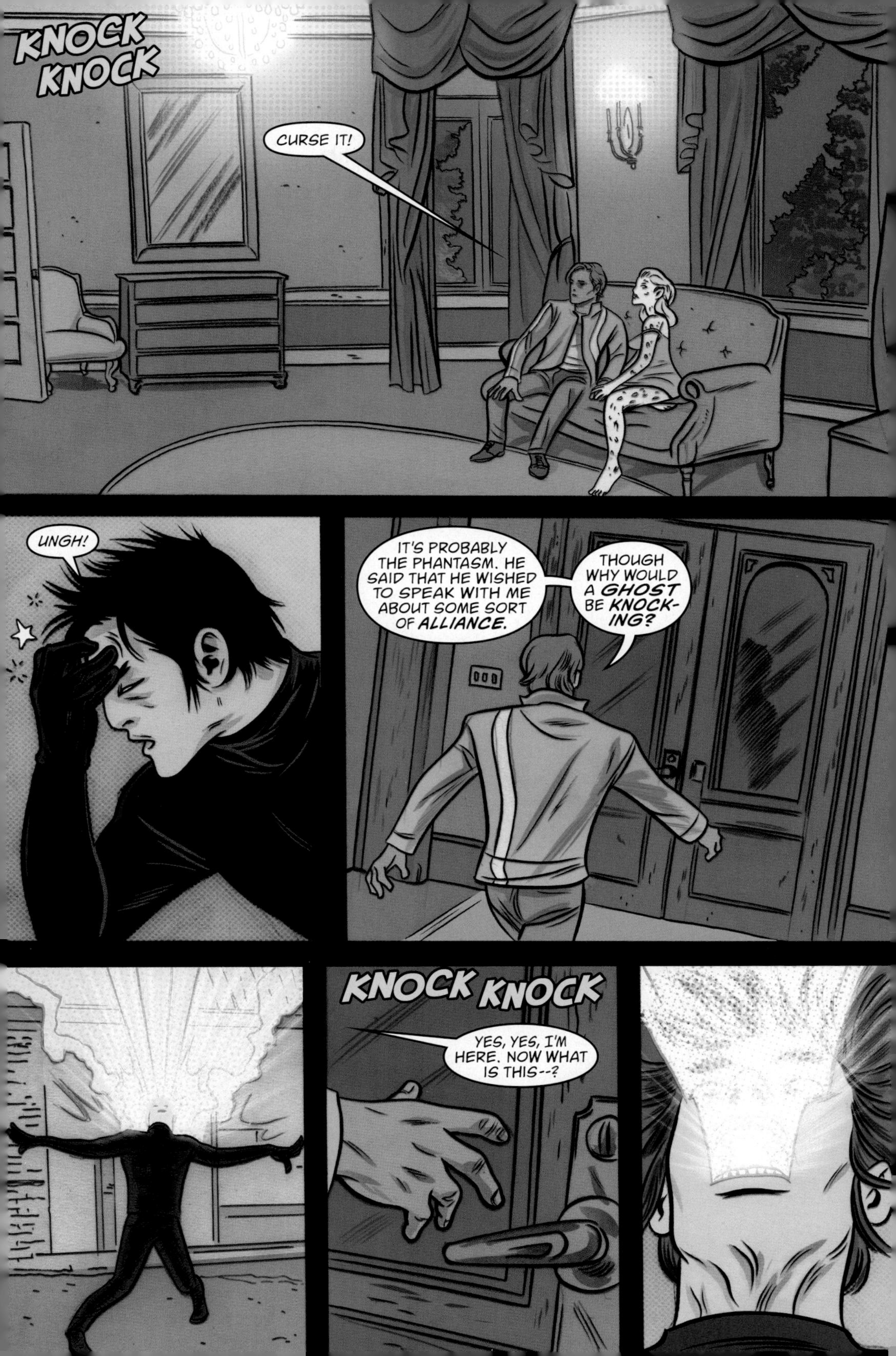
KNOCK KNOCK
CURSE IT!
UNGH!
IT'S PROBABLY THE PHANTASM. HE SAID THAT HE WISHED TO SPEAK WITH ME ABOUT SOME SORT OF ALLIANCE.
THOUGH WHY WOULD A GHOST BE KNOCKING?
KNOCK KNOCK
YES, YES, I'M HERE. NOW WHAT IS THIS--?

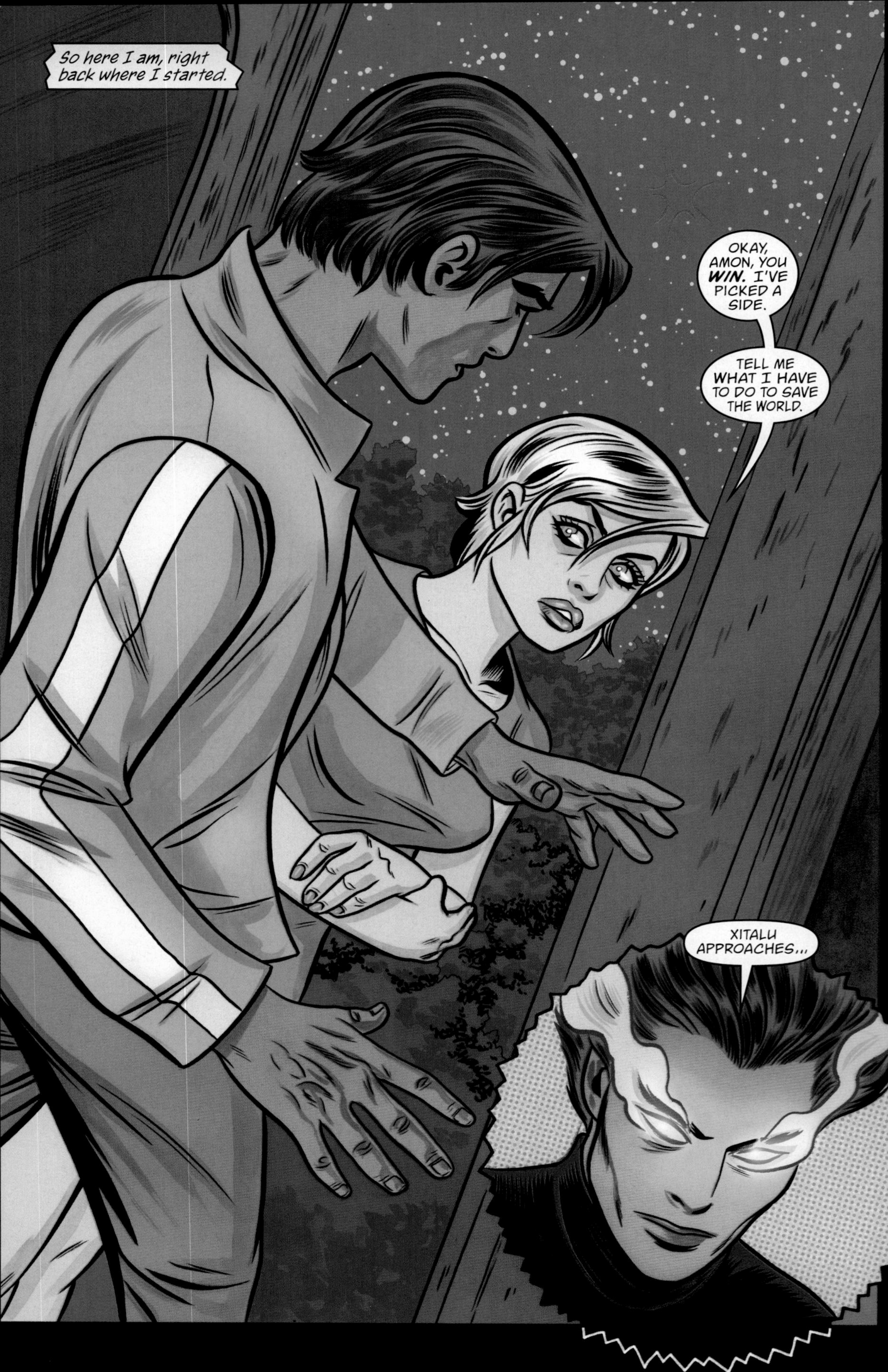

So here I am, right back where I started.
OKAY, AMON, YOU WIN. I'VE PICKED A SIDE.
TELL ME WHAT I HAVE TO DO TO SAVE THE WORLD.
XITALU APPROACHES...

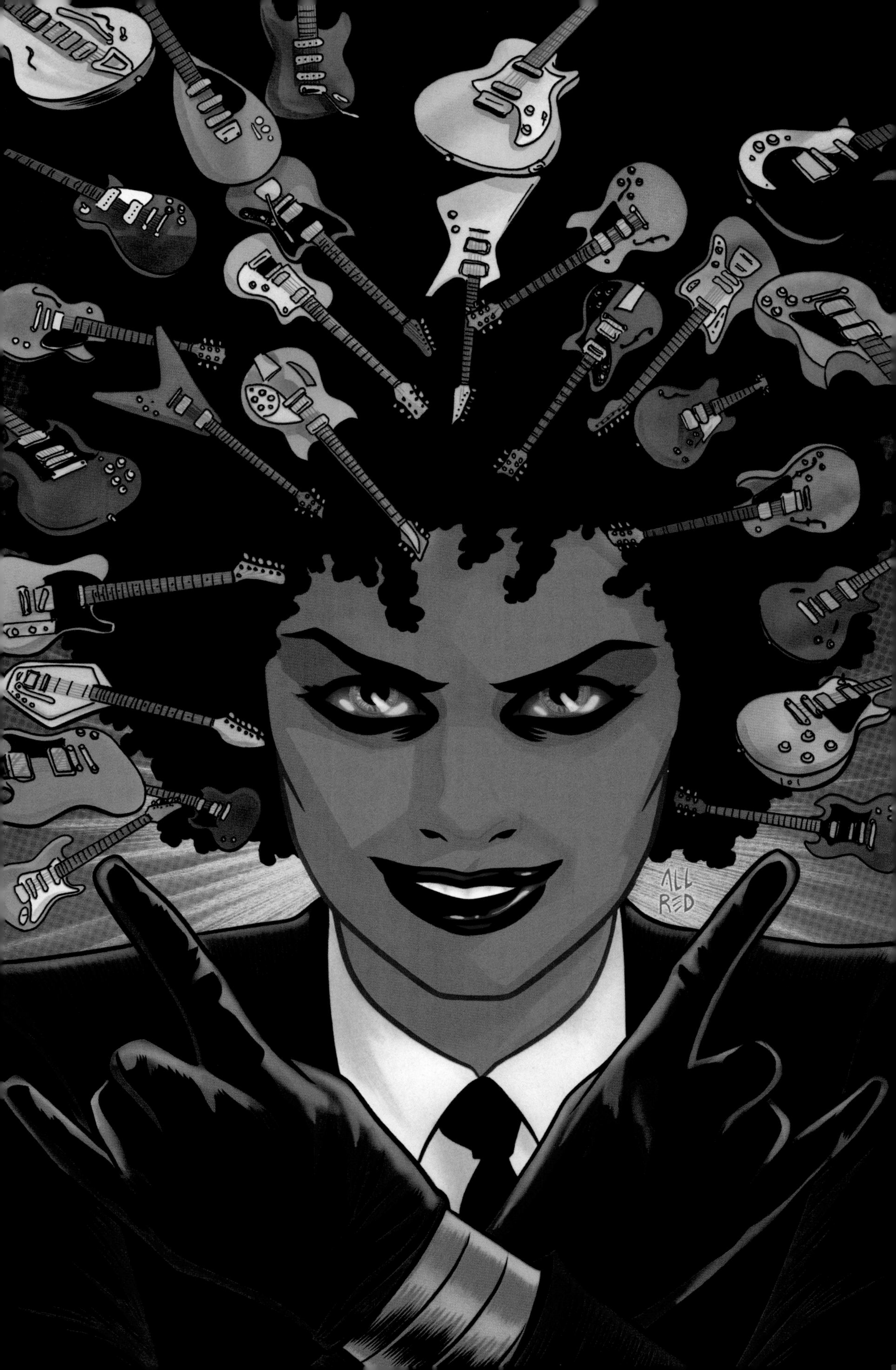
ALL
RED

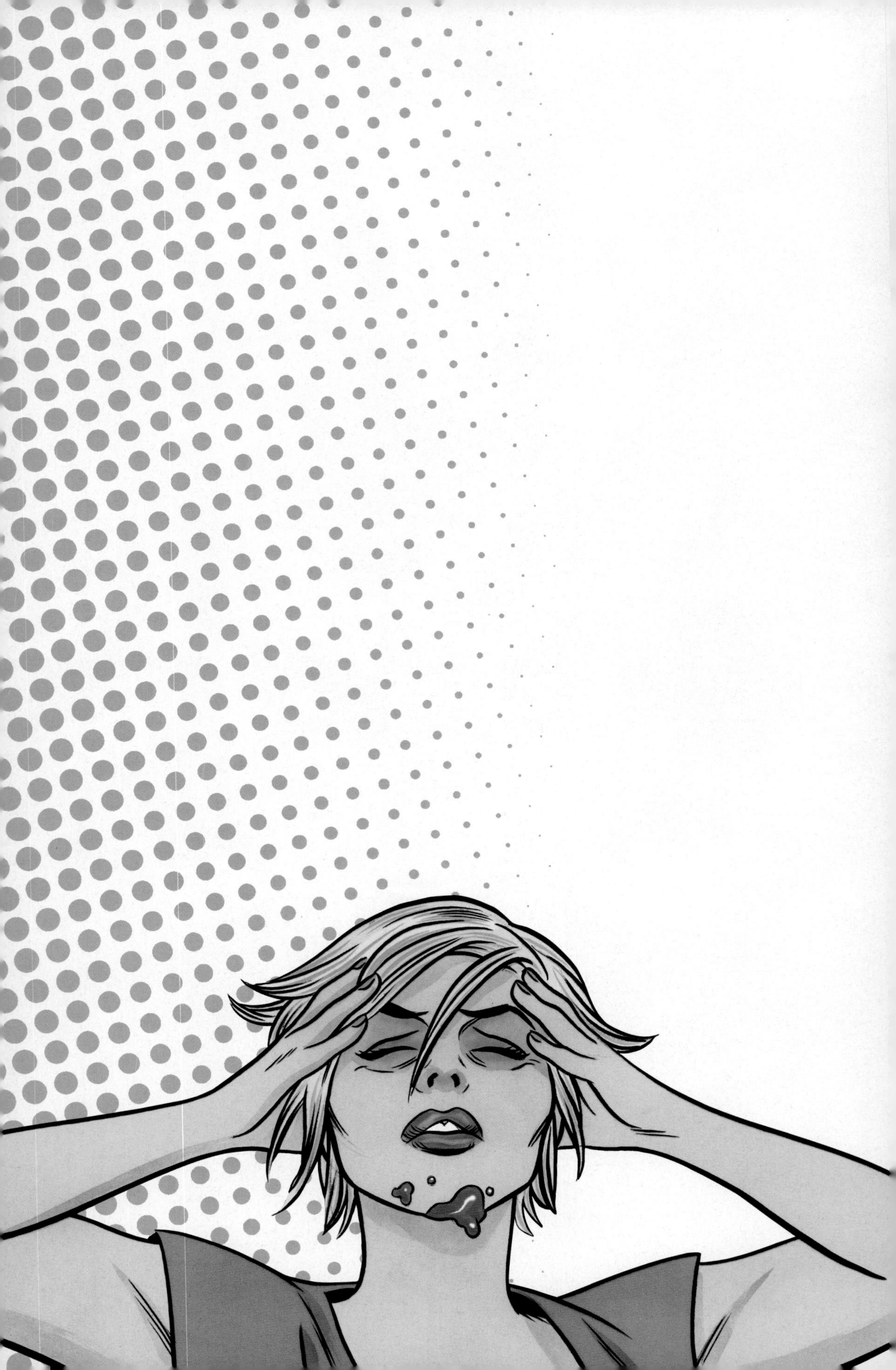

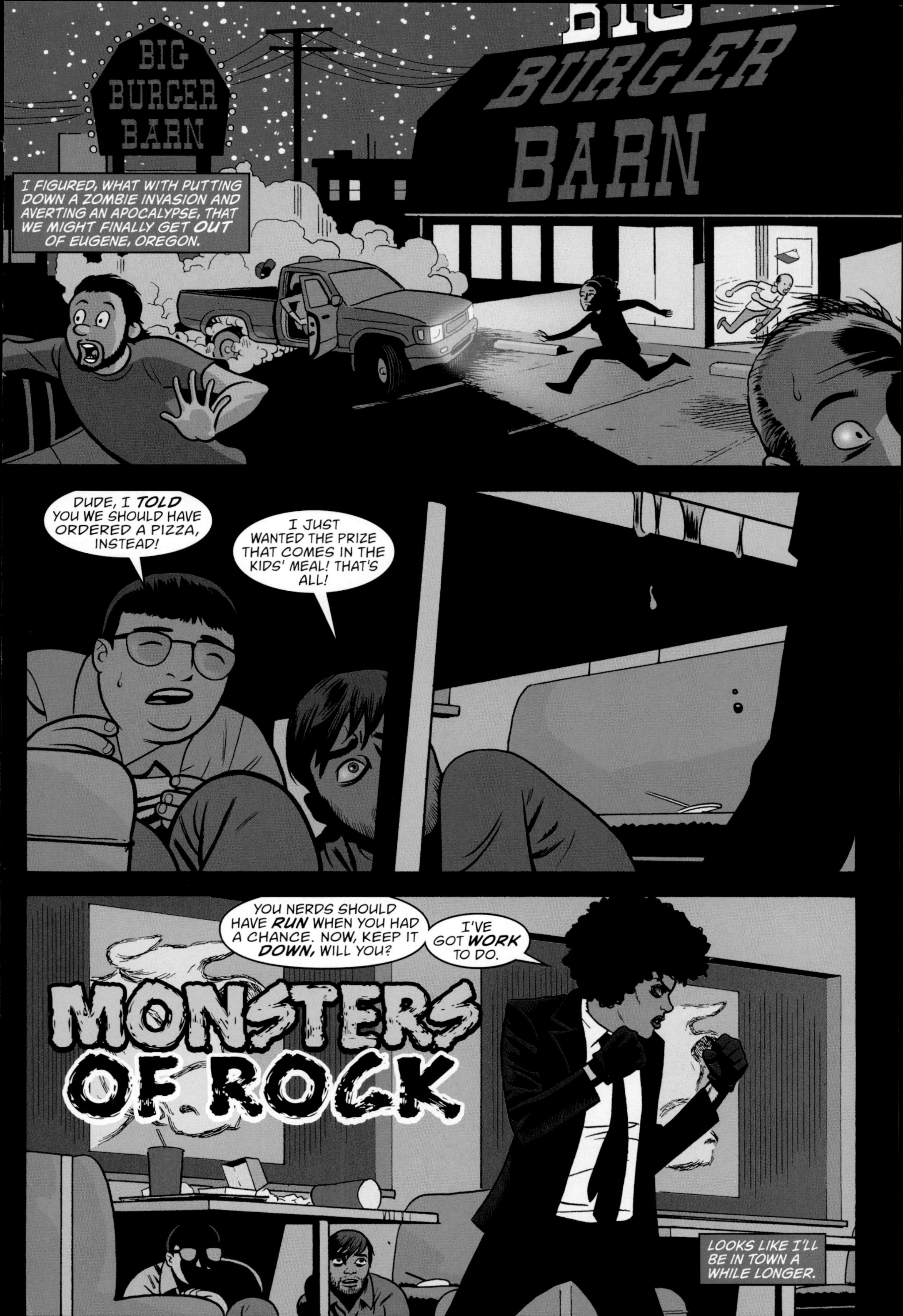
BIG BURGER BARN
BIG BURGER BARN
I FIGURED, WHAT WITH PUTTING DOWN A ZOMBIE INVASION AND AVERTING AN APOCALYPSE, THAT WE MIGHT FINALLY GET OUT OF EUGENE, OREGON.
DUDE, I TOLD YOU WE SHOULD HAVE ORDERED A PIZZA, INSTEAD!
I JUST WANTED THE PRIZE THAT COMES IN THE KIDS' MEAL! THAT'S ALL!
YOU NERDS SHOULD HAVE RUN WHEN YOU HAD A CHANCE. NOW, KEEP IT DOWN, WILL YOU?
I'VE GOT WORK TO DO.
MONSTERS OF ROCK
LOOKS LIKE I'LL BE IN TOWN A WHILE LONGER.

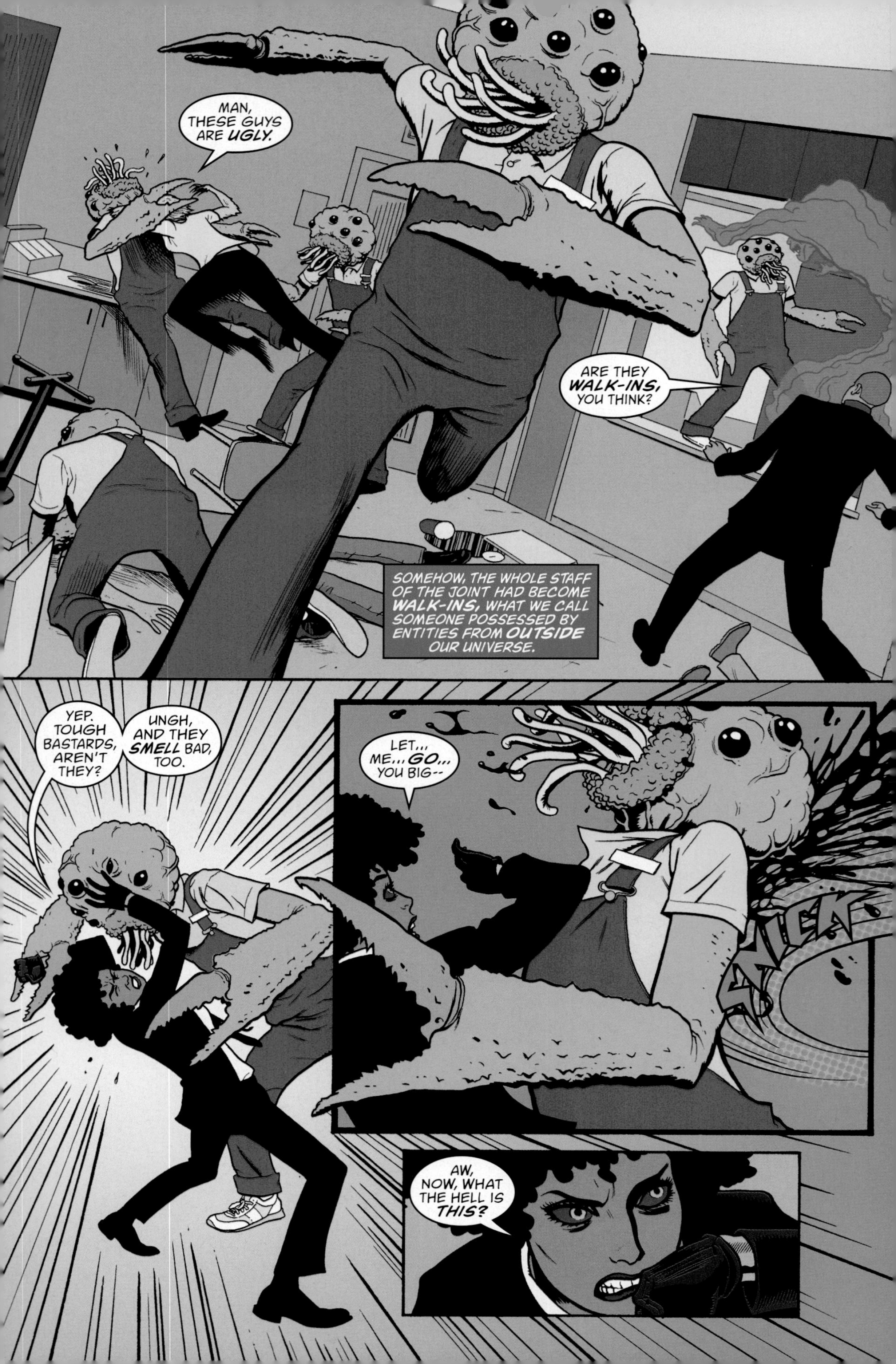
MAN, THESE GUYS ARE UGLY.
ARE THEY WALK-INS, YOU THINK?
SOMEHOW, THE WHOLE STAFF OF THE JOINT HAD BECOME WALK-INS, WHAT WE CALL SOMEONE POSSESSED BY ENTITIES FROM OUTSIDE OUR UNIVERSE.
YEP. TOUGH BASTARDS, AREN'T THEY?
UNGH, AND THEY SMELL BAD, TOO.
LET... ME... GO... YOU BIG--
AW, NOW, WHAT THE HELL IS THIS?

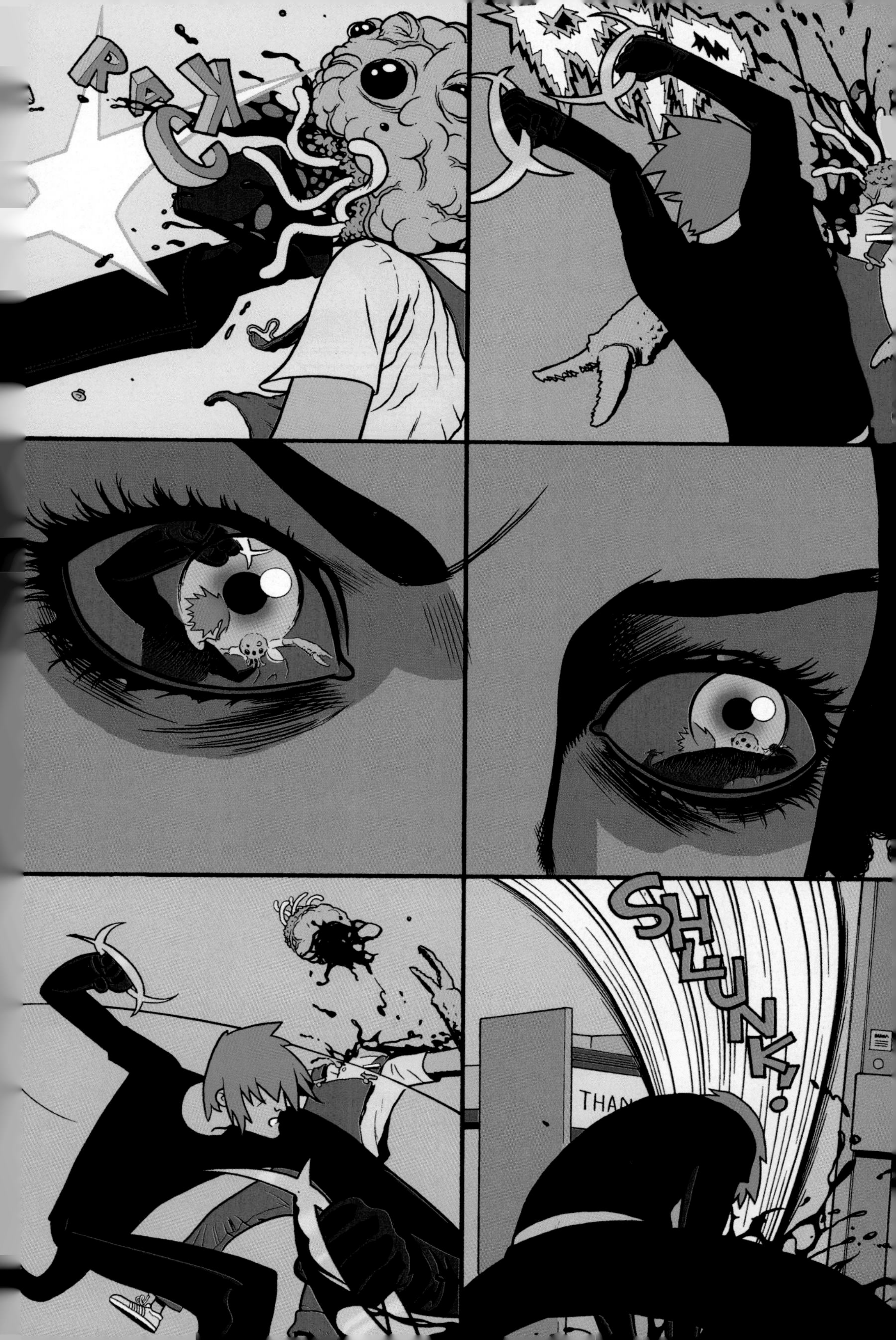
RACK
SHLUNK!
THAN

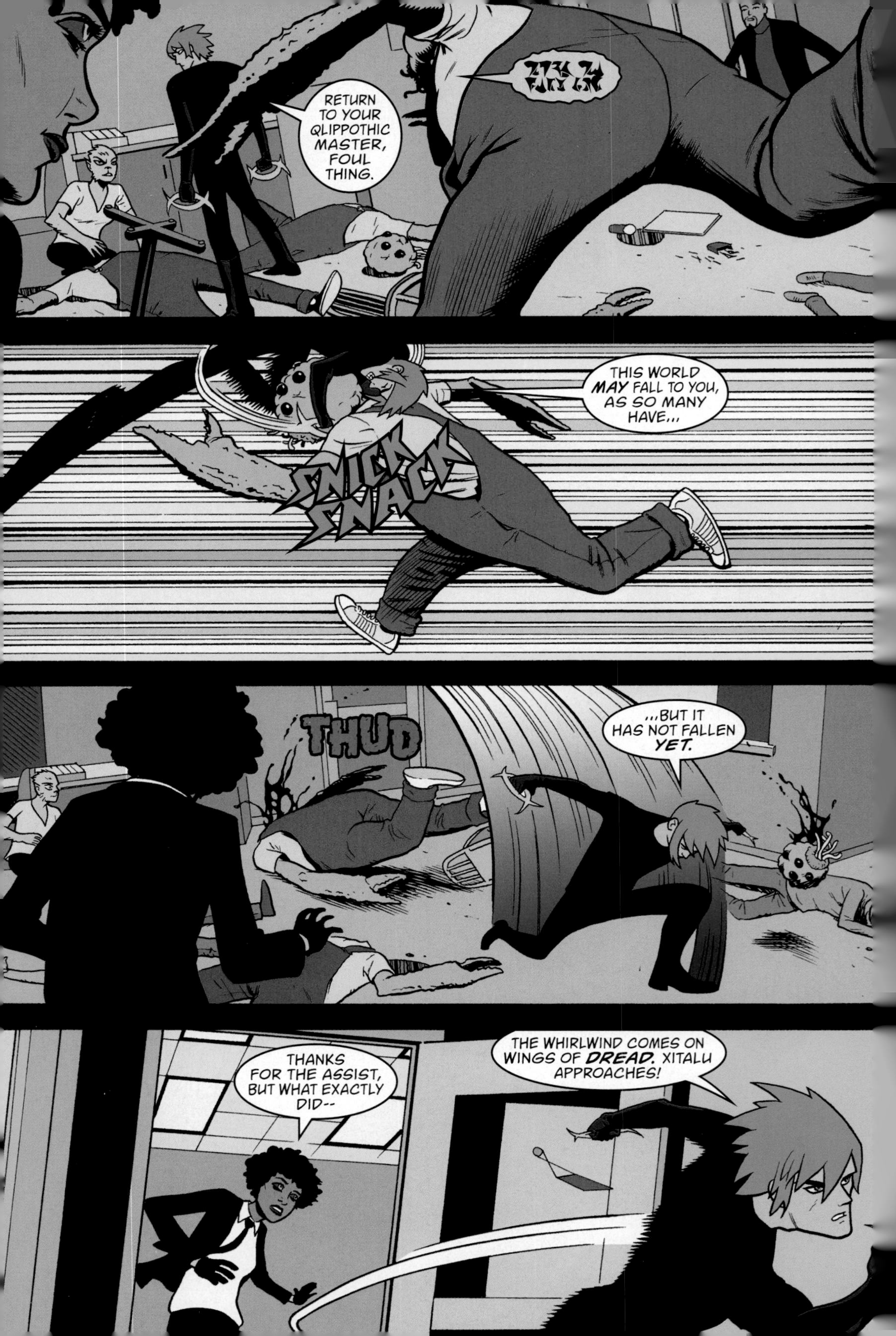
RETURN TO YOUR QLIPPOTHIC MASTER, FOUL THING.
THIS WORLD MAY FALL TO YOU, AS SO MANY HAVE...
SNICK SNACK
THUD
...BUT IT HAS NOT FALLEN YET.
THANKS FOR THE ASSIST, BUT WHAT EXACTLY DID--
THE WHIRLWIND COMES ON WINGS OF DREAD. XITALU APPROACHES!

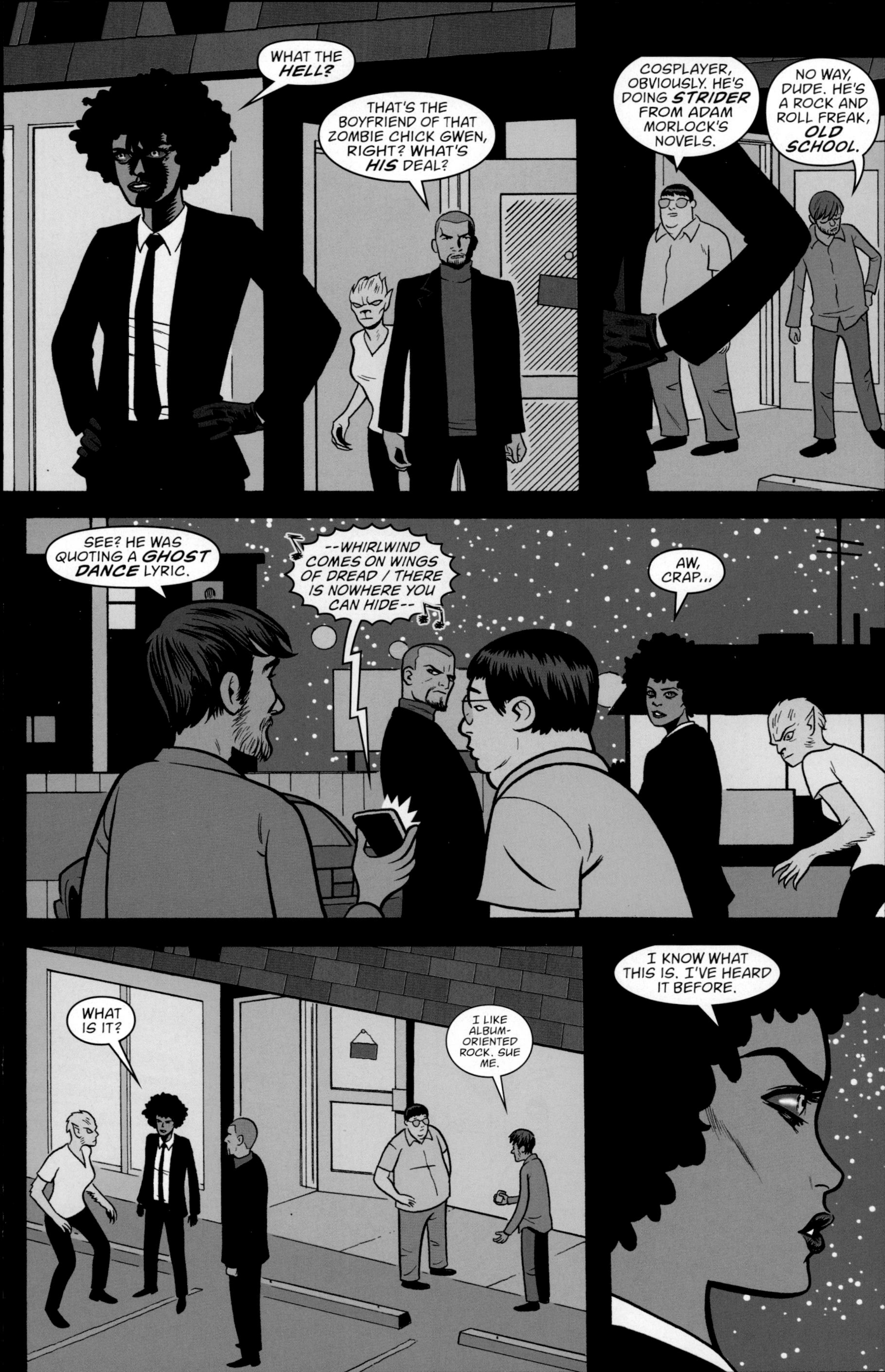
WHAT THE HELL?
THAT'S THE BOYFRIEND OF THAT ZOMBIE CHICK GWEN, RIGHT? WHAT'S HIS DEAL?
COSPLAYER, OBVIOUSLY. HE'S DOING STRIDER FROM ADAM MORLOCK'S NOVELS.
NO WAY, DUDE. HE'S A ROCK AND ROLL FREAK, OLD SCHOOL.
SEE? HE WAS QUOTING A GHOST DANCE LYRIC.
--WHIRLWIND COMES ON WINGS OF DREAD / THERE IS NOWHERE YOU CAN HIDE--
AW, CRAP...
WHAT IS IT?
I LIKE ALBUM-ORIENTED ROCK. SUE ME.
I KNOW WHAT THIS IS. I'VE HEARD IT BEFORE.

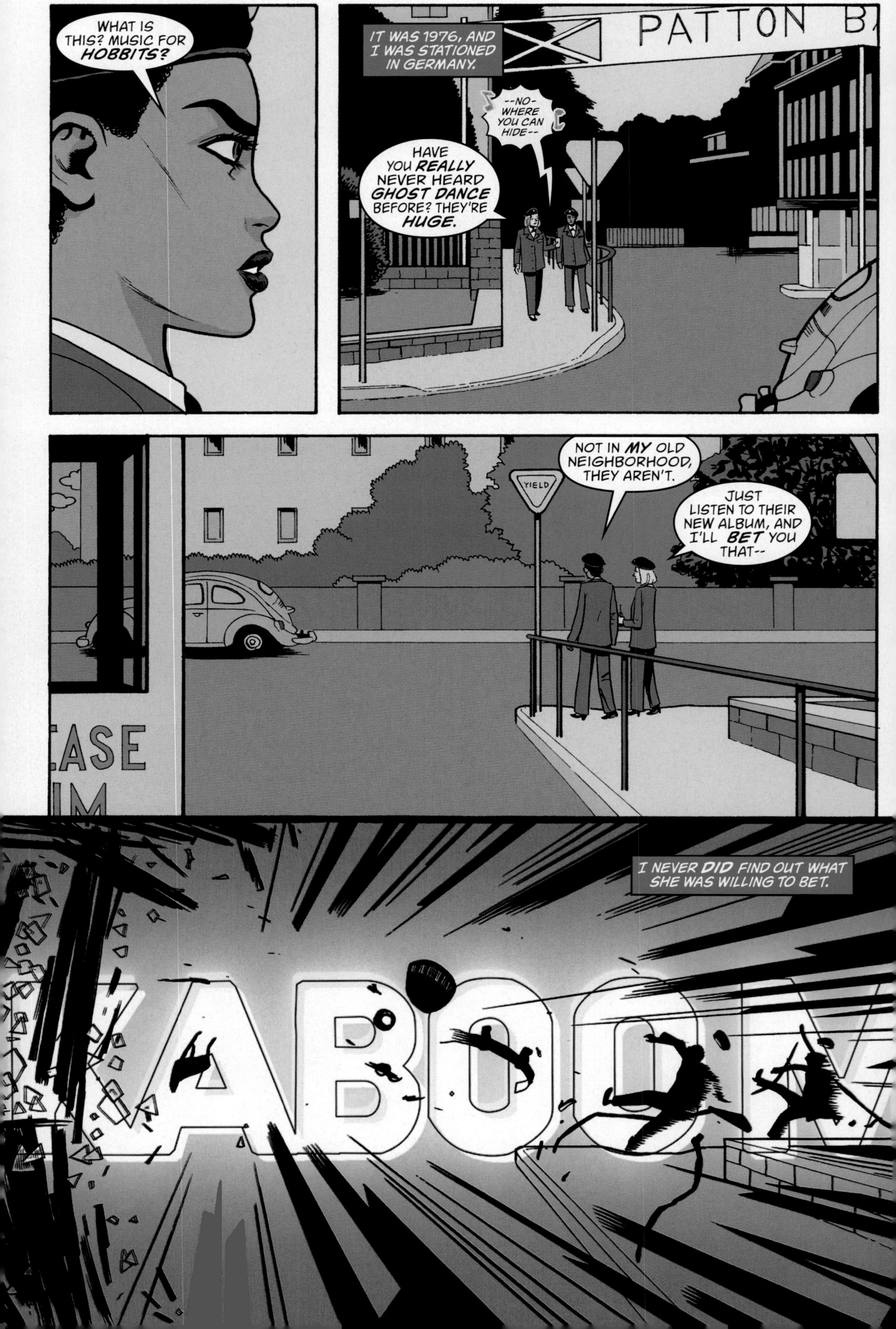
WHAT IS THIS? MUSIC FOR ***HOBBITS?***
PATTON B
IT WAS 1976, AND I WAS STATIONED IN GERMANY.
--NO-WHERE YOU CAN HIDE--
HAVE YOU ***REALLY*** NEVER HEARD ***GHOST DANCE*** BEFORE? THEY'RE ***HUGE.***
YIELD
NOT IN ***MY*** OLD NEIGHBORHOOD, THEY AREN'T.
JUST LISTEN TO THEIR NEW ALBUM, AND I'LL ***BET*** YOU THAT--
*I NEVER **DID** FIND OUT WHAT SHE WAS WILLING TO BET.*

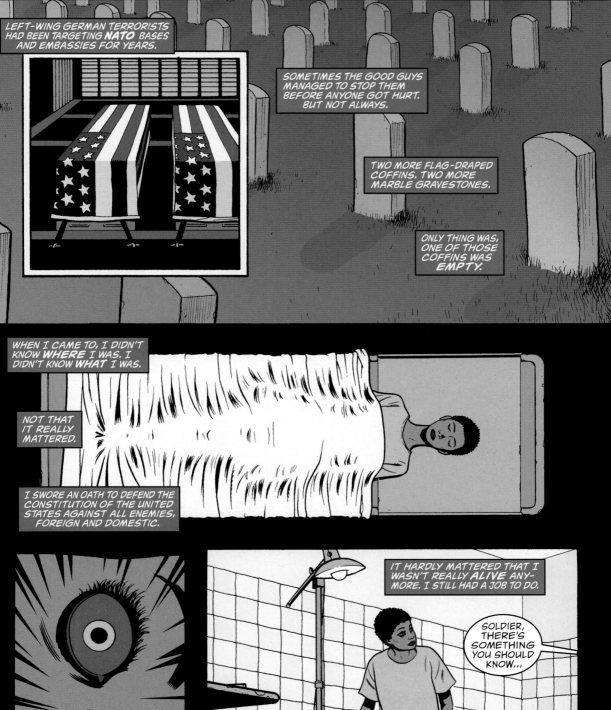

LEFT-WING GERMAN TERRORISTS HAD BEEN TARGETING **NATO** BASES AND EMBASSIES FOR YEARS.

SOMETIMES THE GOOD GUYS MANAGED TO STOP THEM BEFORE ANYONE GOT HURT. BUT NOT ALWAYS.

TWO MORE FLAG-DRAPED COFFINS. TWO MORE MARBLE GRAVESTONES.

ONLY THING WAS, ONE OF THOSE COFFINS WAS **EMPTY**.

WHEN I CAME TO, I DIDN'T KNOW **WHERE** I WAS. I DIDN'T KNOW **WHAT** I WAS.

NOT THAT IT REALLY MATTERED.

I SWORE AN OATH TO DEFEND THE CONSTITUTION OF THE UNITED STATES AGAINST ALL ENEMIES, FOREIGN AND DOMESTIC.

IT HARDLY MATTERED THAT I WASN'T REALLY **ALIVE** ANY-MORE. I STILL HAD A JOB TO DO.

SOLDIER, THERE'S SOMETHING YOU SHOULD KNOW...

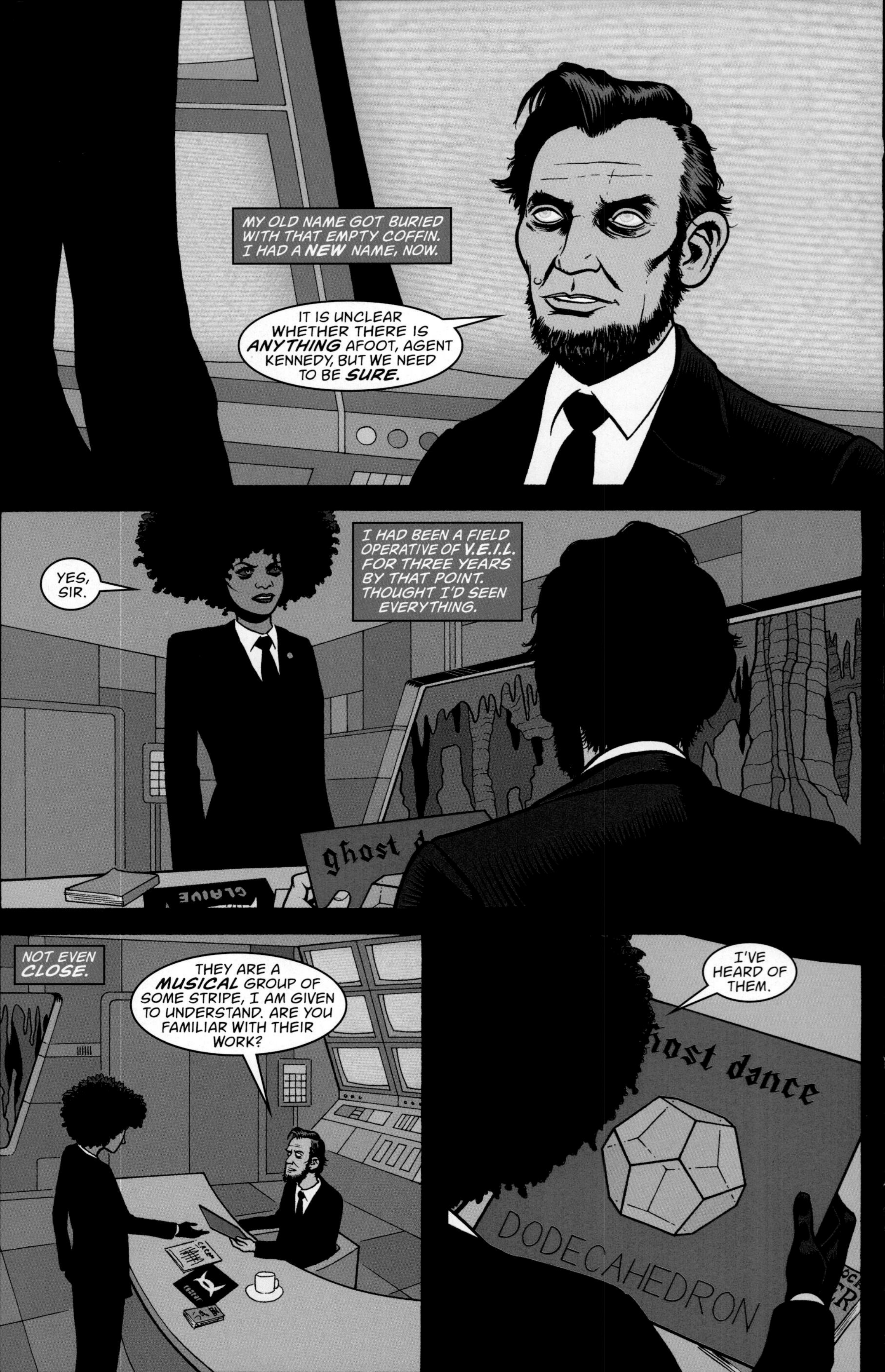
MY OLD NAME GOT BURIED WITH THAT EMPTY COFFIN. I HAD A NEW NAME, NOW.
IT IS UNCLEAR WHETHER THERE IS ANYTHING AFOOT, AGENT KENNEDY, BUT WE NEED TO BE SURE.
YES, SIR.
I HAD BEEN A FIELD OPERATIVE OF V.E.I.L. FOR THREE YEARS BY THAT POINT. THOUGHT I'D SEEN EVERYTHING.
ghost d
CLAIVE
NOT EVEN CLOSE.
THEY ARE A MUSICAL GROUP OF SOME STRIPE, I AM GIVEN TO UNDERSTAND. ARE YOU FAMILIAR WITH THEIR WORK?
I'VE HEARD OF THEM.
host dance
DODECAHEDRON

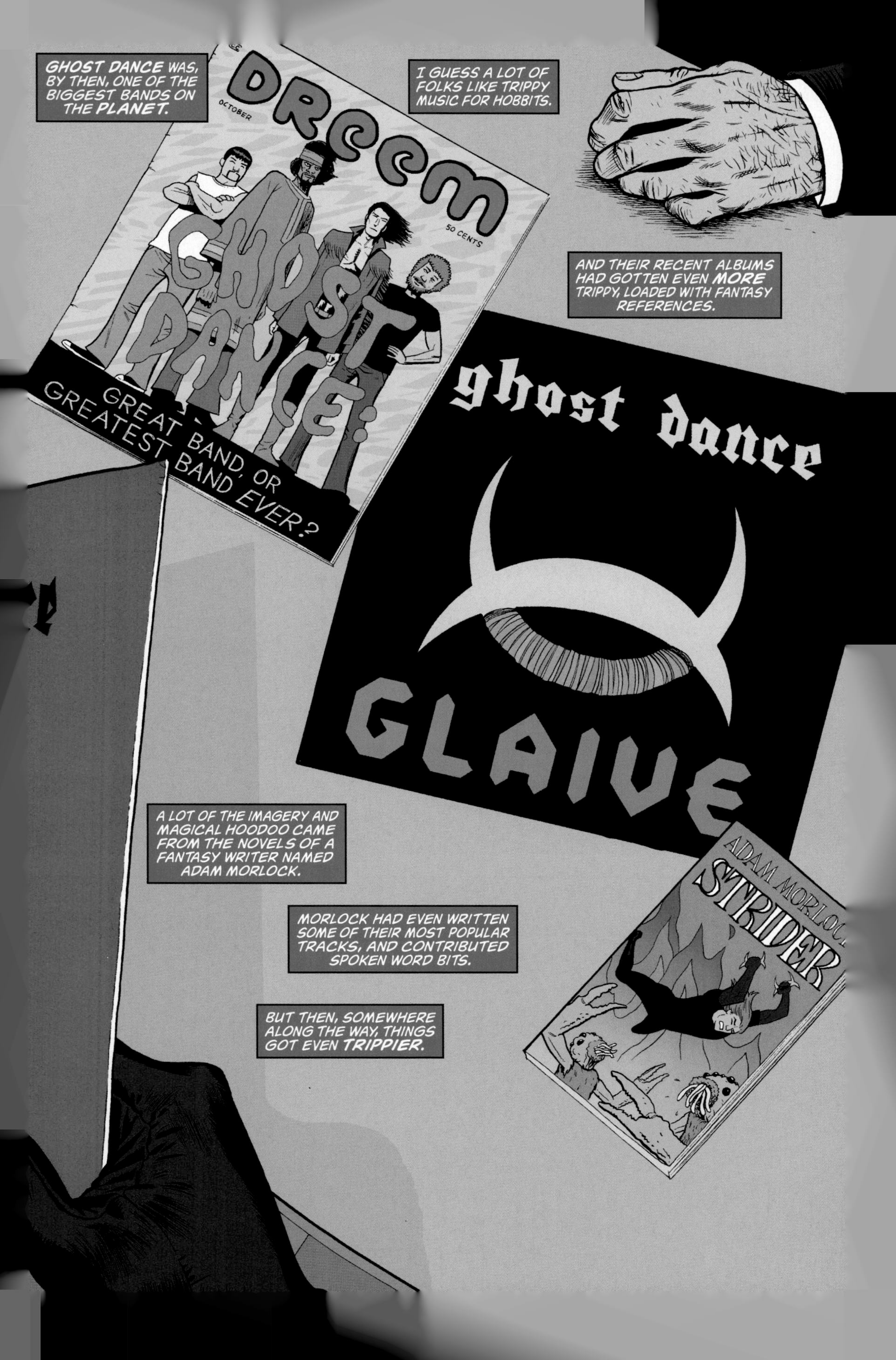

GHOST DANCE WAS, BY THEN, ONE OF THE BIGGEST BANDS ON THE PLANET.
DREEM
OCTOBER
50 CENTS
GHOST DANCE!
GREAT BAND, OR GREATEST BAND EVER?
I GUESS A LOT OF FOLKS LIKE TRIPPY MUSIC FOR HOBBITS.
AND THEIR RECENT ALBUMS HAD GOTTEN EVEN MORE TRIPPY, LOADED WITH FANTASY REFERENCES.
ghost dance
GLAIVE
A LOT OF THE IMAGERY AND MAGICAL HOODOO CAME FROM THE NOVELS OF A FANTASY WRITER NAMED ADAM MORLOCK.
ADAM MORLOCK
STRIDER
MORLOCK HAD EVEN WRITTEN SOME OF THEIR MOST POPULAR TRACKS, AND CONTRIBUTED SPOKEN WORD BITS.
BUT THEN, SOMEWHERE ALONG THE WAY, THINGS GOT EVEN TRIPPIER.

SO I WAS SUPPOSED TO GO CHECK IT OUT.

I CAUGHT UP WITH THE BAND AT CANDLESTICK PARK, BEFORE THE LAST CONCERT OF THEIR INTERNATIONAL CAREER.

LUCKY ME.

--AND ANYTHING YOU CAN TELL ME WILL BE VERY HELPFUL.

I TAKE IT YOU'VE ALL WITNESSED THESE..."MANIFESTA-TIONS"?

YEAH, MAN.

IT SOUNDS CRAZY, BUT THERE WERE THESE, LIKE, LIGHTS. JUST...HANGING ABOVE US.

ALBERT MOON, DRUMS.

AFTER THAT NIGHT, MOON WOULD NEVER PERFORM AGAIN.

HE WOULD GO ON TO BECOME AN AUDIO ENGINEER AND A PRODUCER, OVERSEEING DOZENS OF CHART-TOPPING ALBUMS FOR OTHER ACTS.

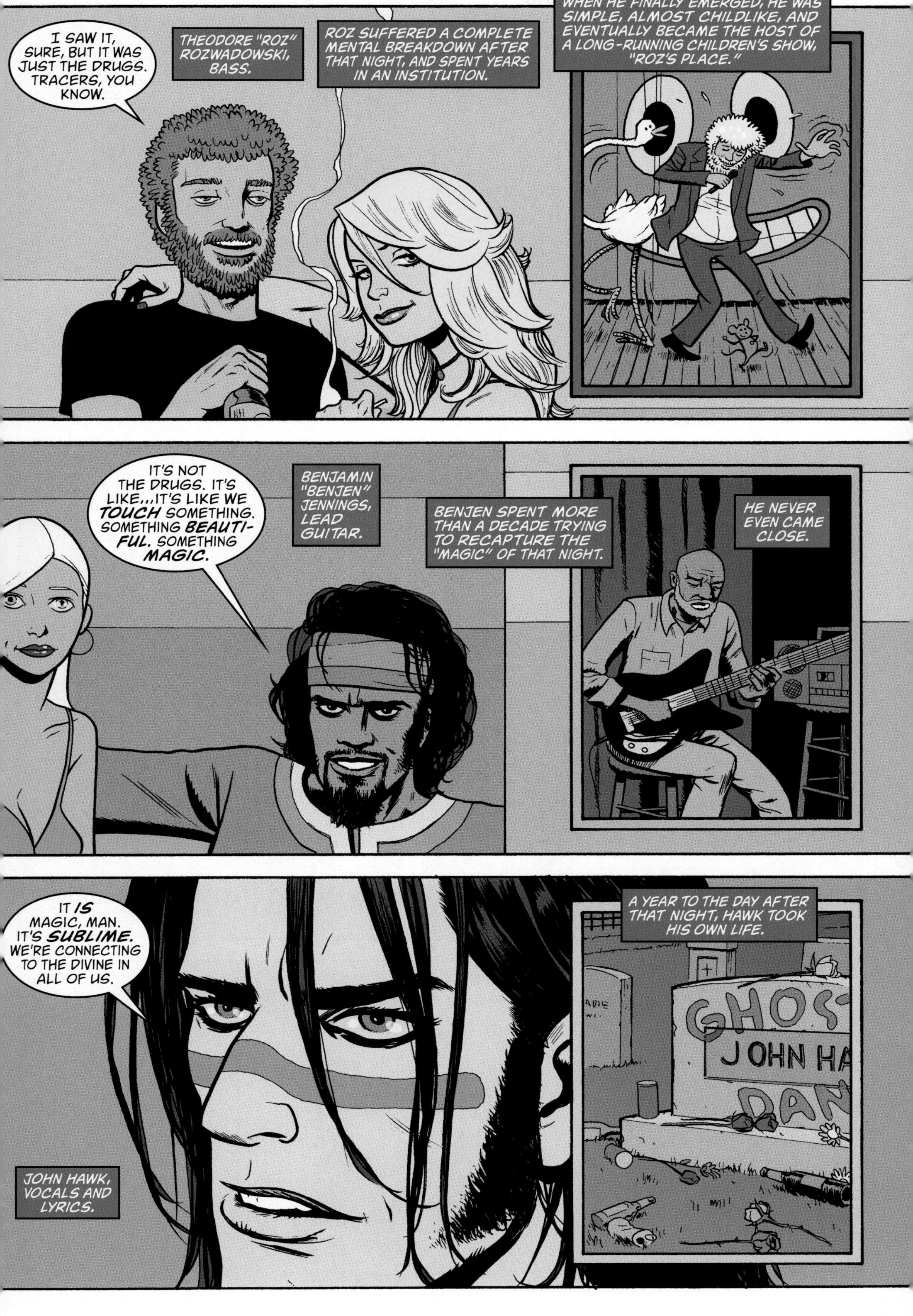
I SAW IT, SURE, BUT IT WAS JUST THE DRUGS. TRACERS, YOU KNOW.
THEODORE "ROZ" ROZWADOWSKI, BASS.
ROZ SUFFERED A COMPLETE MENTAL BREAKDOWN AFTER THAT NIGHT, AND SPENT YEARS IN AN INSTITUTION.
WHEN HE FINALLY EMERGED, HE WAS SIMPLE, ALMOST CHILDLIKE, AND EVENTUALLY BECAME THE HOST OF A LONG-RUNNING CHILDREN'S SHOW, "ROZ'S PLACE."
IT'S NOT THE DRUGS. IT'S LIKE...IT'S LIKE WE TOUCH SOMETHING. SOMETHING BEAUTIFUL. SOMETHING MAGIC.
BENJAMIN "BENJEN" JENNINGS, LEAD GUITAR.
BENJEN SPENT MORE THAN A DECADE TRYING TO RECAPTURE THE "MAGIC" OF THAT NIGHT.
HE NEVER EVEN CAME CLOSE.
IT IS MAGIC, MAN. IT'S SUBLIME. WE'RE CONNECTING TO THE DIVINE IN ALL OF US.
A YEAR TO THE DAY AFTER THAT NIGHT, HAWK TOOK HIS OWN LIFE.
GHOS
JOHN HA
DAN
JOHN HAWK, VOCALS AND LYRICS.

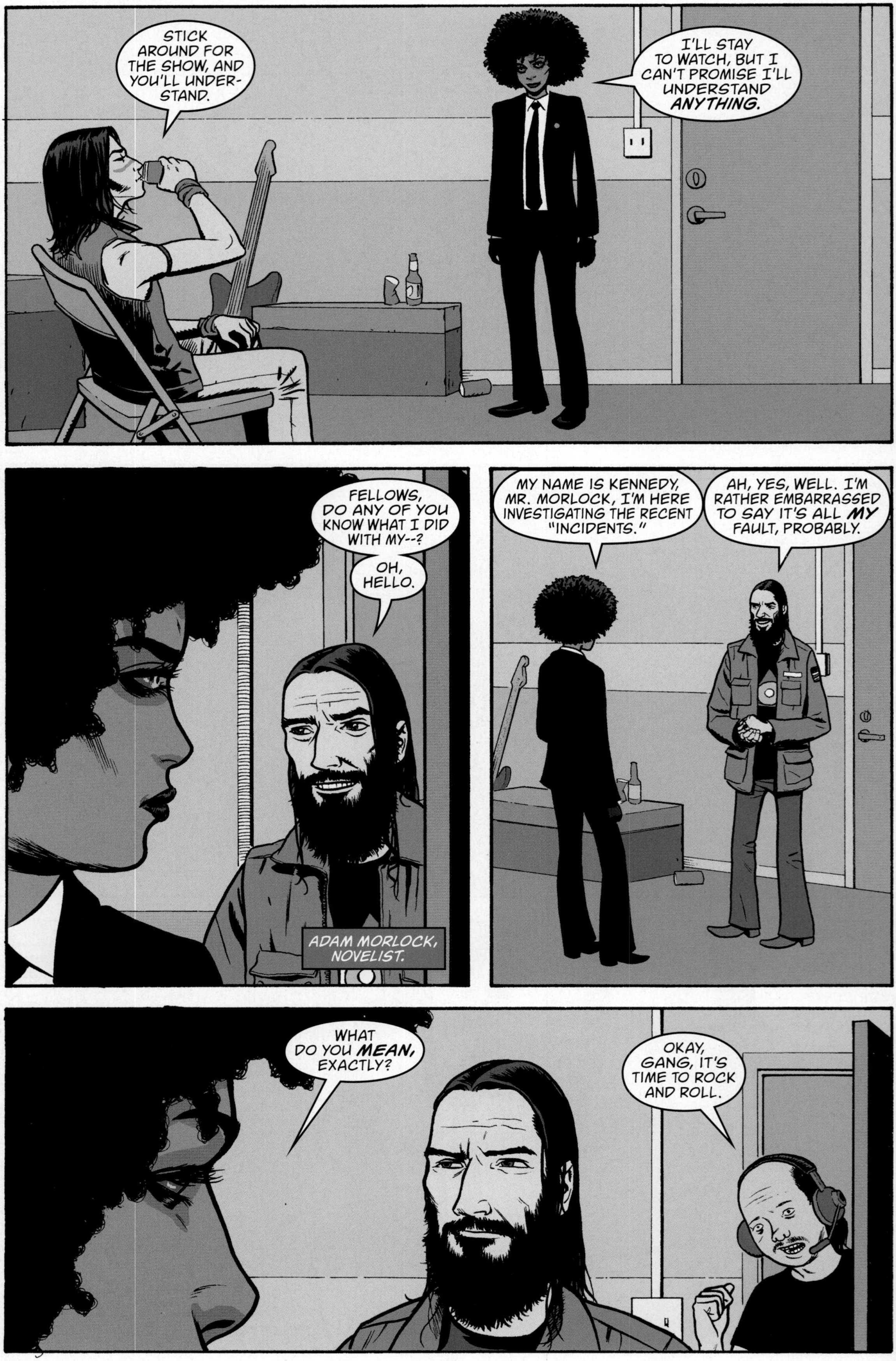
STICK AROUND FOR THE SHOW, AND YOU'LL UNDER-STAND.
I'LL STAY TO WATCH, BUT I CAN'T PROMISE I'LL UNDERSTAND ANYTHING.
FELLOWS, DO ANY OF YOU KNOW WHAT I DID WITH MY--?
OH, HELLO.
ADAM MORLOCK, NOVELIST.
MY NAME IS KENNEDY, MR. MORLOCK, I'M HERE INVESTIGATING THE RECENT "INCIDENTS."
AH, YES, WELL. I'M RATHER EMBARRASSED TO SAY IT'S ALL MY FAULT, PROBABLY.
WHAT DO YOU MEAN, EXACTLY?
OKAY, GANG, IT'S TIME TO ROCK AND ROLL.

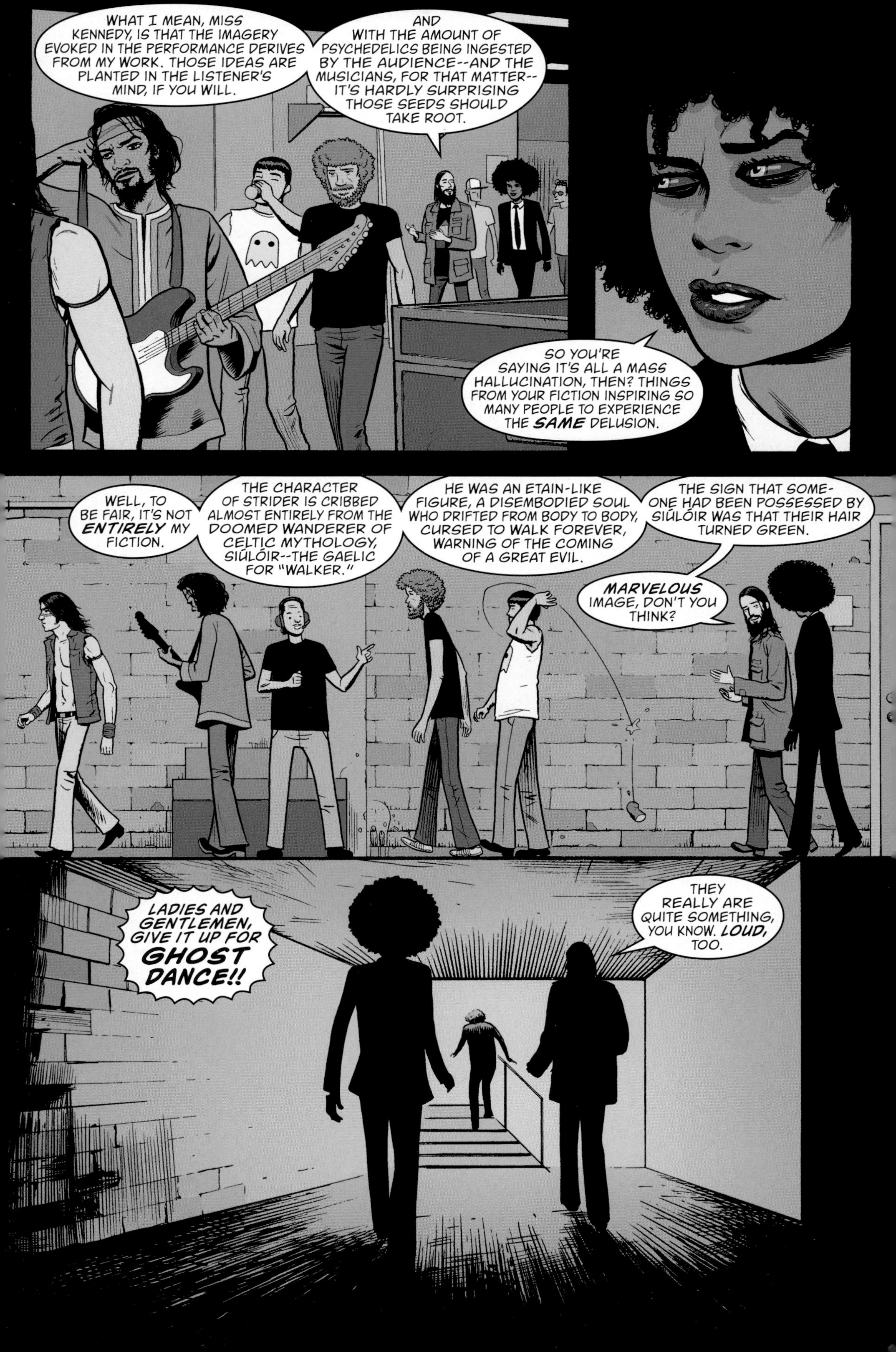

WHAT I MEAN, MISS KENNEDY, IS THAT THE IMAGERY EVOKED IN THE PERFORMANCE DERIVES FROM MY WORK. THOSE IDEAS ARE PLANTED IN THE LISTENER'S MIND, IF YOU WILL.
AND WITH THE AMOUNT OF PSYCHEDELICS BEING INGESTED BY THE AUDIENCE--AND THE MUSICIANS, FOR THAT MATTER--IT'S HARDLY SURPRISING THOSE SEEDS SHOULD TAKE ROOT.
SO YOU'RE SAYING IT'S ALL A MASS HALLUCINATION, THEN? THINGS FROM YOUR FICTION INSPIRING SO MANY PEOPLE TO EXPERIENCE THE **SAME** DELUSION.
WELL, TO BE FAIR, IT'S NOT **ENTIRELY** MY FICTION.
THE CHARACTER OF STRIDER IS CRIBBED ALMOST ENTIRELY FROM THE DOOMED WANDERER OF CELTIC MYTHOLOGY, SIÚLÓIR--THE GAELIC FOR "WALKER."
HE WAS AN ETAIN-LIKE FIGURE, A DISEMBODIED SOUL WHO DRIFTED FROM BODY TO BODY, CURSED TO WALK FOREVER, WARNING OF THE COMING OF A GREAT EVIL.
THE SIGN THAT SOME-ONE HAD BEEN POSSESSED BY SIÚLÓIR WAS THAT THEIR HAIR TURNED GREEN.
MARVELOUS IMAGE, DON'T YOU THINK?
LADIES AND GENTLEMEN, GIVE IT UP FOR **GHOST DANCE!!**
THEY REALLY ARE QUITE SOMETHING, YOU KNOW. **LOUD,** TOO.

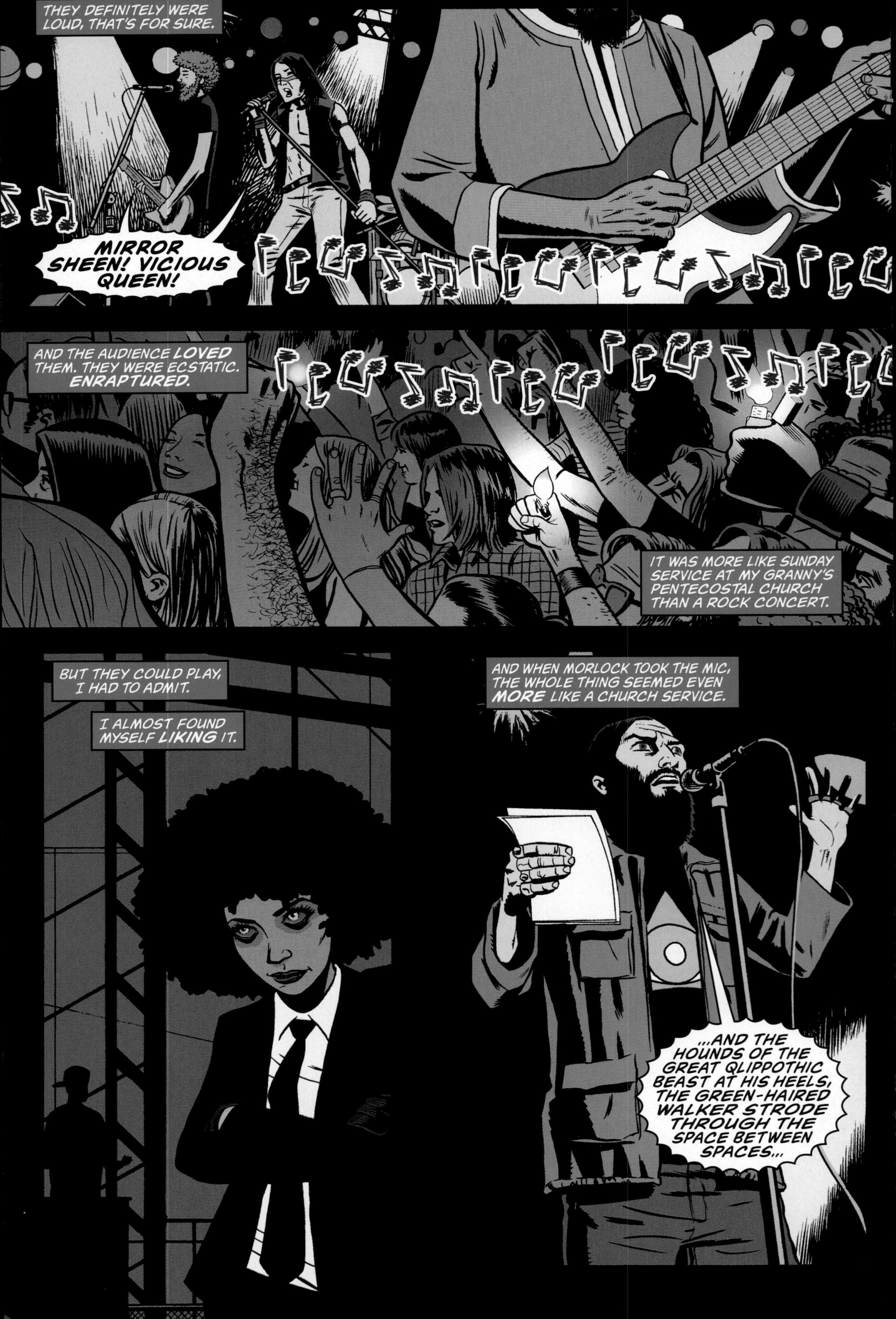
THEY DEFINITELY WERE LOUD, THAT'S FOR SURE.
MIRROR SHEEN! VICIOUS QUEEN!
AND THE AUDIENCE LOVED THEM. THEY WERE ECSTATIC. ENRAPTURED.
IT WAS MORE LIKE SUNDAY SERVICE AT MY GRANNY'S PENTECOSTAL CHURCH THAN A ROCK CONCERT.
BUT THEY COULD PLAY, I HAD TO ADMIT.
I ALMOST FOUND MYSELF LIKING IT.
AND WHEN MORLOCK TOOK THE MIC, THE WHOLE THING SEEMED EVEN MORE LIKE A CHURCH SERVICE.
...AND THE HOUNDS OF THE GREAT QLIPPOTHIC BEAST AT HIS HEELS, THE GREEN-HAIRED WALKER STRODE THROUGH THE SPACE BETWEEN SPACES...

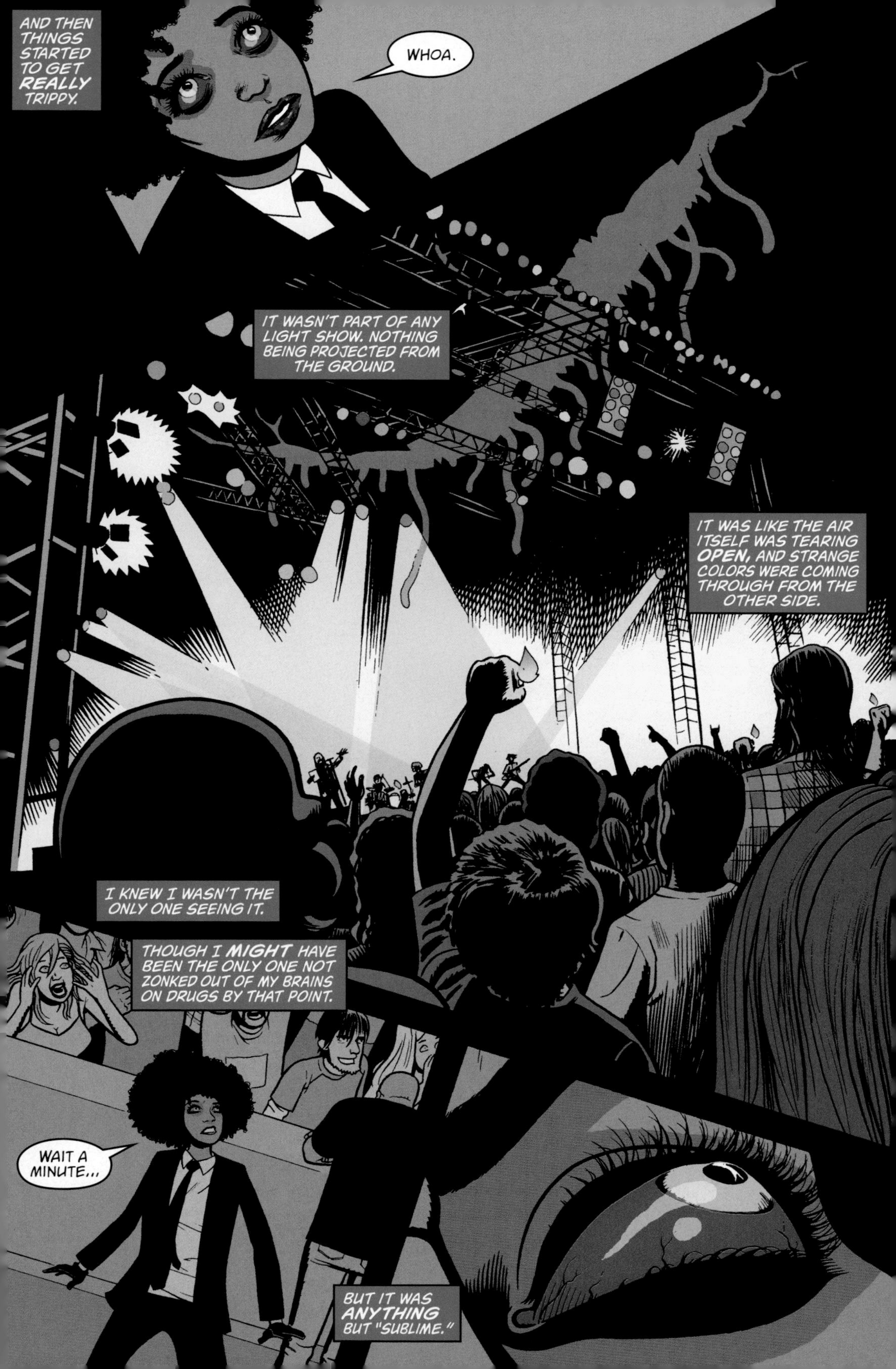

AND THEN THINGS STARTED TO GET REALLY TRIPPY.
WHOA.
IT WASN'T PART OF ANY LIGHT SHOW. NOTHING BEING PROJECTED FROM THE GROUND.
IT WAS LIKE THE AIR ITSELF WAS TEARING OPEN, AND STRANGE COLORS WERE COMING THROUGH FROM THE OTHER SIDE.
I KNEW I WASN'T THE ONLY ONE SEEING IT.
THOUGH I MIGHT HAVE BEEN THE ONLY ONE NOT ZONKED OUT OF MY BRAINS ON DRUGS BY THAT POINT.
WAIT A MINUTE...
BUT IT WAS ANYTHING BUT "SUBLIME."

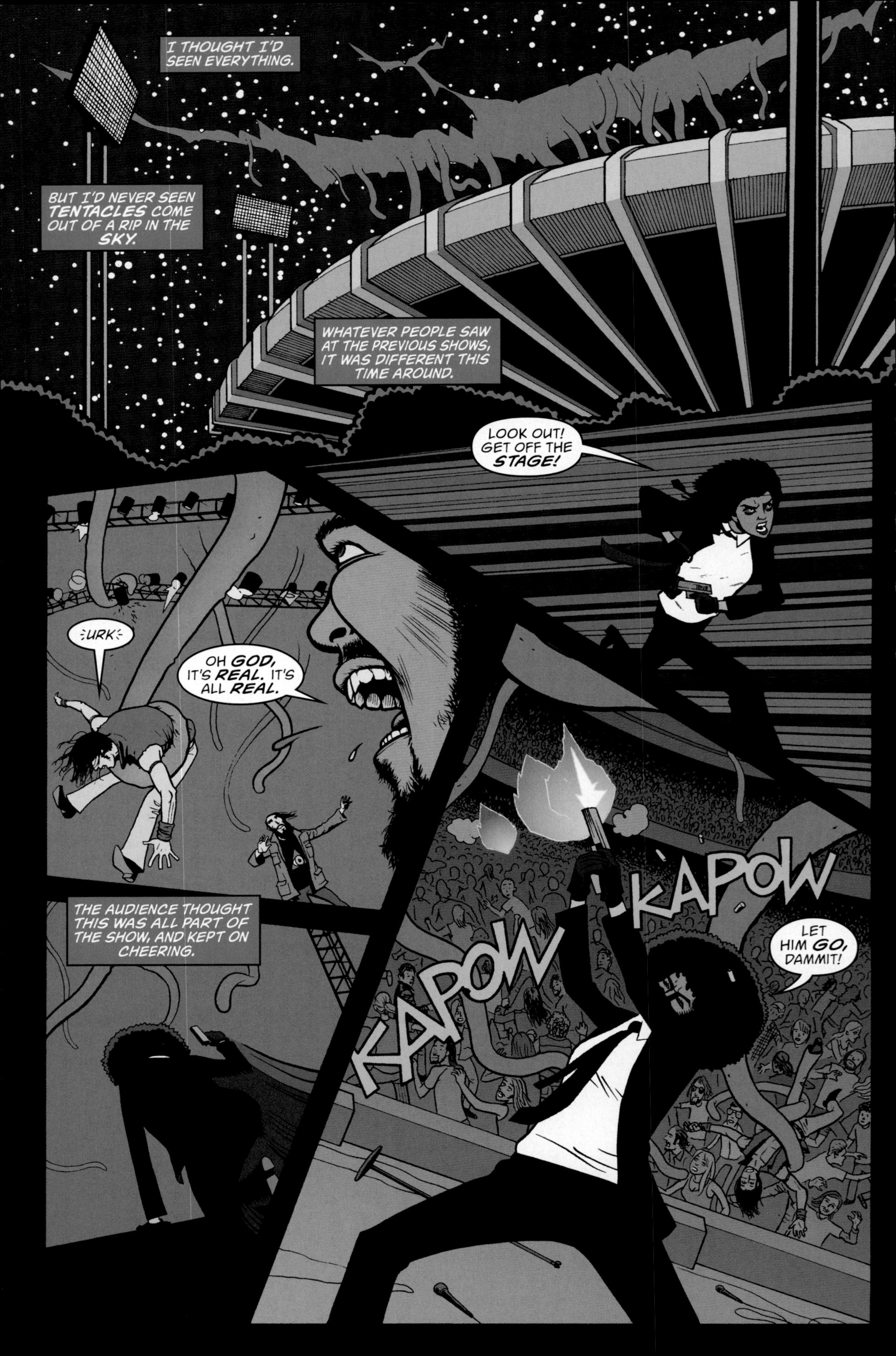
I THOUGHT I'D SEEN EVERYTHING.
BUT I'D NEVER SEEN TENTACLES COME OUT OF A RIP IN THE SKY.
WHATEVER PEOPLE SAW AT THE PREVIOUS SHOWS, IT WAS DIFFERENT THIS TIME AROUND.
LOOK OUT! GET OFF THE STAGE!
URK
OH GOD, IT'S REAL. IT'S ALL REAL.
THE AUDIENCE THOUGHT THIS WAS ALL PART OF THE SHOW, AND KEPT ON CHEERING.
KAPOW
KAPOW
LET HIM GO, DAMMIT!

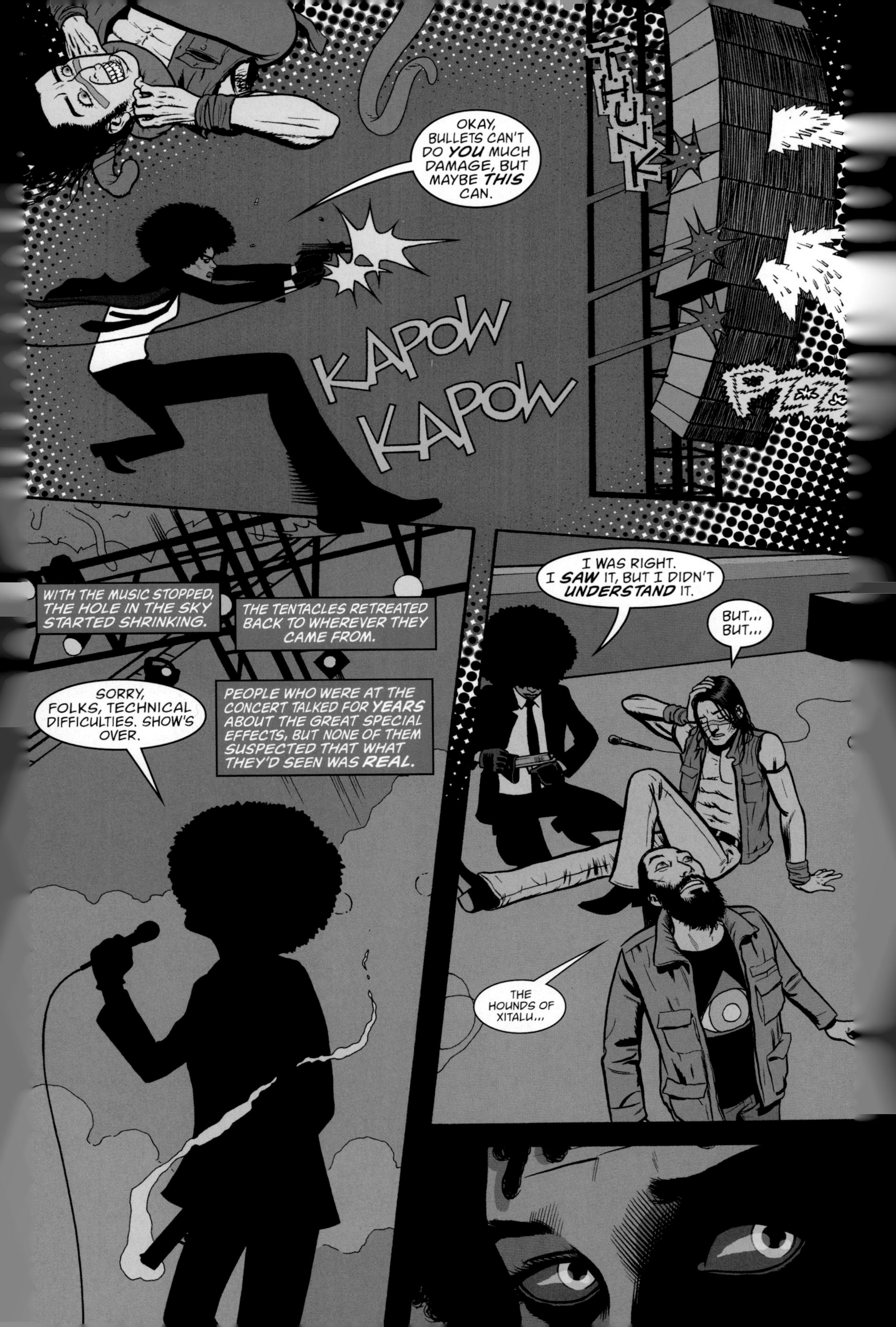
OKAY, BULLETS CAN'T DO YOU MUCH DAMAGE, BUT MAYBE THIS CAN.
THUNK
KAPOW
KAPOW
WITH THE MUSIC STOPPED, THE HOLE IN THE SKY STARTED SHRINKING.
THE TENTACLES RETREATED BACK TO WHEREVER THEY CAME FROM.
SORRY, FOLKS, TECHNICAL DIFFICULTIES. SHOW'S OVER.
PEOPLE WHO WERE AT THE CONCERT TALKED FOR YEARS ABOUT THE GREAT SPECIAL EFFECTS, BUT NONE OF THEM SUSPECTED THAT WHAT THEY'D SEEN WAS REAL.
I WAS RIGHT. I SAW IT, BUT I DIDN'T UNDERSTAND IT.
BUT... BUT...
THE HOUNDS OF XITALU...

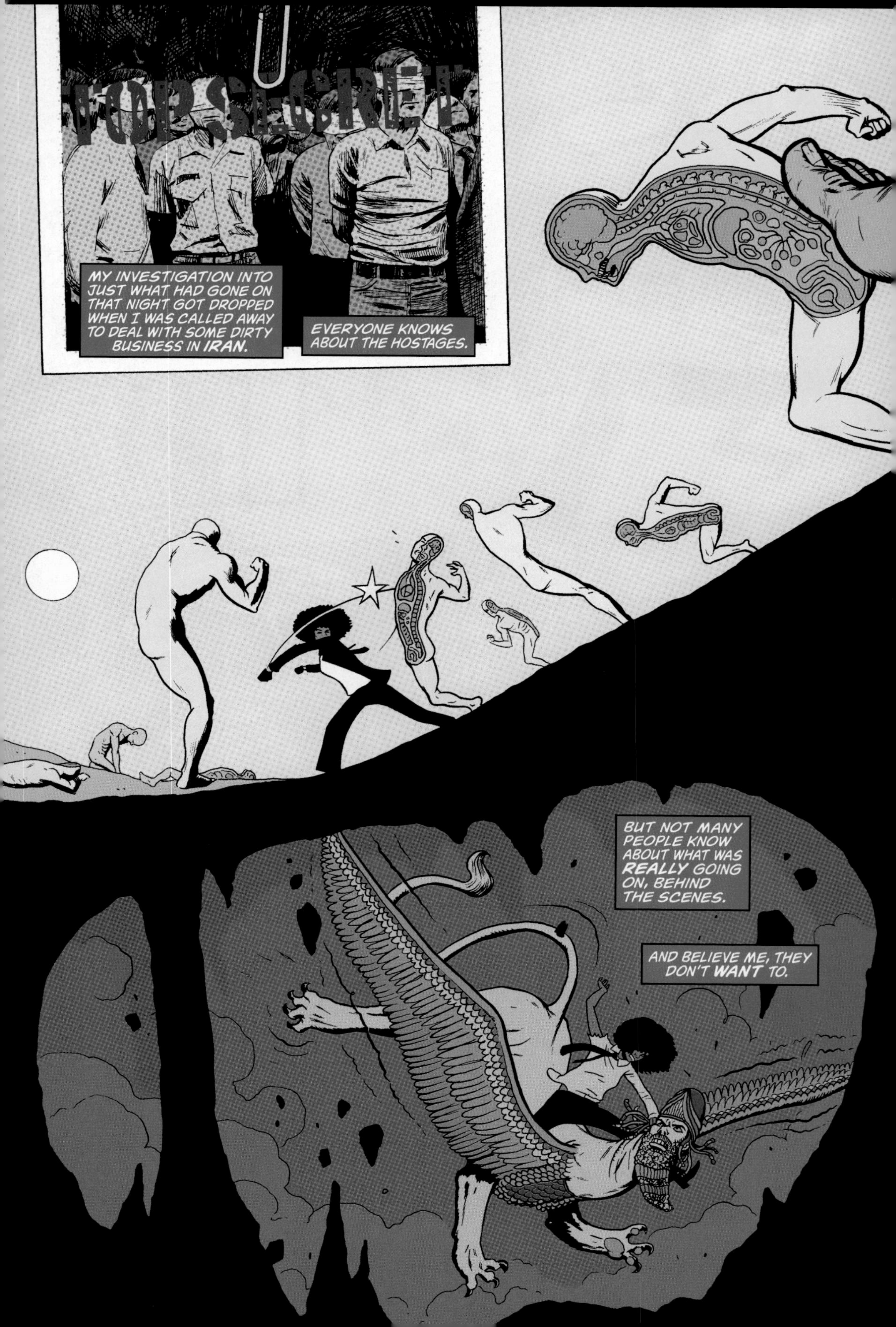

TOP SECRET
MY INVESTIGATION INTO JUST WHAT HAD GONE ON THAT NIGHT GOT DROPPED WHEN I WAS CALLED AWAY TO DEAL WITH SOME DIRTY BUSINESS IN IRAN.
EVERYONE KNOWS ABOUT THE HOSTAGES.
BUT NOT MANY PEOPLE KNOW ABOUT WHAT WAS REALLY GOING ON, BEHIND THE SCENES.
AND BELIEVE ME, THEY DON'T WANT TO.

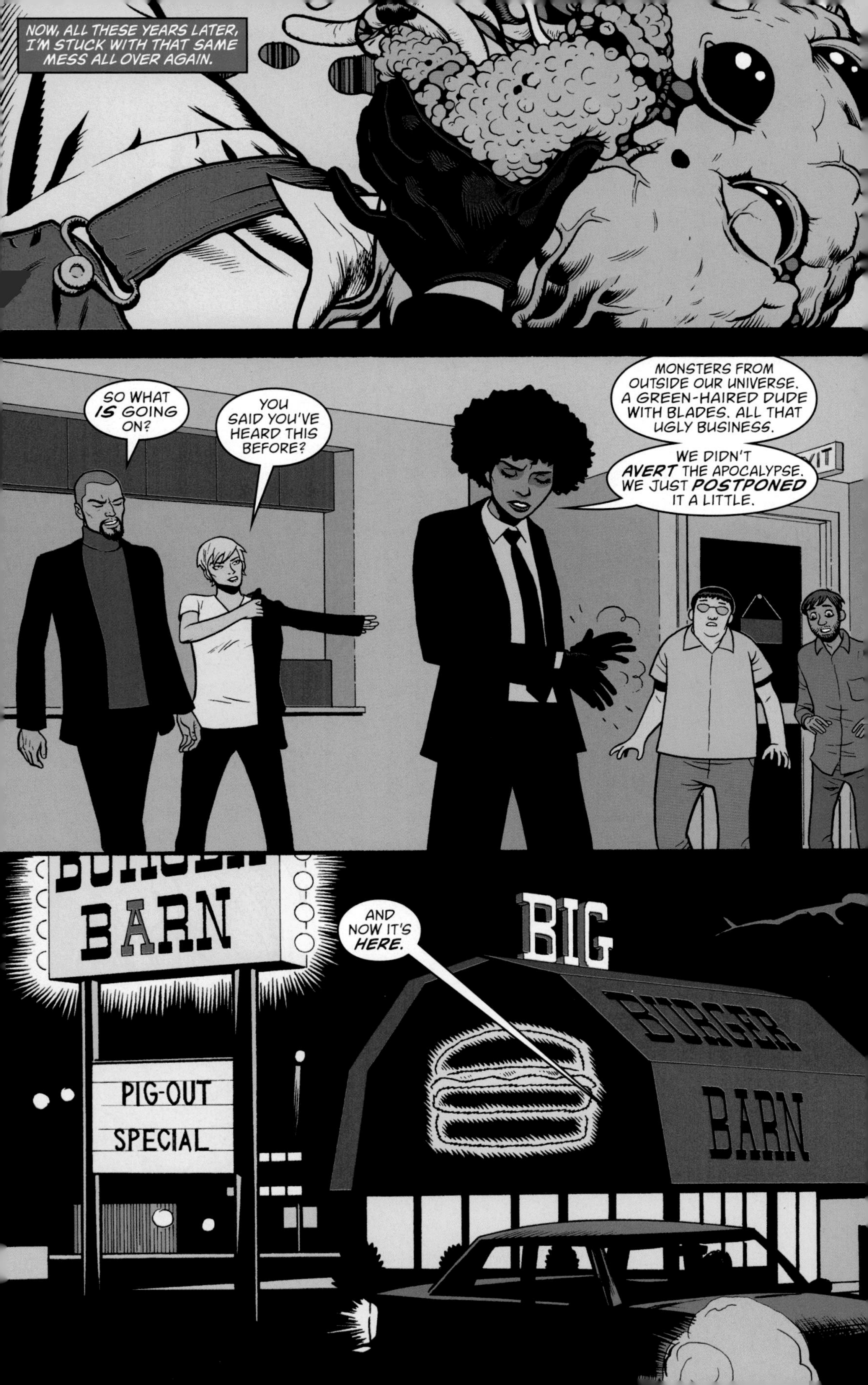
NOW, ALL THESE YEARS LATER, I'M STUCK WITH THAT SAME MESS ALL OVER AGAIN.
SO WHAT *IS* GOING ON?
YOU SAID YOU'VE HEARD THIS BEFORE?
MONSTERS FROM OUTSIDE OUR UNIVERSE. A GREEN-HAIRED DUDE WITH BLADES. ALL THAT UGLY BUSINESS.
WE DIDN'T *AVERT* THE APOCALYPSE. WE JUST *POSTPONED* IT A LITTLE.
BARN
PIG-OUT
SPECIAL
AND NOW IT'S *HERE*.
BIG
BURGER
BARN

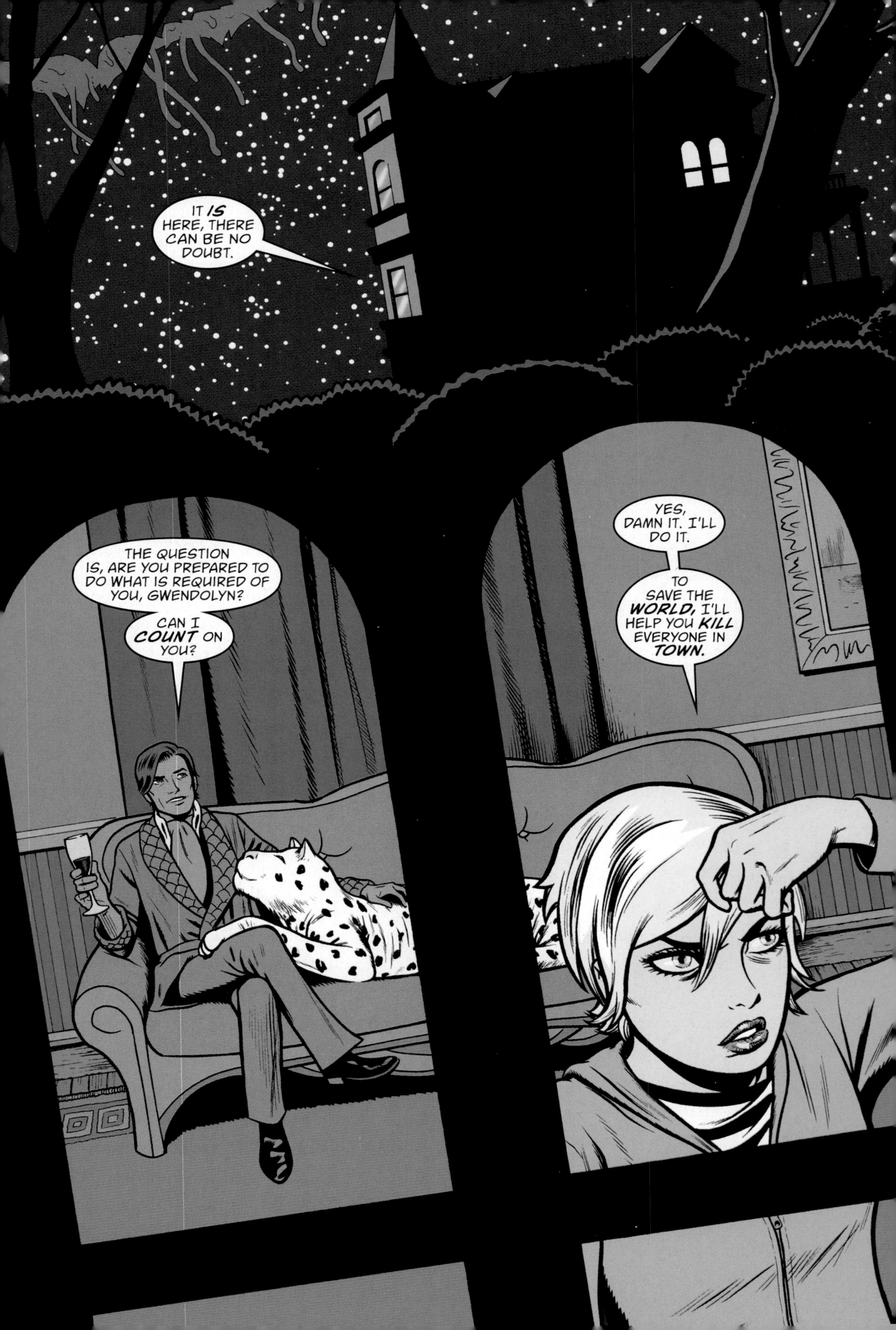
IT IS HERE, THERE CAN BE NO DOUBT.
THE QUESTION IS, ARE YOU PREPARED TO DO WHAT IS REQUIRED OF YOU, GWENDOLYN?
CAN I COUNT ON YOU?
YES, DAMN IT. I'LL DO IT.
TO SAVE THE WORLD, I'LL HELP YOU KILL EVERYONE IN TOWN.

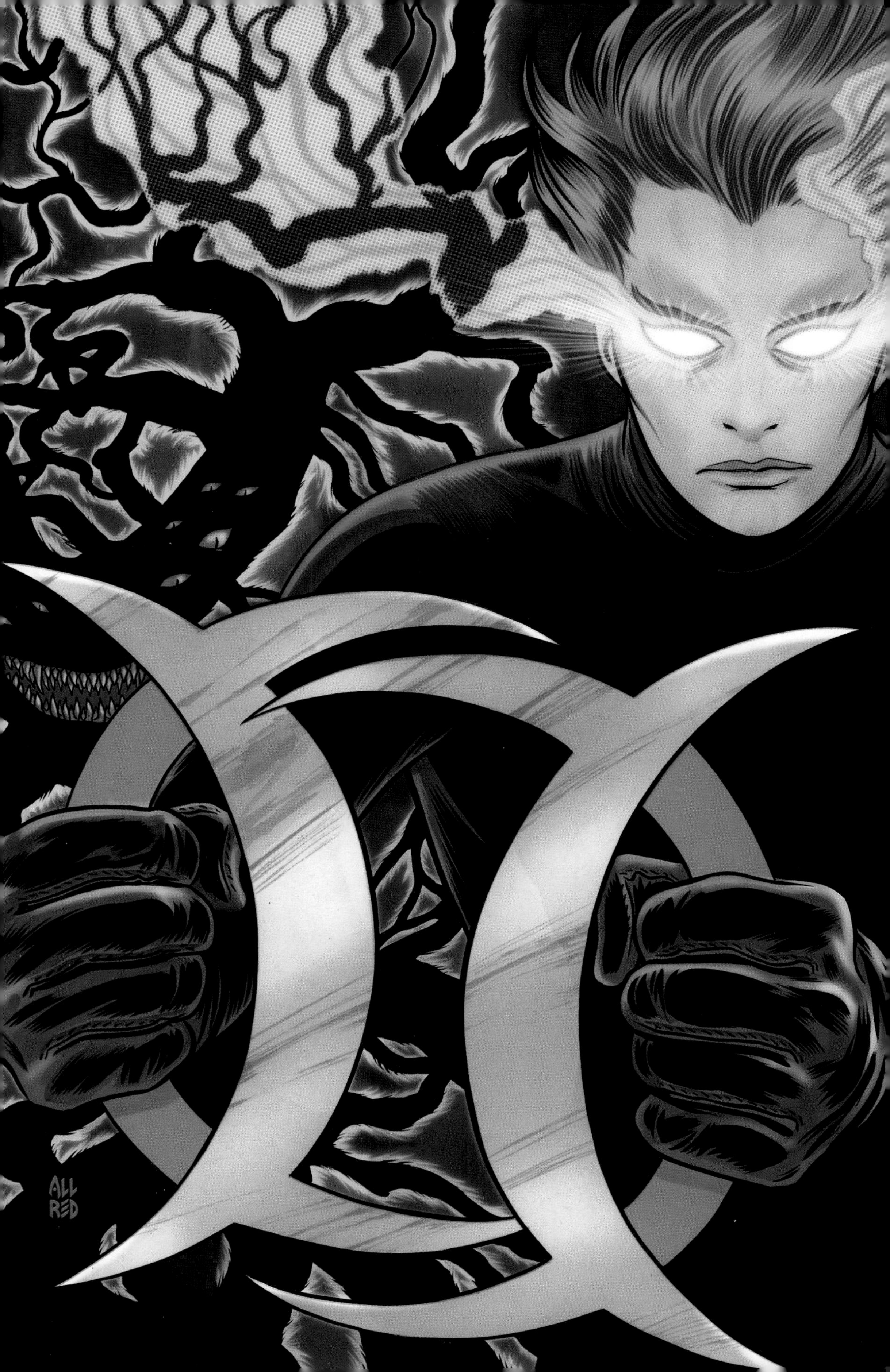
ALLRED

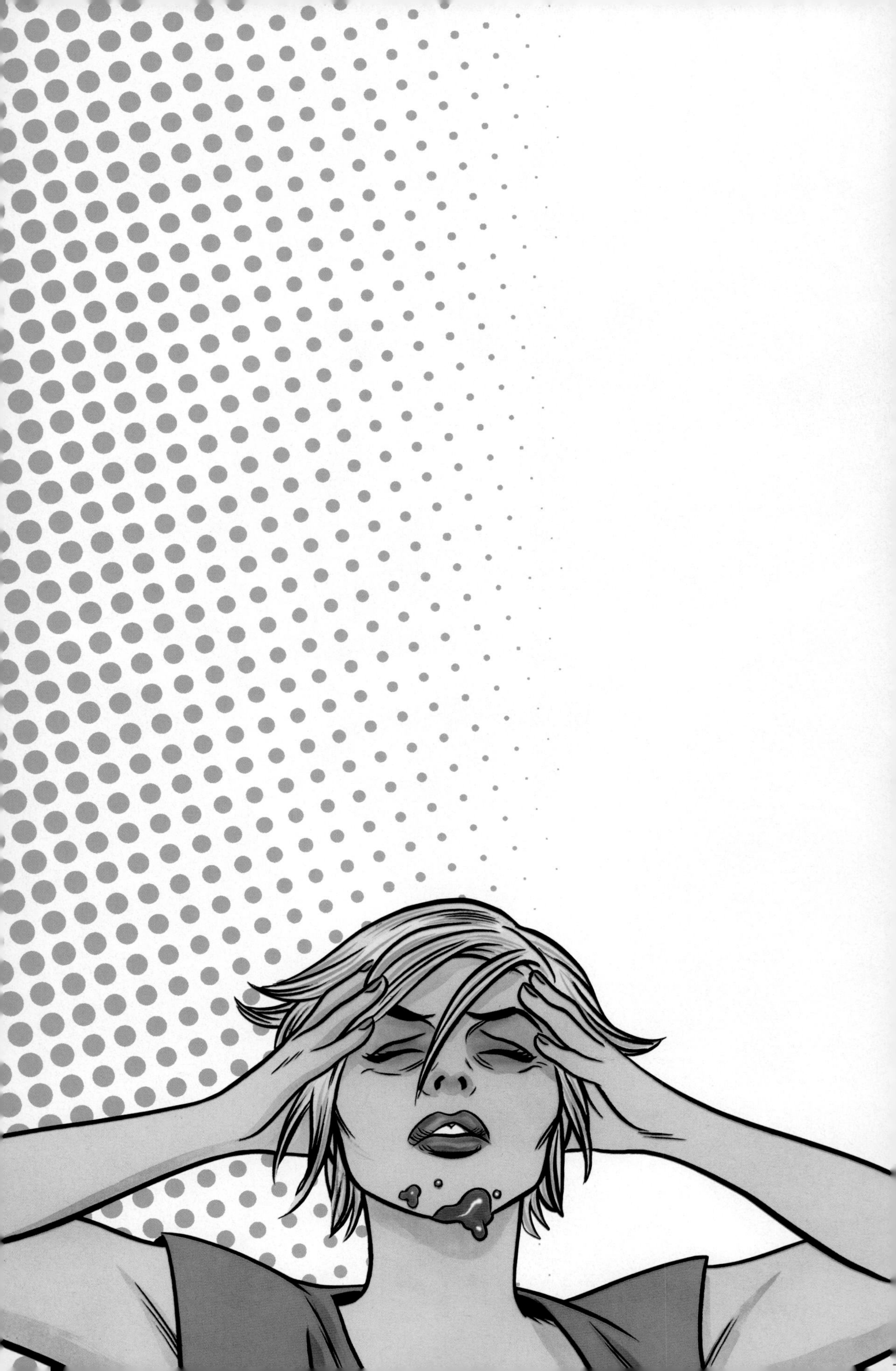

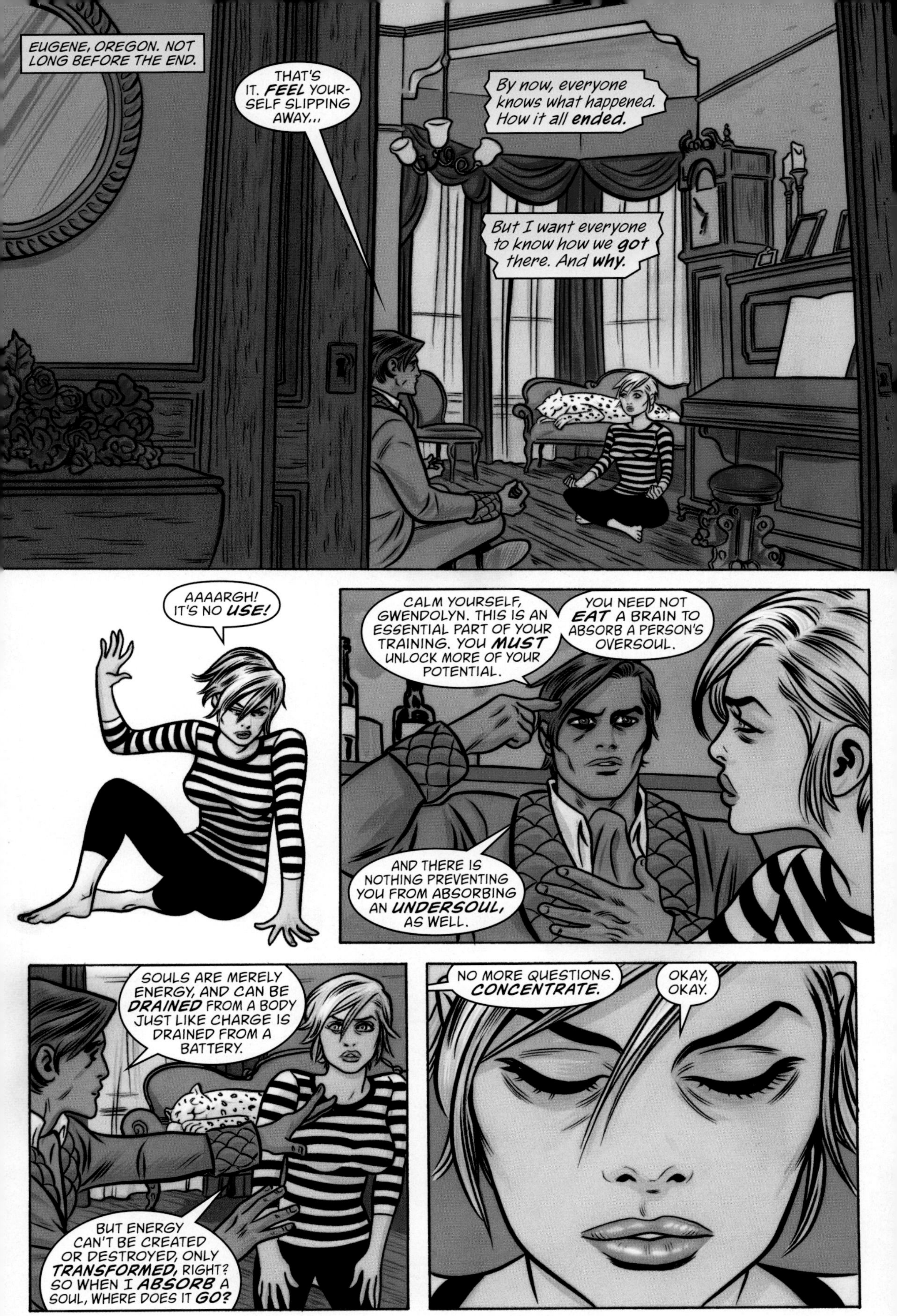
EUGENE, OREGON. NOT LONG BEFORE THE END.
THAT'S IT. FEEL YOURSELF SLIPPING AWAY...
By now, everyone knows what happened. How it all ended.
But I want everyone to know how we got there. And why.
AAAARGH! IT'S NO USE!
CALM YOURSELF, GWENDOLYN. THIS IS AN ESSENTIAL PART OF YOUR TRAINING. YOU MUST UNLOCK MORE OF YOUR POTENTIAL.
YOU NEED NOT EAT A BRAIN TO ABSORB A PERSON'S OVERSOUL.
AND THERE IS NOTHING PREVENTING YOU FROM ABSORBING AN UNDERSOUL, AS WELL.
SOULS ARE MERELY ENERGY, AND CAN BE DRAINED FROM A BODY JUST LIKE CHARGE IS DRAINED FROM A BATTERY.
BUT ENERGY CAN'T BE CREATED OR DESTROYED, ONLY TRANSFORMED, RIGHT? SO WHEN I ABSORB A SOUL, WHERE DOES IT GO?
NO MORE QUESTIONS. CONCENTRATE.
OKAY, OKAY.

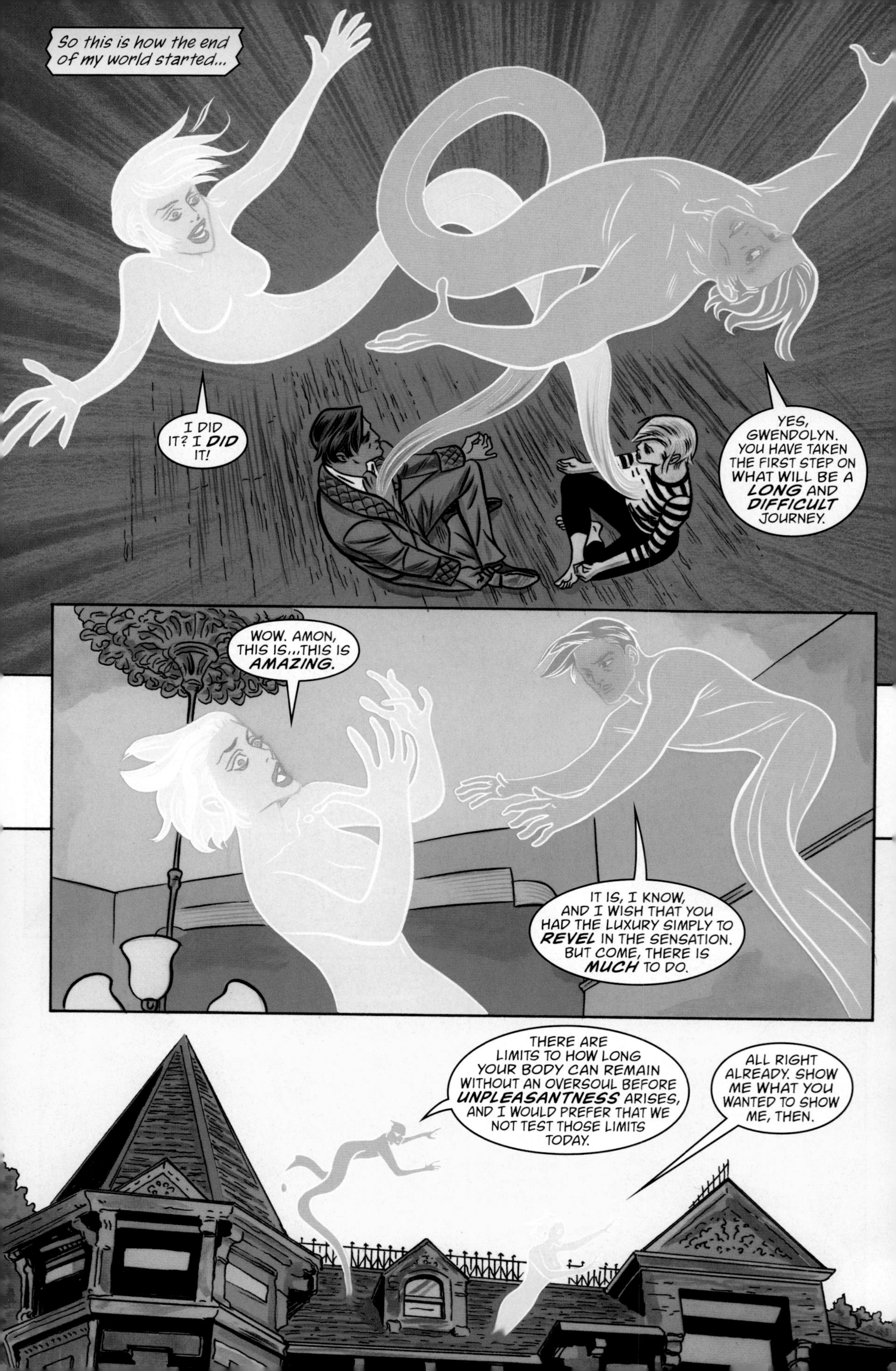

So this is how the end of my world started...
I DID IT? I DID IT!
YES, GWENDOLYN. YOU HAVE TAKEN THE FIRST STEP ON WHAT WILL BE A LONG AND DIFFICULT JOURNEY.
WOW. AMON, THIS IS...THIS IS AMAZING.
IT IS, I KNOW, AND I WISH THAT YOU HAD THE LUXURY SIMPLY TO REVEL IN THE SENSATION. BUT COME, THERE IS MUCH TO DO.
THERE ARE LIMITS TO HOW LONG YOUR BODY CAN REMAIN WITHOUT AN OVERSOUL BEFORE UNPLEASANTNESS ARISES, AND I WOULD PREFER THAT WE NOT TEST THOSE LIMITS TODAY.
ALL RIGHT ALREADY. SHOW ME WHAT YOU WANTED TO SHOW ME, THEN.

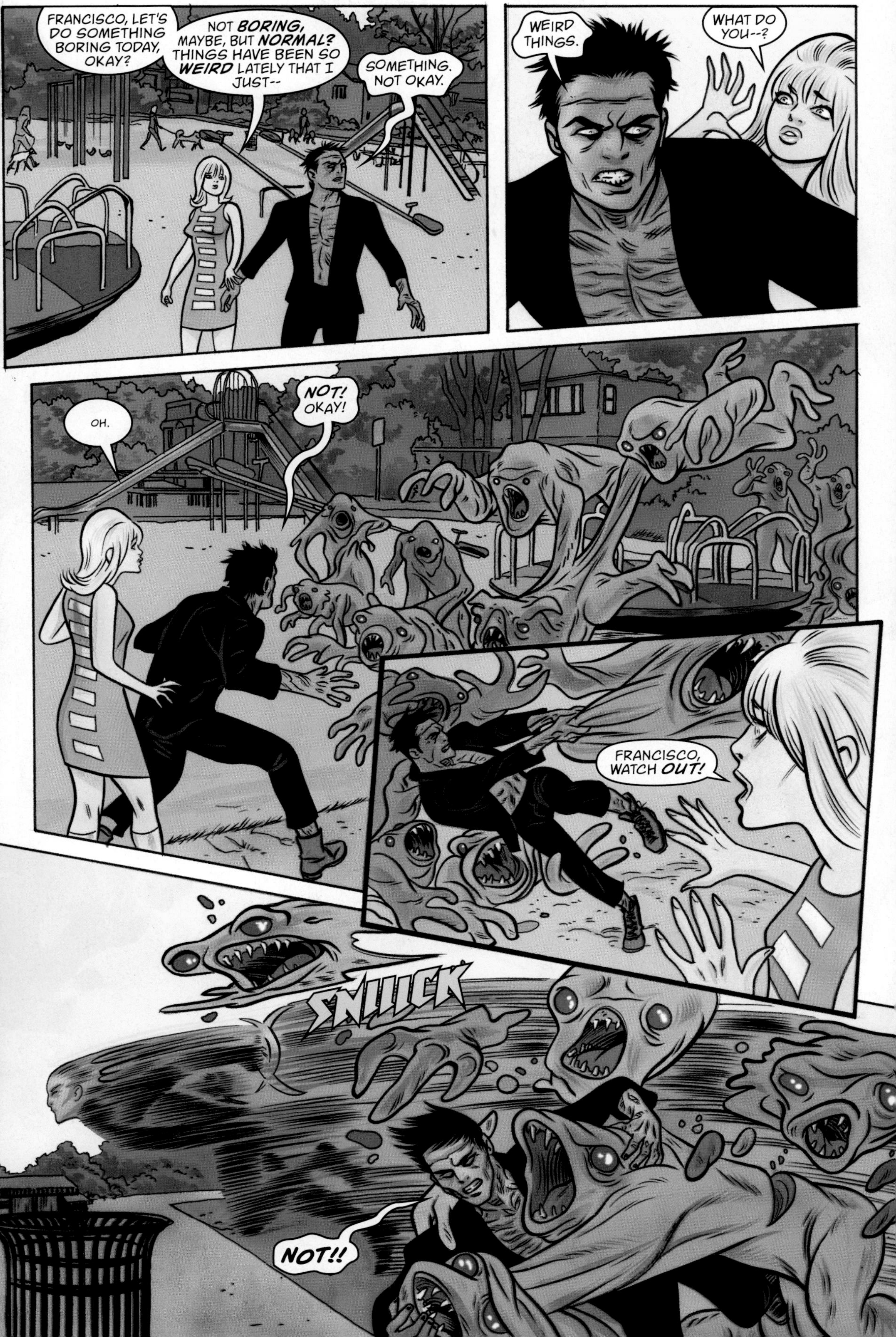

FRANCISCO, LET'S DO SOMETHING BORING TODAY, OKAY?
NOT BORING, MAYBE, BUT NORMAL? THINGS HAVE BEEN SO WEIRD LATELY THAT I JUST--
SOMETHING. NOT OKAY.
WEIRD THINGS.
WHAT DO YOU--?
OH.
NOT! OKAY!
FRANCISCO, WATCH OUT!
SNLLICK
NOT!!

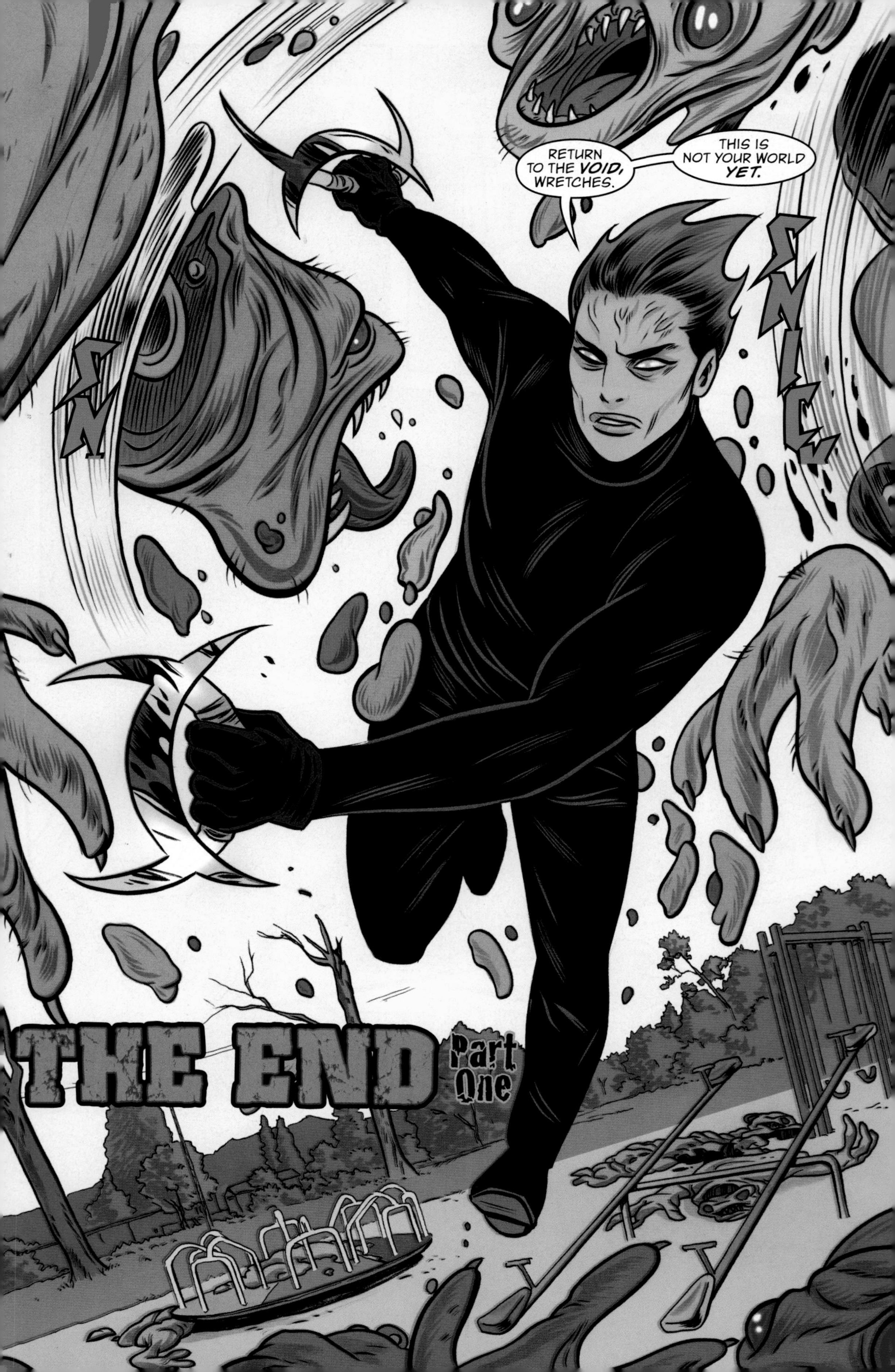
RETURN TO THE VOID, WRETCHES.
THIS IS NOT YOUR WORLD YET.
SNIC
SN
THE END
Part One

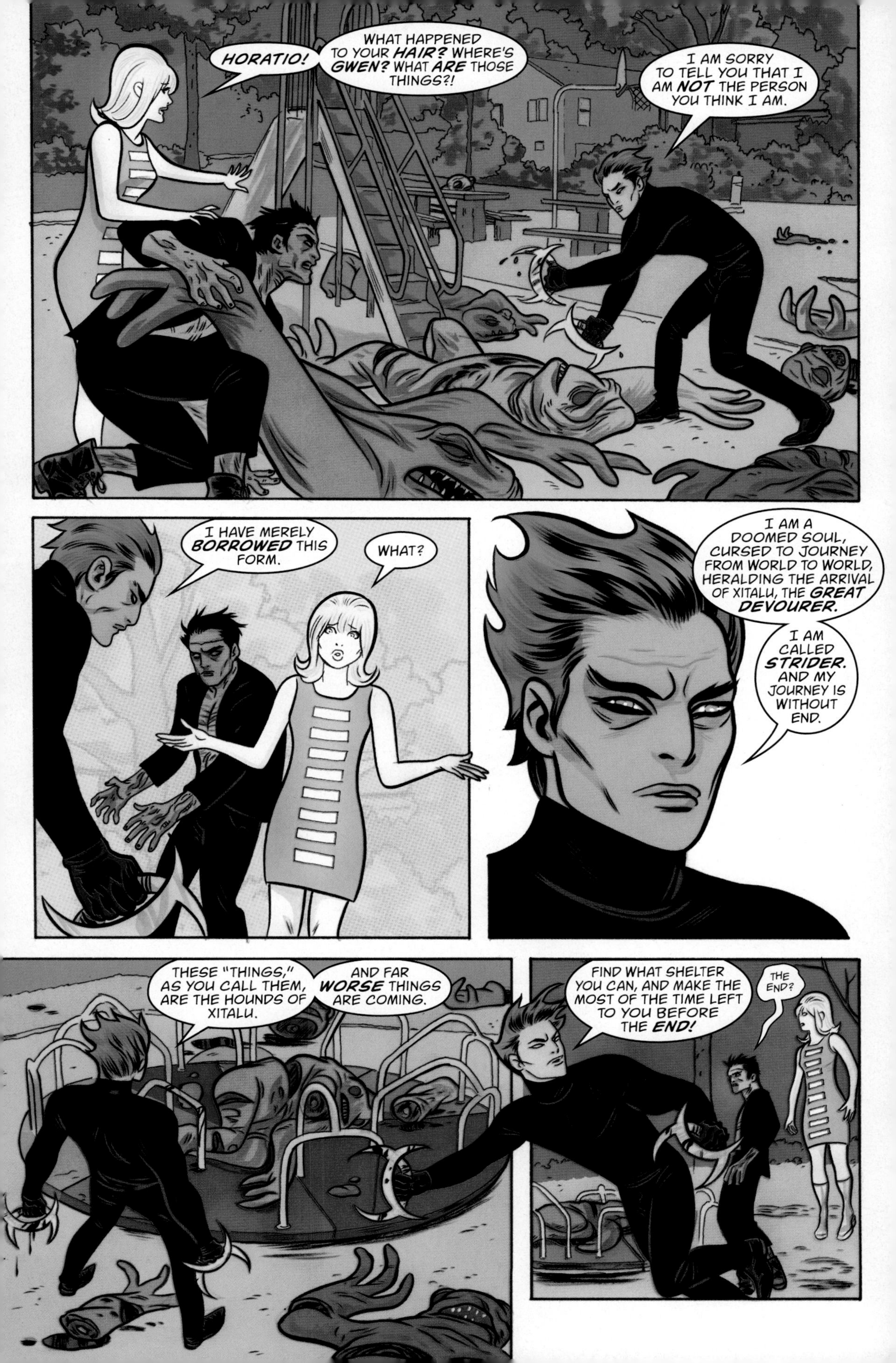
HORATIO!
WHAT HAPPENED TO YOUR HAIR? WHERE'S GWEN? WHAT ARE THOSE THINGS?!
I AM SORRY TO TELL YOU THAT I AM NOT THE PERSON YOU THINK I AM.
I HAVE MERELY BORROWED THIS FORM.
WHAT?
I AM A DOOMED SOUL, CURSED TO JOURNEY FROM WORLD TO WORLD, HERALDING THE ARRIVAL OF XITALU, THE GREAT DEVOURER.
I AM CALLED STRIDER. AND MY JOURNEY IS WITHOUT END.
THESE "THINGS," AS YOU CALL THEM, ARE THE HOUNDS OF XITALU.
AND FAR WORSE THINGS ARE COMING.
FIND WHAT SHELTER YOU CAN, AND MAKE THE MOST OF THE TIME LEFT TO YOU BEFORE THE END!
THE END?

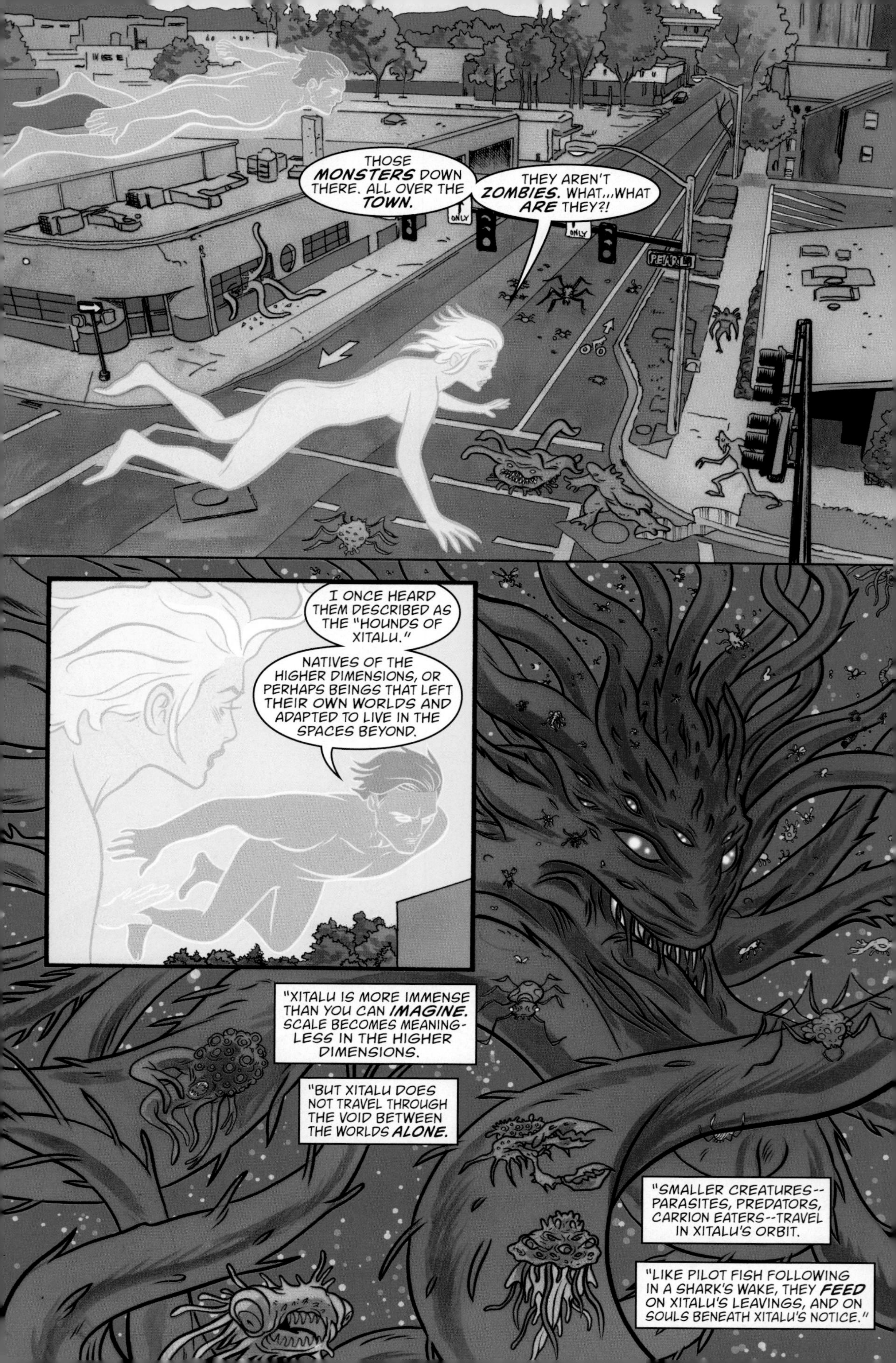

THOSE MONSTERS DOWN THERE. ALL OVER THE TOWN.
THEY AREN'T ZOMBIES. WHAT...WHAT ARE THEY?!
I ONCE HEARD THEM DESCRIBED AS THE "HOUNDS OF XITALU."
NATIVES OF THE HIGHER DIMENSIONS, OR PERHAPS BEINGS THAT LEFT THEIR OWN WORLDS AND ADAPTED TO LIVE IN THE SPACES BEYOND.
"XITALU IS MORE IMMENSE THAN YOU CAN IMAGINE. SCALE BECOMES MEANING-LESS IN THE HIGHER DIMENSIONS.
"BUT XITALU DOES NOT TRAVEL THROUGH THE VOID BETWEEN THE WORLDS ALONE.
"SMALLER CREATURES--PARASITES, PREDATORS, CARRION EATERS--TRAVEL IN XITALU'S ORBIT.
"LIKE PILOT FISH FOLLOWING IN A SHARK'S WAKE, THEY FEED ON XITALU'S LEAVINGS, AND ON SOULS BENEATH XITALU'S NOTICE."

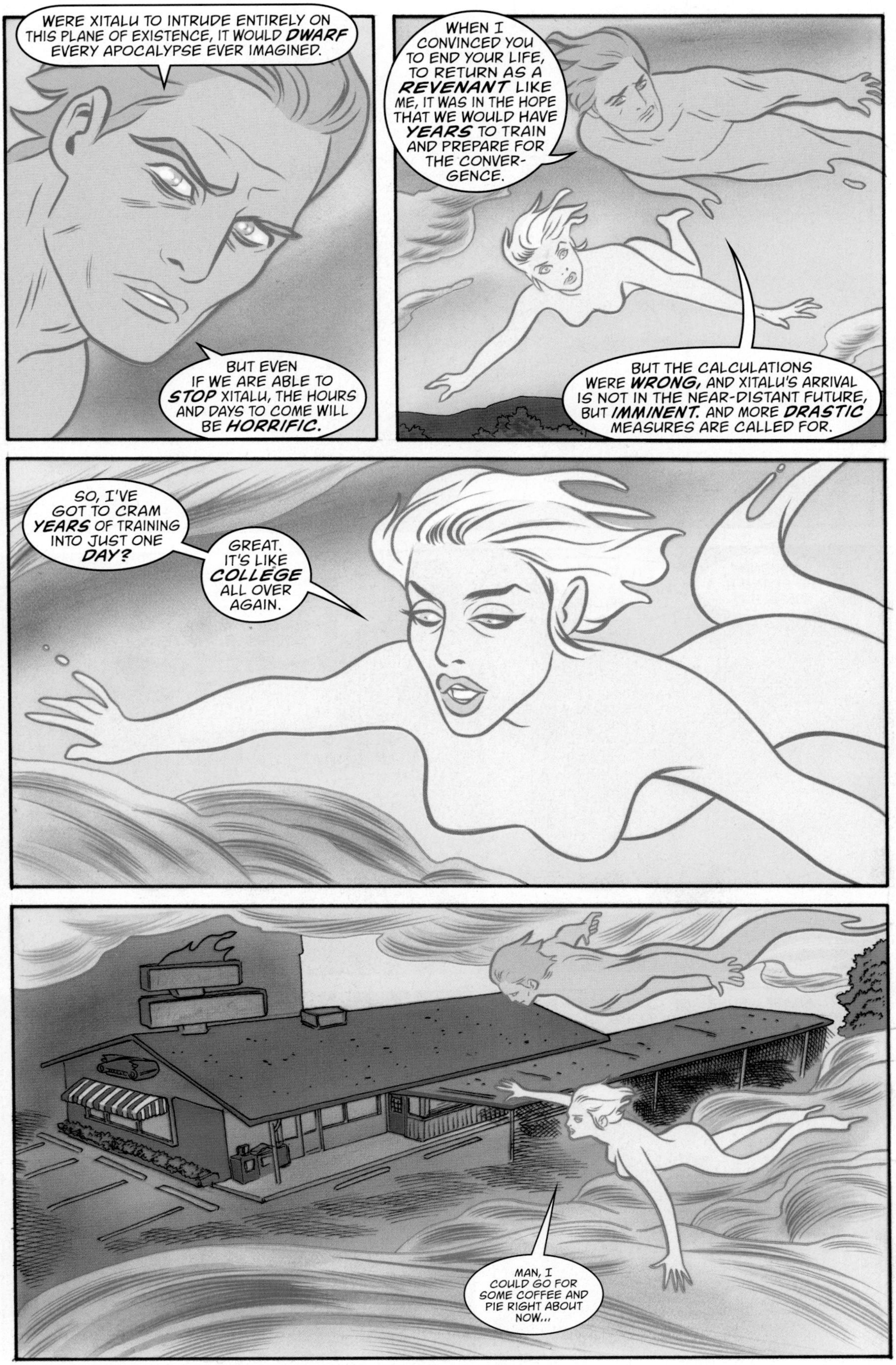
WERE XITALU TO INTRUDE ENTIRELY ON THIS PLANE OF EXISTENCE, IT WOULD DWARF EVERY APOCALYPSE EVER IMAGINED.
BUT EVEN IF WE ARE ABLE TO STOP XITALU, THE HOURS AND DAYS TO COME WILL BE HORRIFIC.
WHEN I CONVINCED YOU TO END YOUR LIFE, TO RETURN AS A REVENANT LIKE ME, IT WAS IN THE HOPE THAT WE WOULD HAVE YEARS TO TRAIN AND PREPARE FOR THE CONVER-GENCE.
BUT THE CALCULATIONS WERE WRONG, AND XITALU'S ARRIVAL IS NOT IN THE NEAR-DISTANT FUTURE, BUT IMMINENT. AND MORE DRASTIC MEASURES ARE CALLED FOR.
SO, I'VE GOT TO CRAM YEARS OF TRAINING INTO JUST ONE DAY?
GREAT. IT'S LIKE COLLEGE ALL OVER AGAIN.
MAN, I COULD GO FOR SOME COFFEE AND PIE RIGHT ABOUT NOW...

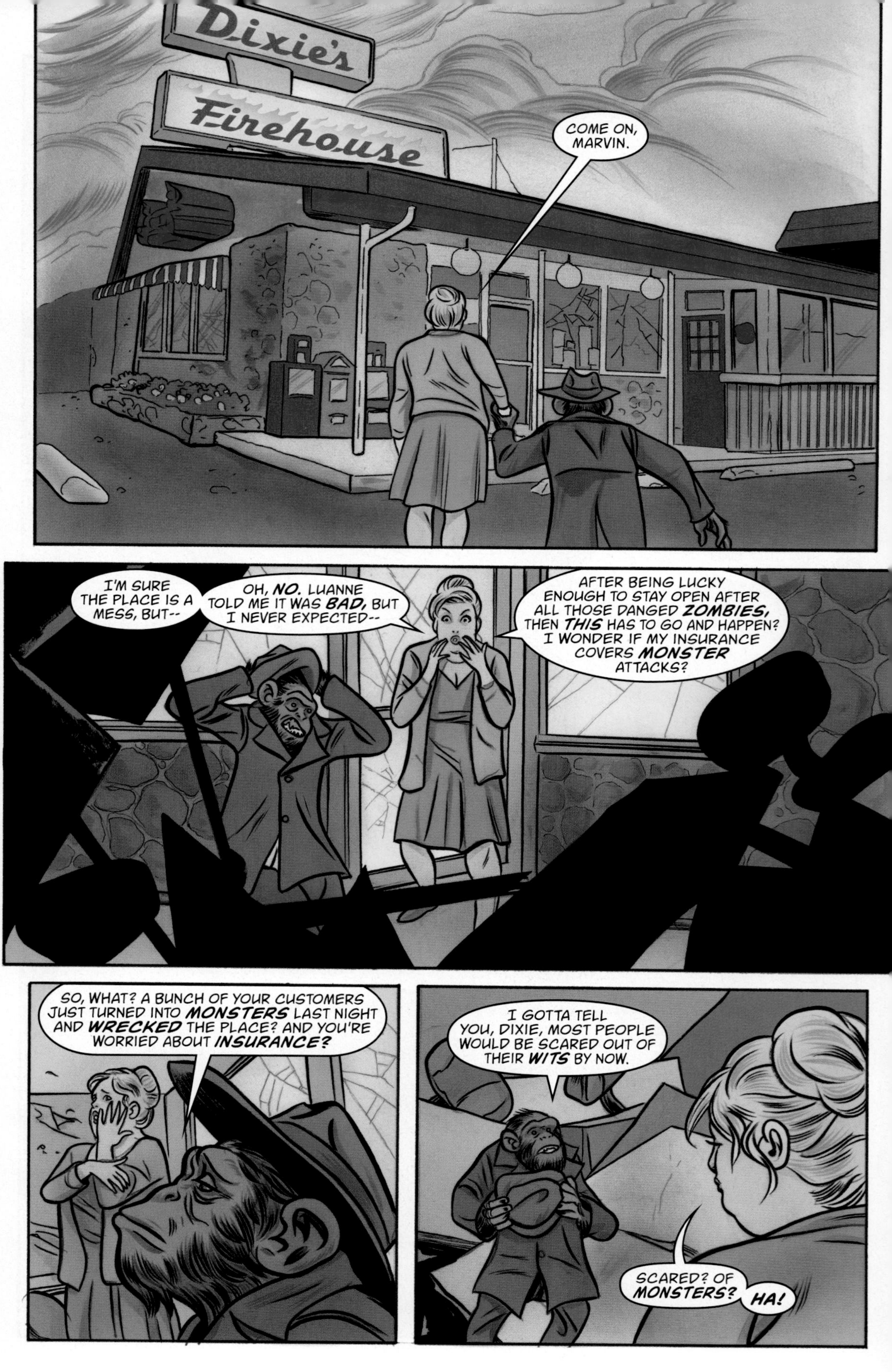
Dixie's
Firehouse
COME ON, MARVIN.
I'M SURE THE PLACE IS A MESS, BUT--
OH, NO. LUANNE TOLD ME IT WAS BAD, BUT I NEVER EXPECTED--
AFTER BEING LUCKY ENOUGH TO STAY OPEN AFTER ALL THOSE DANGED ZOMBIES, THEN THIS HAS TO GO AND HAPPEN? I WONDER IF MY INSURANCE COVERS MONSTER ATTACKS?
SO, WHAT? A BUNCH OF YOUR CUSTOMERS JUST TURNED INTO MONSTERS LAST NIGHT AND WRECKED THE PLACE? AND YOU'RE WORRIED ABOUT INSURANCE?
I GOTTA TELL YOU, DIXIE, MOST PEOPLE WOULD BE SCARED OUT OF THEIR WITS BY NOW.
SCARED? OF MONSTERS?
HA!

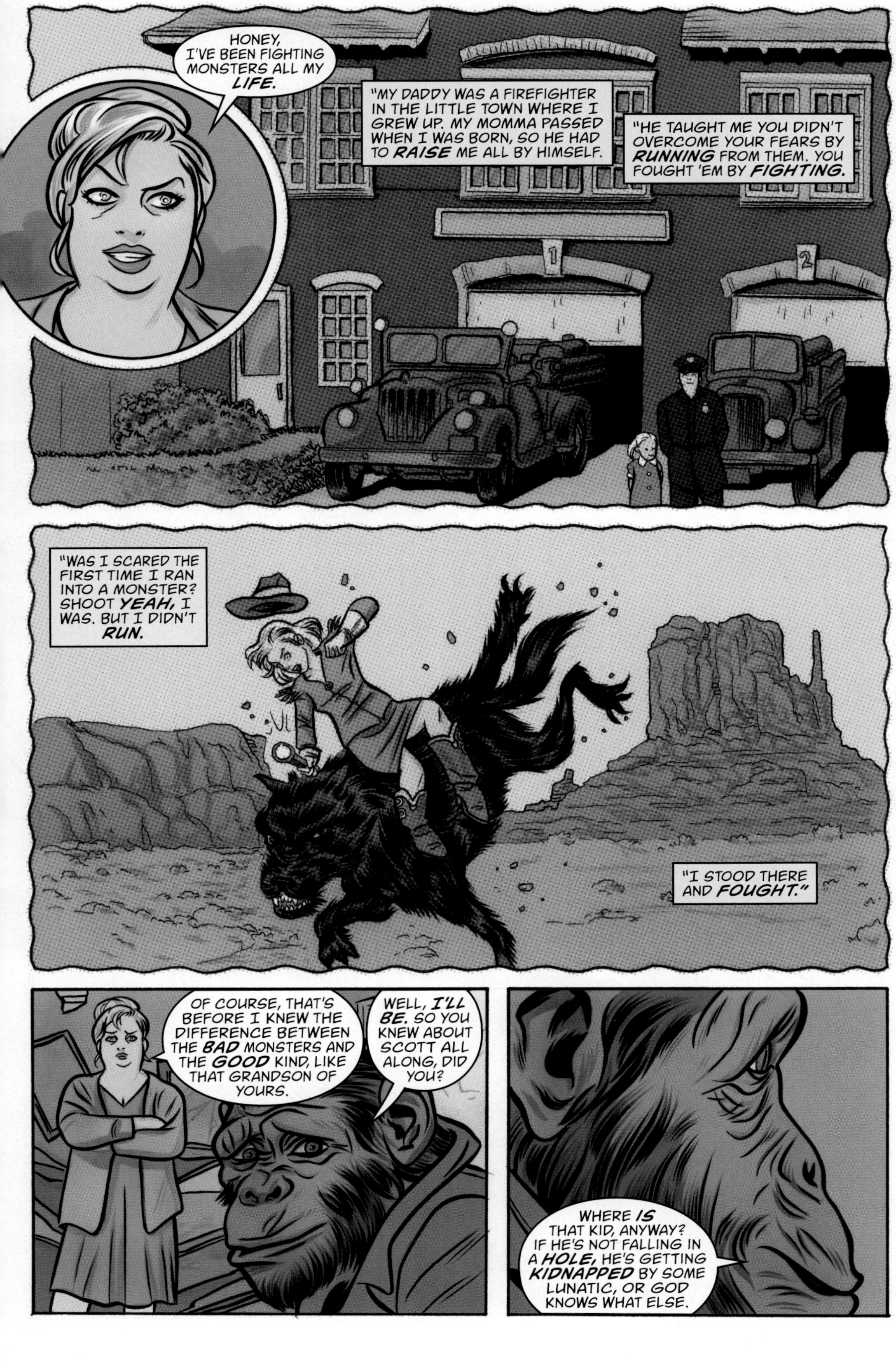
HONEY, I'VE BEEN FIGHTING MONSTERS ALL MY LIFE.
"MY DADDY WAS A FIREFIGHTER IN THE LITTLE TOWN WHERE I GREW UP. MY MOMMA PASSED WHEN I WAS BORN, SO HE HAD TO RAISE ME ALL BY HIMSELF.
"HE TAUGHT ME YOU DIDN'T OVERCOME YOUR FEARS BY RUNNING FROM THEM. YOU FOUGHT 'EM BY FIGHTING.
1
2
"WAS I SCARED THE FIRST TIME I RAN INTO A MONSTER? SHOOT YEAH, I WAS. BUT I DIDN'T RUN.
"I STOOD THERE AND FOUGHT."
OF COURSE, THAT'S BEFORE I KNEW THE DIFFERENCE BETWEEN THE BAD MONSTERS AND THE GOOD KIND, LIKE THAT GRANDSON OF YOURS.
WELL, I'LL BE. SO YOU KNEW ABOUT SCOTT ALL ALONG, DID YOU?
WHERE IS THAT KID, ANYWAY? IF HE'S NOT FALLING IN A HOLE, HE'S GETTING KIDNAPPED BY SOME LUNATIC, OR GOD KNOWS WHAT ELSE.

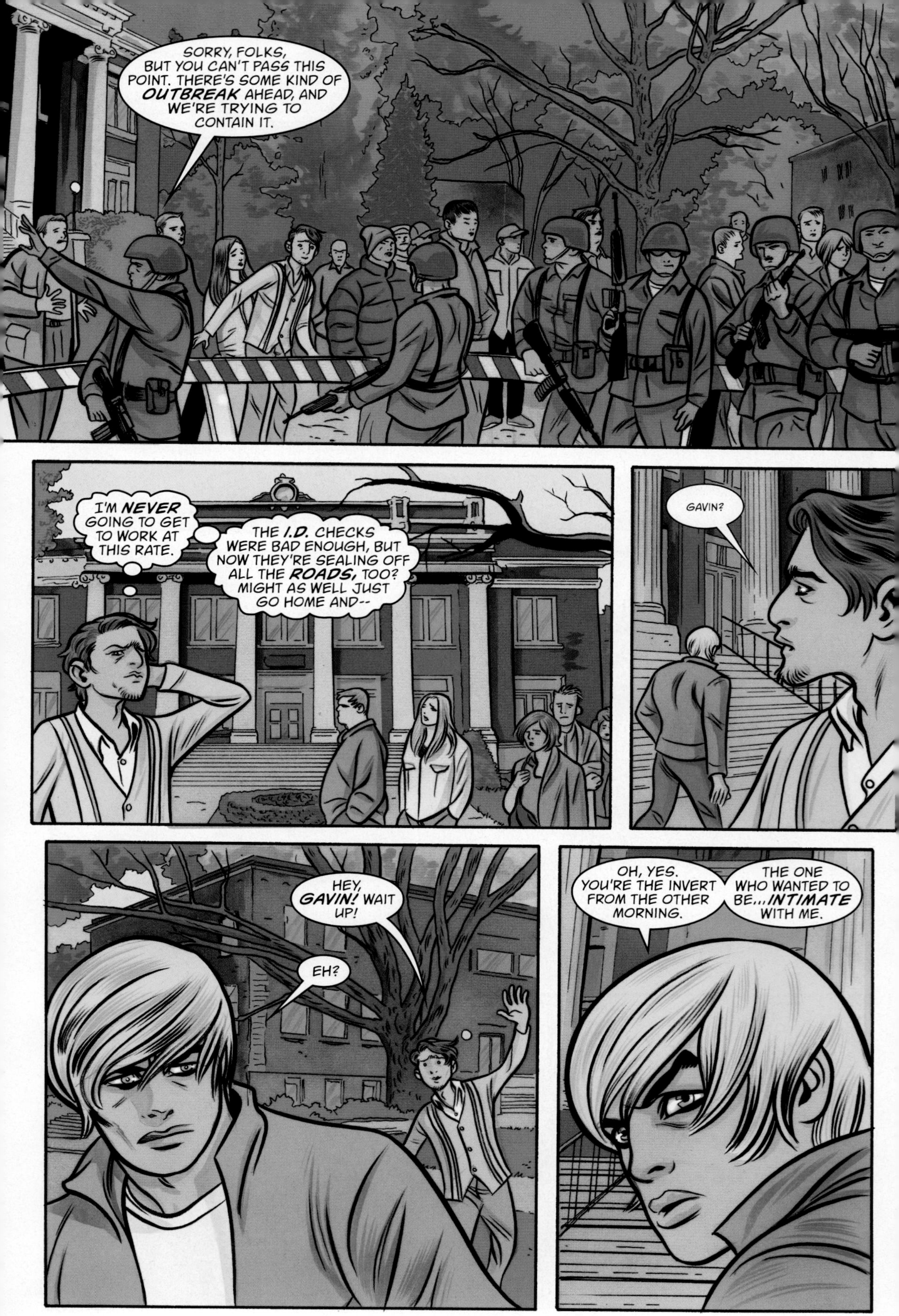
SORRY, FOLKS, BUT YOU CAN'T PASS THIS POINT. THERE'S SOME KIND OF OUTBREAK AHEAD, AND WE'RE TRYING TO CONTAIN IT.
I'M NEVER GOING TO GET TO WORK AT THIS RATE.
THE I.D. CHECKS WERE BAD ENOUGH, BUT NOW THEY'RE SEALING OFF ALL THE ROADS, TOO? MIGHT AS WELL JUST GO HOME AND--
GAVIN?
HEY, GAVIN! WAIT UP!
EH?
OH, YES. YOU'RE THE INVERT FROM THE OTHER MORNING.
THE ONE WHO WANTED TO BE...INTIMATE WITH ME.

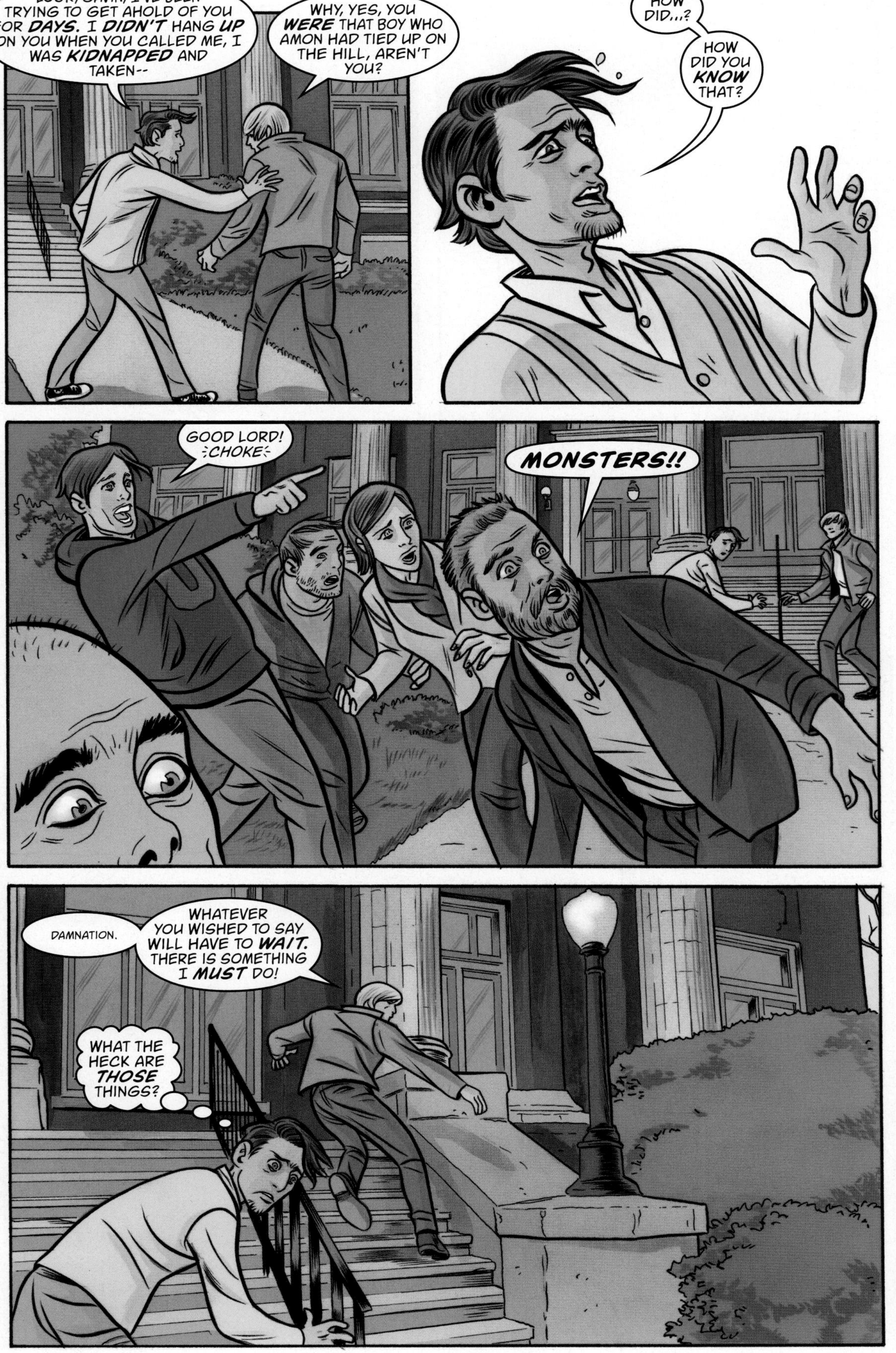
LOOK, GAVIN, I'VE BEEN TRYING TO GET AHOLD OF YOU FOR DAYS. I DIDN'T HANG UP ON YOU WHEN YOU CALLED ME, I WAS KIDNAPPED AND TAKEN--
WHY, YES, YOU WERE THAT BOY WHO AMON HAD TIED UP ON THE HILL, AREN'T YOU?
HOW DID...?
HOW DID YOU KNOW THAT?
GOOD LORD! CHOKE
MONSTERS!!
DAMNATION.
WHATEVER YOU WISHED TO SAY WILL HAVE TO WAIT. THERE IS SOMETHING I MUST DO!
WHAT THE HECK ARE THOSE THINGS?

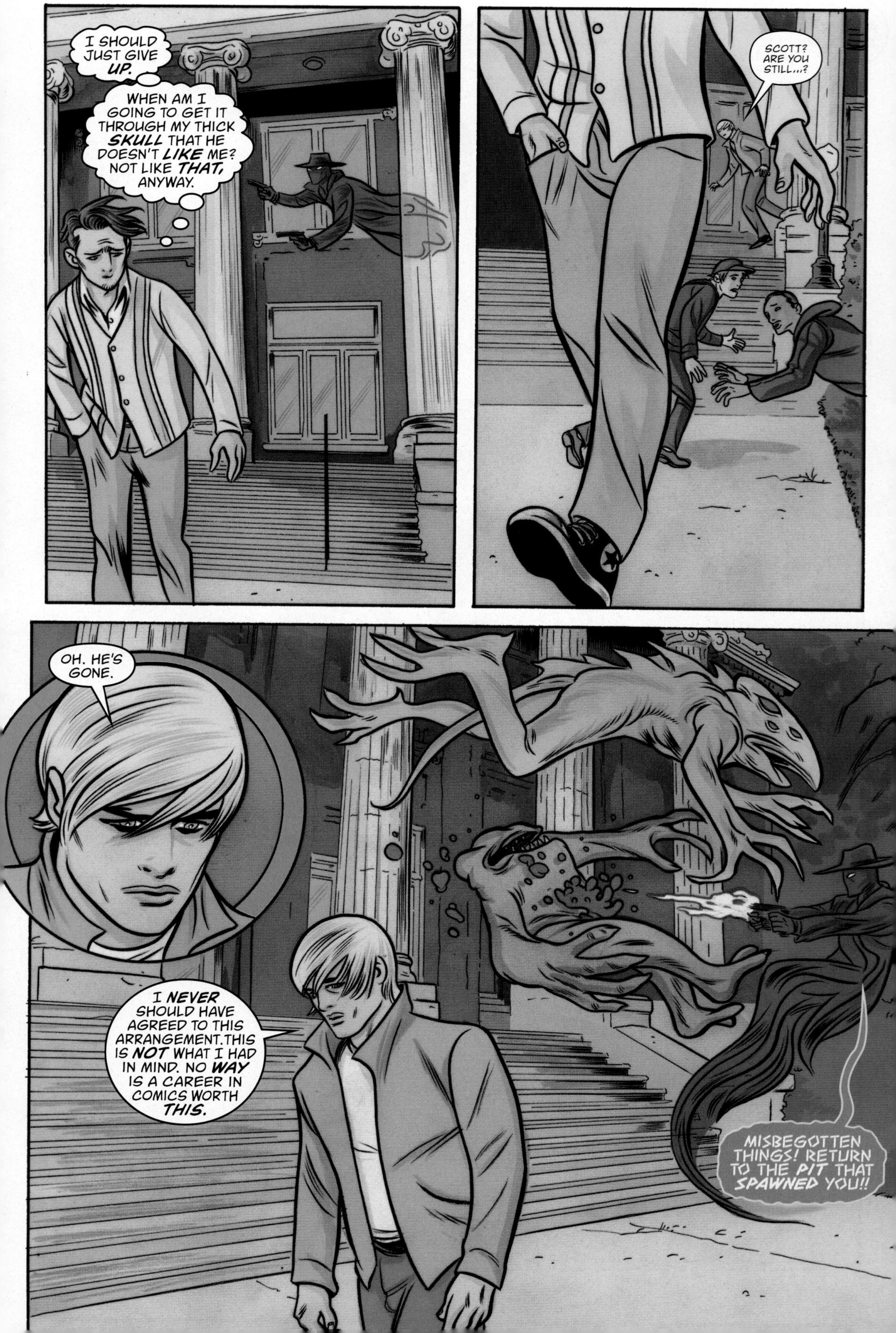

I SHOULD JUST GIVE UP.
WHEN AM I GOING TO GET IT THROUGH MY THICK SKULL THAT HE DOESN'T LIKE ME? NOT LIKE THAT, ANYWAY.
SCOTT? ARE YOU STILL...?
OH. HE'S GONE.
I NEVER SHOULD HAVE AGREED TO THIS ARRANGEMENT. THIS IS NOT WHAT I HAD IN MIND. NO WAY IS A CAREER IN COMICS WORTH THIS.
MISBEGOTTEN THINGS! RETURN TO THE PIT THAT SPAWNED YOU!!

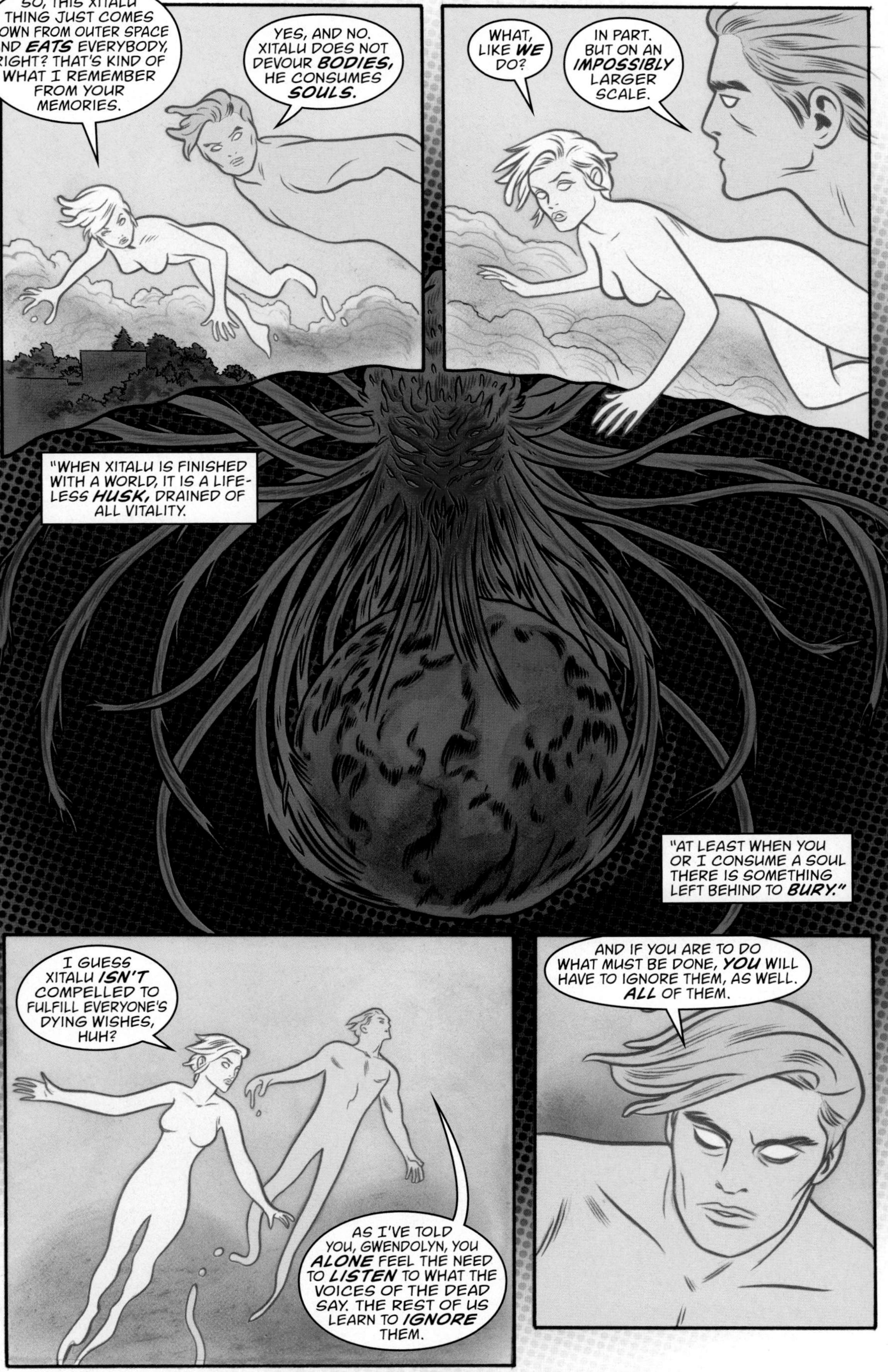
SO, THIS XITALU THING JUST COMES DOWN FROM OUTER SPACE AND EATS EVERYBODY, RIGHT? THAT'S KIND OF WHAT I REMEMBER FROM YOUR MEMORIES.
YES, AND NO. XITALU DOES NOT DEVOUR BODIES, HE CONSUMES SOULS.
WHAT, LIKE WE DO?
IN PART. BUT ON AN IMPOSSIBLY LARGER SCALE.
"WHEN XITALU IS FINISHED WITH A WORLD, IT IS A LIFELESS HUSK, DRAINED OF ALL VITALITY.
"AT LEAST WHEN YOU OR I CONSUME A SOUL THERE IS SOMETHING LEFT BEHIND TO BURY."
I GUESS XITALU ISN'T COMPELLED TO FULFILL EVERYONE'S DYING WISHES, HUH?
AS I'VE TOLD YOU, GWENDOLYN, YOU ALONE FEEL THE NEED TO LISTEN TO WHAT THE VOICES OF THE DEAD SAY. THE REST OF US LEARN TO IGNORE THEM.
AND IF YOU ARE TO DO WHAT MUST BE DONE, YOU WILL HAVE TO IGNORE THEM, AS WELL. ALL OF THEM.

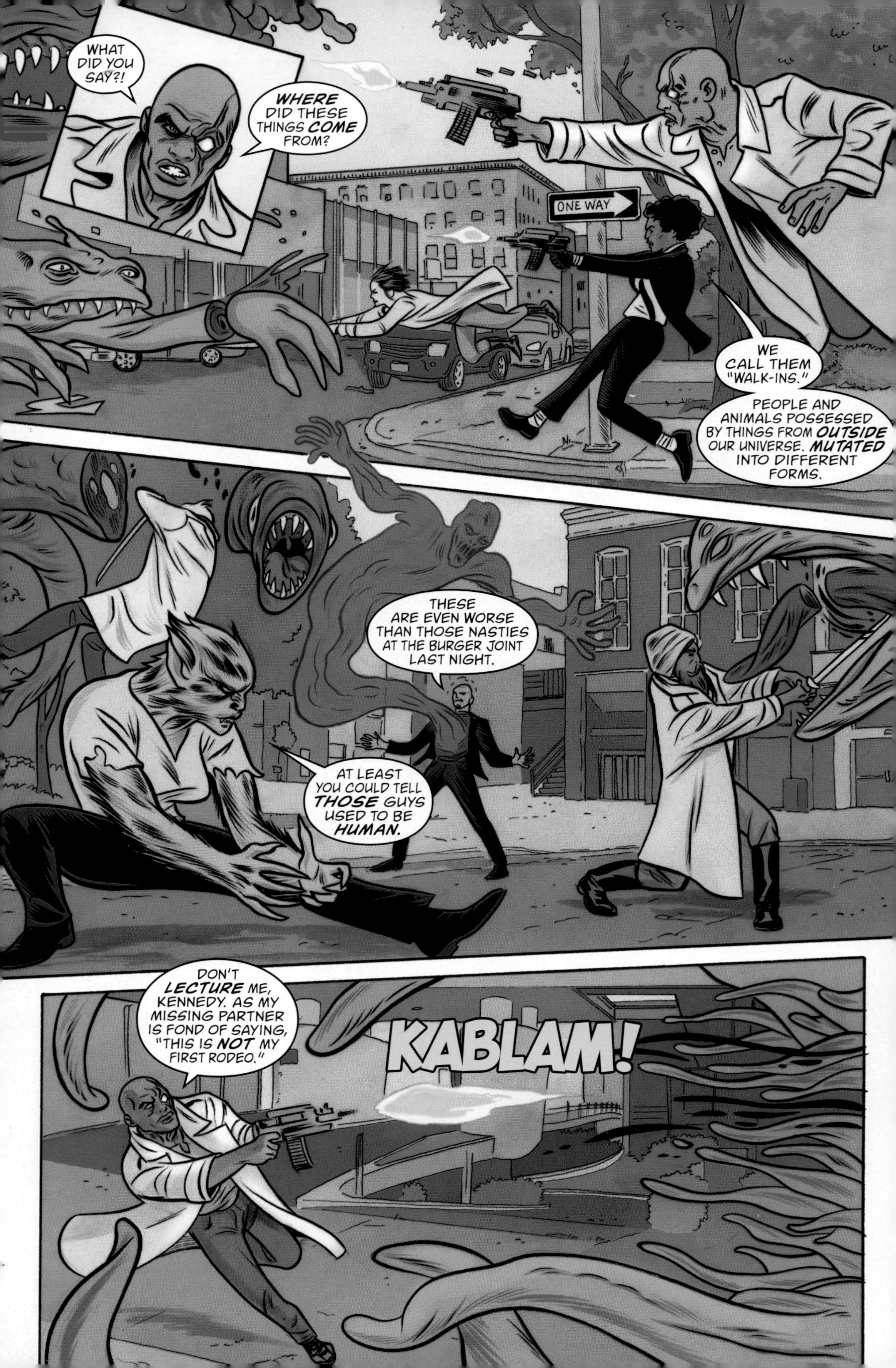

WHAT DID YOU SAY?!
WHERE DID THESE THINGS COME FROM?
ONE WAY
WE CALL THEM "WALK-INS."
PEOPLE AND ANIMALS POSSESSED BY THINGS FROM OUTSIDE OUR UNIVERSE. MUTATED INTO DIFFERENT FORMS.
THESE ARE EVEN WORSE THAN THOSE NASTIES AT THE BURGER JOINT LAST NIGHT.
AT LEAST YOU COULD TELL THOSE GUYS USED TO BE HUMAN.
DON'T LECTURE ME, KENNEDY. AS MY MISSING PARTNER IS FOND OF SAYING, "THIS IS NOT MY FIRST RODEO."
KABLAM!

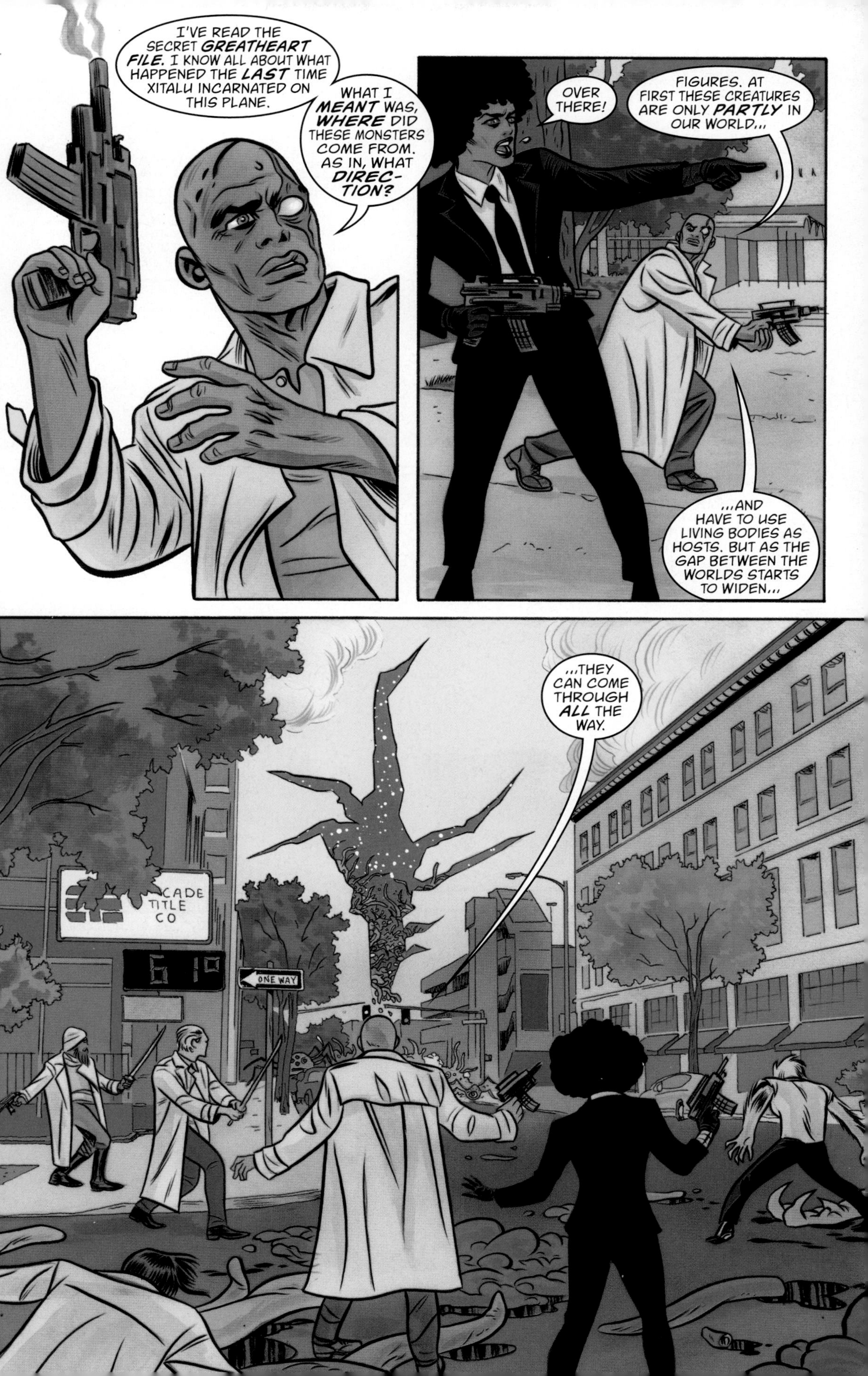
I'VE READ THE SECRET GREATHEART FILE. I KNOW ALL ABOUT WHAT HAPPENED THE LAST TIME XITALU INCARNATED ON THIS PLANE.
WHAT I MEANT WAS, WHERE DID THESE MONSTERS COME FROM. AS IN, WHAT DIREC-TION?
OVER THERE!
FIGURES. AT FIRST THESE CREATURES ARE ONLY PARTLY IN OUR WORLD...
...AND HAVE TO USE LIVING BODIES AS HOSTS. BUT AS THE GAP BETWEEN THE WORLDS STARTS TO WIDEN...
...THEY CAN COME THROUGH ALL THE WAY.
CADE
TITLE
CO
61°
ONE WAY

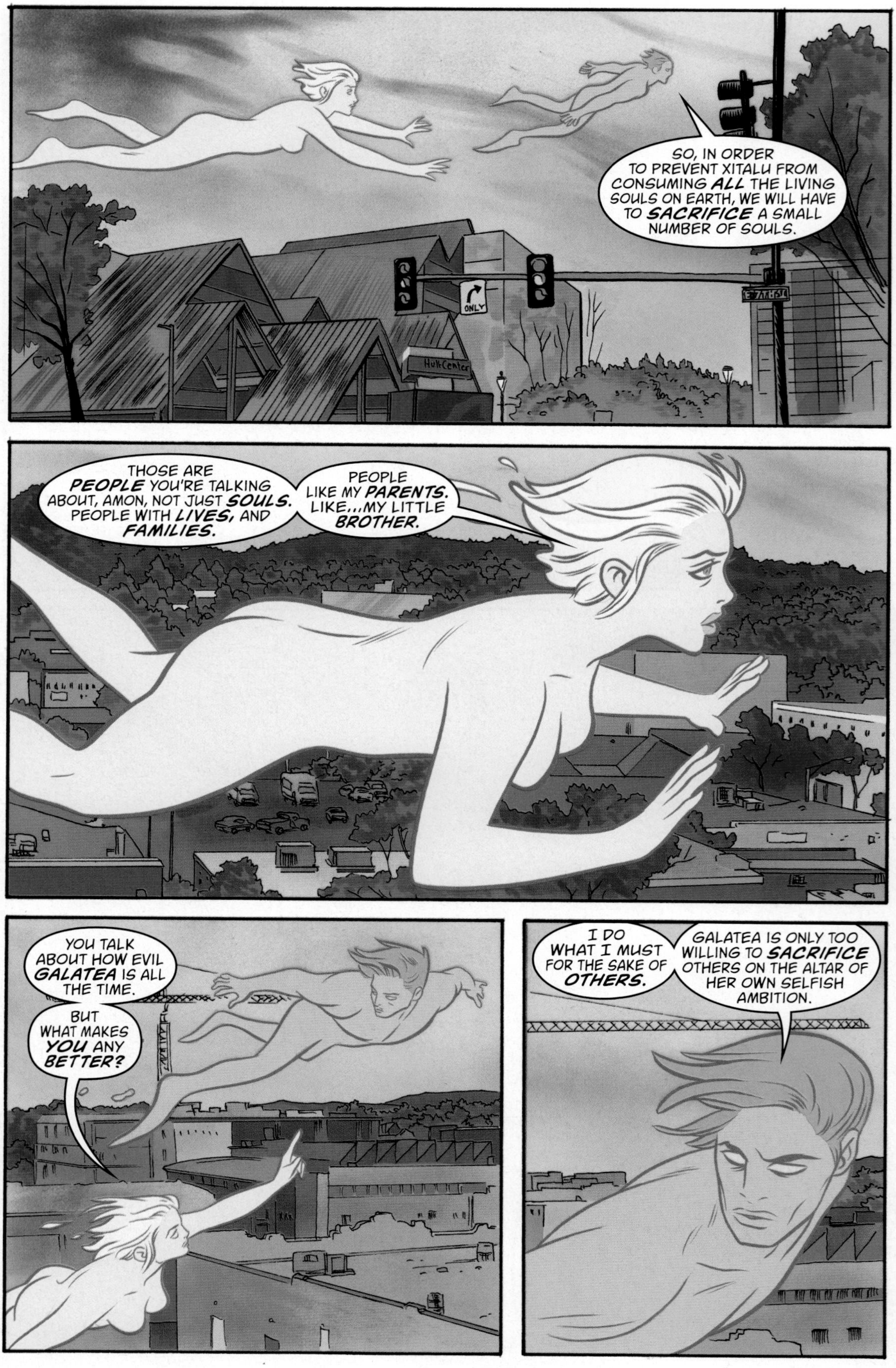
SO, IN ORDER TO PREVENT XITALU FROM CONSUMING ALL THE LIVING SOULS ON EARTH, WE WILL HAVE TO SACRIFICE A SMALL NUMBER OF SOULS.
ONLY
Hult Center
THOSE ARE PEOPLE YOU'RE TALKING ABOUT, AMON, NOT JUST SOULS. PEOPLE WITH LIVES, AND FAMILIES.
PEOPLE LIKE MY PARENTS. LIKE...MY LITTLE BROTHER.
YOU TALK ABOUT HOW EVIL GALATEA IS ALL THE TIME.
BUT WHAT MAKES YOU ANY BETTER?
I DO WHAT I MUST FOR THE SAKE OF OTHERS.
GALATEA IS ONLY TOO WILLING TO SACRIFICE OTHERS ON THE ALTAR OF HER OWN SELFISH AMBITION.

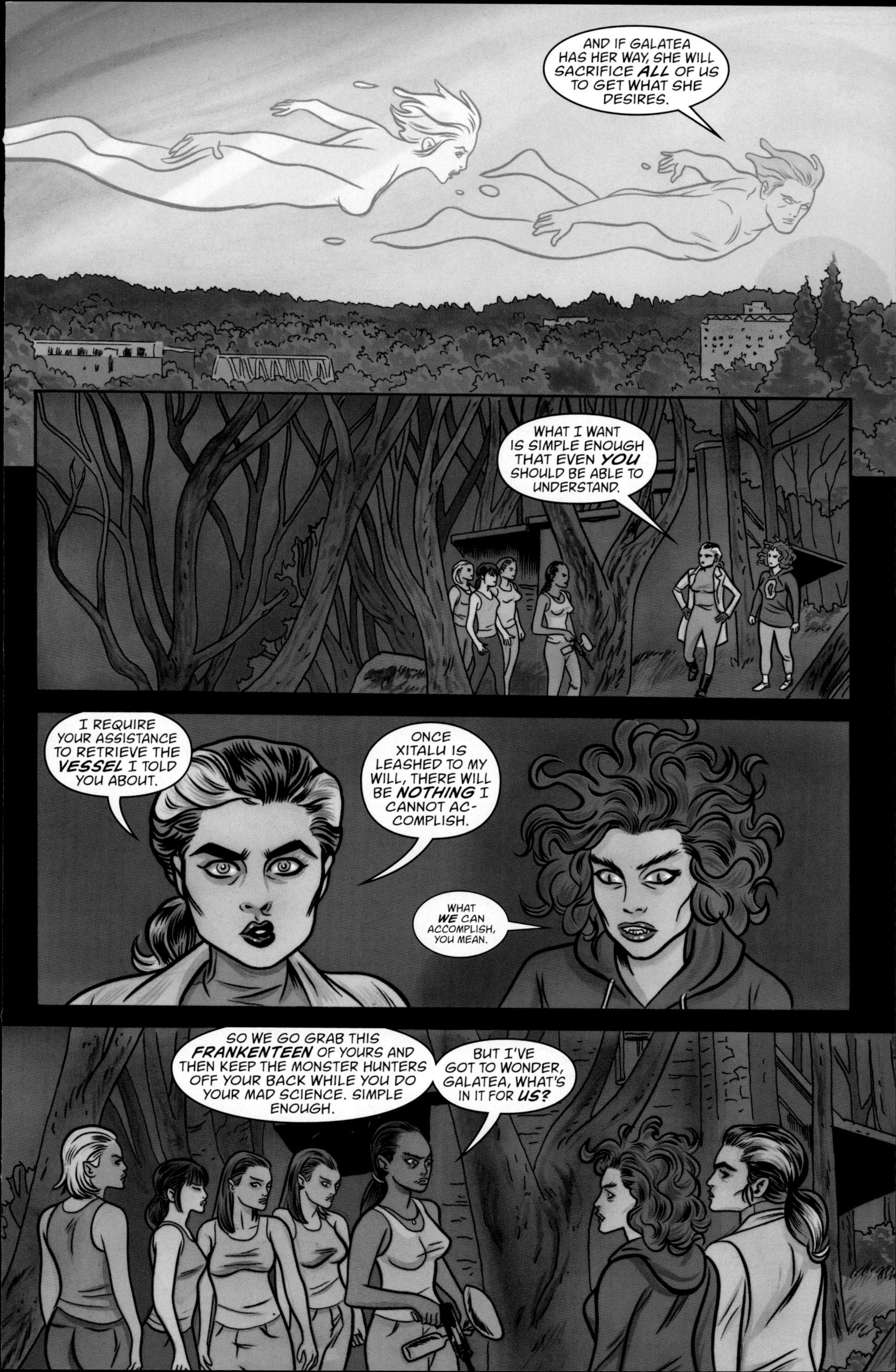
AND IF GALATEA HAS HER WAY, SHE WILL SACRIFICE ALL OF US TO GET WHAT SHE DESIRES.
WHAT I WANT IS SIMPLE ENOUGH THAT EVEN YOU SHOULD BE ABLE TO UNDERSTAND.
I REQUIRE YOUR ASSISTANCE TO RETRIEVE THE VESSEL I TOLD YOU ABOUT.
ONCE XITALU IS LEASHED TO MY WILL, THERE WILL BE NOTHING I CANNOT ACCOMPLISH.
WHAT WE CAN ACCOMPLISH, YOU MEAN.
SO WE GO GRAB THIS FRANKENTEEN OF YOURS AND THEN KEEP THE MONSTER HUNTERS OFF YOUR BACK WHILE YOU DO YOUR MAD SCIENCE. SIMPLE ENOUGH.
BUT I'VE GOT TO WONDER, GALATEA, WHAT'S IN IT FOR US?

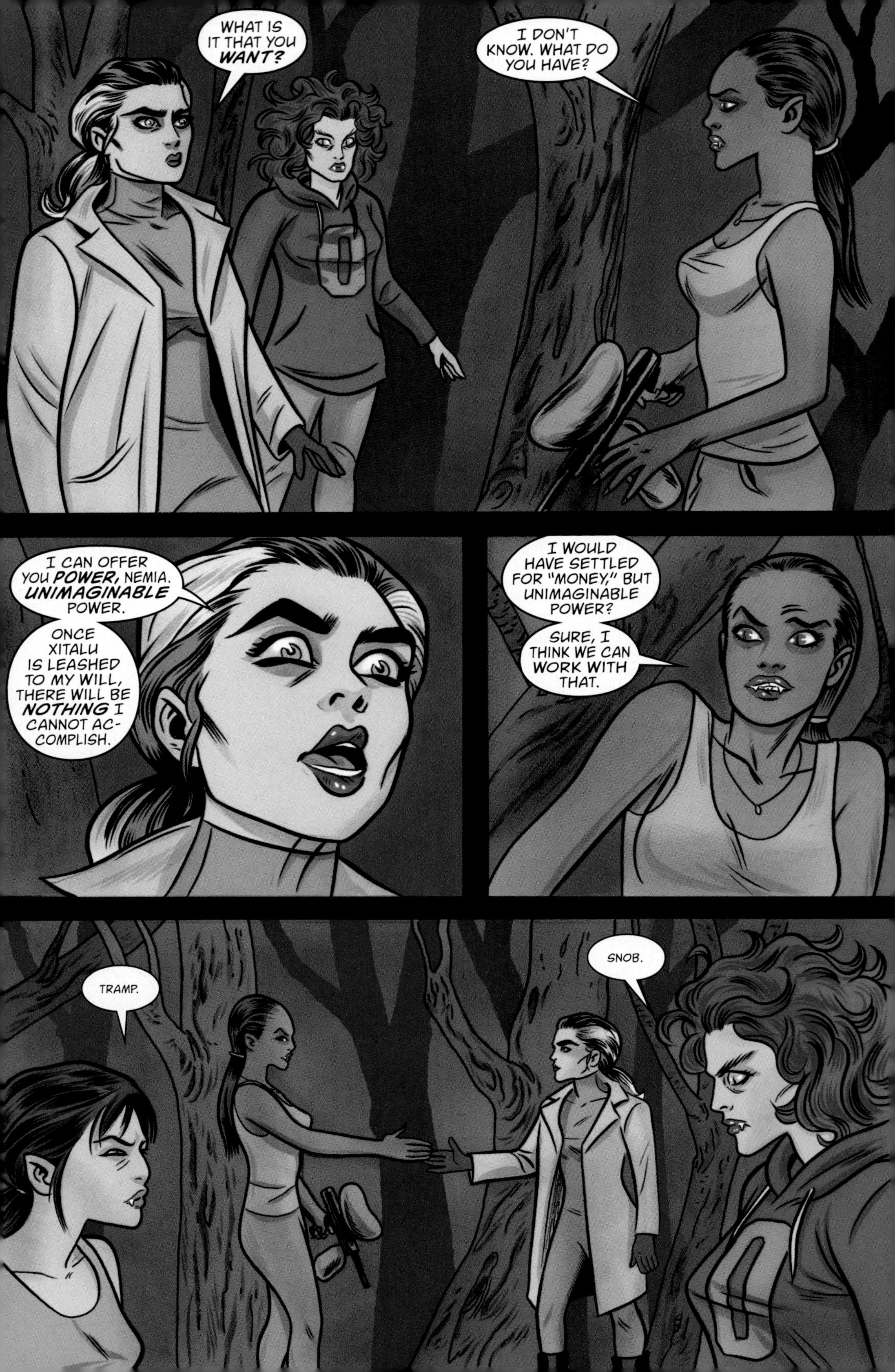
WHAT IS IT THAT YOU WANT?
I DON'T KNOW. WHAT DO YOU HAVE?
I CAN OFFER YOU POWER, NEMIA. UNIMAGINABLE POWER.
ONCE XITALU IS LEASHED TO MY WILL, THERE WILL BE NOTHING I CANNOT AC-COMPLISH.
I WOULD HAVE SETTLED FOR "MONEY," BUT UNIMAGINABLE POWER?
SURE, I THINK WE CAN WORK WITH THAT.
TRAMP.
SNOB.

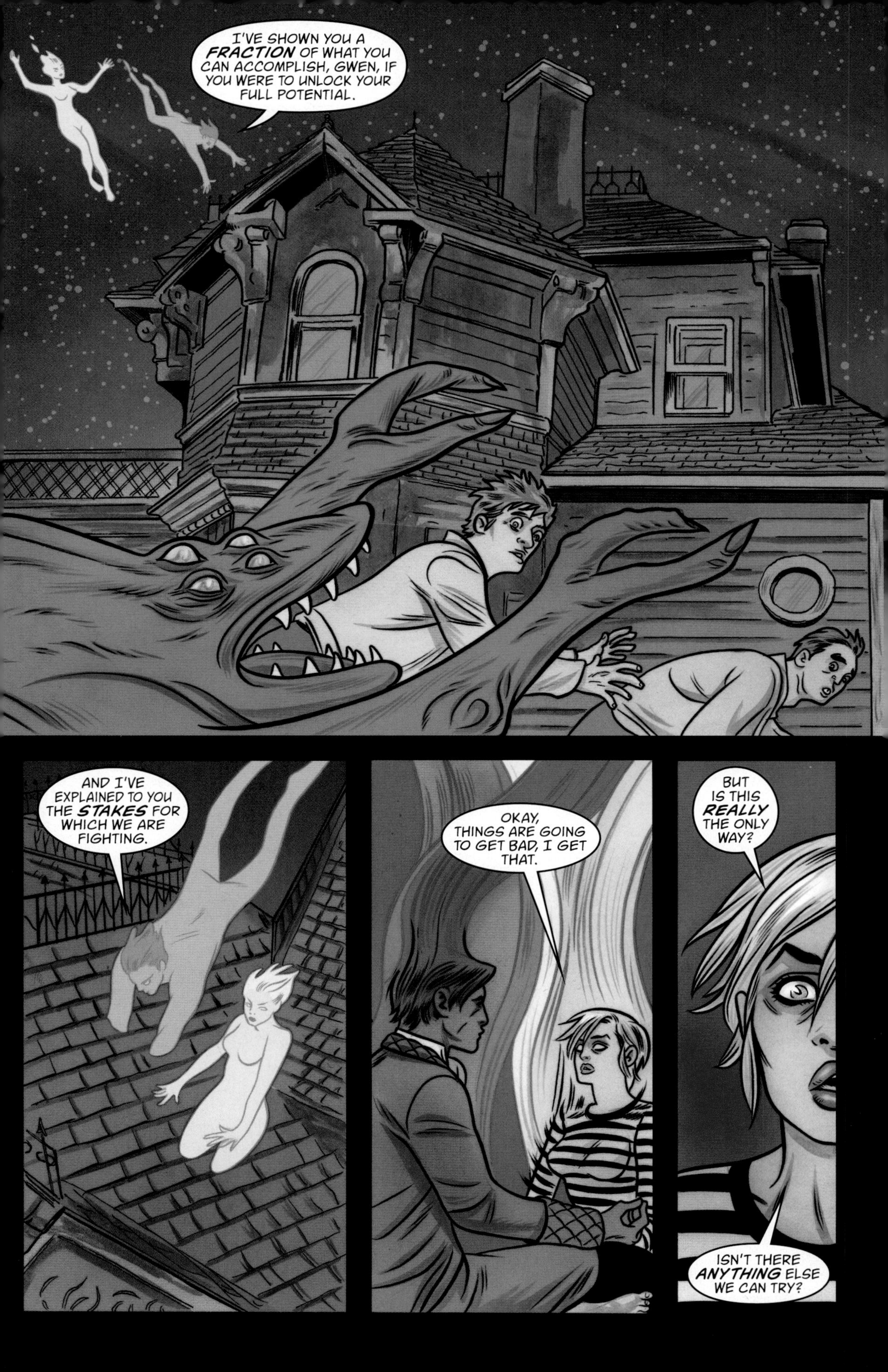
I'VE SHOWN YOU A FRACTION OF WHAT YOU CAN ACCOMPLISH, GWEN, IF YOU WERE TO UNLOCK YOUR FULL POTENTIAL.
AND I'VE EXPLAINED TO YOU THE STAKES FOR WHICH WE ARE FIGHTING.
OKAY, THINGS ARE GOING TO GET BAD, I GET THAT.
BUT IS THIS REALLY THE ONLY WAY?
ISN'T THERE ANYTHING ELSE WE CAN TRY?

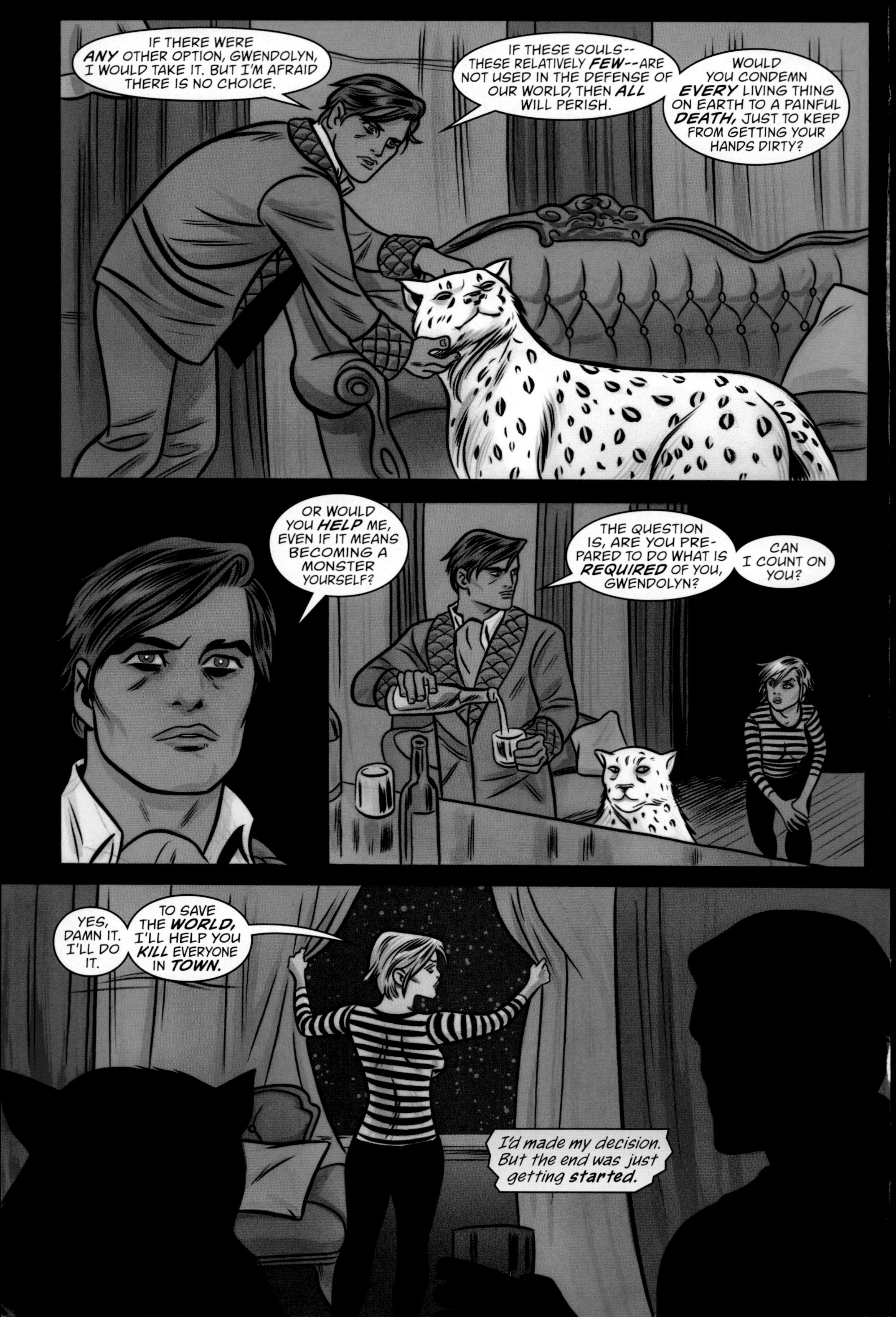
IF THERE WERE ANY OTHER OPTION, GWENDOLYN, I WOULD TAKE IT. BUT I'M AFRAID THERE IS NO CHOICE.
IF THESE SOULS-- THESE RELATIVELY FEW--ARE NOT USED IN THE DEFENSE OF OUR WORLD, THEN ALL WILL PERISH.
WOULD YOU CONDEMN EVERY LIVING THING ON EARTH TO A PAINFUL DEATH, JUST TO KEEP FROM GETTING YOUR HANDS DIRTY?
OR WOULD YOU HELP ME, EVEN IF IT MEANS BECOMING A MONSTER YOURSELF?
THE QUESTION IS, ARE YOU PRE-PARED TO DO WHAT IS REQUIRED OF YOU, GWENDOLYN?
CAN I COUNT ON YOU?
YES, DAMN IT. I'LL DO IT.
TO SAVE THE WORLD, I'LL HELP YOU KILL EVERYONE IN TOWN.
I'd made my decision. But the end was just getting started.

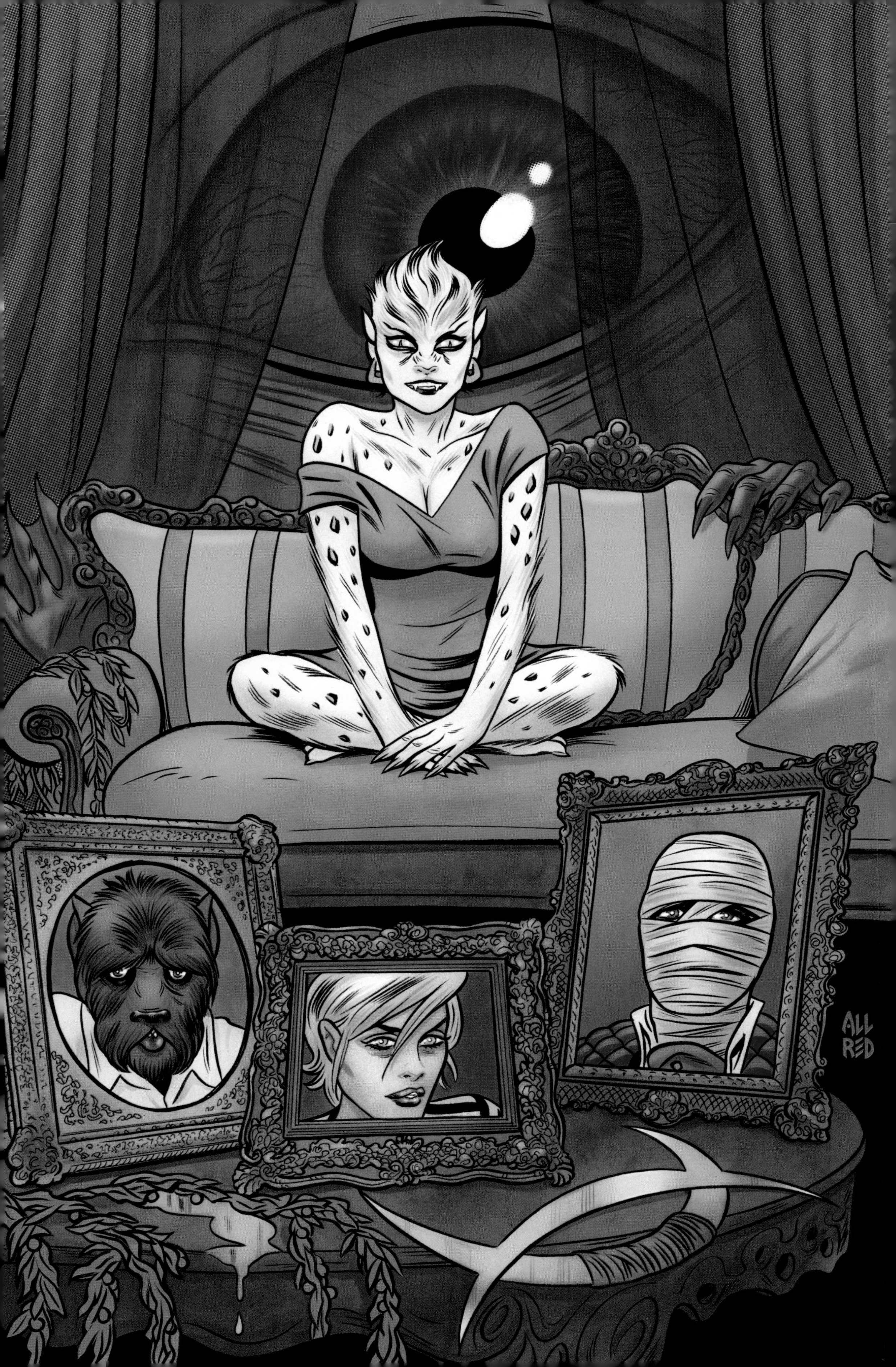
ALL
RED

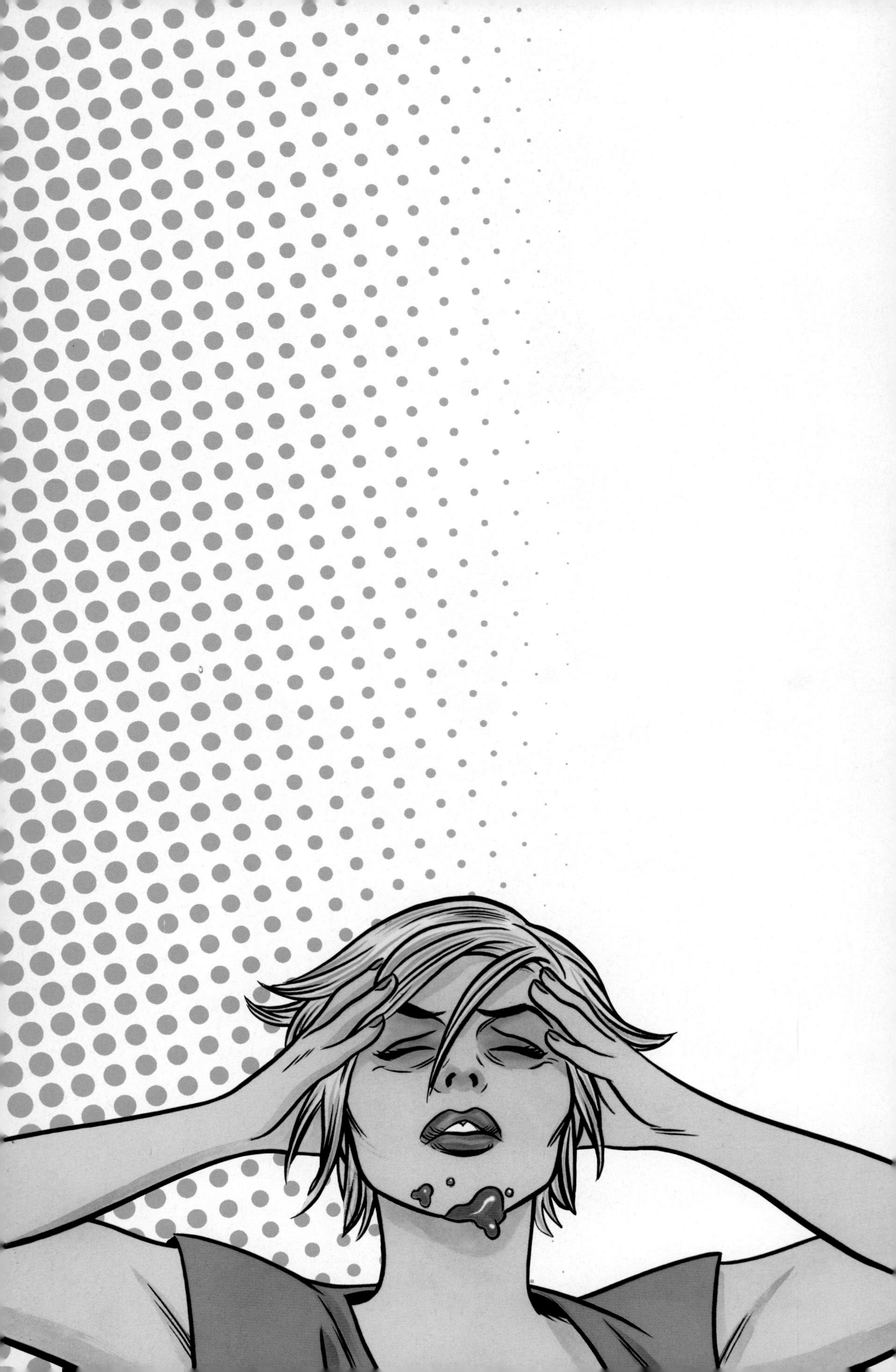

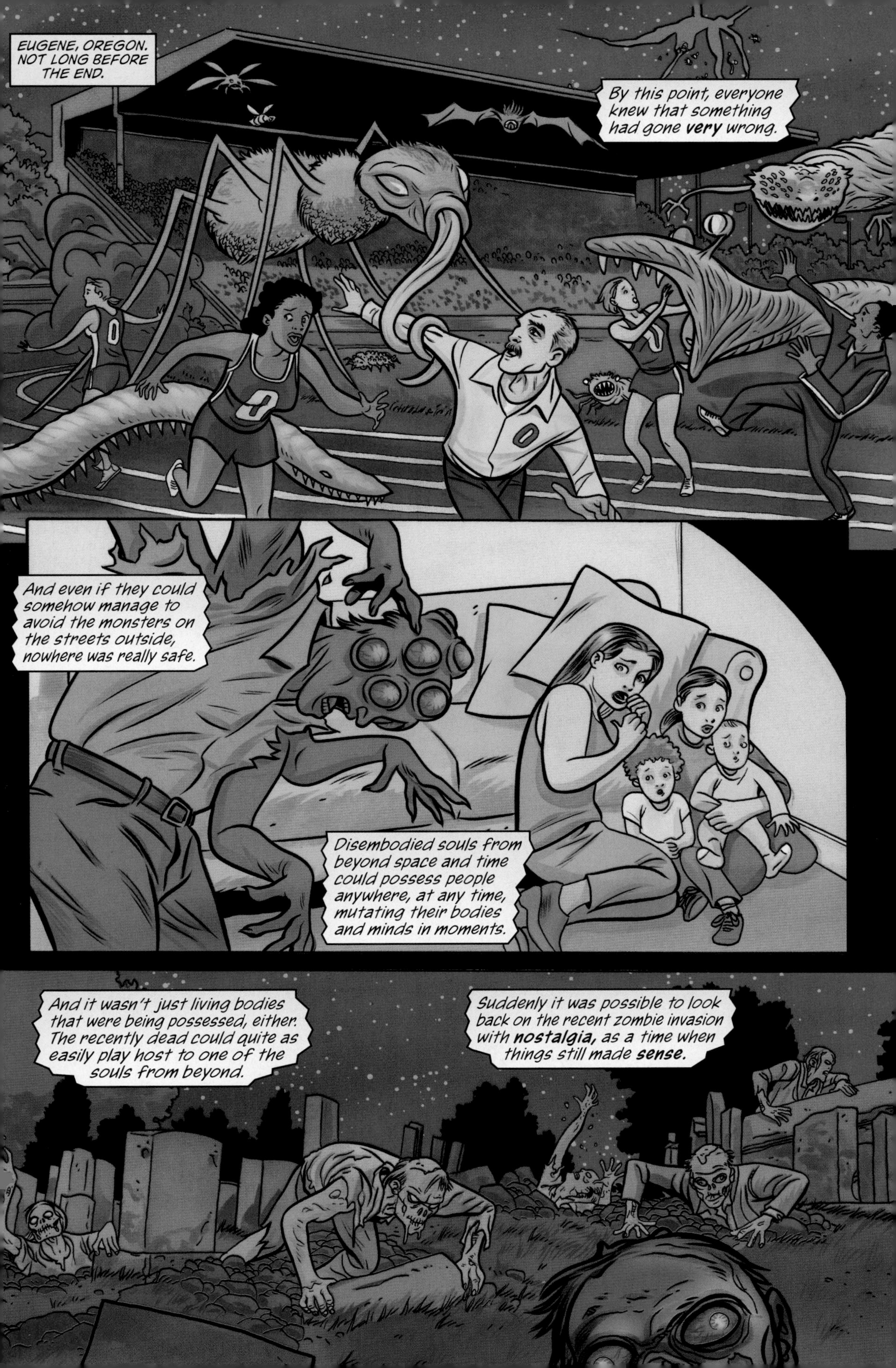
EUGENE, OREGON. NOT LONG BEFORE THE END.
By this point, everyone knew that something had gone **very** wrong.
And even if they could somehow manage to avoid the monsters on the streets outside, nowhere was really safe.
Disembodied souls from beyond space and time could possess people anywhere, at any time, mutating their bodies and minds in moments.
And it wasn't just living bodies that were being possessed, either. The recently dead could quite as easily play host to one of the souls from beyond.
Suddenly it was possible to look back on the recent zombie invasion with **nostalgia**, as a time when things still made **sense**.

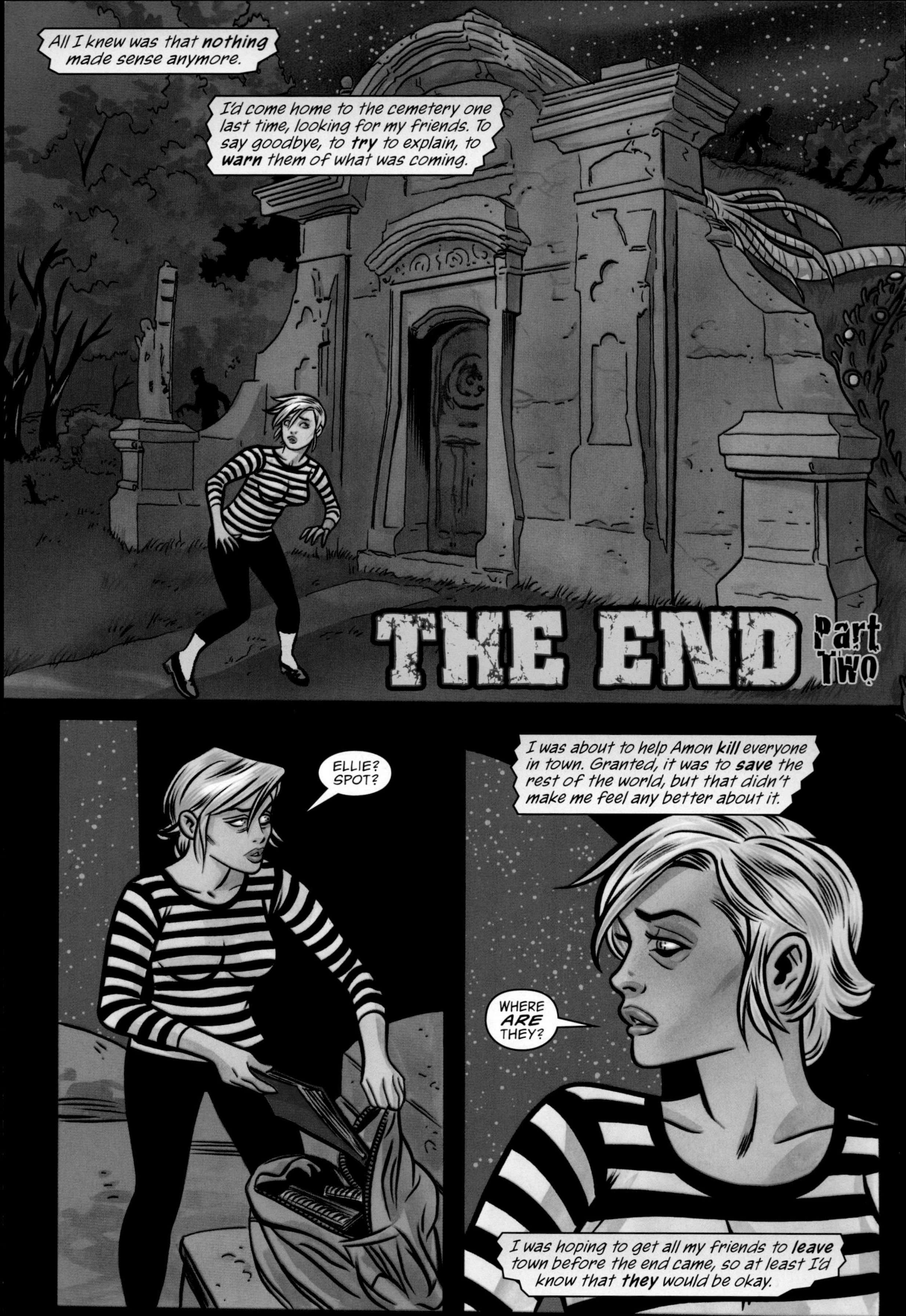
All I knew was that nothing made sense anymore.
I'd come home to the cemetery one last time, looking for my friends. To say goodbye, to try to explain, to warn them of what was coming.
THE END Part TWO
ELLIE? SPOT?
I was about to help Amon kill everyone in town. Granted, it was to save the rest of the world, but that didn't make me feel any better about it.
WHERE ARE THEY?
I was hoping to get all my friends to leave town before the end came, so at least I'd know that they would be okay.

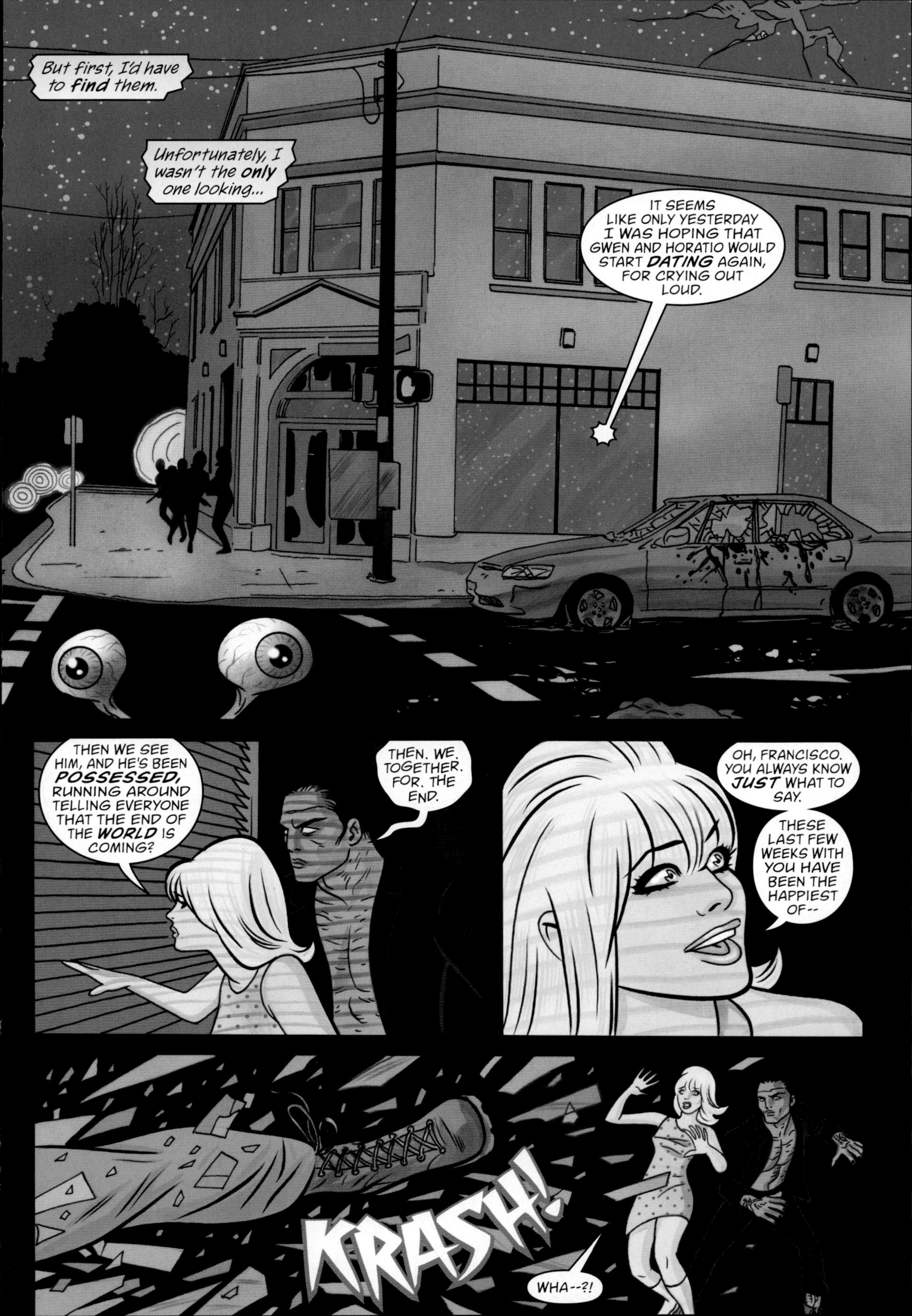
But first, I'd have to **find** them.
Unfortunately, I wasn't the **only** one looking...
IT SEEMS LIKE ONLY YESTERDAY I WAS HOPING THAT GWEN AND HORATIO WOULD START **DATING** AGAIN, FOR CRYING OUT LOUD.
THEN WE SEE HIM, AND HE'S BEEN **POSSESSED,** RUNNING AROUND TELLING EVERYONE THAT THE END OF THE **WORLD** IS COMING?
THEN. WE. TOGETHER. FOR. THE END.
OH, FRANCISCO. YOU ALWAYS KNOW **JUST** WHAT TO SAY.
THESE LAST FEW WEEKS WITH YOU HAVE BEEN THE HAPPIEST OF--
KRASH!
WHA--?!

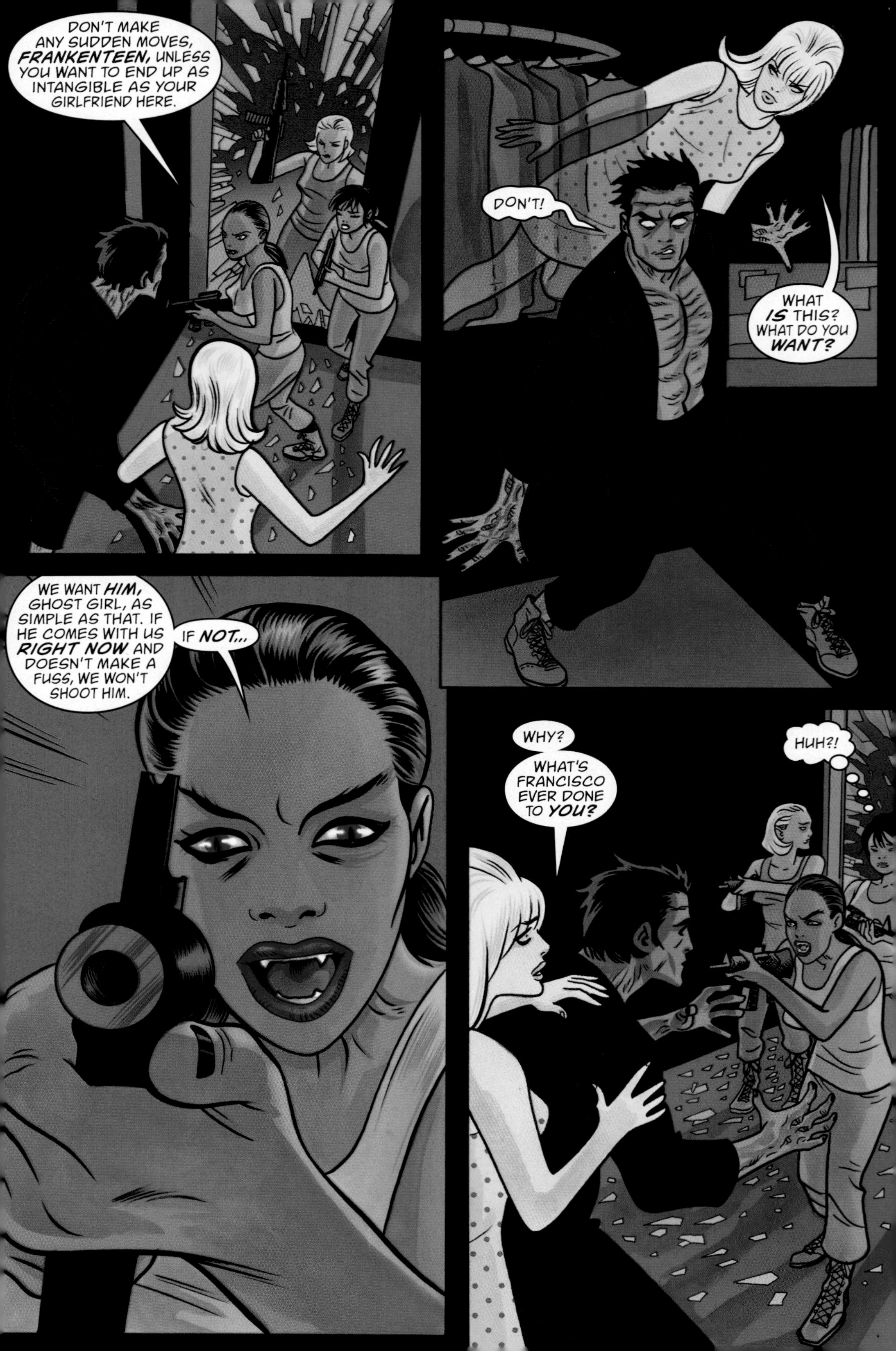
DON'T MAKE ANY SUDDEN MOVES, FRANKENTEEN, UNLESS YOU WANT TO END UP AS INTANGIBLE AS YOUR GIRLFRIEND HERE.
DON'T!
WHAT IS THIS? WHAT DO YOU WANT?
WE WANT HIM, GHOST GIRL, AS SIMPLE AS THAT. IF HE COMES WITH US RIGHT NOW AND DOESN'T MAKE A FUSS, WE WON'T SHOOT HIM.
IF NOT...
WHY?
WHAT'S FRANCISCO EVER DONE TO YOU?
HUH?!

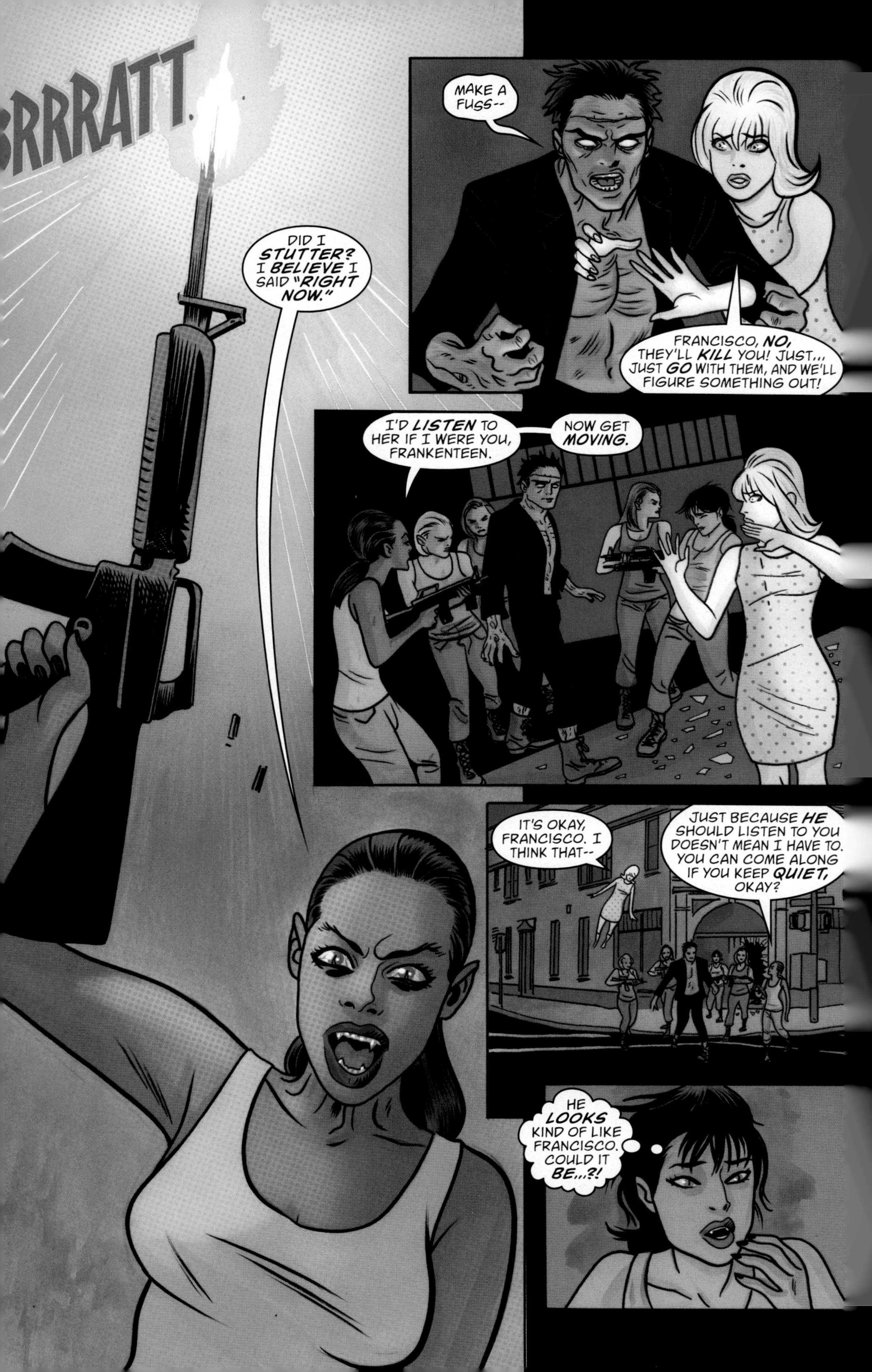

SRRRATT
DID I STUTTER? I BELIEVE I SAID "RIGHT NOW."
MAKE A FUSS--
FRANCISCO, NO, THEY'LL KILL YOU! JUST... JUST GO WITH THEM, AND WE'LL FIGURE SOMETHING OUT!
I'D LISTEN TO HER IF I WERE YOU, FRANKENTEEN.
NOW GET MOVING.
IT'S OKAY, FRANCISCO. I THINK THAT--
JUST BECAUSE HE SHOULD LISTEN TO YOU DOESN'T MEAN I HAVE TO. YOU CAN COME ALONG IF YOU KEEP QUIET, OKAY?
HE LOOKS KIND OF LIKE FRANCISCO. COULD IT BE...?!

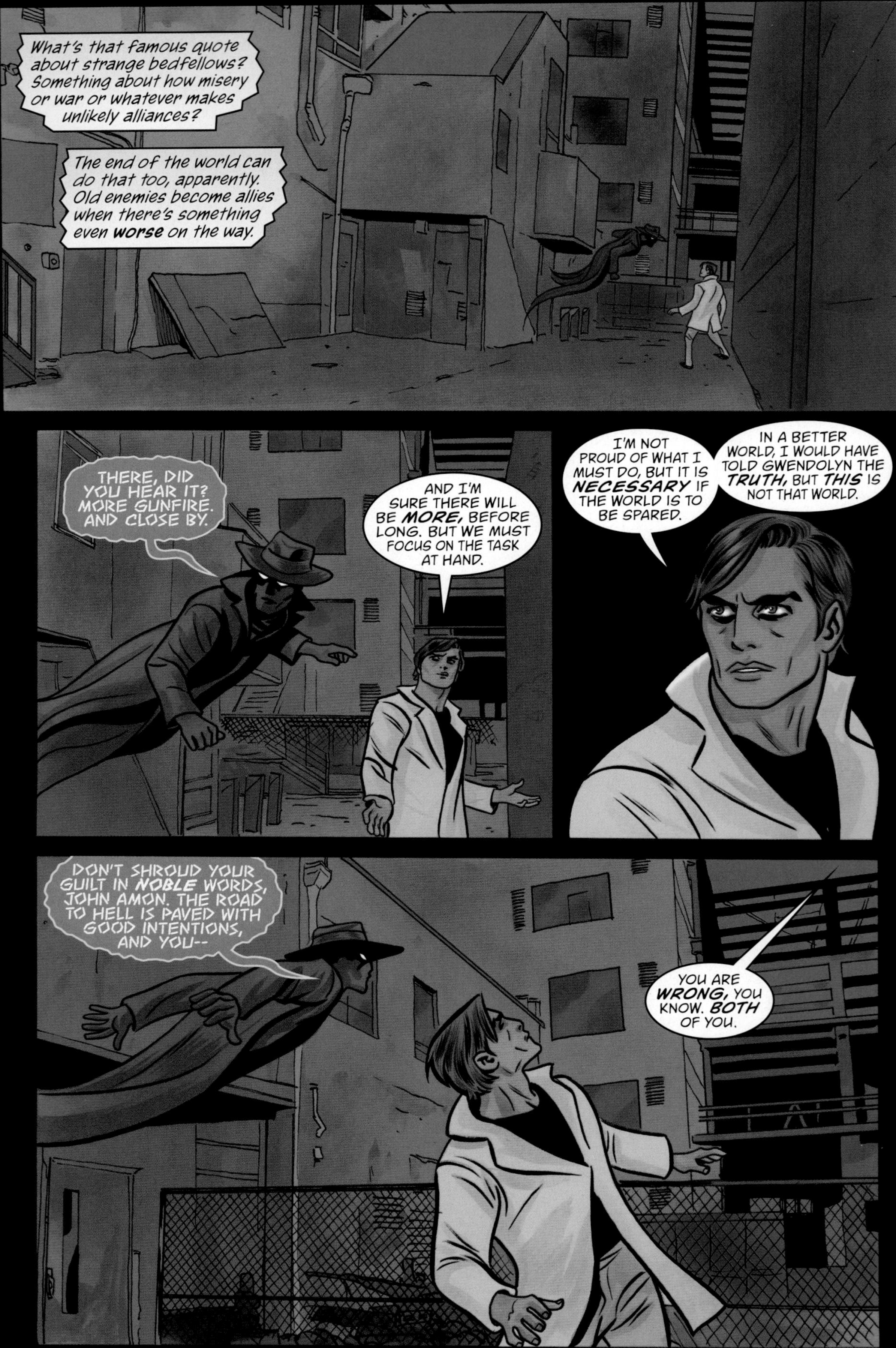
What's that famous quote about strange bedfellows? Something about how misery or war or whatever makes unlikely alliances?
The end of the world can do that too, apparently. Old enemies become allies when there's something even **worse** on the way.
THERE, DID YOU HEAR IT? MORE GUNFIRE. AND CLOSE BY.
AND I'M SURE THERE WILL BE **MORE,** BEFORE LONG. BUT WE MUST FOCUS ON THE TASK AT HAND.
I'M NOT PROUD OF WHAT I MUST DO, BUT IT IS **NECESSARY** IF THE WORLD IS TO BE SPARED.
IN A BETTER WORLD, I WOULD HAVE TOLD GWENDOLYN THE **TRUTH,** BUT **THIS** IS NOT THAT WORLD.
DON'T SHROUD YOUR GUILT IN **NOBLE** WORDS, JOHN AMON. THE ROAD TO HELL IS PAVED WITH GOOD INTENTIONS, AND YOU--
YOU ARE **WRONG,** YOU KNOW. **BOTH** OF YOU.

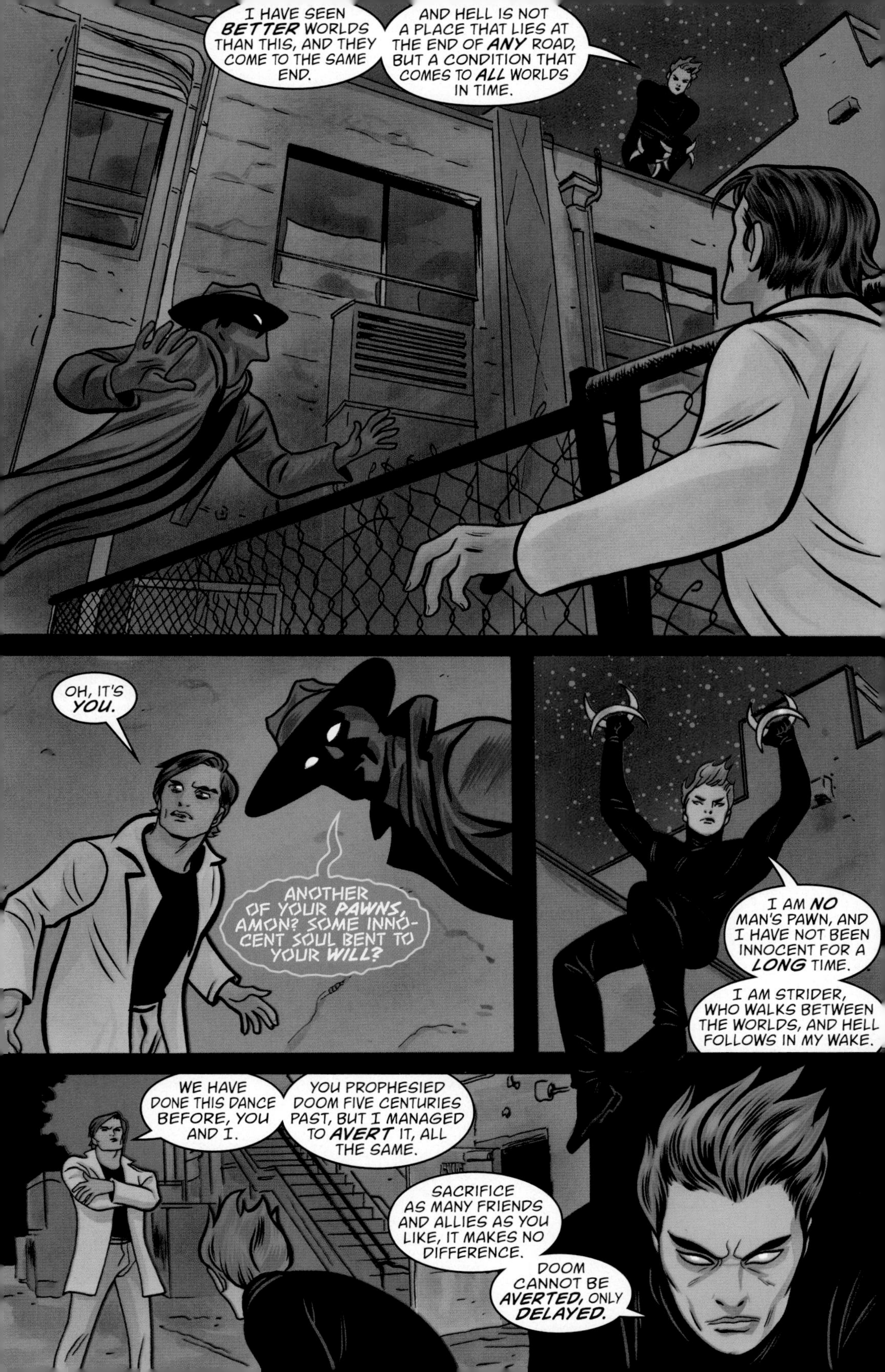
I HAVE SEEN BETTER WORLDS THAN THIS, AND THEY COME TO THE SAME END.
AND HELL IS NOT A PLACE THAT LIES AT THE END OF ANY ROAD, BUT A CONDITION THAT COMES TO ALL WORLDS IN TIME.
OH, IT'S YOU.
ANOTHER OF YOUR PAWNS, AMON? SOME INNO-CENT SOUL BENT TO YOUR WILL?
I AM NO MAN'S PAWN, AND I HAVE NOT BEEN INNOCENT FOR A LONG TIME.
I AM STRIDER, WHO WALKS BETWEEN THE WORLDS, AND HELL FOLLOWS IN MY WAKE.
WE HAVE DONE THIS DANCE BEFORE, YOU AND I.
YOU PROPHESIED DOOM FIVE CENTURIES PAST, BUT I MANAGED TO AVERT IT, ALL THE SAME.
SACRIFICE AS MANY FRIENDS AND ALLIES AS YOU LIKE, IT MAKES NO DIFFERENCE.
DOOM CANNOT BE AVERTED, ONLY DELAYED.

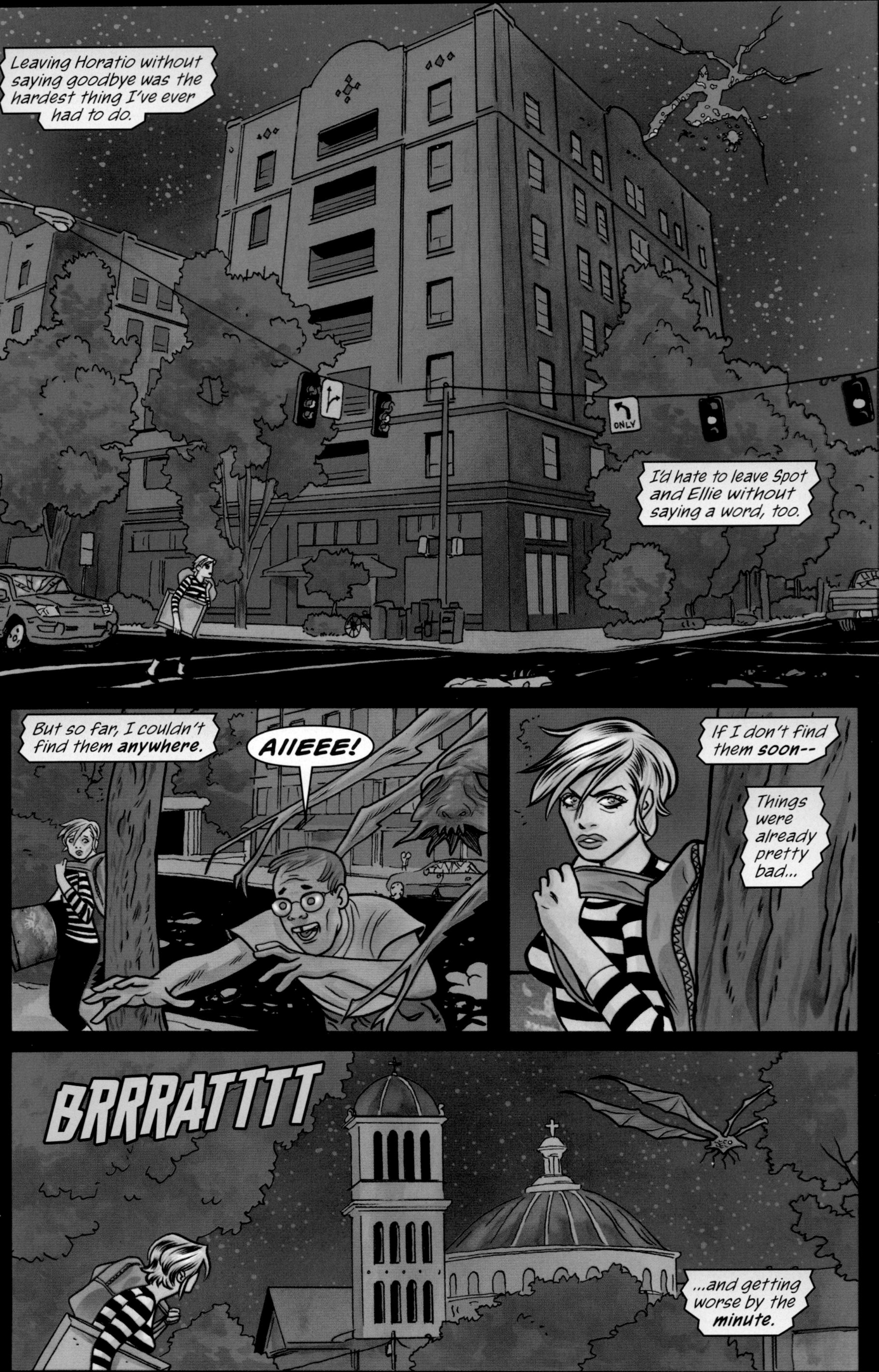

Leaving Horatio without saying goodbye was the hardest thing I've ever had to do.
ONLY
I'd hate to leave Spot and Ellie without saying a word, too.
But so far, I couldn't find them **anywhere**.
AIIEEE!
If I don't find them **soon--**
Things were already pretty bad...
BRRRATTTT
...and getting worse by the **minute.**

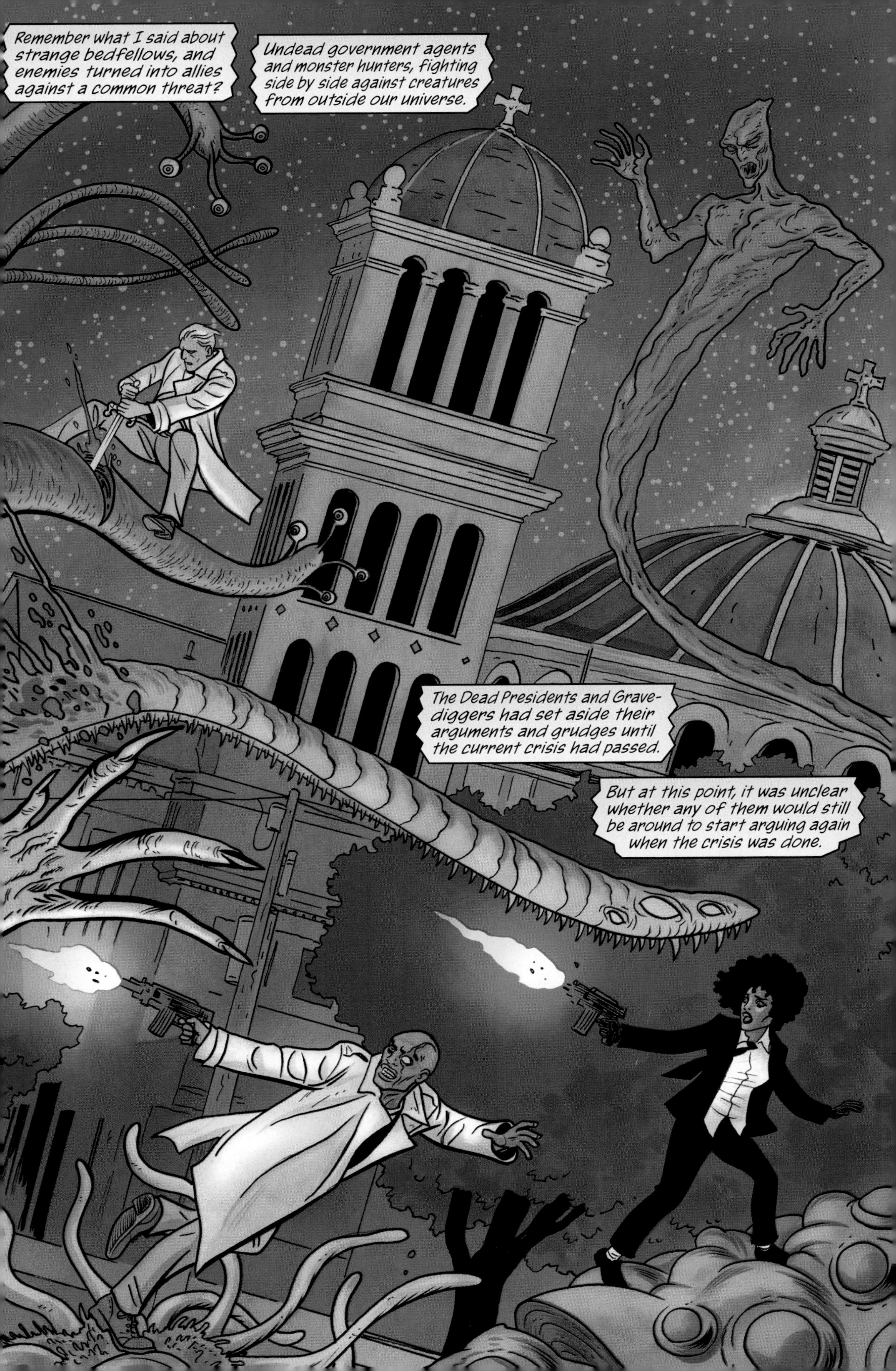
Remember what I said about strange bedfellows, and enemies turned into allies against a common threat?
Undead government agents and monster hunters, fighting side by side against creatures from outside our universe.
The Dead Presidents and Grave-diggers had set aside their arguments and grudges until the current crisis had passed.
But at this point, it was unclear whether any of them would still be around to start arguing again when the crisis was done.

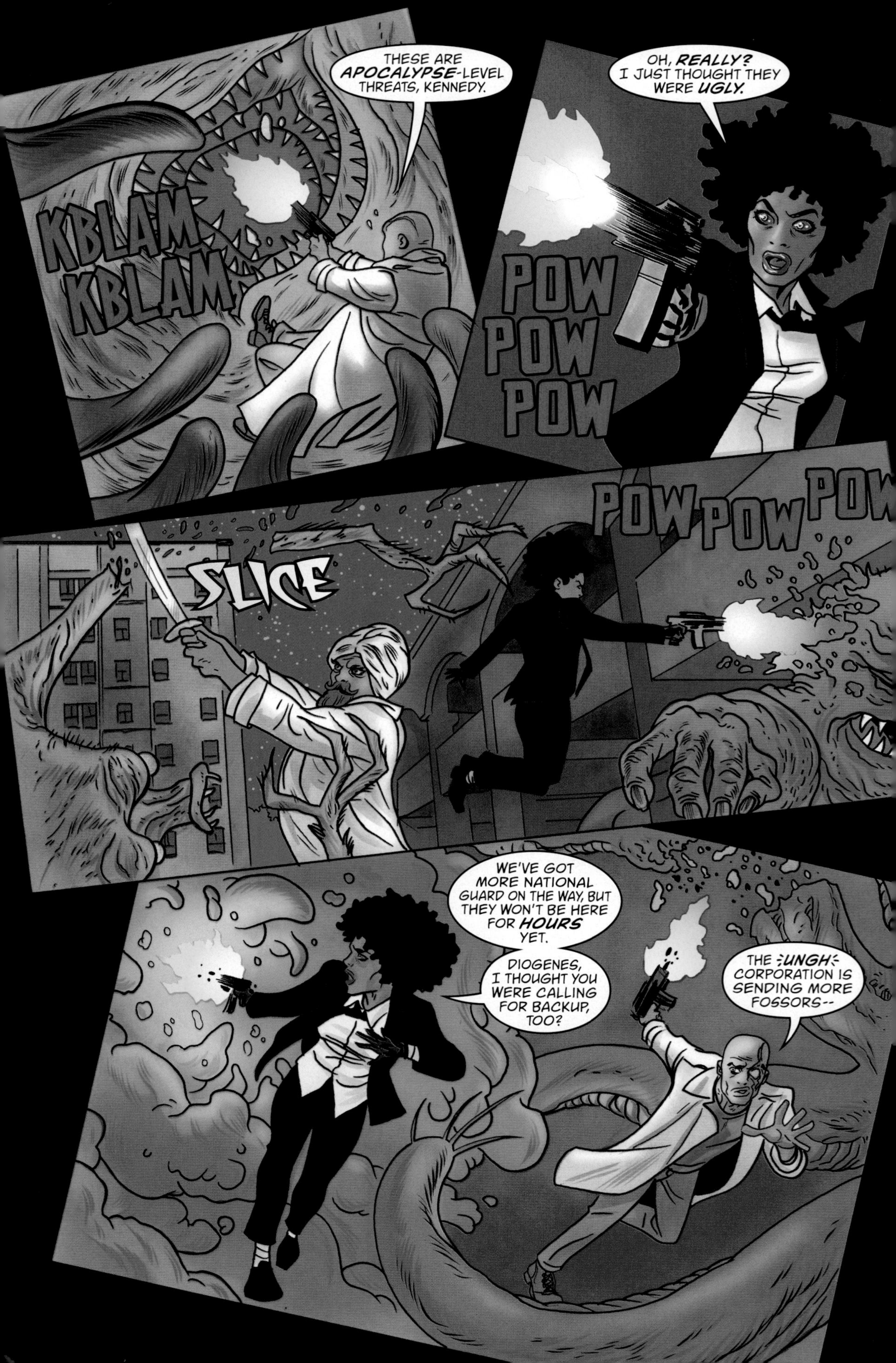
THESE ARE APOCALYPSE-LEVEL THREATS, KENNEDY.
KBLAM KBLAM
OH, REALLY? I JUST THOUGHT THEY WERE UGLY.
POW POW POW
SLICE
POW POW POW
WE'VE GOT MORE NATIONAL GUARD ON THE WAY, BUT THEY WON'T BE HERE FOR HOURS YET.
DIOGENES, I THOUGHT YOU WERE CALLING FOR BACKUP, TOO?
THE UNGH CORPORATION IS SENDING MORE FOSSORS--

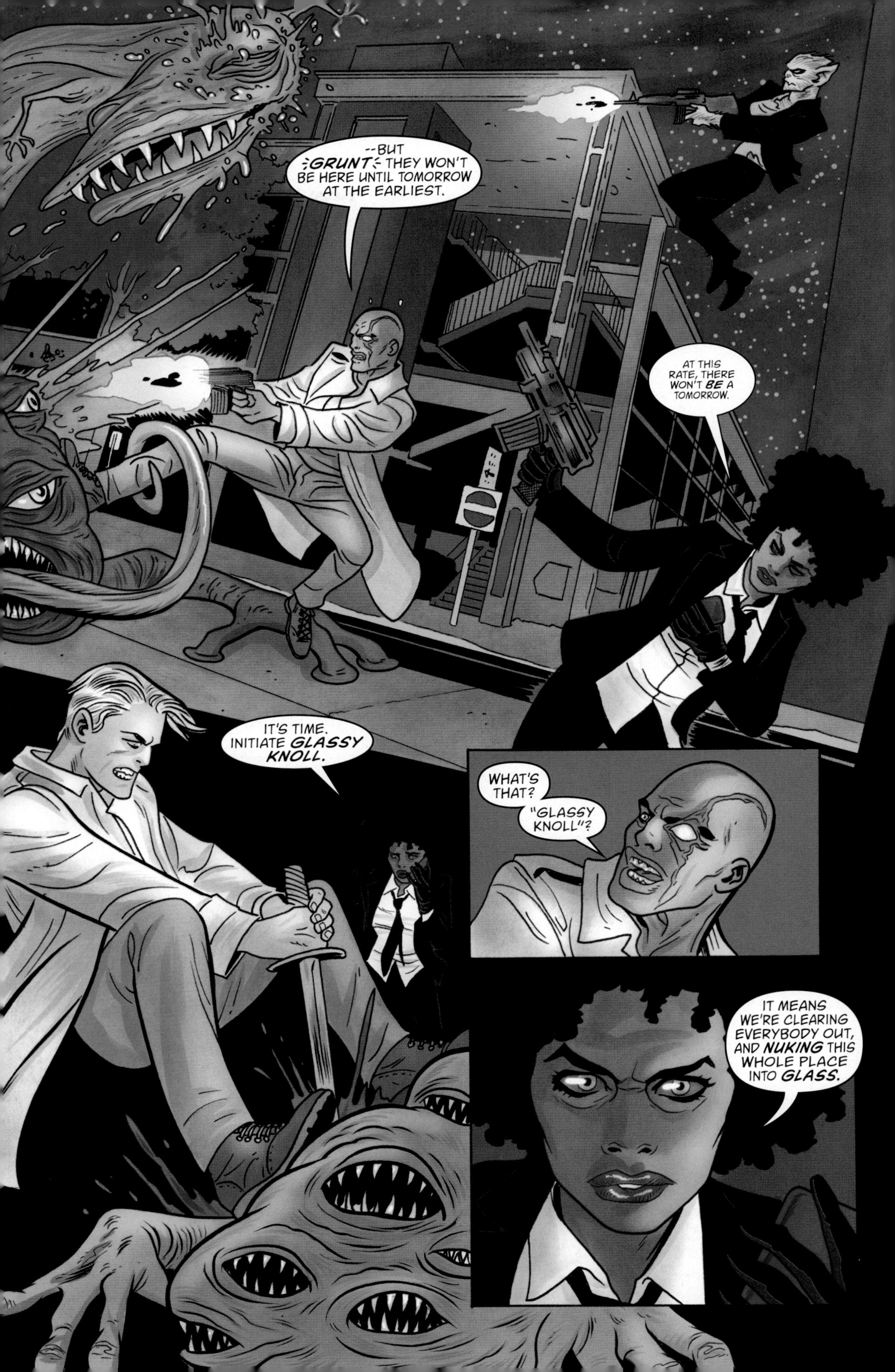
--BUT
GRUNT THEY WON'T BE HERE UNTIL TOMORROW AT THE EARLIEST.
AT THIS RATE, THERE WON'T BE A TOMORROW.
IT'S TIME. INITIATE GLASSY KNOLL.
WHAT'S THAT?
"GLASSY KNOLL"?
IT MEANS WE'RE CLEARING EVERYBODY OUT, AND NUKING THIS WHOLE PLACE INTO GLASS.

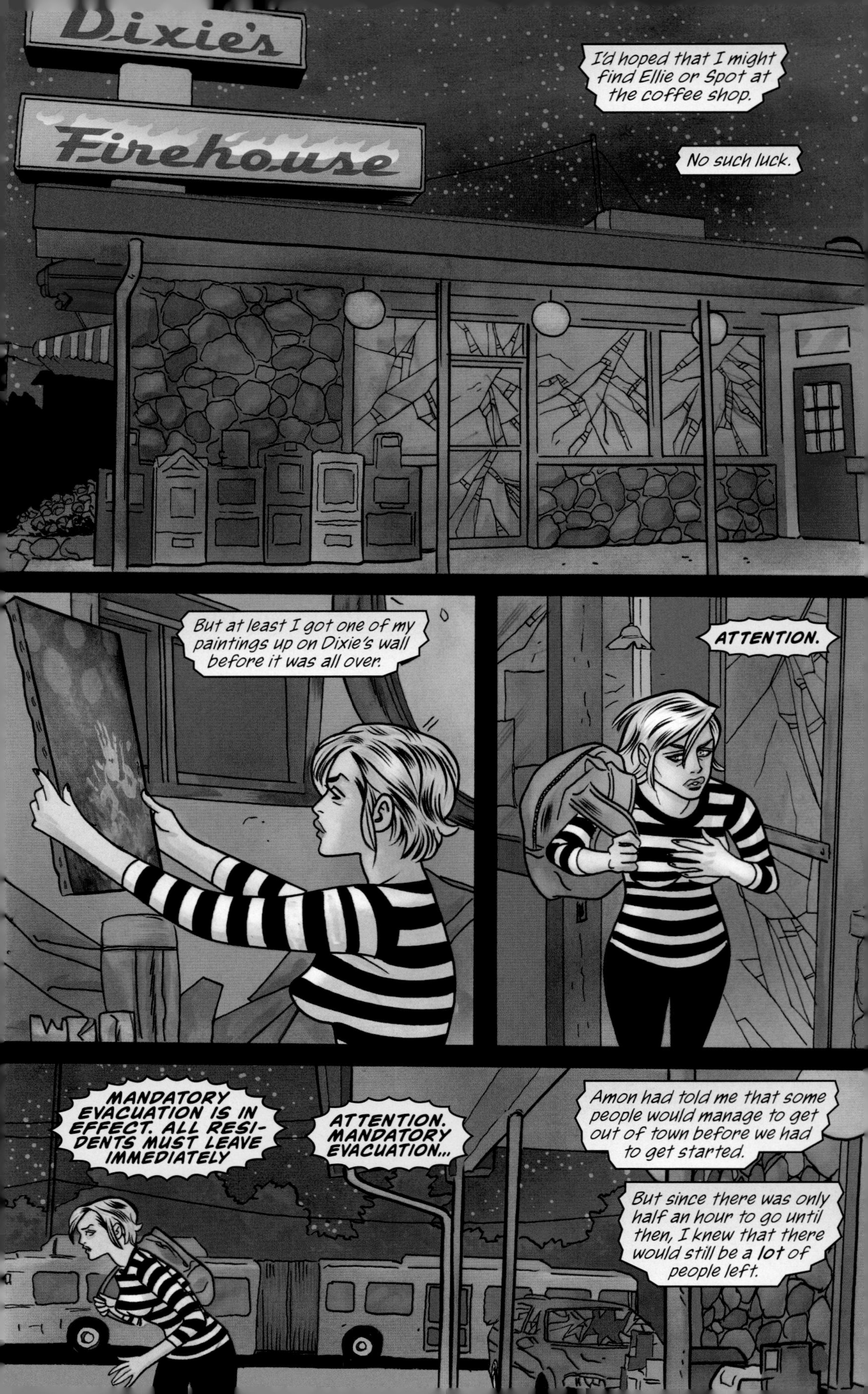
Dixie's
Firehouse
I'd hoped that I might find Ellie or Spot at the coffee shop.
No such luck.
But at least I got one of my paintings up on Dixie's wall before it was all over.
ATTENTION.
MANDATORY EVACUATION IS IN EFFECT. ALL RESIDENTS MUST LEAVE IMMEDIATELY
ATTENTION. MANDATORY EVACUATION...
Amon had told me that some people would manage to get out of town before we had to get started.
But since there was only half an hour to go until then, I knew that there would still be a lot of people left.

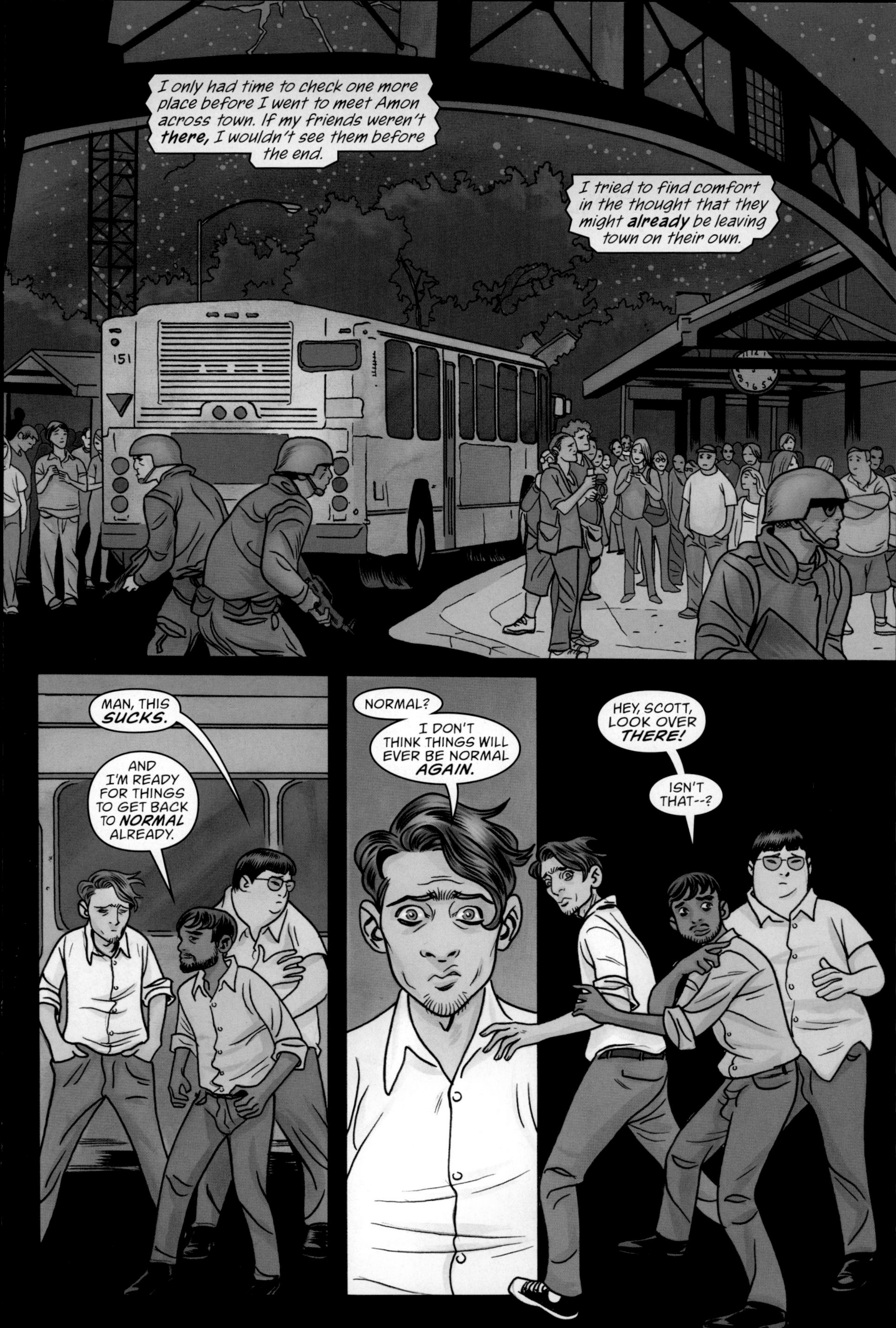
I only had time to check one more place before I went to meet Amon across town. If my friends weren't **there,** I wouldn't see them before the end.
I tried to find comfort in the thought that they might **already** be leaving town on their own.
151
MAN, THIS ***SUCKS.***
AND I'M READY FOR THINGS TO GET BACK TO ***NORMAL*** ALREADY.
NORMAL?
I DON'T THINK THINGS WILL EVER BE NORMAL ***AGAIN.***
HEY, SCOTT, LOOK OVER ***THERE!***
ISN'T THAT--?

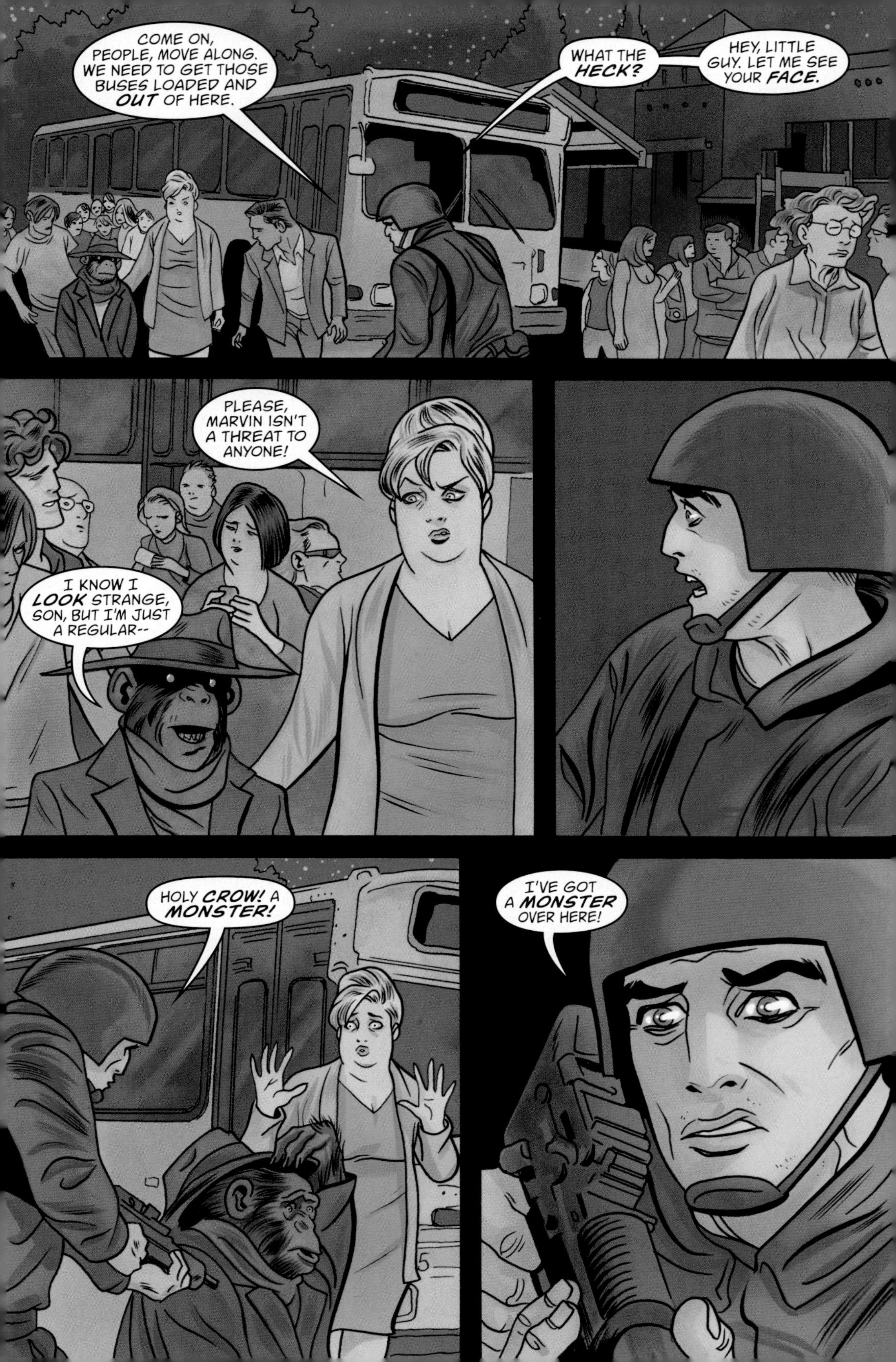
COME ON, PEOPLE, MOVE ALONG. WE NEED TO GET THOSE BUSES LOADED AND OUT OF HERE.
WHAT THE HECK?
HEY, LITTLE GUY. LET ME SEE YOUR FACE.
PLEASE, MARVIN ISN'T A THREAT TO ANYONE!
I KNOW I LOOK STRANGE, SON, BUT I'M JUST A REGULAR--
HOLY CROW! A MONSTER!
I'VE GOT A MONSTER OVER HERE!

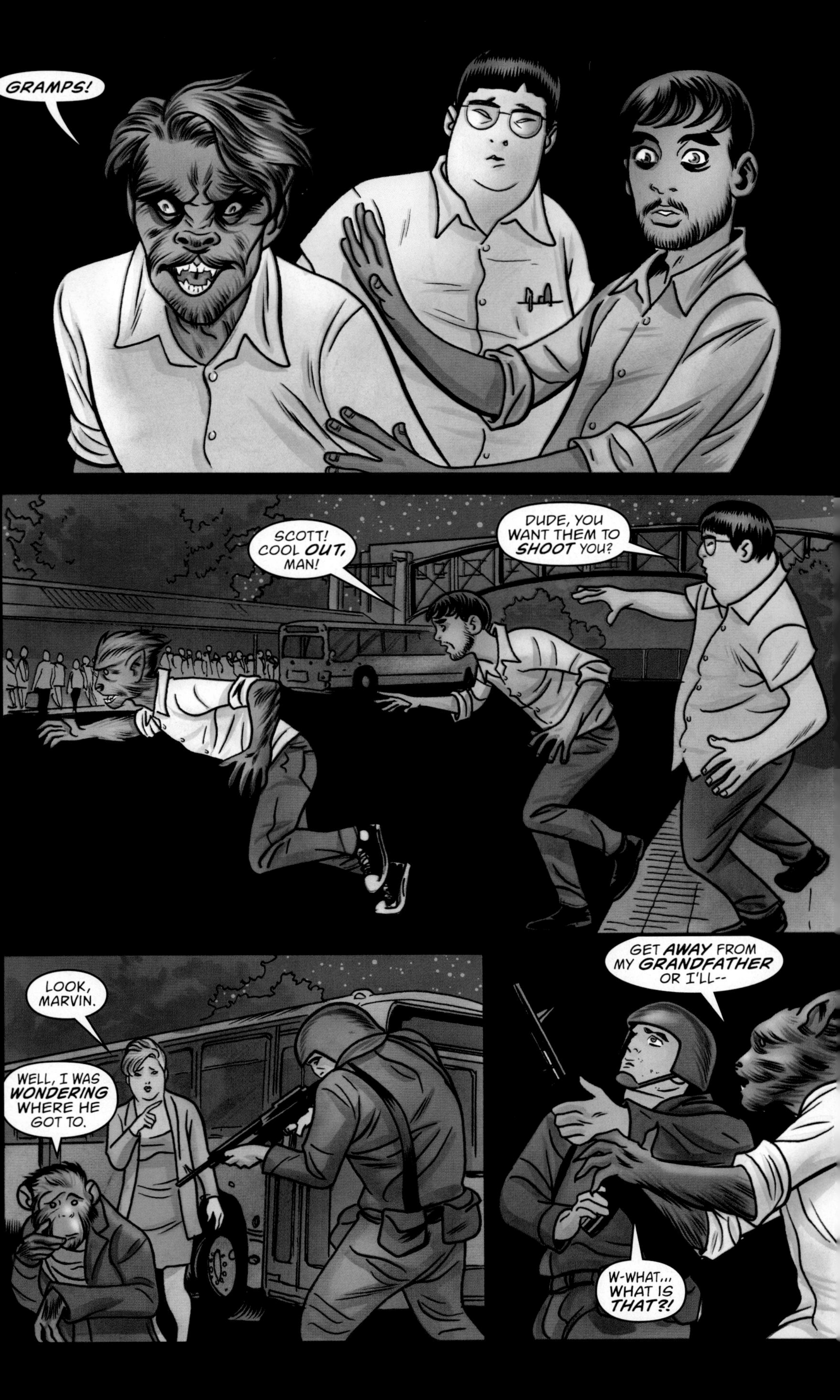
GRAMPS!
SCOTT! COOL OUT, MAN!
DUDE, YOU WANT THEM TO SHOOT YOU?
LOOK, MARVIN.
WELL, I WAS WONDERING WHERE HE GOT TO.
GET AWAY FROM MY GRANDFATHER OR I'LL--
W-WHAT... WHAT IS THAT?!

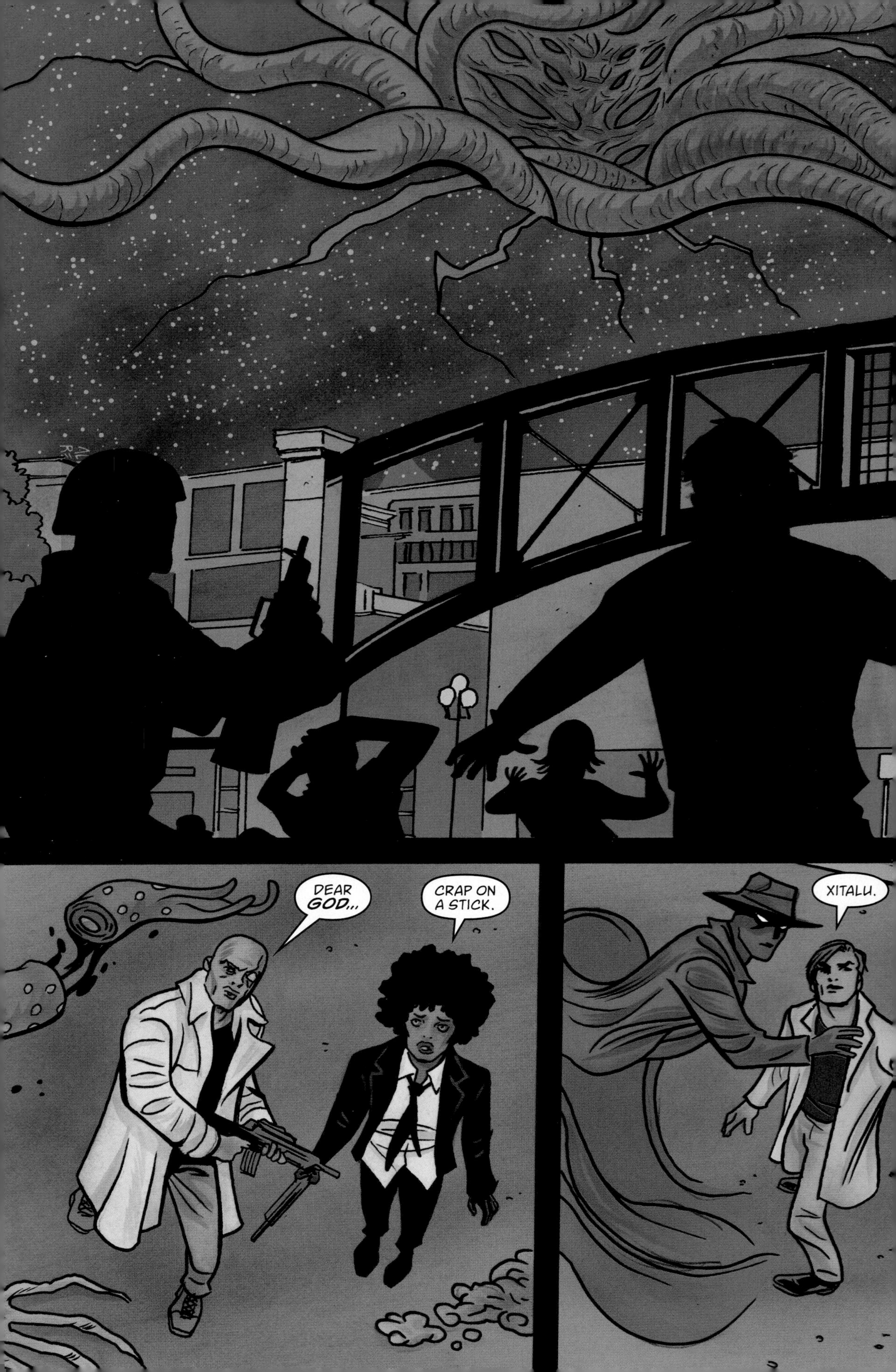
DEAR GOD...
CRAP ON A STICK.
XITALU.

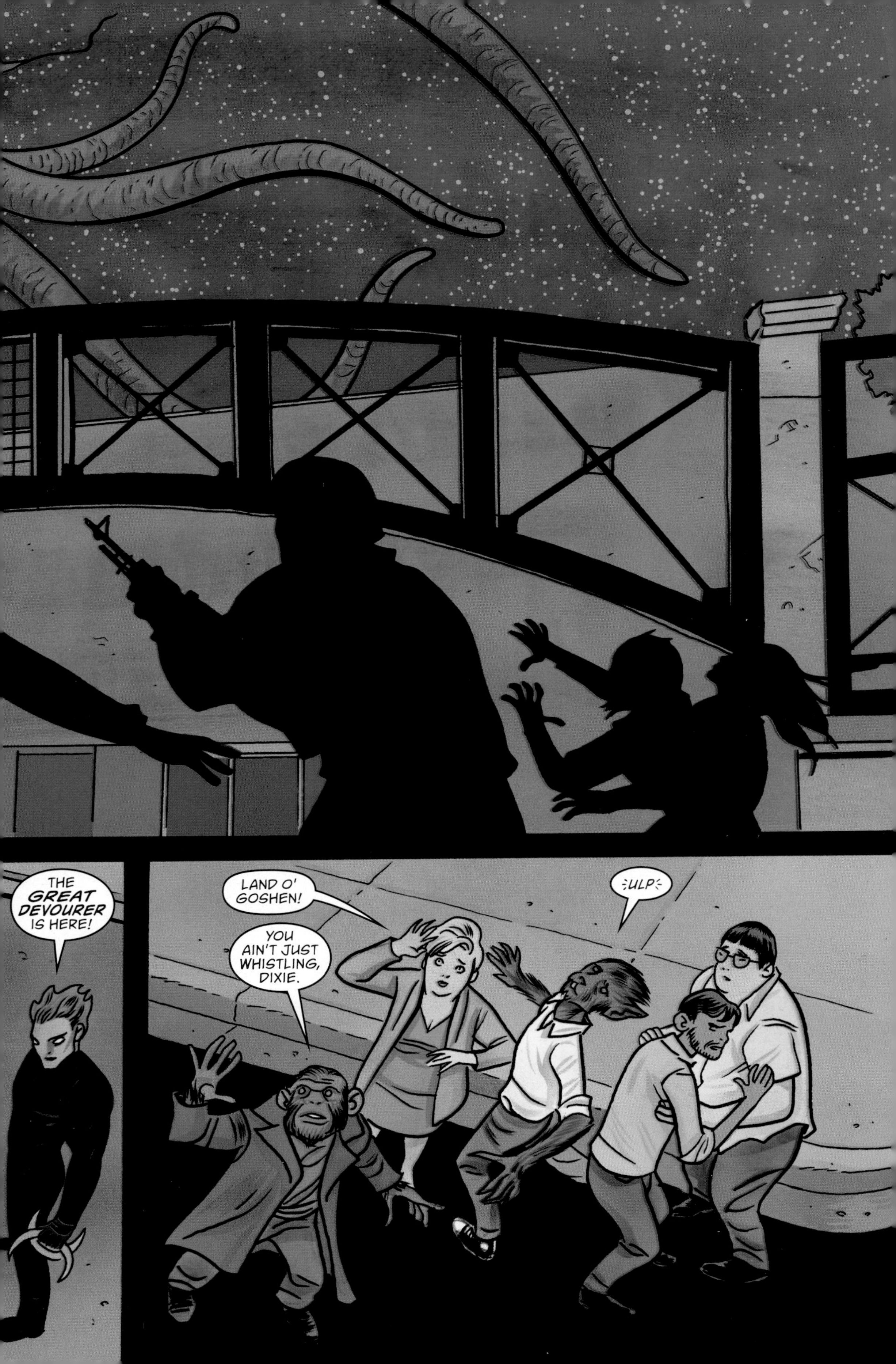
THE GREAT DEVOURER IS HERE!
LAND O' GOSHEN!
YOU AIN'T JUST WHISTLING, DIXIE.
ULP

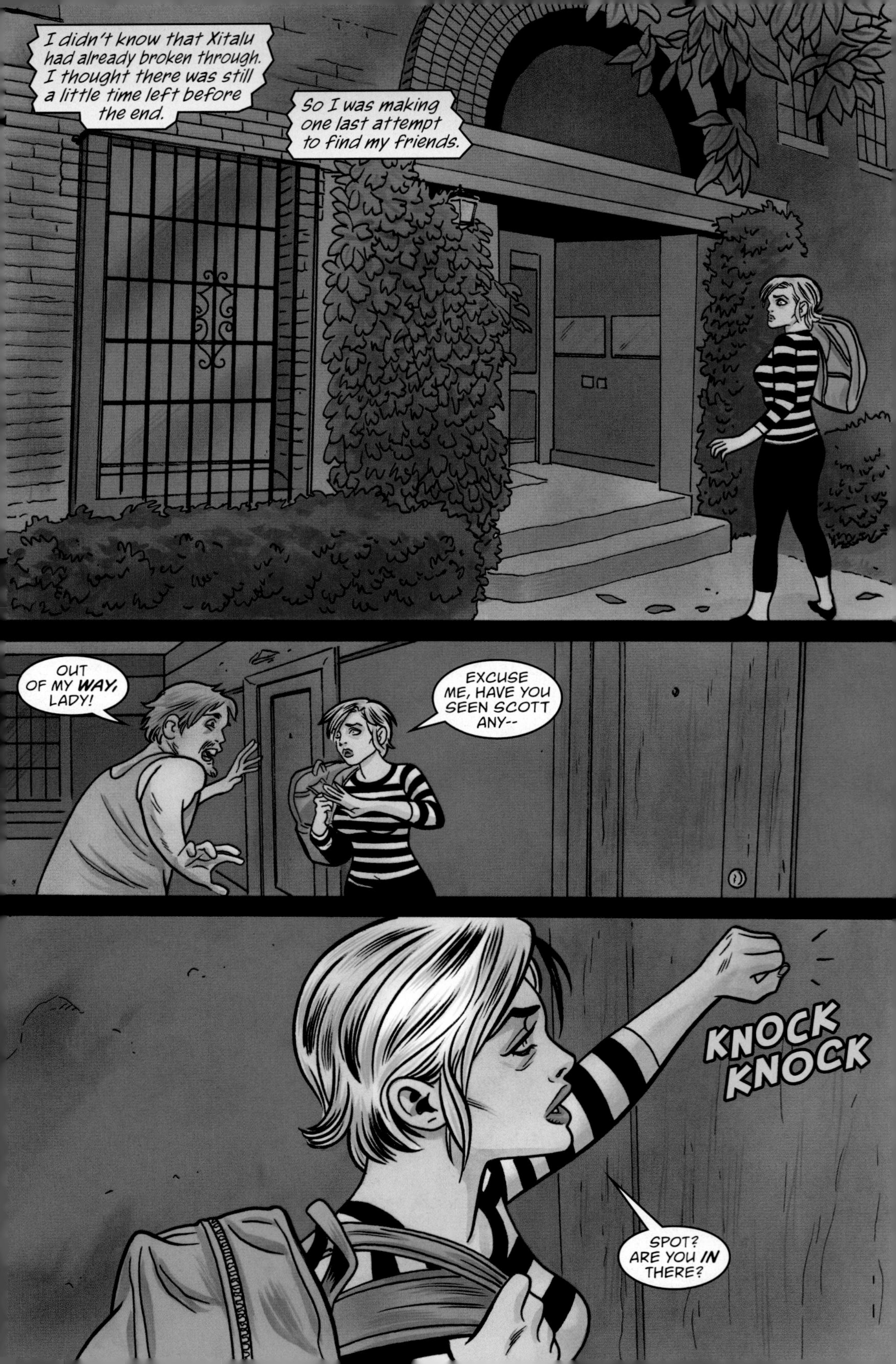
I didn't know that Xitalu had already broken through. I thought there was still a little time left before the end.
So I was making one last attempt to find my friends.
OUT OF MY WAY, LADY!
EXCUSE ME, HAVE YOU SEEN SCOTT ANY--
KNOCK KNOCK
SPOT? ARE YOU IN THERE?

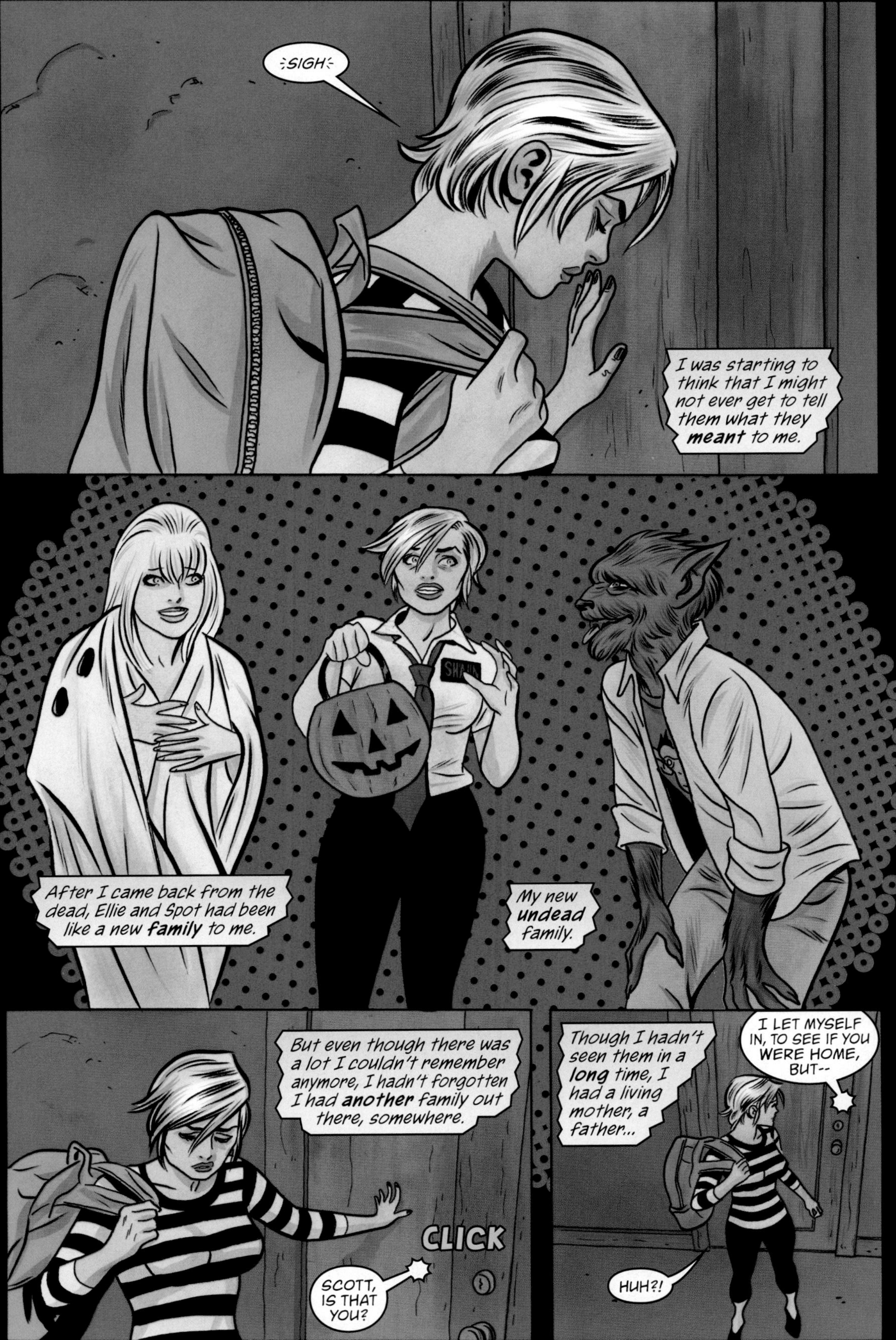
SIGH
I was starting to think that I might not ever get to tell them what they **meant** to me.
After I came back from the dead, Ellie and Spot had been like a new **family** to me.
My new **undead** family.
But even though there was a lot I couldn't remember anymore, I hadn't forgotten I had **another** family out there, somewhere.
CLICK
SCOTT, IS THAT YOU?
Though I hadn't seen them in a **long** time, I had a living mother, a father...
I LET MYSELF IN, TO SEE IF YOU WERE HOME, BUT--
HUH?!

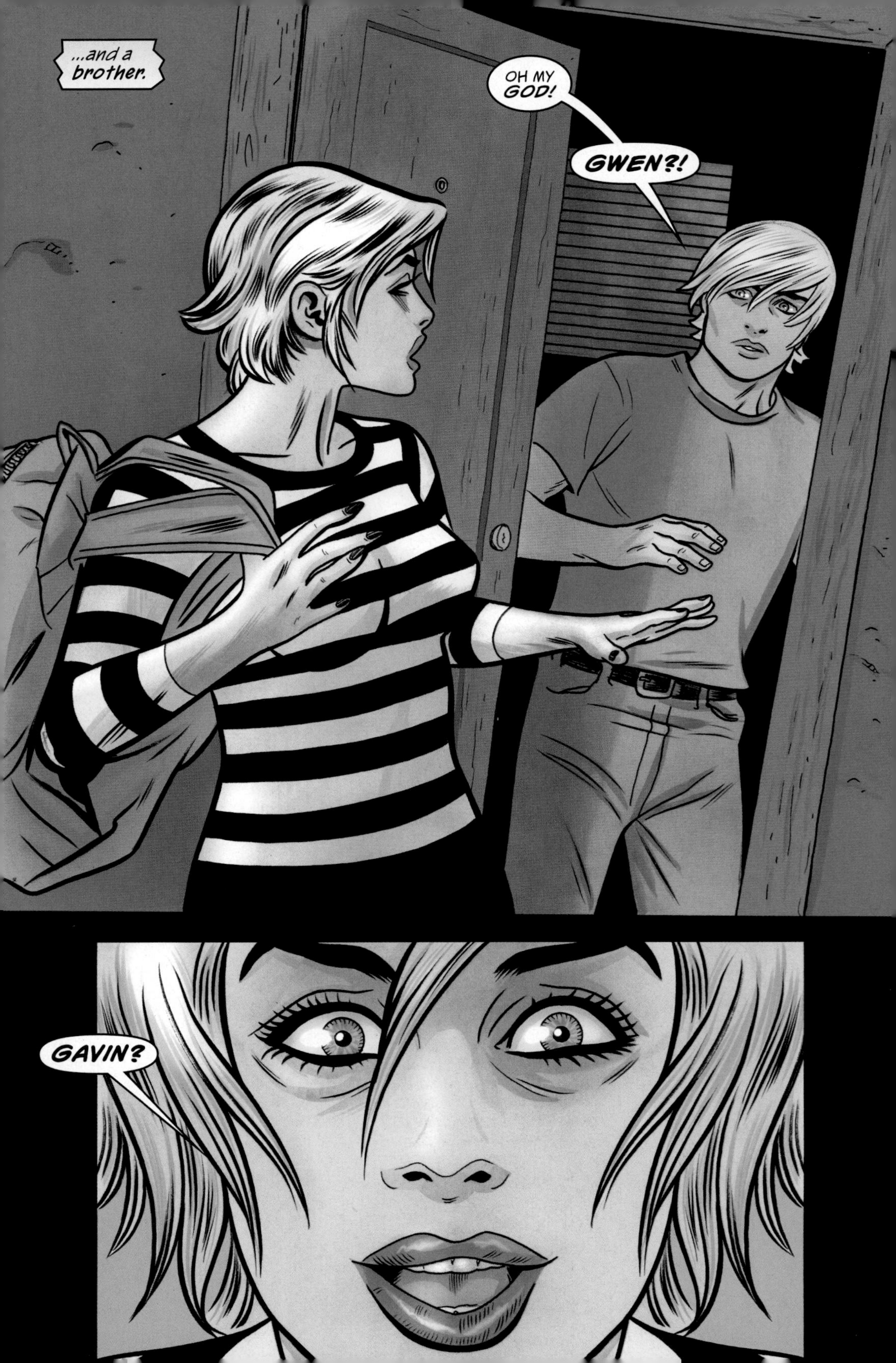
...and a brother.
OH MY GOD!
GWEN?!
GAVIN?

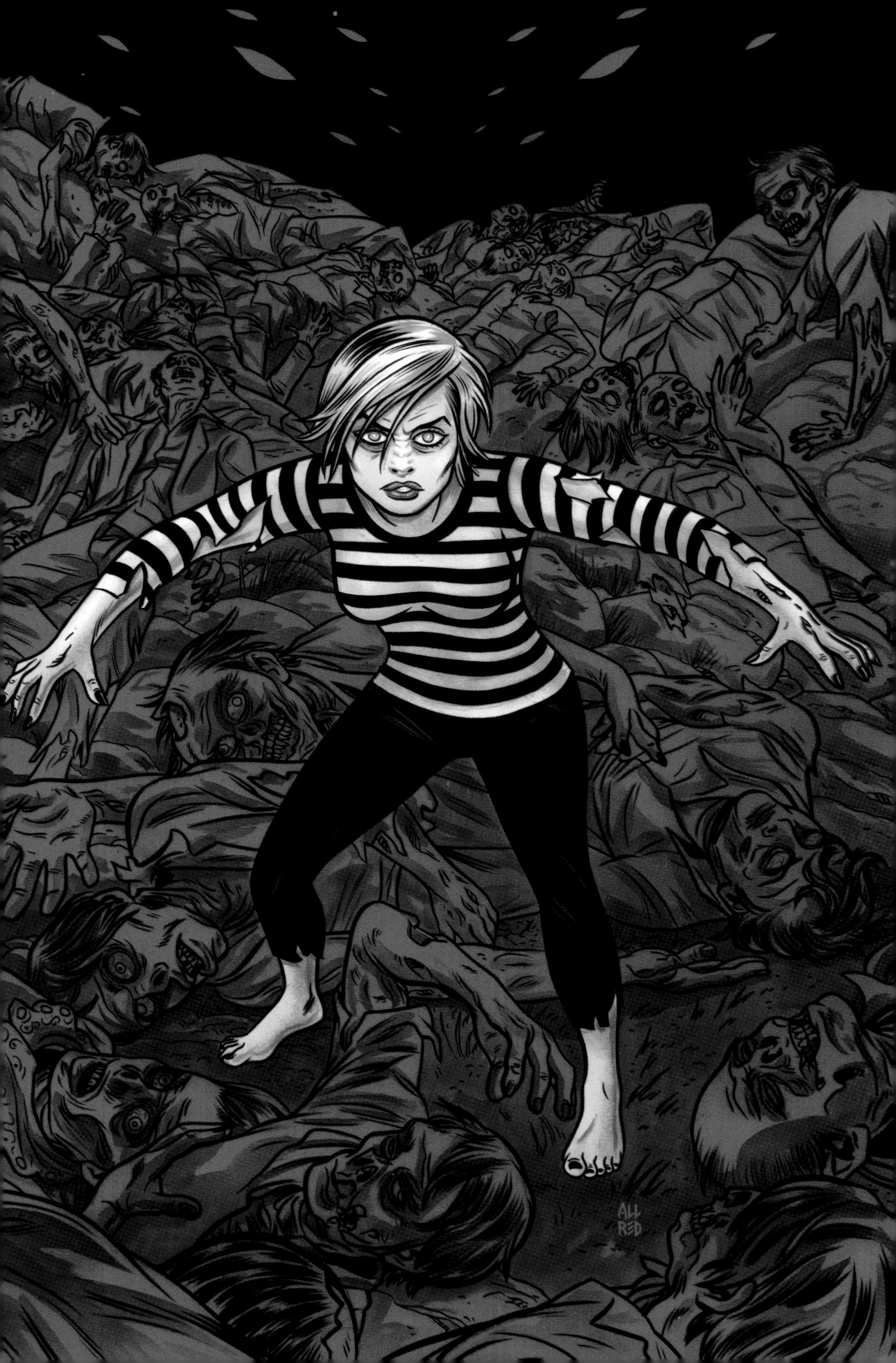
ALL
RED

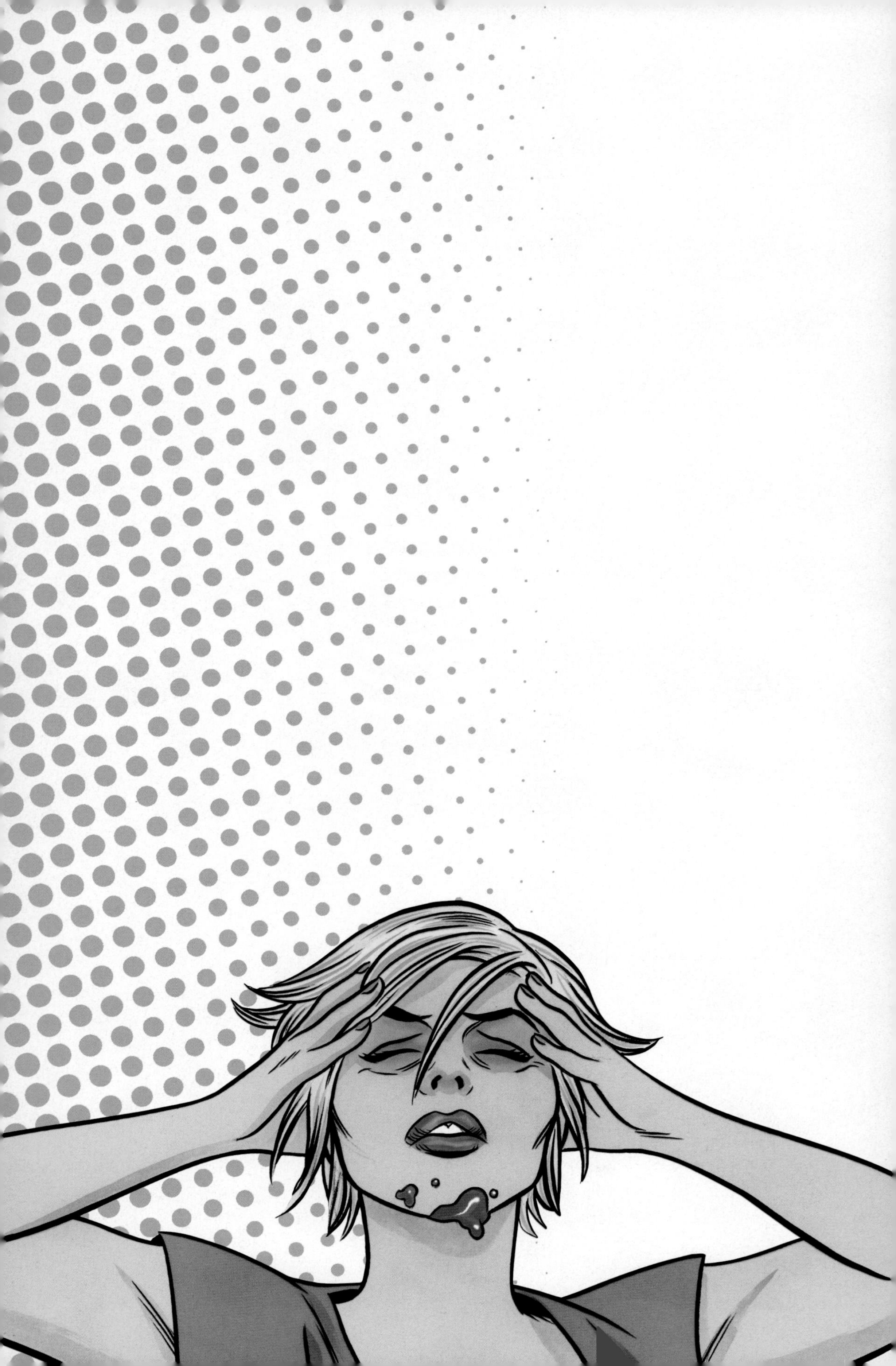

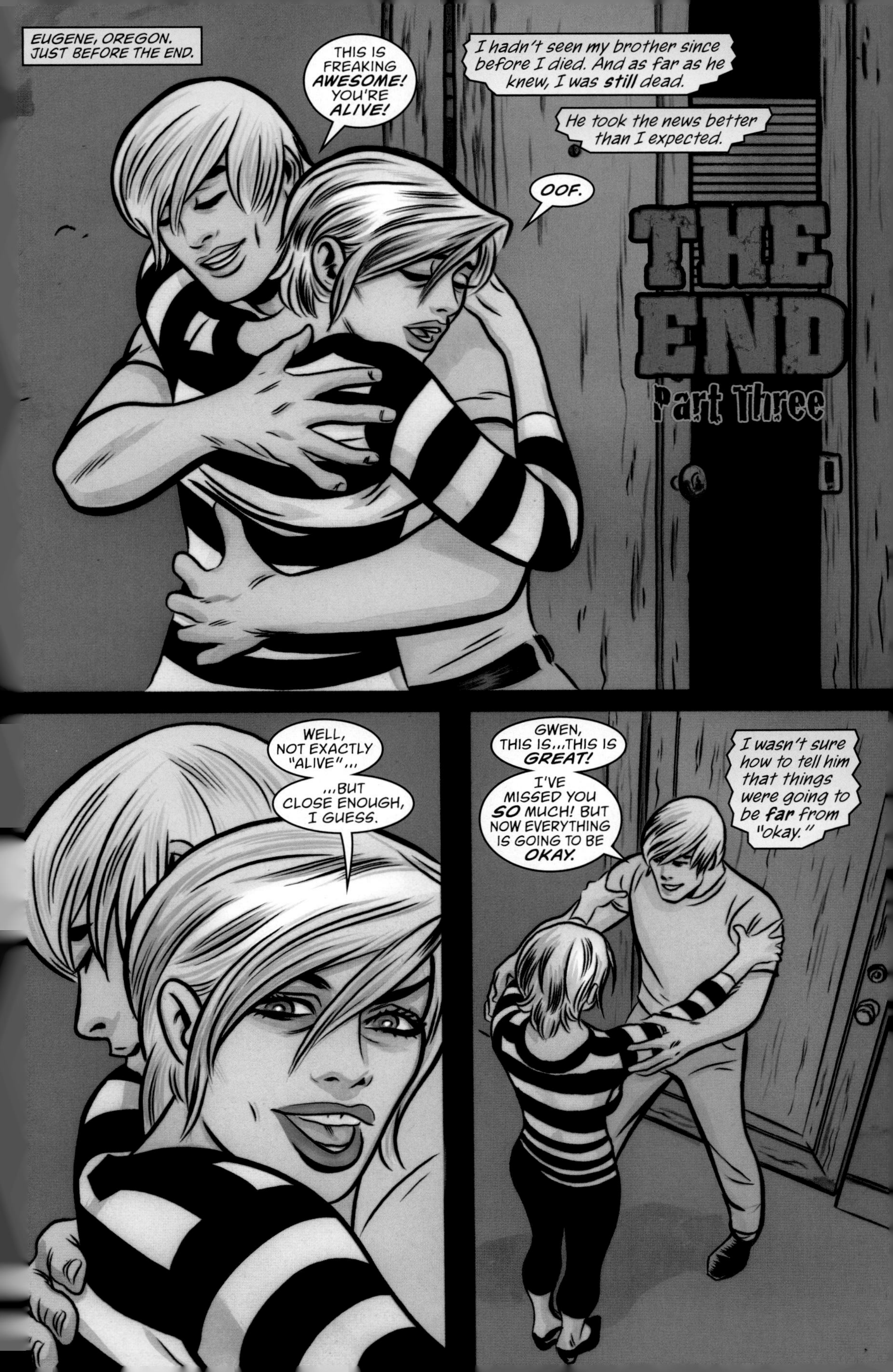
EUGENE, OREGON. JUST BEFORE THE END.
THIS IS FREAKING AWESOME! YOU'RE ALIVE!
I hadn't seen my brother since before I died. And as far as he knew, I was still dead.
He took the news better than I expected.
OOF.
THE END
Part Three
WELL, NOT EXACTLY "ALIVE"...
...BUT CLOSE ENOUGH, I GUESS.
GWEN, THIS IS...THIS IS GREAT!
I'VE MISSED YOU SO MUCH! BUT NOW EVERYTHING IS GOING TO BE OKAY.
I wasn't sure how to tell him that things were going to be far from "okay."

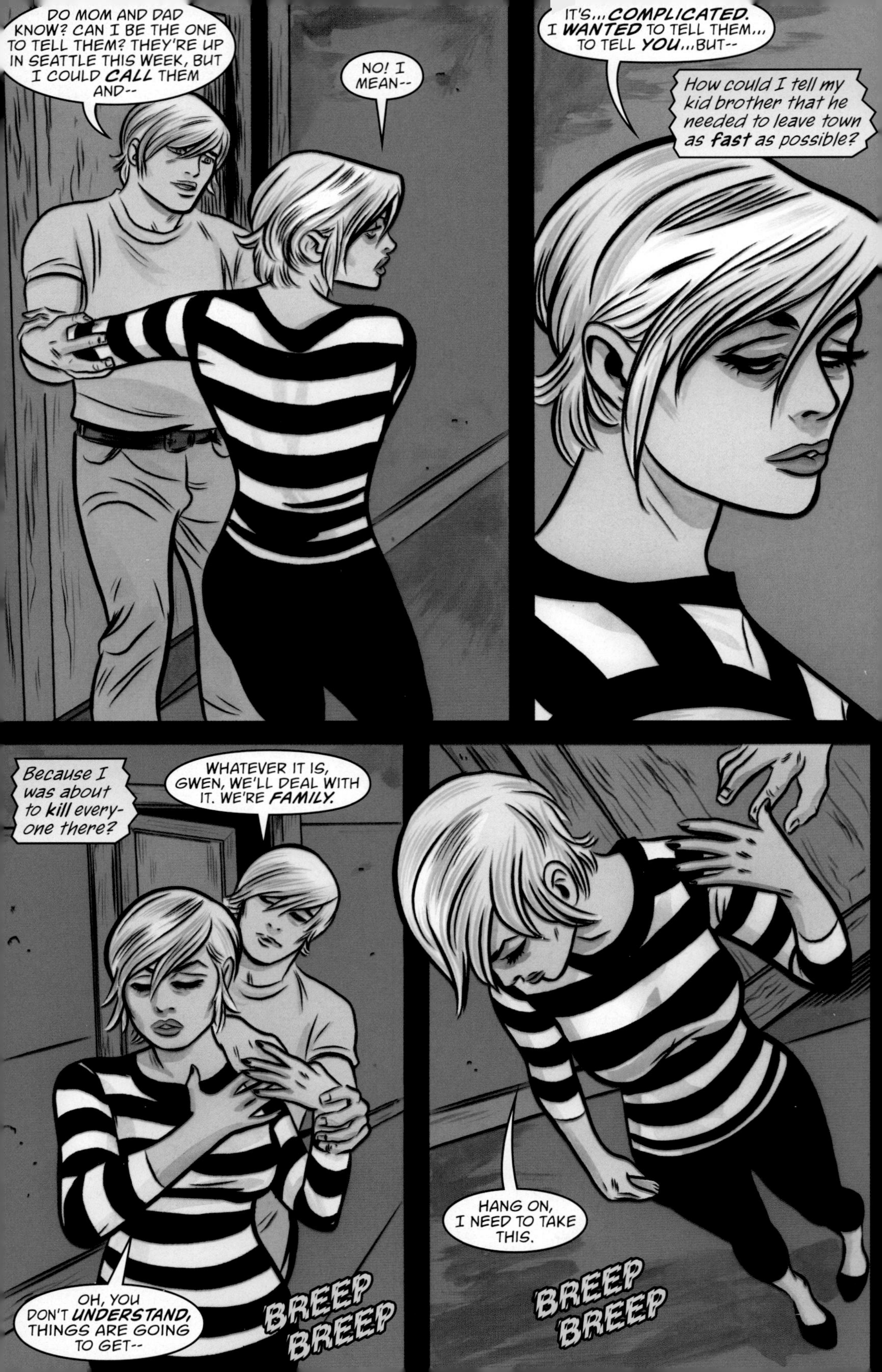
DO MOM AND DAD KNOW? CAN I BE THE ONE TO TELL THEM? THEY'RE UP IN SEATTLE THIS WEEK, BUT I COULD CALL THEM AND--
NO! I MEAN--
IT'S...COMPLICATED. I WANTED TO TELL THEM... TO TELL YOU...BUT--
How could I tell my kid brother that he needed to leave town as fast as possible?
Because I was about to kill every-one there?
WHATEVER IT IS, GWEN, WE'LL DEAL WITH IT. WE'RE FAMILY.
OH, YOU DON'T UNDERSTAND, THINGS ARE GOING TO GET--
BREEP BREEP
HANG ON, I NEED TO TAKE THIS.
BREEP BREEP

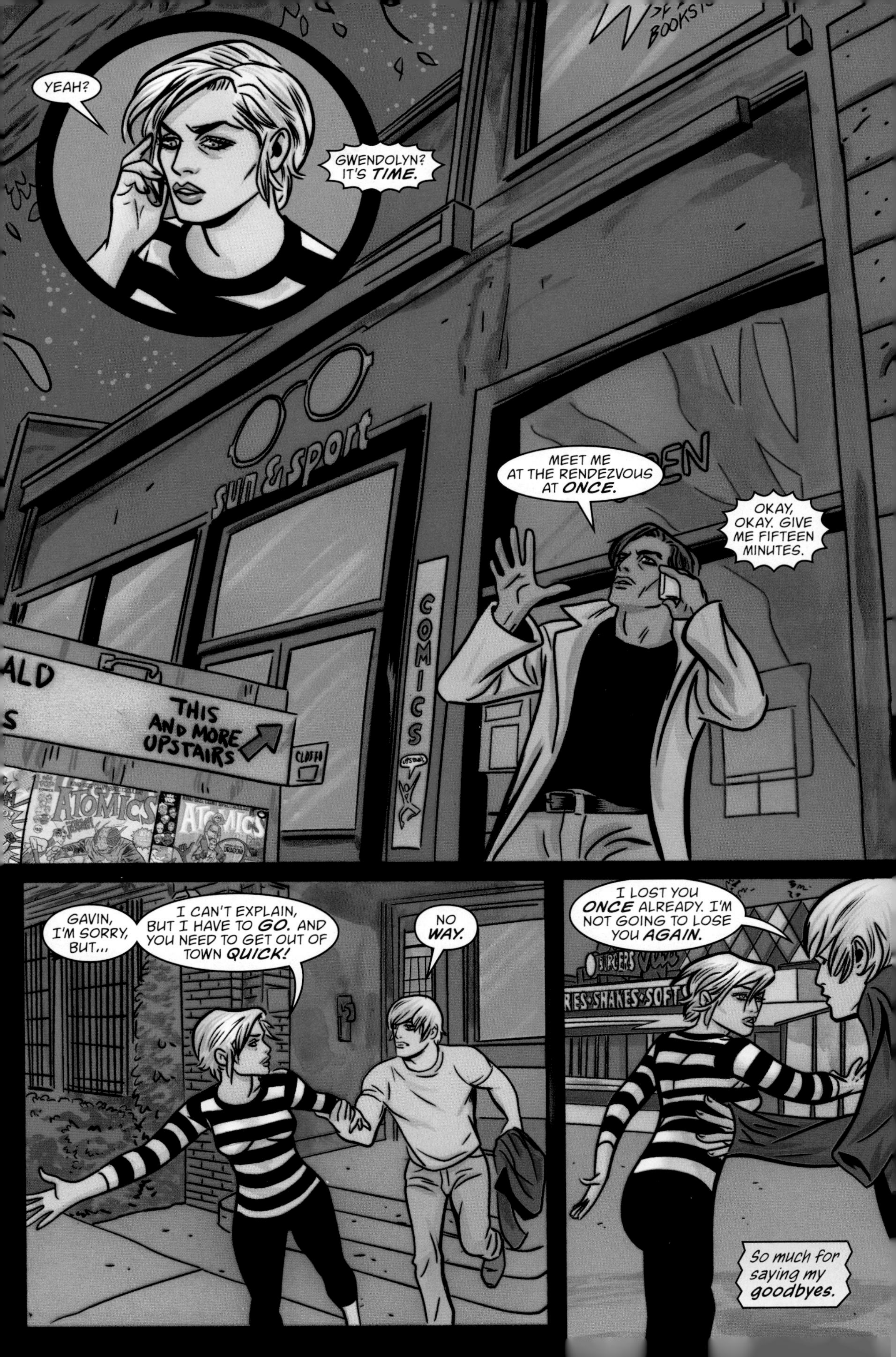

YEAH?
GWENDOLYN? IT'S TIME.
MEET ME AT THE RENDEZVOUS AT ONCE.
OKAY, OKAY. GIVE ME FIFTEEN MINUTES.
SUN & SPORT
COMICS
THIS AND MORE UPSTAIRS
ATOMICS
ATOMICS
GAVIN, I'M SORRY, BUT...
I CAN'T EXPLAIN, BUT I HAVE TO GO. AND YOU NEED TO GET OUT OF TOWN QUICK!
NO WAY.
I LOST YOU ONCE ALREADY. I'M NOT GOING TO LOSE YOU AGAIN.
BURGERS
SHAKES
So much for saying my goodbyes.

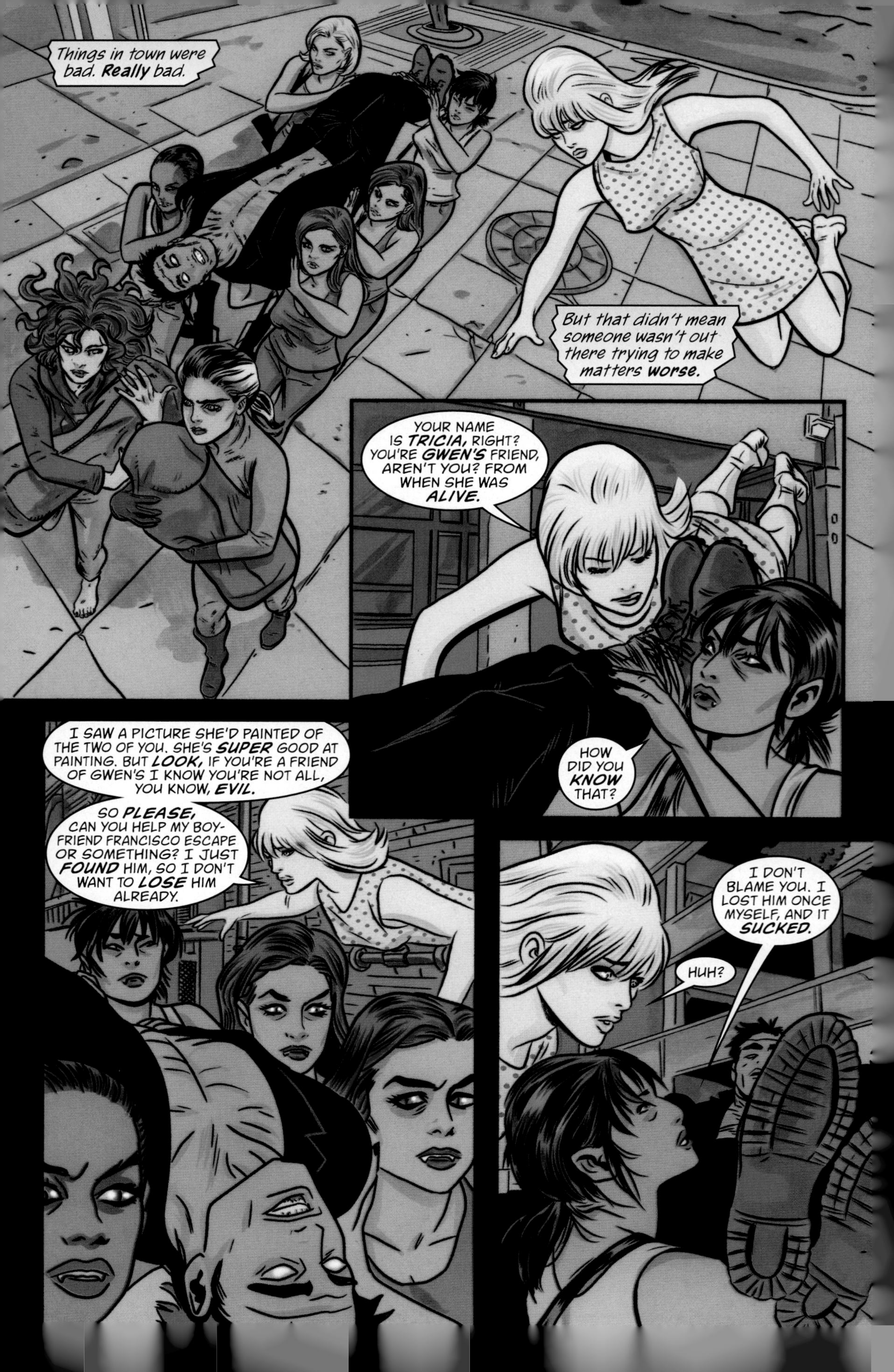
Things in town were bad. **Really** bad.
But that didn't mean someone wasn't out there trying to make matters **worse.**
YOUR NAME IS **TRICIA,** RIGHT? YOU'RE **GWEN'S** FRIEND, AREN'T YOU? FROM WHEN SHE WAS **ALIVE.**
HOW DID YOU **KNOW** THAT?
I SAW A PICTURE SHE'D PAINTED OF THE TWO OF YOU. SHE'S **SUPER** GOOD AT PAINTING. BUT **LOOK,** IF YOU'RE A FRIEND OF GWEN'S I KNOW YOU'RE NOT ALL, YOU KNOW, **EVIL.**
SO **PLEASE,** CAN YOU HELP MY BOY-FRIEND FRANCISCO ESCAPE OR SOMETHING? I JUST **FOUND** HIM, SO I DON'T WANT TO **LOSE** HIM ALREADY.
I DON'T BLAME YOU. I LOST HIM ONCE MYSELF, AND IT **SUCKED.**
HUH?

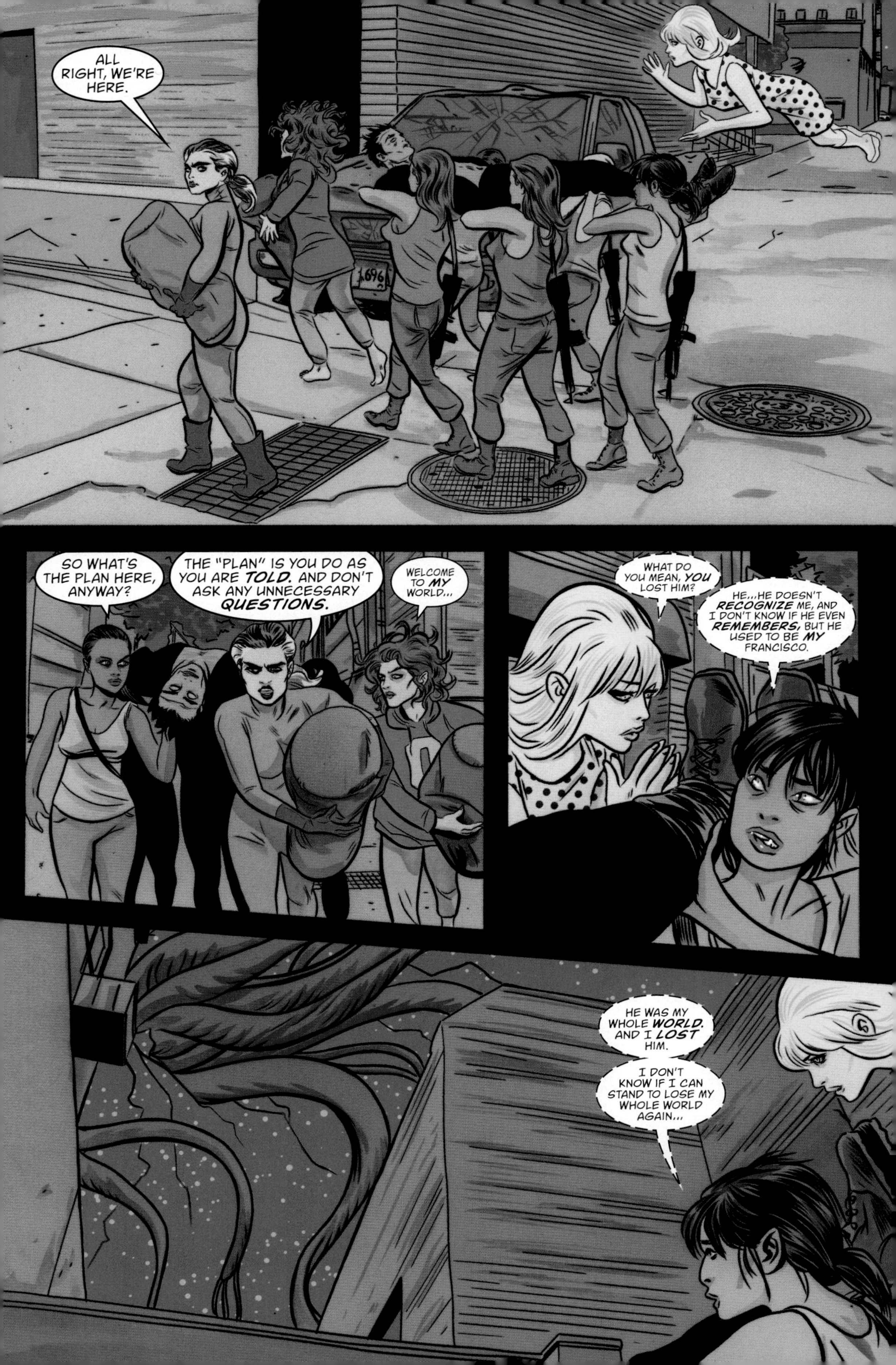

ALL RIGHT, WE'RE HERE.
SO WHAT'S THE PLAN HERE, ANYWAY?
THE "PLAN" IS YOU DO AS YOU ARE TOLD. AND DON'T ASK ANY UNNECESSARY QUESTIONS.
WELCOME TO MY WORLD...
WHAT DO YOU MEAN, YOU LOST HIM?
HE...HE DOESN'T RECOGNIZE ME, AND I DON'T KNOW IF HE EVEN REMEMBERS, BUT HE USED TO BE MY FRANCISCO.
HE WAS MY WHOLE WORLD. AND I LOST HIM.
I DON'T KNOW IF I CAN STAND TO LOSE MY WHOLE WORLD AGAIN...

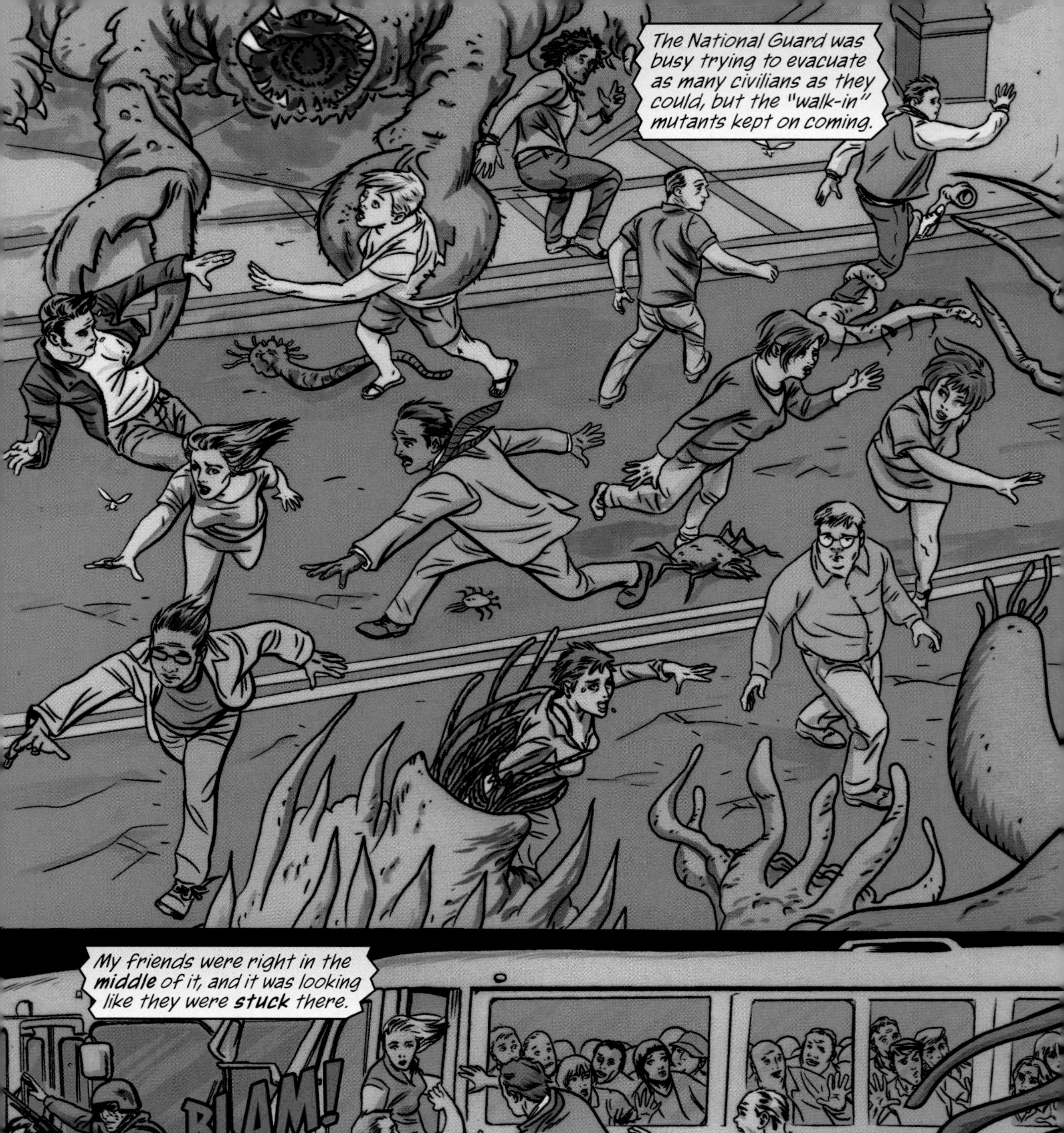
The National Guard was busy trying to evacuate as many civilians as they could, but the "walk-in" mutants kept on coming.

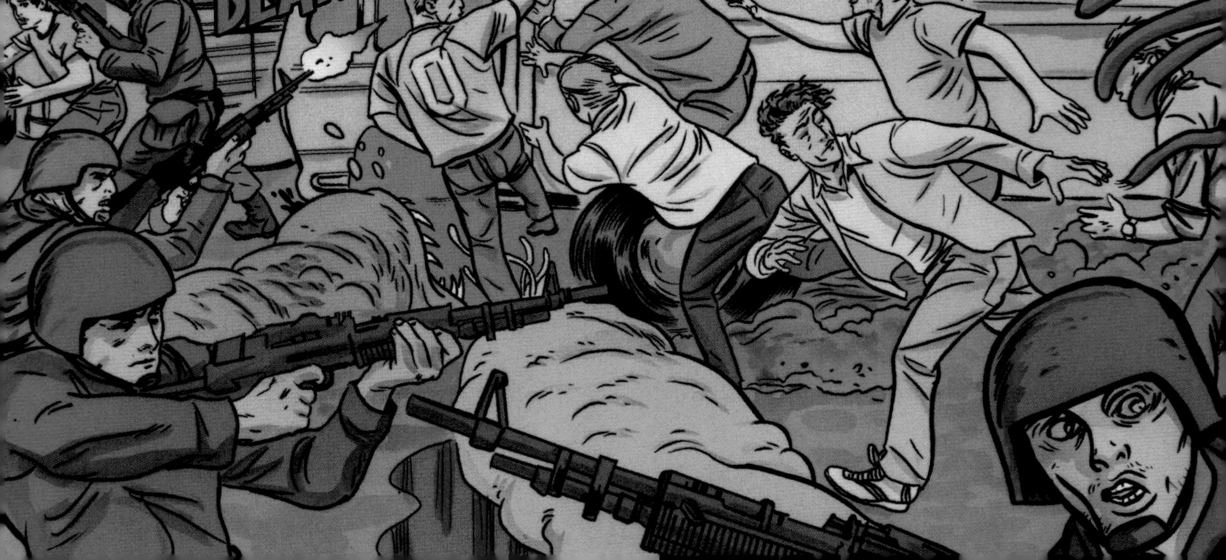
My friends were right in the **middle** of it, and it was looking like they were **stuck** there.
BLAM!

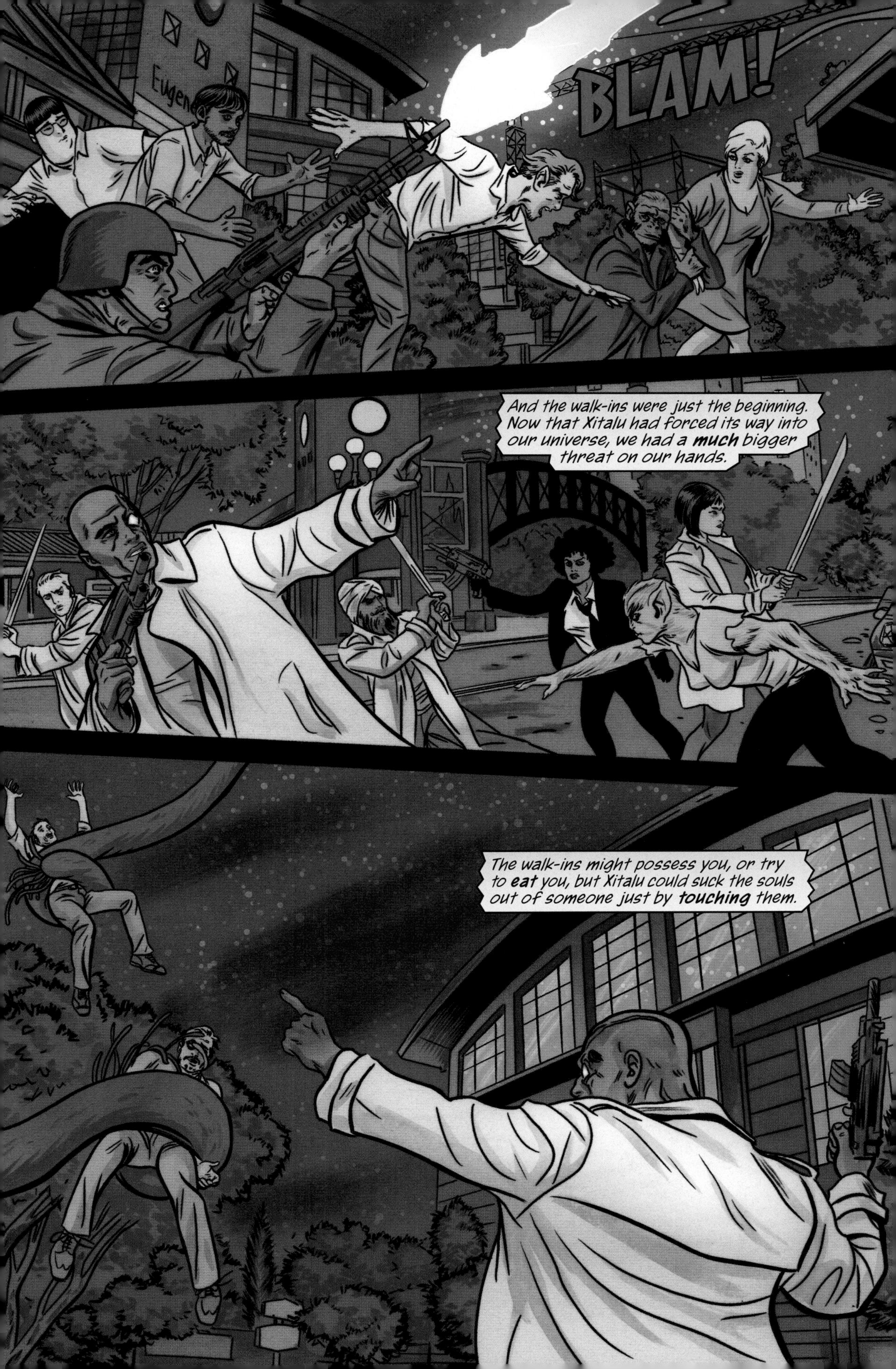
BLAM!
And the walk-ins were just the beginning. Now that Xitalu had forced its way into our universe, we had a **much** bigger threat on our hands.
The walk-ins might possess you, or try to **eat** you, but Xitalu could suck the souls out of someone just by **touching** them.

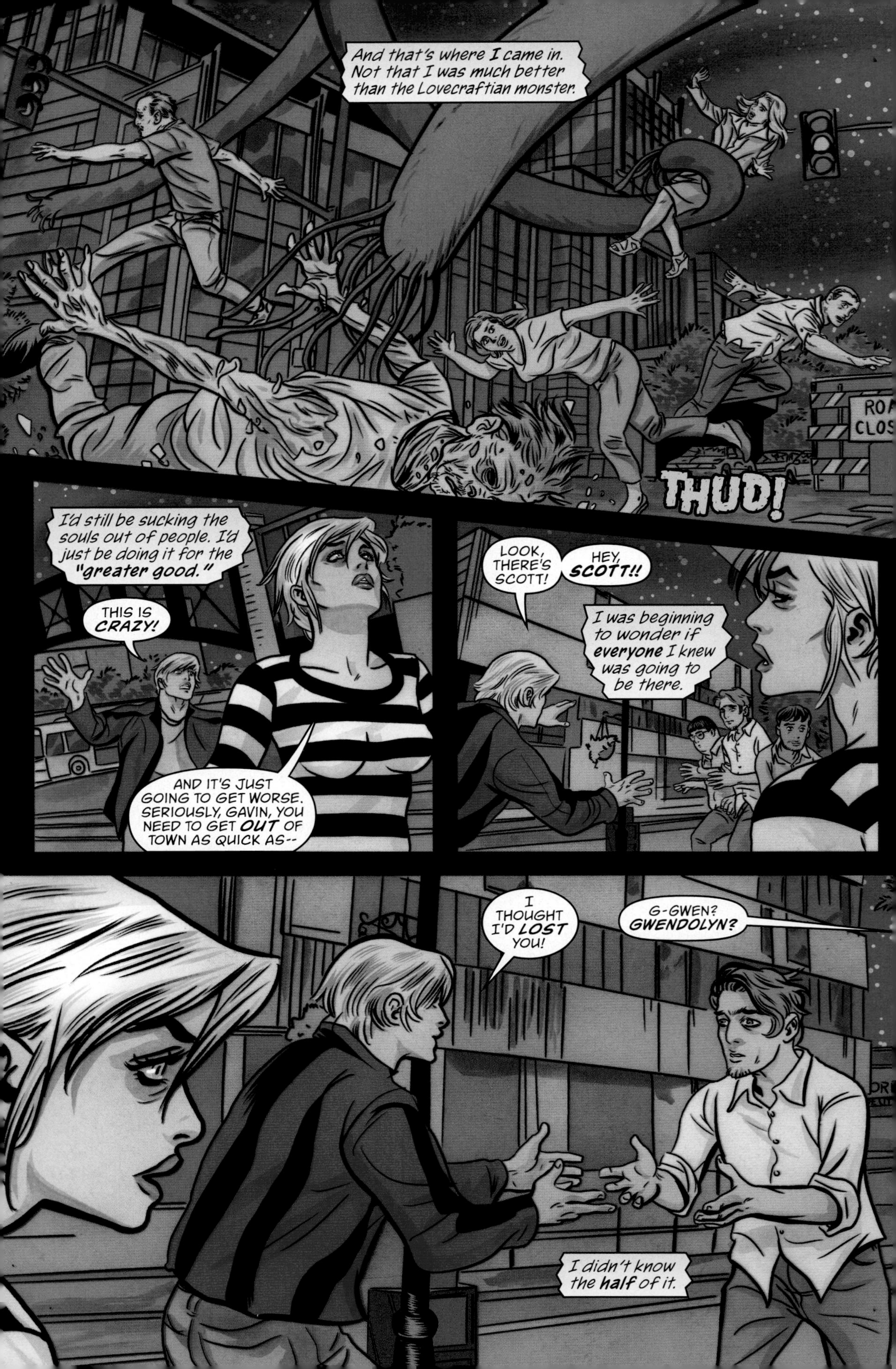

And that's where I came in. Not that I was much better than the Lovecraftian monster.
ROA
CLOS
THUD!
I'd still be sucking the souls out of people. I'd just be doing it for the "greater good."
THIS IS CRAZY!
AND IT'S JUST GOING TO GET WORSE. SERIOUSLY, GAVIN, YOU NEED TO GET OUT OF TOWN AS QUICK AS--
LOOK, THERE'S SCOTT!
HEY, SCOTT!!
I was beginning to wonder if everyone I knew was going to be there.
I THOUGHT I'D LOST YOU!
G-GWEN? GWENDOLYN?
I didn't know the half of it.

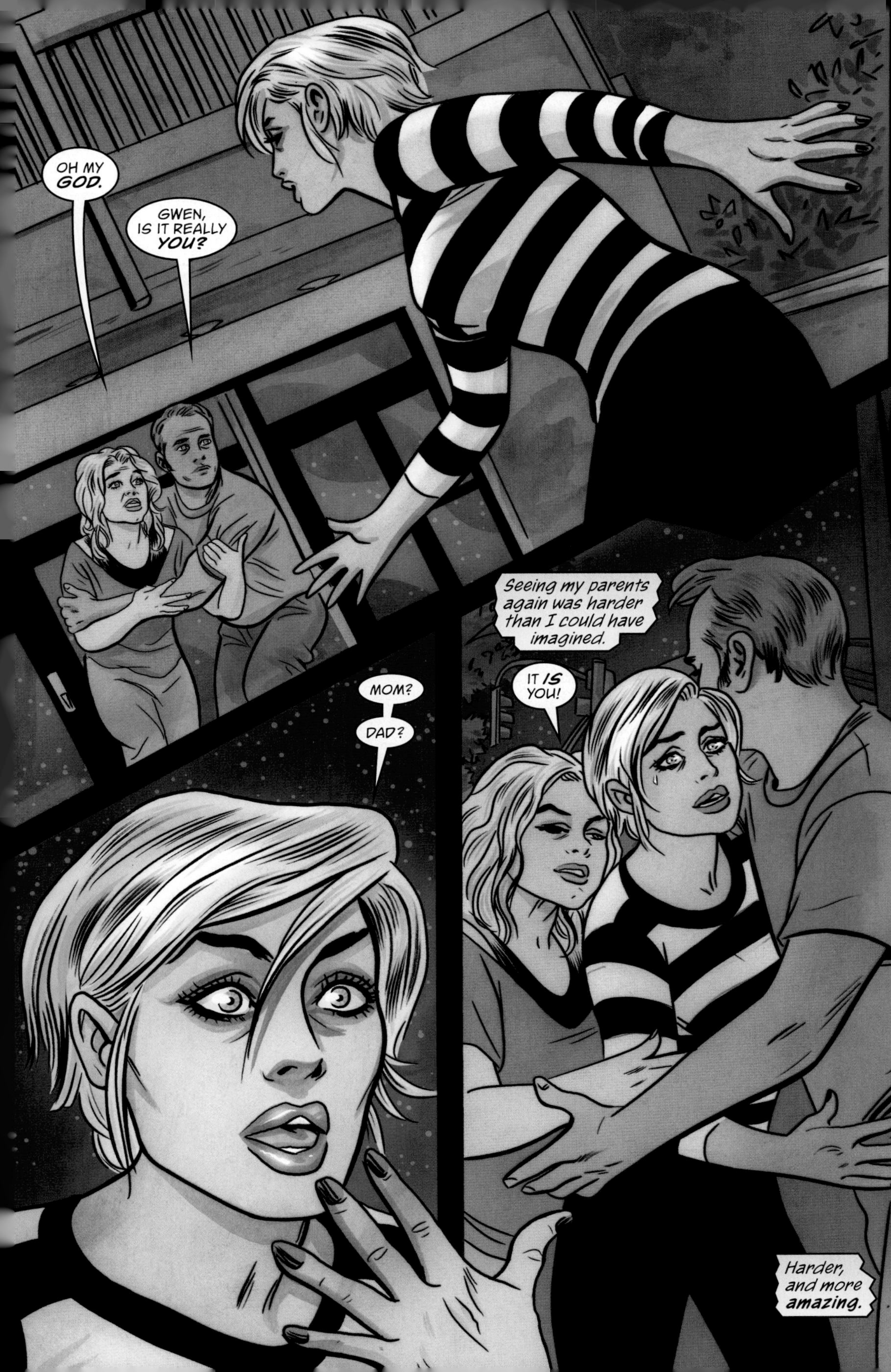

OH MY GOD.
GWEN, IS IT REALLY YOU?
MOM?
DAD?
Seeing my parents again was harder than I could have imagined.
IT IS YOU!
Harder, and more amazing.

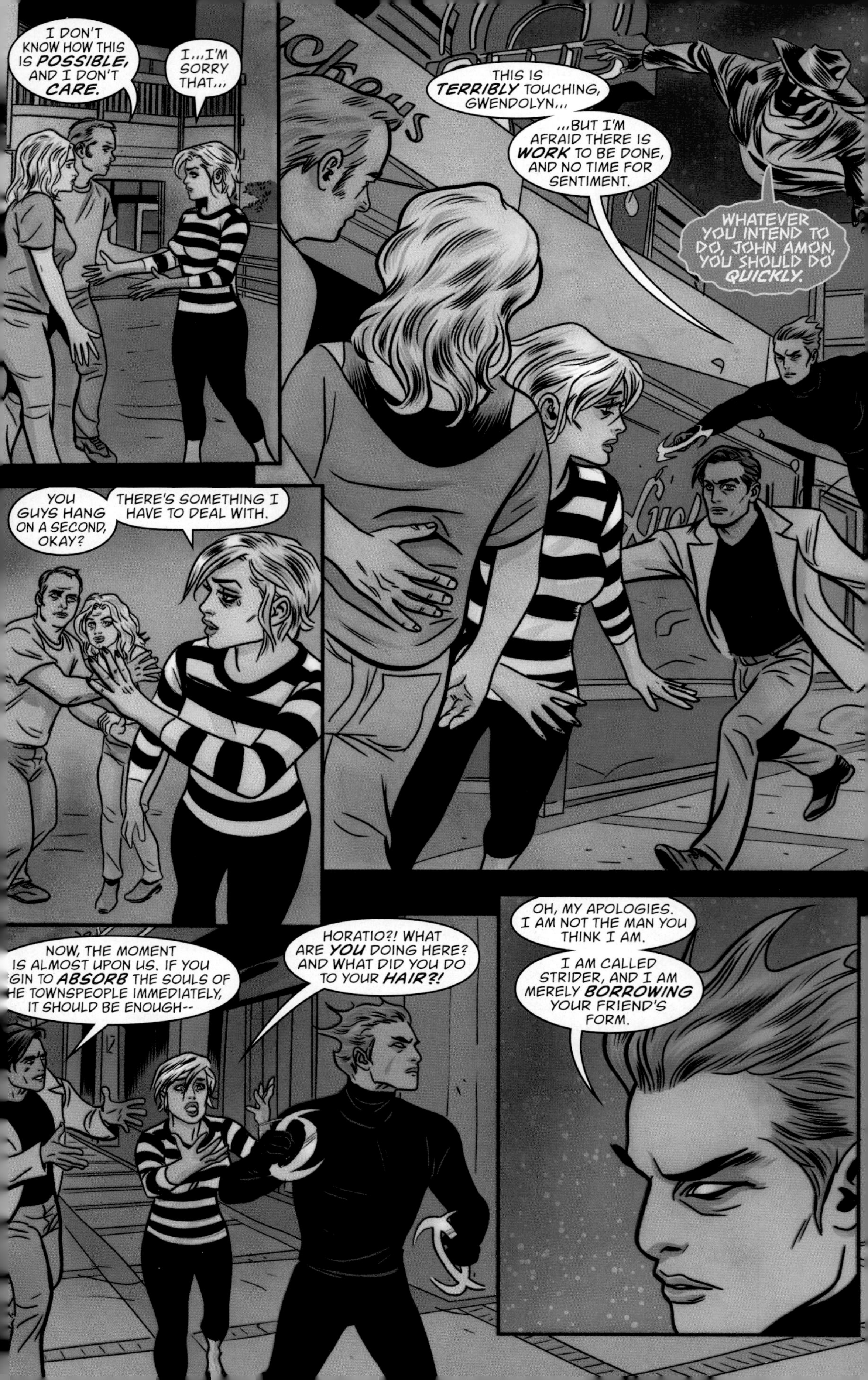

I DON'T KNOW HOW THIS IS POSSIBLE, AND I DON'T CARE.
I...I'M SORRY THAT...
THIS IS TERRIBLY TOUCHING, GWENDOLYN...
...BUT I'M AFRAID THERE IS WORK TO BE DONE, AND NO TIME FOR SENTIMENT.
WHATEVER YOU INTEND TO DO, JOHN AMON, YOU SHOULD DO QUICKLY.
YOU GUYS HANG ON A SECOND, OKAY?
THERE'S SOMETHING I HAVE TO DEAL WITH.
NOW, THE MOMENT IS ALMOST UPON US. IF YOU EGIN TO ABSORB THE SOULS OF HE TOWNSPEOPLE IMMEDIATELY, IT SHOULD BE ENOUGH--
HORATIO?! WHAT ARE YOU DOING HERE? AND WHAT DID YOU DO TO YOUR HAIR?!
OH, MY APOLOGIES. I AM NOT THE MAN YOU THINK I AM.
I AM CALLED STRIDER, AND I AM MERELY BORROWING YOUR FRIEND'S FORM.

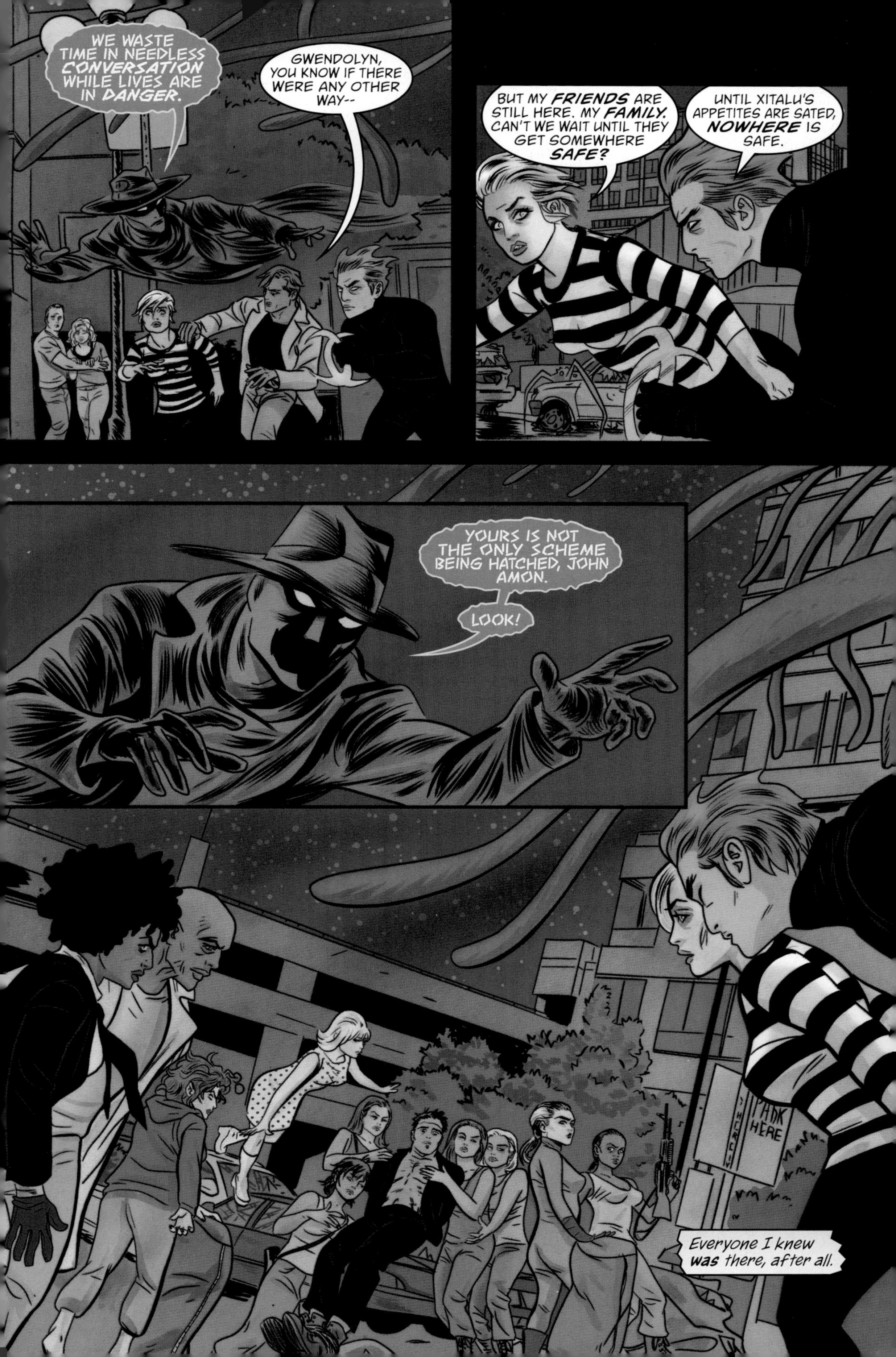
WE WASTE TIME IN NEEDLESS CONVERSATION WHILE LIVES ARE IN DANGER.
GWENDOLYN, YOU KNOW IF THERE WERE ANY OTHER WAY--
BUT MY FRIENDS ARE STILL HERE. MY FAMILY. CAN'T WE WAIT UNTIL THEY GET SOMEWHERE SAFE?
UNTIL XITALU'S APPETITES ARE SATED, NOWHERE IS SAFE.
YOURS IS NOT THE ONLY SCHEME BEING HATCHED, JOHN AMON.
LOOK!
PARK HERE
Everyone I knew was there, after all.

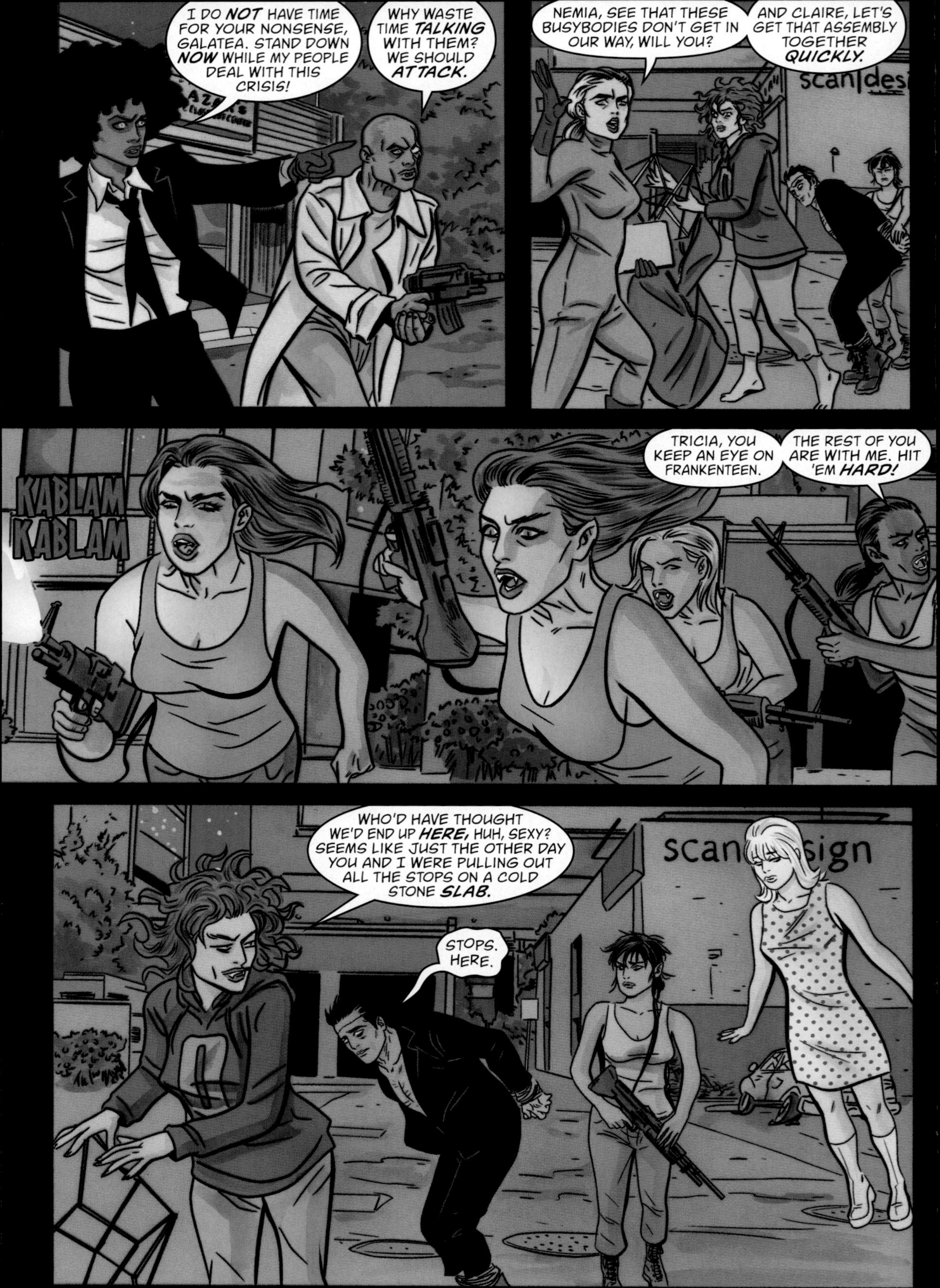

I DO NOT HAVE TIME FOR YOUR NONSENSE, GALATEA. STAND DOWN NOW WHILE MY PEOPLE DEAL WITH THIS CRISIS!
WHY WASTE TIME TALKING WITH THEM? WE SHOULD ATTACK.
NEMIA, SEE THAT THESE BUSYBODIES DON'T GET IN OUR WAY, WILL YOU?
AND CLAIRE, LET'S GET THAT ASSEMBLY TOGETHER QUICKLY.
scan|desi
KABLAM KABLAM
TRICIA, YOU KEEP AN EYE ON FRANKENTEEN.
THE REST OF YOU ARE WITH ME. HIT 'EM HARD!
WHO'D HAVE THOUGHT WE'D END UP HERE, HUH, SEXY? SEEMS LIKE JUST THE OTHER DAY YOU AND I WERE PULLING OUT ALL THE STOPS ON A COLD STONE SLAB.
scan sign
STOPS. HERE.

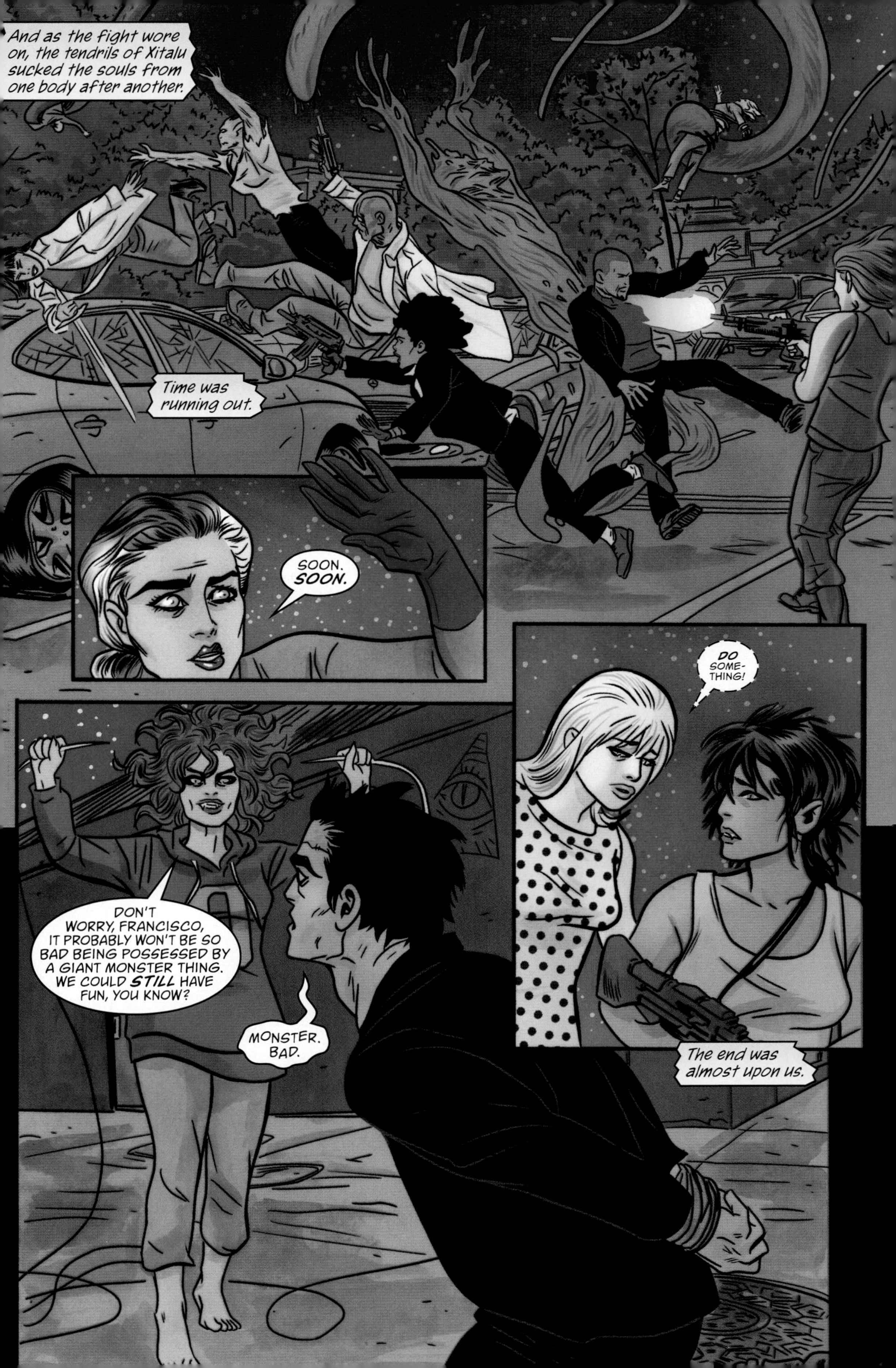

And as the fight wore on, the tendrils of Xitalu sucked the souls from one body after another.
Time was running out.
SOON. SOON.
DO SOMETHING!
DON'T WORRY, FRANCISCO, IT PROBABLY WON'T BE SO BAD BEING POSSESSED BY A GIANT MONSTER THING. WE COULD STILL HAVE FUN, YOU KNOW?
MONSTER. BAD.
The end was almost upon us.

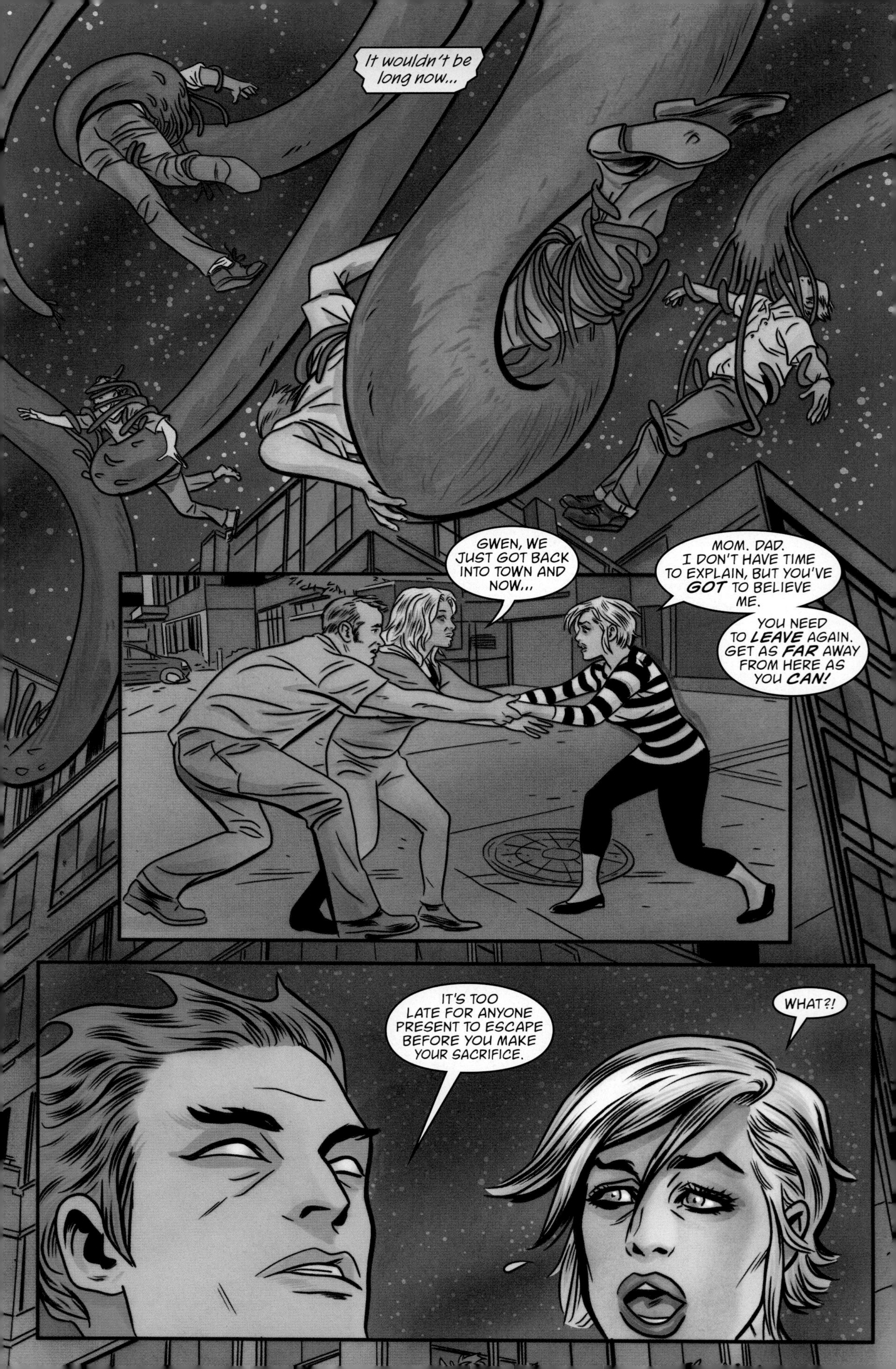

It wouldn't be long now...
GWEN, WE JUST GOT BACK INTO TOWN AND NOW...
MOM. DAD. I DON'T HAVE TIME TO EXPLAIN, BUT YOU'VE GOT TO BELIEVE ME.
YOU NEED TO LEAVE AGAIN. GET AS FAR AWAY FROM HERE AS YOU CAN!
IT'S TOO LATE FOR ANYONE PRESENT TO ESCAPE BEFORE YOU MAKE YOUR SACRIFICE.
WHAT?!

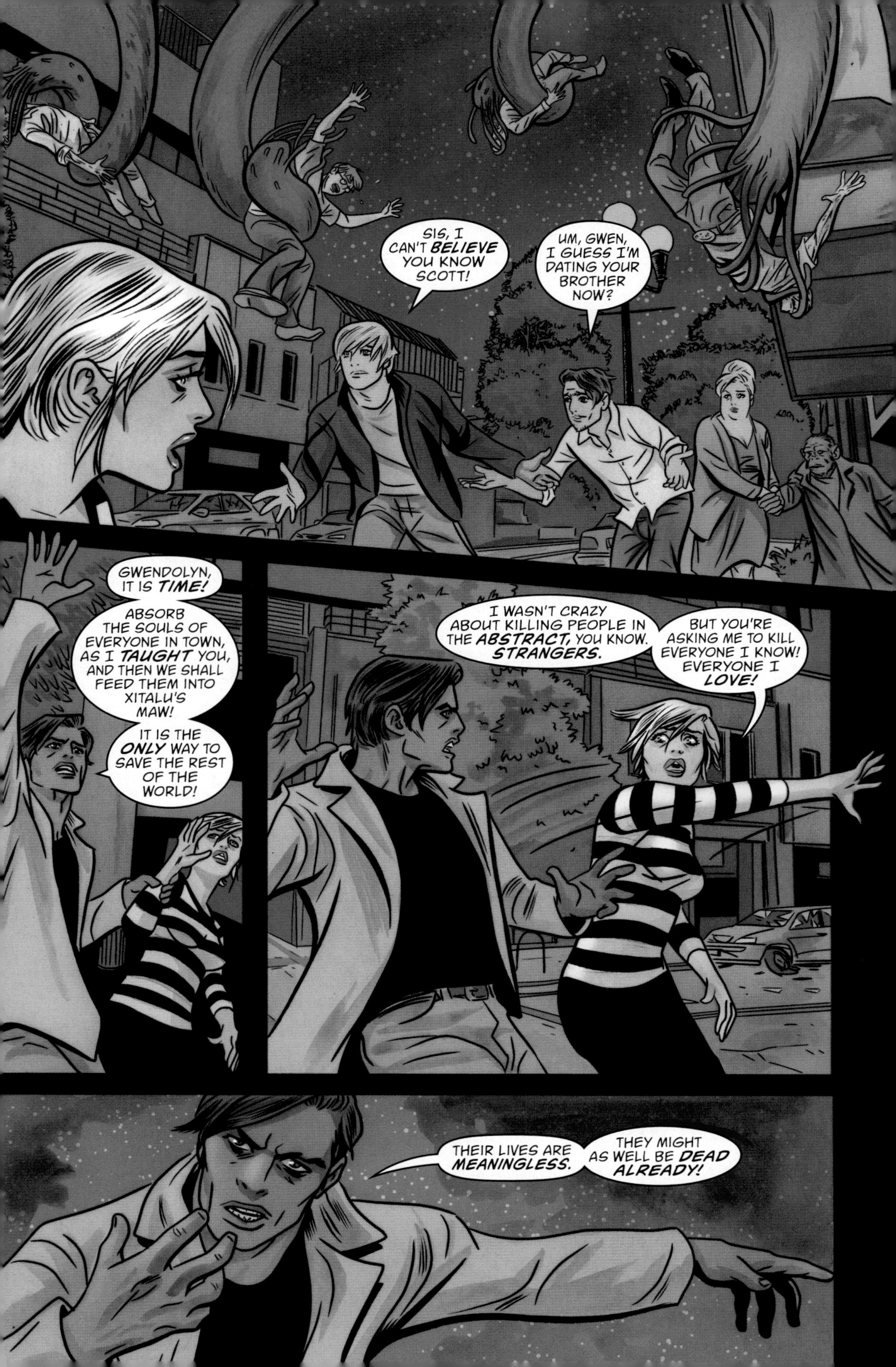
SIS, I CAN'T BELIEVE YOU KNOW SCOTT!
UM, GWEN, I GUESS I'M DATING YOUR BROTHER NOW?
GWENDOLYN, IT IS TIME!
ABSORB THE SOULS OF EVERYONE IN TOWN, AS I TAUGHT YOU, AND THEN WE SHALL FEED THEM INTO XITALU'S MAW!
IT IS THE ONLY WAY TO SAVE THE REST OF THE WORLD!
I WASN'T CRAZY ABOUT KILLING PEOPLE IN THE ABSTRACT, YOU KNOW. STRANGERS.
BUT YOU'RE ASKING ME TO KILL EVERYONE I KNOW! EVERYONE I LOVE!
THEIR LIVES ARE MEANINGLESS.
THEY MIGHT AS WELL BE DEAD ALREADY!

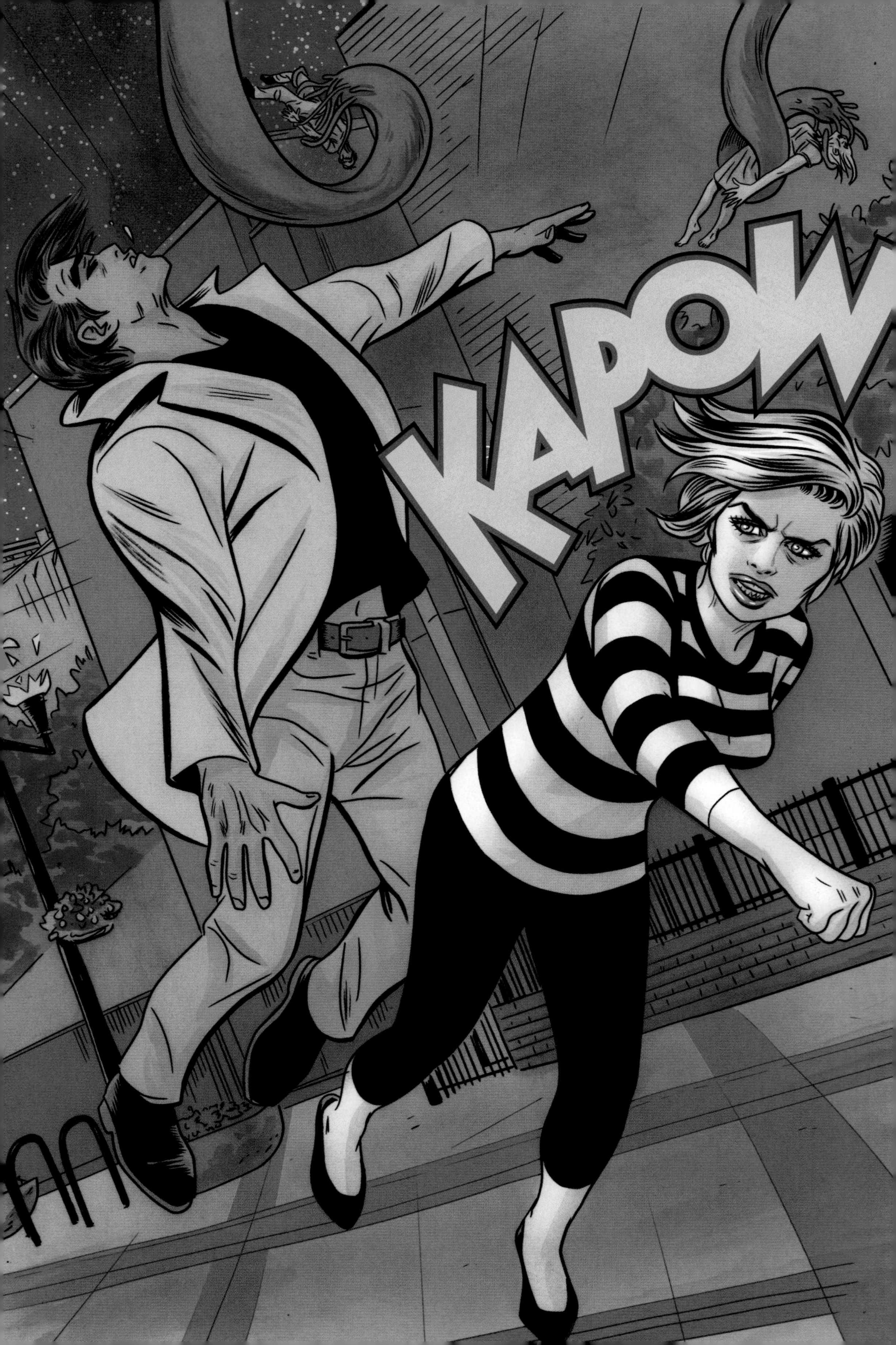
KAPOW

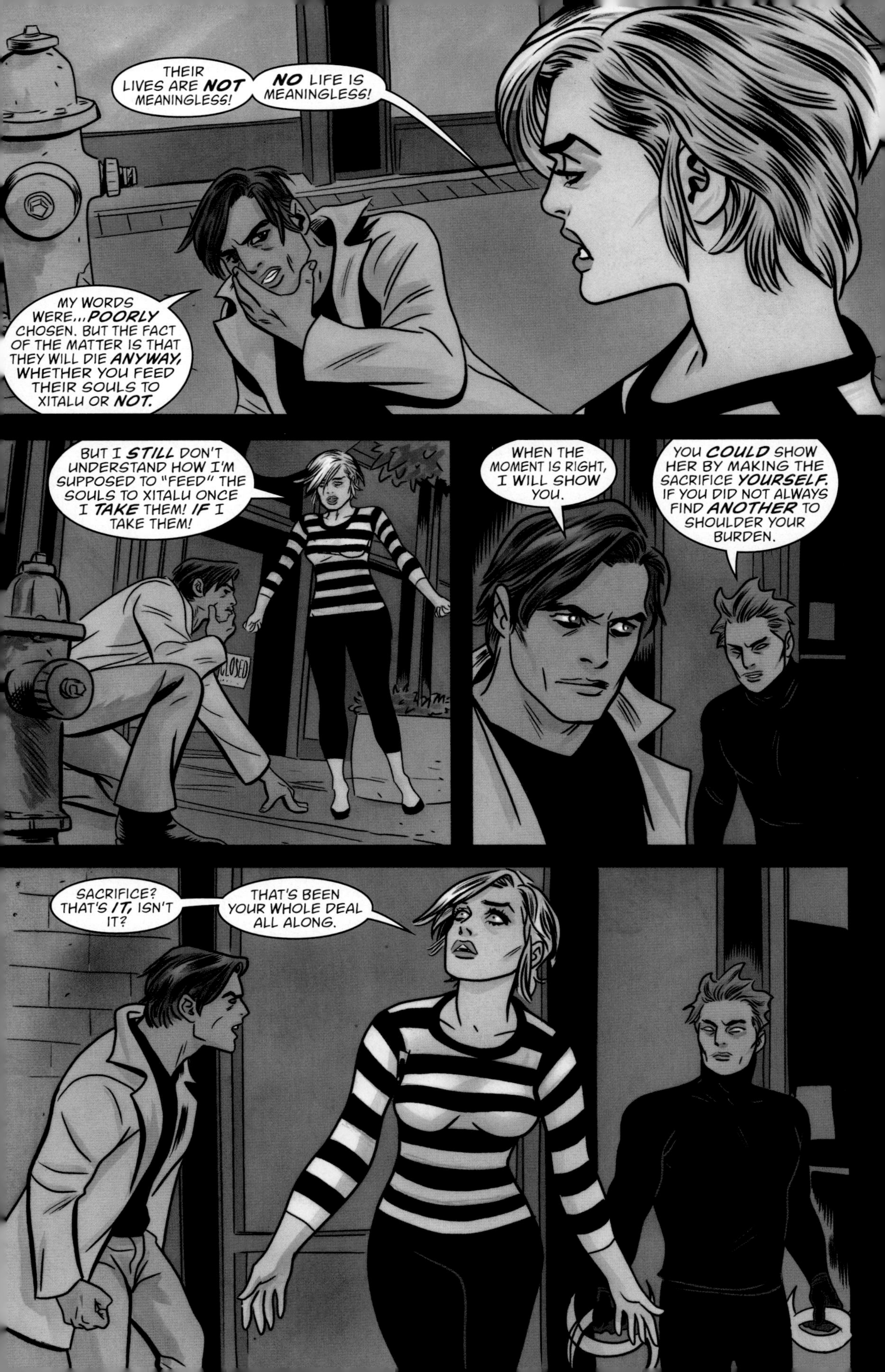
THEIR LIVES ARE NOT MEANINGLESS!
NO LIFE IS MEANINGLESS!
MY WORDS WERE... POORLY CHOSEN. BUT THE FACT OF THE MATTER IS THAT THEY WILL DIE ANYWAY, WHETHER YOU FEED THEIR SOULS TO XITALU OR NOT.
BUT I STILL DON'T UNDERSTAND HOW I'M SUPPOSED TO "FEED" THE SOULS TO XITALU ONCE I TAKE THEM! IF I TAKE THEM!
CLOSED
WHEN THE MOMENT IS RIGHT, I WILL SHOW YOU.
YOU COULD SHOW HER BY MAKING THE SACRIFICE YOURSELF. IF YOU DID NOT ALWAYS FIND ANOTHER TO SHOULDER YOUR BURDEN.
SACRIFICE? THAT'S IT, ISN'T IT?
THAT'S BEEN YOUR WHOLE DEAL ALL ALONG.

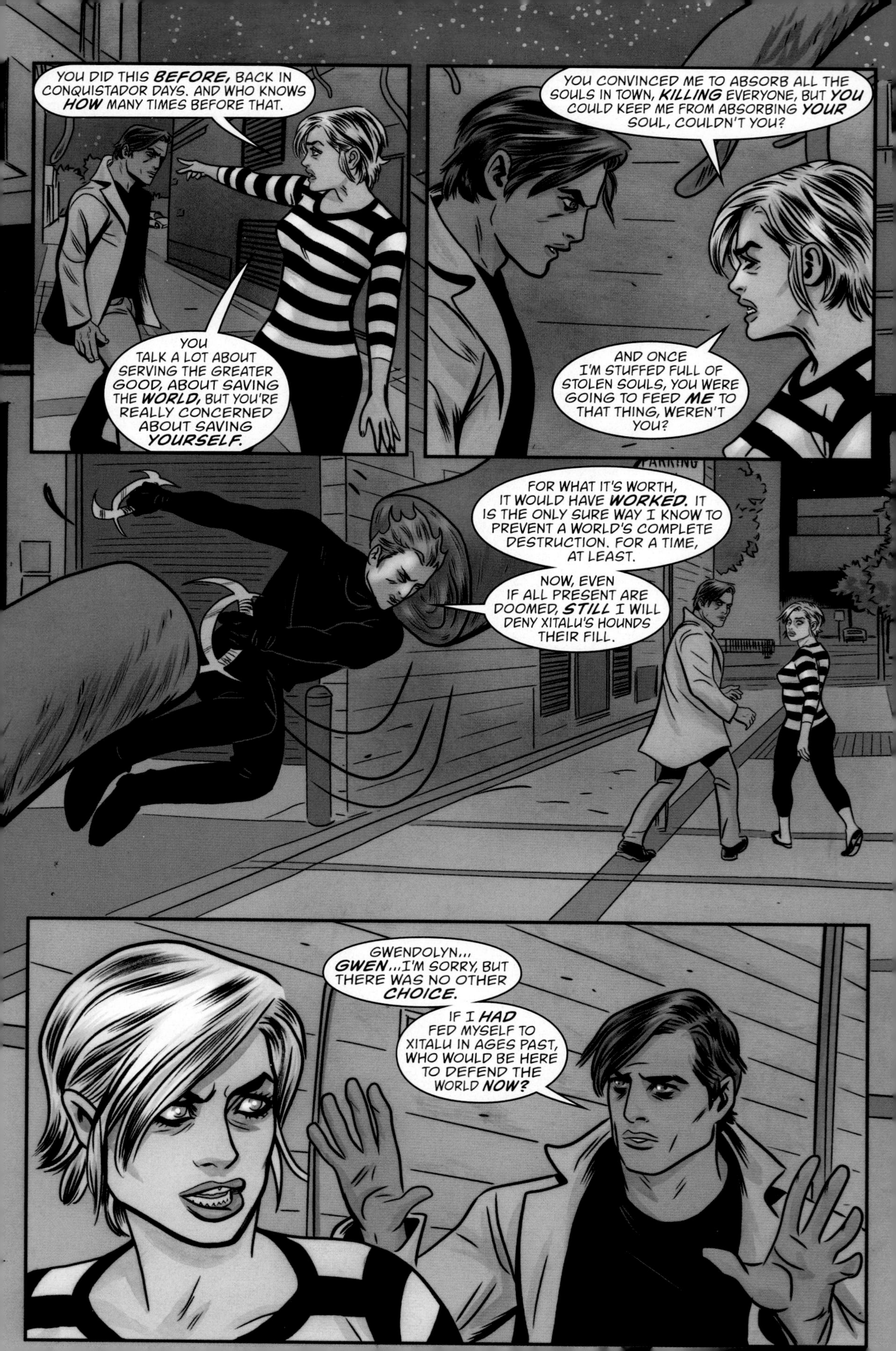

YOU DID THIS BEFORE, BACK IN CONQUISTADOR DAYS. AND WHO KNOWS HOW MANY TIMES BEFORE THAT.
YOU TALK A LOT ABOUT SERVING THE GREATER GOOD, ABOUT SAVING THE WORLD, BUT YOU'RE REALLY CONCERNED ABOUT SAVING YOURSELF.
YOU CONVINCED ME TO ABSORB ALL THE SOULS IN TOWN, KILLING EVERYONE, BUT YOU COULD KEEP ME FROM ABSORBING YOUR SOUL, COULDN'T YOU?
AND ONCE I'M STUFFED FULL OF STOLEN SOULS, YOU WERE GOING TO FEED ME TO THAT THING, WEREN'T YOU?
FOR WHAT IT'S WORTH, IT WOULD HAVE WORKED. IT IS THE ONLY SURE WAY I KNOW TO PREVENT A WORLD'S COMPLETE DESTRUCTION. FOR A TIME, AT LEAST.
NOW, EVEN IF ALL PRESENT ARE DOOMED, STILL I WILL DENY XITALU'S HOUNDS THEIR FILL.
GWENDOLYN... GWEN...I'M SORRY, BUT THERE WAS NO OTHER CHOICE.
IF I HAD FED MYSELF TO XITALU IN AGES PAST, WHO WOULD BE HERE TO DEFEND THE WORLD NOW?

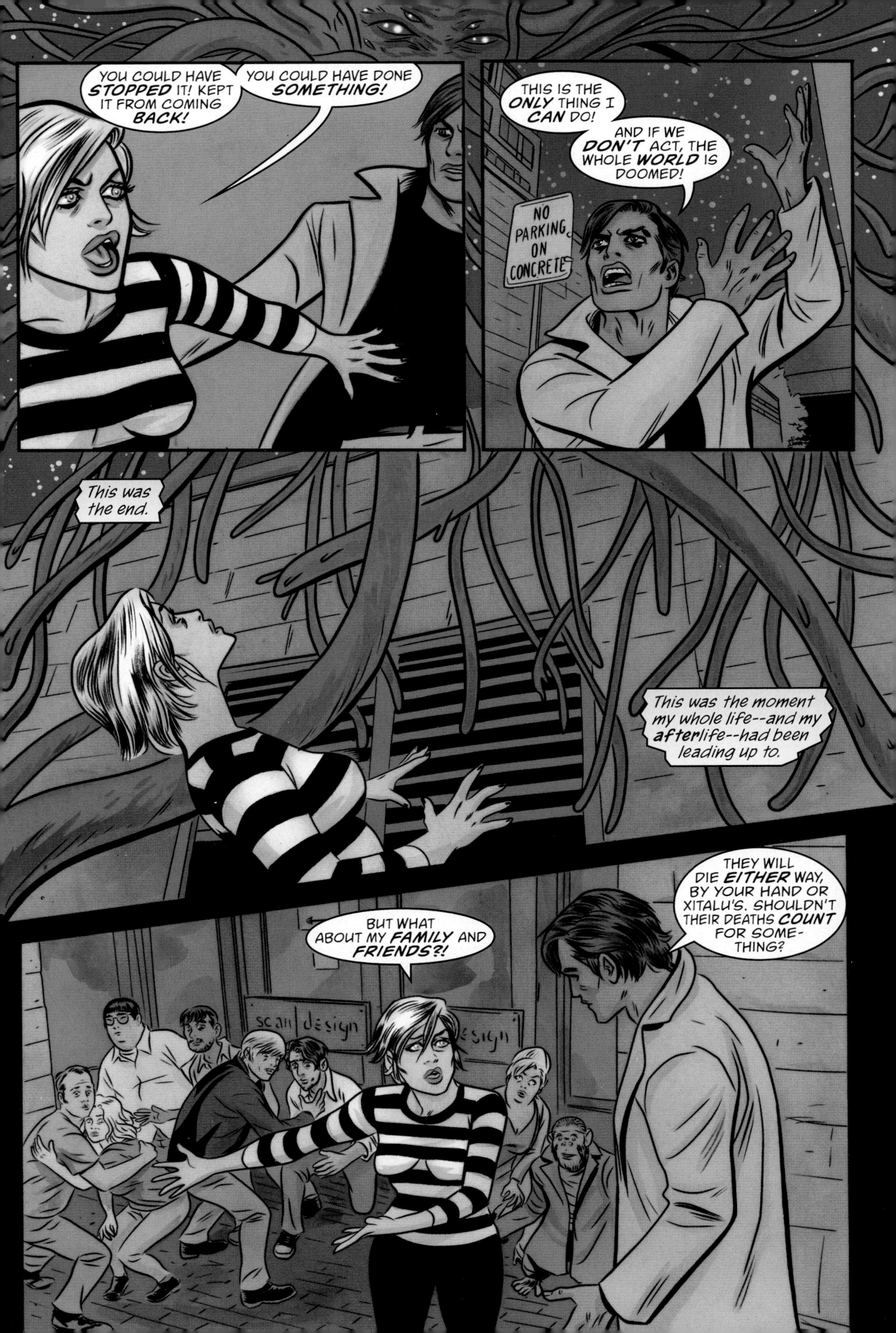
YOU COULD HAVE STOPPED IT! KEPT IT FROM COMING BACK!
YOU COULD HAVE DONE SOMETHING!
THIS IS THE ONLY THING I CAN DO!
AND IF WE DON'T ACT, THE WHOLE WORLD IS DOOMED!
NO PARKING ON CONCRETE
This was the end.
This was the moment my whole life--and my afterlife--had been leading up to.
BUT WHAT ABOUT MY FAMILY AND FRIENDS?!
THEY WILL DIE EITHER WAY, BY YOUR HAND OR XITALU'S. SHOULDN'T THEIR DEATHS COUNT FOR SOME-THING?
scan design
design

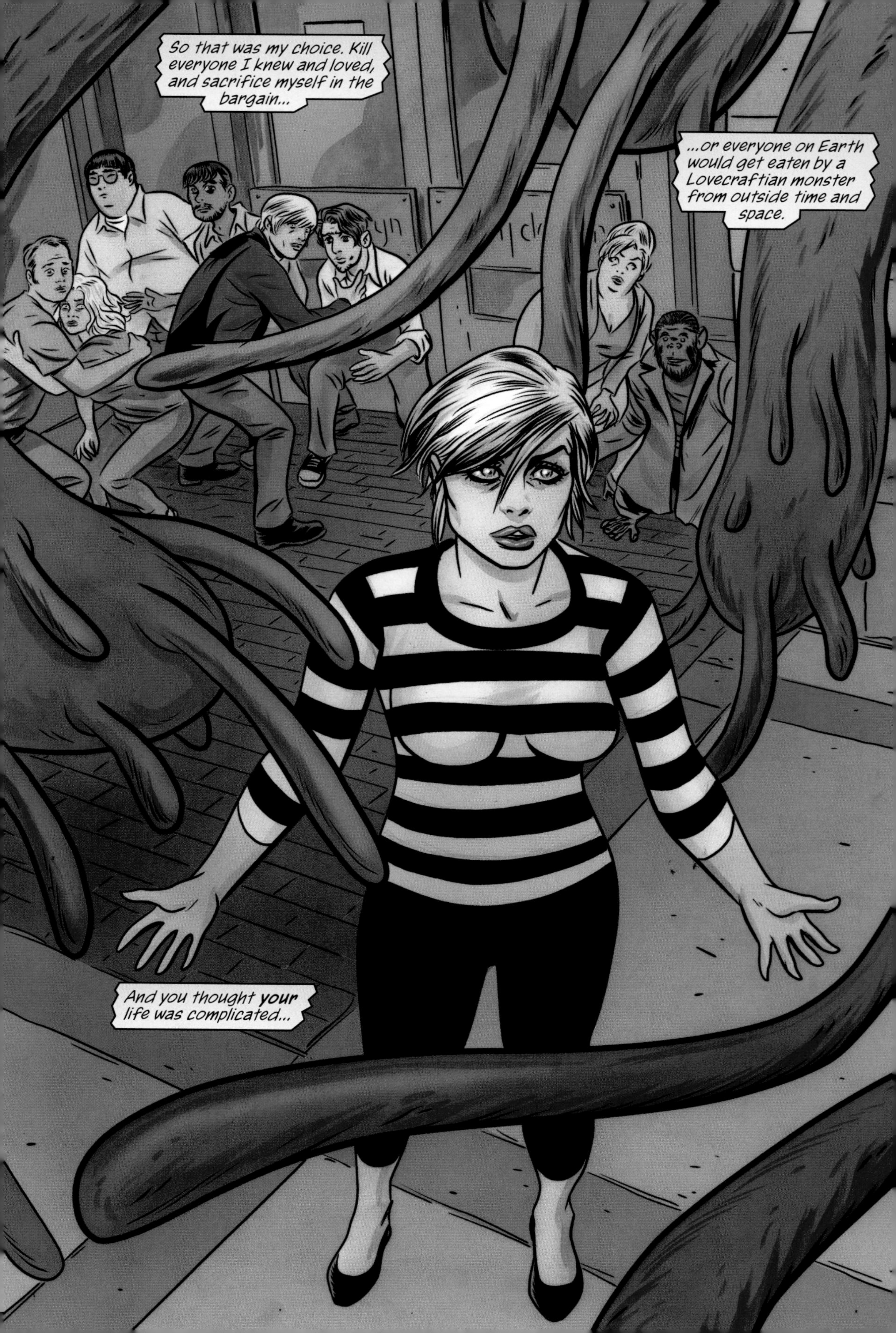
So that was my choice. Kill everyone I knew and loved, and sacrifice myself in the bargain...
...or everyone on Earth would get eaten by a Lovecraftian monster from outside time and space.
And you thought **your** life was complicated...

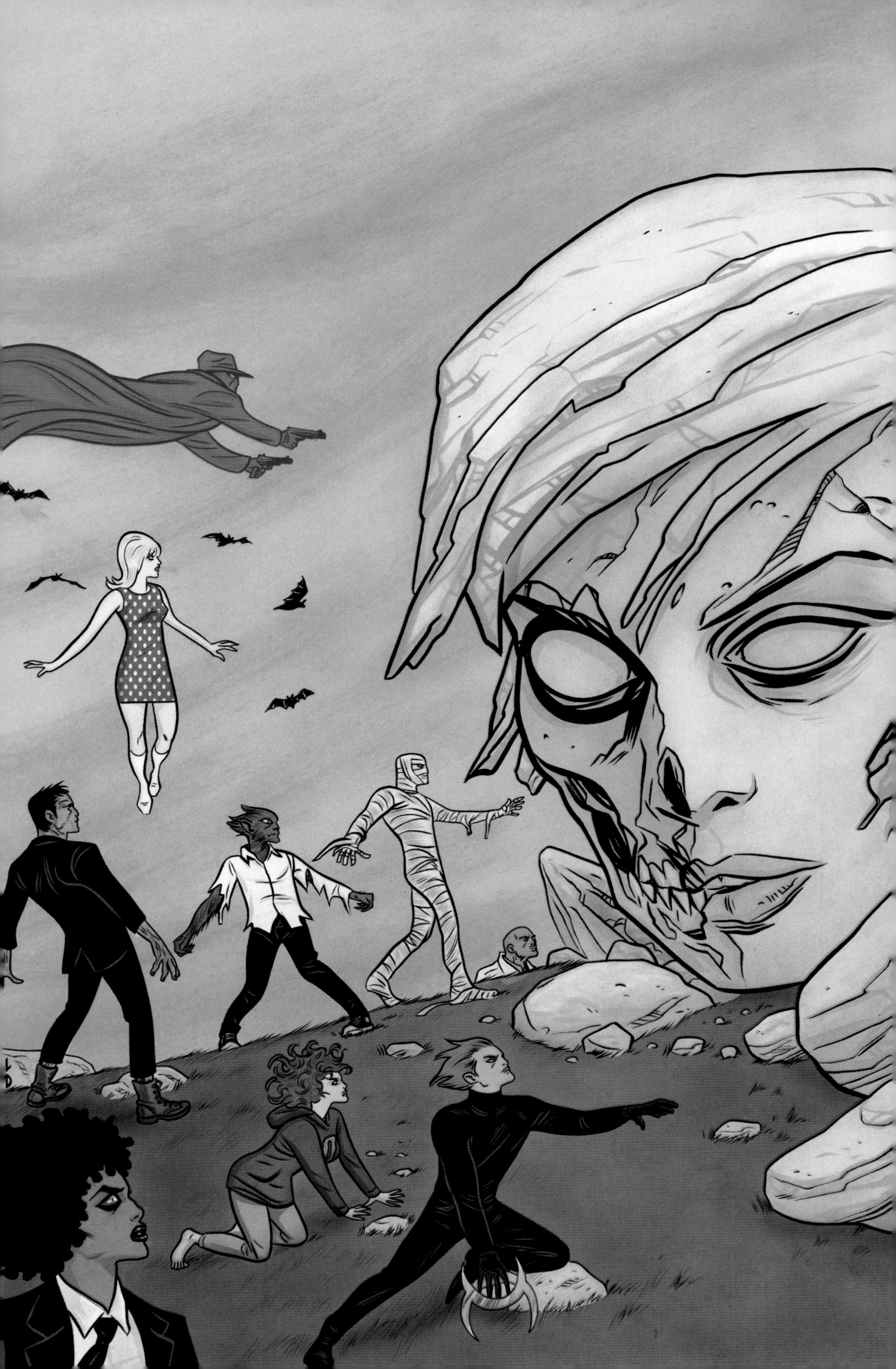

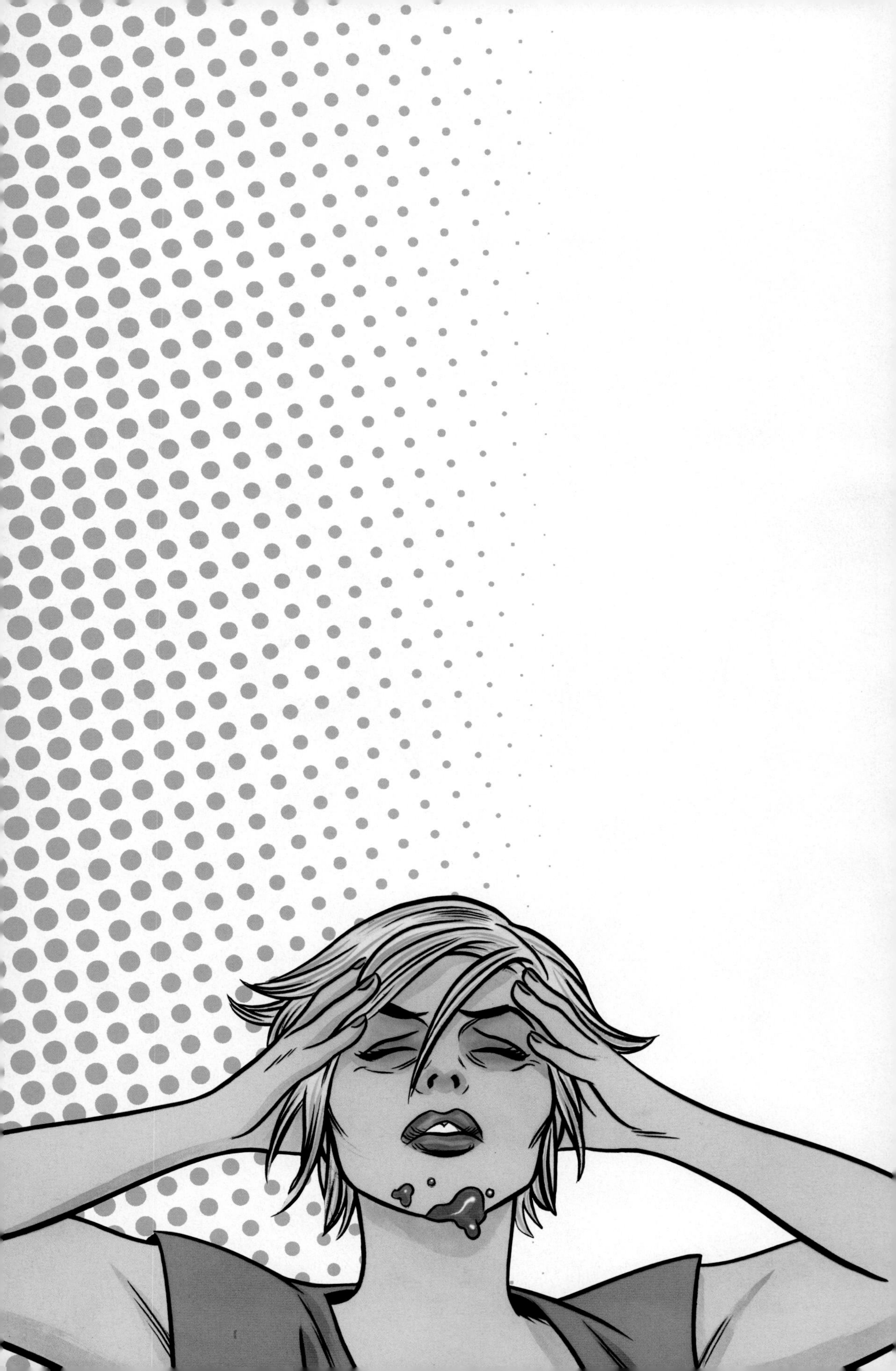

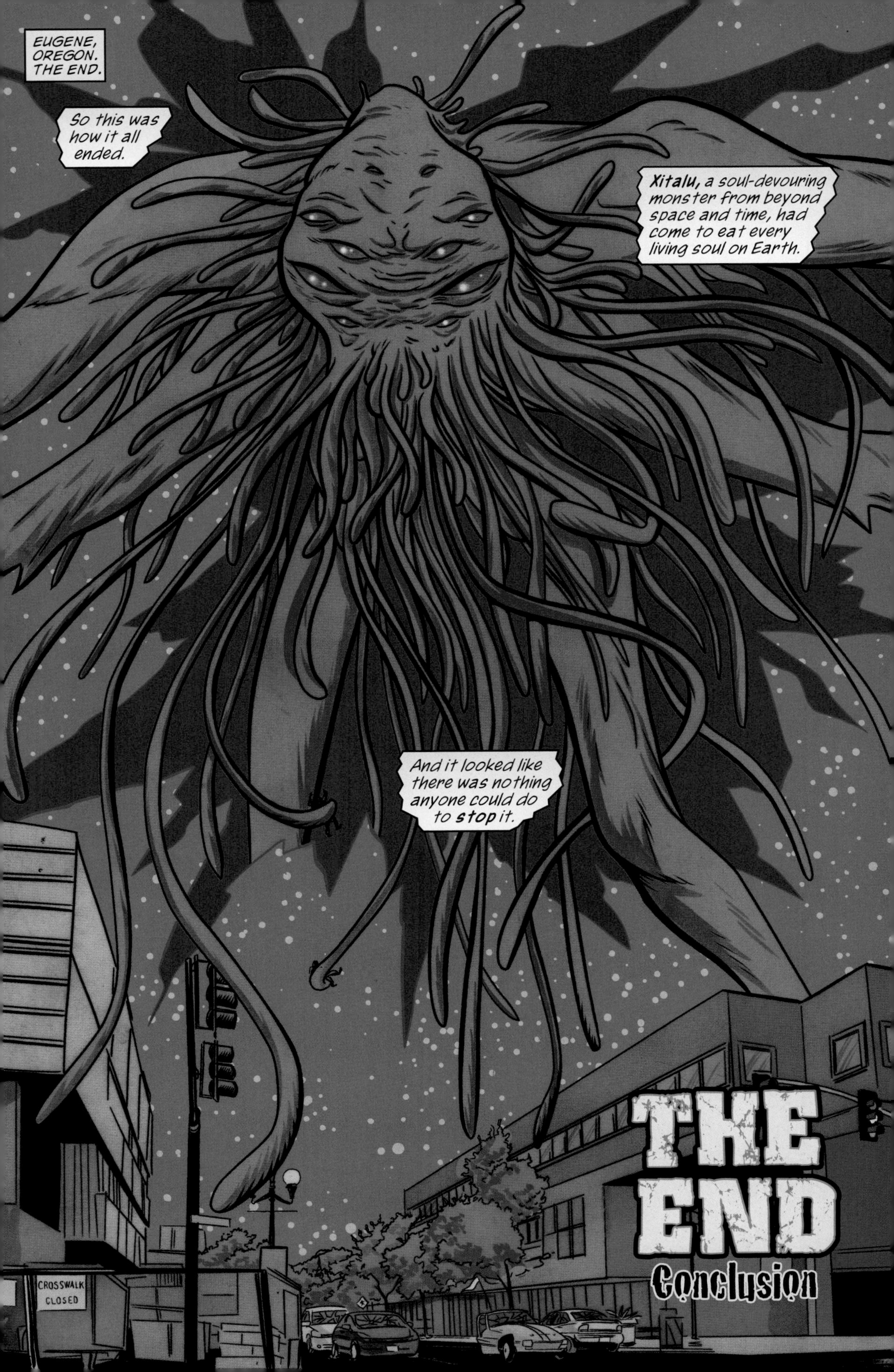
EUGENE, OREGON. THE END.
So this was how it all ended.
Xitalu, a soul-devouring monster from beyond space and time, had come to eat every living soul on Earth.
And it looked like there was nothing anyone could do to stop it.
THE END
Conclusion
CROSSWALK CLOSED

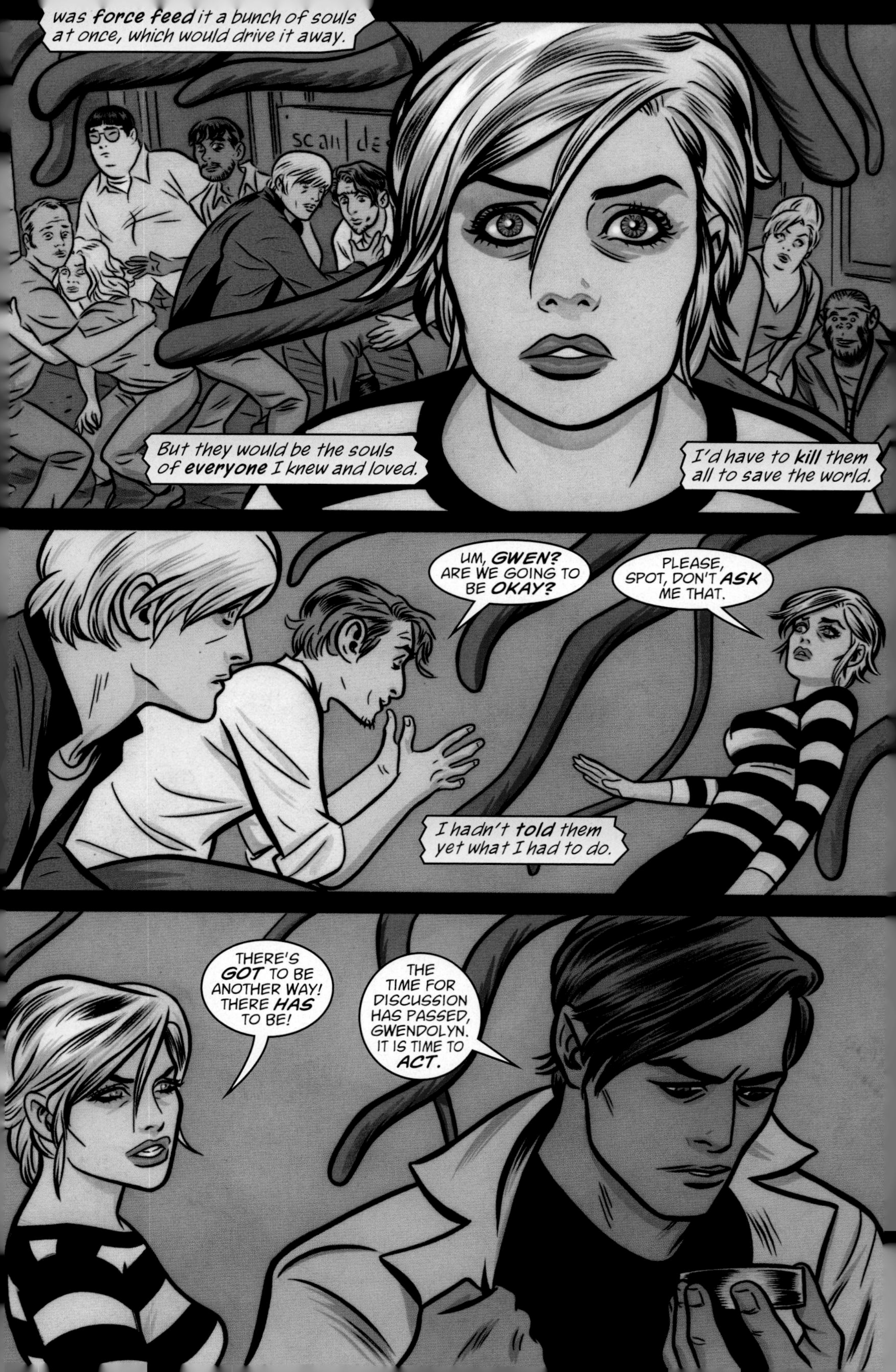
was force feed it a bunch of souls at once, which would drive it away.
scan des
But they would be the souls of everyone I knew and loved.
I'd have to kill them all to save the world.
UM, GWEN? ARE WE GOING TO BE OKAY?
PLEASE, SPOT, DON'T ASK ME THAT.
I hadn't told them yet what I had to do.
THERE'S GOT TO BE ANOTHER WAY! THERE HAS TO BE!
THE TIME FOR DISCUSSION HAS PASSED, GWENDOLYN. IT IS TIME TO ACT.

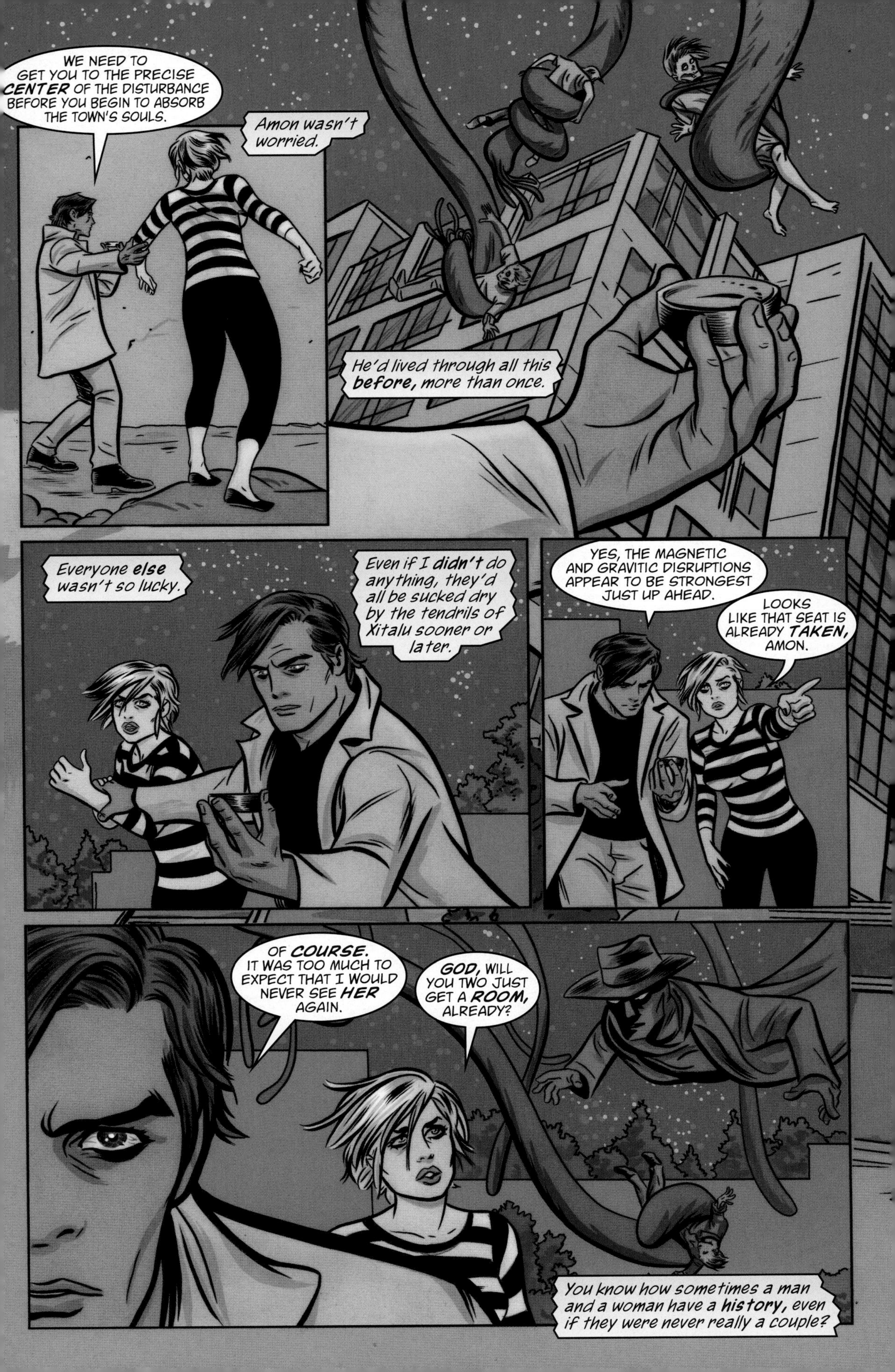

WE NEED TO GET YOU TO THE PRECISE CENTER OF THE DISTURBANCE BEFORE YOU BEGIN TO ABSORB THE TOWN'S SOULS.
Amon wasn't worried.
He'd lived through all this before, more than once.
Everyone else wasn't so lucky.
Even if I didn't do anything, they'd all be sucked dry by the tendrils of Xitalu sooner or later.
YES, THE MAGNETIC AND GRAVITIC DISRUPTIONS APPEAR TO BE STRONGEST JUST UP AHEAD.
LOOKS LIKE THAT SEAT IS ALREADY TAKEN, AMON.
OF COURSE. IT WAS TOO MUCH TO EXPECT THAT I WOULD NEVER SEE HER AGAIN.
GOD, WILL YOU TWO JUST GET A ROOM, ALREADY?
You know how sometimes a man and a woman have a history, even if they were never really a couple?

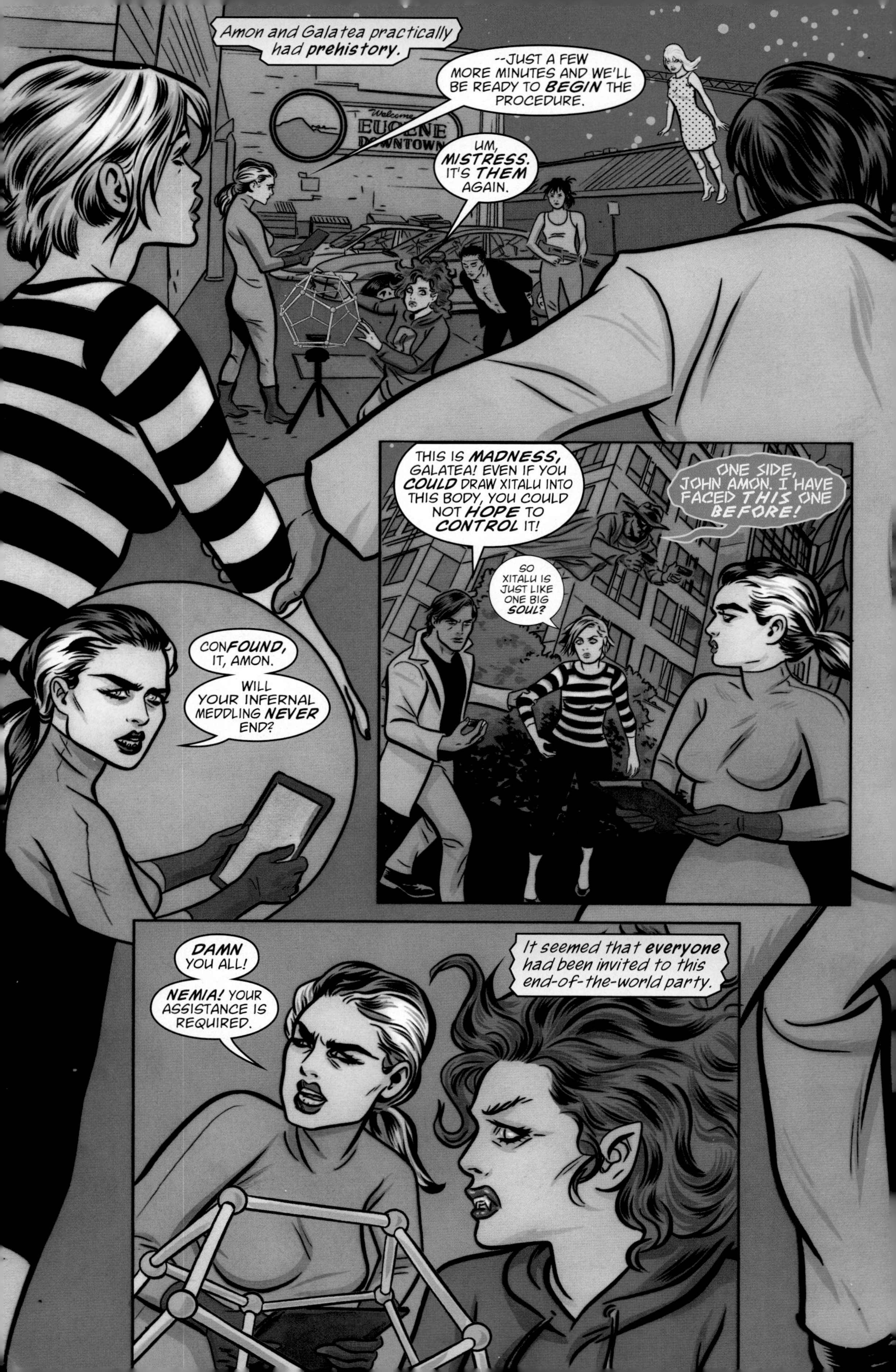
Amon and Galatea practically had prehistory.
--JUST A FEW MORE MINUTES AND WE'LL BE READY TO BEGIN THE PROCEDURE.
Welcome EUGENE DOWNTOWN
UM, MISTRESS. IT'S THEM AGAIN.
THIS IS MADNESS, GALATEA! EVEN IF YOU COULD DRAW XITALU INTO THIS BODY, YOU COULD NOT HOPE TO CONTROL IT!
ONE SIDE, JOHN AMON. I HAVE FACED THIS ONE BEFORE!
SO XITALU IS JUST LIKE ONE BIG SOUL?
CONFOUND, IT, AMON.
WILL YOUR INFERNAL MEDDLING NEVER END?
DAMN YOU ALL!
NEMIA! YOUR ASSISTANCE IS REQUIRED.
It seemed that everyone had been invited to this end-of-the-world party.

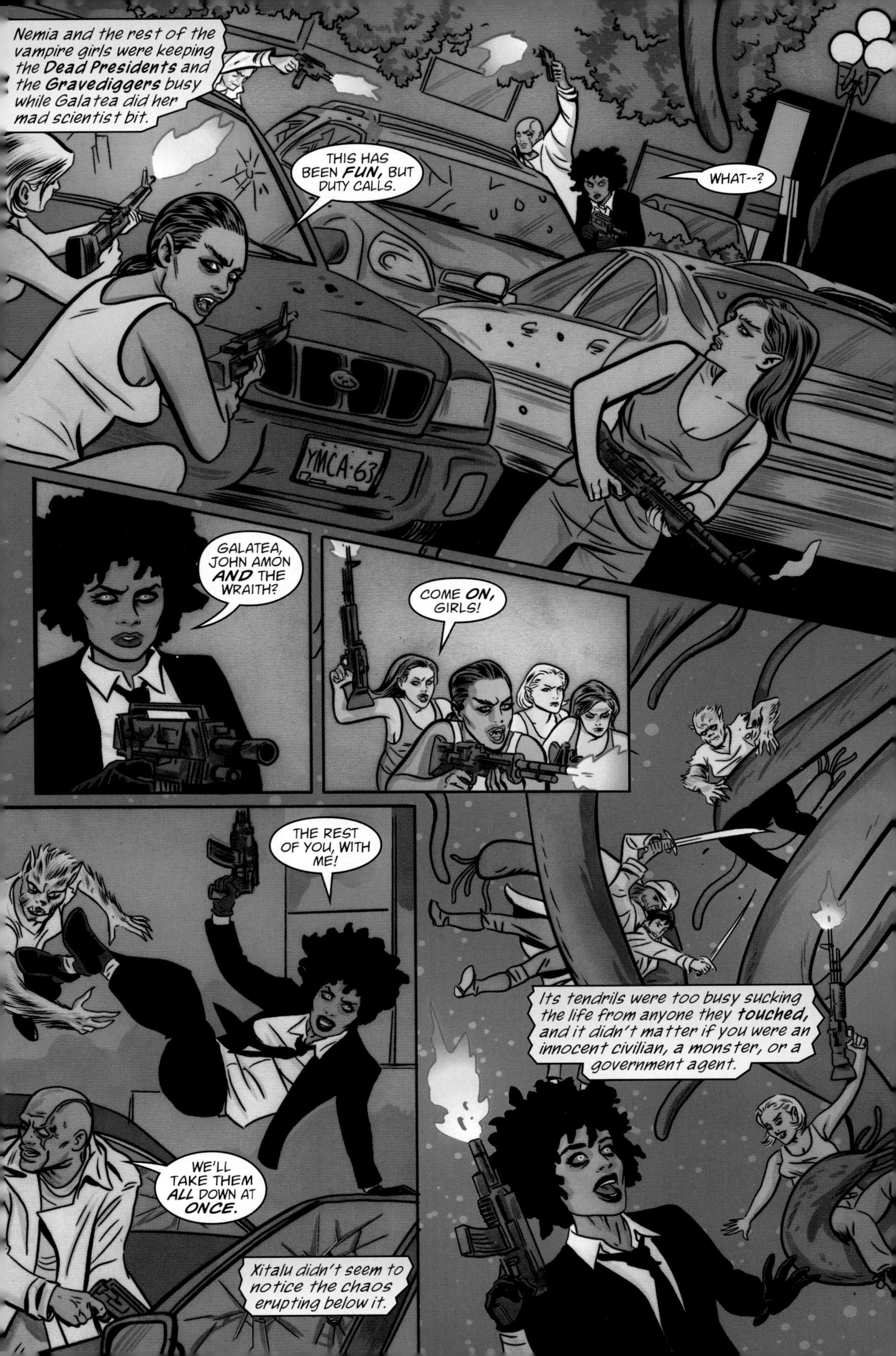
Nemia and the rest of the vampire girls were keeping the **Dead Presidents** and the **Gravediggers** busy while Galatea did her mad scientist bit.
THIS HAS BEEN **FUN,** BUT DUTY CALLS.
WHAT--?
YMCA·63
GALATEA, JOHN AMON **AND** THE WRAITH?
COME **ON,** GIRLS!
THE REST OF YOU, WITH ME!
WE'LL TAKE THEM **ALL** DOWN AT **ONCE**.
Xitalu didn't seem to notice the chaos erupting below it.
Its tendrils were too busy sucking the life from anyone they **touched,** and it didn't matter if you were an innocent civilian, a monster, or a government agent.

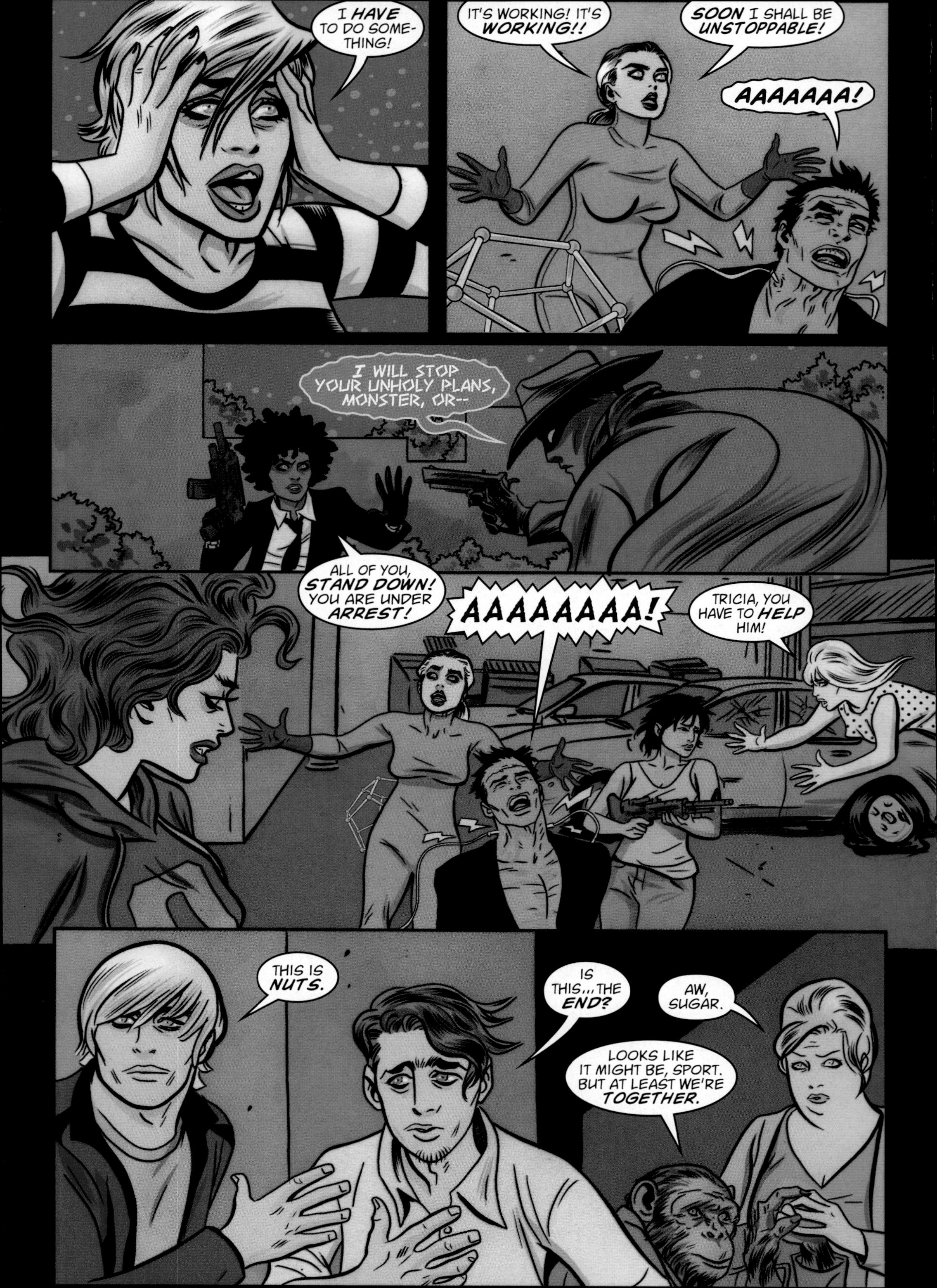
I HAVE TO DO SOME-THING!
IT'S WORKING! IT'S WORKING!!
SOON I SHALL BE UNSTOPPABLE!
AAAAAAA!
I WILL STOP YOUR UNHOLY PLANS, MONSTER, OR--
ALL OF YOU, STAND DOWN! YOU ARE UNDER ARREST!
AAAAAAAA!
TRICIA, YOU HAVE TO HELP HIM!
THIS IS NUTS.
IS THIS... THE END?
AW, SUGAR.
LOOKS LIKE IT MIGHT BE, SPORT. BUT AT LEAST WE'RE TOGETHER.

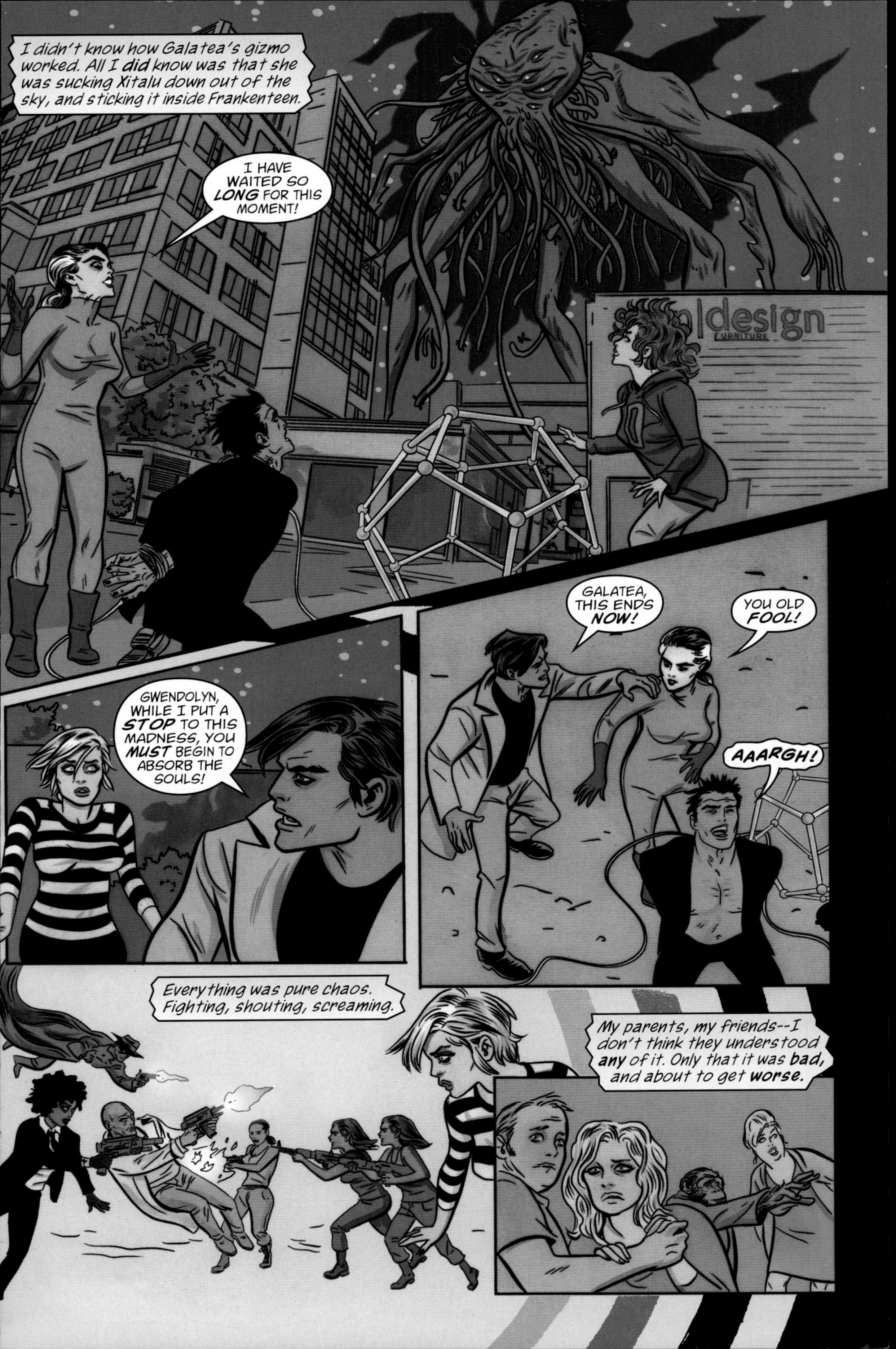
I didn't know how Galatea's gizmo worked. All I did know was that she was sucking Xitalu down out of the sky, and sticking it inside Frankenteen.
I HAVE WAITED SO LONG FOR THIS MOMENT!
GWENDOLYN, WHILE I PUT A STOP TO THIS MADNESS, YOU MUST BEGIN TO ABSORB THE SOULS!
GALATEA, THIS ENDS NOW!
YOU OLD FOOL!
AAARGH!
Everything was pure chaos. Fighting, shouting, screaming.
My parents, my friends--I don't think they understood any of it. Only that it was bad, and about to get worse.

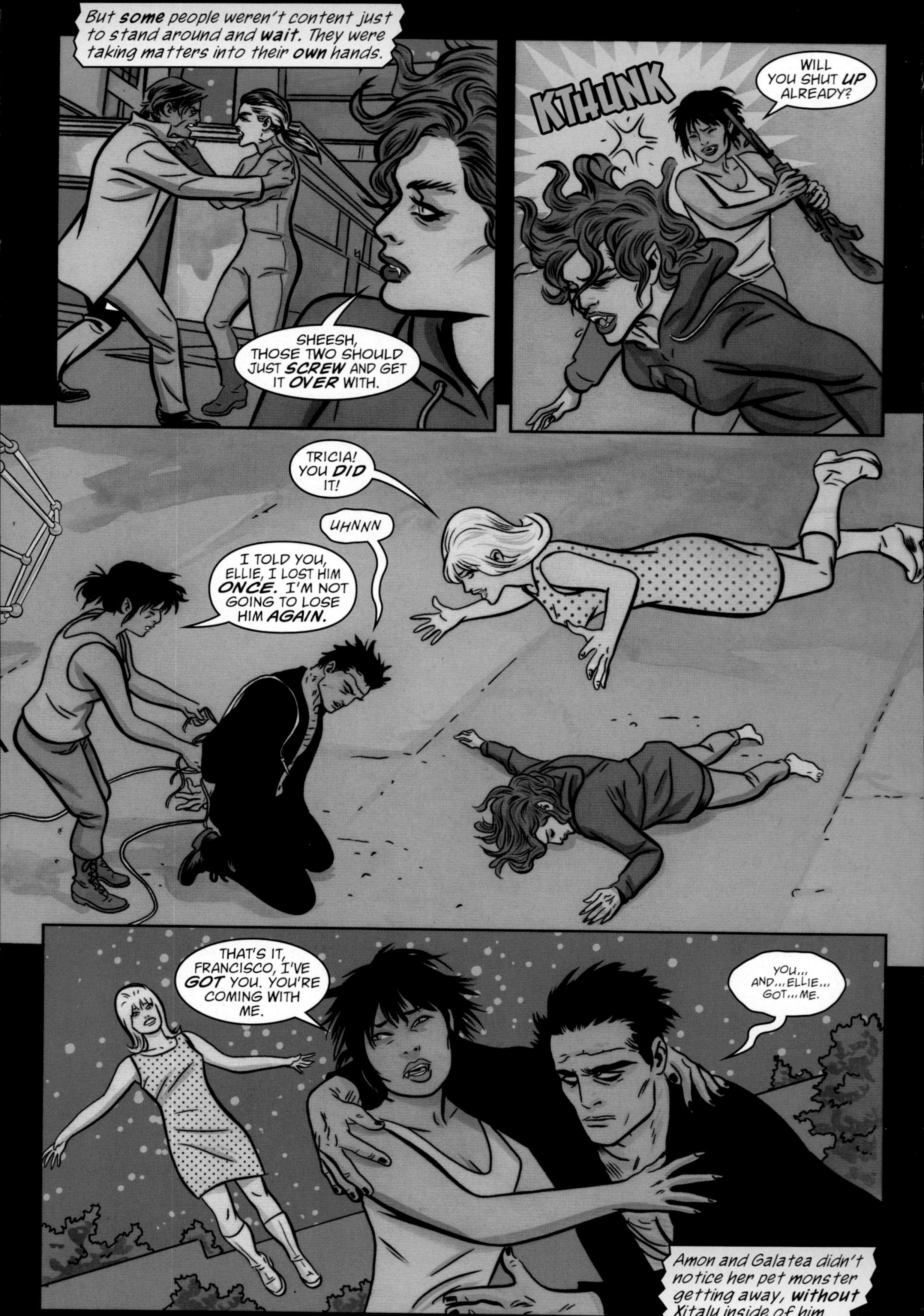
But some people weren't content just to stand around and wait. They were taking matters into their own hands.
SHEESH, THOSE TWO SHOULD JUST SCREW AND GET IT OVER WITH.
KTHUNK
WILL YOU SHUT UP ALREADY?
TRICIA! YOU DID IT!
UHNNN
I TOLD YOU, ELLIE, I LOST HIM ONCE. I'M NOT GOING TO LOSE HIM AGAIN.
THAT'S IT, FRANCISCO, I'VE GOT YOU. YOU'RE COMING WITH ME.
YOU... AND... ELLIE... GOT... ME.
Amon and Galatea didn't notice her pet monster getting away, without

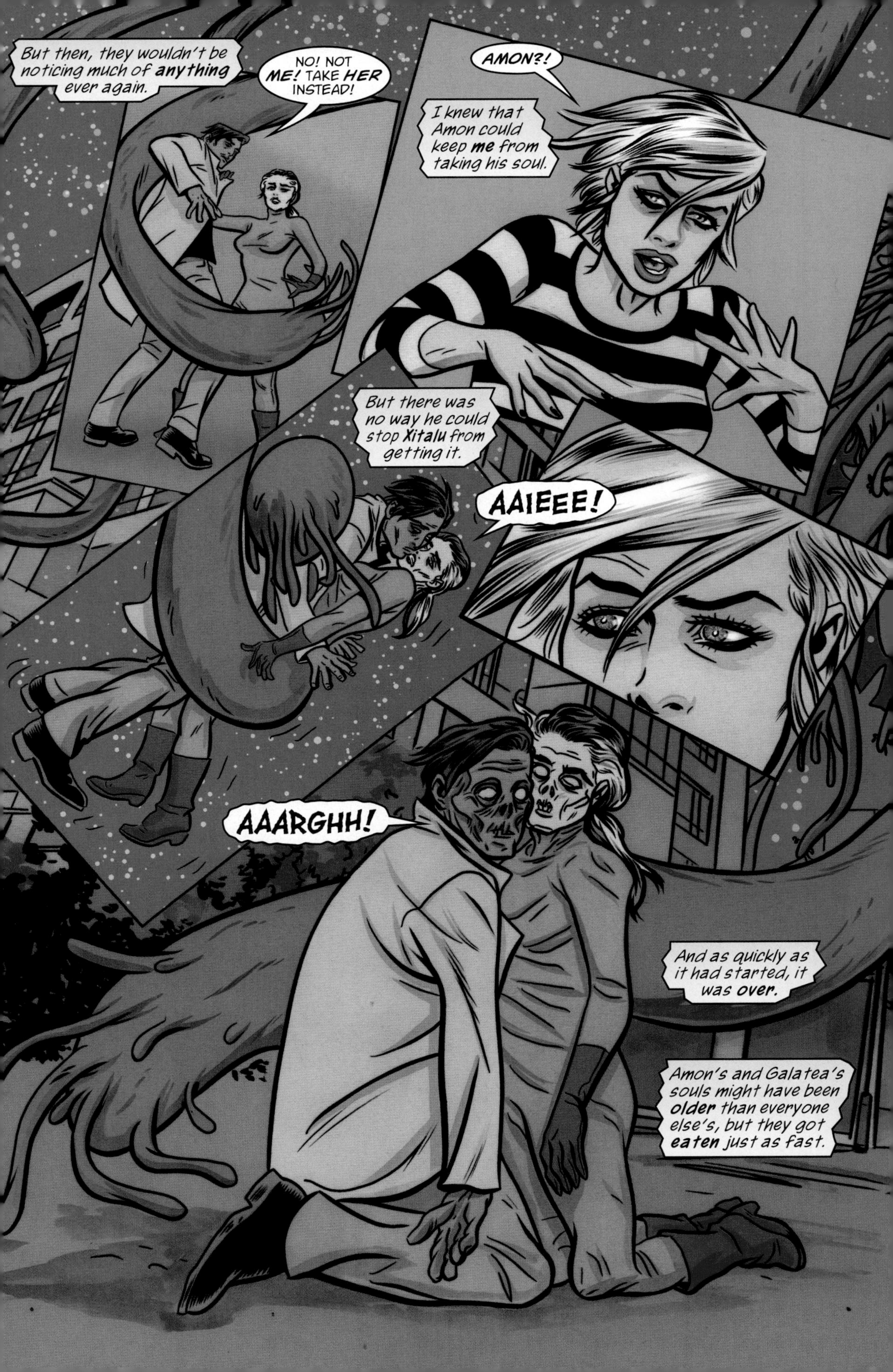

But then, they wouldn't be noticing much of **anything** ever again.
NO! NOT **ME!** TAKE **HER** INSTEAD!
AMON?!
I knew that Amon could keep **me** from taking his soul.
But there was no way he could stop **Xitalu** from getting it.
AAIEEE!
AAARGHH!
And as quickly as it had started, it was **over.**
Amon's and Galatea's souls might have been **older** than everyone else's, but they got **eaten** just as fast.

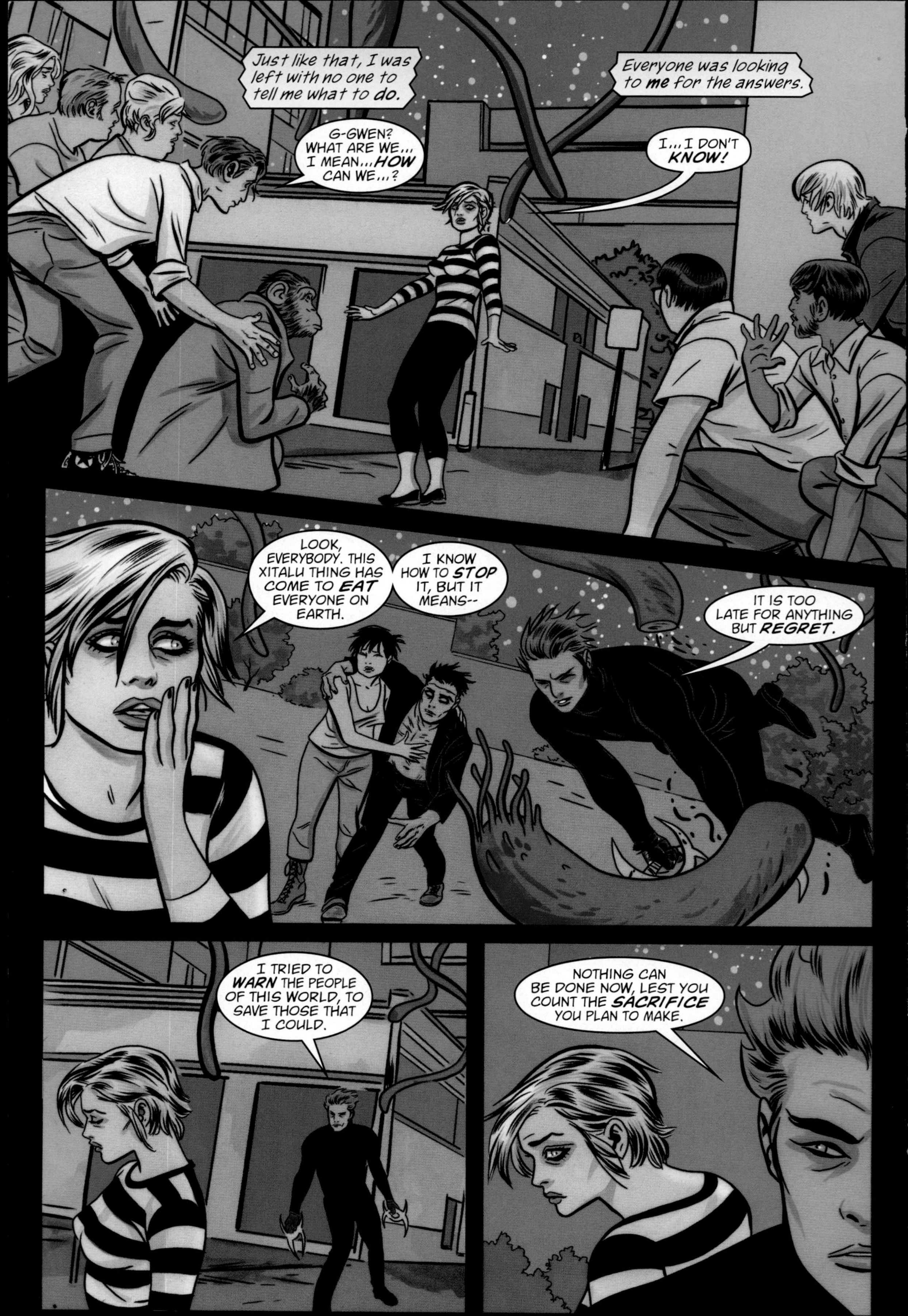
Just like that, I was left with no one to tell me what to do.
G-GWEN? WHAT ARE WE... I MEAN...HOW CAN WE...?
Everyone was looking to me for the answers.
I... I DON'T KNOW!
LOOK, EVERYBODY. THIS XITALU THING HAS COME TO EAT EVERYONE ON EARTH.
I KNOW HOW TO STOP IT, BUT IT MEANS--
IT IS TOO LATE FOR ANYTHING BUT REGRET.
I TRIED TO WARN THE PEOPLE OF THIS WORLD, TO SAVE THOSE THAT I COULD.
NOTHING CAN BE DONE NOW, LEST YOU COUNT THE SACRIFICE YOU PLAN TO MAKE.

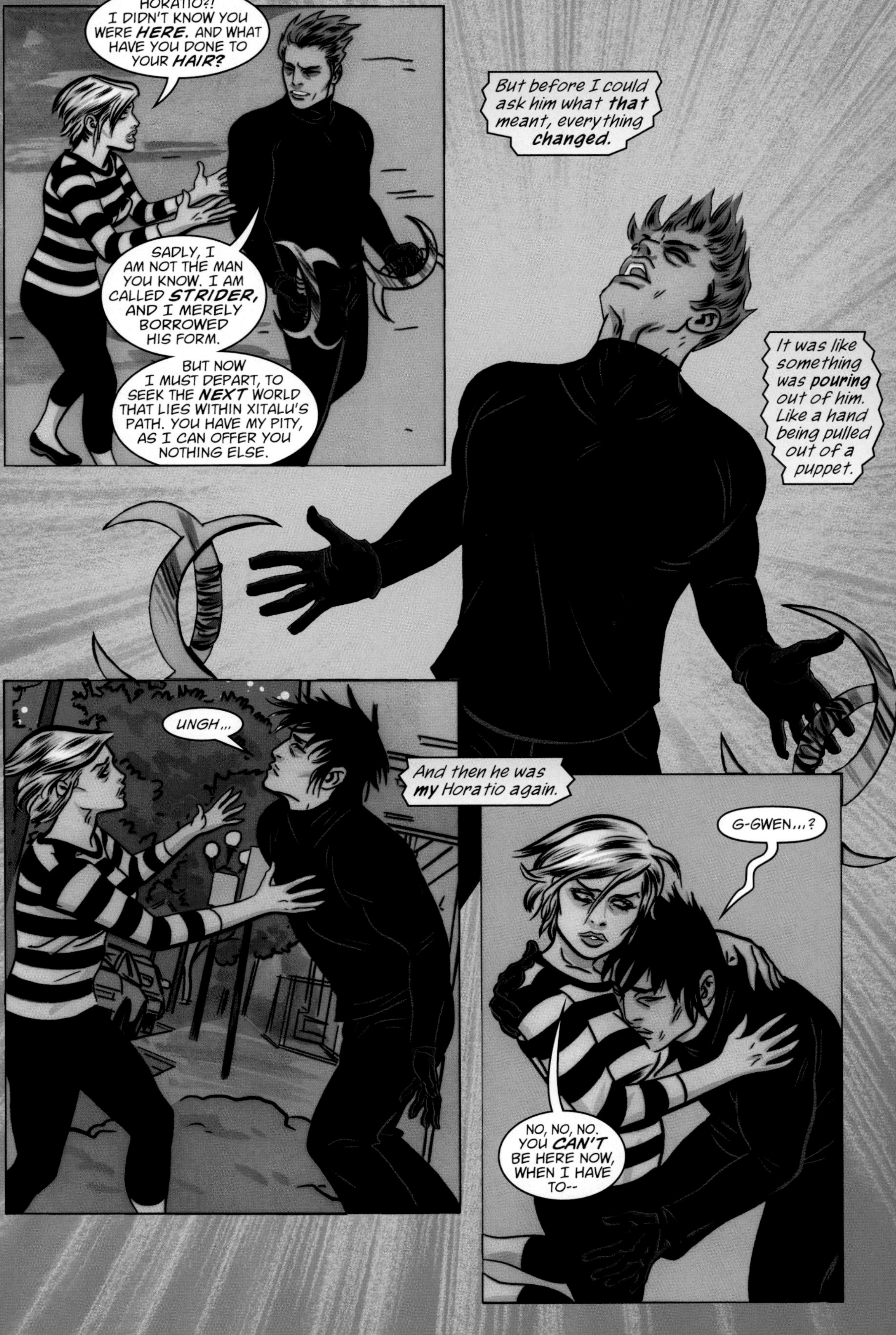
HORATIO?! I DIDN'T KNOW YOU WERE HERE. AND WHAT HAVE YOU DONE TO YOUR HAIR?
SADLY, I AM NOT THE MAN YOU KNOW. I AM CALLED STRIDER, AND I MERELY BORROWED HIS FORM.
BUT NOW I MUST DEPART, TO SEEK THE NEXT WORLD THAT LIES WITHIN XITALU'S PATH. YOU HAVE MY PITY, AS I CAN OFFER YOU NOTHING ELSE.
But before I could ask him what that meant, everything changed.
It was like something was pouring out of him. Like a hand being pulled out of a puppet.
UNGH...
And then he was my Horatio again.
G-GWEN...?
NO, NO, NO. YOU CAN'T BE HERE NOW, WHEN I HAVE TO--

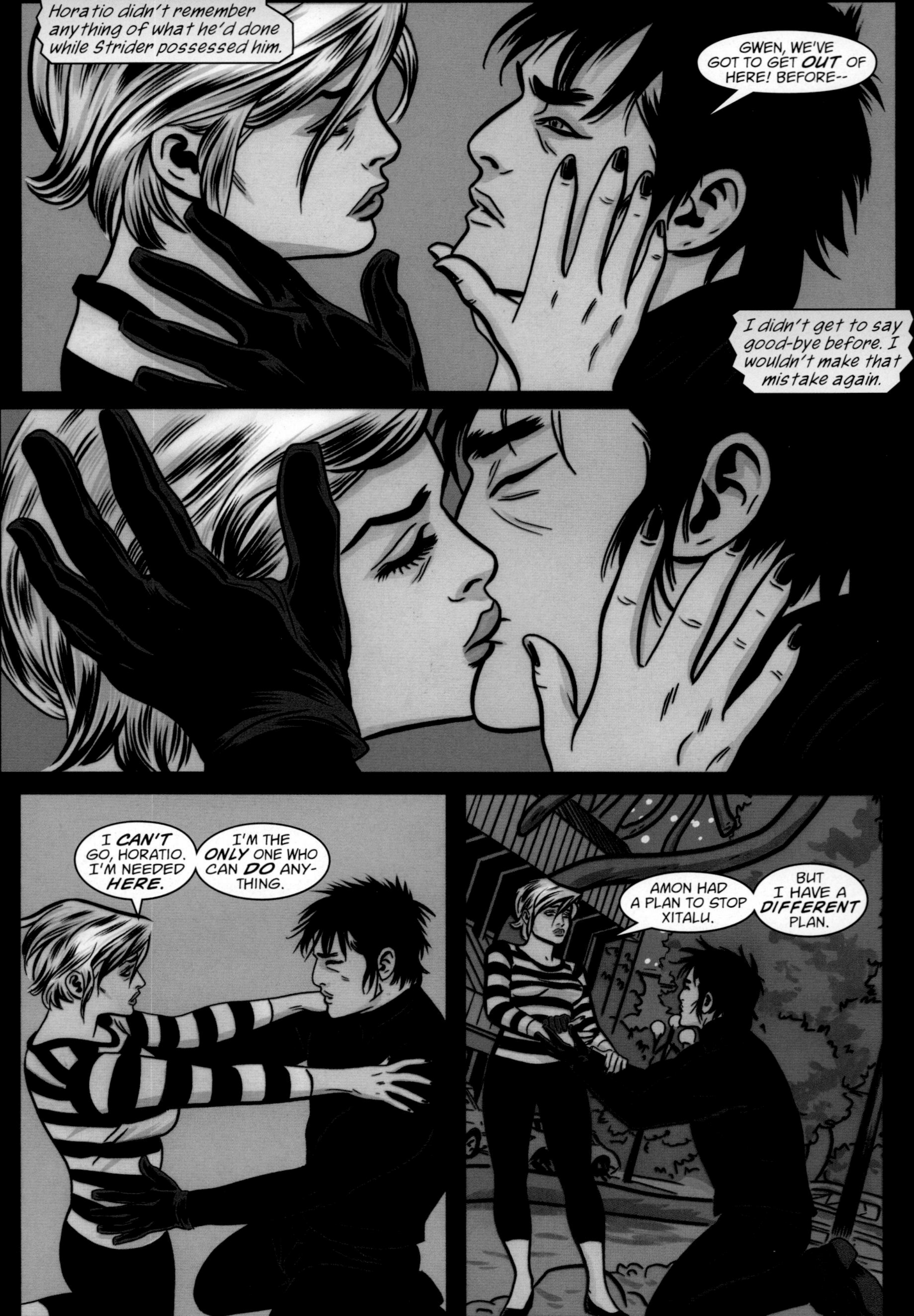
Horatio didn't remember anything of what he'd done while Strider possessed him.
GWEN, WE'VE GOT TO GET **OUT** OF HERE! BEFORE--
I didn't get to say good-bye before. I wouldn't make that mistake again.
I **CAN'T** GO, HORATIO. I'M NEEDED **HERE.**
I'M THE **ONLY** ONE WHO CAN **DO** ANY-THING.
AMON HAD A PLAN TO STOP XITALU.
BUT I HAVE A **DIFFERENT** PLAN.

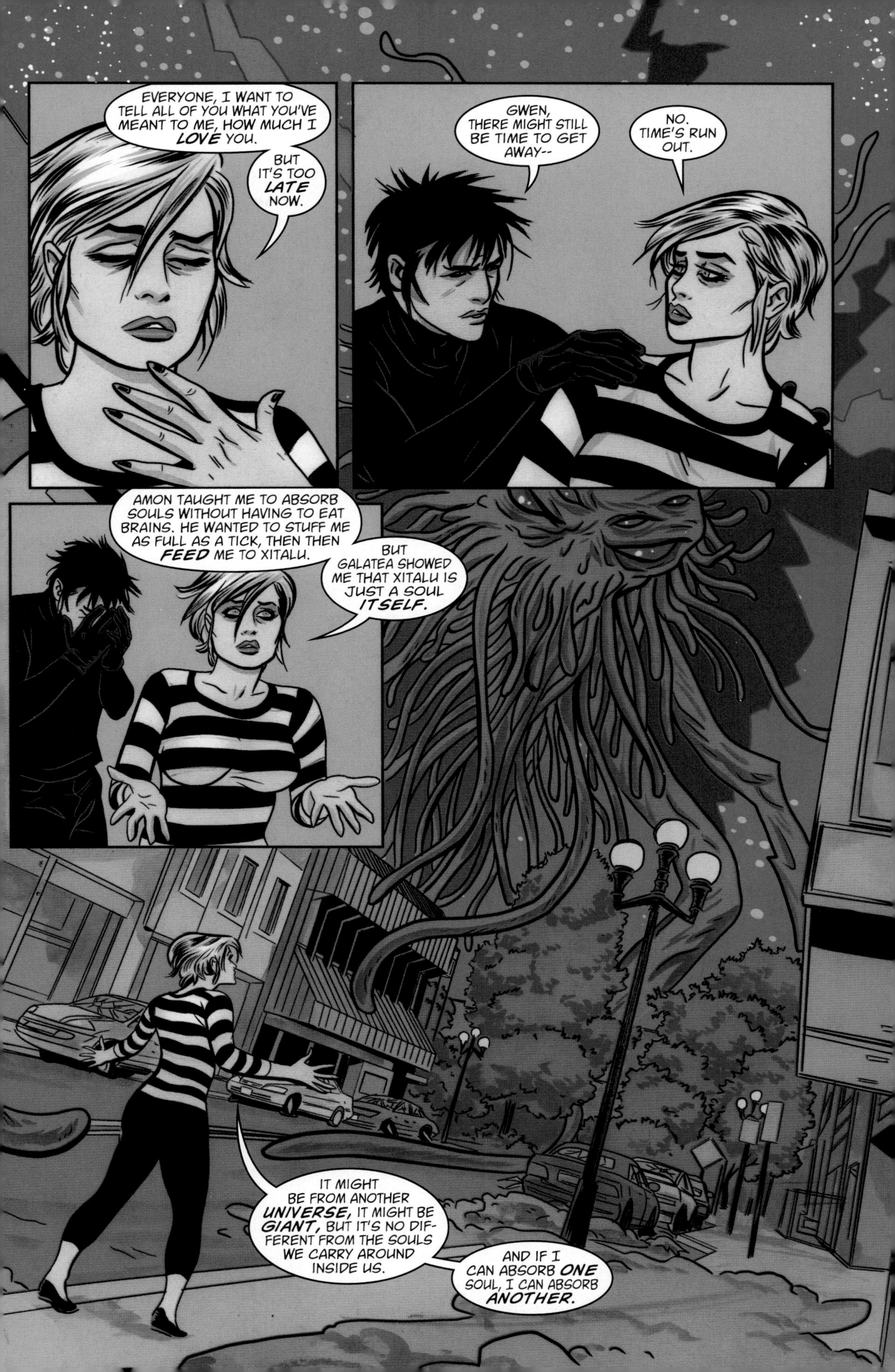
EVERYONE, I WANT TO TELL ALL OF YOU WHAT YOU'VE MEANT TO ME, HOW MUCH I LOVE YOU.
BUT IT'S TOO LATE NOW.
GWEN, THERE MIGHT STILL BE TIME TO GET AWAY--
NO. TIME'S RUN OUT.
AMON TAUGHT ME TO ABSORB SOULS WITHOUT HAVING TO EAT BRAINS. HE WANTED TO STUFF ME AS FULL AS A TICK, THEN THEN FEED ME TO XITALU.
BUT GALATEA SHOWED ME THAT XITALU IS JUST A SOUL ITSELF.
IT MIGHT BE FROM ANOTHER UNIVERSE, IT MIGHT BE GIANT, BUT IT'S NO DIF-FERENT FROM THE SOULS WE CARRY AROUND INSIDE US.
AND IF I CAN ABSORB ONE SOUL, I CAN ABSORB ANOTHER.

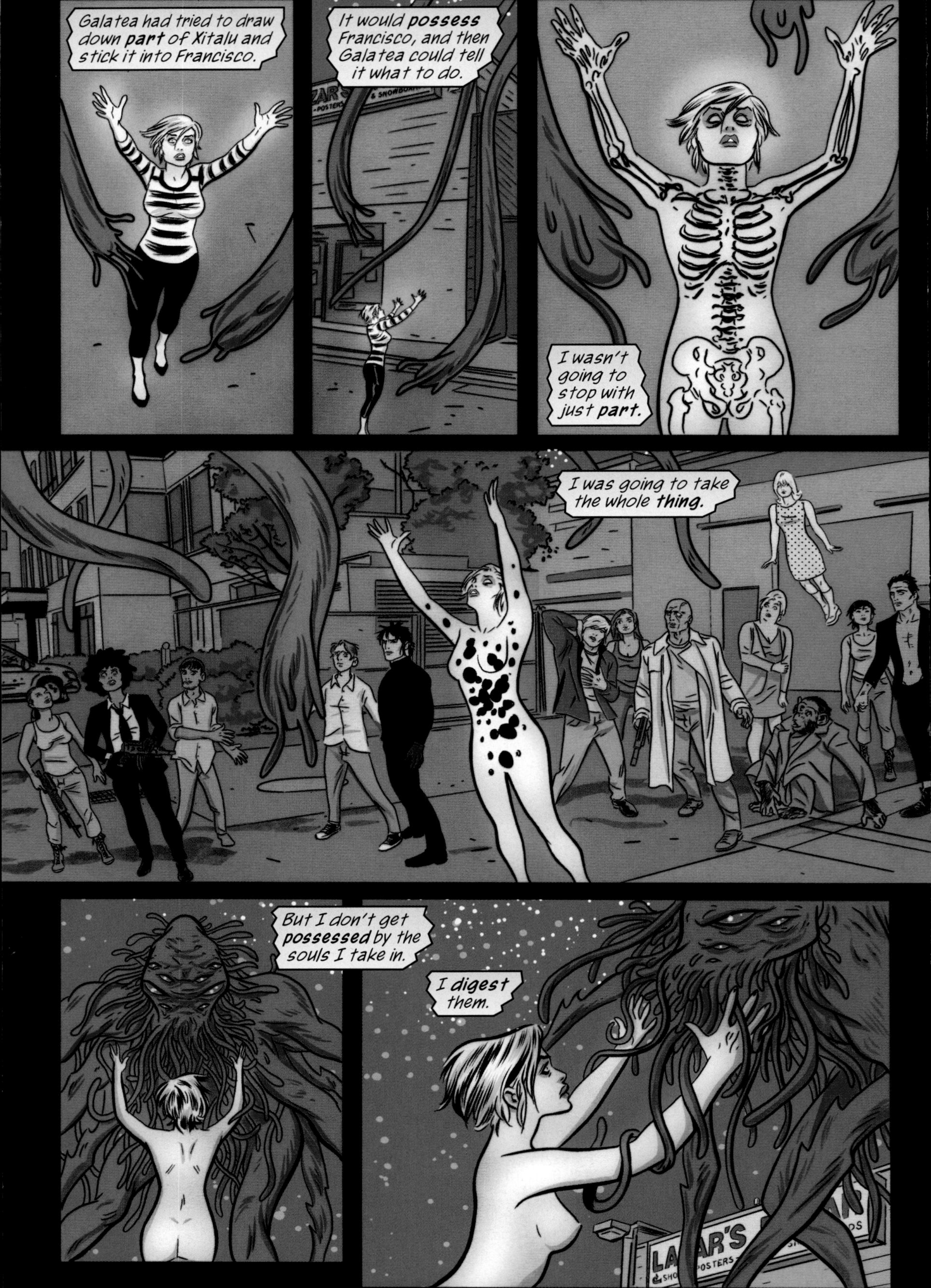
Galatea had tried to draw down part of Xitalu and stick it into Francisco.
It would possess Francisco, and then Galatea could tell it what to do.
I wasn't going to stop with just part.
I was going to take the whole thing.
But I don't get possessed by the souls I take in.
I digest them.

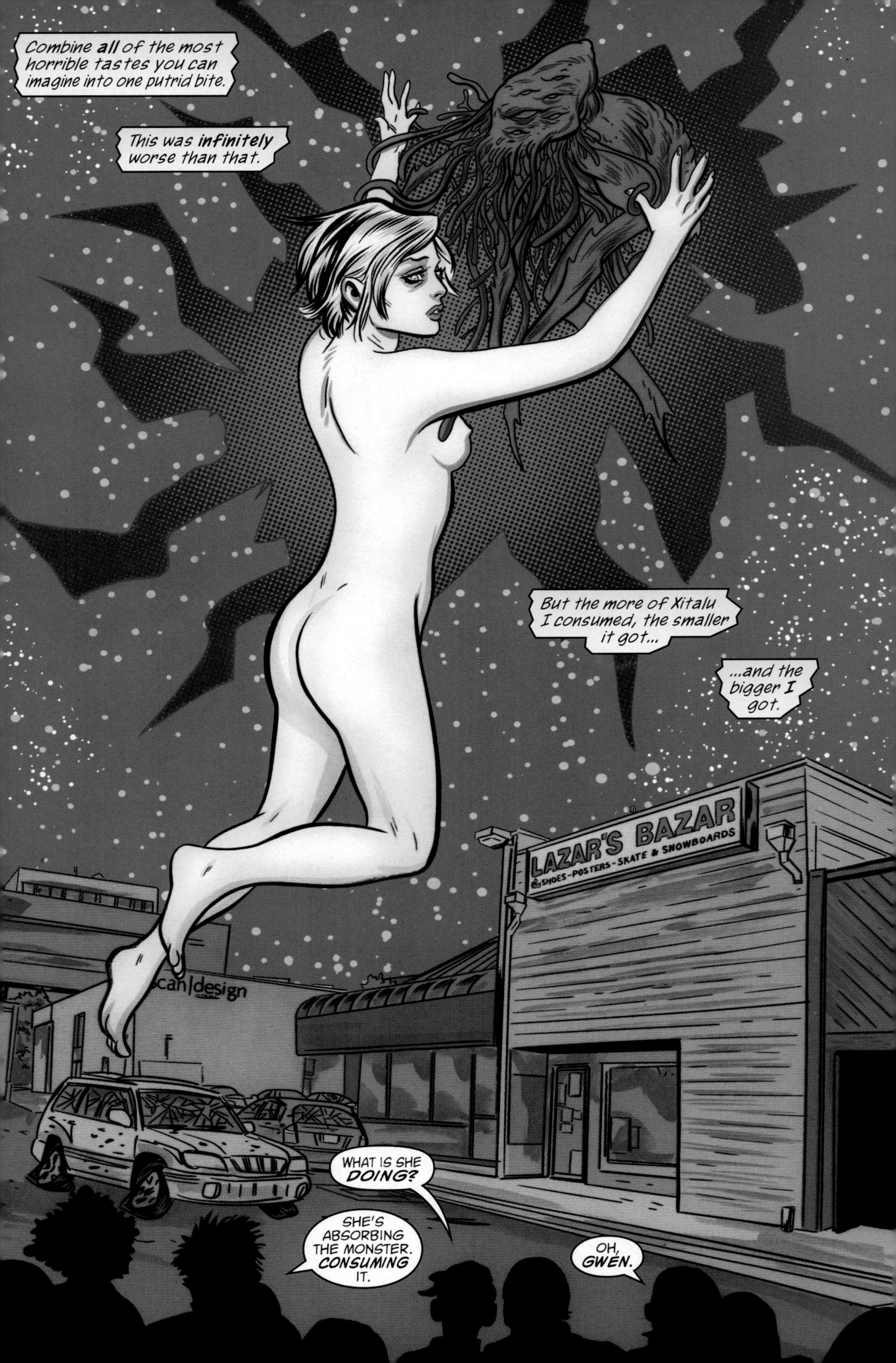
Combine all of the most horrible tastes you can imagine into one putrid bite.
This was infinitely worse than that.
But the more of Xitalu I consumed, the smaller it got...
...and the bigger I got.
LAZAR'S BAZAR
SHOES-POSTERS-SKATE & SNOWBOARDS
scan|design
WHAT IS SHE DOING?
SHE'S ABSORBING THE MONSTER. CONSUMING IT.
OH, GWEN.

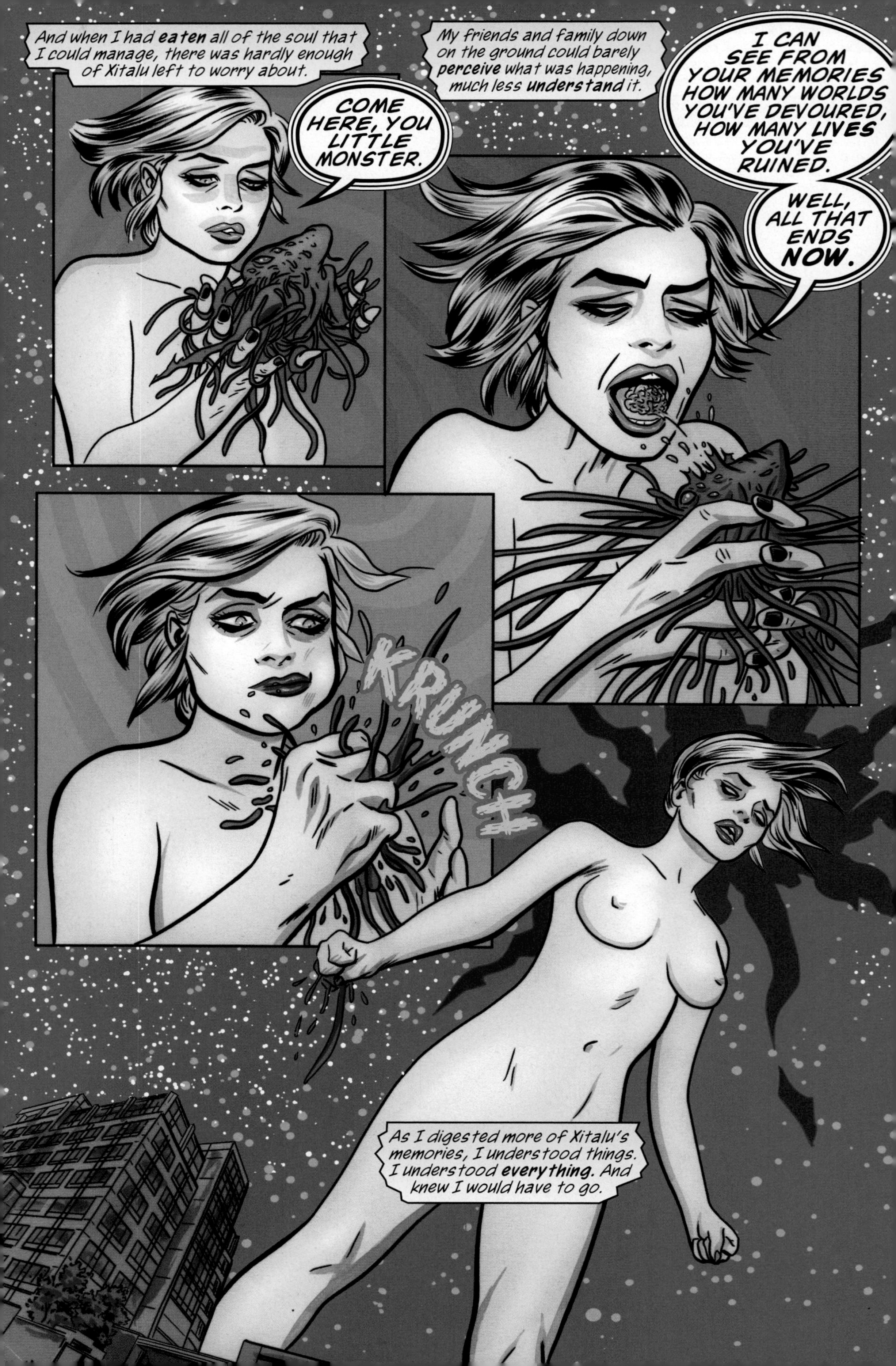
And when I had **eaten** all of the soul that I could manage, there was hardly enough of Xitalu left to worry about.
COME HERE, YOU LITTLE MONSTER.
My friends and family down on the ground could barely **perceive** what was happening, much less **understand** it.
I CAN SEE FROM YOUR MEMORIES HOW MANY WORLDS YOU'VE DEVOURED, HOW MANY **LIVES** YOU'VE RUINED.
WELL, ALL THAT ENDS **NOW.**
KRUNCH
As I digested more of Xitalu's memories, I understood things. I understood **everything.** And knew I would have to go.

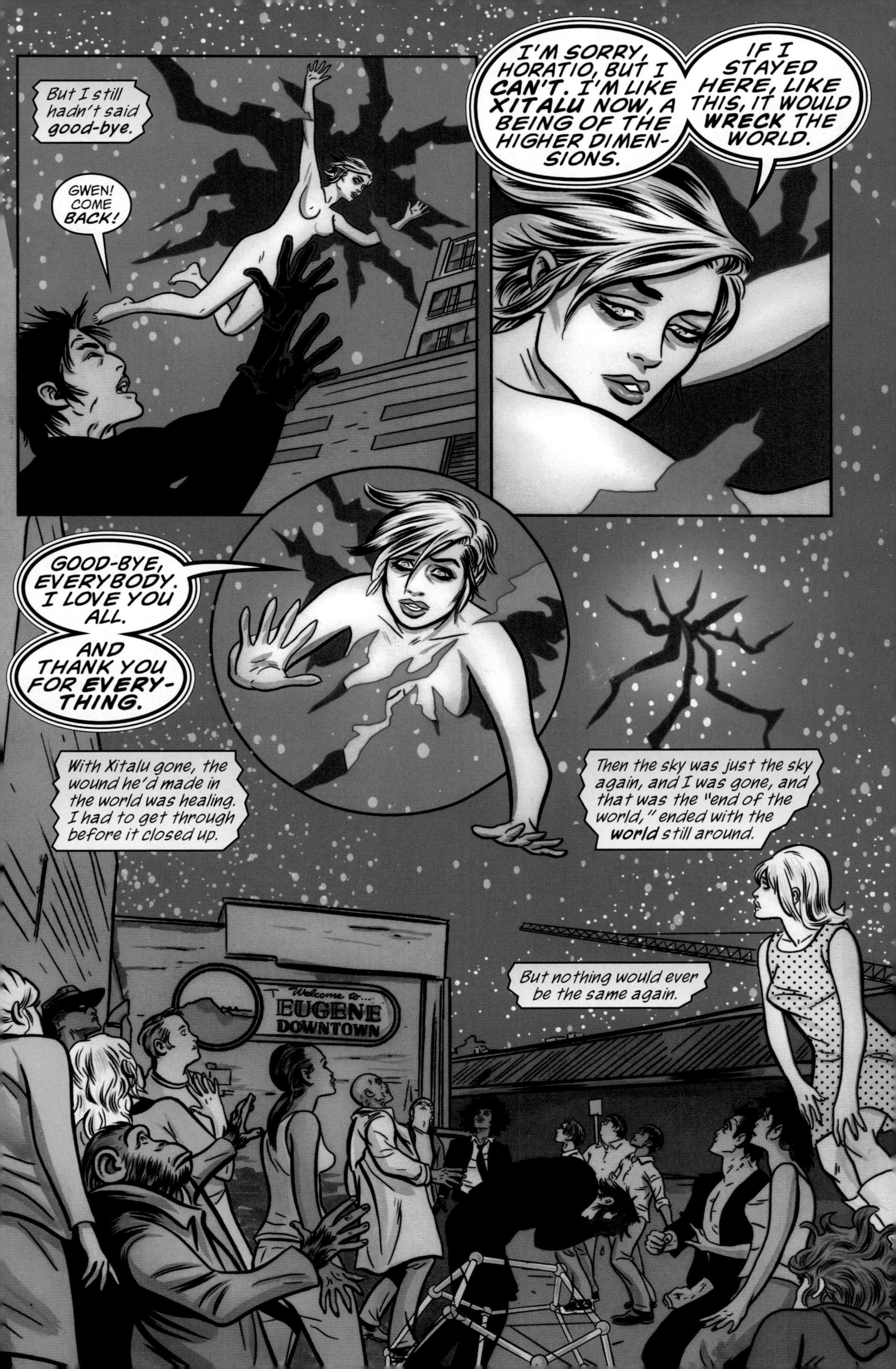
But I still hadn't said good-bye.
GWEN! COME BACK!
I'M SORRY, HORATIO, BUT I CAN'T. I'M LIKE XITALU NOW, A BEING OF THE HIGHER DIMENSIONS.
IF I STAYED HERE, LIKE THIS, IT WOULD WRECK THE WORLD.
GOOD-BYE, EVERYBODY. I LOVE YOU ALL.
AND THANK YOU FOR EVERYTHING.
With Xitalu gone, the wound he'd made in the world was healing. I had to get through before it closed up.
Then the sky was just the sky again, and I was gone, and that was the "end of the world," ended with the world still around.
Welcome to... EUGENE DOWNTOWN
But nothing would ever be the same again.

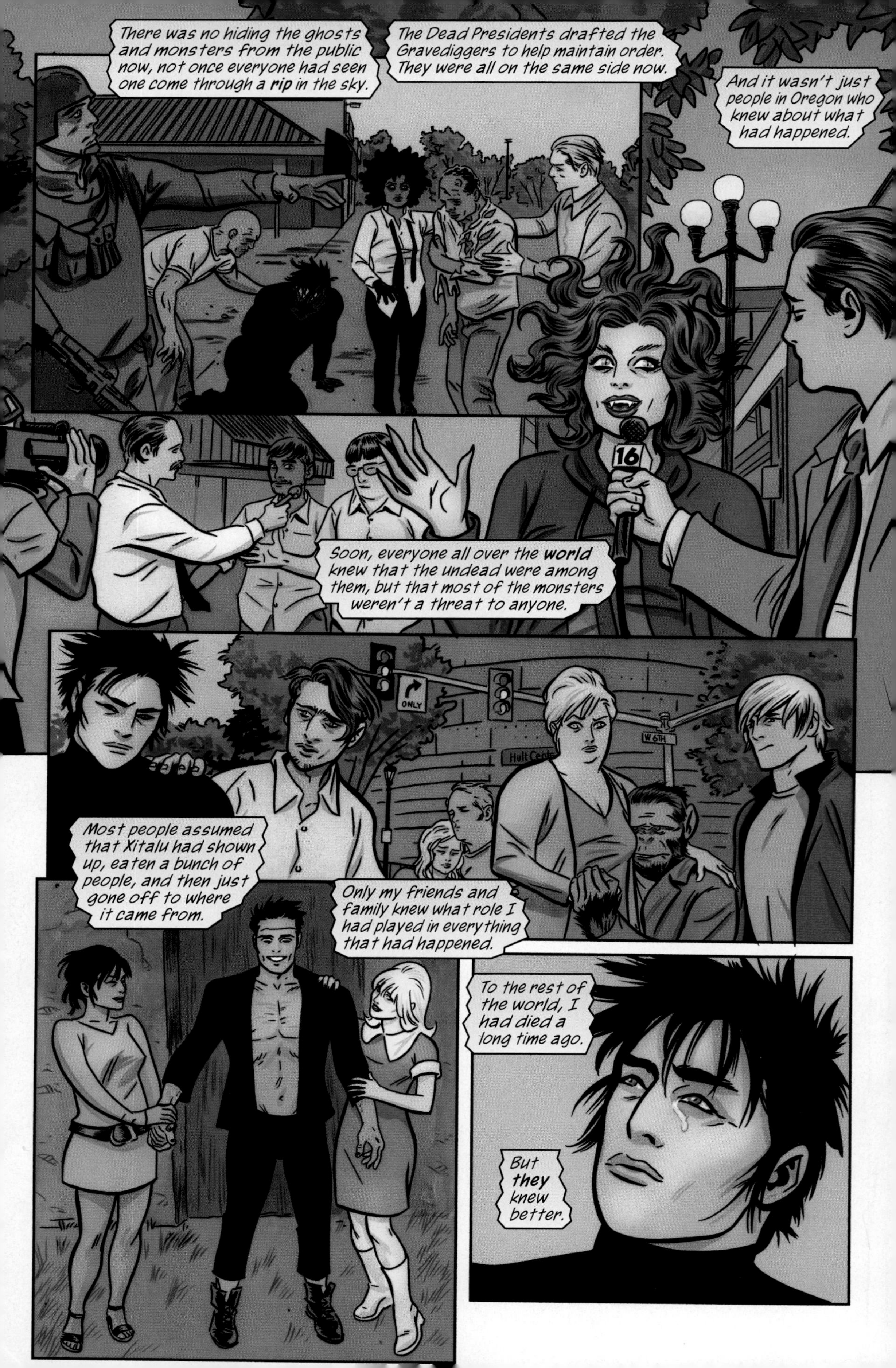
There was no hiding the ghosts and monsters from the public now, not once everyone had seen one come through a rip in the sky.
The Dead Presidents drafted the Gravediggers to help maintain order. They were all on the same side now.
And it wasn't just people in Oregon who knew about what had happened.
16
Soon, everyone all over the world knew that the undead were among them, but that most of the monsters weren't a threat to anyone.
ONLY
W 6TH
Most people assumed that Xitalu had shown up, eaten a bunch of people, and then just gone off to where it came from.
Only my friends and family knew what role I had played in everything that had happened.
To the rest of the world, I had died a long time ago.
But they knew better.

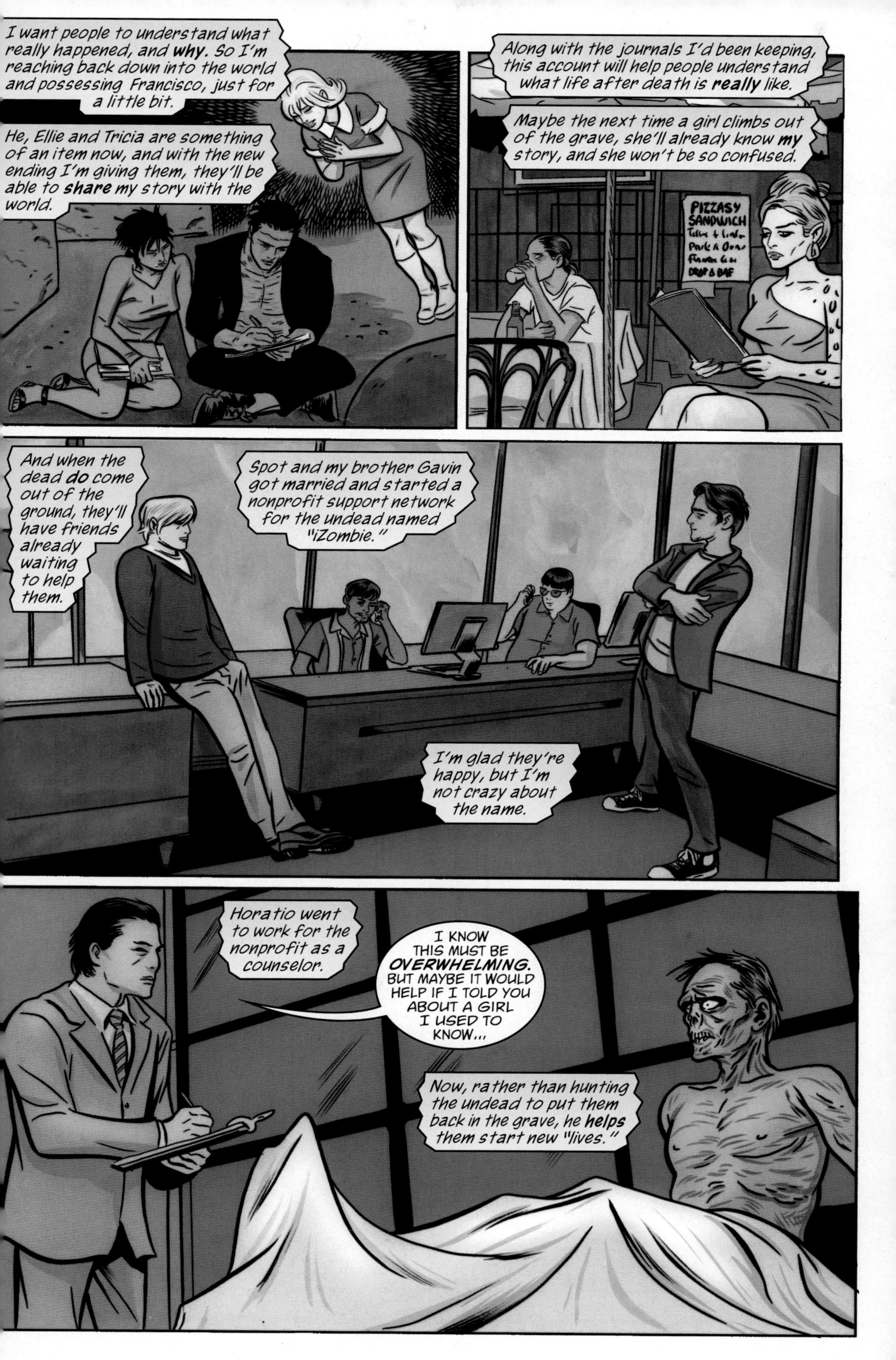
I want people to understand what really happened, and why. So I'm reaching back down into the world and possessing Francisco, just for a little bit.
He, Ellie and Tricia are something of an item now, and with the new ending I'm giving them, they'll be able to share my story with the world.
Along with the journals I'd been keeping, this account will help people understand what life after death is really like.
Maybe the next time a girl climbs out of the grave, she'll already know my story, and she won't be so confused.
PIZZASY
SANDWICH
And when the dead do come out of the ground, they'll have friends already waiting to help them.
Spot and my brother Gavin got married and started a nonprofit support network for the undead named "iZombie."
I'm glad they're happy, but I'm not crazy about the name.
Horatio went to work for the nonprofit as a counselor.
I KNOW THIS MUST BE OVERWHELMING. BUT MAYBE IT WOULD HELP IF I TOLD YOU ABOUT A GIRL I USED TO KNOW...
Now, rather than hunting the undead to put them back in the grave, he helps them start new "lives."

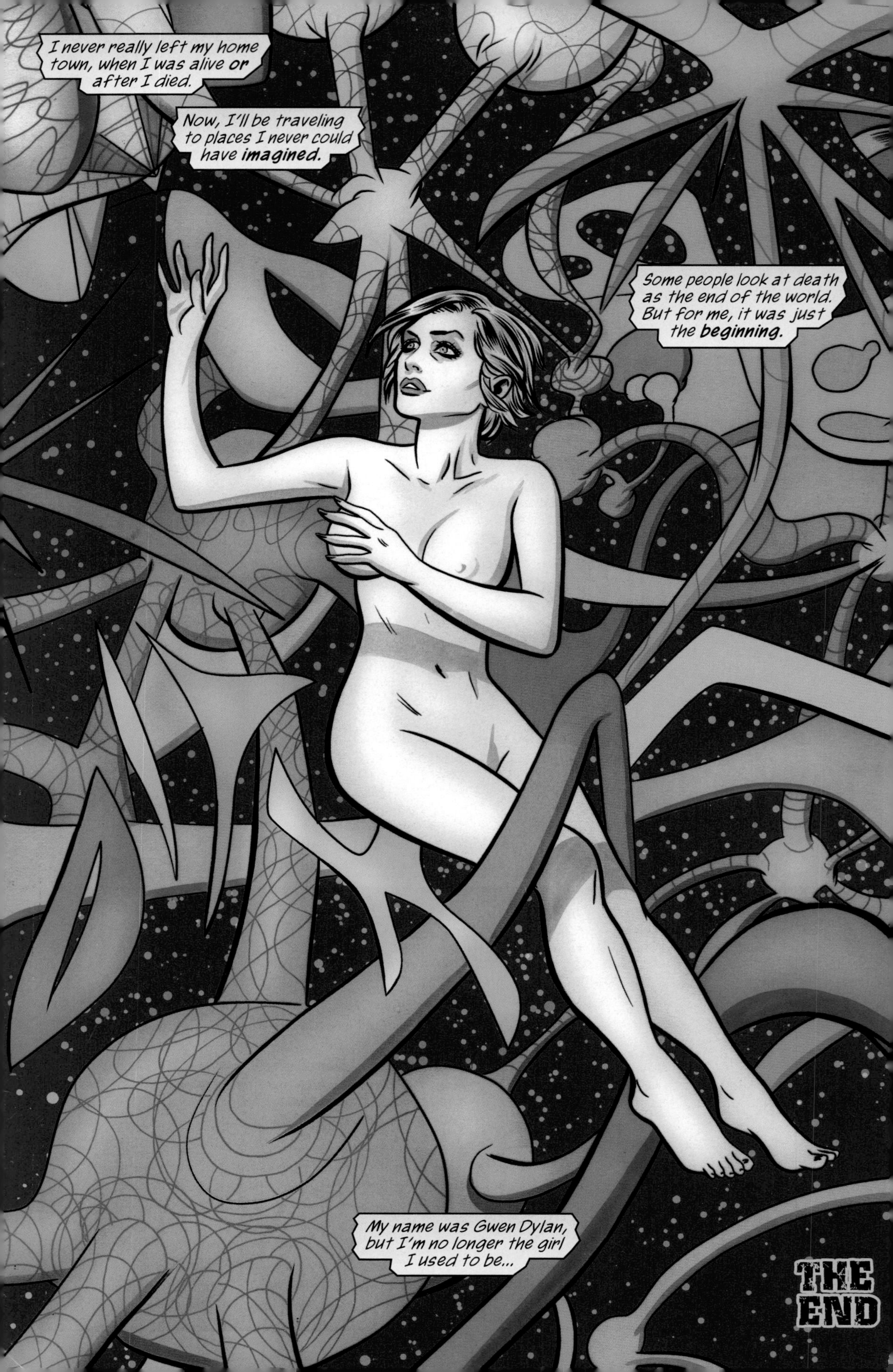
I never really left my home town, when I was alive **or** after I died.
Now, I'll be traveling to places I never could have **imagined.**
Some people look at death as the end of the world. But for me, it was just the **beginning.**
My name was Gwen Dylan, but I'm no longer the girl I used to be...
THE END